KU-576-699

PENGUIN BOOKS

Seven Pillars of Wisdom

Thomas Edward Lawrence was born in Wales in 1888 and educated at Oxford High School and at Jesus and Magdalen Colleges, Oxford. He was later made a research fellow of All Souls College, Oxford. From 1910 to 1914 he was an assistant in the British Museum's excavation of Carchemish on the Euphrates. He was commissioned on the outbreak of the First World War and in 1917 was officially attached to the staff of the Hejaz Expeditionary Force, under General Wingate. In 1918 he was transferred to General Allenby's staff. He attended the Peace Conference in 1919 as one of the British Delegation, and in 1921 and 1922 was Adviser on Arab Affairs in the Middle Eastern Division of the Colonial Office. In 1927, embarrassed with the 'Lawrence of Arabia' legend, he changed his name by Deed Poll to Shaw. He joined the R.A.F. and served as an aircraftman, maintaining in Dorset a cottage which is now National Trust property. He was killed in a motor-cycle accident in 1935. In addition to this book, of which Lawrence lost almost the whole manuscript at Reading Station in 1919, he wrote *Revolt in the Desert* (1927), *The Odyssey of Homer* (1935), a translation in prose, *Crusader Castles* (1936), and *The Mint*, which was published twenty years after his death.

MAP 1

MAP 2

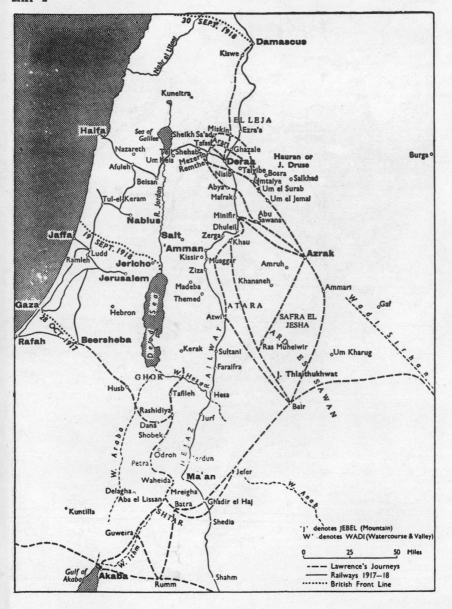

30 SEPT. 1918
Damascus
Kiswe
Kuneitra
EL LEJA
Miskin
Ezra's
Haifa
Sea of
Galilee
Sheikh Sa'ad
Tel Shehab
Tafas
Nazareth
Mezerib
Remtheh
Afuleh
Um Keis
Beisan
Ghazale
Hauran or
J. Druse
Burga
Deraa
Talyibe
Bosra
Nisib
Umtaiye
Salkhad
Abya
Um el Surab
Mafrak
Um el Jemal
Tul-el-Keram
Nablus
Minifir
Abu
Sawana
Jaffa
19 SEPT. 1918
Salt
Dhuleil
Zerga
'Amman
Khau
Azrak
Ludd
Kissir
Muaggar
Amruh
Ramleh
Jericho
Ziza
Jerusalem
Khananeh
Ammari
Madeba
Themed
ATARA
Gaf
Gaza
Hebron
Atwi
SAFRA EL
JESHA
Wadi Sirhan
28 OCT. 1917
Dead Sea
RAILWAY
Ras Muheiwir
Um Kharug
Rafah
Beersheba
Kerak
Sultani
J. Thlaithukhwat
GHOR
W. Hesa
Faraifra
Husb
Tafileh
Hesa
Bair
Rashidiya
Jurf
SAWAN
Dana
Shobek
HEJAZ
W. Araba
Odroh
erdun
Petra
Jefer
Waheida
Ma'an
W. Anab
Delagha
Mreigha
Aba el Lissan
Batra
Ghadir el Haj
Kuntilla
Shedia
'J' denotes JEBEL (Mountain)
W' denotes WADI (Watercourse & Valley)
SHTAR
Guweira
0   25   50 Miles
W. Ithm
Gulf of
Akaba
Akaba
Shahm
Rumm
— — — Lawrence's Journeys
———— Railways 1917–18
· · · · · · British Front Line

MAP 3

MAP 4

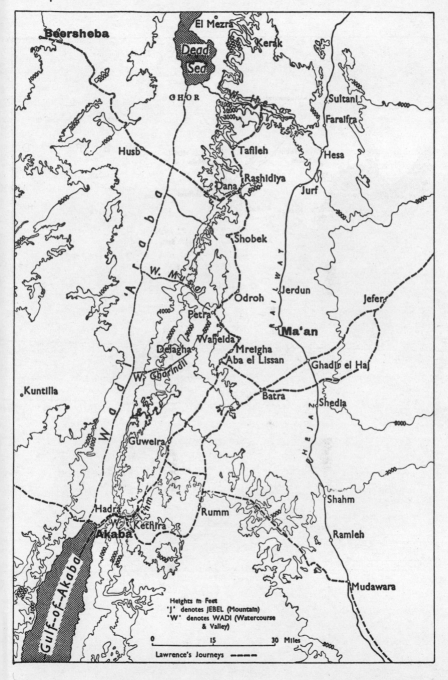

Beersheba

El Mezra

Dead Sea

Kerak

GHOR

Sultani

Faraifra

Husb

Tafileh

Hesa

Rashidiya

Dana

Jurf

W. Araba

Shobek

W. Mu

Odroh

Jerdun

Jefer

Petra

Ma'an

Waheida

Mreigha

Delagha

Aba el Lissan

W. Gharindil

Ghadir el Haj

Kuntilla

Batra

Shedia

HEJAZ RAILWAY

Guweira

Shahm

Hadra

W. Ithm

Kethira

Rumm

Akaba

Ramleh

Gulf of Akaba

Mudawara

Heights in Feet
'J' denotes JEBEL (Mountain)
'W' denotes WADI (Watercourse
& Valley)

0   15   30   Miles

Lawrence's Journeys ------

T. E. LAWRENCE

SEVEN PILLARS
OF WISDOM

A TRIUMPH

PENGUIN BOOKS
IN ASSOCIATION WITH
JONATHAN CAPE

PENGUIN BOOKS

Published by the Penguin Group
Penguin Books Ltd, 80 Strand, London WC2R 0RL, England
Penguin Putnam Inc., 375 Hudson Street, New York, New York 10014, USA
Penguin Books Australia Ltd, 250 Camberwell Road, Camberwell, Victoria 3124, Australia
Penguin Books Canada Ltd, 10 Alcorn Avenue, Toronto, Ontario, Canada M4V 3B2
Penguin Books India (P) Ltd, 11 Community Centre, Panchsheel Park, New Delhi – 110 017, India
Penguin Books (NZ) Ltd, Cnr Rosedale and Airborne Roads, Albany, Auckland, New Zealand
Penguin Books (South Africa) (Pty) Ltd, 24 Sturdee Avenue, Rosebank 2196, South Africa

Penguin Books Ltd, Registered Offices: 80 Strand, London WC2R 0RL, England

www.penguin.com

Privately printed 1926
First published in Great Britain by Jonathan Cape 1935
First published in the United States of America by
Doubleday & Company, Inc. 1935
Published in Penguin Books 1962
Published in Penguin Books in the United States of America by
arrangement with Doubleday & Company, Inc.
Reprinted in Penguin Classics 2000

037

Copyright 1926, 1935 by Doubleday & Company, Inc.
All rights reserved

Printed and bound in Great Britain by Clays Ltd, Elcograf S.p.A.
Set in Monotype Fournier

The maps for this edition were drawn by A. Gatrell

Except in the United States of America, this book is sold subject
to the condition that it shall not, by way of trade or otherwise, be lent,
re-sold, hired out, or otherwise circulated without the publisher's
prior consent in any form of binding or cover other than that in
which it is published and without a similar condition including this
condition being imposed on the subsequent purchaser

ISBN-13: 978–0–141–18276–6

www.greenpenguin.co.uk

MIX
Paper from
responsible sources
FSC® C018179

Penguin Books is committed to a sustainable
future for our business, our readers and our planet.
This book is made from Forest Stewardship
Council™ certified paper.

To S.A.

I loved you, so I drew these tides of men into my hands
and wrote my will across the sky in stars
To earn you Freedom, the seven-pillared worthy house,
that your eyes might be shining for me
When we came.

Death seemed my servant on the road, till we were near
and saw you waiting:
When you smiled, and in sorrowful envy he outran me
and took you apart:
Into his quietness.

Love, the way-weary, groped to your body, our brief wage
ours for the moment
Before earth's soft hand explored your shape, and the blind
worms grew fat upon
Your substance.

Men prayed me that I set our work, the inviolate house,
as a memory of you.
But for fit monument I shattered it, unfinished: and now
The little things creep out to patch themselves hovels
in the marred shadow
Of your gift.

AUTHOR'S PREFACE

Mr Geoffrey Dawson persuaded All Souls College to give me leisure, in 1919-20, to write about the Arab Revolt. Sir Herbert Baker let me live and work in his Westminster houses.

The book so written passed in 1921 into proof: where it was fortunate in the friends who criticized it. Particularly it owes its thanks to Mr and Mrs Bernard Shaw for countless suggestions of great value and diversity: and for all the present semi-colons.

It does not pretend to be impartial. I was fighting for my hand, upon my own midden. Please take it as a personal narrative pieced out of memory. I could not make proper notes: indeed it would have been a breach of my duty to the Arabs if I had picked such flowers while they fought. My superior officers, Wilson, Joyce, Dawnay, Newcombe, and Davenport, could each tell a like tale. The same is true of Stirling, Young, Lloyd, and Maynard: of Buxton and Winterton: of Ross, Stent, and Siddons: of Peake, Hornby, Scott-Higgins, and Garland: of Wordie, Bennett, and MacIndoe: of Bassett, Scott, Goslett, Wood, and Gray: of Hinde, Spence, and Bright: of Brodie and Pascoe, Gilman and Grisenthwaite, Greenhill, Dowsett, and Wade: of Henderson, Leeson, Makins, and Nunan.

And there were many other leaders or lonely fighters to whom this self-regardant picture is not fair. It is still less fair, of course, like all war-stories, to the unnamed rank and file, who miss their share of credit, as they must do, until they can write the despatches.

T. E. S.

Cranwell, 15 August 1926

CONTENTS

LIST OF PLATES

List of Drawings by Eric Kennington

PREFACE BY A. W. LAWRENCE

THE seven pillars of wisdom are first mentioned in the Bible, in the Book of Proverbs (ix. 1).

'Wisdom hath builded a house: she hath hewn out her seven pillars'.

The title was originally applied by the author to a book of his about seven cities. He decided not to publish this early book because he considered it immature, but he transferred the title as a memento.

A four-page leaflet entitled SOME NOTES ON THE WRITING OF THE SEVEN PILLARS OF WISDOM BY T. E. SHAW was issued by my brother to those who bought or were presented with copies of the 1926 edition. It contains the following information:

MANUSCRIPTS

Text I

I WROTE Books 2, 3, 4, 5, 6, 7 and 10 in Paris between February and June of 1919. The Introduction was written between Paris and Egypt on my way out to Cairo by Handley-Page in July and August 1919. Afterwards in England I wrote Book 1: and then lost all but the Introduction and drafts of Books 9 and 10 at Reading Station, while changing trains. This was about Christmas, 1919.

Text I, if completed, would have been about 250,000 words, a little less than the privately printed *Seven Pillars* as subscribers received it. My war-time notes, on which it was largely constructed, were destroyed as each section was finished. Only three people read much of it, before I lost it.

Text II

A month or so later I began, in London, to scribble out what I remembered of the first text. The original Introduction was of course still available. The other ten Books I completed in less than three months, by doing many thousand words at a time, in long sittings. Thus Book VI was written entire between sunrise and sunrise. Naturally the style was careless: and so Text II (though it introduced few new episodes) came to over 400,000 words. I corrected it at intervals throughout 1920, checking it with the files of the *Arab Bulletin*, and with two diaries and some of my surviving field-notes. Though hopelessly bad as a text, it became substantially complete and accurate. All but one page of this text was burned by me in 1922.

Text III

With Text II available on the table, Text III was begun in London, and worked on there, in Jeddah, and in Amman during 1921, and again in London till February 1922. It was composed with great care. This manuscript still exists. It is nearly 330,000 words long.

PRIVATELY PRINTED TEXTS

Oxford 1922

THOUGH the story, as completed in Text III, appeared to me still diffuse and unsatisfactory, yet for security's sake it was set up and printed textually, in sheets, at Oxford in the first quarter of 1922, by care of the *Oxford Times* staff. Since eight copies were required, and the book was very large, printing was preferred to typewriting. Five copies (bound in book form, for the convenience of those former members of the Hejaz Expeditionary Force who undertook to read it critically for me) have not yet (April 1927) been destroyed.

Subscribers' Text 1. xii. 26

This text, as issued to subscribers in December 1926 and January 1927, was a recension of the Oxford sheets of 1922. They were condensed (the single canon of change being literary) during 1923 and 1924 (Royal Tank Corps) and 1925 and 1926 (Royal Air Force) in my spare evenings. Beginners in literature are inclined to fumble with a handful of adjectives round the outline of what they want to describe: but by 1924 I had learnt my first lessons in writing, and was often able to combine two or three of my 1921 phrases into one.

There were four exceptions to the rule of condensation:

i) An incident, of less than a page, was cut out because two seniors of our party thought it unpleasantly unnecessary.

ii) Two characters of Englishmen were modified: one into nothing, because the worm no longer seemed worth treading on: the other into plain praise, because what I had innocently written as complaint was read ambiguously by an authority well able to judge.

iii) One chapter of the Introduction was omitted. My best critic told me it was much inferior to the rest.

iv) Book VIII, intended as a 'flat', to interpose between the comparative excitements of Book VII and the final advance on Damascus, was shortened of an abortive reconnaissance, some 10,000 words long. Several of those who read the Oxford text complained of the inordinate boredom of the 'flat', and upon reflection I agreed with them that it was perhaps too successful.

By thus excising 3 per cent and condensing the rest of the Oxford text a total reduction of 15 per cent was achieved, and the length of the subscribers' text brought down to some 280,000 words. It is swifter and more pungent than the Oxford text; and it would have been improved yet more if I had had leisure to carry the process of revision further.

The *Seven Pillars* was so printed and assembled that nobody but myself knew how many copies were produced. I propose to keep this knowledge to myself. Newspaper statements of 107 copies can be easily disproved, for there were more than 107 subscribers: and in addition I gave away, not perhaps as many copies as I owed, but as many as my bankers could afford, to those who had shared with me in the Arab effort, or in the actual production of the volume.

PUBLISHED TEXTS
New York Text

A PROOF of the subscribers' text was sent to New York, and reprinted there by the George Doran Publishing Company. This was necessary to ensure U.S.A. copyright of the *Seven Pillars*. Ten copies are offered for sale, at a price high enough to prevent their ever being sold.

No further issue of the *Seven Pillars* will be made in my lifetime.

Revolt in the Desert

This abridgement of the *Seven Pillars* contains about 130,000 words. It was made by myself in 1926, with the minimum of necessary adjustment (perhaps three new paragraphs in all) to preserve sense and continuity. Parts of it appeared serially in the *Daily Telegraph* in December 1926. The whole was published in England by Jonathan Cape, and in U.S.A. by Doran in March 1927.

T. E. SHAW

To bring the information up to date, I add that the remaining copies of the Oxford printed Text of 1922 are still in existence, but will not be made public for at least ten years, and then only in a limited edition. *Revolt in the Desert* will not be printed again, at least during the remainder of the legal term of copyright.

The text of the present edition (1935) is identical with that of the thirty-guinea edition of 1926, except for the following omissions and alterations. The omissions are necessary to save hurting the feelings of persons still living; they come on pages 61, 62, and 329 where gaps of the same length are left in the present text. The 1926 edition contains no Chapter XI; the chapters have now been renumbered to remove this anomaly. On p. 300 (line 7) the phrase 'halts to breath' has been changed to 'halts to breathe' in agreement with the corresponding passage in the Oxford Text of 1922, 'we let the camels breathe a little'. On p. 398 (line 14) the word 'Humber' has been printed in italics instead of Roman type, to make the sense clearer; in 1926 the names of some other ships were similarly italicized.

The spelling of Arabic names varies greatly in all editions, and I have made no alterations. It should be explained that only three vowels are recognized in Arabic, and that some of the consonants have no equivalents in English. The general practice of orientalists in recent years has been to adopt one of the various sets of conventional signs for the letters and vowel marks of the Arabic alphabet, transliterating Mohamed as Muhammad, muezzin as mu'edhdhin, and Koran as Qur'an or Kur'an. This method is useful to those who know what it means, but this book follows the old fashion of writing the best phonetic approximations according to ordinary English spelling. The same place-name will be found spelt in several different ways, not only because the sound of many Arabic words can legitimately be represented in English in a variety of ways, but also because the natives of a district often differ as to the pronunciation of any place-name which has not already become famous or fixed by literary usage. (For example a locality near Akaba is called Abu Lissan, Aba el Lissan or Abu Lissal.) A reference by the author to his views on this matter occurs on page 664. I reprint here a series of questions by the publisher and answers by the author concerning the printing of *Revolt in the Desert*.

Q.

I attach a list of queries raised by F. who is reading the proofs. He finds these very clean, but full of inconsistencies in the spelling of proper names, a point which reviewers often take up. Will you annotate it in the margin, so that I can get the proofs straightened?

A.

Annotated: not very helpfully perhaps. Arabic names won't go into English, exactly, for their consonants are not the same as ours, and their vowels, like ours, vary from district to district. There are some 'scientific systems' of transliteration, helpful to people who know enough Arabic not to need helping, but a wash-out for the world. I spell my names anyhow, to show what rot the systems are.

Slip 1. Jeddah and Jidda used impartially throughout. Intentional?

Rather!

Slip 16. Bir Wahei*da*, was Bir Wahei*di*.

Why not? All one place.

Slip 20. Nuri, Emir of the Ruwalla, belongs to the 'chief family of the Rualla'. On Slip 23 'Rualla horse', and Slip 38, 'killed one Rueli'. In all later slips 'Rualla'.

Should have also used Ruwala and Ruala.

Slip 28. The Bisaita is also spelt Biseita.

Good.

Slip 47. Jedha, the she-camel, was Jedhah on Slip 40.

She was a splendid beast.

Slip 53. 'Meleager, the immoral poet'. I have put 'immortal' poet, but the author may mean immoral after all.

Immorality I know. Immortality I cannot judge. As you please: Meleager will not sue us for libel.

Q.	A.
Slip 65. Author is addressed 'Ya Auruns', but on Slip 56 was 'Aurans'.	Also Lurens and Runs: not to mention 'Shaw'. More to follow, if time permits.
Slip 78. Sherif Abd el Mayin of Slip 68 becomes el Main, el Mayein, el Muein, el Mayin, and el Muyein.	Good egg. I call this really ingenious.

A. W. LAWRENCE

POSTSCRIPT

THE subscribers' edition of *Seven Pillars of Wisdom* contained no chapter eleven, for the original first chapter had been omitted in the course of proof-correction, and renumbering proceeded only as far as the next ten. For the first published edition (1935) the chapters were renumbered throughout, so as to remove this anomaly. In this edition the suppressed chapter again appears in its rightful place, but, in order to avoid further renumbering, it has been entitled Introductory Chapter. In 1939, it was included in *Oriental Assembly* among other uncollected writings of T. E. Lawrence, together with a short explanatory note of my own.

A. W. L.

INTRODUCTORY CHAPTER

THE story which follows was first written out in Paris during the Peace Conference, from notes jotted daily on the march, strengthened by some reports sent to my chiefs in Cairo. Afterwards, in the autumn of 1919, this first draft and some of the notes were lost. It seemed to me historically needful to reproduce the tale, as perhaps no one but myself in Feisal's army had thought of writing down at the time what we felt, what we hoped, what we tried. So it was built again with heavy repugnance in London in the winter of 1919-20 from memory and my surviving notes. The record of events was not dulled in me and perhaps few actual mistakes crept in — except in details of dates or numbers — but the outlines and significance of things had lost edge in the haze of new interests.

Dates and places are correct, so far as my notes preserved them: but the personal names are not. Since the adventure some of those who worked with me have buried themselves in the shallow grave of public duty. Free use has been made of their names. Others still possess themselves, and here keep their secrecy. Sometimes one man carried various names. This may hide individuality and make the book a scatter of featureless puppets, rather than a group of living people: but once good is told of a man, and again evil, and some would not thank me for either blame or praise.

This isolated picture throwing the main light upon myself is unfair to my British colleagues. Especially I am most sorry that I have not told what the non-commissioned of us did. They were inarticulate, but wonderful, especially when it is taken into account that they had not the motive, the imaginative vision of the end, which sustained the officers. Unfortunately my concern was limited to this end, and the book is just a designed procession of Arab freedom from Mecca to Damascus. It is intended to rationalize the campaign, that everyone may see how natural the success was and how inevitable, how little dependent on direction or brain, how much less on the outside assistance of the few British. It was an Arab war waged and led by Arabs for an Arab aim in Arabia.

My proper share was a minor one, but because of a fluent pen, a free speech, and a certain adroitness of brain, I took upon myself, as I describe it, a mock primacy. In reality I never had any office among the Arabs: was never in charge of the British mission with them. Wilson, Joyce, Newcombe, Dawnay and Davenport were all over my head. I flattered myself that I was too young, not that they had more heart or mind in the work. I did my best. Wilson, Newcombe, Joyce, Dawnay, Davenport, Buxton, Marshall, Stirling, Young, Maynard, Ross, Scott, Winterton, Lloyd, Wordie, Siddons, Goslett, Stent, Henderson, Spence, Gilman, Garland, Brodie, Makins, Nunan, Leeson, Hornby, Peake, Scott-Higgins, Ramsay, Wood, Hinde, Bright, MacIndoe, Greenhill, Grisenthwaite, Dowsett, Bennett, Wade, Gray, Pascoe and the others also did their best.

It would be impertinent in me to praise them. When I wish to say ill of one outside our number, I do it: though there is less of this than was in my diary, since the passage of time seems to have bleached out men's stains. When I wish to praise outsiders, I do it: but our family affairs are our own. We did what we set out to do, and have the satisfaction of that knowledge. The others have liberty some day to put on record their story, one parallel to mine but not mentioning more of me than I of them, for each of us did his job by himself and as he pleased, hardly seeing his friends.

In these pages the history is not of the Arab movement, but of me in it. It is a narrative of daily life, mean happenings, little people. Here are no lessons for the world, no disclosures to shock peoples. It is filled with trivial things, partly that no one mistake for history the bones from which some day a man may make history, and partly for the pleasure it gave me to recall the fellowship of the revolt. We were fond together, because of the sweep of the open places, the taste of wide winds, the sunlight, and the hopes in which we worked. The morning freshness of the world-to-be intoxicated us. We were wrought up with ideas inexpressible and vaporous, but to be fought for. We lived many lives in those whirling campaigns, never sparing ourselves: yet when we achieved and the new world dawned, the old men came out again and took our victory to re-make in the likeness of the former world they knew. Youth could win, but had not learned to keep: and was pitiably weak against age. We stammered that we had worked for a new heaven and a new earth, and they thanked us kindly and made their peace.

All men dream: but not equally. Those who dream by night in the dusty recesses of their minds wake in the day to find that it was vanity: but the dreamers of the day are dangerous men, for they may act their dream with open eyes, to make it possible. This I did. I meant to make a new nation, to restore a lost influence, to give twenty millions of Semites the foundations on which to build an inspired dream-palace of their national thoughts. So high an aim called out the inherent nobility of their minds, and made them play a generous part in events: but when we won, it was charged against me that the British petrol royalties in Mesopotamia were become dubious, and French Colonial policy ruined in the Levant.

I am afraid that I hope so. We pay for these things too much in honour and in innocent lives. I went up the Tigris with one hundred Devon Territorials, young, clean, delightful fellows, full of the power of happiness and of making women and children glad. By them one saw vividly how great it was to be their kin, and English. And we were casting them by thousands into the fire to the worst of deaths, not to win the war but that the corn and rice and oil of Mesopotamia might be ours. The only need was to defeat our enemies (Turkey among them), and this was at last done in the wisdom of Allenby with less than four hundred killed, by turning to our uses the hands of the oppressed in Turkey. I am proudest of my thirty fights in that I did not have any of our own blood shed. All our subject provinces to me were not worth one dead Englishman.

We were three years over this effort and I have had to hold back many things which may not yet be said. Even so, parts of this book will be new to nearly all who see it, and many will look for familiar things and not find them. Once I reported fully to my chiefs, but learnt that they were rewarding me on my own evidence. This was not as it should be. Honours may be necessary in a professional army, as so many emphatic mentions in despatches, and by enlisting we had put ourselves, willingly or not, in the position of regular soldiers.

For my work on the Arab front I had determined to accept nothing. The Cabinet raised the Arabs to fight for us by definite promises of self-government afterwards. Arabs believe in persons, not in institutions. They saw in me a free agent of the British Government, and demanded from me an endorsement of its written promises. So I had to join the conspiracy, and, for what my word was worth, assured the men of their reward. In our two years' partnership under fire they grew accustomed to believing me and to think my Government, like myself, sincere. In this hope they performed some fine things, but, of course, instead of being proud of what we did together, I was continually and bitterly ashamed.

It was evident from the beginning that if we won the war these promises would be dead paper, and had I been an honest adviser of the Arabs I would have advised them to go home and not risk their lives fighting for such stuff: but I salved myself with the hope that, by leading these Arabs madly in the final victory I would establish them, with arms in their hands, in a position so assured (if not dominant) that expediency would counsel to the Great Powers a fair settlement of their claims. In other words, I presumed (seeing no other leader with the will and power) that I would survive the campaigns, and be able to defeat not merely the Turks on the battlefield, but my own country and its allies in the council-chamber. It was an immodest presumption: it is not yet clear if I succeeded: but it is clear that I had no shadow of leave to engage the Arabs, unknowing, in such hazard. I risked the fraud, on my conviction that Arab help was necessary to our cheap and speedy victory in the East, and that better we win and break our word than lose.

The dismissal of Sir Henry McMahon confirmed my belief in our essential insincerity: but I could not so explain myself to General Wingate while the war lasted, since I was nominally under his orders, and he did not seem sensible of how false his own standing was. The only thing remaining was to refuse rewards for being a successful trickster and, to prevent this unpleasantness arising, I began in my reports to conceal the true stories of things, and to persuade the few Arabs who knew to an equal reticence. In this book also, for the last time, I mean to be my own judge of what to say.

SEVEN PILLARS OF WISDOM

INTRODUCTION

FOUNDATIONS OF REVOLT

Chapters I to VII

SOME *Englishmen, of whom Kitchener was chief,
believed that a rebellion of Arabs against Turks
would enable England, while fighting Germany,
simultaneously to defeat her ally Turkey.*

*Their knowledge of the nature and power and
country of the Arabic-speaking peoples made them
think that the issue of such a rebellion would be
happy: and indicated its character and method.*

*So they allowed it to begin, having obtained for
it formal assurances of help from the British
Government. Yet none the less the rebellion of the
Sherif of Mecca came to most as a surprise, and
found the Allies unready. It aroused mixed
feelings and made strong friends and
strong enemies, amid whose clashing
jealousies its affairs began to
miscarry.*

CHAPTER I

Some of the evil of my tale may have been inherent in our circumstances. For years we lived anyhow with one another in the naked desert, under the indifferent heaven. By day the hot sun fermented us; and we were dizzied by the beating wind. At night we were stained by dew, and shamed into pettiness by the innumerable silences of stars. We were a self-centred army without parade or gesture, devoted to freedom, the second of man's creeds, a purpose so ravenous that it devoured all our strength, a hope so transcendent that our earlier ambitions faded in its glare.

As time went by our need to fight for the ideal increased to an unquestioning possession, riding with spur and rein over our doubts. Willy-nilly it became a faith. We had sold ourselves into its slavery, manacled ourselves together in its chain-gang, bowed ourselves to serve its holiness with all our good and ill content. The mentality of ordinary human slaves is terrible — they have lost the world — and we had surrendered, not body alone, but soul to the overmastering greed of victory. By our own act we were drained of morality, of volition, of responsibility, like dead leaves in the wind.

The everlasting battle stripped from us care of our own lives or of others'. We had ropes about our necks, and on our heads prices which showed that the enemy intended hideous tortures for us if we were caught. Each day some of us passed; and the living knew themselves just sentient puppets on God's stage: indeed, our taskmaster was merciless, merciless, so long as our bruised feet could stagger forward on the road. The weak envied those tired enough to die; for success looked so remote, and failure a near and certain, if sharp, release from toil. We lived always in the stretch or sag of nerves, either on the crest or in the trough of waves of feeling. This impotency was bitter to us, and made us live only for the seen horizon, reckless what spite we inflicted or endured, since physical sensation showed itself meanly transient. Gusts of cruelty, perversions, lusts ran lightly over the surface without troubling us; for the moral laws which had seemed to hedge about these silly accidents must be yet fainter words. We had learned that there were pangs too sharp, griefs too deep, ecstasies too high for our finite selves to register. When emotion reached this pitch the mind choked; and memory went white till the circumstances were humdrum once more.

Such exaltation of thought, while it let adrift the spirit, and gave it licence in strange airs, lost it the old patient rule over the body. The body was too coarse to feel the utmost of our sorrows and of our joys. Therefore, we abandoned it as rubbish: we left it below us to march forward, a breathing simulacrum, on its own unaided level, subject to influences from which in normal times our instincts would have shrunk. The men were young and sturdy; and hot flesh and blood unconsciously claimed a right in them and tormented their bellies with strange longings. Our privations and dangers fanned this virile heat, in a climate as racking as can be conceived. We had no shut places to be alone in, no thick clothes to hide our nature. Man in all things lived candidly with man.

The Arab was by nature continent; and the use of universal marriage had nearly abolished irregular courses in his tribes. The public women of the rare settlements we encountered in our months of wandering would have been nothing to our numbers, even had their raddled meat been palatable to a man of healthy parts. In horror of such sordid commerce our youths began indifferently to slake one another's few needs in their own clean bodies — a cold convenience that, by comparison, seemed sexless and even pure. Later, some began to justify this sterile process, and swore that friends quivering together in the yielding sand with intimate hot limbs in supreme embrace, found there hidden in the darkness a sensual co-efficient of the mental passion which was welding our souls and spirits in one flaming effort. Several, thirsting to punish appetites they could not wholly prevent, took a savage pride in degrading the body, and offered themselves fiercely in any habit which promised physical pain or filth.

I was sent to these Arabs as a stranger, unable to think their thoughts or subscribe their beliefs, but charged by duty to lead them forward and to develop to the highest any movement of theirs profitable to England in her war. If I could not assume their character, I could at least conceal my own, and pass among them without evident friction, neither a discord nor a critic but an unnoticed influence. Since I was their fellow, I will not be their apologist or advocate. Today in my old garments, I could play the bystander, obedient to the sensibilities of our theatre . . . but it is more honest to record that these ideas and actions then passed naturally. What now looks wanton or sadic seemed in the field inevitable, or just unimportant routine.

Blood was always on our hands: we were licensed to it. Wounding and killing seemed ephemeral pains, so very brief and sore was life with us. With the sorrow of living so great, the sorrow of punishment had to be pitiless. We lived for the day and died for it. When there was reason and desire to punish we wrote our lesson with gun or whip immediately in the sullen flesh of the sufferer, and the case was beyond appeal. The desert did not afford the refined slow penalties of courts and gaols.

Of course our rewards and pleasures were as suddenly sweeping as our troubles; but, to me in particular, they bulked less large. Bedouin ways were hard even for those brought up to them, and for strangers terrible: a death in life. When the march or labour ended I had no energy to record sensation, nor while it lasted any leisure to see the spiritual loveliness which sometimes came upon us by the way. In my notes, the cruel rather than the beautiful found place. We no doubt enjoyed more the rare moments of peace and forgetfulness; but I remember more the agony, the terrors, and the mistakes. Our life is not summed up in what I have written (there are things not to be repeated in cold blood for very shame); but what I have written was in and of our life. Pray God that men reading the story will not, for love of the glamour of strangeness, go out to prostitute themselves and their talents in serving another race.

A man who gives himself to be a possession of aliens leads a Yahoo life, having bartered his soul to a brute-master. He is not of them. He may stand against them, persuade himself of a mission, batter and twist them into something which they, of their own accord, would not have been. Then he is exploiting his old environment to press them out of theirs. Or, after my model, he may imitate them so well that they spuriously imitate him back again. Then he is giving away his own environment: pretending to theirs; and pretences are hollow, worthless things. In neither case does he do a thing of himself, nor a thing so clean as to be his own (without thought of conversion), letting them take what action or reaction they please from the silent example.

In my case, the efforts for these years to live in the dress of Arabs, and to imitate their mental foundation, quitted me of my English self, and let me look at the West and its conventions with new eyes: they destroyed it all for me. At the same time I could not sincerely take on the Arab skin: it was an affectation only. Easily was a man made an infidel, but hardly might he be converted to another faith. I had dropped one form and not taken on the other, and was become like Mohammed's coffin in our legend, with a resultant feeling of intense loneliness in life, and a contempt, not for other men, but for all they do. Such detachment came at times to a man exhausted by prolonged physical effort and isolation. His body plodded on mechanically, while his reasonable mind left him, and from without looked down critically on him, wondering what that futile lumber did and why. Sometimes these selves would converse in the void; and then madness was very near, as I believe it would be near the man who could see things through the veils at once of two customs, two educations, two environments.

CHAPTER II

A FIRST difficulty of the Arab movement was to say who the Arabs were. Being a manufactured people, their name had been changing in sense slowly year by year. Once it meant an Arabian. There was a country called Arabia; but this was nothing to the point. There was a language called Arabic; and in it lay the test. It was the current tongue of Syria and Palestine, of Mesopotamia, and of the great peninsula called Arabia on the map. Before the Moslem conquest, these areas were inhabited by diverse peoples, speaking languages of the Arabic family. We called them Semitic, but (as with most scientific terms) incorrectly. However, Arabic, Assyrian, Babylonian, Phoenician, Hebrew, Aramaic and Syriac were related tongues; and indications of common influences in the past, or even of a common origin, were strengthened by our knowledge that the appearances and customs of the present Arabic-speaking peoples of Asia, while as varied as a field-full of poppies, had an equal and essential likeness. We might with perfect propriety call them cousins — and cousins certainly, if sadly, aware of their own relationship.

The Arabic-speaking areas of Asia in this sense were a rough parallelogram. The northern side ran from Alexandretta, on the Mediterranean, across Mesopotamia eastward to the Tigris. The south side was the edge of the Indian Ocean, from Aden to Muscat. On the west it was bounded by the Mediterranean, the Suez Canal, and the Red Sea to Aden. On the east by the Tigris, and the Persian Gulf to Muscat. This square of land, as large as India, formed the homeland of our Semites, in which no foreign race had kept a permanent footing, though Egyptians, Hittites, Philistines, Persians, Greeks, Romans, Turks and Franks had variously tried. All had in the end been broken, and their scattered elements drowned in the strong characteristics of the Semitic race. Semites had sometimes pushed outside this area, and themselves been drowned in the outer world. Egypt, Algiers, Morocco, Malta, Sicily, Spain, Cilicia and France absorbed and obliterated Semitic colonies. Only in Tripoli of Africa, and in the everlasting miracle of Jewry, had distant Semites kept some of their identity and force.

The origin of these peoples was an academic question; but for the understanding of their revolt their present social and political differences were important, and could only be grasped by looking at their geography. This continent of theirs fell into certain great regions, whose gross physical diversities imposed varying habits on the dwellers in them. On the west the parallelogram was framed, from Alexandretta to Aden, by a mountain belt, called (in the north) Syria, and thence progressively southward called Palestine, Midian, Hejaz, and lastly Yemen. It had an average height of perhaps three thousand feet, with peaks of ten to twelve thousand feet. It faced west, was well watered with rain and cloud from the sea, and in general was fully peopled.

Another range of inhabited hills, facing the Indian Ocean, was the south edge of the parallelogram. The eastern frontier was at first an alluvial plain called Mesopotamia, but south of Basra a level littoral, called Kuweit, and Hasa, to Gattar. Much of this plain was peopled. These inhabited hills and plains framed a gulf of thirsty desert, in whose heart was an archipelago of watered and populous oases called Kasim and Aridh. In this group of oases lay the true centre of Arabia, the preserve of its native spirit, and its most conscious individuality. The desert lapped it round and kept it pure of contact.

The desert which performed this great function around the oases, and so made the character of Arabia, varied in nature. South of the oases it appeared to be a pathless sea of sand, stretching nearly to the populous escarpment of the Indian Ocean shore, shutting it out from Arabian history, and from all influence on Arabian morals and politics. Hadhramaut, as they called this southern coast, formed part of the history of the Dutch Indies; and its thought swayed Java rather than Arabia. To the west of the oases, between them and the Hejaz hills, was the Nejd desert, an area of gravel and lava, with little sand in it. To the east of these oases, between them and Kuweit, spread a similar expanse of gravel, but with some great stretches of soft sand, making the road difficult. To the north of the oases lay a belt of sand, and then an immense gravel and lava plain, filling up everything between the eastern edge of Syria and the banks of the Euphrates where Mesopotamia began. The practicability of this northern desert for men and motor-cars enabled the Arab revolt to win its ready success.

The hills of the west and the plains of the east were the parts of Arabia always most populous and active. In particular on the west, the mountains of Syria and Palestine, of Hejaz and Yemen, entered time and again into the current of our European life. Ethically, these fertile healthy hills were in Europe, not in Asia, just as the Arabs looked always to the Mediterranean, not to the Indian Ocean, for their cultural sympathies, for their enterprises, and particularly for their expansions, since the migration problem was the greatest and most complex force in Arabia, and general to it, however it might vary in the different Arabic districts.

In the north (Syria) the birth rate was low in the cities and the death rate high, because of the insanitary conditions and the hectic life led by the majority. Consequently the surplus peasantry found openings in the towns, and were there swallowed up. In the Lebanon, where sanitation had been improved, a greater exodus of youth took place to America each year, threatening (for the first time since Greek days) to change the outlook of an entire district.

In Yemen the solution was different. There was no foreign trade, and no massed industries to accumulate population in unhealthy places. The towns were just market towns, as clean and simple as ordinary villages. Therefore the population slowly increased; the scale of living was brought down very low; and a congestion of numbers was generally felt. They could not emigrate overseas; for the Sudan was even worse country than Arabia, and the few tribes which did venture across were compelled to modify their manner of life and their Semitic culture profoundly, in order to exist. They could not move northward along the hills; for these were barred by the holy town of Mecca and its port Jidda: an alien belt, continually reinforced by strangers from India and Java and Bokhara and Africa, very strong in vitality, violently hostile to the Semitic consciousness, and maintained despite economics and geography and climate by the artificial factor of a world-religion. The congestion of Yemen, therefore, becoming extreme, found its only relief in the east, by forcing the weaker aggregations of its border down and down the slopes of the hills along the Widian, the half-waste district of the great water-bearing valleys of Bisha, Dawasir, Ranya and Taraba which ran out towards the deserts of Nejd. These weaker clans had continually to exchange good springs and fertile palms for poorer springs and scantier palms, till at last they reached an area where a proper agricultural life became impossible. They then began to eke out their precarious husbandry by breeding sheep and camels, and in time came to depend more and more on these herds for their living.

Finally, under a last impulse from the straining population behind them, the border people (now almost wholly pastoral) were flung out of the furthest crazy oasis into the untrodden wilderness as nomads. This process, to be watched today with individual families and tribes to whose marches an exact name and date might be put, must have been going on since the first day of full settlement of Yemen. The Widian below Mecca and Taif are crowded with the memories and place-names of half a hundred tribes which have gone from there, and may be found today in Nejd, in Jebel Shammar, in the Hamad, even on the frontiers of Syria and Mesopotamia. There was the source of migration, the factory of nomads, the springing of the gulf-stream of desert wanderers.

For the people of the desert were as little static as the people of the hills. The economic life of the desert was based on the supply of camels, which were best bred on the rigorous upland pastures with their strong nutritive thorns. By this industry the Bedouins lived; and it in turn moulded their life, apportioned the tribal areas, and kept the clans revolving through their rote of spring, summer and winter pasturages, as the herds cropped the scanty growths of each in turn. The camel markets in Syria, Mesopotamia, and Egypt determined the population which the deserts could support, and regulated strictly their standard of living. So the desert likewise over-peopled itself upon occasion; and then there were heavings and thrustings of the crowded tribes as they elbowed themselves by natural courses towards the light. They might not go south towards the inhospitable sand or sea. They could not turn west; for there the steep hills of Hejaz were thickly lined by mountain peoples taking full advantage of their defensiveness. Sometimes they went towards the central oases of Aridh and Kasim, and if the tribes looking for new homes were strong and vigorous, might succeed in occupying parts of them. If, however, the desert had not this strength, its peoples were pushed gradually north, up between Medina of the Hejaz and Kasim of Nejd, till they found themselves at the fork of two roads. They could strike eastward, by Wadi Rumh or Jebel Shammar, to follow eventually the Batn to Shamiya, where they would become riverine Arabs of the Lower Euphrates; or they could climb by slow degrees, the ladder of western oases — Henakiya, Kheibar, Teima, Jauf, and the Sirhan — till fate saw them nearing Jebel Druse, in Syria, or watering their herds about Tadmor of the northern desert, on their way to Aleppo or Assyria.

Nor then did the pressure cease: the inexorable trend northward continued. The tribes found themselves driven to the very edge of cultivation in Syria or Mesopotamia. Opportunity and their bellies persuaded them of the advantages of possessing goats, and then of possessing sheep; and lastly they began to sow, if only a little barley for their animals. They were now no longer Bedouin, and began to suffer like the villagers from the ravages of the nomads behind. Insensibly, they made common cause with the peasants already on the soil, and found out that they, too, were peasantry. So we see clans, born in the highlands of Yemen, thrust by stronger clans into the desert, where, unwillingly, they became nomad to keep themselves alive. We see them wandering, every year moving a little further north or a little further east as chance has sent them down one or other of the well-roads of the wilderness, till finally this pressure drives them from the desert again into the sown, with the like unwillingness of their first shrinking experiment in nomad life. This was the circulation which kept vigour in the Semitic body. There were few, if indeed there was a single northern Semite, whose ancestors had not at some dark age passed through the desert. The mark of nomadism, that most deep and biting social discipline, was on each of them in his degree.

CHAPTER III

IF tribesman and townsman in Arabic-speaking Asia were not different races, but just men in different social and economic stages, a family resemblance might be expected in the working of their minds, and so it was only reasonable that common elements should appear in the product of all these peoples. In the very outset, at the first meeting with them, was found a universal clearness or hardness of belief, almost mathematical in its limitation, and repellent in its unsympathetic form. Semites had no half-tones in their register of vision. They were a people of primary colours, or rather of black and white, who saw the world always in contour. They were a dogmatic people, despising doubt, our modern crown of thorns. They did not understand our metaphysical difficulties, our introspective questionings. They knew only truth and untruth, belief and unbelief, without our hesitating retinue of finer shades.

This people was black and white, not only in vision, but by inmost furnishing: black and white not merely in clarity, but in apposition. Their thoughts were at ease only in extremes. They inhabited superlatives by choice. Sometimes inconsistents seemed to possess them at once in joint sway; but they never compromised: they pursued the logic of several incompatible opinions to absurd ends, without perceiving the incongruity. With cool head and tranquil judgement, imperturbably unconscious of the flight, they oscillated from asymptote to asymptote.*

They were a limited, narrow-minded people, whose inert intellects lay fallow in incurious resignation. Their imaginations were vivid, but not creative. There was so little Arab art in Asia that they could almost be said to have had no art, though their classes were liberal patrons, and had encouraged whatever talents in architecture, or ceramics, or other handicraft their neighbours and helots displayed. Nor did they handle

*The metaphor of oscillation 'from asymptote to asymptote' originated in a conversation with a friend who tells me that he mistakenly applied the term 'asymptote' to the branches of the hyperbola. — A.W.L.

great industries: they had no organizations of mind or body. They invented no systems of philosophy, no complex mythologies. They steered their course between the idols of the tribe and of the cave. The least morbid of peoples, they had accepted the gift of life unquestioningly, as axiomatic. To them it was a thing inevitable, entailed on man, a usufruct, beyond control. Suicide was a thing impossible, and death no grief.

They were a people of spasms, of upheavals, of ideas, the race of the individual genius. Their movements were the more shocking by contrast with the quietude of every day, their great men greater by contrast with the humanity of their mob. Their convictions were by instinct, their activities intuitional. Their largest manufacture was of creeds: almost they were monopolists of revealed religions. Three of these efforts had endured among them: two of the three had also borne export (in modified forms) to non-Semitic peoples. Christianity, translated into the diverse spirits of Greek and Latin and Teutonic tongues, had conquered Europe and America. Islam in various transformations was subjecting Africa and parts of Asia. These were Semitic successes. Their failures they kept to themselves. The fringes of their deserts were strewn with broken faiths.

It was significant that this wrack of fallen religions lay about the meeting of the desert and the sown. It pointed to the generation of all these creeds. They were assertions, not arguments; so they required a prophet to set them forth. The Arabs said there had been forty thousand prophets: we had record of at least some hundreds. None of them had been of the wilderness; but their lives were after a pattern. Their birth set them in crowded places. An unintelligible passionate yearning drove them out into the desert. There they lived a greater or lesser time in meditation and physical abandonment; and thence they returned with their imagined message articulate, to preach it to their old, and now doubting, associates. The founders of the three great creeds fulfilled this cycle: their possible coincidence was proved a law by the parallel life-histories of the myriad others, the unfortunate who failed, whom we might judge of no less true profession, but for whom time and disillusion had not heaped up dry souls ready to be set on fire. To the thinkers of the town the impulse into Nitria had ever been irresistible, not probably that they found God dwelling there, but that in its solitude they heard more certainly the living word they brought with them.

The common base of all the Semitic creeds, winners or losers, was the ever present idea of world-worthlessness. Their profound reaction from matter led them to preach bareness, renunciation, poverty; and the atmosphere of this invention stifled the minds of the desert pitilessly. A first knowledge of their sense of the purity of rarefaction was given me in early years, when we had ridden far out over the rolling plains of North Syria to a ruin of the Roman period which the Arabs believed was made by a prince of the border as a desert-palace for his queen. The clay of its building was said to have been kneaded for greater richness, not with water, but with the precious essential oils of flowers. My guides, sniffing the air like dogs, led me from crumbling room to room, saying, 'This is jessamine, this violet, this rose'.

But at last Dahoum drew me: 'Come and smell the very sweetest scent of all', and we went into the main lodging, to the gaping window sockets of its eastern face, and there drank with open mouths of the effortless, empty, eddyless wind of the desert, throbbing past. That slow breath had been born somewhere beyond the distant Euphrates and had dragged its way across many days and nights of dead grass, to its first obstacle, the man-made walls of our broken palace. About them it seemed to fret and linger, murmuring in baby-speech. 'This,' they told me, 'is the best: it has no taste.' My Arabs were turning their backs on perfumes and luxuries to choose the things in which mankind had had no share or part.

The Beduin of the desert, born and grown up in it, had embraced with all his soul this nakedness too harsh for volunteers, for the reason, felt but inarticulate, that there he found himself indubitably free. He lost material ties, comforts, all superfluities and other complications to achieve a personal liberty which haunted starvation and death. He saw no virtue in poverty herself: he enjoyed the little vices and luxuries — coffee, fresh water, women — which he could still preserve. In his life he had air and winds, sun and light, open spaces and a great emptiness. There was no human effort, no fecundity in Nature: just the heaven above and the unspotted earth beneath. There unconsciously he came near God. God was to him not anthropomorphic, not tangible, not moral nor ethical, nor concerned with the world or with him, not natural: but the being ἀχρώματος, ἀσχημάτιστος, ἀναφής, thus qualified not by divestiture but by investiture, a comprehending Being, the egg of all activity, with nature and matter just a glass reflecting Him.

The Beduin could not look for God within him: he was too sure that he was within God. He could not conceive anything which was or was not God, Who alone was great; yet there was a homeliness, an every-day-ness of this climatic Arab God, who was their eating and their fighting and their lusting, the commonest of their thoughts, their familiar resource and companion, in a way impossible to those whose God is so wistfully veiled from them by despair of their carnal un-worthiness of Him and by the decorum of formal worship. Arabs felt no incongruity in bringing God into the weaknesses and appetites of their least creditable causes. He was the most familiar of their words; and indeed we lost much eloquence when making Him the shortest and ugliest of our monosyllables.

This creed of the desert seemed inexpressible in words, and indeed in thought. It was easily felt as an influence, and those who went into the desert long enough to forget its open spaces and its emptiness were inevitably thrust upon God as the only refuge and rhythm of being. The Bedawi might be a nominal Sunni, or a nominal Wahabi, or any-thing else in the Semitic compass, and he would take it very lightly, a little in the manner of the watchmen at Zion's gate who drank beer and laughed in Zion because they were Zionists. Each individual nomad had his revealed religion, not oral or traditional or expressed, but instinctive in himself; and so we got all the Semitic creeds with (in character and essence) a stress on the emptiness of the world and the fullness of God; and according to the power and opportunity of the believer was the expression of them.

The desert dweller could not take credit for his belief. He had never been either evangelist or proselyte. He arrived at this intense condensa-tion of himself in God by shutting his eyes to the world, and to all the complex possibilities latent in him which only contact with wealth and temptations could bring forth. He attained a sure trust and a powerful trust, but of how narrow a field! His sterile experience robbed him of

compassion and perverted his human kindness to the image of the waste
in which he hid. Accordingly he hurt himself, not merely to be free,
but to please himself. There followed a delight in pain, a cruelty which
was more to him than goods. The desert Arab found no joy like the
joy of voluntarily holding back. He found luxury in abnegation,
renunciation, self restraint. He made nakedness of the mind as sensuous
as nakedness of the body. He saved his own soul, perhaps, and without
danger, but in a hard selfishness. His desert was made a spiritual ice-
house, in which was preserved intact but unimproved for all ages a
vision of the unity of God. To it sometimes the seekers from the outer
world could escape for a season and look thence in detachment at the
nature of the generation they would convert.

This faith of the desert was impossible in the towns. It was at once
too strange, too simple, too impalpable for export and common use.
The idea, the ground-belief of all Semitic creeds was waiting there,
but it had to be diluted to be made comprehensible to us. The scream of
a bat was too shrill for many ears: the desert spirit escaped through our
coarser texture. The prophets returned from the desert with their
glimpse of God, and through their stained medium (as through a dark
glass) showed something of the majesty and brilliance whose full vision
would blind, deafen, silence us, serve us as it had served the Beduin,
setting him uncouth, a man apart.

The disciples, in the endeavour to strip themselves and their neighbours of all things according to the Master's word, stumbled over human
weaknesses and failed. To live, the villager or townsman must fill
himself each day with the pleasures of acquisition and accumulation,
and by rebound off circumstance become the grossest and most material
of men. The shining contempt of life which led others into the barest
asceticism drove him to despair. He squandered himself heedlessly, as
a spendthrift: ran through his inheritance of flesh in hasty longing for the
end. The Jew in the Metropole at Brighton, the miser, the worshipper
of Adonis, the lecher in the stews of Damascus were alike signs of the
Semitic capacity for enjoyment, and expressions of the same nerve
which gave us at the other pole the self-denial of the Essenes, or the
early Christians, or the first Khalifas, finding the way to heaven fairest
for the poor in spirit. The Semite hovered between lust and self-denial.

Arabs could be swung on an idea as on a cord; for the unpledged allegiance of their minds made them obedient servants. None of them would escape the bond till success had come, and with it responsibility and duty and engagements. Then the idea was gone and the work ended — in ruins. Without a creed they could be taken to the four corners of the world (but not to heaven) by being shown the riches of earth and the pleasures of it; but if on the road, led in this fashion, they met the prophet of an idea, who had nowhere to lay his head and who depended for his food on charity or birds, then they would all leave their wealth for his inspiration. They were incorrigibly children of the idea, feckless and colour-blind, to whom body and spirit were for ever and inevitably opposed. Their mind was strange and dark, full of depressions and exaltations, lacking in rule, but with more of ardour and more fertile in belief than any other in the world. They were a people of starts, for whom the abstract was the strongest motive, the process of infinite courage and variety, and the end nothing. They were as unstable as water, and like water would perhaps finally prevail. Since the dawn of life, in successive waves they had been dashing themselves against the coasts of flesh. Each wave was broken, but, like the sea, wore away ever so little of the granite on which it failed, and some day, ages yet, might roll unchecked over the place where the material world had been, and God would move upon the face of those waters. One such wave (and not the least) I raised and rolled before the breath of an idea, till it reached its crest, and toppled over and fell at Damascus. The wash of that wave, thrown back by the resistance of vested things, will provide the matter of the following wave, when in fullness of time the sea shall be raised once more.

CHAPTER IV

THE first great rush round the Mediterranean had shown the world the power of an excited Arab for a short spell of intense physical activity; but when the effort burned out the lack of endurance and routine in the Semitic mind became as evident. The provinces they had overrun they neglected, out of sheer distaste of system, and had to seek the help of their conquered subjects, or of more vigorous foreigners, to administer their ill-knit and inchoate empires. So, early in the Middle Ages, the Turks found a footing in the Arab States, first as servants, then as helpers, and then as a parasite growth which choked the life out of the old body politic. The last phase was of enmity, when the Hulagus or Timurs sated their blood lust, burning and destroying everything which irked them with a pretension of superiority.

Arab civilizations had been of an abstract nature, moral and intellectual rather than applied; and their lack of public spirit made their excellent private qualities futile. They were fortunate in their epoch: Europe had fallen barbarous; and the memory of Greek and Latin learning was fading from men's minds. By contrast the imitative exercise of the Arabs seemed cultured, their mental activity progressive, their state prosperous. They had performed real service in preserving something of a classical past for a medieval future.

With the coming of the Turks this happiness became a dream. By stages the Semites of Asia passed under their yoke, and found it a slow death. Their goods were stripped from them; and their spirits shrivelled in the numbing breath of a military Government. Turkish rule was gendarme rule, and Turkish political theory as crude as its practice. The Turks taught the Arabs that the interests of a sect were higher than those of patriotism: that the petty concerns of the province were more than nationality. They led them by subtle dissensions to distrust one another. Even the Arabic language was banished from courts and offices, from the Government service, and from superior schools. Arabs might only serve the State by sacrifice of their racial characteristics. These measures were not accepted quietly. Semitic tenacity showed itself in the many rebellions of Syria, Mesopotamia and Arabia against the grosser forms of Turkish penetration; and resistance was also made to the more insidious attempts at absorption. The Arabs would not give up their rich and flexible tongue for crude Turkish: instead, they filled Turkish with Arabic words, and held to the treasures of their own literature.

They lost their geographical sense, and their racial and political and historical memories; but they clung the more tightly to their language, and erected it almost into a fatherland of its own. The first duty of every Moslem was to study the Koran, the sacred book of Islam, and incidentally the greatest Arab literary monument. The knowledge that this religion was his own, and that only he was perfectly qualified to understand and practise it, gave every Arab a standard by which to judge the banal achievements of the Turk.

Then came the Turkish revolution, the fall of Abdul Hamid, and the supremacy of the Young Turks. The horizon momentarily broadened for the Arabs. The Young-Turk movement was a revolt against the hierarchic conception of Islam and the pan-Islamic theories of the old Sultan, who had aspired, by making himself spiritual director of the Moslem world, to be also (beyond appeal) its director in temporal affairs. These young politicians rebelled and threw him into prison, under the impulse of constitutional theories of a sovereign state. So, at a time when Western Europe was just beginning to climb out of nationality into internationality, and to rumble with wars far removed from problems of race, Western Asia began to climb out of catholicism into nationalist politics, and to dream of wars for self-government and self-sovereignty, instead of for faith or dogma. This tendency had broken out first and most strongly in the Near East, in the little Balkan States, and had sustained them through an almost unparalleled martyrdom to their goal of separation from Turkey. Later there had been nationalist movements in Egypt, in India, in Persia, and finally in Constantinople, where they were fortified and made pointed by the new American ideas in education: ideas which, when released in the old high Oriental atmosphere, made an explosive mixture. The American schools, teaching by the method of inquiry, encouraged scientific detachment and free exchange of views. Quite without intention they taught revolution, since it was impossible for an individual to be modern in Turkey and at the same time loyal, if he had been born of one of the subject races — Greeks, Arabs, Kurds, Armenians or Albanians — over whom the Turks were so long helped to keep dominion.

The Young Turks, in the confidence of their first success, were carried away by the logic of their principles, and as protest against Pan-Islam preached Ottoman brotherhood. The gullible subject races — far more numerous than the Turks themselves — believed that they were called upon to co-operate in building a new East. Rushing to the task (full of Herbert Spencer and Alexander Hamilton) they laid down platforms of sweeping ideas, and hailed the Turks as partners. The Turks, terrified at the forces they had let loose, drew the fires as suddenly as they had stoked them. Turkey made Turkish for the Turks — *Yeni-Turan* — became the cry. Later on, this policy would turn them towards the rescue of their irredenti — the Turkish populations subject to Russia in Central Asia; but, first of all, they must purge their Empire of such irritating subject races as resisted the ruling stamp. The Arabs, the largest alien component of Turkey, must first be dealt with. Accordingly the Arab deputies were scattered, the Arab societies forbidden, the Arab notables proscribed. Arabic manifestations and the Arabic language were suppressed by Enver Pasha more sternly than by Abdul Hamid before him.

However, the Arabs had tasted freedom: they could not change their ideas as quickly as their conduct; and the stiffer spirits among them were not easily to be put down. They read the Turkish papers, putting 'Arab' for 'Turk' in the patriotic exhortations. Suppression charged them with unhealthy violence. Deprived of constitutional outlets they became revolutionary. The Arab societies went underground, and changed from liberal clubs into conspiracies. The Akhua, the Arab mother society, was publicly dissolved. It was replaced in Mesopotamia by the dangerous Ahad, a very secret brotherhood, limited almost entirely to Arab officers in the Turkish Army, who swore to acquire the military knowledge of their masters, and to turn it against them, in the service of the Arab people, when the moment of rebellion came.

It was a large society, with a sure base in the wild part of Southern Irak, where Sayid Taleb, the young John Wilkes of the Arab movement, held the power in his unprincipled fingers. To it belonged seven out of every ten Mesopotamian-born officers; and their counsel was so well kept that members of it held high command in Turkey to the last. When the crash came, and Allenby rode across Armageddon and Turkey fell, one vice-president of the society was commanding the broken fragments of the Palestine armies on the retreat, and another was directing the Turkish forces across-Jordan in the Amman area. Yet later, after the armistice, great places in the Turkish service were still held by men ready to turn on their masters at a word from their Arab leaders. To most of them the word was never given; for those societies were pro-Arab only, willing to fight for nothing but Arab independence; and they could see no advantage in supporting the Allies rather than the Turks, since they did not believe our assurances that we would leave them free. Indeed, many of them preferred an Arabia united by Turkey in miserable subjection, to an Arabia divided up and slothful under the easier control of several European powers in spheres of influence.

Greater than the Ahad was the Fetah, the society of freedom in Syria. The landowners, the writers, the doctors, the great public servants linked themselves in this society with a common oath, passwords, signs, a press and a central treasury, to ruin the Turkish Empire. With the noisy facility of the Syrian — an ape-like people having much of the Japanese quickness, but shallow — they speedily built up a formidable organization. They looked outside for help, and expected freedom to come by entreaty, not by sacrifice. They corresponded with Egypt, with the Ahad (whose members, with true Mesopotamian dourness, rather despised them), with the Sherif of Mecca, and with Great Britain: everywhere seeking the ally to serve their turn. They also were deadly secret; and the Government, though it suspected their existence, could find no credible evidence of their leaders or membership. It had to hold its hand until it could strike with evidence enough to satisfy the English and French diplomats who acted as modern public opinion in Turkey. The war in 1914 withdrew these agents, and left the Turkish Government free to strike.

Mobilization put all power into the hands of those members —

Enver, Talaat and Jemal — who were at once the most ruthless, the most logical, and the most ambitious of the Young Turks. They set themselves to stamp out all non-Turkish currents in the State, especially Arab and Armenian nationalism. For the first step they found a specious and convenient weapon in the secret papers of a French Consul in Syria, who left behind him in his Consulate copies of correspondence (about Arab freedom) which had passed between him and an Arab club, not connected with the Fetah but made up of the more talkative and less formidable *intelligenzia* of the Syrian coast. The Turks, of course, were delighted; for 'colonial' aggression in North Africa had given the French a black reputation in the Arabic-speaking Moslem world; and it served Jemal well to show his co-religionists that these Arab nationalists were infidel enough to prefer France to Turkey.

In Syria, of course, his disclosures had little novelty; but the members of the society were known and respected, if somewhat academic, persons; and their arrest and condemnation, and the crop of deportations, exiles, and executions to which their trial led, moved the country to its depths, and taught the Arabs of the Fetah that if they did not profit by their lesson the fate of the Armenians would be upon them. The Armenians had been well armed and organized; but their leaders had failed them. They had been disarmed and destroyed piecemeal, the men by massacre, the women and children by being driven and over-driven along the wintry roads into the desert, naked and hungry, the common prey of any passer-by, until death took them. The Young Turks had killed the Armenians, not because they were Christians, but because they were Armenians; and for the same reason they herded Arab Moslems and Arab Christians into the same prison, and hanged them together on the same scaffold. Jemal Pasha united all classes, conditions and creeds in Syria, under pressure of a common misery and peril, and so made a concerted revolt possible.

The Turks suspected the Arab officers and soldiers in the Army, and hoped to use against them the scattering tactics which had served against the Armenians. At first transport difficulties stood in their way; and there came a dangerous concentration of Arab divisions (nearly one third of the original Turkish Army was Arabic speaking) in North

Syria early in 1915. They broke these up when possible, marching them off to Europe, to the Dardanelles, to the Caucasus, or the Canal — anywhere, so long as they were put quickly into the firing-line, or withdrawn far from the sight and help of their compatriots. A Holy War was proclaimed to give the 'Union and Progress' banner something of the traditional sanctity of the Caliph's battle-order in the eyes of the old clerical elements; and the Sherif of Mecca was invited — or rather ordered — to echo the cry.

CHAPTER V

THE position of the Sherif of Mecca had long been anomalous. The title of 'Sherif' implied descent from the prophet Mohammed through his daughter Fatima, and Hassan, her elder son. Authentic Sherifs were inscribed on the family tree — an immense roll preserved at Mecca, in custody of the Emir of Mecca, the elected Sherif of Sherifs, supposed to be the senior and noblest of all. The prophet's family had held temporal rule in Mecca for the last nine hundred years, and counted some two thousand persons.

The old Ottoman Governments regarded this clan of manticratic peers with a mixture of reverence and distrust. Since they were too strong to be destroyed, the Sultan salved his dignity by solemnly confirming their Emir in place. This empty approval acquired dignity by lapse of time, until the new holder began to feel that it added a final seal to his election. At last the Turks found that they needed the Hejaz under their unquestioned sway as part of the stage furniture for their new pan-Islamic notion. The fortuitous opening of the Suez Canal enabled them to garrison the Holy Cities. They projected the Hejaz Railway, and increased Turkish influence among the tribes by money, intrigue, and armed expeditions.

As the Sultan grew stronger there he ventured to assert himself more and more alongside the Sherif, even in Mecca itself, and upon occasion ventured to depose a Sherif too magnificent for his views, and to appoint a successor from a rival family of the clan in hopes of winning the usual advantages from dissension. Finally, Abdul Hamid took away some of the family to Constantinople into honourable captivity. Amongst these was Hussein ibn Ali, the future ruler, who was held a prisoner for nearly eighteen years. He took the opportunity to provide his sons — Ali, Abdulla, Feisal, and Zeid — with the modern education and experience which afterwards enabled them to lead the Arab armies to success.

When Abdul Hamid fell, the less wily Young Turks reversed his policy and sent back Sherif Hussein to Mecca as Emir. He at once set to

work unobtrusively to restore the power of the Emirate, and strengthened himself on the old basis, keeping the while close and friendly touch
with Constantinople through his sons, Abdulla, vice-chairman of the
Turkish House, and Feisal, member for Jidda. They kept him informed
of political opinion in the capital until war broke out, when they
returned in haste to Mecca.

The outbreak of war made trouble in the Hejaz. The pilgrimage
ceased, and with it the revenues and business of the Holy Cities. There
was reason to fear that the Indian food-ships would cease to come (since
the Sherif became technically an enemy subject); and as the province
produced almost no food of its own, it would be precariously dependent
on the goodwill of the Turks, who might starve it by closing the Hejaz
Railway. Hussein had never been entirely at the Turks' mercy before;
and at this unhappy moment they particularly needed his adherence to
their 'Jehad', the Holy War of all Moslems against Christianity.

To become popularly effective this must be endorsed by Mecca; and
if endorsed it might plunge the East in blood. Hussein was honourable,
shrewd, obstinate and deeply pious. He felt that the Holy War was
doctrinally incompatible with an aggressive war, and absurd with a
Christian ally: Germany. So he refused the Turkish demand, and made
at the same time a dignified appeal to the Allies not to starve his province for what was in no way his people's fault. The Turks in reply at
once instituted a partial blockade of the Hejaz by controlling the traffic
on the pilgrim railway. The British left his coast open to specially-
regulated food vessels.

The Turkish demand was, however, not the only one which the
Sherif received. In January 1915, Yisin, head of the Mesopotamian
officers, Ali Riza, head of the Damascus officers, and Abd el Ghani el
Areisi, for the Syrian civilians, sent down to him a concrete proposal for a military mutiny in Syria against the Turks. The oppressed
people of Mesopotamia and Syria, the committees of the Ahad and the
Fetah, were calling out to him as the Father of the Arabs, the Moslem of
Moslems, their greatest prince, their oldest notable, to save them from
the sinister designs of Talaat and Jemal.

Hussein, as politician, as prince, as Moslem, as modernist, and as
nationalist, was forced to listen to their appeal. He sent Feysul, his third

son, to Damascus, to discuss their projects as his representative, and
to make a report. He sent Ali, his eldest son, to Medina, with orders to
raise quietly, on any excuse he pleased, troops from villagers and tribesmen of the Hejaz, and to hold them ready for action if Feisal called.
Abdulla, his politic second son, was to sound the British by letter,
to learn what would be their attitude towards a possible Arab revolt
against Turkey.

Feisal reported in January 1915, that local conditions were good, but
that the general war was not going well for their hopes. In Damascus
were three divisions of Arab troops ready for rebellion. In Aleppo two
other divisions, riddled with Arab nationalism, were sure to join in if
the others began. There was only one Turkish division this side of the
Taurus, so that it was certain that the rebels would get possession of
Syria at the first effort. On the other hand, public opinion was less
ready for extreme measures, and the military class quite sure that
Germany would win the war and win it soon. If, however, the Allies
landed their Australian Expedition (preparing in Egypt) at Alexandretta,
and so covered the Syrian flank, then it would be wise and safe to risk
a final German victory and the need to make a previous separate peace
with the Turks.

Delay followed, as the Allies went to the Dardanelles, and not to
Alexandretta. Feisal went after them to get first-hand knowledge of
Gallipoli conditons, since a breakdown of Turkey would be the Arab
signal. Then followed stagnation through the months of the Dardanelles campaign. In that slaughter-house the remaining Ottoman first-
line army was destroyed. The disaster to Turkey of the accumulated
losses was so great that Feisal came back to Syria, judging it a possible
moment in which to strike, but found that meanwhile the local situation had become unfavourable.

His Syrian supporters were under arrest or in hiding, and their
friends being hanged in scores on political charges. He found the well-
disposed Arab divisions either exiled to distant fronts, or broken up in
drafts and distributed among Turkish units. The Arab peasantry were
in the grip of Turkish military service, and Syria prostrate before the
merciless Jemal Pasha. His assets had disappeared.

He wrote to his father counselling further delay, till England should be ready and Turkey in extremities. Unfortunately, England was in a deplorable condition. Her forces were falling back shattered from the Dardanelles. The slow-drawn agony of Kut was in its last stage; and the Senussi rising, coincident with the entry of Bulgaria, threatened her on new flanks.

Feysul's position was hazardous in the extreme. He was at the mercy of the members of the secret society, whose president he had been before the war. He had to live as the guest of Jemal Pasha, in Damascus, rubbing up his military knowledge; for his brother Ali was raising the troops in Hejaz on the pretext that he and Feisal would lead them against the Suez Canal to help the Turks. So Feisal, as a good Ottoman and officer in the Turkish service, had to live at headquarters, and endure acquiescingly the insults and indignities heaped upon his race by the bully Jemal in his cups.

Jemal would send for Feisal and take him to the hanging of his Syrian friends. These victims of justice dared not show that they knew Feisal's real hopes, any more than he dared show his mind by word or look, since disclosure would have condemned his family and perhaps their race to the same fate. Only once did he burst out that these executions would cost Jemal all that he was trying to avoid; and it took the intercessions of his Constantinople friends, chief men in Turkey, to save him from the price of these rash words.

Feisal's correspondence with his father was an adventure in itself. They communicated by means of old retainers of the family, men above suspicion, who went up and down the Hejaz Railway, carrying letters in sword-hilts, in cakes, sewn between the soles of sandals, or in invisible writings on the wrappers of harmless packages. In all of them Feisal reported unfavourable things, and begged his father to postpone action till a wiser time.

Hussein, however, was not a whit cast down by Emir Feisal's discouragements. The Young Turks in his eyes were so many godless transgressors of their creed and their human duty — traitors to the spirit of the time, and to the highest interests of Islam. Though an old man of sixty-five, he was cheerfully determined to wage war against them, relying upon justice to cover the cost. Hussein trusted so much in God that he let his military sense lie fallow, and thought Hejaz able to fight it out with Turkey on a fair field. So he sent Abd el Kader el Abdu to Feisal with a letter that all was now ready for inspection by him in Medina before the troops started for the front. Feisal informed Jemal, and asked leave to go down, but, to his dismay, Jemal replied that Enver Pasha, the Generalissimo, was on his way to the province, and that they would visit Medina together and inspect them. Feisal had planned to raise his father's crimson banner as soon as he arrived in Medina, and so to take the Turks unawares; and here he was going to be saddled with two uninvited guests to whom, by the Arab law of hospitality, he could do no harm, and who would probably delay his action so long that the whole secret of the revolt would be in jeopardy!

In the end matters passed off well, though the irony of the review was terrible. Enver, Jemal and Feisal watched the troops wheeling and turning in the dusty plain outside the city gate, rushing up and down in mimic camel-battle, or spurring their horses in the javelin game after immemorial Arab fashion. 'And are all these volunteers for the Holy War?' asked Enver at last, turning to Feisal. 'Yes,' said Feisal. 'Willing to fight to the death against the enemies of the faithful?' 'Yes,' said Feisal again; and then the Arab chiefs came up to be presented, and Sherif Ali ibn el Hussein, of Modhig, drew him aside whispering, 'My Lord, shall we kill them now?' and Feisal said, 'No, they are our guests.'

The Sheikhs protested further; for they believed that so they could finish off the war in two blows. They were determined to force Feisal's hand; and he had to go among them, just out of earshot but in full view, and plead for the lives of the Turkish dictators, who had murdered his best friends on the scaffold. In the end he had to make excuses, take the party back quickly to Medina, picket the banqueting hall with his own slaves, and escort Enver and Jemal back to Damascus to save them from death on the way. He explained this laboured courtesy by the plea that it was the Arab manner to devote everything to guests; but Enver and Jemal, being deeply suspicious of what they had seen, imposed a strict blockade of the Hejaz, and ordered large Turkish reinforcements thither. They wanted to detain Feisal in Damascus; but telegrams came from Medina claiming his immediate return to prevent disorder, and, reluctantly, Jemal let him go on condition that his suite remained behind as hostages.

Feisal found Medina full of Turkish troops, with the staff and head-quarters of the Twelfth Army Corps under Fakhri Pasha, the courage-ous old butcher who had bloodily 'purified' Zeitun and Urfa of Armenians. Clearly the Turks had taken warning, and Feisal's hope of a surprise rush, winning success almost without a shot, had become impossible. However, it was too late for prudence. From Damascus four days later his suite took horse and rode out east into the desert to take refuge with Nuri Shaalan, the Beduin chieftain; and the same day Feisal showed his hand. When he raised the Arab flag, the pan-Islamic supra-national State, for which Abdul Hamid had massacred and worked and died, and the German hope of the co-operation of Islam in the world-plans of the Kaiser, passed into the realm of dreams. By the mere fact of his rebellion the Sherif had closed these two fantastic chapters of history.

Rebellion was the gravest step which political men could take, and the success or failure of the Arab revolt was a gamble too hazardous for prophecy. Yet, for once, fortune favoured the bold player, and the Arab epic tossed up its stormy road from birth through weakness, pain and doubt, to red victory. It was the just end to an adventure which had dared so much, but after the victory there came a slow time of disillusion, and then a night in which the fighting men found that all their hopes had failed them. Now, at last, may there have come to them the white peace of the end, in the knowledge that they achieved a deathless thing, a lucent inspiration to the children of their race.

CHAPTER VI

I HAD been many years going up and down the Semitic East before the war, learning the manners of the villagers and tribesmen and citizens of Syria and Mesopotamia. My poverty had constrained me to mix with the humbler classes, those seldom met by European travellers, and thus my experiences gave me an unusual angle of view, which enabled me to understand and think for the ignorant many as well as for the more enlightened whose rare opinions mattered, not so much for the day, as for the morrow. In addition, I had seen something of the political forces working in the minds of the Middle East, and especially had noted everywhere sure signs of the decay of imperial Turkey.

Turkey was dying of overstrain, of the attempt, with diminished resources, to hold, on traditional terms, the whole Empire bequeathed to it. The sword had been the virtue of the children of Othman, and swords had passed out of fashion nowadays, in favour of deadlier and more scientific weapons. Life was growing too complicated for this child-like people, whose strength had lain in simplicity, and patience, and in their capacity for sacrifice. They were the slowest of the races of Western Asia, little fitted to adapt themselves to new sciences of government and life, still less to invent any new arts for themselves. Their administration had become perforce an affair of files and tele-grams, of high finance, eugenics, calculations. Inevitably the old governors, who had governed by force of hand or force of character, illiterate, direct, personal, had to pass away. The rule was transferred to new men, with agility and suppleness to stoop to machinery. The shallow and half-polished committee of the Young Turks were descendants of Greeks, Albanians, Circassians, Bulgars, Armenians, Jews — anything but Seljuks or Ottomans. The commons ceased to feel in tune with their governors, whose culture was Levantine, and whose political theory was French. Turkey was decaying; and only the knife might keep health in her.

Loving the old ways steadily, the Anatolian remained a beast of burden in his village and an uncomplaining soldier abroad, while the subject races of the Empire, who formed nearly seven-tenths of its total population, grew daily in strength and knowledge; for their lack of tradition and responsibility, as well as their lighter and quicker minds, disposed them to accept new ideas. The former natural awe and supremacy of the Turkish name began to fade in the face of wider comparison. This changing balance of Turkey and the subject provinces involved growing garrisons if the old ground was to be retained. Tripoli, Albania, Thrace, Yemen, Hejaz, Syria, Mesopotamia, Kurdistan, Armenia, were all outgoing accounts, burdens on the peasants of Anatolia, yearly devouring a larger draft. The burden fell heaviest on the poor villages, and each year made these poor villages yet more poor.

The conscripts took their fate unquestioning: resignedly, after the custom of Turkish peasantry. They were like sheep, neutrals without vice or virtue. Left alone, they did nothing, or perhaps sat dully on the ground. Ordered to be kind, and without haste they were as good friends and as generous enemies as might be found. Ordered to outrage their fathers or disembowel their mothers, they did it as calmly as they did nothing, or did well. There was about them a hopeless, fever-wasted lack of initiative, which made them the most biddable, most enduring, and least spirited soldiers in the world.

Such men were natural victims of their showy-vicious Levantine officers, to be driven to death or thrown away by neglect without reckoning. Indeed, we found them just kept chopping-blocks of their commanders' viler passions. So cheap did they rate them, that in connection with them they used none of the ordinary precautions. Medical examination of some batches of Turkish prisoners found nearly half of them with unnaturally acquired venereal disease. Pox and its like were not understood in the country; and the infection ran from one to another through the battalion, where the conscripts served for six or seven years, till at the end of their period the survivors, if they came from decent homes, were ashamed to return, and drifted either into the gendarmerie service, or, as broken men, into casual labour about the towns; and so the birth-rate fell. The Turkish peasantry in Anatolia were dying of their military service.

We could see that a new factor was needed in the East, some power or race which would outweigh the Turks in numbers, in output, and in mental activity. No encouragement was given us by history to think that these qualities could be supplied ready-made from Europe. The efforts of European Powers to keep a footing in the Asiatic Levant had been uniformly disastrous, and we disliked no Western people enough to inveigle them into further attempts. Our successor and solution must be local; and fortunately the standard of efficiency required was local also. The competition would be with Turkey; and Turkey was rotten.

Some of us judged that there was latent power enough and to spare in the Arabic peoples (the greatest component of the old Turkish Empire), a prolific Semitic agglomeration, great in religious thought, reasonably industrious, mercantile, politic, yet solvent rather than dominant in character. They had served a term of five hundred years under the Turkish harrow, and had begun to dream of liberty; so when at last England fell out with Turkey, and war was let loose in the East and West at once, we who believed we held an indication of the future set out to bend England's efforts towards fostering the new Arabic world in hither Asia.

We were not many; and nearly all of us rallied round Clayton, the chief of Intelligence, civil and military, in Egypt. Clayton made the perfect leader for such a band of wild men as we were. He was calm, detached, clear-sighted, of unconscious courage in assuming responsibility. He gave an open run to his subordinates. His own views were general, like his knowledge; and he worked by influence rather than by loud direction. It was not easy to descry his influence. He was like water, or permeating oil, creeping silently and insistently through everything. It was not possible to say where Clayton was and was not, and how much really belonged to him. He never visibly led; but his ideas were abreast of those who did: he impressed men by his sobriety, and by a certain quiet and stately moderation of hope. In practical matters he was loose, irregular, untidy, a man with whom independent men could bear.

The first of us was Ronald Storrs, Oriental Secretary of the Residency, the most brilliant Englishman in the Near East, and subtly efficient, despite his diversion of energy in love of music and letters, of sculpture, painting, of whatever was beautiful in the world's fruit. None the less, Storrs sowed what we reaped, and was always first, and the great man among us. His shadow would have covered our work and British policy in the East like a cloak, had he been able to deny himself the world, and to prepare his mind and body with the sternness of an athlete for a great fight.

George Lloyd entered our number. He gave confidence, and with his knowledge of money, proved a sure guide through the subways of trade and politics, and a prophet upon the future arteries of the Middle East. We would not have done so much so soon without his partnership; but he was a restless soul, avid rather to taste than to exhaust. To him many things were needful; and so he would not stay very long with us. He did not see how much we liked him.

Then there was the imaginative advocate of unconvincing world-movements, Mark Sykes: also a bundle of prejudices, intuitions, half-sciences. His ideas were of the outside; and he lacked patience to test his materials before choosing his style of building. He would take an aspect of the truth, detach it from its circumstances, inflate it, twist and model it, until its old likeness and its new unlikeness together drew a laugh; and laughs were his triumphs. His instincts lay in parody: by choice he was a caricaturist rather than an artist, even in statesmanship. He saw the odd in everything, and missed the even. He would sketch out in a few dashes a new world, all out of scale, but vivid as a vision of some sides of the thing we hoped. His help did us good and harm. For this his last week in Paris tried to atone. He had returned from a period of political duty in Syria, after his awful realization of the true shape of his dreams, to say gallantly, 'I was wrong: here is the truth'. His former friends would not see his new earnestness, and thought him fickle and in error; and very soon he died. It was a tragedy of tragedies, for the Arab sake.

Not a wild man, but *Mentor* to all of us was Hogarth, our father confessor and adviser, who brought us the parallels and lessons of history, and moderation, and courage. To the outsiders he was peacemaker (I was all claws and teeth, and had a devil), and made us favoured and listened to, for his weighty judgement. He had a delicate sense of value, and would present clearly to us the forces hidden behind the lousy rags and festering skins which we knew as Arabs. Hogarth was our referee, and our untiring historian, who gave us his great knowledge and careful wisdom even in the smallest things, because he believed in what we were making. Behind him stood Cornwallis, a man rude to look upon, but apparently forged from one of those incredible metals with a melting-point of thousands of degrees. So he could remain for months hotter than other men's white-heat, and yet look cold and hard. Behind him again were others, Newcombe, Parker, Herbert, Graves, all of the creed, and labouring stoutly after their fashion.

We called ourselves 'Intrusive' as a band; for we meant to break into the accepted halls of English foreign policy, and build a new people in the East, despite the rails laid down for us by our ancestors. Therefore from our hybrid intelligence office in Cairo (a jangling place which for its incessant bells and bustle and running to and fro, was likened by Aubrey Herbert to an oriental railway station) we began to work upon all chiefs, far and near. Sir Henry McMahon, High Commissioner in Egypt, was, of course, our first effort; and his shrewd insight and tried, experienced mind understood our design at once and judged it good. Others, like Wemyss, Neil Malcolm, Wingate, supported us in their pleasure at seeing the war turned constructive. Their advocacy confirmed in Lord Kitchener the favourable impression he had derived years before when Sherif Abdulla appealed to him in Egypt; and so McMahon at last achieved our foundation stone, the understanding with the Sherif of Mecca.

But before this we had had hopes of Mesopotamia. The beginning of the Arab Independence Movement had been there, under the vigorous but unscrupulous impulse of Seyid Taleb, and later of Yasin el Hashimi and the military league. Aziz el Masri, Enver's rival, who was living, much indebted to us, in Egypt, was an idol of the Arab officers. He was approached by Lord Kitchener in the first days of the war, with the hope of winning the Turkish Mesopotamian forces to our side. Unfortunately Britain was bursting then with confidence in an easy and early victory: the smashing of Turkey was called a promenade. So the Indian Government was adverse to any pledges to the Arab nationalists which

might limit their ambitions to make the intended Mesopotamian
colony play the self-sacrificing role of a Burma for the general good.
It broke off negotiations, rejected Aziz, and interned Sayid Taleb, who
had placed himself in our hands.

By brute force it marched then into Basra. The enemy troops in
Irak were nearly all Arabs in the unenviable predicament of having to
fight on behalf of their secular oppressors against a people long en-
visaged as liberators, but who obstinately refused to play the part. As
may be imagined, they fought very badly. Our forces won battle after
battle till we came to think an Indian army better than a Turkish army.
There followed our rash advance to Ctesiphon, where we met native
Turkish troops whose full heart was in the game, and were abruptly
checked. We fell back, dazed; and the long misery of Kut began.

Meanwhile, our Government had repented, and, for reasons not un-
connected with the fall of Erzerum, sent me to Mesopotamia to see
what could be done by indirect means to relieve the beleaguered garrison. The local British had the strongest objection to my coming; and
two Generals of them were good enough to explain to me that my
mission (which they did not really know) was dishonourable to a soldier
(which I was not). As a matter of fact it was too late for action, with
Kut just dying; and in consequence I did nothing of what it was in my
mind and power to do.

The conditions were ideal for an Arab movement. The people of
Nejef and Kerbela, far in the rear of Halil Pasha's army, were in revolt
against him. The surviving Arabs in Halil's army were, on his own confession, openly disloyal to Turkey. The tribes of the Hai and Euphrates
would have turned our way had they seen signs of grace in the British.
Had we published the promises made to the Sherif, or even the proclamation afterwards posted in captured Bagdad, and followed it up,
enough local fighting men would have joined us to harry the Turkish
line of communication between Bagdad and Kut. A few weeks of that,
and the enemy would either have been forced to raise the siege and
retire, or have themselves suffered investment, outside Kut, nearly as
stringent as the investment of Townshend within it. Time to develop
such a scheme could easily have been gained. Had the British headquarters in Mesopotamia obtained from the War Office eight more

aeroplanes to increase the daily carriage of food to the garrison of Kut, Townshend's resistance might have been indefinitely prolonged. His defence was Turkishly impregnable; and only blunders within and without forced surrender upon him.

However, as this was not the way of the directing parties there, I returned at once to Egypt; and till the end of the war the British in Mesopotamia remained substantially an alien force invading enemy territory, with the local people passively neutral or sullenly against them, and in consequence had not the freedom of movement and elasticity of Allenby in Syria, who entered the country as a friend, with the local people actively on his side. The factors of numbers, climate and communications favoured us in Mesopotamia more than in Syria; and our higher command was, after the beginning, no less efficient and experienced. But their casualty lists compared with Allenby's, their wood-chopping tactics compared with his rapier-play, showed how formidably an adverse political situation was able to cramp a purely military operation.

CHAPTER VII

OUR check in Mesopotamia was a disappointment to us; but McMahon continued his negotiations with Mecca, and finally brought them to success despite the evacuation of Gallipoli, the surrender of Kut, and the generally unfortunate aspect of the war at the moment. Few people, even of those who knew all the negotiations, had really believed that the Sherif would fight; consequently his eventual rebellion and opening of his coast to our ships and help took us and them by surprise.

We found our difficulties then only beginning. The credit of the new factor was to McMahon and Clayton: professional jealousies immediately raised their heads. Sir Archibald Murray, the General in Egypt, wanted, naturally enough, no competitors, and no competing campaigns in his sphere. He disliked the civil power, which had so long kept the peace between himself and General Maxwell. He could not be entrusted with the Arabian affair; for neither he nor his staff had the ethnological competence needed to deal with so curious a problem. On the other hand, he could make the spectacle of the High Commission running a private war sufficiently ridiculous. His was a very nervous mind, fanciful and essentially competitive. When confronted with what he considered a rival show, he bent his very considerable powers to crab it.

He found help in his Chief of Staff, General Lynden Bell, a red soldier, with an instinctive shuddering away from politicians, and a conscientiously assumed heartiness. His military conception of the loyalties of his office involved him in a chameleon-like attempt to imitate the frailties as well as the virtues of his chief.

Two of the General Staff officers followed their leaders full cry; and so the unfortunate McMahon found himself deprived of Army help and reduced to waging his war in Arabia with the assistance of his Foreign Office Attachés. Even these proved not all quite loyal to him.

Some appeared to resent a war which allowed outsiders to thrust into their business. Also their training in

suppression, by which alone the daily trivialities of diplomacy were made
to look like man's work, had so sunk into them that when the more
important thing arrived, they made it trivial. Their feebleness of tone,
and niggling dishonesties to one another, angered the military to disgust;
and were bad for us, too, since they patently let down the High Commissioner, whose boots the G——s were not good enough to clean.

Wingate, who had complete confidence in his own grasp of the
situation in the Middle East, foresaw credit and great profit for the
country in the Arab development; but as criticism slowly beat up
against McMahon he dissociated himself from him, and London began
to hint that better use might be made by an experienced hand of so
subtle and involved a skein.

However it was, things in the Hejaz went from bad to worse. No
proper liaison was provided for the Arab forces in the field, no military
information was given the Sherifs, no tactical advice or strategy was
suggested, no attempt made to find out the local conditions and adapt
existing Allied resources in material to suit their needs. The French
Military Mission (which Clayton's prudence had suggested be sent to
Hejaz to soothe our very suspicious allies by taking them behind the
scenes and giving them a purpose there), was permitted to carry on an
elaborate intrigue against Sherif Hussein in his towns of Jidda and
Mecca, and to propose to him and to the British authorities measures that
must have ruined his cause in the eyes of all Moslems. Wingate now in
military control of our co-operation with the Sherif, was induced to
land some foreign troops at Rabegh, half-way between Medina and
Mecca, for the defence of Mecca and to hold up the further advance of
the reinvigorated Turks from Medina. McMahon, in the multitude of
counsellors, became confused, and gave a handle to Murray to cry out
against his inconsistencies. The Arab Revolt became discredited; and
Staff Officers in Egypt gleefully prophesied to us its near failure and the
stretching of Sherif Hussein's neck on a Turkish scaffold.

My private position was not easy. As Staff Captain under Clayton
in Sir Archibald Murray's Intelligence Section, I was charged with the
'distribution' of the Turkish Army and the preparation of maps. By
natural inclination I had added to them the invention of the Arab
Bulletin, a secret weekly record of Middle-Eastern politics; and of
necessity Clayton came more and more to need me in the military wing

of the Arab Bureau, the tiny intelligence and war staff for foreign affairs, which he was now organizing for McMahon. Eventually Clayton was driven out of the General Staff; and Colonel Holdich, Murray's intelligence officer at Ismailia, took his place in command of us. His first intention was to retain my services; and since he clearly did not need me, I interpreted this, not without some friendly evidence, as a method of keeping me away from the Arab affair. I decided that I must escape at once, if ever. A straight request was refused; so I took to stratagems. I became, on the telephone (G.H.Q. were at Ismailia, and I in Cairo) quite intolerable to the Staff on the Canal. I took every opportunity to rub into them their comparative ignorance and inefficiency in the department of intelligence (not difficult!) and irritated them yet further by literary airs, correcting Shavian split infinitives and tautologies in their reports.

In a few days they were bubbling over on my account, and at last determined to endure me no longer. I took this strategic opportunity to ask for ten days' leave, saying that Storrs was going down to Jidda on business with the Grand Sherif, and that I would like a holiday and joy-ride in the Red Sea with him. They did not love Storrs, and were glad to get rid of me for the moment. So they agreed at once, and began to prepare against my return some official shelf for me. Needless to say, I had no intention of giving them such a chance; for, while very ready to hire my body out on petty service, I hesitated to throw my mind frivolously away. So I went to Clayton and confessed my affairs; and he arranged for the Residency to make telegraphic application to the Foreign Office for my transfer to the Arab Bureau. The Foreign Office would treat directly with the War Office; and the Egypt command would not hear of it, till all was ended.

Storrs and I then marched off together, happily. In the East they swore that by three sides was the decent way across a square; and my trick to escape was in this sense oriental. But I justified myself by my confidence in the final success of the Arab Revolt if properly advised. I had been a mover in its beginning: my hopes lay in it. The fatalistic subordination of a professional soldier (intrigue being unknown in the British army) would have made a proper officer sit down and watch his plan of campaign wrecked by men who thought nothing of it, and to whose spirit it made no appeal. *Non nobis, Domine.*

BOOK I

THE DISCOVERY OF FEISAL

Chapters VIII to XVI

I HAD *believed these misfortunes of the Revolt to be due mainly to faulty leadership, or rather to the lack of leadership, Arab and English. So I went down to Arabia to see and consider its great men. The first, the Sherif of Mecca, we knew to be aged. I found Abdulla too clever, Ali too clean, Zeid too cool.*

Then I rode up-country to Feisal, and found in him the leader with the necessary fire, and yet with reason to give effect to our science. His tribesmen seemed sufficient instrument, and his hills to provide natural advantage. So I returned pleased and confident to Egypt, and told my chiefs how Mecca was defended not by the obstacle of Rabegh, but by the flank-threat of Feisal in Jebel Subh.

CHAPTER VIII

Waiting off Suez was the *Lama*, a small converted liner; and in her we left immediately. Such short voyages on warships were delicious interludes for us passengers. On this occasion, however, there was some embarrassment. Our mixed party seemed to disturb the ship's company in their own element. The juniors had turned out of their berths to give us night space, and by day we filled their living rooms with irregular talk. Storrs' intolerant brain seldom stooped to company. But to-day he was more abrupt than usual. He turned twice around the decks, sniffed, 'No one worth talking to', and sat down in one of the two comfortable armchairs, to begin a discussion of Debussy with Aziz el Masri (in the other). Aziz, the Arab-Circassian ex-colonel in the Turkish Army, now general in the Sherifian Army, was on his way to discuss with the Emir of Mecca the equipment and standing of the Arab regulars he was forming at Rabegh. A few minutes later they had left Debussy, and were depreciating Wagner: Aziz in fluent German, and Storrs in German, French and Arabic. The ship's officers found the whole conversation unnecessary.

We had the accustomed calm run to Jidda, in the delightful Red Sea climate, never too hot while the ship was moving. By day we lay in shadow; and for great part of the glorious nights we would tramp up and down the wet decks under the stars in the steaming breath of the southern wind. But when at last we anchored in the outer harbour, off the white town hung between the blazing sky and its reflection in the mirage which swept and rolled over the wide lagoon, then the heat of Arabia came out like a drawn sword and struck us speechless. It was mid-day; and the noon sun in the East, like moonlight, put to sleep the colours. There were only lights and shadows, the white houses and black gaps of streets: in front, the pallid lustre of the haze shimmering upon the inner harbour: behind, the dazzle of league after league of featureless sand, running up to an edge of low hills, faintly suggested in the far away mist of heat.

Just north of Jidda was a second group of black-white buildings, moving up and down like pistons in the mirage, as the ship rolled at anchor and the intermittent wind shifted the heat waves in the air. It looked and felt horrible. We began to regret that the inaccessibility which made the Hejaz militarily a safe theatre of revolt involved bad climate and unwholesomeness.

However, Colonel Wilson, British representative with the new Arab state, had sent his launch to meet us; and we had to go ashore to learn the reality of the men levitating in that mirage. Half an hour later Ruhi, Consular Oriental assistant, was grinning a delighted welcome to his old patron Storrs, (Ruhi the ingenious, more like a mandrake than a man), while the newly-appointed Syrian police and harbour officers, with a scratch guard of honour, lined the Customs Wharf in salutation of Aziz el Masri. Sherif Abdulla, the second son of the old man of Mecca, was reported just arriving in the town. He it was we had to meet; so our coming was auspiciously timed.

We walked past the white masonry of the still-building water gate, and through the oppressive alley of the food market on our way to the Consulate. In the air, from the men to the dates and back to the meat, squadrons of flies like particles of dust danced up and down the sun-shafts which stabbed into the darkest corners of the booths through torn places in the wood and sackcloth awnings overhead. The atmosphere was like a bath. The scarlet leathers of the armchair on the *Lama's* deck had dyed Storrs' white tunic and trousers as bright as themselves in their damp contact of the last four days, and now the sweat running in his clothes began to shine like varnish through the stain. I was so fascinated watching him that I never noticed the deepened brown of my khaki drill wherever it touched my body. He was wondering if the walk to the Consulate was long enough to wet me a decent, solid, harmonious colour; and I was wondering if all he ever sat on would grow scarlet as himself.

We reached the Consulate too soon for either hope; and there in a shaded room with an open lattice behind him sat Wilson, prepared to welcome the sea breeze, which had lagged these last few days. He received us stiffly, being of the honest, downright Englishmen, to whom Storrs was suspect, if only for his artistic sense: while his contact with me in Cairo had been a short difference of opinion as to whether native clothes were an indignity for us. I had called them uncomfortable merely. To him they were wrong. Wilson, however, despite his personal feelings, was all for the game. He had made preparations for the coming interview with Abdulla, and was ready to afford every help he could. Besides, we were his guests; and the splendid hospitality of the East was near his spirit.

Abdulla, on a white mare, came to us softly with a bevy of richly-armed slaves on foot about him, through the silent respectful salutes of the town. He was flushed with his success at Taif, and happy. I was seeing him for the first time, while Storrs was an old friend, and on the best of terms; yet, before long, as they spoke together, I began to suspect him of a constant cheerfulness. His eyes had a confirmed twinkle; and though only thirty-five, he was putting on flesh. It might be due to too much laughter. Life seemed very merry for Abdulla. He was short, strong, fair-skinned, with a carefully trimmed brown beard, masking his round smooth face and short lips. In manner he was open, or affected openness, and was charming on acquaintance. He stood not on ceremony, but jested with all comers in most easy fashion: yet, when we fell into serious talk, the veil of humour seemed to fade away. He then chose his words, and argued shrewdly. Of course, he was in discussion with Storrs, who demanded a high standard from his opponent.

The Arabs thought Abdulla a far-seeing statesman and an astute politician. Astute he certainly was, but not greatly enough to convince us always of his sincerity. His ambition was patent. Rumour made him the brain of his father and of the Arab revolt; but he seemed too easy for that. His object was, of course, the winning of Arab independence and the building up of Arab nations, but he meant to keep the direction of the new states in the family. So he watched us, and played through us to the British gallery.

On our part, I was playing for effect, watching, criticizing him. The Sherif's rebellion had been unsatisfactory for the last few months: (standing still, which, with an irregular war, was the prelude to disaster): and my suspicion was that its lack was leadership: not intellect, nor judgement, nor political wisdom, but the flame of enthusiasm, that would set the desert on fire. My visit was mainly to find the yet unknown master-spirit of the affair, and measure his capacity to carry the revolt to the goal I had conceived for it. As our conversation continued, I became more and more sure that Abdulla was too balanced, too cool, too humorous to be a prophet: especially the armed prophet who, if history be true, succeeded in revolutions. His value would come perhaps in the peace after success. During the physical struggle, when singleness of eye and magnetism, devotion and self-sacrifice were needed, Abdulla would be a tool too complex for a simple purpose, though he could not be ignored, even now.

We talked to him first about the state of Jidda, to put him at ease by discussing at this first of our interviews the unnecessary subject of the Sherif's administration. He replied that the war was yet too much with them for civil government. They had inherited the Turkish system in the towns, and were continuing it on a more modest scale. The Turkish Government was often not unkind to strong men, who obtained considerable licence on terms. Consequently, some of the licensees in Hejaz regretted the coming of a native ruler. Particularly in Mecca and Jidda public opinion was against an Arab state. The mass of citizens were foreigners — Egyptians, Indians, Javanese, Africans, and others — quite unable to sympathize with the Arab aspirations, especially as voiced by Beduin; for the Beduin lived on what he could exact from the stranger on his roads, or in his valleys; and he and the townsman bore each other a perpetual grudge.

The Beduins were the only fighting men the Sherif had got; and on their help the revolt depended. He was arming them freely, paying many of them for their service in his forces, feeding their families while they were from home, and hiring from them their transport camels to maintain his armies in the field. Accordingly, the country was prosperous, while the towns went short.

Another grievance in the towns was in the matter of law. The Turkish civil code had been abolished, and a return made to the old religious law, the undiluted Koranic procedure of the Arab Kadi. Abdulla explained to us, with a giggle, that when there was time they would discover in the Koran such opinions and judgements as were required to make it suitable for modern commercial operations, like

banking and exchange. Meanwhile, of course, what townsmen lost by
the abolition of the civil law, the Beduins gained. Sherif Hussein had
silently sanctioned the restoration of the old tribal order. Beduins at
odds with one another pleaded their own cases before the tribal lawman, an office hereditary in one most-respected family, and recognized
by the payment of a goat per household as yearly due. Judgement was
based on custom, by quoting from a great body of remembered precedent. It was delivered publicly without fee. In cases between men of
different tribes, the lawman was selected by mutual consent, or recourse
was had to the lawman of a third tribe. If the case were contentious and
difficult, the judge was supported by a jury of four — two nominated
by plaintiff from the ranks of defendant's family, and two by defendant
from plaintiff's family. Decisions were always unanimous.

We contemplated the vision Abdulla drew for us, with sad thoughts
of the Garden of Eden and all that Eve, now lying in her tomb just
outside the wall, had lost for average humanity; and then Storrs
brought me into the discussion by asking Abdulla to give us his views
on the state of the campaign for my benefit, and for communication to
headquarters in Egypt. Abdulla at once grew serious, and said that he
wanted to urge upon the British their immediate and very personal
concern in the matter, which he tabulated so:—

By our neglect to cut the Hejaz Railway, the Turks had been able
to collect transport and supplies for the reinforcement of Medina.

Feisal had been driven back from the town; and the enemy was
preparing a mobile column of all arms for an advance on Rabegh.

The Arabs in the hills across their road were by our neglect too weak
in supplies, machine guns and artillery to defend them long.

Hussein Mabeirig, chief of the Masruh Harb, had joined the Turks.
If the Medina column advanced, the Harb would join it.

It would only remain for his father to put himself at the head of his
own people of Mecca and to die fighting before the Holy City.

At this moment the telephone rang: the Grand Sherif wanted to
speak to Abdulla. He was told of the point our conversation had
reached, and at once confirmed that he would so act in the extremity.
The Turks would enter Mecca over his dead body. The telephone
rang off; and Abdulla, smiling a little, asked, to prevent such a disaster,

that a British brigade, if possible of Moslem troops, be kept at Suez, with transport to rush it to Rabegh as soon as the Turks debouched from Medina in their attack. What did we think of the proposal?

I replied; first, historically, that Sherif Hussein had asked us not to cut the Hejaz line, since he would need it for his victorious advance into Syria; second, practically, that the dynamite we sent down for demolitions had been returned by him with a note that it was too dangerous for Arab use; third, specifically, that we had had no demands for equipment from Feisal.

With regard to the brigade for Rabegh, it was a complicated question. Shipping was precious; and we could not hold empty transport indefinitely at Suez. We had no Moslem units in our Army. A British brigade was a cumbersome affair, and would take long to embark and disembark. The Rabegh position was large. A brigade would hardly hold it and would be quite unable to detach a force to prevent a Turkish column slipping past it inland. The most they could do would be to defend the beach, under a ship's guns and the ship could do that as well without the troops.

Abdulla replied that ships were insufficient morally, as the Dardanelles fighting had destroyed the old legend of the British Navy and its omnipotence. No Turks could slip past Rabegh; for it was the only water supply in the district, and they must water at its wells. The earmarking of a brigade and transports need be only temporary; for he was taking his victorious Taif troops up the eastern road from Mecca to Medina. As soon as he was in position, he would give orders to Ali and Feisal, who would close in from the south and west, and their combined forces would deliver a grand attack in which Medina would, please God, be taken. Meanwhile, Aziz el Masri was moulding the volunteers from Mesopotamia and Syria into battalions at Rabegh. When we had added the Arab prisoners of war from India and Egypt, there would be enough to take over the duties momentarily allotted to the British brigade.

I said that I would represent his views to Egypt, but that the British were reluctant to spare troops from the vital defence of Egypt (though he was not to imagine that the Canal was in any danger from the Turks) and, still more, to send Christians to defend the people of the

Holy City against their enemies; as some Moslems in India, who considered the Turkish Government had an imprescriptible right to the Haramein, would misrepresent our motives and action. I thought that I might perhaps urge his opinions more powerfully if I was able to report on the Rabegh question in the light of my own knowledge of the position and local feeling. I would also like to see Feisal, and talk over with him his needs and the prospects of a prolonged defence of his hills by the tribesmen if we strengthened them materially. I would like to ride from Rabegh up the Sultani road towards Medina as far as Feisal's camp.

Storrs then came in and supported me with all his might, urging the vital importance of full and early information from a trained observer for the British Commander-in-Chief in Egypt, and showing that his sending down me, his best qualified and most indispensable staff officer, proved the serious consideration being given to Arabian affairs by Sir Archibald Murray. Abdulla went to the telephone and tried to get his father's consent to my going up country. The Sherif viewed the proposal with grave distrust. Abdulla argued the point, made some advantage, and transferred the mouthpiece to Storrs, who turned all his diplomacy on the old man. Storrs in full blast was a delight to listen to in the mere matter of Arabic speech, and also a lesson to every Englishman alive of how to deal with suspicious or unwilling Orientals. It was nearly impossible to resist him for more than a few minutes, and in this case also he had his way. The Sherif asked again for Abdulla, and authorized him to write to Ali, and suggest that if he thought fit, and if conditions were normal, I might be allowed to proceed to Feisal in Jebel Subh; and Abdulla, under Storrs' influence, transformed this guarded message into direct written instructions to Ali to mount me as well and as quickly as possible, and convey me, by sure hand, to Feisal's camp. This being all I wanted, and half what Storrs wanted, we adjourned for lunch.

CHAPTER IX

JEDDAH had pleased us, on our way to the Consulate: so after lunch, when it was a little cooler, or at least when the sun was not so high, we wandered out to see the sights under the guidance of Young, Wilson's assistant, a man who found good in many old things, but little good in things now being made.

It was indeed a remarkable town. The streets were alleys, wood roofed in the main bazaar, but elsewhere open to the sky in the little gap between the tops of the lofty white-walled houses. These were built four or five stories high, of coral rag tied with square beams and decorated by wide bow-windows running from ground to roof in grey wooden panels. There was no glass in Jidda, but a profusion of good lattices, and some very delicate shallow chiselling on the panels of window casings. The doors were heavy two-leaved slabs of teak-wood, deeply carved, often with wickets in them; and they had rich hinges and ring-knockers of hammered iron. There was much moulded or cut plastering, and on the older houses fine stone heads and jambs to the windows looking on the inner courts.

The work of architecture was like crazy Elizabethan half-timber work, in the elaborate Cheshire fashion, but gone gimcrack to an incredible degree. House-fronts were fretted, pierced and pargetted till they looked as though cut out of cardboard for a romantic stage-setting. Every storey jutted, every window leaned one way or other; often the very walls sloped. It was like a dead city, so clean underfoot, and so quiet. Its winding, even streets were floored with damp sand solidified by time and as silent to the tread as any carpet. The lattices and wall-returns deadened all reverberation of voice. There were no carts, nor any streets wide enough for carts, no shod animals, no bustle anywhere. Everything was hushed, strained, even furtive. The doors of houses shut softly as we passed. There were no loud dogs, no crying children: indeed, except in the bazaar, still half asleep, there were few wayfarers of any kind; and the rare people we did meet, all thin, and as it were wasted by disease, with scarred, hairless faces and screwed-up eyes, slipped past us quickly and cautiously, not looking at us. Their skimp, white robes, shaven polls with little skull-caps, red cotton shoulder-shawls, and bare feet were so same as to be almost a uniform.

The atmosphere was oppressive, deadly. There seemed no life in it. It was not burning hot, but held a moisture and sense of great age and exhaustion such as seemed to belong to no other place: not a passion of smells like Smyrna, Naples or Marseilles, but a feeling of long use, of the exhalations of many people, of continued bath-heat and sweat. One would say that for years Jidda had not been swept through by a firm breeze: that its streets kept their air from year's end to year's end, from the day they were built for so long as the houses should endure. There was nothing in the bazaars to buy.

In the evening the telephone rang; and the Sherif called Storrs to the instrument. He asked if we would not like to listen to his band. Storrs, in astonishment, asked What band? and congratulated his holiness on having advanced so far towards urbanity. The Sherif explained that the headquarters of the Hejaz Command under the Turks had had a brass band, which played each night to the Governor General; and when the Governor General was captured by Abdulla at Taif his band was captured with him. The other prisoners were sent to Egypt for internment; but the band was excepted. It was held in Mecca to give music to the victors. Sherif Hussein laid his receiver on the table of his reception hall, and we, called solemnly one by one to the telephone, heard the band in the Palace at Mecca forty-five miles away. Storrs expressed the general gratification; and the Sherif, increasing his bounty replied that the band should be sent down by forced march to Jidda, to play in our courtyard also. 'And,' said he, 'you may then do me the pleasure of ringing me up from your end, that I may share your satisfaction.'

Next day Storrs visited Abdulla in his tent out by Eve's Tomb; and together they inspected the hospital, the barracks, the town offices, and partook of the hospitality of the Mayor and the Governor. In the intervals of duty they talked about money, and the Sherif's title, and his relations with the other Princes of Arabia, and the general course of the war: all the commonplaces that should pass between envoys of two Governments. It was tedious, and for the most part I held myself excused, as after a conversation in the morning I had made up my mind that Abdulla was not the necessary leader. We had asked him to sketch the genesis of the Arab movement: and his reply illuminated his character. He had begun by a long description of Talaat, the first Turk to speak to him with concern of the restlessness of Hejaz. He wanted it properly subdued, and military service, as elsewhere in the Empire, introduced.

Abdulla, to forestall him, had made a plan of peaceful insurrection for Hejaz, and, after sounding Kitchener without profit, had dated it provisionally for 1915. He had meant to call out the tribes during the feast, and lay hold of the pilgrims. They would have included many of the chief men of Turkey besides leading Moslems of Egypt, India, Java, Eritrea, and Algiers. With these thousands of hostages in his hands he had expected to win the notice of the Great Powers concerned. He thought they would bring pressure on the Porte to secure the release of their nationals. The Porte, powerless to deal with Hejaz militarily, would either have made concessions to the Sherif or have confessed its powerlessness to the foreign States. In the latter event, Abdulla would have approached them direct, ready to meet their demands in return for a guarantee of immunity from Turkey. I did not like his scheme, and was glad when he said with almost a sneer that Feisal in fear had begged his father not to follow it. This sounded good for Feisal, towards whom my hopes of a great leader were now slowly turning.

In the evening Abdulla came to dine with Colonel Wilson. We received him in the courtyard on the house steps. Behind him were his brilliant household servants and slaves, and behind them a pale crew of bearded, emaciated men with woe-begone faces, wearing tatters of military uniform, and carrying tarnished brass instruments of music. Abdulla waved his hand towards them and crowed with delight, 'My Band'. We sat them on benches in the forecourt, and Wilson sent them cigarettes, while we went up to the dining room, where the shuttered balcony was opened right out, hungrily, for a sea breeze. As we sat down, the band, under the guns and swords of Abdulla's retainers, began, each instrument apart, to play heartbroken Turkish airs. Our ears ached with noise; but Abdulla beamed.

Curious the party was. Abdulla himself, Vice-President *in partibus* of the Turkish Chamber and now Foreign Minister of the rebel Arab State; Wilson, Governor of the Red Sea Province of the Sudan, and His Majesty's Minister with the Sherif of Mecca; Storrs, Oriental Secretary successively to Gorst, Kitchener and McMahon in Cairo; Young, Cochrane, and myself, hangers-on of the staff; Sayed Ali, a general in the Egyptian Army, commander of the detachment sent over by the Sirdar to help the first efforts of the Arabs; Aziz el Masri, now Chief of Staff of the Arab regular army, but in old days Enver's rival, leader of the Turkish and Senussi forces against the Italians, chief conspirator of the Arab officers in the Turkish army against the Committee of Union and Progress, a man condemned to death by the Turks for obeying the Treaty of Lausanne, and saved by *The Times* and Lord Kitchener.

We got tired of Turkish music, and asked for German. Aziz stepped out on the balcony and called down to the bandsmen in Turkish to play us something foreign. They struck shakily into 'Deutschland über Alles' just as the Sherif came to his telephone in Mecca to listen to the music of our feast. We asked for more German music; and they played 'Eine feste Burg'. Then in the midst they died away into flabby discords of drums. The parchment had stretched in the damp air of Jidda. They cried for fire; and Wilson's servants and Abdulla's bodyguard brought them piles of straw and packing cases. They warmed the drums, turning them round and round before the blaze, and then broke into what they said was the Hymn of Hate, though no one could recognize a European progression in it all. Sayed Ali turned to Abdulla and said, 'It is a death march'. Abdulla's eyes widened; but Storrs who spoke in quickly to the rescue turned the moment to laughter; and we sent out rewards with the leavings of the feast to the sorrowful musicians, who could take no pleasure in our praises, but begged to be sent home. Next morning I left Jidda by ship for Rabegh.

CHAPTER X

MOORED in Rabegh lay the *Northbrook*, an Indian Marine ship. On board was Colonel Parker, our liaison officer with Sherif Ali, to whom he sent my letter from Abdulla, giving Ali the father's 'orders' to send me at once up to Feisal. Ali was staggered at their tenor, but could not help himself; for his only telegraph to Mecca was by the ship's wireless, and he was ashamed to send personal remonstrances through us. So he made the best of it, and prepared for me his own splendid riding-camel, saddled with his own saddle, and hung with luxurious housings and cushions of Nejd leatherwork pieced and inlaid in various colours, with plaited fringes and nets embroidered with metal tissues. As a trustworthy man he chose out Tafas el Raashid, a Hawazim Harb tribesman, with his son, to guide me to Feisal's camp.

He did all this with the better grace for the countenance of Nuri Said, the Bagdadi staff officer, whom I had befriended once in Cairo when he was ill. Nuri was now second in command of the regular force which Aziz el Masri was raising and training here. Another friend at court was Faiz el Ghusein, a secretary. He was a Sulut Sheikh from the Hauran, and a former official of the Turkish Government, who had escaped across Armenia during the war, and had eventually reached Miss Gertrude Bell in Basra. She had sent him on to me with a warm recommendation.

To Ali himself I took a great fancy. He was of middle height, thin and looking already more than his thirty-seven years. He stooped a little. His skin was sallow, his eyes large and deep and brown, his nose thin and rather hooked, his mouth sad and drooping. He had a spare black beard and very delicate hands. His manner was dignified and admirable, but direct; and he struck me as a pleasant gentleman, conscientious, without great force of character, nervous, and rather tired. His physical weakness (he was consumptive) made him subject to quick fits of shaking passion, preceded and followed by long moods of infirm obstinacy. He was bookish, learned in law and religion, and

pious almost to fanaticism. He was too conscious of his high heritage
to be ambitious; and his nature was too clean to see or suspect interested
motives in those about him. Consequently he was much the prey of any
constant companion, and too sensitive to advice for a great leader,
though his purity of intention and conduct gained him the love of
those who came into direct contact with him. If Feisal should turn out
to be no prophet, the revolt would make shift well enough with Ali
for its head. I thought him more definitely Arab than Abdulla, or
than Zeid, his young half-brother, who was helping him at Rabegh,
and came down with Ali and Nuri and Aziz to the palm-groves to
see me start. Zeid was a shy, white, beardless lad of perhaps nineteen,
calm and flippant, no zealot for the revolt. Indeed, his mother was
Turkish; and he had been brought up in the harem, so that he could
hardly feel great sympathy with an Arab revival; but he did his best
this day to be pleasant, and surpassed Ali, perhaps because his feelings
were not much outraged at the departure of a Christian into the Holy
Province under the auspices of the Emir of Mecca. Zeid, of course,
was even less than Abdulla the born leader of my quest. Yet I liked
him, and could see that he would be a decided man when he had found
himself.

Ali would not let me start till after sunset, lest any of his followers
see me leave the camp. He kept my journey a secret even from his
slaves, and gave me an Arab cloak and headcloth to wrap round myself
and my uniform, that I might present a proper silhouette in the dark
upon my camel. I had no food with me; so he instructed Tafas to get
something to eat at Bir el Sheikh, the first settlement, some sixty miles
out, and charged him most stringently to keep me from questioning
and curiosity on the way, and to avoid all camps and encounters. The
Masruh Harb, who inhabited Rabegh and district, paid only lip-service
to the Sherif. Their real allegiance was to Hussein Mabeirig, the
ambitious sheikh of the clan, who was jealous of the Emir of Mecca
and had fallen out with him. He was now a fugitive, living in the hills
to the East, and was known to be in touch with the Turks. His people
were not notably pro-Turkish, but owed him obedience. If he had
heard of my departure he might well have ordered a band of them
to stop me on my way through his district.

Tafas was a Hazimi, of the Beni Salem branch of Harb, and so not on good terms with the Masruh. This inclined him towards me; and when he had once accepted the charge of escorting me to Feisal, we could trust him. The fidelity of road-companions was most dear to Arab tribesmen. The guide had to answer to a sentimental public with his life for that of his fellow. One Harbi, who promised to take Huber to Medina and broke his word and killed him on the road near Rabegh, when he found out that he was a Christian, was ostracized by public opinion, and, in spite of the religious prejudices in his favour, had ever since lived miserably alone in the hills, cut off from friendly intercourse, and refused permission to marry any daughter of the tribe. So we could depend upon the good will of Tafas and his son, Abdulla; and Ali endeavoured by detailed instructions to ensure that their performance should be as good as their intention.

We marched through the palm-groves which lay like a girdle about the scattered houses of Rabegh village, and then out under the stars along the Tehama, the sandy and featureless strip of desert bordering the western coast of Arabia between sea-beach and littoral hills, for hundreds of monotonous miles. In day-time this low plain was insufferably hot, and its waterless character made it a forbidding road; yet it was inevitable, since the more fruitful hills were too rugged to afford passage north and south for loaded animals.

The cool of the night was pleasant after the day of checks and discussions which had so dragged at Rabegh. Tafas led on without speaking, and the camels went silently over the soft flat sand. My thoughts as we went were how this was the pilgrim road, down which, for uncounted generations, the people of the north had come to visit the Holy City, bearing with them gifts of faith for the shrine; and it seemed that the Arab revolt might be in a sense a return pilgrimage, to take back to the north, to Syria, an ideal for an ideal, a belief in liberty for their past belief in a revelation.

We endured for some hours, without variety except at times when the camels plunged and strained a little and the saddles creaked: indications that the soft plain had merged into beds of drift-sand, dotted with tiny scrub, and therefore uneven going, since the plants collected little mounds about their roots, and the eddies of the sea-winds scooped hollows in the intervening spaces. Camels appeared not sure-footed in the dark, and the starlit sand carried little shadow, so that hummocks and holes were difficult to see. Before midnight we halted, and I rolled myself tighter in my cloak, and chose a hollow of my own size and shape, and slept well in it till nearly dawn.

As soon as he felt the air growing chill with the coming change, Tafas got up, and two minutes later we were swinging forward again. An hour after it grew bright, as we climbed a low neck of lava drowned nearly to the top with blown sand. This joined a small flow near the shore to the main Hejaz lava-field, whose western edge ran up upon our right hand, and caused the coast road to lie where it did. The neck was stony, but brief: on each side the blue lava humped itself into low shoulders, from which, so Tafas said, it was possible to see ships sailing on the sea. Pilgrims had built cairns here by the road. Sometimes they were individual piles, of just three stones set up one above the other: sometimes they were common heaps, to which any disposed passer-by might add his stone — not reasonably nor with known motive, but because others did, and perhaps they knew.

Beyond the ridge the path descended into a broad open place, the Masturah, or plain by which Wadi Fura flowed into the sea. Seaming its surface with innumerable interwoven channels of loose stone, a few inches deep, were the beds of the flood water, on those rare occasions when there was rain in the Tareif and the courses raged like rivers to the sea. The delta here was about six miles wide. Down some part of it water flowed for an hour or two, or even for a day or two, every so many years. Underground there was plenty of moisture, protected by the overlying sand from the sun-heat; and thorn trees and loose scrub profited by it and flourished. Some of the trunks were a foot through: their height might be twenty feet. The trees and bushes stood some-what apart, in clusters, their lower branches cropped by the hungry camels. So they looked cared for, and had a premeditated air, which felt strange in the wilderness, more especially as the Tehama hitherto had been a sober bareness.

Two hours up-stream, so Tafas told me, was the throat where Wadi Fura issued from the last granite hills, and there had been built a little village, Khoreiba, of running water channels and wells and palm-groves, inhabited by a small population of freedmen engaged in date husbandry. This was important. We had not understood that the bed of Wadi Fura served as a direct road from near Medina to the neighbourhood of Rabegh. It lay so far south and east of Feisal's supposed position in the hills that he could hardly be said to cover it. Also Abdulla had not warned us of the existence of Khoreiba, though it materially affected the Rabegh question, by affording the enemy a possible watering-place, safe from our interference, and from the guns of our warships. At Khoreiba the Turks could concentrate a large force to attack our proposed brigade in Rabegh.

In reply to further questions, Tafas disclosed that at Hajar, east of Rabegh in the hills, was yet another supply of water, in the hands of the Masruh, and now the headquarters of Hussein Mabeirig, their Turcophil chief. The Turks could make that their next stage from Khoreiba towards Mecca, leaving Rabegh unmolested and harmless on their flank. This meant that the asked-for British Brigade would be unable to save Mecca from the Turks. For that purpose would be required a force with a front or a radius of action of some twenty miles, in order to deny all three water-supplies to the enemy.

Meanwhile in the early sunlight we lifted our camels to a steady trot across the good going of these shingle-beds among the trees, making for Masturah well, the first stage out from Rabegh on the pilgrim road. There we would water and halt a little. My camel was a delight to me, for I had not been on such an animal before. There were no good camels in Egypt; and those of the Sinai Desert, while hardy and strong, were not taught to pace fair and softly and swiftly, like these rich mounts of the Arabian princes.

Yet her accomplishments were to-day largely wasted, since they were reserved for riders who had the knack and asked for them, and not for me, who expected to be carried, and had no sense of how to ride. It was easy to sit on a camel's back without falling off, but very difficult to understand and get the best out of her so as to do long journeys without fatiguing either rider or beast. Tafas gave me hints as we went: indeed, it was one of the few subjects on which he would speak. His orders to preserve me from contact with the world seemed to have closed even his mouth. A pity, for his dialect interested me.

Quite close to the north bank of the Masturah, we found the well. Beside it were some decayed stone walls which had been a hut, and opposite it some little shelters of branches and palm-leaves, under which a few Beduin were sitting. We did not greet them. Instead, Tafas turned across to the ruinous walls, and dismounted; and I sat in their shade while he and Abdulla watered the animals, and drew a drink for themselves and for me. The well was old, and broad, with a good stone steyning, and a strong coping round the top. It was about twenty feet deep; and for the convenience of travellers without ropes, like ourselves, a square chimney had been contrived in the masonry, with foot and hand holds in the corners, so that a man might descend to the water, and fill his goat-skin.

Idle hands had flung so many stones down the shaft, that half the bottom of the well was choked, and the water not abundant. Abdulla tied his flowing sleeves about his shoulders; tucked his gown under his cartridge belt; and clambered nimbly down and up, bringing each time four or five gallons which he poured for our camels into a stone trough beside the well. They drank about five gallons each, for they had been watered at Rabegh a day back. Then we let them moon about a little, while we sat in peace, breathing the light wind coming off the sea. Abdulla smoked a cigarette as reward for his exertions.

Some Harb came up, driving a large herd of brood camels, and began to water them, having sent one man down the well to fill their large leather bucket, which the others drew up hand over hand with a loud staccato chant. We watched them, without intercourse; for these were Masruh, and we Beni Salem; and while the two clans were now at peace, and might pass through each other's districts, this was only a temporary accommodation to further the Sherifs' war against the Turks, and had little depth of goodwill in it.

As we watched, two riders, trotting light and fast on thoroughbred camels, drew towards us from the north. Both were young. One was dressed in rich Cashmere robes and heavy silk embroidered head-cloth. The other was plainer, in white cotton, with a red cotton head-dress. They halted beside the well; and the more splendid one slipped gracefully to the ground without kneeling his camel, and threw his halter to his companion, saying, carelessly, 'Water them while I go over there and rest'. Then he strolled across and sat down under our wall, after glancing at us with affected unconcern. He offered a cigarette, just rolled and licked, saying, 'Your presence is from Syria?' I parried politely, suggesting that he was from Mecca, to which he likewise made no direct reply. We spoke a little of the war and of the leanness of the Masruh she-camels.

Meanwhile the other rider stood by, vacantly holding the halters, waiting perhaps for the Harb to finish watering their herd before taking his turn. The young lord cried, 'What is it, Mustafa? Water them at once'. The servant came up to say dismally, 'They will not let me'. 'God's mercy!' shouted his master furiously, as he scrambled to his feet and hit the unfortunate Mustafa three or four sharp blows about the head and shoulders with his riding-stick. 'Go and ask them.' Mustafa looked hurt, astonished, and angry as though he would hit back, but thought better of it, and ran to the well.

The Harb, shocked, in pity made a place for him, and let his two camels drink from their water-trough. They whispered, 'Who is he?' and Mustapha said, 'Our Lord's cousin from Mecca'. At once they ran and untied a bundle from one of their saddles, and spread from it before the two riding camels fodder of the green leaves and buds of the thorn trees. They were used to gather this by striking the low bushes with a heavy staff, till the broken tips of the branches rained down on a cloth stretched over the ground beneath.

The young Sherif watched them contentedly. When his camel had fed, he climbed slowly and without apparent effort up its neck into the saddle, where he settled himself leisurely, and took an unctuous fare-well of us, asking God to requite the Arabs bountifully. They wished him a good journey; and he started southward, while Abdulla brought our camels, and we went off northward. Ten minutes later I heard a chuckle from old Tafas, and saw wrinkles of delight between his grizzled beard and moustache.

'What is upon you, Tafas?' said I.

'My Lord, you saw those two riders at the well?'

'The Sherif and his servant?'

'Yes; but they were Sherif Ali ibn el Hussein of Modhig, and his cousin, Sherif Mohsin, lords of the Harith, who are blood enemies of the Masruh. They feared they would be delayed or driven off the water if the Arabs knew them. So they pretended to be master and servant from Mecca. Did you see how Mohsin raged when Ali beat him? Ali is a devil. While only eleven years old he escaped from his father's house to his uncle, a robber of pilgrims by trade; and with him he lived by his hands for many months, till his father caught him. He was with our lord Feisal from the first day's battle in Medina, and led the Ateiba in the plains round Aar and Bir Derwish. It was all camel-fighting; and Ali would have no man with him who could not do as he did, run beside his camel, and leap with one hand into the saddle, carrying his rifle. The children of Harith are children of battle.' For the first time the old man's mouth was full of words.

CHAPTER XI

WHILE he spoke we scoured along the dazzling plain, now nearly bare of trees, and turning slowly softer under foot. At first it had been grey shingle, packed like gravel. Then the sand increased and the stones grew rarer, till we could distinguish the colours of the separate flakes, porphyry, green schist, basalt. At last it was nearly pure white sand, under which lay a harder stratum. Such going was like a pile carpet for our camels' running. The particles of sand were clean and polished, and caught the blaze of sun like little diamonds in a reflection so fierce, that after a while I could not endure it. I frowned hard, and pulled the head-cloth forward in a peak over my eyes, and beneath them, too, like a beaver, trying to shut out the heat which rose in glassy waves off the ground, and beat up against my face. Eighty miles in front of us, the huge peak of Rudhwa behind Yenbo was looming and fading in the dazzle of vapour which hid its foot. Quite near in the plain rose the little shapeless hills of Hesna, which seemed to block the way. To our right was the steep ridge of Beni Ayub, toothed and narrow like a saw-blade, the first edge of the sheaf of mountains between the Tehama and the high scarp of the tableland about Medina. These Tareif Beni Ayub fell away on their north into a blue series of smaller hills, soft in character, behind which lofty range after range in a jagged stairway, red now the sun grew low, climbed up to the towering central mass of Jebel Subh with its fantastic granite spires.

A little later we turned to the right, off the pilgrim road, and took a short cut across gradually rising ground of flat basalt ridges, buried in sand till only their topmost piles showed above the surface. It held moisture enough to be well grown over with hard wiry grass and shrubs up and down the slopes, on which a few sheep and goats were pasturing. There Tafas showed me a stone, which was the limit of the district of the Masruh, and told me with grim pleasure that he was now at home, in his tribal property, and might come off his guard.

Men have looked upon the desert as barren land, the free holding of whoever chose; but in fact each hill and valley in it had a man who was its acknowledged owner and would quickly assert the right of his family or clan to it, against aggression. Even the wells and trees had their masters, who allowed men to make firewood of the one and drink of the other freely, as much as was required for their need, but who would instantly check anyone trying to turn the property to account and to exploit it or its products among others for private benefit. The desert was held in a crazed communism by which Nature and the elements were for the free use of every known friendly person for his own purposes and no more. Logical outcomes were the reduction of this licence to privilege by the men of the desert, and their hardness to strangers unprovided with introduction or guarantee, since the common security lay in the common responsibility of kinsmen. Tafas, in his own country, could bear the burden of my safe-keeping lightly.

The valleys were becoming sharply marked, with clean beds of sand and shingle, and an occasional large boulder brought down by a flood. There were many broom bushes, restfully grey and green to the eye, and good for fuel, though useless as pasture. We ascended steadily till we rejoined the main track of the pilgrim road. Along this we held our way till sunset, when we came into sight of the hamlet of Bir el Sheikh. In the first dark as the supper fires were lighted we rode down its wide open street and halted. Tafas went into one of the twenty miserable huts, and in a few whispered words and long silences bought flour, of which with water he kneaded a dough cake two inches thick and eight inches across. This he buried in the ashes of a brushwood fire, provided for him by a Subh woman whom he seemed to know. When the cake was warmed he drew it out of the fire, and clapped it to shake off the dust; then we shared it together, while Abdulla went away to buy himself tobacco.

They told me the place had two stone-lined wells at the bottom of the southward slope, but I felt disinclined to go and look at them, for the long ride that day had tired my unaccustomed muscles, and the heat of the plain had been painful. My skin was blistered by it, and my eyes ached with the glare of light striking up at a sharp angle from the silver sand, and from the shining pebbles. The last two years I had spent in Cairo, at a desk all day or thinking hard in a little overcrowded office full of distracting noises, with a hundred rushing things to say, but no bodily need except to come and go each day between office and hotel. In consequence the novelty of this change was severe, since time had not been given me gradually to accustom myself to the pestilent beating of the Arabian sun, and the long monotony of camel pacing. There was to be another stage to-night, and a long day to-morrow before Feisal's camp would be reached.

So I was grateful for the cooking and the marketing, which spent one hour, and for the second hour of rest after it which we took by common consent; and sorry when it ended, and we re-mounted, and rode in pitch darkness up valleys and down valleys, passing in and out of bands of air, which were hot in the confined hollows, but fresh and stirring in the open places. The ground under foot must have been sandy, because the silence of our passage hurt my straining ears, and smooth, for I was always falling asleep in the saddle, to wake a few seconds later suddenly and sickeningly, as I clutched by instinct at the saddle post to recover my balance which had been thrown out by some irregular stride of the animal. It was too dark, and the forms of the country were too neutral, to hold my heavy-lashed, peering eyes. At length we stopped for good, long after midnight; and I was rolled up in my cloak and asleep in a most comfortable little sand-grave before Tafas had done knee-haltering my camel.

Three hours later we were on the move again, helped now by the last shining of the moon. We marched down Wadi Mared, the night of it dead, hot, silent, and on each side sharp-pointed hills standing up black and white in the exhausted air. There were many trees. Dawn finally came to us as we passed out of the narrows into a broad place, over whose flat floor an uneasy wind span circles, capriciously in the dust. The day strengthened always, and now showed Bir ibn Hassani just to our right. The trim settlement of absurd little houses, brown and white, holding together for security's sake, looked doll-like and more lonely than the desert, in the immense shadow of the dark precipice of Subh, behind. While we watched it, hoping to see life at its doors, the sun was rushing up, and the fretted cliffs, those thousands of feet above our heads, became outlined in hard refracted shafts of white light against a sky still sallow with the transient dawn.

We rode on across the great valley. A camel-rider, garrulous and old, came out from the houses and jogged over to join us. He named himself Khallaf, too friendly-like. His salutation came after a pause in a trite stream of chat; and when it was returned he tried to force us into conversation. However, Tafas grudged his company, and gave him short answers. Khallaf persisted, and finally, to improve his footing, bent down and burrowed in his saddle pouch till he found a small covered pot of enamelled iron, containing a liberal portion of the staple of travel in the Hejaz. This was the unleavened dough cake of yesterday, but crumbled between the fingers while still warm, and moistened with liquid butter till its particles would fall apart only reluctantly. It was then sweetened for eating with ground sugar, and scooped up like damp sawdust in pressed pellets with the fingers.

I ate a little, on this my first attempt, while Tafas and Abdulla played at it vigorously; so for his bounty Khallaf went half-hungry: deservedly, for it was thought effeminate by the Arabs to carry a provision of food for a little journey of one hundred miles. We were now fellows, and the chat began again while Khallaf told us about the last fighting, and a reverse Feisal had had the day before. It seemed he had been beaten out of Kheif in the head of Wadi Safra, and was now at Hamra, only a little way in front of us; or at least Khallaf thought he was there: we might learn for sure in Wasta, the next village on our road. The fighting had not been severe; but the few casualties were all among the tribesmen of Tafas and Khallaf; and the names and hurts of each were told in order.

Meanwhile I looked about, interested to find myself in a new country. The sand and detritus of last night and of Bir el Sheikh had vanished. We were marching up a valley, from two hundred to five hundred yards in width, of shingle and light soil, quite firm, with occasional knolls of shattered green stone cropping out in its midst. There were many thorn trees, some of them woody acacias, thirty feet and more in height, beautifully green, with enough of tamarisk and soft scrub to give the whole a charming, well kept, park-like air, now in the long soft shadows of the early morning. The swept ground was so flat and clean, the pebbles so variegated, their colours so joyously blended that they gave a sense of design to the landscape; and this feeling was strengthened by the straight lines and sharpness of the hills.

They rose on each hand regularly, precipices a thousand feet in height, of granite-brown and dark porphyry-coloured rock, with pink stains; and by a strange fortune these glowing hills rested on hundred-foot bases of the cross-grained stone, whose unusual colour suggested a thin growth of moss.

We rode along this beautiful place for about seven miles, to a low watershed, crossed by a wall of granite slivers, now little more than a shapeless heap, but once no doubt a barrier. It ran from cliff to cliff, and even far up the hill-sides, wherever the slopes were not too steep to climb. In the centre, where the road passed, had been two small enclosures like pounds. I asked Khallaf the purpose of the wall. He replied that he had been in Damascus and Constantinople and Cairo, and had many friends among the great men of Egypt. Did I know any of the English there? Khallaf seemed curious about my intentions and my history. He tried to trip me in Egyptian phrases. When I answered in the dialect of Aleppo he spoke of prominent Syrians of his acquaintance. I knew them, too; and he switched off into local politics, asking careful questions, delicately and indirectly, about the Sherif and his sons, and what I thought Feisal was going to do. I understood less of this than he, and parried inconsequentially. Tafas came to my rescue, and changed the subject. Afterwards we knew that Khallaf was in Turkish pay, and used to send frequent reports of what came past Bir ibn Hassani for the Arab forces.

Across the wall we were in an affluent of Wadi Safra, a more wasted and stony valley among less brilliant hills. It ran into another, far down which to the west lay a cluster of dark palm-trees, which the Arabs said was Jedida, one of the slave villages in Wadi Safra. We turned to the right, across another saddle, and then downhill for a few miles to a corner of tall cliffs. We rounded this and found ourselves suddenly in Wadi Safra, the valley of our seeking, and in the midst of Wasta, its largest village. Wasta seemed to be many nests of houses, clinging to the hill-sides each side the torrent-bed on banks of alluvial soil, or standing on detritus islands between the various deep-swept channels whose sum made up the parent valley.

Riding between two or three of these built-up islands, we made for the far bank of the valley. On our way was the main bed of the winter floods, a sweep of white shingle and boulders, quite flat. Down its middle, from palm-grove on the one side to palm-grove on the other, lay a reach of clear water, perhaps two hundred yards long and twelve feet wide, sand-bottomed, and bordered on each brink by a ten-foot lawn of thick grass and flowers. On it we halted a moment to let our camels put their heads down and drink their fill, and the relief of the grass to our eyes after the day-long hard glitter of the pebbles was so sudden that involuntarily I glanced up to see if a cloud had not covered the face of the sun.

We rode up the stream to the garden from which it ran sparkling in a stone-lined channel; and then we turned along the mud wall of the garden in the shadow of its palms, to another of the detached hamlets. Tafas led the way up its little street (the houses were so low that from our saddles we looked down upon their clay roofs), and near one of the larger houses stopped and beat upon the door of an uncovered court. A slave opened to us, and we dismounted in privacy. Tafas haltered the camels, loosed their girths, and strewed before them green fodder from a fragrant pile beside the gate. Then he led me into the guest-room of the house, a dark clean little mud-brick place, roofed with half palm-logs under hammered earth. We sat down on the palm-leaf mat which ran along the dais. The day in this stifling valley had grown very hot; and gradually we lay back side by side. Then the hum of the bees in the gardens without, and of the flies hovering over our veiled faces within, lulled us into sleep.

CHAPTER XII

BEFORE we awoke, a meal of bread and dates had been prepared for us by the people of the house. The dates were new, meltingly sweet and good, like none I had ever tasted. The owner of the property, a Harbi, was, with his neighbours, away serving Feisal; and his women and children were tenting in the hills with the camels. At the most, the tribal Arabs of Wadi Safra lived in their villages five months a year. For the other seasons the gardens were entrusted to slaves, negroes like the grown lads who brought in the tray to us, and whose thick limbs and plump shining bodies looked curiously out of place among the bird-like Arabs. Khallaf told me these blacks were originally from Africa, brought over as children by their nominal Takruri fathers, and sold during the pilgrimage, in Mecca. When grown strong they were worth from fifty to eighty pounds apiece, and were looked after carefully as befitted their price. Some became house or body servants with their masters; but the majority were sent out to the palm villages of these feverish valleys of running water, whose climate was too bad for Arab labour, but where they flourished and built themselves solid houses, and mated with women slaves, and did all the manual work of the holding.

They were very numerous — for instance, there were thirteen villages of them side by side in this Wadi Safra — so they formed a society of their own, and lived much at their pleasure. Their work was hard, but the supervision loose, and escape easy. Their legal status was bad, for they had no appeal to tribal justice, or even to the Sherif's courts; but public opinion and self-interest deprecated any cruelty towards them, and the tenet of the faith that to enlarge a slave is a good deed, meant in practice that nearly all gained freedom in the end. They made pocket-money during their service, if they were ingenious. Those I saw had property, and declared themselves contented. They grew melons, marrows, cucumber, grapes and tobacco for their own account, in addition to the dates, whose surplus was sent across to the Sudan by sailing dhow, and there exchanged for corn, clothing and the luxuries of Africa or Europe.

After the midday heat was passed we mounted again, and rode up the clear, slow rivulet till it was hidden within the palm-gardens, behind their low boundary walls of sun-dried clay. In and out between the tree roots were dug little canals a foot or two deep, so contrived that the stream might be let into them from the stone channel and each tree watered in its turn. The head of water was owned by the community, and shared out among the landowners for so many minutes or hours daily or weekly according to the traditional use. The water was a little brackish, as was needful for the best palms; but it was sweet enough in the wells of private water in the groves. These wells were very frequent, and found water three or four feet below the surface.

Our way took us through the central village and its market street. There was little in the shops; and all the place felt decayed. A generation ago Wasta was populous (they said of a thousand houses); but one day there rolled a huge wall of water down Wadi Safra, the embankments of many palm-gardens were breached, and the palm trees swept away. Some of the islands on which houses had stood for centuries were submerged, and the mud houses melted back again into mud, killing or drowning the unfortunate slaves within. The men could have been replaced, and the trees, had the soil remained; but the gardens had been built up of earth carefully won from the normal freshets by years of labour, and this wave of water — eight feet deep, running in a race for three days — reduced the plots in its track to their primordial banks of stones.

A little above Wasta we came to Kharma, a tiny settlement with rich palm groves, where a tributary ran in from the north. Beyond Kharma the valley widened somewhat, to an average of perhaps four hundred yards, with a bed of fine shingle and sand, laid very smooth by the winter rains. The walls were of bare red and black rock, whose edges and ridges were sharp as knife blades, and reflected the sun like metal. They made the freshness of the trees and grass seem luxurious. We now saw parties of Feisal's soldiers, and grazing herds of their saddle camels. Before we reached Hamra every nook in the rocks or clump of trees was a bivouac. They cried cheery greetings to Tafas, who came to life again, waving back and calling to them, while he pressed on quickly to end his duty towards me.

Hamra opened on our left. It seemed a village of about one hundred houses, buried in gardens among mounds of earth some twenty feet in height. We forded a little stream, and went up a walled path between trees to the top of one of these mounds, where we made our camels kneel by the yard-gate of a long, low house. Tafas said something to a slave who stood there with silver-hilted sword in hand. He led me to an inner court, on whose further side, framed between the uprights of a black doorway, stood a white figure waiting tensely for me. I felt at first glance that this was the man I had come to Arabia to seek — the leader who would bring the Arab Revolt to full glory. Feisal looked very tall and pillar-like, very slender, in his long white silk robes and his brown head-cloth bound with a brilliant scarlet and gold cord. His eyelids were dropped; and his black beard and colourless face were like a mask against the strange, still watchfulness of his body. His hands were crossed in front of him on his dagger.

I greeted him. He made way for me into the room, and sat down on his carpet near the door. As my eyes grew accustomed to the shade, they saw that the little room held many silent figures, looking at me or at Feisal steadily. He remained staring down at his hands, which were twisting slowly about his dagger. At last he inquired softly how I had found the journey. I spoke of the heat and he asked how long from Rabegh, commenting that I had ridden fast for the season.

'And do you like our place here in Wadi Safra?'

'Well; but it is far from Damascus.'

The word had fallen like a sword in their midst. There was a quiver. Then everybody present stiffened where he sat, and held his breath for a silent minute. Some, perhaps, were dreaming of far off success: others may have thought it a reflection on their late defeat. Feisal at length lifted his eyes, smiling at me, and said, 'Praise be to God, there are Turks nearer us than that'. We all smiled with him; and I rose and excused myself for the moment.

CHAPTER XIII

UNDER tall arcades of palms with ribbed and groined branches, in a soft meadow, I found the trim camp of Egyptian Army soldiers with Nafi Bey, their Egyptian major, sent lately from the Sudan by Sir Reginald Wingate to help the Arab rebellion. They comprised a mountain battery and some machine-guns, and looked smarter than they felt. Nafi himself was an amiable fellow, kind and hospitable to me in spite of weak health and his resentment at having been sent so far away into the desert to serve in an unnecessary and toilsome war.

Egyptians, being home-loving persons and comfortable, found strangeness always a misery. In this bad instance they suffered hardship for a philanthropic end, which made it harder. They were fighting the Turks, for whom they had a sentimental regard, on behalf of the Arabs, an alien people speaking a language kindred to their own, but appearing therefore all the more unlike in character, and crude in life. The Arabs seemed hostile to the material blessings of civilization rather than appreciative of them. They met with a ribald hoot well-meaning attempts to furnish their bareness.

Englishmen being sure of their own absolute excellence would persist in help without grumbling overmuch; but the Egyptians lost faith. They had neither that collective sense of duty towards their State, nor that feeling of individual obligation to push struggling humanity up its road. The vicarious policemanship which was the strongest emotion of Englishmen towards another man's muddle, in their case was replaced by the instinct to pass by as discreetly far as possible on the other side. So, though all was well with these soldiers, and they had abundant rations and good health and no casualties, yet they found fault with the handling of the universe, and hoped this unexpected Englishman had come to set it right.

Feisal was announced with Maulud el Mukhlus, the Arab zealot of Tekrit, who, for rampant nationalism, had been twice degraded in the Turkish Army, and had spent an exile of two years in Nejd as a secretary with Ibn Rashid. He had commanded the Turkish cavalry before

Shaiba, and had been taken by us there. As soon as he heard of the rebellion of the Sherif he had volunteered for him, and had been the first regular officer to join Feisal. He was now nominally his A.D.C.

Bitterly he complained that they were in every way ill-equipped. This was the main cause of their present plight. They got thirty thousand pounds a month from the Sherif, but little flour and rice, little barley, few rifles, insufficient ammunition, no machine-guns, no mountain guns, no technical help, no information.

I stopped Maulud there and said that my coming was expressly to learn what they lacked and to report it, but that I could work with them only if they would explain to me their general situation. Feisal agreed, and began to sketch to me the history of their revolt from its absolute beginning.

The first rush on Medina had been a desperate business. The Arabs were ill-armed and short of ammunition, the Turks in great force, since Fakhri's detachment had just arrived and the troops to escort von Stotzingen to Yemen were still in the town. At the height of the crisis the Beni Ali broke; and the Arabs were thrust out beyond the walls. The Turks then opened fire on them with their artillery; and the Arabs, unused to this new arm, became terrified. The Ageyl and Ateiba got into safety and refused to move out again. Feisal and Ali ibn el Hussein vainly rode about in front of their men in the open, to show them that the bursting shells were not as fatal as they sounded. The demoralization deepened.

Sections of Beni Ali tribesmen approached the Turkish command with an offer to surrender, if their villages were spared. Fakhri played with them, and in the ensuing lull of hostilities surrounded the Awali suburb with his troops: then suddenly he ordered them to carry it by assault and to massacre every living thing within its walls. Hundreds of the inhabitants were raped and butchered, the houses fired, and living and dead alike thrown back into the flames. Fakhri and his men had served together and had learned the arts of both the slow and the fast kill upon the Armenians in the North.

This bitter taste of the Turkish mode of war sent a shock across Arabia; for the first rule of Arab war was that women were inviolable: the second that the lives and honour of children too young to fight with men were to be spared: the third, that property impossible to carry off should be left undamaged. The Arabs with Feisal perceived that they were opposed to new customs, and fell back out of touch to gain time to readjust themselves. There could no longer be any question of submission: the sack of Awali had opened blood feud upon blood feud, and put on them the duty of fighting to the end of their force: but it was plain now that it would be a long affair, and that with muzzle-loading guns for sole weapons, they could hardly expect to win.

So they fell back from the level plains about Medina into the hills across the Sultani-road, about Aar and Raha and Bir Abbas, where they rested a little, while Ali and Feisal sent messenger after messenger down to Rabegh, their sea-base, to learn when fresh stores and money and arms might be expected. The revolt had begun haphazard, on their father's explicit orders, and the old man, too independent to take his sons into his full confidence, had not worked out with them any arrangements for prolonging it. So the reply was only a little food. Later some Japanese rifles, most of them broken, were received. Such barrels as were still whole were so foul that the too-eager Arabs burst them on the first trial. No money was sent up at all: to take its place Feisal filled a decent chest with stones, had it locked and corded carefully, guarded on each daily march by his own slaves, and introduced meticulously into his tent each night. By such theatricals the brothers tried to hold a melting force.

At last Ali went down to Rabegh to inquire what was wrong with the organization. He found that Hussein Mabeirig, the local chief, had made up his mind that the Turks would be victorious (he had tried conclusions with them twice himself and had the worst of it), and accordingly decided theirs was the best cause to follow. As the stores for the Sherif were landed by the British he appropriated them and stored them away secretly in his own houses. Ali made a demonstration, and sent urgent messages for his half-brother Zeid to join him from Jidda with reinforcements. Hussein, in fear, slipped off to the hills, an outlaw. The two Sherifs took possession of his villages. In them they found great stores of arms, and food enough for their armies for a month. The temptation of a spell of leisured ease was too much for them: they settled down in Rabegh.

This left Feisal alone up country, and he soon found himself isolated, in a hollow situation, driven to depend upon his native resources. He bore it for a time, but in August took advantage of the visit of Colonel Wilson to the newly-conquered Yenbo, to come down and give a full explanation of his urgent needs. Wilson was impressed with him and his story, and at once promised him a battery of mountain guns and some maxims, to be handled by men and officers of the Egyptian Army garrison in the Sudan. This explained the presence of Nafi Bey and his units.

The Arabs rejoiced when they came, and believed they were now equals of the Turk; but the four guns were twenty-year-old Krupps, with a range of only three thousand yards; and their crews were not eager enough in brain and spirit for irregular fighting. However, they went forward with the mob and drove in the Turkish outposts, and then their supports, until Fakhri, becoming seriously alarmed, came down himself, inspected the front, and at once reinforced the threatened detachment at Bir Abbas to some three thousand strong. The Turks had field guns and howitzers with them, and the added advantage of high ground for observation. They began to worry the Arabs by indirect fire, and nearly dropped a shell on Feisal's tent while all the head men were conferring within. The Egyptian gunners were asked to return the fire and smother the enemy guns. They had to plead that their weapons were useless, since they could not carry the nine thousand yards. They were derided; and the Arabs ran back again into the defiles.

Feisal was deeply discouraged. His men were tired. He had lost many of them. His only effective tactics against the enemy had been to chase in suddenly upon their rear by fast mounted charges, and many camels had been killed, or wounded or worn out in these expensive measures. He demurred to carrying the whole war upon his own neck while Abdulla delayed in Mecca, and Ali and Zeid at Rabegh. Finally he withdrew the bulk of his forces, leaving the Harb sub-tribes who lived by Bir Abbas to keep up pressure on the Turkish supply columns and communications by a repeated series of such raids as those which he himself found impossible to maintain.

Yet he had no fear that the Turks would again come forward against

him suddenly. His failure to make any impression on them had not
imbued him with the smallest respect for them. His late retirement to
Hamra was not forced: it was a gesture of disgust because he was
bored by his obvious impotence, and was determined for a little while
to have the dignity of rest.

After all, the two sides were still untried. The armament of the
Turks made them so superior at long range that the Arabs never got to
grips. For this reason most of the hand-to-hand fighting had taken
place at night, when the guns were blinded. To my ears they sounded
oddly primitive battles, with torrents of words on both sides in a
preliminary match of wits. After the foulest insults of the languages
they knew would come the climax, when the Turks in frenzy called the
Arabs 'English', and the Arabs screamed back 'German' at them. There
were, of course, no Germans in the Hejaz, and I was the first Englishman; but each party loved cursing, and any epithet would sting on the
tongues of such artists.

I asked Feisal what his plans were now. He said that till Medina fell
they were inevitably tied down there in Hejaz dancing to Fakhri's tune.
In his opinion the Turks were aiming at the recapture of Mecca. The
bulk of their strength was now in a mobile column, which they could
move towards Rabegh by a choice of routes which kept the Arabs in
constant alarm. A passive defence of the Subh hills had shown that the
Arabs did not shine as passive resisters. When the enemy moved they
must be countered by an offensive.

Feisal meant to retire further yet, to the Wadi Yenbo border of the
great Juheina tribe. With fresh levies from them he would march
eastwards towards the Hejaz Railway behind Medina, at the moment
when Abdulla was advancing by the lava-desert to attack Medina from
the East. He hoped that Ali would go up simultaneously from Rabegh,
while Zeid moved into Wadi Safra to engage the big Turkish force at
Bir Abbas, and keep it out of the main battle. By this plan Medina
would be threatened or attacked on all sides at once. Whatever the
success of the attack, the concentration from three sides would at least
break up the prepared Turkish push-outwards on the fourth, and give
Rabegh and the southern Hejaz a breathing space to equip themselves
for effective defence, or counter-attack.

Maulud, who had sat fidgeting through our long, slow talk, could no longer restrain himself and cried out, 'Don't write a history of us. The needful thing is to fight and fight and kill them. Give me a battery of Schneider mountain guns and machine-guns, and I will finish this off for you. We talk and talk and do nothing.' I replied as warmly; and Maulud, a magnificent fighter, who regarded a battle won as a battle wasted if he did not show some wound to prove his part in it, took me up. We wrangled while Feisal sat by and grinned delightedly at us.

This talk had been for him a holiday. He was encouraged even by the trifle of my coming; for he was a man of moods, flickering between glory and despair, and just now dead-tired. He looked years older than thirty-one; and his dark, appealing eyes, set a little sloping in his face, were bloodshot, and his hollow cheeks deeply lined and puckered with reflection. His nature grudged thinking, for it crippled his speed in action: the labour of it shrivelled his features into swift lines of pain. In appearance he was tall, graceful and vigorous, with the most beautiful gait, and a royal dignity of head and shoulders. Of course he knew it, and a great part of his public expression was by sign and gesture.

His movements were impetuous. He showed himself hot-tempered and sensitive, even unreasonable, and he ran off soon on tangents. Appetite and physical weakness were mated in him, with the spur of courage. His personal charm, his imprudence, the pathetic hint of frailty as the sole reserve of this proud character made him the idol of his followers. One never asked if he were scrupulous; but later he showed that he could return trust for trust, suspicion for suspicion. He was fuller of wit than of humour.

His training in Abdul Hamid's entourage had made him past-master in diplomacy. His military service with the Turks had given him a working knowledge of tactics. His life in Constantinople and in the Turkish Parliament had made him familiar with European questions and manners. He was a careful judge of men. If he had the strength to realize his dreams he would go very far, for he was wrapped up in his work and lived for nothing else; but the fear was that he would wear himself out by trying to seem to aim always a little higher than the truth, or that he would die of too much action. His men told me how, after a long spell of fighting, in which he had to guard himself, and lead the charges, and control and encourage them, he had collapsed physically and was carried away from his victory, unconscious, with the foam flecking his lips.

Meanwhile, here, as it seemed, was offered to our hand, which had only to be big enough to take it, a prophet who, if veiled, would give cogent form to the idea behind the activity of the Arab revolt. It was all and more than we had hoped for, much more than our halting course deserved. The aim of my trip was fulfilled.

My duty was now to take the shortest road to Egypt with the news: and the knowledge gained that evening in the palm wood grew and blossomed in my mind into a thousand branches, laden with fruit and shady leaves, beneath which I sat and half-listened and saw visions, while the twilight deepened, and the night; until a line of slaves with lamps came down the winding paths between the palm trunks, and with Feisal and Maulud we walked back through the gardens to the little house, with its courts still full of waiting people, and to the hot inner room in which the familiars were assembled; and there we sat down together to the smoking bowl of rice and meat set upon the food-carpet for our supper by the slaves.

CHAPTER XIV

So mixed was the company, Sherifs, Meccans, sheikhs of the Juheina and Ateiba, Mesopotamians, Ageyl, that I threw apples of discord, inflammatory subjects of talk amongst them, to sound their mettle and beliefs without delay. Feisal, smoking innumerable cigarettes, kept command of the conversation even at its hottest, and it was fine to watch him do it. He showed full mastery of tact, with a real power of disposing men's feelings to his wish. Storrs was as efficient; but Storrs paraded his strength, exhibiting all the cleverness and machinery, the movements of his hands which made the creatures dance. Feisal seemed to govern his men unconsciously: hardly to know how he stamped his mind on them, hardly to care whether they obeyed. It was as great art as Storrs'; and it concealed itself, for Feisal was born to it.

The Arabs loved him openly: indeed, these chance meetings made clear how to the tribes the Sherif and his sons were heroic. Sherif Hussein (Sayidna as they called him) was outwardly so clean and gentle-mannered as to seem weak; but this appearance hid a crafty policy, deep ambition, and an un-Arabian foresight, strength of character and obstinacy. His interest in natural history reinforced his sporting instincts, and made him (when he pleased) a fair copy of a Beduin prince, while his Circassian mother had endowed him with qualities foreign to both Turk and Arab, and he displayed considerable astuteness in turning now one, now another of his inherited assets to present advantage.

Yet the school of Turkish politics was so ignoble that not even the best could graduate from it unaffected. Hussein when young had been honest, outspoken . . . and he learned not merely to suppress his speech, but to use speech to conceal his honest purpose. The art, over-indulged, became a vice from which he could not free himself. In old age ambiguity covered his every communication. Like a cloud it hid his decision of character, his worldly wisdom, his cheerful strength. Many denied him such qualities: but history gave proof.

One instance of his worldly wisdom was the upbringing of his sons. The Sultan had made them live in Constantinople to receive a Turkish education. Sherif Hussein saw to it that the education was general and good. When they came back to the Hejaz as young effendis in European clothes with Turkish manners, the father ordered them into Arab dress; and, to rub up their Arabic, gave them Meccan companions and sent them out into the wilds, with the Camel Corps, to patrol the pilgrim roads.

The young men thought it might be an amusing trip, but were dashed when their father forbade them special food, bedding, or soft-padded saddles. He would not let them back to Mecca, but kept them out for months in all seasons guarding the roads by day and by night, handling every variety of man and learning fresh methods of riding and fighting. Soon they hardened, and became self-reliant, with that blend of native intelligence and vigour which so often comes in a crossed stock. Their formidable family group was admired and efficient, but curiously isolated in their world. They were natives of no country, lovers of no private plot of ground. They had no real confidants or ministers; and no one of them seemed open to another, or to the father, of whom they stood in awe.

The debate after supper was an animated one. In my character as a Syrian I made sympathetic reference to the Arab leaders who had been executed in Damascus by Jemal Pasha. They took me up sharply: the published papers had disclosed that these men were in touch with foreign Governments, and ready to accept French or British suzerainty as the price of help. This was a crime against Arab nationality, and Jemal had only executed the implied sentence. Feisal smiled, almost winked, at me. 'You see,' he explained, 'we are now of necessity tied to the British. We are delighted to be their friends, grateful for their help, expectant of our future profit. But we are not British subjects. We would be more at ease if they were not such disproportionate allies.'

I told a story of Abdulla el Raashid, on the way up to Hamra. He had groaned to me of the British sailors coming ashore each day at Rabegh. 'Soon they will stay nights, and then they will live here always, and take the country.' To cheer him I had spoken of millions of Englishmen now ashore in France, and of the French not afraid.

Whereat he had turned on me scornfully, asking if I meant to compare France with the land of Hejaz!

Feisal mused a little and said, 'I am not a Hejazi by upbringing; and yet, by God, I am jealous for it. And though I know the British do not want it, yet what can I say, when they took the Sudan, also not wanting it? They hunger for desolate lands, to build them up; and so, perhaps, one day Arabia will seem to them precious. Your good and my good, perhaps they are different, and either forced good or forced evil will make a people cry with pain. Does the ore admire the flame which transforms it? There is no reason for offence, but a people too weak are clamant over their little own. Our race will have a cripple's temper till it has found its feet.'

The ragged, lousy tribesmen who had eaten with us astonished me by their familiar understanding of intense political nationality, an abstract idea they could hardly have caught from the educated classes of the Hejaz towns, from those Hindus, Javanese, Bokhariots, Sudanese, Turks, out of sympathy with Arab ideals, and indeed just then suffering a little from the force of local sentiment, springing too high after its sudden escape from Turkish control. Sherif Hussein had had the worldly wisdom to base his precepts on the instinctive belief of the Arabs that they were of the salt of the earth and self-sufficient. Then, enabled by his alliance with us to back his doctrine by arms and money, he was assured of success.

Of course, this success was not level throughout. The great body of Sherifs, eight hundred or nine hundred of them, understood his nationalistic doctrine and were his missionaries, successful missionaries thanks to the revered descent from the Prophet, which gave them the power to hold men's minds, and to direct their courses into the willing quietness of eventual obedience.

The tribes had followed the smoke of their racial fanaticism. The towns might sigh for the cloying inactivity of Ottoman rule: the tribes were convinced that they had made a free and Arab Government, and that each of them was It. They were independent and would enjoy themselves — a conviction and resolution which might have led to anarchy, if they had not made more stringent the family tie, and the bonds of kin-responsibility. But this entailed a negation of central power. The Sherif might have legal sovereignty abroad, if he liked the high-sounding toy; but home affairs were to be customary. The problem of the foreign theorists — 'Is Damascus to rule the Hejaz, or can Hejaz rule Damascus?' did not trouble them at all, for they would not have it set. The Semites' idea of nationality was the independence of clans and villages, and their ideal of national union was episodic combined resistance to an intruder. Constructive policies, an organized state, an extended empire, were not so much beyond their sight as hateful in it. They were fighting to get rid of Empire, not to win it.

The feeling of the Syrians and Mesopotamians in these Arab armies was indirect. They believed that by fighting in the local ranks, even here in Hejaz, they were vindicating the general rights of all Arabs to national existence; and without envisaging one State, or even a confederation of States, they were definitely looking northward, wishing to add an autonomous Damascus and Bagdad to the Arab family. They were weak in material resources, and even after success would be, since their world was agricultural and pastoral, without minerals, and could never be strong in modern armaments. Were it otherwise, we should have had to pause before evoking in the strategic centre of the Middle East new national movements of such abounding vigour.

Of religious fanaticism there was little trace. The Sherif refused in round terms to give a religious twist to his rebellion. His fighting creed was nationality. The tribes knew that the Turks were Moslems, and thought that the Germans were probably true friends of Islam. They knew that the British were Christians, and that the British were their allies. In the circumstances, their religion would not have been of much help to them, and they had put it aside. 'Christian fights Christian, so why should not Mohammedans do the same? What we want is a Government which speaks our own language of Arabic and will let us live in peace. Also we hate those Turks.'

CHAPTER XV

NEXT morning I was up early and out among Feisal's troops towards the side of Kheif, by myself, trying to feel the pulse of their opinions in a moment, by such tricks as those played upon their chiefs the night before. Time was of the essence of my effort, for it was necessary to gain in ten days the impressions which would ordinarily have been the fruit of weeks of observing, in my crab-fashion, that sideways-slipping affair of the senses. Normally I would go along all day, with the sounds immediate, but blind to every detail, only generally aware that there were things red, or things grey, or clear things about me. To-day my eyes had to be switched straight to my brain, that I might note a thing or two the more clearly by contrast with the former mistiness. Such things were nearly always shapes: rocks and trees, or men's bodies in repose or movement: not small things like flowers, nor qualities like colour.

Yet here was strong need of a lively reporter. In this drab war the least irregularity was a joy to all, and McMahon's strongest course was to exploit the latent imagination of the General Staff. I believed in the Arab movement, and was confident, before ever I came, that in it was the idea to tear Turkey into pieces; but others in Egypt lacked faith, and had been taught nothing intelligent of the Arabs in the field. By noting down something of the spirit of these romantics in the hills about the Holy Cities I might gain the sympathy of Cairo for the further measures necessary to help them.

The men received me cheerfully. Beneath every great rock or bush they sprawled like lazy scorpions, resting from the heat, and refreshing their brown limbs with the early coolness of the shaded stone. Because of my khaki they took me for a Turk-trained officer who had deserted to them, and were profuse in good-humoured but ghastly suggestions of how they should treat me. Most of them were young, though the term 'fighting man' in the Hejaz meant anyone between twelve and sixty sane enough to shoot. They were a tough-looking crowd, dark-coloured, some negroid. They were physically thin, but exquisitely made, moving with an oiled activity altogether delightful to watch. It did not seem possible that men could be hardier or harder. They would ride immense distances day after day, run through sand and over rocks bare-foot in the heat for hours without pain, and climb their hills like goats. Their clothing was mainly a loose shirt, with sometimes short cotton drawers, and a head-shawl usually of red cloth, which acted towel or handkerchief or sack as required. They were corrugated with bandoliers and fired joy-shots when they could.

They were in wild spirits, shouting that the war might last ten years. It was the fattest time the hills had ever known. The Sherif was feeding not only the fighting men, but their families, and paying two pounds a month for a man, four for a camel. Nothing else would have performed the miracle of keeping a tribal army in the field for five months on end. It was our habit to sneer at Oriental soldiers' love of pay; but the Hejaz campaign was a good example of the limitations of that argument. The Turks were offering great bribes, and obtaining little service — no active service. The Arabs took their money, and gave gratifying assurances in exchange; yet these very tribes would be meanwhile in touch with Feisal, who obtained service for his payment. The Turks cut the throats of their prisoners with knives, as though they were butchering sheep. Feisal offered a reward of a pound a head for prisoners, and had many carried in to him unhurt. He also paid for captured mules or rifles.

The actual contingents were continually shifting, in obedience to the rule of flesh. A family would own a rifle, and the sons serve in turn for a few days each. Married men alternated between camp and wife, and sometimes a whole clan would become bored and take a rest. Consequently the paid men were more than those mobilized; and policy often gave to great sheikhs, as wages, money that was a polite bribe for friendly countenance. Feisal's eight thousand men were one in ten camel-corps and the rest hill-men. They served only under their tribal sheikhs, and near home, arranging their own food and transport. Nominally each sheikh had a hundred followers. Sherifs acted as group leaders, in virtue of their privileged position, which raised them above the jealousies which shackled the tribesmen.

Blood feuds were nominally healed, and really suspended in the

Sherifian area: Billi and Juheina, Ateiba and Ageyl living and fighting side by side in Feisal's army. All the same, the members of one tribe were shy of those of another, and within the tribe no man would quite trust his neighbour. Each might be, usually was, whole-hearted against the Turk, but perhaps not quite to the point of failing to work off a family grudge upon a family enemy in the field. Consequently they could not attack. One company of Turks firmly entrenched in open country could have defied the entire army of them; and a pitched defeat, with its casualties, would have ended the war by sheer horror.

I concluded that the tribesmen were good for defence only. Their acquisitive recklessness made them keen on booty, and whetted them to tear up railways, plunder caravans, and steal camels; but they were too free-minded to endure command, or to fight in team. A man who could fight well by himself made generally a bad soldier, and these champions seemed to me no material for our drilling; but if we strengthened them by light automatic guns of the Lewis type, to be handled by themselves, they might be capable of holding their hills and serving as an efficient screen behind which we could build up, perhaps at Rabegh, an Arab regular mobile column, capable of meeting a Turkish force (distracted by guerilla warfare) on terms, and of defeating it piecemeal. For such a body of real soldiers no recruits would be forthcoming from Hejaz. It would have to be formed of the heavy unwarlike Syrian and Mesopotamian towns-folk already in our hands, and officered by Arabic-speaking officers trained in the Turkish army, men of the type and history of Aziz el Masri or Maulud. They would eventually finish the war by striking while the tribesmen skirmished about, and hindered and distracted the Turks by their pin-prick raids.

The Hejaz war, meanwhile, would be one of dervishes against regular troops. It was the fight of a rocky, mountainous, barren country (reinforced by a wild horde of mountaineers) against an enemy so enriched in equipment by the Germans as almost to have lost virtue for rough-and-tumble war. The hill-belt was a paradise for snipers; and Arabs were artists in sniping. Two or three hundred determined men knowing the ranges should hold any section of them; because the slopes were too steep for escalade. The valleys, which were the only practicable roads, for miles and miles were not so much valleys as chasms or gorges, sometimes two hundred yards across, but sometimes only twenty, full of twists and turns, one thousand or four thousand feet deep, barren of cover, and flanked each side by pitiless granite, basalt and porphyry, not in polished slopes, but serrated and split and piled up in thousands of jagged heaps of fragments as hard as metal and nearly as sharp.

It seemed to my unaccustomed eyes impossible that, without treachery on the part of the mountain tribes, the Turks could dare to break their way through. Even with treachery as an ally, to pass the hills would be dangerous. The enemy would never be sure that the fickle population might not turn again; and to have such a labyrinth of defiles in the rear, across the communications, would be worse than having it in front. Without the friendship of the tribes, the Turks would own only the ground on which their soldiers stood; and lines so long and complex would soak up thousands of men in a fortnight, and leave none in the battle-front.

The sole disquieting feature was the very real success of the Turks in frightening the Arabs by artillery. Aziz el Masri in the Turk-Italian war in Tripoli had found the same terror, but had found also that it wore off. We might hope that the same would happen here; but for the moment the sound of a fired cannon sent every man within earshot behind cover. They thought weapons destructive in proportion to their noise. They were not afraid of bullets, not indeed overmuch of dying: just the manner of death by shell-fire was unendurable. It seemed to me that their moral confidence was to be restored only by having guns, useful or useless, but noisy, on their side. From the magnificent Feisal down to the most naked stripling in the army the theme was artillery, artillery, artillery.

When I told them of the landing of the five-inch howitzers at Rabegh they rejoiced. Such news nearly balanced in their minds the check of their last retreat down Wadi Safra. The guns would be of no real use to them: indeed, it seemed to me that they would do the Arabs positive harm; for their virtues lay in mobility and intelligence, and by giving them guns we hampered their movements and efficiency. Only if we did not give them guns they would quit.

At these close quarters the bigness of the revolt impressed me. This

well-peopled province, from Um Lejj to Kunfida, more than a fortnight's camel march, had suddenly changed its character from a rout
of casual nomad pilferers to an eruption against Turkey, fighting her,
not certainly in our manner, but fiercely enough, in spite of the religion
which was to raise the East against us in a holy war. Beyond anything
calculable in figures, we had let loose a passion of anti-Turkish feeling
which, embittered as it had been by generations of subjection, might
die very hard. There was among the tribes in the fighting zone a
nervous enthusiasm common, I suppose, to all national risings, but
strangely disquieting to one from a land so long delivered that national
freedom had become like the water in our mouths, tasteless.

Later I saw Feisal again, and promised to do my best for him. My
chiefs would arrange a base at Yenbo, where the stores and supplies he
needed would be put ashore for his exclusive use. We would try to
get him officer-volunteers from among the prisoners of war captured in
Mesopotamia or on the Canal. We would form gun crews and
machine-gun crews from the rank and file in the internment camps, and
provide them with such mountain guns and light machine-guns as
were obtainable in Egypt. Lastly, I would advise that British Army
officers, professionals, be sent down to act as advisers and liaison
officers with him in the field.

This time our talk was of the pleasantest, and ended in warm thanks
from him, and an invitation to return as soon as might be. I explained
that my duties in Cairo excluded field work, but perhaps my chiefs
would let me pay a second visit later on, when his present wants were
filled and his movement was going forward prosperously. Meanwhile
I would ask for facilities to go down to Yenbo, for Egypt, that I might
get things on foot promptly. He at once appointed me an escort of
fourteen Juheina Sherifs, all kinsmen of Mohamed Ali ibn Beidawi,
the Emir of the Juheina. They were to deliver me intact in Yenbo to
Sheikh Abd el Kadir el Abdo, its Governor.

CHAPTER XVI

LEAVING Hamra as dusk fell, we marched back down Wadi Safra until opposite Kharma, where we turned to the right up the side valley. It was closely grown with stiff brushwood through which we drove our camels strenuously, having tucked up the streamers of our saddle-bags to save them from being shredded by the thorns. Two miles later we began to climb the narrow pass of Dhifran, which gave evidence even by night of labour expended on the road. It had been artificially smoothed, and the stones piled at each side into a heavy wall of protection against the rush of water in the rains. Parts had been graded, and were at times carried on a causeway built seemingly six or eight feet high, of great blocks of uncut stone: but it had been breached at every turn by torrents, and was in terrible ruin.

The ascent lasted perhaps for a mile; and the steep descent on the other side was about the same. Then we got to the level and found ourselves in a much broken country of ridges, with an intricate net of wadies whose main flow was apparently towards the south-west. The going was good for our camels. We rode for about seven miles in the dark, and came to a well, Bir el Murra, in a valley bed under a very low bluff, on whose head the square courses of a small fort of ashlar stood out against the starry sky. Conceivably both fort and causeway had been built by an Egyptian Mameluke for the passage of his pilgrim-caravan from Yenbo.

We halted there for the night, sleeping for six hours, a long luxury upon the road, though this rest was broken twice by challenges from half-seen mounted parties who had found our bivouac. Afterwards we wandered among more small ridges until the dawn showed gentle valleys of sand with strange hills of lava hemming us about. The lava here was not the blue-black cinder-stone of the fields about Rabegh: it was rust-coloured, and piled in huge crags of flowing surface and bent and twisted texture, as though played with oddly while yet soft. The sand, at first a carpet about the foot of the dolerite, gradually gained on it. The hills got lower, with the sand banked up against them in greater drifts, till even the crests were sand-spattered, and at last drowned beyond sight. So, as the sun became high and painfully fierce, we led out upon a waste of dunes, rolling southward for miles down hill to the misty sea, where it lay grey-blue in the false distance of the heat.

The dunes were narrow. By half-past seven we were on a staring plain of glassy sand mixed with shingle, overspread by tall scrub and thorn bushes, with some good acacia trees. We rode very fast across this, myself in some discomfort; for I was not a skilled rider: the movement exhausted me, while sweat ran down my forehead and dripped smartingly into my gritty, sun-cracked eyelids. Sweat was actually welcome when a drop fell from the end of a tuft of hair, to strike on the cheek cold and sudden and unexpected like a splash; but these refreshments were too few to pay for the pain of heat. We pressed on, while the sand yielded to pure shingle, and that again hardened into the bed of a great valley, running down by shallow, interwoven mouths towards the sea.

We crossed over a rise, and from the far side opened a wide view, which was the delta of Wadi Yenbo, the largest valley of Northern Hejaz. It seemed a vivid copse of tamarisk and thorn. To the right, some miles up the valley, showed darkly the palm-groves of Nakhl Mubarak, a village and gardens of the Beni Ibrahim Juheina. In the distance, ahead of us, lay the massive Jebel Rudhwa, brooding always so instantly over Yenbo, though more than twenty miles away. We had seen it from Masturah, for it was one of the great hills of Hejaz, the more wonderful because it lifted itself in one clear edge from flat Tehama to crest. My companions felt at home in its protection; so, as the plain was now dancing with unbearable heat, we took shade under the branches of a leafy acacia beside the path, and slumbered through the middle day.

In the afternoon we watered our camels at a brackish little water hole in the sand bed of a branch watercourse, before a trim hedge of the feathery tamarisk, and then pushed on for two more happy hours. At last we halted for the night in typical Tehama country of bare slowly-swelling sand and shingle ridges, with shallow valleys.

The Sherifs lit a fire of aromatic wood to bake bread and boil coffee;

and we slept sweetly with the salt sea air cool on our chafed faces. We rose at two in the morning, and raced our camels over a featureless plain of hard shingle and wet sand to Yenbo, which stood up with walls and towers on a reef of coral rag twenty feet above our level. They took me straight through the gates by crumbling, empty streets — Yenbo had been half a city of the dead since the Hejaz Railway opened — to the house of Abd el Kader, Feisal's agent, a well-informed, efficient, quiet and dignified person, with whom we had had correspondence when he was postmaster in Mecca, and the Survey in Egypt had been making stamps for the new State. He had just been transferred here.

With Abd el Kader, in his picturesque rambling house looking over the deserted square, whence so many Medina caravans had started, I stayed four days waiting for the ship, which seemed as if it might fail me at the rendezvous. However, at last the *Suva* appeared, with Captain Boyle, who took me back to Jidda. It was my first meeting with Boyle. He had done much in the beginning of the revolt, and was to do much more for the future: but I failed to make a good return impression. I was travel-stained and had no baggage with me. Worst of all I wore a native head-cloth, put on as a compliment to the Arabs. Boyle disapproved.

Our persistence in the hat (due to a misunderstanding of the ways of heat-stroke) had led the East to see significance in it, and after long thought their wisest brains concluded that Christians wore the hideous thing that its broad brim might interpose between their weak eyes and the uncongenial sight of God. So it reminded Islam continually that God was miscalled and misliked by Christians. The British thought this prejudice reprehensible (quite unlike our hatred of a head-cloth) one to be corrected at any price. If the people would not have us hatted, they should not have us any way. Now as it happened I had been educated in Syria before the war to wear the entire Arab outfit when necessary without strangeness, or sense of being socially compromised. The skirts were a nuisance in running up stairs, but the head-cloth was even convenient in such a climate. So I had accepted it when I rode inland, and must now cling to it under fire of naval disapproval, till some shop should sell me a cap.

In Jidda was the *Euryalus*, with Admiral Wemyss, bound for Port

Sudan that Sir Rosslyn might visit Sir Reginald Wingate at Khartum. Sir Reginald, as Sirdar of the Egyptian Army, had been put in command of the British military side of the Arab adventure in place of Sir Henry McMahon, who continued to direct its politics; and it was necessary for me to see him, to impart my impressions to him. So I begged the Admiral for a passage over sea, and a place in his train to Khartum. This he readily granted, after cross-questioning me himself at length.

I found that his active and broad intelligence had engaged his interest in the Arab Revolt from the beginning. He had come down again and again in his flagship to lend a hand when things were critical, and had gone out of his way twenty times to help the shore, which properly was Army business. He had given the Arabs guns and machine-guns, landing parties and technical help, with unlimited transport and naval co-operation, always making a real pleasure of requests, and fulfilling them in overflowing measure.

Had it not been for Admiral Wemyss' good will, and prescience, and the admirable way in which Captain Boyle carried out his wishes, the jealousy of Sir Archibald Murray might have wrecked the Sherif's rebellion at its start. As it was, Sir Rosslyn Wemyss acted godfather till the Arabs were on their feet; when he went to London; and Allenby, coming out fresh to Egypt, found the Arabs a factor on his battle front, and put the energies and resources of the Army at their disposal. This was opportune, and a fortunate twist of the whirligig; for Admiral Wemyss' successor in the naval command in Egypt was not considered helpful by the other services, though apparently he treated them no worse than he treated his own subordinates. A hard task, of course, to succeed Wemyss.

In Port Sudan we saw two British officers of the Egyptian Army waiting to embark for Rabegh. They were to command the Egyptian troops in Hejaz, and to do their best to help Aziz el Masri organize the Arab Regular Force, which was going to end the war from Rabegh. This was my first meeting with Joyce and Davenport, the two Englishmen to whom the Arab cause owed the greater part of its foreign debt of gratitude. Joyce worked for long beside me. Of Davenport's successes in the south we heard by constant report.

Khartum felt cool after Arabia, and nerved me to show Sir Reginald Wingate my long reports written in those days of waiting at Yenbo. I urged that the situation seemed full of promise. The main need was skilled assistance; and the campaign should go prosperously if some regular British officers, professionally competent and speaking Arabic, were attached to the Arab leaders as technical advisers, to keep us in proper touch.

Wingate was glad to hear a hopeful view. The Arab Revolt had been his dream for years. While I was at Khartum chance gave him the power to play the main part in it; for the workings against Sir Henry McMahon came to a head, were successful, and ended in his recall to England. Sir Reginald Wingate was ordered down to Egypt in his stead. So after two or three comfortable days in Khartum, resting and reading the *Morte d'Arthur* in the hospitable palace, I went down towards Cairo, feeling that the responsible person had all my news. The Nile trip became a holiday.

Egypt was, as usual, in the throes of a Rabegh question. Some aeroplanes were being sent there; and it was being argued whether to send a brigade of troops after them or not. The head of the French Military Mission at Jidda, Colonel Bremond (Wilson's counterpart, but with more authority; for he was a practising light in native warfare, a success in French Africa, and an ex-chief of staff of a Corps on the Somme), strongly urged the landing of Allied forces in Hejaz. To tempt us he had brought to Suez some artillery, some machine-guns, and some cavalry and infantry, all Algerian Moslem rank and file, with French officers. These added to the British troops would give the force an international flavour.

Bremond's specious appreciation of the danger of the state of affairs in Arabia gained upon Sir Reginald. Wingate was a British General, commander of a nominal expeditionary force, the Hejaz Force, which in reality comprised a few liaison officers and a handful of storemen and instructors. If Bremond got his way he would be G.O.C. of a genuine brigade of mixed British and French troops, with all its pleasant machinery of responsibility and despatches, and its prospect of increment and official recognition. Consequently he wrote a guarded despatch, half-tending towards direct interference.

As my experience of Arab feeling in the Harb country had given me strong opinions on the Rabegh question (indeed, most of my opinions were strong), I wrote for General Clayton, to whose Arab Bureau I was now formally transferred, a violent memorandum on the whole subject. Clayton was pleased with my view that the tribes might defend Rabegh for months if lent advice and guns, but that they would certainly scatter to their tents again as soon as they heard of the landing of foreigners in force. Further, that the intervention-plans were technically unsound, for a brigade would be quite insufficient to defend the position, to forbid the neighbouring water-supplies to the Turks, and to block their road towards Mecca. I accused Colonel Bremond of having motives of his own, not military, nor taking account of Arab interests and of the importance of the revolt to us; and quoted his words and acts in Hejaz as evidence against him. They gave just plausible colour to my charge.

Clayton took the memorandum to Sir Archibald Murray, who, liking its acidity and force, promptly wired it all home to London as proof that the Arab experts asking this sacrifice of valuable troops from him were divided about its wisdom and honesty, even in their own camp. London asked for explanations; and the atmosphere slowly cleared, though in a less acute form the Rabegh question lingered for two months more.

My popularity with the Staff in Egypt, due to the sudden help I had lent to Sir Archibald's prejudices, was novel and rather amusing. They began to be polite to me, and to say that I was observant, with a pungent style, and character. They pointed out how good of them it was to spare me to the Arab cause in its difficulties. I was sent for by the Commander-in-Chief, but on my way to him was intercepted by a waiting and agitated aide, and led first into the presence of the Chief of Staff, General Lynden Bell. To such an extent had he felt it his duty to support Sir Archibald in his whimsies that people generally confounded the two as one enemy. So I was astonished when, as I came in, he jumped to his feet, leaped forward, and gripped me by the shoulder, hissing, 'Now you're not to frighten him: don't you forget what I say!'

My face probably showed bewilderment, for his one eye turned bland and he made me sit down, and talked nicely about Oxford, and what fun undergrads had, and the interest of my report of life in Feisal's ranks, and his hope that I would go back there to carry on what I had so well begun, mixing these amiabilities with remarks of how nervous the Commander-in-Chief was, and how worried about everything, and the need there was for me to give him a reassuring picture of affairs, and yet not a rosy picture, since they could not afford excursions either way.

I was hugely amused, inwardly, and promised to be good, but pointed out that my object was to secure the extra stores and arms and officers the Arabs needed, and how for this end I must enlist the interest, and, if necessary (for I would stick at nothing in the way of duty), even the excitement of the Commander-in-Chief; whereupon General Lynden Bell took me up, saying that supplies were his part, and in them he did everything without reference, and he thought he might at once, here and now, admit his new determination to do all he could for us.

I think he kept his word and was fair to us thereafter. I was very soothing to his chief.

BOOK II

OPENING THE ARAB OFFENSIVE

Chapters XVII to XXVII

MY *chiefs were astonished at such favourable news, but promised help, and meanwhile sent me back, much against my will, into Arabia. I reached Feisal's camp on the day the Turks carried the defences of Jebel Subh. By their so doing the entire basis of my confidence in a tribal war was destroyed.*

We havered for a while by Yenbo, hoping to retrieve the position: but the tribesmen proved to be useless for assault, and we saw that if the Revolt was to endure we must invent a new plan of campaign at once.

This was hazardous, as the promised British military experts had not yet arrived. However, we decided that to regain the initiative we must ignore the main body of the enemy, and concentrate far off on his railway flank. The first step towards this was to move our base to Wejh: which we proceeded to do in the grand manner.

CHAPTER XVII

CLAYTON a few days later told me to return to Arabia and Feisal. This being much against my grain I urged my complete unfitness for the job: said I hated responsibility — obviously the position of a conscientious adviser would be responsible — and that in all my life objects had been gladder to me than persons, and ideas than objects. So the duty of succeeding with men, of disposing them to any purpose, would be doubly hard to me. They were not my medium: I was not practised in that technique. I was unlike a soldier: hated soldiering. Of course, I had read the usual books (too many books), Clausewitz and Jomini, Mahan and Foch, had played at Napoleon's campaigns, worked at Hannibal's tactics, and the wars of Belisarius, like any other man at Oxford; but I had never thought myself into the mind of a real commander compelled to fight a compaign of his own.

Last of all I reminded Clayton, relevantly, that the Sirdar had telegraphed to London for certain regular officers competent to direct the Arab war. The reply was that they might be months arriving, and meanwhile Feisal must be linked to us, and his needs promptly notified to Egypt. So I had to go; leaving to others the Arab Bulletin I had founded, the maps I wished to draw, and the file of the war-changes of the Turkish Army, all fascinating activities in which my training helped me; to take up a role for which I felt no inclination. As our revolt succeeded, onlookers have praised its leadership: but behind the scenes lay all the vices of amateur control, experimental councils, divisions, whimsicality.

My journey was to Yenbo, now the special base of Feisal's army, where Garland single-handed was teaching the Sherifians how to blow up railways with dynamite, and how to keep army stores in systematic order. The first activity was the better. Garland was an enquirer in physics, and had years of practical knowledge of explosives. He had his own devices for mining trains and felling telegraphs and cutting metals; and his knowledge of Arabic and freedom from the theories of the ordinary sapper-school enabled him to teach the art of demolition to unlettered Beduin in a quick and ready way. His pupils admired a man who was never at a loss.

Incidentally he taught me to be familiar with high explosive. Sappers handled it like a sacrament, but Garland would shovel a handful of detonators into his pocket, with a string of primers, fuse, and fusees, and jump gaily on his camel for a week's ride to the Hejaz Railway. His health was poor and the climate made him regularly ill. A weak heart troubled him after any strenuous effort or crisis; but he treated these troubles as freely as he did detonators, and persisted till he had derailed the first train and broken the first culvert in Arabia. Shortly afterwards he died.

Things in Hejaz had changed a good deal in the elapsed month. Pursuing his former plan, Feisal had moved to Wadi Yenbo, and was trying to make safe his rear before going up to attack the railway in the grand manner. To relieve him of the burdensome Harb tribes, his young half-brother Zeid was on the way up from Rabegh to Wadi Safra, as a nominal subordinate of Sherif Ali. The advanced Harb clans were efficiently harrying the Turkish communications between Medina and Bir Abbas. They sent in to Feisal nearly every day a little convoy of captured camels, or rifles picked up after an engagement, or prisoners, or deserters.

Rabegh, shaken by the first appearance of Turkish aeroplanes on November the seventh, had been reassured by the arrival of a flight of four British aeroplanes, B.E. machines, under Major Ross, who spoke Arabic so adeptly and was so splendid a leader that there could be no two minds as to the wise direction of his help. More guns came in week by week, till there were twenty-three, mostly obsolete, and of fourteen patterns. Ali had about three thousand Arab infantry; of whom two thousand were regulars in khaki, under Aziz el Masri. With them were nine hundred camel corps, and three hundred Egyptian troops. French gunners were promised.

Sherif Abdulla had at last left Mecca, on November the twelfth. A fortnight later he was much where he had meant to be, south, east and north-east of Medina, able to cut off its supplies from Kasim and Kuweit. Abdulla had about four thousand men with him, but only three machine-guns, and ten inefficient mountain guns captured at Taif and Mecca. Consequently he was not strong enough to carry out his further plan of a concerted attack on Medina with Ali and Feisal. He could only blockade it, and for this purpose posted himself at Henakiyeh, a desert place, eighty miles north-east of Medina, where he was too far away to be very useful.

The matter of the stores in the Yenbo base was being well handled. Garland had left the checking and issuing of them to Abd el Kader, Feisal's governor, who was systematic and quick. His efficiency was a great comfort to us, since it enabled us to keep our attention on more active things. Feisal was organizing his peasants, his slaves, and his paupers into formal battalions, an irregular imitation of the new model army of Aziz at Rabegh. Garland held bombing classes, fired guns, repaired machine-guns, wheels, and harness, and was armourer for them all. The feeling was busy and confident.

Feisal, who had not yet acted on our reminders of the importance of Wejh, was imagining an expedition of the Juheina to take it. Meanwhile he was in touch with the Billi, the numerous tribe with headquarters in Wejh, and he hoped for support from them. Their paramount Sheikh, Suleiman Rifada, was temporizing, being really hostile; for the Turks had made him Pasha and decorated him; but his cousin Hamid was in arms for the Sherif, and had just captured a gratifying little caravan of seventy camels on the way from El Ula, with stores for the Turkish garrison of Wejh. As I was starting for Kheif Hussein to press the Wejh plan again on Feisal, news came in of a Turkish repulse near Bir ibn Hassani. A reconnaissance of their cavalry and camel corps had been pushed too far into the hills, and the Arabs had caught it and scattered it. Better and better yet.

CHAPTER XVIII

So I made a happy start with my sponsor for the journey, Sherif Abd el Kerim el Beidawi, half-brother of Mohammed, Emir of the Juheina, but, to my astonishment, of pure Abyssinian type. They told me later that his mother had been a slave-girl married by the old Emir late in life. Abd el Kerim was a man of middle height, thin and coal black, but debonair, twenty-six years old; though he looked less, and had only a tiny tuft of beard on his sharp chin. He was restless and active, endowed with an easy, salacious humour. He hated the Turks, who had despised him for his colour (Arabs had little colour-feeling against Africans: it was the Indian who evoked their race-dislike), and was very merry and intimate with me. With him were three or four of his men, all well mounted; and we had a rapid journey, for Abd el Kerim was a famous rider who took pride in covering his stages at three times the normal speed. It was not my camel, and the weather was cool and clouded, with a taste of rain. So I had no objection.

After starting, we cantered for three unbroken hours. That had shaken down our bellies far enough for us to hold more food, and we stopped and ate bread and drank coffee till sunset, while Abd el Kerim rolled about his carpet in a dog-fight with one of the men. When he was exhausted he sat up; and they told stories and japed, till they were breathed enough to get up and dance. Everything was very free, very good-tempered, and not at all dignified.

When we re-started, an hour's mad race in the dusk brought us to the end of the Tehama, and to the foot of a low range of rock and sand. A month ago, coming from Hamra, we had passed south of this: now we crossed it, going up Wadi Agida, a narrow, winding, sandy valley between the hills. Because it had run in flood a few days earlier, the going was firm for our panting camels; but the ascent was steep and we had to take it at walking pace. This pleased me, but so angered Abd el Kerim, that when, in a short hour, we reached the watershed he thrust his mount forward again and led us at break-neck speed down hill in the yielding night (a fair road, fortunately, with sand and pebbles underfoot) for half an hour, when the land flattened out, and we came to the outlying plantations of Nakhl Mubarak, chief date-gardens of the southern Juheina.

As we got near we saw through the palm-trees flame, and the flame-lit smoke of many fires, while the hollow ground re-echoed with the roaring of thousands of excited camels, and volleying of shots or shoutings in the darkness of lost men, who sought through the crowd to rejoin their friends. As we had heard in Yenbo that the Nekhl were deserted, this tumult meant something strange, perhaps hostile. We crept quietly past an end of the grove and along a narrow street between man-high mud walls, to a silent group of houses. Abd el Kerim forced the courtyard door of the first on our left, led the camels within, and hobbled them down by the walls that they might remain unseen. Then he slipped a cartridge into the breech of his rifle and stole off on tiptoe down the street towards the noise to find out what was happening. We waited for him, the sweat of the ride slowly drying in our clothes as we sat there in the chill night, watching.

He came back after half an hour to say that Feisal with his camel corps had just arrived, and we were to go down and join him. So we led the camels out and mounted; and rode in file down another lane on a bank between houses, with a sunk garden of palms on our right. Its end was filled with a solid crowd of Arabs and camels, mixed together in the wildest confusion, and all crying aloud. We pressed through them, and down a ramp suddenly into the bed of Wadi Yenbo, a broad, open space: how broad could only be guessed from the irregular lines of watch-fires glimmering over it to a great distance. Also it was very damp; with slime, the relic of a shallow flood two days before, yet covering its stones. Our camels found it slippery under foot and began to move timidly.

We had no opportunity to notice this, or indeed anything, just now, except the mass of Feisal's army, filling the valley from side to side. There were hundreds of fires of thorn-wood, and round them were Arabs making coffee or eating, or sleeping muffled like dead men in their cloaks, packed together closely in the confusion of camels. So many camels in company made a mess indescribable, couched as they were or tied down all over the camping ground, with more ever coming in, and the old ones leaping up on three legs to join them, roaring with hunger and agitation. Patrols were going out, caravans being unloaded, and dozens of Egyptian mules bucking angrily over the middle of the scene.

We ploughed our way through this din, and in an island of calm at the very centre of the valley bed found Sherif Feisal. We halted our camels by his side. On his carpet, spread barely over the stones, he was sitting between Sherif Sharraf, the Kaimmakam both of the Imaret and of Taif, his cousin, and Maulud, the rugged, slashing old Mesopotamian patriot, now acting as his A.D.C. In front of him knelt a secretary taking down an order, and beyond him another reading reports aloud by the light of a silvered lamp which a slave was holding. The night was windless, the air heavy, and the unshielded flame poised there stiff and straight.

Feisal, quiet as ever, welcomed me with a smile until he could finish his dictation. After it he apologized for my disorderly reception, and waved the slaves back to give us privacy. As they retired with the onlookers, a wild camel leaped into the open space in front of us, plunging and trumpeting. Maulud dashed at its head to drag it away; but it dragged him instead; and, its load of grass ropes for camel fodder coming untied, there poured down over the taciturn Sharraf, the lamp, and myself, an avalanche of hay. 'God be praised,' said Feisal gravely, 'that it was neither butter nor bags of gold.' Then he explained to me what unexpected things had happened in the last twenty-four hours on the battle front.

The Turks had slipped round the head of the Arab barrier forces in Wadi Safra by a side road in the hills, and had cut their retreat. The Harb, in a panic, had melted into the ravines on each side, and escaped through them in parties of twos and threes, anxious for their threatened families. The Turkish mounted men poured down the empty valley and over the Dhifran Pass to Bir Said, where Ghalib Bey, their commander, nearly caught the unsuspecting Zeid asleep in his tent. However, warning came just in time. With the help of Sherif Abdulla ibn Thawab, an old Harith campaigner, Emir Zeid held up the enemy attack for long enough to get some of his tents and baggage packed on camels and driven away. Then he escaped himself; but his force melted into a loose mob of fugitives riding wildly through the night towards Yenbo.

Thereby the road to Yenbo was laid open to the Turks, and Feisal had rushed down here only an hour before our arrival, with five thousand men, to protect his base until something properly defensive could be arranged. His spy system was breaking down: the Harb, having lost their wits in the darkness, were bringing in wild and contradictory reports from one side and another about the strength of the Turks and their movements and intention. He had no idea whether they would strike at Yenbo or be content with holding the passes from Wadi Yenbo into Wadi Safra while they threw the bulk of their forces down the coast towards Rabegh and Mecca. The situation would be serious either way: the best that could happen would be if Feisal's presence here attracted them, and caused them to lose more days trying to catch his field army while we strengthened Yenbo. Meanwhile, he was doing all he could, quite cheerfully; so I sat down and listened to the news; or to the petitions, complaints and difficulties being brought in and settled by him summarily.

Sharraf beside me worked a busy tooth-stick back and forward along his gleaming jaws, speaking only once or twice an hour, in reproof of too-urgent suitors. Maulud ever and again leaned over to me, round Feisal's neutral body, eagerly repeating for our joint benefit any word of a report which might be turned to favour the launching of an instant and formal counter-attack.

This lasted till half-past four in the morning. It grew very cold as the damp of the valley rose through the carpet and soaked our clothes. The camp gradually stilled as the tired men and animals went one by one to sleep; a white mist collected softly over them and in it the fires became slow pillars of smoke. Immediately behind us, rising out of the bed of mist, Jebel Rudhwa, more steep and rugged than ever, was brought so close by the hushed moonlight that it seemed hanging over our heads.

Feisal at last finished the urgent work. We ate half-a-dozen dates, a frigid comfort, and curled up on the wet carpet. As I lay there in a shiver, I saw the Biasha guards creep up and spread their cloaks gently over Feisal, when they were sure that he was sleeping.

An hour later we got up stiffly in the false dawn (too cold to go on pretending and lying down) and the slaves lit a fire of palm-ribs to warm us, while Sharraf and myself searched for food and fuel enough for the moment. Messengers were still coming in from all sides with evil rumours of an immediate attack; and the camp was not far off panic. So Feisal decided to move to another position, partly because we should be washed out of this one if it rained anywhere in the hills, and partly to occupy his men's minds and work off their restlessness.

When his drums began to beat, the camels were loaded hurriedly. After the second signal everyone leaped into the saddle and drew off to left or right, leaving a broad lane up which Feisal rode, on his mare, with Sharraf a pace behind him, and then Ali, the standard-bearer, a splendid wild man from Nejd, with his hawk's face framed in long plaits of jet-black hair falling downward from his temples. Ali was dressed garishly, and rode a tall camel. Behind him were all the mob of sherifs and sheikhs and slaves — and myself — pell-mell. There were eight hundred in the bodyguard that morning.

Feisal rode up and down looking for a place to camp, and at last stopped on the further side of a little open valley just north of Nakhl Mubarak village; though the houses were so buried in the trees that few of them could be seen from outside. On the south bank of this valley, beneath some rocky knolls, Feisal pitched his two plain tents. Sharraf had his personal tent also; and some of the other chiefs came and lived by us. The guard put up their booths and shelters; and the Egyptian gunners halted lower down on our side, and dressed their twenty tents beautifully in line, to look very military. So in a little while we were populous, if hardly imposing in detail.

CHAPTER XIX

WE stayed here two days, most of which I spent in Feisal's company, and so got a deeper experience of his method of command, at an interesting season when the morale of his men was suffering heavily from the scare reports brought in, and from the defection of the Northern Harb. Feisal, fighting to make up their lost spirits, did it most surely by lending of his own to everyone within reach. He was accessible to all who stood outside his tent and waited for notice; and he never cut short petitions, even when men came in chorus with their grief in a song of many verses, and sang them around us in the dark. He listened always, and if he did not settle the case himself called Sharraf or Faiz to arrange it for him. This extreme patience was a further lesson to me of what native headship in Arabia meant.

His self-control seemed equally great. When Mirzuk el Tikheimi, his guest-master, came in from Zeid to explain the shameful story of their rout, Feisal just laughed at him in public and sent him aside to wait while he saw the sheikhs of the Harb and the Ageyl whose carelessness had been mainly responsible for the disaster. These he rallied gently, chaffing them for having done this or that, for having inflicted such losses or lost so much. Then he called back Mirzuk and lowered the tent-flap: a sign that there was private business to be done. I thought of the meaning of Feisal's name (the sword flashing downward in the stroke) and feared a scene, but he made room for Mirzuk on his carpet, and said, 'Come! tell us more of your "nights" and marvels of the battle: amuse us'. Mirzuk, a good-looking, clever lad (a little too sharp-featured) falling into the spirit of the thing, began, in his broad, Ateibi twang, to draw for us word-pictures of young Zeid in flight; of the terror of Ibn Thawab, that famous brigand; and, ultimate disgrace, of how the venerable el Hussein, father of Sherif Ali, the Harithi, had lost his coffee-pots!

Feisal, in speaking, had a rich musical voice, and used it carefully upon his men. To them he talked in tribal dialect, but with a curious, hesitant manner, as though faltering painfully among phrases, looking inward for the just word. His thought, perhaps, moved only by a little in front of his speech, for the phrases at last chosen were usually the simplest, which gave an effect emotional and sincere. It seemed possible, so thin was the screen of words, to see the pure and the very brave spirit shining out.

At other times he was full of humour — that invariable magnet of Arab goodwill. He spoke one night to the Rifaa sheikhs when he sent them forward to occupy the plain this side of Bir el Fagir, a tangled country of acacia and tamarisk thickets on the imperceptible watershed of the long depression uniting Bruka and Bir Said. He told them gently that the Turks were coming on, and that it was their duty to hold them up and give God the credit of their victory; adding that this would become impossible if they went to sleep. The old men — and in Arabia elders mattered more than youths — broke out into delighted speech, and, after saying that God would give him a victory, or rather two victories, capped their wishes with a prayer that his life might be prolonged in the accumulation of an unprecedented number of victories. What was better, they kept effective watch all night, in the strength of his exhortation.

The routine of our life in camp was simple. Just before daybreak the army Imam used to climb to the head of the little hill above the sleeping army, and thence utter an astounding call to prayer. His voice was harsh and very powerful, and the hollow, like a sounding-board, threw echoes at the hills which returned them with indignant interest. We were effectually roused, whether we prayed or cursed. As soon as he ended, Feisal's Imam cried gently and musically from just outside the tent. In a minute, one of Feisal's five slaves (all freed men, but refusing discharge till it was their pleasure: since it was good and not unprofitable to be my lord's servant) came round to Sharraf and myself with sweetened coffee. Sugar for the first cup in the chill of dawn was considered fit.

An hour or so later, the flap of Feisal's sleeping tent would be thrown back: his invitation to callers from the household. There would be four or five present; and after the morning's news a tray of breakfast would be carried in. The staple of this was dates in Wadi Yenbo; sometimes Feisal's Circassian grandmother would send him a box of her famous spiced cakes from Mecca; and sometimes Hejris, the body slave, would give us odd biscuits and cereals of his own trying. After breakfast we would play with bitter coffee and sweet tea in alternation, while Feisal's correspondence was dealt with by dictation to his secretaries. One of these was Faiz el Ghusein the adventurous; another was the Imam, a sad-faced person made conspicuous in the army by the baggy umbrella hanging from his saddle-bow. Occasionally a man was given private audience at this hour, but seldom; as the sleeping tent was strictly for the Sherif's own use. It was an ordinary bell tent, furnished with cigarettes, a camp-bed, a fairly good Kurd rug, a poor Shirazi, and the delightful old Baluch prayer-carpet on which he prayed.

At about eight o'clock in the morning, Feisal would buckle on his ceremonial dagger and walk across to the reception tent, which was floored with two horrible kilims. Feisal would sit down at the end of the tent facing the open side, and we with our backs against the wall, in a semicircle out from him. The slaves brought up the rear, and clustered round the open wall of the tent to control the besetting suppliants who lay on the sand in the tent-mouth, or beyond, waiting their turn. If possible, business was got through by noon, when the Emir liked to rise.

We of the household, and any guests, then reassembled in the living tent; and Hejris and Salem carried in the luncheon tray, on which were as many dishes as circumstances permitted. Feisal was an inordinate smoker, but a very light eater, and he used to make-believe with his fingers or a spoon among the beans, lentils, spinach, rice, and sweet cakes till he judged that we had had enough, when at a wave of his hand the tray would disappear, as other slaves walked forward to pour water for our fingers at the tent door. Fat men, like Mohammed Ibn Shefia, made a comic grievance of the Emir's quick and delicate meals, and would have food of their own prepared for them when they came away. After lunch we would talk a little, while sucking up two cups of coffee, and savouring two glasses full of syrup-like green tea. Then till two in the afternoon the curtain of the living tent was down, signifying that Feisal was sleeping, or reading, or doing private business. Afterwards he would sit again in the reception tent till he had finished with all who wanted him. I never saw an Arab leave him dissatisfied or hurt

— a tribute to his tact and to his memory; for he seemed never to halt for loss of a fact, nor to stumble over a relationship.

If there were time after second audience, he would walk with his friends, talking of horses or plants, looking at camels, or asking someone the names of the visible land features. The sunset prayer was at times public, though Feisal was not outwardly very pious. After it he saw people individually in the living tent, planning the night's reconnaissances and patrols — for most of the field-work was done after dark. Between six and seven there was brought in the evening meal, to which all present in headquarters were called by the slaves. It resembled the lunch, except that cubes of boiled mutton were sorted through the great tray of rice, *Medfa el Suhur*, the mainstay of appetite. We observed silence till all had eaten.

This meal ended our day, save for the stealthy offering by a bare-footed slave of a tray of tea-glasses at protracted intervals. Feisal did not sleep till very late, and never betrayed a wish to hasten our going. In the evening he relaxed as far as possible and avoided avoidable work. He would send out for some local sheikh to tell stories of the district, and histories of the tribe and its genealogy; or the tribal poets would sing us their war narratives: long traditional forms with stock epithets, stock sentiments, stock incidents grafted afresh on the efforts of each generation. Feisal was passionately fond of Arabic poetry, and would often provoke recitations, judging and rewarding the best verses of the night. Very rarely he would play chess, with the unthinking directness of a fencer, and brilliantly. Sometimes, perhaps for my benefit, he told stories of what he had seen in Syria, and scraps of Turkish secret history, or family affairs. I learned much of the men and parties in the Hejaz from his lips.

CHAPTER XX

SUDDENLY Feisal asked me if I would wear Arab clothes like his own while in the camp. I should find it better for my own part, since it was a comfortable dress in which to live Arab-fashion as we must do. Besides, the tribesmen would then understand how to take me. The only wearers of khaki in their experience had been Turkish officers, before whom they took up an instinctive defence. If I wore Meccan clothes, they would behave to me as though I were really one of the leaders; and I might slip in and out of Feisal's tent without making a sensation which he had to explain away each time to strangers.

I agreed at once, very gladly; for army uniform was abominable when camel-riding, or when sitting about on the ground; and the Arab things, which I had learned to manage before the war, were cleaner and more decent in the desert. Hejris was pleased, too, and exercised his fancy in fitting me out in splendid white silk and gold-embroidered wedding garments which had been sent to Feisal lately (was it a hint?) by his great-aunt in Mecca. I took a stroll in the new looseness of them round the palm-gardens of Mubarak and Bruka, to accustom myself to their feel.

These villages were pleasant little places, built of mud brick on the high earth mounds encircling the palm-gardens. Nakhl Mubarak lay to the north, and Bruka just south of it across a thorny valley. The houses were small, mud-washed inside, cool, and very clean, furnished with a mat or two, a coffee mortar, and food pots and trays. The narrow streets were shaded by an occasional well-grown tree. The earth embankments round the cultivated areas were sometimes fifty feet in height, and had been for the most part artificially formed from the surplus earth dug out between the trees, from household rubbish and from stones gathered out of the Wadi.

The banks were to defend the crops from flood. Wadi Yenbo otherwise would soon have filled the gardens, since these, to be irrigable, must be below the valley floor. The narrow plots were divided by fences of palm-ribs or by mud walls, with narrow streams of sweet water in raised channels round them. Each garden gate was over water, with a bridge of three or four parallel palm-logs built up to it for the passage of donkeys or camels. Each plot had a mud sluice, scooped away when its turn for watering came. The palms, regularly planted in ordered lines and well cared for, were the main crop; but between them were grown barley, radishes, marrows, cucumbers, tobacco and henna. Villages higher up Wadi Yenbo were cool enough to grow grapes.

Feisal's stand in Nakhl Mubarak could in the nature of things only be a pause, and I felt that I had better get back to Yenbo, to think seriously about our amphibious defence of this port, the Navy having promised its every help. We settled that I should consult Zeid, and act with him as seemed best. Feisal gave me a magnificent bay camel for the trip back. We marched through the Agida hills by a new road, Wadi Messarih, because of a scare of Turkish patrols on the more direct line. Bedr ibn Shefia was with me; and we did the distance gently in a single stage of six hours, getting to Yenbo before dawn. Being tired after three strenuous days of little sleep among constant alarms and excitements I went straight to Garland's empty house (he was living on board ship in the harbour) and fell asleep on a bench; but afterwards I was called out again by the news that Sherif Zeid was coming, and went down to the walls to see the beaten force ride in.

There were about eight hundred of them, quiet, but in no other way mortified by their shame. Zeid himself seemed finely indifferent. As he entered the town he turned and cried to Abd el Kadir, the Governor, riding behind him, 'Why, your town is ruinous! I must telegraph to my father for forty masons to repair the public buildings.' And this actually he did. I had telegraphed to Captain Boyle that Yenbo was gravely threatened, and Boyle at once replied that his fleet would be there in time, if not sooner. This readiness was an opportune consolation: worse news came along next day. The Turks, by throwing a strong force forward from Bir Said against Nakhl Mubarak, had closed with Feisal's levies while they were yet unsteady. After a short fight, Feisal had broken off, yielded his ground, and was retreating here. Our war seemed entering its last act. I took my camera, and from the parapet of the Medina gate got a fine photograph of the brothers coming in. Feisal had nearly two thousand men with him, but none of the Juheina tribesmen. It looked like treachery and a real defection of the tribes, things which both of us had ruled out of court as impossible.

I called at once at his house and he told me the history. The Turks had come on with three battalions and a number of mule-mounted infantry and camelry. Their command was in the hands of Ghalib Bey, who handled his troops with great keenness, acting as he did under the eye of the Corps Commander. Fakhru Pasha privately accompanied the expedition, whose guide and go-between with the Arabs was Dakhil-Allah el Kadhi, the hereditary law-giver of the Juheina, a rival of Sherif Mohammed Ali el Beidawi, and after him the second man in the tribe.

They got across Wadi Yenbo to the groves of Bruka in their first onset, and thus threatened the Arab communications with Yenbo. They were also able to shell Nakhl Mubarak freely with their seven guns. Feisal was not a whit dismayed, but threw out the Juheina on his left to work down the great valley. His centre and right he kept in Nakhl Mubarak, and he sent the Egyptian artillery to take post in Jebel Agida, to deny that to the Turks. Then he opened fire on Bruka with his own two fifteen-pounders.

Rasim, a Syrian officer, formerly a battery commander in the Turkish Army, was fighting these two guns; and he made a great demonstration with them. They had been sent down as a gift from Egypt, anyhow, old rubbish thought serviceable for the wild Arabs, just as the sixty thousand rifles supplied the Sherif were condemned weapons, relics of the Gallipoli campaign. So Rasim had no sights, nor range-finder, no range tables, no high explosive.

His distance might have been six thousand yards; but the fuses of his shrapnel were Boer War antiquities, full of green mould, and, if they burst, it was sometimes short in the air, and sometimes grazing. However, he had no means of getting his ammunition away if things went wrong, so he blazed off at speed, shouting with laughter at this fashion of making war; and the tribesmen seeing the commandant so merry took heart of grace themselves. 'By God,' said one, 'those are the real guns: the Importance of their noise!' Rasim swore that the Turks were dying in heaps; and the Arabs charged forward warmly at his word.

Things were going well; and Feisal had the hope of a decisive success when suddenly his left wing in the valley wavered, halted; finally it turned its back on the enemy and retired tumultuously to the camping ground. Feisal, in the centre, galloped to Rasim and cried that the Juheina had broken and he was to save the guns. Rasim yoked up the teams and trotted away to Wadi Agida, wherein the Egyptians were taking counsel pavidly with one another. After him streamed the Ageyl and the Atban, the men of Ibn Shefia, the Harb and Biasha. Feisal and his household composed the rear, and in deliberate procession they moved down towards Yenbo, leaving the Juheina with the Turks on the battlefield.

As I was still hearing of this sad end and cursing with him the traitor Beidawi brothers, there was a stir about the door, and Abd el Kerim broke through the slaves, swung up to the dais, kissed Feisal's head-rope in salutation, and sat down beside us. Feisal with a gasping stare at him, said, 'How?' and Abd el Kerim explained their dismay at the sudden flight of Feisal, and how he with his brother and their gallant men had fought the Turks for the whole night, alone, without artillery, till the palm-groves became untenable and they too had been driven through Wadi Agida. His brother, with half the manhood of the tribe, was just entering the gate. The others had fallen back up Wadi Yenbo for water.

'And why did you retire to the camp-ground behind us during the battle?' asked Feisal. 'Only to make ourselves a cup of coffee,' said Abd el Kerim. 'We had fought from sunrise and it was dusk: we were very tired and thirsty.' Feisal and I lay back and laughed: then we went to see what could be done to save the town.

The first step was simple. We sent all the Juheina back to Wadi Yenbo with orders to mass at Kheif, and keep up a steady pressure on the Turkish line of communications. They were also to push sniping parties down the Agida hills. This diversion would hold up so many of the Turks that they would be unable to bring against Yenbo a force superior in number to the defenders, who in addition had the advantage of a good position. The town on the top of its flat reef of coral rose perhaps twenty feet above the sea, and was compassed by water on two sides. The other two sides looked over flat stretches of sand, soft in places, destitute of cover for miles, and with no fresh water upon them anywhere. In daylight, if defended by artillery and machine-gun fire, they should be impregnable.

The artillery was arriving every minute; for Boyle, as usual far better than his word, had concentrated five ships on us in less than twenty-four hours. He put the monitor *M.31*, whose shallow draught fitted her for the job, in the end of the south-eastern creek of the harbour, whence she could rake the probable direction of a Turkish advance with her six-inch guns. Crocker, her captain, was very anxious to let off those itching guns. The larger ships were moored to fire over the town at longer range, or to rake the other flank from the northern harbour. The searchlights of *Dufferin* and *M.31* crossed on the plain beyond the town.

The Arabs, delighted to count up the quantity of vessels in the harbour, were prepared to contribute their part to the night's entertainment. They gave us good hope there would be no further panic: but to reassure them fully they needed some sort of rampart to defend, mediæval fashion: it was no good digging trenches, partly because the ground was coral rock, and, besides, they had no experience of trenches and might not have manned them confidently. So we took the crumbling, salt-riddled wall of the place, doubled it with a second, packed earth between the two, and raised them till our sixteenth-century bastions were rifle-proof at least, and probably proof against the Turkish mountain guns. Outside the bastions we put barbed wire, festooned between cisterns on the rain catchments beyond the walls. We dug in machine-gun nests in the best angles, and manned them with Feisal's regular gunners. The Egyptians, like everyone else given a place in the scheme, were gratifyingly happy. Garland was engineer-in-chief and chief adviser.

After sun-down the town quivered with suppressed excitement. So long as the day lasted there had been shouts and joy-shots and wild bursts of frenzy among the workmen; but when dark came, they went back to feed and a hush fell. Nearly everyone sat up that night. There was one alarm about eleven o'clock. Our outposts had met the enemy only three miles outside the town. Garland, with a crier, went through the few streets, and called the garrison. They tumbled straight out and went to their places in dead silence without a shot or a loose shout. The seamen on the minaret sent warning to the ships, whose combined searchlights began slowly to traverse the plain in complex intersections, drawing pencils of wheeling light across the flats which the attacking force must cross. However, no sign was made and no cause given us to open fire.

Afterwards, old Dakhil Allah told me he had guided the Turks down to rush Yenbo in the dark that they might stamp out Feisal's army once for all; but their hearts had failed them at the silence and the blaze of lighted ships from end to end of the harbour, with the eerie beams of the searchlights revealing the bleakness of the glacis they would have to cross. So they turned back: and that night, I believe, the Turks lost their war. Personally, I was on the *Suva*, to be undisturbed, and sleeping splendidly at last; so I was grateful to Dakhil Allah for the prudence which he preached the Turks, as though we might perhaps have won a glorious victory, I was ready to give much more for just that eight hours' unbroken rest.

CHAPTER XXI

NEXT day the crisis had passed: the Turks had clearly failed. The Juheina were active in their flank position from Wadi Yenbo. Garland's architectural efforts about the town became impressive. Sir Archibald Murray, to whom Feisal had appealed for a demonstration in Sinai to prevent further withdrawals of Turks for service at Medina, sent back an encouraging reply, and everybody was breathing easily. A few days later Boyle dispersed the ships, promising another lightning concentration upon another warning; and I took the opportunity to go down to Rabegh, where I met Colonel Bremond, the great bearded chief of the French Military Mission, and the only real soldier in Hejaz. He was still using his French detachment in Suez as a lever to move a British Brigade into Rabegh; and, since he suspected I was not wholly of his party, he made an effort to convert me.

In the course of the argument which followed, I said something about the need of soon attacking Medina; for, with the rest of the British, I believed that the fall of Medina was a necessary preliminary to any further progress of the Arab Revolt. He took me up sharply, saying that it was in no wise proper for the Arabs to take Medina. In his view, the Arab Movement had attained its maximum utility by the mere rebellion in Mecca; and military operations against Turkey were better in the unaided hands of Great Britain and France. He wished to land Allied troops at Rabegh, because it would quench the ardour of the tribes by making the Sherif suspect in their eyes. The foreign troops would then be his main defence, and his preservation be our work and option, until at the end of the war, when Turkey was defeated, the victorious Powers could extract Medina by treaty from the Sultan, and confer it upon Hussein, with the legal sovereignty of Hejaz, as his rewards for faithful service.

I had not his light confidence in our being strong enough to dispense with small allies; so I said shortly that my opinions were opposed to his. I laid the greatest weight on the immediate conquest of Medina, and was advising Feisal to seize Wejh, in order to prolong his threat against the railway. In sum, to my mind, the Arab Movement would not justify its creation if the enthusiasm of it did not carry the Arabs into Damascus.

This was unwelcome to him; for the Sykes-Picot Treaty of 1916 between France and England had been drawn by Sykes for this very eventuality; and, to reward it, stipulated the establishment of independent Arab states in Damascus, Aleppo and Mosul, districts which would otherwise fall to the unrestricted control of France. Neither Sykes nor Picot had believed the thing really possible; but I knew that it was, and believed that after it the vigour of the Arab Movement would prevent the creation — by us or others — in Western Asia of unduly 'colonial' schemes of exploitation.

Bremond took refuge in his technical sphere, and assured me, on his honour as a staff-officer, that for Feisal to leave Yenbo and go to Wejh was military suicide; but I saw no force in the arguments which he threw at me volubly; and told him so. It was a curious interview, that, between an old soldier and a young man in fancy dress; and it left a bad taste in my mouth. The Colonel, like his countrymen, was a realist in love, and war. Even in situations of poetry the French remained incorrigible prose-writers, seeing by the directly-thrown light of reason and understanding, not through the half-closed eye, mistily, by things' essential radiance, in the manner of the imaginative British: so the two races worked ill together on a great undertaking. However, I controlled myself enough not to tell any Arab of the conversation, but sent a full account of it to Colonel Wilson, who was shortly coming up to see Feisal for a discussion of the Wejh prospect in all its bearings.

Before Wilson arrived the centre of Turkish gravity changed abruptly. Fakhri Pasha had seen the hopelessness of attacking Yenbo, or of driving after the intangible Juheina in Kheif Hussein. Also he was being violently bombed in Nakhl Mubarak itself by a pair of British seaplanes which did hardy flights over the desert and got well into the enemy on two occasions, despite their shrapnel.

Consequently he decided to fall back in a hurry on Bir Said, leaving a small force there to check the Juheina, and to move down the Sultani road towards Rabegh with the bulk of his men. These changes were no doubt partly impelled by the unusual vigour of Ali at Rabegh. As soon as Ali had heard of Zeid's defeat he had sent him reinforcements and guns; and when Feisal himself collapsed he decided to move north with all his army, to attack the Turks in Wadi Safra and draw them off Yenbo. Ali had nearly seven thousand men; and Feisal felt that if the move was synchronized with one on his part, Fakhri's force might be crushed between them in the hills. He telegraphed, suggesting this, asking for a delay of a few days till his shaken men were ready.

Ali was strung up and would not wait. Feisal therefore rushed Zeid out to Masahali in Wadi Yenbo to make preparations. When these were complete he sent Zeid on to occupy Bir Said, which was done successfully. He then ordered the Juheina forward in support. They demurred; for ibn Beidawi was jealous of Feisal's growing power among his tribes, and wanted to keep himself indispensable. Feisal rode unattended to Nakhl Mubarak, and in one night convinced the Juheina that he was their leader. Next morning they were all moving, while he went on to collect the northern Harb on the Tasha Pass to interrupt the Turkish retreat in Wadi Safra. He had nearly six thousand men; and if Ali took the southern bank of the valley the weak Turks would be between two fires.

Unfortunately it did not happen. When actually on the move he heard from Ali that, after a peaceful recovery of Bir ibn Hassani, his men had been shaken by false reports of disloyalty among the Subh, and had fallen back in rapid disorder to Rabegh.

In this ominous pause Colonel Wilson came up to Yenbo to persuade us of the necessity of an immediate operation against Wejh. An amended plan had been drawn up whereby Feisal would take the whole force of the Juheina, and his permanent battalions, against Wejh with the maximum of naval help. This strength would make success reasonably sure, but it left Yenbo empty and defenceless. For the moment Feisal dreaded incurring such a risk. He pointed out, not unreasonably, that the Turks in his neighbourhood were still mobile; that Ali's force had proved hollow, unlikely to defend even Rabegh against serious attack; and that, as Rabegh was the bulwark of Mecca, sooner than see it lost he must throw away Yenbo and ferry himself and men thither to die fighting on its beach.

To reassure him, Wilson painted the Rabegh force in warm colours.

Feisal checked his sincerity by asking for his personal word that the Rabegh garrison, with British naval help, would resist enemy attack till Wejh fell. Wilson looked for support round the silent deck of the *Dufferin* (on which we were conferring), and nobly gave the required assurance: a wise gamble, since without it Feisal would not move; and this diversion against Wejh, the only offensive in the Arabs' power, was their last chance not so much of securing a convincing siege of Medina, as of preventing the Turkish capture of Mecca. A few days later he strengthened himself by sending Feisal direct orders from his father, the Sherif, to proceed to Wejh at once, with all his available troops.

Meanwhile the Rabegh situation grew worse. The enemy in Wadi Safra and the Sultani road were estimated at nearly five thousand men. The Harb of the north were suppliant to them for preservation of their palm-groves. The Harb of the south, those of Hussein Mabeirig, notoriously waited their advance to attack the Sherifians in the rear. At a conference of Wilson, Bremond, Joyce, Ross and others, held in Rabegh on Christmas Eve, it was decided to lay out on the beach by the aerodrome a small position, capable of being held under the ship's guns by the Egyptians, the Flying Corps and a seamen's landing party from the *Minerva*, for the few hours needed to embark or destroy the stores. The Turks were advancing step by step; and the place was not in condition to resist one well-handled battalion supported by field artillery.

However, Fakhri was too slow. He did not pass Bir el Sheikh in any force till near the end of the first week in January, and seven days later was still not ready to attack Khoreiba, where Ali had an outpost of a few hundred men. The patrols were in touch; and an assault was daily expected, but as regularly delayed.

In truth the Turks were meeting with unguessed difficulties. Their headquarters were faced by a heavy sick rate among the men, and a growing weakness of the animals: both symptoms of overwork and lack of decent food. Always the activity of the tribesmen behind their back hampered them. Clans might sometimes fall away from the Arab cause, but did not therefore become trustworthy adherents of the Turks, who soon found themselves in ubiquitously hostile country. The tribal raids in the first fortnight of January caused them average daily losses of forty camels and some twenty men killed and wounded, with corresponding expense in stores.

These raids might occur at any point from ten miles seaward of Medina itself for the next seventy miles through the hills. They illustrated the obstacles in the way of the new Turkish Army with its half-Germanized complexity of equipment, when, from a distant rail-head with no made roads, it tried to advance through extremely rugged and hostile country. The administrative developments of scientific war had clogged its mobility and destroyed its dash; and troubles grew in geometrical rather than arithmetical progression for each new mile its commanding officers put between themselves and Medina, their ill-found, insecure and inconvenient base.

The situation was so unpromising for the Turks that Fakhri was probably half glad when the forthcoming sudden moves of Abdulla and Feisal in the last days of 1916 altered the strategic conception of the Hejaz war, and hurried the Mecca expedition (after January the eighteenth 1917) back from the Sultani and the Fara and the Gaha roads, back from Wadi Safra, to hold a passive defence of trenches within sight of the walls of Medina; a static position which endured till the Armistice ended the war and involved Turkey in the dismal surrender of the Holy City and its helpless garrison.

CHAPTER XXII

FEISAL was a fine, hot workman, whole-heartedly doing a thing when he had agreed to it. He had pledged his word that he would go at once to Wejh; so he and I sat down together on new-year's day for consideration of what this move meant to us and to the Turks. Around us, stretching up and down the Wadi Yenbo for miles, in little groups round palm-gardens, under the thicker trees, and in all the side tributaries, wherever there was shelter from the sun and rain, or good grazing for the camels, were the soldiers of our army. The mountaineers, half-naked footmen, had grown few. Most of the six thousand present were mounted men of substance. Their coffee hearths were outlined from afar by the camel saddles, pitched in circles round the fire as elbow-rests for men reclining between meals. The Arabs' physical perfection let them lie relaxed to the stony ground like lizards, moulding themselves to its roughness in corpse-like abandon.

They were quiet but confident. Some, who had been serving Feisal for six months or more, had lost that pristine heat of eagerness which had so thrilled me in Hamra; but they had gained experience in compensation; and staying-power in the ideal was fatter and more important for us than an early fierceness. Their patriotism was now conscious; and their attendance grew more regular as the distance from their homes increased. Tribal independence of orders was still maintained; but they had achieved a mild routine in camp life and on the march. When the Sherif came near they fell into a ragged line, and together made the bow and sweep of the arm to the lips, which was the official salute. They did not oil their guns: they said lest the sand clog them; also they had no oil, and it was better rubbed in to soften wind-chaps on their skin; but the guns were decently kept, and some of the owners could shoot at long range.

In mass they were not formidable, since they had no corporate spirit, nor discipline nor mutual confidence. The smaller the unit the better its performance. A thousand were a mob, ineffective against a company of trained Turks: but three or four Arabs in their hills would stop a dozen Turks. Napoleon remarked this of the Mamelukes. We were yet too breathless to turn our hasty practice into principle: our tactics were empirical snatchings of the first means to escape difficulty. But we were learning like our men.

From the battle of Nakhl Mubarak we abandoned the brigading of Egyptian troops with irregulars. We embarked the Egyptian officers and men, after turning over their complete equipment to Rasim, Feisal's gunner, and Abdulla el Deleimi, his machine-gun officer. They built up Arab companies out of local material, with a stiffening of Turk-trained Syrian and Mesopotamian deserters. Maulud, the fire-eating A.D.C., begged fifty mules off me, put across them fifty of his trained infantrymen, and told them they were cavalry. He was a martinet, and a born mounted officer, and by his spartan exercises the much-beaten mule-riders grew painfully into excellent soldiers, instantly obedient and capable of formal attack! They were prodigies in the Arab ranks. We telegraphed for another fifty mules, to double the dose of mounted infantry, since the value of so tough a unit for reconnaissance was obvious.

Feisal suggested taking nearly all the Juheina to Wejh with him and adding to them enough of the Harb and Billi, Ateiba and Ageyl to give the mass a many-tribed character. We wanted this march, which would be in its way a closing act of the war in Northern Hejaz, to send a rumour through the length and breadth of Western Arabia. It was to be the biggest operation of the Arabs in their memory; dismissing those who saw it to their homes, with a sense that their world had changed indeed; so that there would be no more silly defections and jealousies of clans behind us in future, to cripple us with family politics in the middle of our fighting.

Not that we expected immediate opposition. We bothered to take this unwieldy mob with us to Wejh, in the teeth of efficiency and experience, just because there was no fighting in the bill. We had intangible assets on our side. In the first place, the Turks had now engaged their surplus strength in attacking Rabegh, or rather in prolonging their occupied area so as to attack Rabegh. It would take them days to transfer back north. Then the Turks were stupid, and we reckoned on their not hearing all at once of our move, and on their not believing its first tale, and not seeing till later what chances it had given them. If we did our march in three weeks we should probably take Wejh by surprise. Lastly, we might develop the sporadic raiding activity of the Harb into conscious operations, to take booty, if possible, in order to be self-supporting; but primarily to lock up large numbers of Turks in defence positions. Zeid agreed to go down to Rabegh to organize similar pin-pricks in the Turks' rear. I gave him letters to the captain of the *Dufferin*, the Yenbo guardship, which would ensure him a quick passage down: for all who knew of the Wejh scheme were agog to help it.

To exercise my own hand in the raiding genre I took a test party of thirty-five Mahamid with me from Nakhl Mubarak, on the second day of 1917, to the old blockhouse-well of my first journey from Rabegh to Yenbo. When dark came we dismounted, and left our camels with ten men to guard them against possible Turkish patrols. The rest of us climbed up Dhifran: a painful climb, for the hills were of knife-sharp strata turned on edge and running in oblique lines from crest to foot. They gave abundance of broken surface, but no sure grip, for the stone was so minutely cracked that any segment would come away from its matrix, in the hand.

The head of Dhifran was cold and misty, and time dragged till dawn. We disposed ourselves in crevices of the rock, and at last saw the tips of bell-tents three hundred yards away beneath us to the right, behind a spur. We could not get a full view, so contented ourselves with putting bullets through their tops. A crowd of Turks turned out and leaped like stags into their trenches. They were very fast targets, and probably suffered little. In return they opened rapid fire in every direction, and made a terrific row; as if signalling the Hamra force to turn out in their help. As the enemy were already more than ten to one, the reinforcements might have prevented our retreat: so we crawled gently back till we could rush down into the first valley, where we fell over two scared Turks, unbuttoned, at their morning exercise. They were ragged, but something to show, and we dragged them homeward, where their news proved useful.

Feisal was still nervous over abandoning Yenbo, hitherto his indispensable base, and the second sea-port of Hejaz: and when casting

about for further expedients to distract the Turks from its occupation
we suddenly remembered Sidi Abdulla in Henakiyeh. He had some
five thousand irregulars, and a few guns and machine-guns, and the
reputation of his successful (if too slow) siege of Taif. It seemed a
shame to leave him wasting in the middle of the wilderness. A first
idea was that he might come to Kheibar, to threaten the railway north
of Medina: but Feisal improved my plan vastly, by remembering
Wadi Ais, the historic valley of springs and palm-villages flowing
through the impregnable Juheina hills from behind Rudhwa eastward
to the Hamdh valley near Hedia. It lay just one hundred kilometres
north of Medina, a direct threat on Fakhri's railway communications
with Damascus. From it Abdulla could keep up his arranged blockade
of Medina from the east, against caravans from the Persian Gulf. Also
it was near Yenbo, which could easily feed him there with munitions
and supplies.

The proposal was obviously an inspiration and we sent off Raja el
Khuluwi at once to put it to Abdulla. So sure were we of his adopting
it that we urged Feisal to move away from Wadi Yenbo northward on
the first stage to Wejh, without waiting a reply.

CHAPTER XXIII

H E agreed, and we took the wide upper road through Wadi
Messarih, for Owais, a group of wells about fifteen miles to
the north of Yenbo. The hills were beautiful to-day. The rains
of December had been abundant, and the warm sun after them had
deceived the earth into believing it was spring. So a thin grass had
come up in all the hollows and flat places. The blades (single, straight
and very slender) shot up between the stones. If a man bent over from
his saddle and looked downward he would see no new colour in the
ground; but, by looking forward, and getting a distant slope at a flat
angle with his eye, he could feel a lively mist of pale green here and
there over the surface of slate-blue and brown-red rock. In places the
growth was strong, and our painstaking camels had become prosperous,
grazing on it.

The starting signal went, but only for us and the Ageyl. The other
units of the army, standing each man by his couched camel, lined up
beside our road, and, as Feisal came near, saluted him in silence. He
called back cheerfully, 'Peace upon you', and each head sheikh returned
the phrase. When we had passed they mounted, taking the time from
their chiefs, and so the forces behind us swelled till there was a line of
men and camels winding along the narrow pass towards the watershed
for as far back as the eye reached.

Feisal's greetings had been the only sounds before we reached the
crest of the rise where the valley opened out and became a gentle
forward slope of soft shingle and flint bedded in sand: but there ibn
Dakhil, the keen sheikh of Russ, who had raised this contingent of
Ageyl two years before to aid Turkey, and had brought it over with
him intact to the Sherif when the revolt came, dropped back a pace or
two, marshalled our following into a broad column of ordered ranks,
and made the drums strike up. Everyone burst out singing a full-
throated song in honour of Emir Feisal and his family.

The march became rather splendid and barbaric. First rode Feisal in
white, then Sharraf at his right in red head-cloth and henna-dyed tunic

and cloak, myself on his left in white and scarlet, behind us three banners of faded crimson silk with gilt spikes, behind them the drummers playing a march, and behind them again the wild mass of twelve hundred bouncing camels of the bodyguard, packed as closely as they could move, the men in every variety of coloured clothes and the camels nearly as brilliant in their trappings. We filled the valley to its banks with our flashing stream.

At the mouth of Messarih, a messenger rode up with letters to Feisal from Abd el Kader, in Yenbo. Among them was one three days' old for me from the *Dufferin* to say that she would not embark Zeid till she had seen me and heard details of the local situation. She was in the Sherm, a lonely creek eight miles up the coast from the port, where the officers could play cricket on the beach without the plague of flies pervading Yenbo. Of course, they cut themselves off from news by staying so far away: it was a point of old friction between us. Her well-meaning commander had not the breadth of Boyle, the fiery politician and revolutionary constitutionalist, nor the brain of Linberry, of the *Hardinge*, who filled himself with the shore gossip of every port he touched, and who took pains to understand the nature of all classes on his beat.

Apparently I had better race off to *Dufferin* and regulate affairs. Zeid was a nice fellow, but would assuredly do something quaint in his enforced holiday; and we needed peace just then. Feisal sent some Ageyl with me and we made speed for Yenbo: indeed, I got there in three hours, leaving my disgusted escort (who said they would wear out neither camels nor bottoms for my impatience) half way back on the road across the plain so wearily well known to me. The sun, which had been delightful overhead in the hills, now, in the evening, shone straight into our faces with a white fury, before which I had to press my hand as shield over my eyes. Feisal had given me a racing camel (a present from the Emir of Nejd to his father), the finest and roughest animal I had ridden. Later she died of overwork, mange, and necessary neglect on the road to Akaba.

On arrival in Yenbo things were not as expected. Zeid had been embarked, and the *Dufferin* had started that morning for Rabegh. So I sat down to count what we needed of naval help on the way to Wejh, and to scheme out means of transport. Feisal had promised to wait at Owais till he got my report that everything was ready.

The first check was a conflict between the civil and military powers. Abd el Kader, the energetic but temperamental governor, had been cluttered up with duties as our base grew in size, till Feisal added to him a military commandant, Tewfik Bey, a Syrian from Homs, to care for ordnance stores. Unfortunately, there was no arbiter to define ordnance stores. That morning they fell out over empty arms-chests. Abd el Kadir locked the store and went to lunch. Tewfik came down to the quay with four men, a machine-gun and a sledge hammer, and opened the door. Abd el Kader got into a boat, and rowed out to the British guardship — the tiny *Espiegle* — and told her embarrassed but hospitable captain that he had come to stay. His servant brought him food from the shore and he slept the night in a camp-bed on the quarter-deck.

I wanted to hurry, so began to solve the deadlock by making Abd el Kadir write to Feisal for his decision and by making Tewfik hand over the store to me. We brought the trawler *Arethusa* near the sloop, that Abd el Kader might direct the loading of the disputed chests from his ship, and lastly brought Tewfik off to the *Espiegle* for a temporary reconciliation. It was made easy by an accident, for, as Tewfik saluted his guard of honour at the gangway (not strictly regular, this guard, but politic), his face beamed and he said: 'This ship captured me at Kurna', pointing to the trophy of the nameplate of the Turkish gunboat *Marmaris*, which the *Espiegle* had sunk in action on the Tigris. Abd el Kadir was as interested in the tale as Tewfik, and the trouble ceased.

Sharraf came into Yenbo next day as Emir, in Feisal's place. He was a powerful man, perhaps the most capable of all the Sherifs in the army, but devoid of ambition: acting out of duty, not from impulse. He was rich, and had been for years chief justice of the Sherif's court. He knew and handled tribesmen better than any man, and they feared him, for he was severe and impartial, and his face was sinister, with a left eyebrow which drooped (the effect of an old blow) and gave him an air of forbidding hardness. The surgeon of the *Suva* operated on the eye and repaired much of the damage, but the face remained one to rebuke liberties or weakness. I found him good to work with, very clearheaded, wise and kind, with a pleasant smile — his mouth became soft then, while his eyes remained terrible — and a determination to do fittingly, always.

We agreed that the risk of the fall of Yenbo while we hunted Wejh was great, and that it would be wise to empty it of stores. Boyle gave me an opportunity by signalling that either *Dufferin* or *Hardinge* would be made available for transport. I replied that as difficulties would be severe I preferred *Hardinge*! Captain Warren, whose ship intercepted the message, felt it superfluous, but it brought along *Hardinge* in the best temper two days later. She was an Indian troop-ship, and her lowest troop-deck had great square ports along the water level. Linberry opened these for us, and we stuffed straight in eight thousand rifles, three million rounds of ammunition, thousands of shells, quantities of rice and flour, a shed-full of uniforms, two tons of high explosive, and all our petrol, pell-mell. It was like posting letters in a box. In no time she had taken a thousand tons of stuff.

Boyle came in eager for news. He promised the *Hardinge* as depot ship throughout, to land food and water whenever needed, and this solved the main difficulty. The Navy were already collecting. Half the Red Sea Fleet would be present. The admiral was expected and landing parties were being drilled on every ship. Everyone was dyeing white duck khaki-coloured, or sharpening bayonets, or practising with rifles.

I hoped silently, in their despite, that there would be no fighting. Feisal had nearly ten thousand men, enough to fill the whole Billi country with armed parties and carry off everything not too heavy or too hot. The Billi knew it, and were now profuse in their loyalties to the Sherif, completely converted to Arab nationality.

It was sure that we would take Wejh: the fear was lest numbers of Feisal's host die of hunger or thirst on the way. Supply was my business, and rather a responsibility. However, the country to Um Lejj, half way, was friendly: nothing tragic could happen so far as that: therefore, we sent word to Feisal that all was ready, and he left Owais on the very day that Abdulla replied welcoming the Ais plan and promising an immediate start thither. The same day came news of my relief. Newcombe, the regular colonel being sent to Hejaz as chief of our military mission, had arrived in Egypt, and his two staff officers, Cox and Vickery, were actually on their way down the Red Sea, to join this expedition.

Boyle took me to Um Lejj in the *Suva*, and we went ashore to get the news. The sheikh told us that Feisal would arrive to-day, at Bir el Waheidi, the water supply, four miles inland. We sent up a message for him and then walked over to the fort which Boyle had shelled some months before from the *Fox*. It was just a rubble barrack, and Boyle looked at the ruins and said: 'I'm rather ashamed of myself for smashing such a potty place.' He was a very professional officer, alert, business-like and official; sometimes a little intolerant of easy-going things and people. Red-haired men are seldom patient. 'Ginger Boyle', as they called him, was warm.

While we were looking over the ruins four grey ragged elders of the village came up and asked leave to speak. They said that some months before a sudden two-funnelled ship had come up and destroyed their fort. They were now required to re-build it for the police of the Arab Government. Might they ask the generous captain of this peace-able one-funnelled ship for a little timber, or for other material help towards the restoration? Boyle was restless at their long speech, and snapped at me, 'What is it? What do they want?' I said, 'Nothing; they were describing the terrible effect of the *Fox's* bombardment.' Boyle looked round him for a moment and smiled grimly, 'It's a fair mess'.

Next day Vickery arrived. He was a gunner, and in his ten years' service in the Sudan had learned Arabic, both literary and colloquial, so well that he would quit us of all need of an interpreter. We arranged to go up with Boyle to Feisal's camp to make the time-table for the attack, and after lunch Englishmen and Arabs got to work and dis-cussed the remaining march to Wejh.

We decided to break the army into sections: and that these should proceed independently to our concentration place of Abu Zereibat in Hamdh, after which there was no water before Wejh; but Boyle agreed that the *Hardinge* should take station for a single night in Sherm Habban — supposed to be a possible harbour — and land twenty tons of water for us on the beach. So that was settled.

For the attack on Wejh we offered Boyle an Arab landing party of several hundred Harb and Juheina peasantry and freed men, under Saleh ibn Shefia, a negroid boy of good courage (with the faculty of friendliness) who kept his men in reasonable order by conjurations and appeals, and never minded how much his own dignity was outraged by them or by us. Boyle accepted them and decided to put them on another deck of the many-stomached *Hardinge*. They, with the naval party, would land north of the town, where the Turks had no post to block a landing, and whence Wejh and its harbour were best turned.

Boyle would have at least six ships, with fifty guns to occupy the Turks' minds, and a seaplane ship to direct the guns. We would be at Abu Zereibat on the twentieth of the month: at Habban for the *Hardinge's* water on the twenty-second: and the landing party should go ashore at dawn on the twenty-third, by which time our mounted men would have closed all roads of escape from the town.

The news from Rabegh was good; and the Turks had made no attempt to profit by the nakedness of Yenbo. These were our hazards, and when Boyle's wireless set them at rest we were mightily encouraged. Abdulla was almost in Ais: we were half-way to Wejh: the initiative had passed to the Arabs. I was so joyous that for a moment I forgot my self-control, and said exultingly that in a year we would be tapping on the gates of Damascus. A chill came over the feeling in the tent and my hopefulness died. Later, I heard that Vickery had gone to Boyle and vehemently condemned me as a braggart and visionary; but, though the outburst was foolish, it was not an impossible dream, for five months later I was in Damascus, and a year after that I was its *de facto* Governor.

Vickery had disappointed me, and I had angered him. He knew I was militarily incompetent and thought me politically absurd. I knew he was the trained soldier our cause needed, and yet he seemed blind to its power. The Arabs nearly made shipwreck through this blindness of European advisers, who would not see that rebellion was not war: indeed, was more of the nature of peace — a national strike perhaps. The conjunction of Semites, an idea, and an armed prophet held illimitable possibilities; in skilled hands it would have been, not Damascus, but Constantinople which was reached in 1918.

CHAPTER XXIV

EARLY next morning, having seen that the *Hardinge* was unloading without friction, I went ashore to Sheikh Yusuf, and found him helping his Bisha police, the frightened villagers and a squad of old Maulud's men to throw a quick barricade across the end of the main street. He told me that fifty wild mules, without halter or bridle or saddle, had been loosed on shore that morning from a ship. By luck rather than skill they had been stampeded into the market-place: the exits were now safely barred, and there they must remain, ramping about the stalls, till Maulud, to whom they were addressed, invented saddlery in the wilderness. This was the second batch of fifty mules for the mounted unit, and by the chance of our fear at Yenbo we, fortunately, had spare ropes and bits enough for them on board the *Hardinge*. So by noon the shops were again open, and the damage paid for.

I went to Feisal's camp, which was busy. Some of the tribes were drawing a month's wages; all were getting eight days' food; tents and heavy baggage were being stored; and the last arrangement for the march being made. I sat and listened to the chatter of the staff: Faiz el Ghusein, Beduin sheikh, Turkish official, chronicler of the Armenian massacres, now secretary; Nesib el Bekri, Damascene land-owner, and Feisal's host in Syria, now exiled from his country with a death-sentence over him; Sami, Nesib's brother, graduate of the Law School, and now assistant paymaster; Shefik el Eyr, ex-journalist, now assistant secretary, a little white-faced man, and furtive, with a whispering manner, honest in his patriotism, but in life perverse, and so a nasty colleague.

Hassan Sharaf, the headquarters' doctor, a noble man who had put not merely his life, but his purse to service in the Arab cause, was plaintive with excess of disgust at finding his phials smashed and their drugs confounded in the bottom of his chest. Shefik rallying him, said, 'Do you expect a rebellion to be comfortable?' and the contrast with the pale misery of their manner delighted us. In hardships the humour of triteness outweighed a whole world of wit.

With Feisal in the evening we talked of the coming marches. The first stage was short: to Semna, where were palm-groves and wells of abundant water. After that there was choice of ways, to be determined only when our scouts returned with reports as to ponded rain-water. By the coast, the straight road, it was sixty dry miles to the next well. and our multitude of footmen would find that long.

The army at Bir el Waheida amounted to five thousand one hundred camel-riders, and five thousand three hundred men on foot, with four Krupp mountain guns, and ten machine-guns: and for transport we had three hundred and eighty baggage camels. Everything was cut to the lowest, far below the standard of the Turks. Our start was set for January the eighteenth just after noon, and punctually by lunch-time Feisal's work was finished. We were a merry party: Feisal himself, relaxed after responsibility, Abd el Kerim, never very serious, Sherif Jabar, Nasib and Sami, Shefik, Hassan Sharaf and myself. After lunch the tent was struck. We went to our camels, where they were couched in a circle, saddled and loaded, each held short by the slave standing on its doubled fore-leg. The kettle drummer, waiting beside ibn Dakhil, who commanded the bodyguard, rolled his drum seven or eight times, and everything became still. We watched Feisal. He got up from his rug, on which he had been saying a last word to Abd el Kerim, caught the saddle-pommels in his hands, put his knee on the side and said aloud, 'Make God your agent'. The slave released the camel, which sprang up. When it was on its feet Feisal passed his other leg across its back, swept his skirts and his cloak under him by a wave of the arm, and settled himself in the saddle.

As his camel moved we had jumped for ours, and the whole mob rose together, some of the beasts roaring, but the most quiet, as trained she-camels should be. Only a young animal, a male or ill-bred, would grumble on the road, and self-respecting Beduins did not ride such, since the noise might give them away by night or in surprise attacks. The camels took their first abrupt steps, and we riders had quickly to hook our legs round the front cantles, and pick up the head-stalls to check the pace. We then looked where Feisal was, and tapped our mounts' heads gently round, and pressed them on the shoulders with our bare feet till they were in line beside him. Ibn Dakhil came up, and after a glance at the country and the direction of march passed a short order for the Ageyl to arrange themselves in wings, out to right and left of us for two or three hundred yards, camel marching by camel in line as near as the accidents underfoot permitted. The manœuvre was neatly done.

These Ageyl were Nejd townsmen, the youth of Aneyza, Boreida or Russ, who had contracted for service as regular camel corps for a term of years. They were young, from sixteen to twenty-five, and nice fellows, large-eyed, cheery, a bit educated, catholic, intelligent, good companions on the road. There was seldom a heavy one. Even in repose (when most Eastern faces emptied themselves of life) these lads remained keen-looking and handsome. They talked a delicate and elastic Arabic, and were mannered, often foppish, in habit. The docility and reasonableness of their town-bred minds made them look after themselves and their masters without reiterated instructions. Their fathers dealt in camels, and they had followed the trade from infancy; consequently they wandered instinctively, like Beduin; while the decadent softness in their nature made them biddable, tolerant of the harshness and physical punishment which in the East were the outward proofs of discipline. They were essentially submissive; yet had the nature of soldiers, and fought with brains and courage when familiarly led.

Not being a tribe, they had no blood enemies, but passed freely in the desert: the carrying trade and chaffer of the interior lay in their hands. The gains of the desert were poor, but enough to tempt them abroad, since the conditions of their home-life were uncomfortable. The Wahabis, followers of a fanatical Moslem heresy, had imposed their strict rules on easy and civilized Kasim. In Kasim there was but little coffee-hospitality, much prayer and fasting, no tobacco, no artistic dalliance with women, no silk clothes, no gold and silver head-ropes or ornaments. Everything was forcibly pious or forcibly puritanical.

It was a natural phenomenon, this periodic rise at intervals of little more than a century, of ascetic creeds in Central Arabia. Always the votaries found their neighbours' beliefs cluttered with inessential things, which became impious in the hot imagination of their preachers. Again and again they had arisen, had taken possession, soul and body, of the tribes, and had dashed themselves to pieces on the urban Semites,

merchants and concupiscent men of the world. About their comfortable possessions the new creeds ebbed and flowed like the tides or the
changing seasons, each movement with the seeds of early death in its
excess of rightness. Doubtless they must recur so long as the causes —
sun, moon, wind, acting in the emptiness of open spaces, weigh without
check on the unhurried and uncumbered minds of the desert-dwellers.

However, this afternoon the Ageyl were not thinking of God, but of
us, and as Ibn Dakhil ranged them to the right and left they fell eagerly
into rank. There came a warning patter from the drums and the poet
of the right wing burst into strident song, a single invented couplet, of
Feisal and the pleasure he would afford us at Wejh. The right wing
listened to the verse intently, took it up and sang it together once, twice
and three times, with pride and self-satisfaction and derision. However,
before they could brandish it a fourth time the poet of the left wing
broke out in extempore reply, in the same metre, in answering rhyme,
and capping the sentiment. The left wing cheered it in a roar of
triumph, the drums tapped again, the standard-bearers threw out their
great crimson banners, and the whole guard, right, left and centre,
broke together into the rousing regimental chorus,

> 'I've lost Britain, and I've lost Gaul,
> I've lost Rome, and, worst of all,
> I've lost Lalage—'

only it was Nejd they had lost, and the women of the Maabda, and their
future lay from Jidda towards Suez. Yet it was a good song, with a
rhythmical beat which the camels loved, so that they put down their
heads, stretched their necks out far and with lengthened pace shuffled
forward musingly while it lasted.

Our road to-day was easy for them, since it was over firm sand slopes,
long, slowly-rising waves of dunes, bare-backed, but for scrub in the
folds, or barren palm-trees solitary in the moist depressions. Afterwards in a broad flat, two horsemen came cantering across from the left
to greet Feisal. I knew the first one, dirty old blear-eyed Mohammed
Ali el Beidawi, Emir of the Juheina: but the second looked strange.
When he came nearer I saw he was in khaki uniform, with a cloak to
cover it and a silk head-cloth and head-rope, much awry. He looked

up, and there was Newcombe's red and peeling face, with straining eyes and vehement mouth, a strong, humorous grin between the jaws. He had arrived at Um Lejj this morning, and hearing we were only just off, had seized Sheikh Yusuf's fastest horse and galloped after us.

I offered him my spare camel and an introduction to Feisal, whom he greeted like an old school-friend; and at once they plunged into the midst of things, suggesting, debating, planning at lightning speed. Newcombe's initial velocity was enormous, and the freshness of the day and the life and happiness of the Army gave inspiration to the march and brought the future bubbling out of us without pain.

We passed Ghowashia, a ragged grove of palms, and marched over a lava-field easily, its roughnesses being drowned in sand just deep enough to smooth them, but not deep enough to be too soft. The tops of the highest lava-piles showed through. An hour later we came suddenly to a crest which dropped as a sand slope, abrupt and swept and straight enough to be called a sand-cliff, into a broad splendid valley of rounded pebbles. This was Semna, and our road went down the steep, through terraces of palms.

The wind had been following our march, and so it was very still and warm at bottom of the valley in lee of the great bank of sand. Here was our water, and here we would halt till the scouts returned from seeking rain-pools in front of us; for so Abd el Kerim, our chief guide, had advised. We rode the four hundred yards across the valley and up the further slopes till we were safe from floods, and there Feisal tapped his camel lightly on the neck till she sank to her knees with a scrape of shingle pushed aside, and settled herself. Hejris spread the carpet for us, and with the other Sherifs we sat and jested while the coffee was made hot.

I maintained against Feisal the greatness of Ibrahim Pasha, leader of Milli-Kurds, in North Mesopotamia. When he was to march, his women rose before dawn, and footing noiselessly overhead on the taut tentcloth, unskewered the strips of it, while others beneath held and removed the poles till all was struck and divided into camel-loads, and loaded. Then they drove off, so that the Pasha awoke alone on his pallet in the open air where at night he had lain down in the rich inner compartment of his palace-tent.

He would get up at leisure and drink coffee on his carpet: and afterwards the horses would be brought, and they would ride towards the new camping ground. But if on his way he thirsted he would crisp his fingers to the servants, and the coffee man would ride up beside him with his pots ready and his brazier burning on a copper bracket of the saddle, to serve the cup on the march without breaking stride; and at sunset they would find the women waiting in the erected tent, as it had been on the evening before.

To-day had a grey weather, so strange after the many thronging suns, that Newcombe and I walked stooping to look where our shadows had gone, as we talked of what I hoped, and of what he wanted. They were the same thing, so we had brain-leisure to note Semna and its fine groves of cared-for palms between little hedges of dead thorn; with here and there huts of reed and palm-rib, to shelter the owners and their families at times of fertilization and harvest. In the lowest gardens and in the valley bed were the shallow wood-lined wells, whose water was, they said, fairly sweet and never-failing: but so little fluent that to water our host of camels took the night.

Feisal wrote letters from Semna to twenty-five leaders of the Billi and Howeitat and Beni Atiyeh, saying that he with his army would be instantly in Wejh and they must see to it. Mohammed Ali bestirred himself, and since almost all our men were of his tribe, was useful in arranging the detachments and detailing them their routes for the morrow. Our water-scouts had come in, to report shallow pools at two points well-spaced on the coast road. After cross-questioning them we decided to send four sections that way, and the other five by the hills: in such a fashion we thought we should arrive soonest and safest at Abu Zereibat.

The route was not easy to decide with the poor help of the Musa Juheina, our informants. They seemed to have no unit of time smaller than the half-day, or of distance between the span and the stage; and a stage might be from six to sixteen hours according to the man's will and camel. Intercommunication between our units was hindered because often there was no one who could read or write, in either. Delay, confusion, hunger and thirst marred this expedition. These might have been avoided had time let us examine the route beforehand. The animals were without food for nearly three days, and the men marched the last fifty miles on half a gallon of water, with nothing to eat. It did not in any way dim their spirit, and they trotted into Wejh gaily enough, hoarsely singing, and executing mock charges: but Feisal said that another hot and barren midday would have broken both their speed and their energy.

When business ended, Newcombe and I went off to sleep in the tent Feisal had lent us as a special luxury. Baggage conditions were so hard and important for us that we rich took pride in faring like the men, who could not transport unnecessary things: and never before had I had a tent of my own. We pitched it at the very edge of a bluff of the foothills; a bluff no wider than the tent and rounded, so that the slope went straight down from the pegs of the door-flap. There we found sitting and waiting for us Abd el Kerim, the young Beidawi Sherif, wrapped up to the eyes in his head-cloth and cloak, since the evening was chill and threatened rain. He had come to ask me for a mule, with saddle and bridle. The smart appearance of Maulud's little company in breeches and puttees, and their fine new animals in the market at Um Lejj, had roused his desire.

I played with his eagerness, and put him off, advancing a condition that he should ask me after our successful arrival at Wejh; and with this he was content. We hungered for sleep, and at last he rose to go, but, chancing to look across the valley, saw the hollows beneath and about us winking with the faint camp-fires of the scattered contingents. He called me out to look, and swept his arm round, saying half-sadly, 'We are no longer Arabs but a People'.

He was half-proud too, for the advance on Wejh was their biggest effort; the first time in memory that the manhood of a tribe, with transport, arms, and food for two hundred miles, had left its district and marched into another's territory without the hope of plunder or the stimulus of blood feud. Abd el Kerim was glad that his tribe had shown this new spirit of service, but also sorry; for to him the joys of life were a fast camel, the best weapons, and a short sharp raid against his neighbour's herd: and the gradual achievement of Feisal's ambition was making such joys less and less easy for the responsible.

CHAPTER XXV

D URING the morning it rained persistently; and we were glad to see more water coming to us, and so comfortable in the tents at Semna that we delayed our start till the sun shone again in the early afternoon. Then we rode westward down the valley in the fresh light. First behind us came the Ageyl. After them Abd el Kerim led his Gufa men, about seven hundred of them mounted, with more than that number following afoot. They were dressed in white, with large head-shawls of red and black striped cotton, and they waved green palm-branches instead of banners.

Next to them rode Sherif Mohammed Ali abu Sharrain, an old patriarch with a long, curling grey beard and an upright carriage of himself. His three hundred riders were Ashraf, of the Aiaishi (Juheina) stock, known Sherifs, but only acknowledged in the mass, since they had not inscribed pedigrees. They wore rusty-red tunics henna-dyed, under black cloaks, and carried swords. Each had a slave crouched behind him on the crupper to help him with rifle and dagger in the fight, and to watch his camel and cook for him on the road. The slaves, as befitted slaves of poor masters, were very little dressed. Their strong, black legs gripped the camels' woolly sides as in a vice, to lessen the shocks inevitable on their bony perches, while they had knotted up their rags of shirts into the plaited thong about their loins to save them from the fouling of the camels and their staling on the march. Semna water was medicinal, and our animals' dung flowed like green soup down their hocks that day.

Behind the Ashraf came the crimson banner of our last tribal detachment, the Rifaa, under Owdi ibn Zuweid, the old wheedling sea-pirate who had robbed the Stotzingen Mission and thrown their wireless and their Indian servants into the sea at Yenbo. The sharks presumably refused the wireless, but we had spent fruitless hours dragging for it in the harbour. Owdi still wore a long, rich, fur-lined German officer's greatcoat, a garment little suited to the climate but, as he

157

insisted, magnificent booty. He had about a thousand men, three-quarters of them on foot, and next him marched Rasim, the gunner commandant, with his four old Krupp guns on the pack-mules, just as we had lifted them from the Egyptian Army.

Rasim was a sardonic Damascene, who rose laughing to every crisis and slunk about sore-headed with grievances when things went well. On this day there were dreadful murmurings, for alongside him rode Abdulla el Deleimi, in charge of machine-guns, a quick, clever, super-ficial but attractive officer, much of the professional type, whose great joy was to develop some rankling sorrow in Rasim till it discharged full blast on Feisal or myself. To-day I helped him by smiling to Rasim that we were moving at intervals of a quarter-day in echelon of sub-tribes. Rasim looked over the new-washed underwood, where raindrops glistened in the light of the sun setting redly across the waves below a ceiling of clouds, and looked too at the wild mob of Beduins racing here and there on foot after birds and rabbits and giant lizards and jerboas and one another; and assented sourly, saying that he too would shortly become a sub-tribe, and echelon himself half a day to one side or other, and be quit of flies.

At first starting a man in the crowd had shot a hare from the saddle, but because of the risk of wild shooting Feisal had then forbidden it, and those later put up by our camels' feet were chased with sticks. We laughed at the sudden commotion in the marching companies: cries, and camels swerving violently, their riders leaping off and laying out wildly with their canes to kill or to be pickers-up of a kill. Feisal was happy to see the army win so much meat, but disgusted at the shameless Juheina appetite for lizards and jerboas.

We rode over the flat sand, among the thorn trees, which here were plentiful and large, till we came out on the sea-beach and turned north-ward along a broad, well-beaten track, the Egyptian pilgrim road. It ran within fifty yards of the sea, and we could go up it thirty or forty singing files abreast. An old lava-bed half buried in sand jutted out from the hills four or five miles inland, and made a promontory. The road cut across this, but at the near side were some mud flats, on which shallow reaches of water burned in the last light of the west. This was our expected stage, and Feisal signalled the halt. We got off our camels and stretched ourselves, sat down or walked before supper to the sea and bathed by hundreds, a splashing, screaming, mob of fish-like naked men of all earth's colours.

Supper was to look forward to, as a Juheina that afternoon had shot a gazelle for Feisal. Gazelle meat we found better than any other in the desert, because this beast, however barren the land and dry the water-holes, seemed to own always a fat juicy body.

The meal was the expected success. We retired early, feeling too full: but soon after Newcombe and myself had stretched out in our tent we were quickened by a wave of excitement travelling up the lines; running camels, shots, and shouts. A breathless slave thrust his head under the flap crying, 'News! news! Sherif Bey is taken'. I jumped up and ran through the gathering crowd to Feisal's tent, which was already beset by friends and servants. With Feisal sat, portentously and un-naturally collected in the din, Raja, the tribesman who had taken to Abdulla word to move into Wadi Ais. Feisal was radiant, his eyes swollen with joy, as he jumped up and shouted to me through the voices, 'Abdulla has captured Eshref Bey'. Then I knew how big and good the event was.

Eshref was a notorious adventurer in the lower levels of Turkish politics. In his boyhood, near his Smyrna home, he had been just a brigand, but with years he became a revolutionary, and when he was finally captured Abd el Hamid exiled him to Medina for five coloured years. At first he was closely confined there, but one day he broke the privy window and escaped to Shehad, the bibulous Emir, in his suburb of Awali. Shahad, was, as usual, at war with the Turks and gave him sanctuary; but Eshref, finding life dull, at last borrowed a fine mare and rode to the Turkish barracks. On its square was the officer-son of his enemy the Governor drilling a company of gendarmes. He galloped him down, slung him across his saddle, and made away before the astonished police could protest.

He took to Jebel Ohod, an uninhabited place, driving his prisoner before him, calling him his ass, and lading upon him thirty loaves and the skins of water necessary for their nourishment. To recover his son, the Pasha gave Eshref liberty on parole and five hundred pounds. He bought camels, a tent, and a wife, and wandered among the tribes till the Young Turk revolution. Then he reappeared in Constantinople and became a bravo, doing Enver's murders. His services earned the appointment of inspector of refugee-relief in Macedonia, and he retired a year later with an assured income from landed estate.

When war broke out he went down to Medina with funds, and letters from the Sultan to Arabian neutrals; his mission being to open communications with the isolated Turkish garrison in Yemen. His track on the first stage of the journey had happened to cross Abdulla's, on his way to Wadi Ais, near Kheibar, and some of the Arabs, watching their camels during a midday halt, had been stopped by Eshref's men and questioned. They said they were Heteym, and Abdulla's army a supply caravan going to Medina. Eshref released one with orders to bring the rest for examination, and this man told Abdulla of soldiers camped up on the hill.

Abdulla was puzzled and sent horsemen to investigate. A minute later he was startled by the sudden chatter of a machine-gun. He leaped to the conclusion that the Turks had sent out a flying column to cut him off, and ordered his mounted men to charge them desperately. They galloped over the machine-gun, with few casualties, and scattered the Turks. Eshref fled on foot to the hill-top. Abdulla offered a reward of a thousand pounds for him; and near dusk he was found, wounded, and captured by Sherif Fauzan el Harith, in a stiff fight.

In the baggage were twenty thousand pounds in coins, robes of honour, costly presents, some interesting papers, and camel loads of rifles and pistols. Abdulla wrote an exultant letter to Fakhri Pasha, (telling him of the capture), and nailed it to an uprooted telegraph pole between the metals, when he crossed the railway next night on his unimpeded way to Wadi Ais. Raja had left him there, camped in quiet and in ease. The news was a double fortune for us.

Between the joyful men slipped the sad figure of the Iman, who raised his hand. Silence fell for an instant. 'Hear me,' he said, and intoned an ode in praise of the event, to the effect that Abdulla was especially favoured, and had attained quickly to the glory which Feisal was winning slowly but surely by hard work. The poem was creditable as the issue of only sixteen minutes, and the poet was rewarded in gold.

Then Feisal saw a gaudy jewelled dagger at Raja's belt. Raja stammered it was Eshref's. Feisal threw him his own and pulled the other off, to give it in the end to Colonel Wilson. 'What did my brother say to Eshref?' 'Is this your return for our hospitality?' While Eshref had replied like Suckling, 'I can fight, Whether I am i' the wrong or right, Devoutly!'

'How many millions did the Arabs get?' gasped greedy old Mohammed Ali, when he heard of Abdulla to the elbows in the captured chest, flinging gold by handfuls to the tribes. Raja was everywhere in hot demand, and he slept a richer man that night, deservedly, for Abdulla's march to Ais made the Medina situation sure. With Murray pressing in Sinai, Feisal nearing Wejh, and Abdulla between Wejh and Medina, the position of the Turks in Arabia became defensive only. The tide of our ill-fortune had turned; and the camp seeing our glad faces was noisy until dawn.

Next day we rode easily. A breakfast suggested itself, upon our finding some more little water-pools, in a bare valley flowing down from El Sukhur, a group of three extraordinary hills like granite bubbles blown through the earth. The journey was pleasant, for it was cool; there were a lot of us; and we two Englishmen had a tent in which we could shut ourselves up and be alone. A weariness of the desert was the living always in company, each of the party hearing all that was said and seeing all that was done by the others day and night. Yet the craving for solitude seemed part of the delusion of self-sufficiency, a factitious making-rare of the person to enhance its strangeness in its own estimation. To have privacy, as Newcombe and I had, was ten thousand times more restful than the open life, but the work suffered by the creation of such a bar between the leaders and men. Among the Arabs there were no distinctions, traditional or natural, except the unconscious power given a famous sheikh by virtue of his accomplishment; and they taught me that no man could be their leader except he ate the ranks' food, wore their clothes, lived level with them, and yet appeared better in himself.

In the morning we pressed towards Abu Zereibat with the early sun incandescent in a cloudless sky, and the usual eye-racking dazzle and dance of sunbeams on polished sand or polished flint. Our path rose slightly at a sharp limestone ridge with eroded flanks, and we looked over a sweeping fall of bare, black gravel between us and the sea, which now lay about eight miles to the westward: but invisible.

Once we halted and began to feel that a great depression lay in front of us; but not till two in the afternoon after we had crossed a basalt outcrop did we look out over a trough fifteen miles across, which was Wadi Hamdh, escaped from the hills. On the north-west spread the great delta through which Hamdh spilled itself by twenty mouths; and we saw the dark lines, which were thickets of scrub in the flood channels of the dried beds, twisting in and out across the flat from the hill-edge beneath us, till they were lost in the sun-haze twenty miles away beyond us to our left, near the invisible sea. Behind Hamdh rose sheer from the plain a double hill, Jebel Raal: hog-backed but for a gash which split it in the middle. To our eyes, sated with small things, it was a fair sight, this end of a dry river longer than the Tigris; the greatest valley in Arabia, first understood by Doughty, and as yet unexplored; while Raal was a fine hill, sharp and distinctive, which did honour to the Hamdh.

Full of expectation we rode down the gravel slopes, on which tufts of grass became more frequent, till at three o'clock we entered the Wadi itself. It proved a bed about a mile wide, filled with clumps of *asla* bushes, round which clung sandy hillocks each a few feet high. Their sand was not pure, but seamed with lines of dry and brittle clay, last indications of old flood levels. These divided them sharply into layers, rotten with salty mud and flaking away, so that our camels sank in, fetlock-deep, with a crunching noise like breaking pastry. The dust rose up in thick clouds, thickened yet more by the sunlight held in them; for the dead air of the hollow was a-dazzle.

The ranks behind could not see where they were going, which was difficult for them, as the hillocks came closer together, and the river-bed slit into a maze of shallow channels, the work of partial floods year after year. Before we gained the middle of the valley everything was overgrown by brushwood, which sprouted sideways from the mounds and laced one to another with tangled twigs as dry, dusty and brittle as old bone. We tucked in the streamers of our gaudy saddle-bags, to

prevent their being jerked off by the bushes, drew cloaks tight over our
clothes, bent our heads down to guard our eyes and crashed through
like a storm amongst reeds. The dust was blinding and choking, and
the snapping of the branches, grumbles of the camels, shouts and
laughter of the men, made a rare adventure.

CHAPTER XXVI

BEFORE we quite reached the far bank the ground suddenly cleared at a clay bottom, in which stood a deep brown water-pool, eighty yards long and about fifteen yards wide. This was the flood water of the Abu Zereibat, our goal. We went a few yards further, through the last scrub, and reached the open north bank where Feisal had appointed the camp. It was a huge plain of sand and flints, running to the very feet of Raal, with room on it for all the armies of Arabia. So we stopped our camels, and the slaves unloaded them and set up the tents; while we walked back to see the mules, thirsty after their long day's march, rush with the foot-soldiers into the pond, kicking and splashing with pleasure in the sweet water. The abundance of fuel was an added happiness, and in whatever place they chose to camp each group of friends had a roaring fire — very welcome, as a wet evening mist rose eight feet out of the ground and our woollen cloaks stiffened and grew cold with its silver beads in their coarse woof.

It was a black night, moonless, but above the fog very brilliant with stars. On a little mound near our tents we collected and looked over the rolling white seas of fog. Out of it arose tent-peaks, and tall spires of melting smoke, which became luminous underneath when the flames licked higher into the clean air, as if driven by the noises of the unseen army. Old Auda ibn Zuweid corrected me gravely when I said this to him, telling me, 'It is not an army, it is a world which is moving on Wejh'. I rejoiced at his insistence, for it had been to create this very feeling that we had hampered ourselves with an unwieldy crowd of men on so difficult a march.

That evening the Billi began to come in to us shyly, and swear fealty, for the Hamdh Valley was their boundary. Amongst them Hamid el Rifada rode up with a numerous company to pay his respects to Feisal. He told us that his cousin, Suleiman Pasha, the paramount of the tribe, was at Abu Ajaj, fifteen miles north of us, trying desperately for once to make up the mind which had chopped and balanced profitably throughout a long life. Then, without warning or parade, Sherif Nasir of Medina came in. Feisal leaped up and embraced him, and led him over to us.

Nasir made a splendid impression, much as we had heard, and much as we were expecting of him. He was the opener of roads, the fore-runner of Feisal's movement, the man who had fired his first shot in Medina, and who was to fire our last shot at Muslimieh beyond Aleppo on the day that Turkey asked for an armistice, and from beginning to end all that could be told of him was good.

He was a brother of Shehad, the Emir of Medina. Their family was descended from Hussein, the younger of Ali's children, and they were the only descendants of Hussein considered Ashraf, not Saada. They were Shias, and had been since the days of Kerbela, and in Hejaz were respected only second to the Emirs of Mecca. Nasir himself was a man of gardens, whose lot had been unwilling war since boyhood. He was now about twenty-seven. His low, broad forehead matched his sensitive eyes, while his weak pleasant mouth and small chin were clearly seen through a clipped black beard.

He had been up here for two months, containing Wejh, and his last news was that the outpost of Turkish camel corps upon our road had withdrawn that morning towards the main defensive position.

We slept late the following day, to brace ourselves for the necessary hours of talk. Feisal carried most of this upon his own shoulders. Nasir supported him as second in command, and the Beidawi brothers sat by to help. The day was bright and warm, threatening to be hot later, and Newcombe and I wandered about looking at the watering, the men, and the constant affluence of newcomers. When the sun was high a great cloud of dust from the east heralded a larger party and we walked back to the tents to see Mirzuk el Tikheimi, Feisal's sharp, mouse-featured guest-master, ride in. He led his clansmen of the Juheina past the Emir at a canter, to make a show. They stifled us with their dust, for his van of a dozen sheikhs carrying a large red flag and a large white flag drew their swords and charged round and round our tents. We admired neither their riding nor their mares; perhaps because they were a nuisance to us.

About noon the Wuld Mohammed Harb, and the mounted men of the ibn Shefia battalion came in: three hundred men, under Sheikh

Salih and Mohammed ibn Shefia. Mohammed was a tubby, vulgar little man of fifty-five, common-sensible and energetic. He was rapidly making a name for himself in the Arab army, for he would get done any manual work. His men were the sweepings of Wadi Yenbo, landless and without family, or labouring Yenbo townsmen, hampered by no inherited dignity. They were more docile than any other of our troops except the white-handed Ageyl who were too beautiful to be made into labourers.

We were already two days behind our promise to the Navy, and Newcombe decided to ride ahead this night to Habban. There he would meet Boyle and explain that we must fail the *Hardinge* at the rendezvous, but would be glad if she could return there on the evening of the twenty-fourth, when we should arrive much in need of water. He would also see if the naval attack could not be delayed till the twenty-fifth to preserve the joint scheme.

After dark there came a message from Suleiman Rifada, with a gift-camel for Feisal to keep if he were friendly, and to send back if hostile. Feisal was vexed, and protested his inability to understand so feeble a man. Nasir asserted, 'Oh, it's because he eats fish. Fish swells the head, and such behaviour follows'. The Syrians and Mesopotamians, and men of Jidda and Yenbo laughed loudly, to shew that they did not share this belief of the upland Arab, that a man of his hands was disgraced by tasting the three mean foods — chickens, eggs and fish. Feisal said, with mock gravity, 'You insult the company, we like fish'. Others protested, 'We abandon it, and take refuge in God', and Mirzuk to change the current said, 'Suleiman is an unnatural birth, neither raw nor ripe'.

In the morning, early, we marched in a straggle for three hours down Wadi Hamdh. Then the valley went to the left, and we struck out across a hollow, desolate, featureless region. To-day was cold: a hard north wind drove into our faces down the grey coast. As we marched we heard intermittent heavy firing from the direction of Wejh, and feared that the Navy had lost patience and were acting without us. However, we could not make up the days we had wasted, so we pushed on for the whole dull stage, crossing affluent after affluent of Hamdh. The plain was striped with these wadies, all shallow and straight and bare, as many and as intricate as the veins in a leaf. At last we re-entered Hamdh, at Kurna, and though its clay bottoms held only mud, decided to camp.

While we were settling in there was a sudden rush. Camels had been seen pasturing away to the east, and the energetic of the Juheina streamed out, captured them, and drove them in. Feisal was furious, and shouted to them to stop, but they were too excited to hear him. He snatched his rifle, and shot at the nearest man; who, in fear, tumbled out of his saddle, so that the others checked their course. Feisal had them up before him, laid about the principals with his camel-stick, and impounded the stolen camels and those of the thieves till the whole tally was complete. Then he handed the beasts back to their Billi owners. Had he not done so it would have involved the Juheina in a private war with the Billi, our hoped-for allies of the morrow, and might have checked extension beyond Wejh. Our success lay in bond to such trifles.

Next morning we made for the beach, and up it to Habban at four o'clock. The *Hardinge* was duly there, to our relief, and landing water: although the shallow bay gave little shelter, and the rough sea rolling in made boat-work hazardous. We reserved first call for the mules, and gave what water was left to the more thirsty of the footmen; but it was a difficult night, and crowds of suffering men lingered jostling about the tanks in the rays of the searchlight, hoping for another drink, if the sailors should venture in again.

I went on board, and heard that the naval attack had been carried out as though the land army were present, since Boyle feared the Turks would run away if he waited. As a matter of fact, the day we reached Abu Zereibat, Ahmed Tewfik Bey, Turkish Governor, had addressed the garrison, saying that Wejh must be held to the last drop of blood. Then at dusk he had got on to his camel and ridden off to the railway with the few mounted men fit for flight. The two hundred infantry determined to do his abandoned duty against the landing party; but they were out-numbered three to one, and the naval gun-fire was too heavy to let them make proper use of their positions. So far as the *Hardinge* knew, the fighting was not ended, but Wejh town had been occupied by seamen and Saleh's Arabs.

CHAPTER XXVII

PROFITABLE rumours excited the army, which began to trickle off northward soon after midnight. At dawn we rallied the various contingents on Wadi Miya, twelve miles south of the town, and advanced on it in order, meeting a few scattered Turks, of whom one party put up a short resistance. The Ageyl dismounted, to strip off their cloaks, head-cloths and shirts; and went on in brown half-nakedness, which they said would ensure clean wounds if they were hit: also their precious clothes would not be damaged. Ibn Dakhil in command obtained a quiet regularity of obedience. They advanced by alternate companies, in open order, at intervals of four or five yards, with even-numbered companies in support, making good use of the poor cover which existed.

It was pretty to look at the neat, brown men in the sunlit sandy valley, with the turquoise pool of salt water in the midst to set off the crimson banners which two standard bearers carried in the van. They went along in a steady lope, covering the ground at nearly six miles an hour, dead silent, and reached and climbed the ridge without a shot fired. So we knew the work had been finished for us and trotted forward to find the boy Saleh, son of ibn Shefia, in possession of the town. He told us that his casualties had been nearly twenty killed; and later we heard that a British lieutenant of the Air Service had been mortally wounded in a seaplane reconnaissance, and one British seaman hurt in the foot.

Vickery, who had directed the battle, was satisfied, but I could not share his satisfaction. To me an unnecessary action, or shot, or casualty, was not only waste but sin. I was unable to take the professional view that all successful actions were gains. Our rebels were not materials, like soldiers, but friends of ours, trusting our leadership. We were not in command nationally, but by invitation; and our men were volunteers, individuals, local men, relatives, so that a death was a personal sorrow to many in the army. Even from the purely military point of view the assault seemed to me a blunder.

The two hundred Turks in Wejh had no transport and no food, and if left alone a few days must have surrendered. Had they escaped, it would not have mattered the value of an Arab life. We wanted Wejh as a base against the railway and to extend our front; the smashing and killing in it had been wanton.

The place was inconveniently smashed. Its townspeople had been warned by Feisal of the coming attack, and advised either to forestall it by revolt or to clear out; but they were mostly Egyptians from Kosseir, who preferred the Turks to us, and decided to wait the issue; so the Shefia men and the Biasha found the houses packed with fair booty and made a sweep of it. They robbed the shops, broke open doors, searched every room, smashed chests and cupboards, tore down all fixed fittings, and slit each mattress and pillow for hidden treasure; while the fire of the fleet punched large holes in every prominent wall or building.

Our main difficulty was the landing of stores. The *Fox* had sunk the local lighters and rowing boats and there was no sort of quay; but the resourceful *Hardinge* thrust herself into the harbour (which was wide enough but much too short) and landed our stuff in her own cutters. We raised a tired working party of ibn Shefia followers, and with their clumsy or languid help got enough food into the place for the moment's needs. The townspeople had returned hungry, and furious at the state of what had been their property; and began their revenge by stealing everything unguarded, even slitting open the rice-bags on the beach and carrying away quantities in their held-up skirts. Feisal corrected this by making the pitiless Maulud Town-governor. He brought in his rough-riders and in one day of wholesale arrest and summary punishment persuaded everyone to leave things alone. After that Wejh had the silence of fear.

Even in the few days which elapsed before I left for Cairo the profits of our spectacular march began to come in. The Arab movement had now no opponent in Western Arabia, and had passed beyond danger of collapse. The vexed Rabegh question died: and we had learnt the first rules of Beduin warfare. When regarded backward from our benefits of new knowledge the deaths of those regretted twenty men in the Wejh streets seemed not so terrible. Vickery's impatience was justified, perhaps, in cold blood.

BOOK III

A RAILWAY DIVERSION

Chapters XXVIII to XXXVIII

OUR *taking Wejh had the wished effect upon the Turks, who abandoned their advance towards Mecca for a passive defence of Medina and its Railway. Our experts made plans for attacking them.*

The Germans saw the danger of envelopment, and persuaded Enver to order the instant evacuation of Medina. Sir Archibald Murray begged us to put in a sustained attack to destroy the retreating enemy.

Feisal was soon ready in his part: and I went off to Abdulla to get his co-operation. On the way I fell sick and while lying alone with empty hands was driven to think about the campaign. Thinking convinced me that our recent practice had been better than our theory.

So on recovery I did little to the Railway, but went back to Wejh with novel ideas. I tried to make the others admit them, and adopt deployment as our ruling principle; and to put preaching even before fighting. They preferred the limited and direct objective of Medina. So I decided to slip off to Akaba by myself on test of my own theory.

CHAPTER XXVIII

IN Cairo the yet-hot authorities promised gold, rifles, mules, more machine-guns, and mountain guns; but these last, of course, we never got. The gun question was an eternal torment. Because of the hilly, trackless country, field guns were no use to us; and the British Army had no mountain guns except the Indian ten-pounder, which was serviceable only against bows and arrows. Bremond had some excellent Schneider sixty-fives at Suez, with Algerian gunners, but he regarded them principally as his lever to move allied troops into Arabia. When we asked him to send them down to us with or without men, he would reply, first that the Arabs would not treat the crews properly, and then that they would not treat the guns properly. His price was a British brigade for Rabegh; and we would not pay it.

He feared to make the Arab Army formidable — an argument one could understand — but the case of the British Government was incomprehensible. It was not ill-will, for they gave us all else we wanted; nor was it niggardliness, for their total help to the Arabs, in materials and money, exceeded ten millions. I believed it was sheer stupidity. But it was maddening to be unequal to many enterprises and to fail in others, for the technical reason that we could not keep down the Turkish artillery because its guns outranged ours by three or four thousand yards. In the end, happily, Bremond over-reached himself, after keeping his batteries idle for a year at Suez. Major Cousse, his successor, ordered them down to us, and by their help we entered Damascus. During that idle year they had been, to each Arab officer who entered Suez, a silent incontrovertible proof of French malice towards the Arab movement.

We received a great reinforcement to our cause in Jaafar Pasha, a Bagdadi officer from the Turkish Army. After distinguished service in the German and Turkish armies, he had been chosen by Enver to organize the levies of the Sheikh el Senussi. He went there by submarine, made a decent force of the wild men, and showed tactical ability against the British in two battles. Then he was captured and lodged in the citadel at Cairo with the other officer prisoners of war. He escaped one night, slipping down a blanket-rope towards the moat; but the blankets failed under the strain, and in the fall he hurt his ankle, and was re-taken helpless. In hospital he gave his parole, and was enlarged after paying for the torn blanket. But one day he read in an Arabic newspaper of the Sherif's revolt, and of the execution by the Turks of prominent Arab Nationalists — his friends — and realized that he had been on the wrong side.

Feisal had heard of him, of course, and wanted him as commander-in-chief of his regular troops, whose improvement was now our main effort. We knew that Jaafar was one of the few men with enough of reputation and personality to weld their difficult and reciprocally disagreeable elements into an army. King Hussein, however, would not have it. He was old and narrow, and disliked Mesopotamians and Syrians: Mecca must deliver Damascus. He refused the services of Jaafar. Feisal had to accept him on his own responsibility.

In Cairo were Hogarth and George Lloyd, and Storrs and Deedes, and many old friends. Beyond them the circle of Arabian well-wishers was now strangely increased. In the army our shares rose as we showed profits. Lynden Bell stood firmly our friend and swore that method was coming out of the Arab madness. Sir Archibald Murray realized with a sudden shock that more Turkish troops were fighting the Arabs than were fighting him, and began to remember how he had always favoured the Arab revolt. Admiral Wemyss was as ready to help now as he had been in our hard days round Rabegh. Sir Reginald Wingate, High Commissioner in Egypt, was happy in the success of the work he had advocated for years. I grudged him this happiness; for McMahon who took the actual risk of starting it, had been broken just before prosperity began. However, that was hardly Wingate's fault.

In the midst of my touching the slender stops of all these quills there came a rude surprise. Colonel Bremond called to felicitate me on the capture of Wejh, saying that it confirmed his belief in my military talent and encouraged him to expect my help in an extension of our success. He wanted to occupy Akaba with an Anglo-French force and naval help. He pointed out the importance of Akaba, the only Turkish port left in the Red Sea, the nearest to the Suez Canal, the nearest to the

Hejaz Railway, on the left flank of the Beersheba army; suggesting its occupation by a composite brigade, which should advance up Wadi Itm for a crushing blow at Maan. He began to enlarge on the nature of the ground.

I told him that I knew Akaba from before the war, and felt that his scheme was technically impossible. We could take the beach of the gulf; but our forces there, as unfavourably placed as on a Gallipoli beach, would be under observation and gun-fire from the coastal hills: and these granite hills, thousands of feet high, were impracticable for heavy troops: the passes through them being formidable defiles, very costly to assault or to cover. In my opinion, Akaba, whose importance was all and more than he said, would be best taken by Arab irregulars descending from the interior without naval help.

Bremond did not tell me (but I knew) that he wanted the landing at Akaba to head off the Arab movement, by getting a mixed force in front of them (as at Rabegh), so that they might be confined to Arabia, and compelled to waste their efforts against Medina. The Arabs still feared that the Sherif's alliance with us was based on a secret agreement to sell them at the end, and such a Christian invasion would have confirmed these fears and destroyed their co-operation. For my part, I did not tell Bremond (but he knew) that I meant to defeat his efforts and to take the Arabs soon into Damascus. It amused me, this childishly-conceived rivalry of vital aims, but he ended his talk ominously by saying that, anyhow, he was going down to put the scheme to Feisal in Wejh.

Now, I had not warned Feisal that Bremond was a politician. Newcombe was in Wejh, with his friendly desire to get moves on. We had not talked over the problem of Akaba. Feisal knew neither its terrain nor its tribes. Keenness and ignorance would lend an ear favourable to the proposal. It seemed best for me to hurry down there and put my side on its guard, so I left the same afternoon for Suez and sailed that night. Two days later, in Wejh, I explained myself; so that when Bremond came after ten days and opened his heart, or part of it, to Feisal, his tactics were returned to him with improvements.

The Frenchman began by presenting six Hotchkiss automatics complete with instructors. This was a noble gift; but Feisal took the opportunity to ask him to increase his bounty by a battery of the quick-firing mountain guns at Suez, explaining that he had been sorry to leave the Yenbo area for Wejh, since Wejh was so much further from his objective — Medina — but it was really impossible for him to assault the Turks (who had French artillery) with rifles or with the old guns supplied him by the British Army. His men had not the technical excellence to make a bad tool prevail over a good one. He had to exploit his only advantages — numbers and mobility — and, unless his equipment could be improved, there was no saying where this protraction of his front might end!

Bremond tried to turn it off by belittling guns as useless for Hejaz warfare (quite right, this, practically). But it would end the war at once if Feisal made his men climb about the country like goats and tear up the railway. Feisal, angry at the metaphor (impolite in Arabic), looked at Bremond's six feet of comfortable body, and asked if he had ever tried to 'goat' himself. Bremond referred gallantly to the question of Akaba, and the real danger to the Arabs in the Turks remaining there: insisting that the British, who had the means for an expedition thither, should be pressed to undertake it. Feisal, in reply, gave him a geographical sketch of the land behind Akaba (I recognized the less dashing part of it myself) and explained the tribal difficulties and the food problem — all the points which made it a serious obstacle. He ended by saying that, after the cloud of orders, counter-orders and confusion over the allied troops for Rabegh, he really had not the face to approach Sir Archibald Murray so soon with another request for an excursion.

Bremond had to retire from the battle in good order, getting in a Parthian shot at me, where I sat spitefully smiling, by begging Feisal to insist that the British armoured cars in Suez be sent down to Wejh. But even this was a boomerang, since they had started! After he had gone, I returned to Cairo for a cheerful week, in which I gave my betters much good advice. Murray, who had growlingly earmarked Tullibardine's brigade for Akaba, approved me still further when I declared against that side-show too. Then to Wejh.

CHAPTER XXIX

LIFE in Wejh was interesting. We had now set our camp in order. Feisal pitched his tents (here an opulent group: living tents, reception tents, staff tents, guest tents, servants') about a mile from the sea, on the edge of the coral shelf which ran up gently from the beach till it ended in a steep drop facing east and south over broad valleys radiating star-like from the land-locked harbour. The tents of soldiers and tribesmen were grouped in these sandy valleys, leaving the chill height for ourselves; and very delightful in the evening we northerners found it when the breeze from the sea carried us a murmur of the waves, faint and far off, like the echo of traffic up a by-street in London.

Immediately beneath us were the Ageyl, an irregular close group of tents. South of these were Rasim's artillery; and by him for company, Abdulla's machine-gunners, in regular lines, with their animals picketed out in those formal rows which were incense to the professional officer and convenient if space were precious. Further out the market was set plainly on the ground, a boiling swell of men always about the goods. The scattered tents and shelters of the tribesmen filled each gully or windless place. Beyond the last of them lay open country, with camel-parties coming in and out by the straggling palms of the nearest, too-brackish well. As background were the foothills, reefs and clusters like ruined castles, thrown up craggily to the horizon of the coastal range.

As it was the custom in Wejh to camp wide apart, very wide apart, my life was spent in moving back and forth, to Feisal's tents, to the English tents, to the Egyptian Army tents, to the town, the port, the wireless station, tramping all day restlessly up and down these coral paths in sandals or barefoot, hardening my feet, getting by slow degrees the power to walk with little pain over sharp and burning ground, tempering my already trained body for greater endeavour.

Poor Arabs wondered why I had no mare; and I forbore to puzzle them by incomprehensible talk of hardening myself, or confess I would rather walk than ride for sparing of animals: yet the first was true and the second true. Something hurtful to my pride, disagreeable, rose at the sight of these lower forms of life. Their existence struck a servile reflection upon our human kind: the style in which a God would look on us; and to make use of them, to lie under an avoidable obligation to them, seemed to me shameful. It was as with the negroes, tomtom playing themselves to red madness each night under the ridge. Their faces, being clearly different from our own, were tolerable; but it hurt that they should possess exact counterparts of all our bodies.

Feisal, within, laboured day and night at his politics, in which so few of us could help. Outside, the crowd employed and diverted us with parades, joy-shooting, and marches of victory. Also there were accidents. Once a group, playing behind our tents, set off a seaplane bomb, dud relic of Boyle's capture of the town. In the explosion their limbs were scattered about the camp, marking the canvas with red splashes which soon turned a dull brown and then faded pale. Feisal had the tents changed and ordered the bloody ones to be destroyed: the frugal slaves washed them. Another day a tent took fire, and part-roasted three of our guests. The camp crowded round and roared with laughter till the fire died down, and then, rather shamefacedly, we cared for their hurts. The third day, a mare was wounded by a falling joy-bullet, and many tents were pierced.

One night the Ageyl mutinied against their commandant, ibn Dakhil, for fining them too generally and flogging them too severely. They rushed his tent, howling and shooting, threw his things about and beat his servants. That not being enough to blunt their fury, they began to remember Yenbo, and went off to kill the Ateiba. Feisal from our bluff saw their torches and ran barefoot among them, laying on with the flat of his sword like four men. His fury delayed them while the slaves and horsemen, calling for help, dashed downhill with rushes and shouts and blows of sheathed swords. One gave him a horse on which he charged down the ringleaders, while we dispersed groups by firing Very lights into their clothing. Only two were killed and thirty wounded. Ibn Dakhil resigned next day.

Murray had given us two armoured-cars, Rolls-Royces, released from the campaign in East Africa. Gilman and Wade commanded, and their crews were British, men from the A.S.C. to drive and from the Machine Gun Corps to shoot. Having them in Wejh made things more difficult for us, because the food we had been eating and the water we had been drinking were at once medically condemned; but English company was a balancing pleasure, and the occupation of pushing cars and motor-bicycles through the desperate sand about Wejh was great. The fierce difficulty of driving across country gave the men arms like boxers, so that they swung their shoulders professionally as they walked. With time they became skilled, developing a style and art of sand-driving, which got them carefully over the better ground and rushed them at speed over soft places. One of these soft places was the last twenty miles of plain in front of Jebal Raal. The cars used to cross it in little more than half an hour, leaping from ridge to ridge of the dunes and swaying dangerously around their curves. The Arabs loved the new toys. Bicycles they called devil-horses, the children of cars, which themselves were sons and daughters of trains. It gave us three generations of mechanical transport.

The Navy added greatly to our interests in Wejh. The *Espiegle* was sent by Boyle as station ship, with the delightful orders to 'do everything in her power to co-operate in the many plans which would be suggested to her by Colonel Newcombe, while letting it be clearly seen that she was conferring a favour'. Her commander Fitzmaurice (a good name in Turkey), was the soul of hospitality and found quiet amusement in our work on shore. He helped us in a thousand ways; above all in signalling; for he was a wireless expert, and one day at noon the *Northbrook* came in and landed an army wireless set, on a light lorry, for us. As there was no one to explain it, we were at a loss; but Fitzmaurice raced ashore with half his crew, ran the car to a fitting site, rigged the masts professionally, started the engine, and connected up to such effect that before sunset he had called the astonished *Northbrook* and held a long conversation with her operator. The station increased the efficiency of the base at Wejh and was busy day and night, filling the Red Sea with messages in three tongues, and twenty different sorts of army cypher-codes.

CHAPTER XXX

FAKHRI Pasha was still playing our game. He held an entrenched line around Medina, just far enough to make it impossible for the Arabs to shell the city. (Such an attempt was never made or imagined.) The other troops were being distributed along the railway, in strong garrisons at all water stations between Medina and Tebuk, and in smaller posts between these garrisons, so that daily patrols might guarantee the track. In short, he had fallen back on as stupid a defensive as could be conceived. Garland had gone south-east from Wejh, and Newcombe north-east, to pick holes in it with high explosives. They would cut rails and bridges, and place automatic mines for running trains.

The Arabs had passed from doubt to violent optimism, and were promising exemplary service. Feisal enrolled most of the Billi, and the Moahib, which made him master of Arabia between the railway and the sea. He then sent the Juheina to Abdulla in Wadi Ais.

He could now prepare to deal solemnly with the Hejaz Railway; but with a practice better than my principles, I begged him first to delay in Wejh and set marching an intense movement among the tribes beyond us, that in the future our revolt might be extended, and the railway threatened from Tebuk (our present limit of influence) northward as far as Maan. My vision of the course of the Arab war was still purblind. I had not seen that the preaching was victory and the fighting a delusion. For the moment, I roped them together, and, as Feisal fortunately liked changing men's minds rather than breaking railways, the preaching went the better.

With his northern neighbours, the coastal Howeitat, he had already made a beginning: but we now sent to the Beni Atiyeh, a stronger people to the north-east; and gained a great step when the chief, Asi ibn Atiyeh, came in and swore allegiance. His main motive was jealousy of his brothers, so that we did not expect from him active help; but the bread and salt with him gave us freedom of movement across his tribe's territory. Beyond lay various tribes owning obedience to

Nuri Shaalan, the great Emir of the Ruwalla, who, after the Sherif and ibn Saud and ibn Rashid, was the fourth figure among the precarious princes of the desert.

Nuri was an old man, who had ruled his Anazeh tribesmen for thirty years. His was the chief family of the Rualla, but Nuri had no precedence among them at birth, nor was he loved, nor a great man of battle. His leadership had been acquired by sheer force of character. To gain it he had killed two of his brothers. Later he had added Sherarat and others to the number of his followers, and in all their desert his word was absolute law. He had none of the wheedling diplomacy of the ordinary sheikh; a word, and there was an end of opposition, or of his opponent. All feared and obeyed him; to use his roads we must have his countenance.

Fortunately, this was easy. Feisal had secured it years ago, and had retained it by interchange of gifts from Medina and Yenbo. Now, from Wejh, Fais el Ghusein went up to him and on the way crossed ibn Dughmi, one of the chief men of the Ruwalla, coming down to us with the desirable gift of some hundreds of good baggage camels. Nuri, of course, still kept friendly with the Turks. Damascus and Bagdad were his markets, and they could have half-starved his tribe in three months, had they suspected him; but we knew that when the moment came we should have his armed help, and till then anything short of a breach with Turkey.

His favour would open to us the Sirhan, a famous roadway, camping ground, and chain of water-holes, which in a series of linked depressions extended from Jauf, Nuri's capital, in the south-east, northwards to Azrak, near Jebel Druse, in Syria. It was the freedom of the Sirhan we needed to reach the tents of the Eastern Howeitat, those famous abu Tayi, of whom Auda, the greatest fighting man in northern Arabia, was chief. Only by means of Auda abu Tayi could we swing the tribes from Maan to Akaba so violently in our favour that they would help us take Akaba and its hills from their Turkish garrisons: only with his active support could we venture to thrust out from Wejh on the long trek to Maan. Since our Yenbo days we had been longing for him and trying to win him to our cause.

We made a great step forward at Wejh; ibn Zaal, his cousin and a war-leader of the abu Tayi, arrived on the seventeenth of February, which was in all respects a fortunate day. At dawn there came in five chief men of the Sherarat from the desert east of Tebuk, bringing a present of eggs of the Arabian ostrich, plentiful in their little-frequented desert. After them, the slaves showed in Dhaif-Allah, abu Tiyur, a cousin of Hamd ibn Jazi, paramount of the central Howeitat of the Maan plateau. These were numerous and powerful; splendid fighters; but blood enemies of their cousins, the nomad abu Tayi, because of an old-grounded quarrel between Auda and Hamd. We were proud to see them coming thus far to greet us, yet not content, for they were less fit than the abu Tayi for our purposed attack against Akaba.

On their heels came a cousin of Nawwaf, Nuri Shaalan's eldest son, with a mare sent by Nawwaf to Feisal. The Shaalan and the Jazi, being hostile, hardened eyes at one another; so we divided the parties and improvised a new guest-camp. After the Rualla, was announced the abu Tageiga chief of the sedentary Howeitat of the coast. He brought his tribe's respectful homage and the spoils of Dhaba and Moweilleh, the two last Turkish outlets on the Red Sea. Room was made for him on Feisal's carpet, and the warmest thanks rendered him for his tribe's activity; which carried us to the borders of Akaba, by tracks too rough for operations of force, but convenient for preaching and still more so for getting news.

In the afternoon, ibn Zaal arrived, with ten other of Auda's chief followers. He kissed Feisal's hand once for Auda and then once for himself, and, sitting back, declared that he came from Auda to present his salutations and to ask for orders. Feisal, with policy, controlled his outward joy, and introduced him gravely to his blood enemies, the Jazi Howeitat. Ibn Zaal acknowledged them distantly. Later, we held great private conversations with him and dismissed him with rich gifts, richer promises, and Feisal's own message to Auda that his mind would not be smooth till he had seen him face to face in Wejh. Auda was an immense chivalrous name, but an unknown quantity to us, and in so vital a matter as Akaba we could not afford a mistake. He must come down that we might weigh him, and frame our future plans actually in his presence, and with his help.

Except that all its events were happy, this day was not essentially unlike Feisal's every day. The rush of news made my diary fat. The roads to Wejh swarmed with envoys and volunteers and great sheikhs riding in to swear allegiance. The contagion of their constant passage made the lukewarm Billi ever more profitable to us. Feisal swore new adherents solemnly on the Koran between his hands, 'to wait while he waited, march when he marched, to yield obedience to no Turk, to deal kindly with all who spoke Arabic (whether Bagdadi, Aleppine, Syrian, or pure-blooded) and to put independence above life, family, and goods'.

He also began to confront them at once, in his presence, with their tribal enemies, and to compose their feuds. An account of profit and loss would be struck between the parties, with Feisal modulating and interceding between them, and often paying the balance, or contributing towards it from his own funds, to hurry on the pact. During two years Feisal so laboured daily, putting together and arranging in their natural order the innumerable tiny pieces which made up Arabian society, and combining them into his one design of war against the Turks. There was no blood feud left active in any of the districts through which he had passed, and he was Court of Appeal, ultimate and unchallenged, for western Arabia.

He showed himself worthy of this achievement. He never gave a partial decision, nor a decision so impracticably just that it must lead to disorder. No Arab ever impugned his judgements, or questioned his wisdom and competence in tribal business. By patiently sifting out right and wrong, by his tact, his wonderful memory, he gained authority over the nomads from Medina to Damascus and beyond. He was recognized as a force transcending tribe, superseding blood chiefs, greater than jealousies. The Arab movement became in the best sense national, since within it all Arabs were at one, and for it private interests must be set aside; and in this movement chief place, by right of application and by right of ability, had been properly earned by the man who filled it for those few weeks of triumph and longer months of disillusion after Damascus had been set free.

CHAPTER XXXI

URGENT messages from Clayton broke across this cheerful work with orders to wait in Wejh for two days and meet the *Nur el Bahr*, an Egyptian patrol ship, coming down with news. I was not well and waited with more excellent grace. She arrived on the proper day, and disembarked MacRury, who gave me a copy of long telegraphic instructions from Jemal Pasha to Fakhri in Medina. These, emanating from Enver and the German staff in Constantinople, ordered the instant abandonment of Medina, and evacuation of the troops by route march in mass, first to Hedia, thence to El Ula, thence to Tebuk, and finally to Maan, where a fresh rail-head and entrenched position would be constituted.

This move would have suited the Arabs excellently; but our army of Egypt was perturbed at the prospect of twenty-five thousand Anatolian troops, with far more than the usual artillery of a corps, descending suddenly on the Beersheba front. Clayton, in his letter, told me the development was to be treated with the utmost concern, and every effort made to capture Medina, or to destroy the garrison when they came out. Newcombe was on the line, doing a vigorous demolition-series, so that the moment's responsibility fell on me. I feared that little could be done in time, for the message was days old, and the evacuation timed to begin at once.

We told Feisal the frank position, and that Allied interests in this case demanded the sacrifice, or at least the postponement of immediate advantage to the Arabs. He rose, as ever, to a proposition of honour, and agreed instantly to do his best. We worked out our possible resources and arranged to move them into contact with the railway. Sherif Mastur, an honest, quiet old man, and Rasim, with tribesmen, mule-mounted infantry, and a gun, were to proceed directly to Fagair, the first good water-base north of Wadi Ais, to hold up our first section of railway, from Abdulla's area northward.

Ali ibn el Hussein, from Jeida, would attack the next section of line northward from Mastur. We told ibn Mahanna to get close to El Ula, and watch it. We ordered Sherif Nasir to stay near Kalaat el Muadhd-ham, and keep his men in hand for an effort. I wrote asking Newcombe to come in for news. Old Mohammed Ali was to move from Dhaba to an oasis near Tebuk, so that if the evacuation got so far we should be ready. All our hundred and fifty miles of line would thus be beset, while Feisal himself, at Wejh, stood ready to bring help to whatever sector most needed him.

My part was to go off to Abdulla in Wadi Ais, to find out why he had done nothing for two months, and to persuade him, if the Turks came out, to go straight at them. I hoped we might deter them from moving by making so many small raids on this lengthy line that traffic would be seriously disorganized, and the collection of the necessary food-dumps for the army at each main stage be impracticable. The Medina force, being short of animal transport, could carry little with them. Enver had instructed them to put guns and stores on trains; and to enclose these trains in their columns and march together up the rail-way. It was an unprecedented manœuvre, and if we gained ten days to get in place, and they then attempted anything so silly, we should have a chance of destroying them all.

Next day I left Wejh, ill and unfit for a long march, while Feisal in his haste and many preoccupations had chosen me a travelling party of queer fellows. There were four Rifaa and one Merawi Juheina as guides, and Arslan, a Syrian soldier-servant, who prepared bread and rice for me and acted besides as butt to the Arabs; four Ageyl, a Moor, and an Ateibi, Suleiman. The camels, thin with the bad grazing of this dry Billi territory, would have to go slowly.

Delay after delay took place in our starting, until nine at night, and then we moved unwillingly: but I was determined to get clear of Wejh somehow before morning. So we went four hours and slept. Next day we did two stages of five hours each, and camped at Abu Zereibat, in our old ground of the winter. The great pool had shrunk little in the two months, but was noticeably more salt. A few weeks later it was unfit to drink. A shallow well near by was said to afford tolerable water. I did not look for it, since boils on my back and heavy fever made painful the jolting of the camel, and I was tired.

Long before dawn we rode away, and having crossed Hamdh got

confused in the broken surfaces of Agunna, an area of low hills. When day broke we recovered direction and went over a watershed steeply down into El Khubt, a hill-locked plain extending to the Sukhur, the granite bubbles of hills which had been prominent on our road up from Um Lejj. The ground was luxuriant with colocynth, whose runners and fruits looked festive in the early light. The Juheina said both leaves and stalks were excellent food for such horses as would eat them, and defended from thirst for many hours. The Ageyl said that the best aperient was to drink camel-milk from cups of the scooped-out rind. The Ateibi said that he was sufficiently moved if he just rubbed the juice of the fruit on the soles of his feet. The Moor Hamed said that the dried pith made good tinder. On one point however they were all agreed, that the whole plant was useless or poisonous as fodder for camels.

This talk carried us across the Khubt, a pleasant three miles, and through a low ridge into a second smaller section. We now saw that, of the Sukhur, two stood together to the north-east, great grey striated piles of volcanic rock, reddish coloured where protected from the burning of the sun and the bruising of sandy winds. The third Sakhara, which stood a little apart, was the bubble rock which had roused my curiosity. Seen from near by, it more resembled a huge football half-buried in the ground. It, too, was brown in colour. The south and east faces were quite smooth and unbroken, and its regular, domed head was polished and shining and had fine cracks running up and over it like stitched seams: altogether one of the strangest hills in Hejaz, a country of strange hills. We rode gently towards it, through a thin shower of rain which came slanting strangely and beautifully across the sunlight. Our path took us between the Sakhara and the Sukhur by a narrow gorge with sandy floor and steep bare walls. Its head was rough. We had to scramble up shelves of coarse-faced stone, and along a great fault in the hill-side between two tilted red reefs of hard rock. The summit of the pass was a knife-edge, and from it we went down an encumbered gap, half-blocked by one fallen boulder which had been hammered over with the tribal marks of all the generations of men who had used this road. Afterwards there opened tree-grown spaces, collecting grounds in winter for the sheets of rain which poured off the glazed sides of the Sukhur. There were granite outcrops here and there, and a fine silver sand underfoot in the still damp water-channels. The drainage was towards Heiran.

We then entered a wild confusion of granite shards, piled up haphazard into low mounds, in and out of which we wandered any way we could find practicable going for our hesitating camels. Soon after noon this gave place to a broad wooded valley, up which we rode for an hour, till our troubles began again; for we had to dismount and lead our animals up a narrow hill-path with broken steps of rock so polished by long years of passing feet that they were dangerous in wet weather. They took us over a great shoulder of the hills and down among more small mounds and valleys, and afterwards by another rocky zigzag descent into a torrent-bed. This soon became too confined to admit the passage of laden camels, and the path left it to cling precariously to the hill-side with a cliff above and cliff below. After fifteen minutes of this we were glad to reach a high saddle on which former travellers had piled little cairns of commemoration and thankfulness. Of such a nature had been the road-side cairns of Masturah, on my first Arabian journey, from Rabegh to Feisal.

We stopped to add one to the number, and then rode down a sandy valley into Wadi Hanbag, a large, well-wooded tributary of Hamdh. After the broken country in which we had been prisoned for hours, the openness of Hanbag was refreshing. Its clean white bed swept on northward through the trees in a fine curve under precipitous hills of red and brown, with views for a mile or two up and down its course. There were green weeds and grass growing on the lower sand-slopes of the tributary, and we stopped there for half an hour to let our starved camels eat the juicy, healthy stuff.

They had not so enjoyed themselves since Bir el Waheidi, and tore at it ravenously, stowing it away unchewed inside them, pending a fit time for leisurely digestion. We then crossed the valley to a great branch opposite our entry. This Wadi Kitan was also beautiful. Its shingle face, without loose rocks, was plentifully grown over with trees. On the right were low hills, on the left great heights called the Jidhwa, in parallel ridges of steep broken granite, very red now that the sun was setting amid massed cloud-banks of boding rain.

At last we camped, and when the camels were unloaded and driven out to pasture, I lay down under the rocks and rested. My body was very sore with headache and high fever, the accompaniments of a sharp attack of dysentery which had troubled me along the march and had laid me out twice that day in short fainting fits, when the more difficult parts of the climb had asked too much of my strength. Dysentery of this Arabian coast sort used to fall like a hammer blow, and crush its victims for a few hours, after which the extreme effects passed off; but it left men curiously tired, and subject for some weeks to sudden breaks of nerve.

My followers had been quarrelling all day; and while I was lying near the rocks a shot was fired. I paid no attention; for there were hares and birds in the valley; but a little later Suleiman roused me and made me follow him across the valley to an opposite bay in the rocks, where one of the Ageyl, a Boreida man, was lying stone dead with a bullet through his temples. The shot must have been fired from close by; because the skin was burnt about one wound. The remaining Ageyl were running frantically about; and when I asked what it was Ali, their head man, said that Hamed the Moor had done the murder. I suspected Suleiman, because of the feud between the Atban and Ageyl which had burned up in Yenbo and Wejh; but Ali assured me that Suleiman had been with him three hundred yards further up the valley gathering sticks when the shot was fired. I sent all out to search for Hamed, and crawled back to the baggage, feeling that it need not have happened this day of all days when I was in pain.

As I lay there I heard a rustle, and opened my eyes slowly upon Hamed's back as he stooped over his saddle-bags, which lay just beyond my rock. I covered him with a pistol and then spoke. He had put down his rifle to lift the gear; and was at my mercy till the others came. We held a court at once; and after a while Hamed confessed that, he and Salem having had words, he had seen red and shot him suddenly. Our inquiry ended. The Ageyl, as relatives of the dead man, demanded blood for blood. The others supported them; and I tried vainly to talk the gentle Ali round. My head was aching with fever and I could not think; but hardly even in health, with all eloquence, could I have begged Hamed off; for Salem had been a friendly fellow and his sudden murder a wanton crime.

Then rose up the horror which would make civilized man shun justice like a plague if he had not the needy to serve him as hangmen for wages. There were other Moroccans in our army; and to let the Ageyl kill one in feud meant reprisals by which our unity would have been endangered. It must be a formal execution, and at last, desperately, I told Hamed that he must die for punishment, and laid the burden of his killing on myself. Perhaps they would count me not qualified for feud. At least no revenge could lie against my followers; for I was a stranger and kinless.

I made him enter a narrow gully of the spur, a dank twilight place overgrown with woods. Its sandy bed had been pitted by trickles of water down the cliffs in the late rain. At the end it shrank to a crack a few inches wide. The walls were vertical. I stood in the entrance and gave him a few moments' delay which he spent crying on the ground. Then I made him rise and shot him through the chest. He fell down on the weeds shrieking, with the blood coming out in spurts over his clothes, and jerked about till he rolled nearly to where I was. I fired again, but was shaking so that I only broke his wrist. He went on calling out, less loudly, now lying on his back with his feet towards me, and I leant forward and shot him for the last time in the thick of his neck under the jaw. His body shivered a little, and I called the Ageyl; who buried him in the gully where he was. Afterwards the wakeful night dragged over me, till, hours before dawn, I had the men up and made them load, in my longing to be set free of Wadi Kitan. They had to lift me into the saddle.

CHAPTER XXXII

DAWN found us crossing a steep short pass out of Wadi Kitan into the main drainage valley of these succeeding hills. We turned aside into Wadi Reimi, a tributary, to get water. There was no proper well, only a seepage hole in the stony bed of the valley; and we found it partly by our noses: though the taste, while as foul, was curiously unlike the smell. We refilled our water-skins. Arslan baked bread, and we rested for two hours. Then we went on through Wadi Amk, an easy green valley which made comfortable marching for the camels.

When the Amk turned westward we crossed it, going up between piles of the warped grey granite (like cold toffee) which was common up-country in the Hejaz. The defile culminated at the foot of a natural ramp and staircase: badly broken, twisting, and difficult for camels, but short. Afterwards we were in an open valley for an hour, with low hills to the right and mountains to the left. There were water pools in the crags, and Merawin tents under the fine trees which studded the flat. The fertility of the slopes was great: on them grazed flocks of sheep and goats. We got milk from the Arabs: the first milk my Ageyl had been given in the two years of drought.

The track out of the valley when we reached its head was execrable, and the descent beyond into Wadi Marrakh almost dangerous; but the view from the crest compensated us. Wadi Marrakh, a broad, peaceful avenue, ran between two regular straight walls of hills to a circus four miles off where valleys from left, right and front seemed to meet. Artificial heaps of uncut stone were piled about the approach. As we entered it, we saw that the grey hill-walls swept back on each side in a half-circle. Before us, to the south, the curve was barred across by a straight wall or step of blue-black lava, standing over a little grove of thorn trees. We made for these and lay down in their thin shade, grateful in such sultry air for any pretence of coolness.

The day, now at its zenith, was very hot; and my weakness had so increased that my head hardly held up against it. The puffs of feverish wind pressed like scorching hands against our faces, burning our eyes. My pain made me breathe in gasps through the mouth; the wind cracked my lips and seared my throat till I was too dry to talk, and drinking became sore; yet I always needed to drink, as my thirst would not let me lie still and get the peace I longed for. The flies were a plague.

The bed of the valley was of fine quartz gravel and white sand. Its glitter thrust itself between our eyelids; and the level of the ground seemed to dance as the wind moved the white tips of stubble grass to and fro. The camels loved this grass, which grew in tufts, about sixteen inches high, on slate-green stalks. They gulped down great quantities of it until the men drove them in and couched them by me. At the moment I hated the beasts, for too much food made their breath stink; and they rumblingly belched up a new mouthful from their stomachs each time they had chewed and swallowed the last, till a green slaver flooded out between their loose lips over the side teeth, and dripped down their sagging chins.

Lying angrily there, I threw a stone at the nearest, which got up and wavered about behind my head: finally it straddled its back legs and staled in wide, bitter jets; and I was so far gone with the heat and weakness and pain that I just lay there and cried about it unhelping. The men had gone to make a fire and cook a gazelle one of them had fortunately shot; and I realized that on another day this halt would have been pleasant to me; for the hills were very strange and their colours vivid. The base had the warm grey of old stored sunlight; while about their crests ran narrow veins of granite-coloured stone, generally in pairs, following the contour of the skyline like the rusted metals of an abandoned scenic railway. Arslan said the hills were combed like cocks, a sharper observation.

After the men had fed we re-mounted, and easily climbed the first wave of the lava flood. It was short, as was the second, on the top of which lay a broad terrace with an alluvial plot of sand and gravel in its midst. The lava was a nearly clean floor of iron-red rock-cinders, over which were scattered fields of loose stone. The third and other steps ascended to the south of us: but we turned east, up Wadi Gara.

Gara had, perhaps, been a granite valley down whose middle the lava had flowed, slowly filling it, and arching itself up in a central heap. On each side were deep troughs, between the lava and the hill-side. Rain water flooded these as often as storms burst in the hills. The lava flow, as it coagulated, had been twisted like a rope, cracked, and bent back irregularly upon itself. The surface was loose with fragments through which many generations of camel parties had worn an inadequate and painful track.

We struggled along for hours, going slowly, our camels wincing at every stride as the sharp edges slipped beneath their tender feet. The paths were only to be seen by the droppings along them, and by the slightly bluer surfaces of the rubbed stones. The Arabs declared them impassable after dark, which was to be believed, for we risked laming our beasts each time our impatience made us urge them on. Just before five in the afternoon, however, the way got easier. We seemed to be near the head of the valley, which grew narrow. Before us on the right, an exact cone-crater, with tidy furrows scoring it from lip to foot, promised good going; for it was made of black ash, clean as though sifted, with here and there a bank of harder soil, and cinders. Beyond it was another lava-field, older perhaps than the valleys, for its stones were smoothed, and between them were straths of flat earth, rank with weeds. In among these open spaces were Beduin tents, whose owners ran to us when they saw us coming; and, taking our head-stalls with hospitable force, led us in.

They proved to be Sheikh Fahad el Hansha and his men: old and garrulous warriors who had marched with us to Wejh, and had been with Garland on that great occasion when his first automatic mine had succeeded under a troop train near Toweira station. Fahad would not hear of my resting quietly outside his tent, but with the reckless equality of the desert men urged me into an unfortunate place inside among his own vermin. There he plied me with bowl after bowl of diuretic camel-milk between questions about Europe, my home tribe, the English camel-pasturages, the war in the Hejaz and the wars elsewhere, Egypt and Damascus, how Feisal was, why did we seek Abdulla, and by what perversity did I remain Christian, when their hearts and hands waited to welcome me to the Faith?

So passed long hours till ten at night, when the guest-sheep was carried in, dismembered royally over a huge pile of buttered rice. I ate as manners demanded, twisted myself up in my cloak, and slept; my bodily exhaustion, after those hours of the worst imaginable marching, proofing me against the onslaught of lice and fleas. The illness, however, had stimulated my ordinarily sluggish fancy, which ran riot this night in dreams of wandering naked for a dark eternity over interminable lava (like scrambled egg gone iron-blue, and very wrong), sharp as insect-bites underfoot; and with some horror, perhaps a dead Moor, always climbing after us.

In the morning we woke early and refreshed, with our clothes stinging-full of fiery points feeding on us. After one more bowl of milk proffered us by the eager Fahad, I was able to walk unaided to my camel and mount her actively. We rode up the last piece of Wadi Gara to the crest, among cones of black cinders from a crater to the south. Thence we turned to a branch valley, ending in a steep and rocky chimney, up which we pulled our camels.

Beyond we had an easy descent into Wadi Murrmiya, whose middle bristled with lava like galvanized iron, on each side of which there were smooth sandy beds, good going. After a while we came to a fault in the flow, which served as a track to the other side. By it we crossed over, finding the lava pocketed with soils apparently of extreme richness, for in them were leafy trees and lawns of real grass, starred with flowers, the best grazing of all our ride, looking the more wonderfully green because of the blue-black twisted crusts of rock about. The lava had changed its character. Here were no piles of loose stones, as big as a skull or a man's hand, rubbed and rounded together; but bunched and crystallized fronds of metallic rock, altogether impassable for bare feet.

Another watershed conducted us to an open place where the Jeheina had ploughed some eight acres of the thin soil below a thicket of scrub. They said there were like it in the neighbourhood other fields, silent witnesses to the courage and persistence of the Arabs. It was called Wadi Chetf, and after it was another broken river of lava, the worst yet encountered. A shadowy path zigzagged across it. We lost one camel with a broken fore-leg, the result of a stumble in a pot-hole; and the many bones which lay about showed that we were not the only party to suffer misfortune in the passage. However, this ended our lava, according to the guides, and we went thence forward along easy valleys with finally a long run up a gentle slope till dusk. The going was so good and the cool of the day so freshened me that we did not halt at nightfall, after our habit, but pushed on for an hour across the basin of Murrmiya into the basin of Wadi Ais, and there, by Tleih, we stopped for our last camp in the open.

I rejoiced that we were so nearly in, for fever was heavy on me. I was afraid that perhaps I was going to be really ill, and the prospect of falling into the well-meaning hands of tribesmen in such a state was not pleasant. Their treatment of every sickness was to burn holes in the patient's body at some spot believed to be the complement of the part affected. It was a cure tolerable to such as had faith in it, but torture to the unbelieving: to incur it unwillingly would be silly, and yet certain; for the Arabs' good intentions, selfish as their good digestions, would never heed a sick man's protesting.

The morning was easy, over open valleys and gentle rides into Wadi Ais. We arrived at Abu Markha, its nearest watering-place, just a few minutes after Sherif Abdulla had dismounted there, and while he was ordering his tents to be pitched in an acacia glade beyond the well. He was leaving his old camp at Bir el Amri, lower down the valley, as he had left Murabba, his camp before, because the ground had been fouled by the careless multitude of his men and animals. I gave him the documents from Feisal, explaining the situation in Medina, and the need we had of haste to block the railway. I thought he took it coolly; but, without argument, went on to say that I was a little tired after my journey, and with his permission would lie down and sleep a while. He pitched me a tent next his great marquee, and I went into it and rested myself at last. It had been a struggle against faintness day-long in the saddle to get here at all: and now the strain was ended with the delivery of my message, I felt that another hour would have brought the breaking point.

CHAPTER XXXIII

ABOUT ten days I lay in that tent, suffering a bodily weakness which made my animal self crawl away and hide till the shame was passed. As usual in such circumstances my mind cleared, my senses became more acute, and I began at last to think consecutively of the Arab Revolt, as an accustomed duty to rest upon against the pain. It should have been thought out long before, but at my first landing in Hejaz there had been a crying need for action, and we had done what seemed to instinct best, not probing into the why, nor formulating what we really wanted at the end of all. Instinct thus abused without a basis of past knowledge and reflection had grown intuitive, feminine, and was now bleaching my confidence; so in this forced inaction I looked for the equation between my book-reading and my movements, and spent the intervals of uneasy sleeps and dreams in plucking at the tangle of our present.

As I have shown, I was unfortunately as much in command of the campaign as I pleased, and was untrained. In military theory I was tolerably read, my Oxford curiosity having taken me past Napoleon to Clausewitz and his school, to Caemmerer and Moltke, and the recent Frenchmen. They had all seemed to be one-sided; and after looking at Jomini and Willisen, I had found broader principles in Saxe and Guibert and the eighteenth century. However, Clausewitz was intellectually so much the master of them, and his book so logical and fascinating, that unconsciously I accepted his finality, until a comparison of Kuhne and Foch disgusted me with soldiers, wearied me of their officious glory, making me critical of all their light. In any case, my interest had been abstract, concerned with the theory and philosophy of warfare especially from the metaphysical side.

Now, in the field everything had been concrete, particularly the tiresome problem of Medina; and to distract myself from that I began to recall suitable maxims on the conduct of modern, scientific war. But they would not fit, and it worried me. Hitherto, Medina had been an obsession for us all; but now that I was ill, its image was not clear, whether it was that we were near to it (one seldom liked the attainable), or whether it was that my eyes were misty with too constant staring at the butt. One afternoon I woke from a hot sleep, running with sweat and pricking with flies, and wondered what on earth was the good of Medina to us? Its harmfulness had been patent when we were at Yenbo and the Turks in it were going to Mecca: but we had changed all that by our march to Wejh. To-day we were blockading the railway, and they only defending it. The garrison of Medina, reduced to an inoffensive size, were sitting in trenches destroying their own power of movement by eating the transport they could no longer feed. We had taken away their power to harm us, and yet wanted to take away their town. It was not a base for us like Wejh, nor a threat like Wadi Ais. What on earth did we want it for?

The camp was bestirring itself after the torpor of the midday hours; and noises from the world outside began to filter in to me past the yellow lining of the tent-canvas, whose every hole and tear was stabbed through by a long dagger of sunlight. I heard the stamping and snorting of the horses plagued with flies where they stood in the shadow of the trees, the complaint of camels, the ringing of coffee mortars, distant shots. To their burden I began to drum out the aim in war. The books gave it pat — the destruction of the armed forces of the enemy by the one process — battle. Victory could be purchased only by blood. This was a hard saying for us. As the Arabs had no organized forces, a Turkish Foch would have no aim. The Arabs would not endure casualties. How would our Clausewitz buy his victory? Von der Goltz had seemed to go deeper, saying it was necessary not to annihilate the enemy, but to break his courage. Only we showed no prospect of ever breaking anybody's courage.

However, Goltz was a humbug, and these wise men must be talking metaphors; for we were indubitably winning our war; and as I pondered slowly, it dawned on me that we had won the Hejaz war. Out of every thousand square miles of Hejaz nine hundred and ninety-nine were now free. Did my provoked jape at Vickery, that rebellion was more like peace than like war, hold as much truth as haste? Perhaps in war the absolute did rule, but for peace a majority was good enough. If we held the rest, the Turks were welcome to the tiny fraction on which they

stood, till peace or Doomsday showed them the futility of clinging to
our window-pane.

I brushed off the same flies once more from my face patiently,
content to know that the Hejaz War was won and finished with: won
from the day we took Wejh, if we had had wit to see it. Then I broke
the thread of my argument again to listen. The distant shots had grown
and tied themselves into long, ragged volleys. They ceased. I strained
my ears for the other sounds which I knew would follow. Sure enough
across the silence came a rustle like the dragging of a skirt over the
flints, around the thin walls of my tent. A pause, while the camel-riders
drew up: and then the soggy tapping of canes on the thick of the beasts'
necks to make them kneel.

They knelt without noise: and I timed it in my memory: first the
hesitation, as the camels, looking down, felt the soil with one foot for a
soft place; then the muffled thud and the sudden loosening of breath as
they dropped on their fore-legs, since this party had come far and were
tired; then the shuffle as the hind legs were folded in, and the rocking
as they tossed from side to side thrusting outward with their knees to
bury them in the cooler subsoil below the burning flints, while the
riders, with a quick soft patter of bare feet, like birds over the ground,
were led off tacitly either to the coffee hearth or to Abdulla's tent,
according to their business. The camels would rest there, uneasily
switching their tails across the shingle till their masters were free and
looked to their stabling.

I had made a comfortable beginning of doctrine, but was left still to
find an alternative end and means of war. Ours seemed unlike the
ritual of which Foch was priest; and I recalled him, to see a difference
in kind between him and us. In his modern war — absolute war he
called it — two nations professing incompatible philosophies put them
to the test of force. Philosophically, it was idiotic, for while opinions
were arguable, convictions needed shooting to be cured; and the
struggle could end only when the supporters of the one immaterial
principle had no more means of resistance against the supporters of the
other. It sounded like a twentieth-century restatement of the wars of
religion, whose logical end was utter destruction of one creed, and
whose protagonists believed that God's judgement would prevail. This

might do for France and Germany, but would not represent the British attitude. Our Army was not intelligently maintaining a philosophic conception in Flanders or on the Canal. Efforts to make our men hate the enemy usually made them hate the fighting. Indeed Foch had knocked out his own argument by saying that such war depended on levy in mass, and was impossible with professional armies; while the old army was still the British ideal, and its manner the ambition of our ranks and our files. To me the Foch war seemed only an exterminative variety, no more absolute than another. One could as explicably call it 'murder war'. Clausewitz enumerated all sorts of war . . . personal wars, joint-proxy duels, for dynastic reasons . . . expulsive wars, in party politics . . . commercial wars, for trade objects . . . two wars seemed seldom alike. Often the parties did not know their aim, and blundered till the march of events took control. Victory in general habit leaned to the clear-sighted, though fortune and superior intelligence could make a sad muddle of nature's 'inexorable' law.

I wondered why Feisal wanted to fight the Turks, and why the Arabs helped him, and saw that their aim was geographical, to extrude the Turk from all Arabic-speaking lands in Asia. Their peace ideal of liberty could exercise itself only so. In pursuit of the ideal conditions we might kill Turks, because we disliked them very much; but the killing was a pure luxury. If they would go quietly the war would end. If not, we would urge them, or try to drive them out. In the last resort, we should be compelled to the desperate course of blood and the maxims of 'murder war', but as cheaply as could be for ourselves, since the Arabs fought for freedom, and that was a pleasure to be tasted only by a man alive. Posterity was a chilly thing to work for, no matter how much a man happened to love his own, or other people's already-produced children.

At this point a slave slapped my tent-door, and asked if the Emir might call. So I struggled into more clothes, and crawled over to his great tent to sound the depth of motive in him. It was a comfortable place, luxuriously shaded and carpeted deep in strident rugs, the aniline-dyed spoils of Hussein Mabeirig's house in Rabegh. Abdulla passed most of his day in it, laughing with his friends, and playing games with Mohammed Hassan, the court jester. I set the ball of conversation rolling between him and Shakir and the chance sheikhs, among whom was the fire-hearted Ferhan el Aida, the son of Doughty's Motlog; and I was rewarded, for Abdullas' words were definite. He contrasted his hearer's present independence with their past servitude to Turkey, and roundly said that talk of Turkish heresy, or the immoral doctrine of *Yeni-Turan*, or the illegitimate Caliphate was beside the point. It was Arab country, and the Turks were in it: that was the one issue. My argument preened itself.

The next day a great complication of boils developed out, to conceal my lessened fever, and to chain me down yet longer in impotence upon my face in this stinking tent. When it grew too hot for dreamless dozing, I picked up my tangle again, and went on ravelling it out, considering now the whole house of war in its structural aspect, which was strategy, in its arrangements, which were tactics, and in the sentiment of its inhabitants, which was psychology; for my personal duty was command, and the commander, like the master architect, was responsible for all.

The first confusion was the false antithesis between strategy, the aim in war, the synoptic regard seeing each part relative to the whole, and tactics, the means towards a strategic end, the particular steps of its staircase. They seemed only points of view from which to ponder the elements of war, the Algebraical element of things, a Biological element of lives, and the Psychological element of ideas.

The algebraical element looked to me a pure science, subject to mathematical law, inhuman. It dealt with known variables, fixed conditions, space and time, inorganic things like hills and climates and railways, with mankind in type-masses too great for individual variety, with all artificial aids and the extensions given our faculties by mechanical invention. It was essentially formulable.

Here was a pompous, professorial beginning. My wits, hostile to the abstract, took refuge in Arabia again. Translated into Arabic, the algebraic factor would first take practical account of the area we wished to deliver, and I began idly to calculate how many square miles: sixty: eighty: one hundred: perhaps one hundred and forty thousand square miles. And how would the Turks defend all that? No doubt by a trench line across the bottom, if we came like an army with banners;

but suppose we were (as we might be) an influence, an idea, a thing intangible, invulnerable, without front or back, drifting about like a gas? Armies were like plants, immobile, firm-rooted, nourished through long stems to the head. We might be a vapour, blowing where we listed. Our kingdoms lay in each man's mind; and as we wanted nothing material to live on, so we might offer nothing material to the killing. It seemed a regular soldier might be helpless without a target, owning only what he sat on, and subjugating only what, by order, he could poke his rifle at.

Then I figured out how many men they would need to sit on all this ground, to save it from our attack-in-depth, sedition putting up her head in every unoccupied one of those hundred thousand square miles. I knew the Turkish Army exactly, and even allowing for their recent extension of faculty by aeroplanes and guns and armoured trains (which made the earth a smaller battlefield) still it seemed they would have need of a fortified post every four square miles, and a post could not be less than twenty men. If so, they would need six hundred thousand men to meet the illwills of all the Arab peoples, combined with the active hostility of a few zealots.

How many zealots could we have? At present we had nearly fifty thousand: sufficient for the day. It seemed the assets in this element of war were ours. If we realized our raw materials and were apt with them, then climate, railway, desert, and technical weapons could also be attached to our interests. The Turks were stupid; the Germans behind them dogmatical. They would believe that rebellion was absolute like war, and deal with it on the analogy of war. Analogy in human things was fudge, anyhow; and war upon rebellion was messy and slow, like eating soup with a knife.

This was enough of the concrete; so I sheered off ἐπιστήμη, the mathematical element, and plunged into the nature of the biological factor in command. Its crisis seemed to be the breaking point, life and death, or less finally, wear and tear. The war-philosophers had properly made an art of it, and had elevated one item, 'effusion of blood', to the height of an essential, which became humanity in battle, an act touching every side of our corporal being, and very warm. A line of variability. Man, persisted like leaven through its estimates, making them irregular.

The components were sensitive and illogical, and generals guarded themselves by the device of a reserve, the significant medium of their art. Goltz had said that if you knew the enemy's strength, and he was fully deployed, then you could dispense with a reserve: but this was never. The possibility of accident, of some flaw in materials was always in the general's mind, and the reserve unconsciously held to meet it.

The 'felt' element in troops, not expressible in figures, had to be guessed at by the equivalent of Plato's δόξα, and the greatest commander of men was he whose intuitions most nearly happened. Nine-tenths of tactics were certain enough to be teachable in schools; but the irrational tenth was like the kingfisher flashing across the pool, and in it lay the test of generals. It could be ensued only by instinct (sharpened by thought practising the stroke) until at the crisis it came naturally, a reflex. There had been men whose δόξα so nearly approached perfection that by its road they reached the certainty of ἐπιστήμη. The Greeks might have called such genius for command νόησις had they bothered to rationalize revolt.

My mind see-sawed back to apply this to ourselves, and at once knew that it was not bounded by mankind, that it applied also to materials. In Turkey things were scarce and precious, men less esteemed than equipment. Our cue was to destroy, not the Turk's army, but his minerals. The death of a Turkish bridge or rail, machine or gun or charge of high explosive, was more profitable to us than the death of a Turk. In the Arab Army at the moment we were chary both of materials and of men. Governments saw men only in mass; but our men, being irregulars, were not formations, but individuals. An individual death, like a pebble dropped in water, might make but a brief hole; yet rings of sorrow widened out therefrom. We could not afford casualties.

Materials were easier to replace. It was our obvious policy to be superior in some one tangible branch; gun-cotton or machine-guns or whatever could be made decisive. Orthodoxy had laid down the maxim, applied to men, of being superior at the critical point and moment of attack. We might be superior in equipment in one dominant moment or respect; and for both things and men we might give the doctrine a twisted negative side, for cheapness' sake, and be weaker than the enemy everywhere except in that one point or matter. The decision of what was critical would always be ours. Most wars were wars of contact, both forces striving into touch to avoid tactical surprise. Ours should be a war of detachment. We were to contain the enemy by the silent threat of a vast unknown desert, not disclosing ourselves till we attacked. The attack might be nominal, directed not against him, but against his stuff; so it would not seek either his strength or his weakness, but his most accessible material. In railway-cutting it would be usually an empty stretch of rail; and the more empty, the greater the tactical success. We might turn our average into a rule (not a law, since war was antinomian) and develop a habit of never engaging the enemy. This would chime with the numerical plea for never affording a target. Many Turks on our front had no chance all the war to fire on us, and we were never on the defensive except by accident and in error.

The corollary of such a rule was perfect 'intelligence', so that we could plan in certainty. The chief agent must be the general's head; and his understanding must be faultless, leaving no room for chance. Morale, if built on knowledge, was broken by ignorance. When we knew all about the enemy we should be comfortable. We must take more pains in the service of news than any regular staff.

I was getting through my subject. The algebraical factor had been translated into terms of Arabia, and fitted like a glove. It promised victory. The biological factor had dictated to us a development of the tactical line most in accord with the genius of our tribesmen. There remained the psychological element to build up an apt shape. I went to Xenophon and stole, to name it, his word *diathetics*, which had been the art of Cyrus before he struck.

Of this our 'propaganda' was the stained and ignoble offspring. It was the pathic, almost the ethical, in war. Some of it concerned the crowd, an adjustment of its spirit to the point where it became useful to exploit in action, and the pre-direction of this changing spirit to a certain end. Some of it concerned the individual, and then it became a rare art of human kindness, transcending, by purposed emotion, the gradual logical sequence of the mind. It was more subtle than tactics, and better worth doing, because it dealt with uncontrollables, with subjects incapable of direct command. It considered the capacity for mood of our men, their complexities and mutability, and the cultivation of whatever in them promised to profit our intention. We had to arrange their minds in order of battle just as carefully and as formally as other officers would arrange their bodies. And not only our own men's minds, though naturally they came first. We must also arrange the minds of the enemy, so far as we could reach them; then those other minds of the nation supporting us behind the firing line, since more than half the battle passed there in the back; then the minds of the enemy nation waiting the verdict; and of the neutrals looking on; circle beyond circle.

There were many humiliating material limits, but no moral impossibilities; so that the scope of our diathetical activities was unbounded. On it we should mainly depend for the means of victory on the Arab front: and the novelty of it was our advantage. The printing press, and each newly-discovered method of communication favoured the intellectual above the physical, civilization paying the mind always from the body's funds. We kindergarten soldiers were beginning our art of war in the atmosphere of the twentieth century, receiving our weapons without prejudice. To the regular officer, with the tradition of forty generations of service behind him, the antique arms were the most honoured. As we had seldom to concern ourselves with what our men did, but always with what they thought, the diathetic for us would be more than half the command. In Europe it was set a little aside, and entrusted to men outside the General Staff. In Asia the regular elements were so weak that irregulars could not let the metaphysical weapon rust unused.

Battles in Arabia were a mistake, since we profited in them only by the ammunition the enemy fired off. Napoleon had said it was rare to find generals willing to fight battles; but the curse of this war was that so few would do anything else. Saxe had told us that irrational battles were the refuges of fools: rather they seemed to me impositions on the side which believed itself weaker, hazards made unavoidable either by lack of land room or by the need to defend a material property dearer than the lives of soldiers. We had nothing material to lose, so our best line was to defend nothing and to shoot nothing. Our cards were speed and time, not hitting power. The invention of bully beef had profited us more than the invention of gunpowder, but gave us strategical, rather than tactical strength, since in Arabia range was more than force, space greater than the power of armies.

I had now been eight days lying in this remote tent, keeping my ideas general,* till my brain, sick of unsupported thinking, had to be dragged to its work by an effort of will, and went off into a doze whenever that effort was relaxed. The fever passed: my dysentery ceased; and with restored strength the present again became actual to me. Facts concrete and pertinent thrust themselves into my reveries; and my inconstant wit bore aside towards all these roads of escape. So I hurried into line my shadowy principles, to have them once precise before my power to evoke them faded.

It seemed to me proven that our rebellion had an unassailable base, guarded not only from attack, but from the fear of attack. It had a sophisticated alien enemy, disposed as an army of occupation in an area greater than could be dominated effectively from fortified posts. It had a friendly population, of which some two in the hundred were active, and the rest quietly sympathetic to the point of not betraying the movements of the minority. The active rebels had the virtues of secrecy and self-control, and the qualities of speed, endurance and independence of arteries of supply. They had technical equipment enough to paralyse the enemy's communications. A province would be won when we had taught the civilians in it to die for our ideal of freedom. The presence of the enemy was secondary. Final victory seemed certain, if the war lasted long enough for us to work it out.

---

* Not perhaps as successfully as here. I thought out my problems mainly in terms of Hejaz, illustrated by what I knew of its men and its geography. These would have been too long if written down; and the argument has been compressed into an abstract form in which it smells more of the lamp than of the field. All military writing does, worse luck.

CHAPTER XXXIV

OBVIOUSLY I was well again, and I remembered the reason of my journey to Wadi Ais. The Turks meant to march out of Medina, and Sir Archibald Murray wanted us to attack them in professional form. It was irksome that he should come butting into our show from Egypt, asking from us alien activities. Yet the British were the bigger; and the Arabs lived only by grace of their shadow. We were yoked to Sir Archibald Murray, and must work with him, to the point of sacrificing our non-essential interests for his, if they would not be reconciled. At the same time we could not possibly act alike. Feisal might be a free gas: Sir Archibald's army, probably the most cumbrous in the world, had to be laboriously pushed forward on its belly. It was ridiculous to suppose it could keep pace with ethical conceptions as nimble as the Arab Movement: doubtful even if it would understand them. However, perhaps by hindering the railway we could frighten the Turks off their plan to evacuate Medina, and give them reason to remain in the town on the defensive: a conclusion highly serviceable to both Arabs and English, though possibly neither would see it, yet.

Accordingly, I wandered into Abdulla's tent, announcing my complete recovery and an ambition to do something to the Hejaz railway. Here were men, guns, machine-guns, explosives and automatic mines: enough for a main effort. But Abdulla was apathetic. He wanted to talk about the Royal families of Europe, or the Battle of the Somme: the slow march of his own war bored him. However, Sherif Shakir, his cousin and second in command, was fired to enthusiasm, and secured us licence to do our worst. Shakir loved the Ateiba, and swore they were the best tribe on earth; so we settled to take mostly Ateiba with us. Then we thought we might have a mountain gun, one of the Egyptian Army Krupp veterans, which had been sent by Feisal to Abdulla from Wejh as a present.

Shakir promised to collect the force, and we agreed that I should go in front (gently, as befitted my weakness) and search for a target. The nearest and biggest was Aba el Naam Station. With me went Raho, Algerian officer in the French Army, and member of Bremond's mission, a very hard-working and honest fellow. Our guide was Mohammed el Kadhi, whose old father, Dakhil-Allah, hereditary lawman of the Juheina, had guided the Turks down to Yenbo last December. Mohammed was eighteen, solid and silent natured. Sherif Fauzan el Harith, the famous warrior who had captured Eshref at Janbila, escorted us, with about twenty Ateiba and five or six Juheina adventurers.

We left on March the twenty-sixth, while Sir Archibald Murray was attacking Gaza; and rode down Wadi Ais; but after three hours the heat proved too much for me, and we stopped by a great sidr tree (lote or ju-jube, but the fruit was scarce) and rested under it the midday hours. Sidr trees cast heavy shade: there was a cool east wind, and few flies. Wadi Ais was luxuriant with thorn trees and grass, and its air full of white butterflies and scents of wild flowers; so that we did not remount till late in the afternoon, and then did only a short march, leaving Wadi Ais by the right, after passing in an angle of the valley a ruined terrace and cistern. Once there had been villages in this part, with the underground waters carefully employed in their frequent gardens; but now it was waste.

The following morning we had two hours' rough riding around the spurs of Jebel Serd into Wadi Turaa, a historic valley, linked by an easy pass to Wadi Yenbo. We spent this midday also under a tree, near some Juheina tents, where Mohammed guested while we slept. Then we rode on rather crookedly for two more hours, and camped after dark. By ill luck an early spring scorpion stung me severely on the left hand while I lay down to sleep. The place swelled up; and my arm became stiff and sore.

At five next morning, after a long night, we restarted, and passed through the last hills, out into the Jurf, an undulating open space which ran up southward to Jebel Antar, a crater with a split and castellated top, making it a landmark. We turned half-right in the plain, to get under cover of the low hills which screened it from Wadi Hamdh, in whose bed the railway lay. Behind these hills we rode southward till opposite Aba el Naam. There we halted to camp, close to the enemy but quite in safety. The hill-top commanded them; and we climbed it before sunset for a first view of the station.

The hill was, perhaps, six hundred feet high and steep, and I made many stages of it, resting on my way up: but the sight from the top was good. The railway was some three miles off. The station had a pair of large, two-storied houses of basalt, a circular water-tower, and other buildings. There were bell-tents, huts and trenches, but no sign of guns. We could see about three hundred men in all.

We heard that the Turks patrolled their neighbourhood actively at night. A bad habit this: so we sent off two men to lie by each block-house, and fire a few shots after dark. The enemy, thinking it a prelude to attack, stood-to in their trenches all night, while we were comfortably sleeping; but the cold woke us early with a restless dawn wind blowing across the Jurf, and singing in the great trees round our camp. As we climbed to our observation point the sun conquered the clouds and an hour later it grew very hot.

We lay like lizards in the long grass round the stones of the foremost cairn upon the hill-top and saw the garrison parade. Three hundred and ninety-nine infantry, little toy men, ran about when the bugle sounded, and formed up in stiff lines below the black building till there was more bugling: then they scattered, and after a few minutes the smoke of cooking fires went up. A herd of sheep and goats in charge of a little ragged boy issued out towards us. Before he reached the foot of the hills there came a loud whistling down the valley from the north, and a tiny, picture-book train rolled slowly into view across the hollow sounding bridge and halted just outside the station, panting out white puffs of steam.

The shepherd lad held on steadily, driving his goats with shrill cries up our hill for the better pasture on the western side. We sent two Juheina down behind a ridge beyond sight of the enemy, and they ran from each side and caught him. The lad was of the outcast Heteym, pariahs of the desert, whose poor children were commonly sent on hire as shepherds to the tribes about them. This one cried continually, and made efforts to escape as often as he saw his goats straying uncared-for about the hill. In the end the men lost patience and tied him up roughly, when he screamed for terror that they would kill him.

Fauzan had great ado to make him quiet, and then questioned him about his Turkish masters. But all his thoughts were for the flock: his eyes followed them miserably while the tears made edged and crooked tracks down his dirty face.

Shepherds were a class apart. For the ordinary Arab the hearth was a university, about which their world passed and where they heard the best talk, the news of their tribe, its poems, histories, love tales, lawsuits and bargainings. By such constant sharing in the hearth councils they grew up masters of expression, dialecticians, orators, able to sit with dignity in any gathering and never at a loss for moving words. The shepherds missed the whole of this. From infancy they followed their calling, which took them in all seasons and weathers, day and night, into the hills and condemned them to loneliness and brute company. In the wilderness, among the dry bones of nature, they grew up natural, knowing nothing of man and his affairs; hardly sane in ordinary talk; but very wise in plants, wild animals and the habits of their own goats and sheep, whose milk was their chief sustenance. With manhood they became sullen, while a few turned dangerously savage, more animal than man, haunting the flocks, and finding the satisfaction of their adult appetites in them, to the exclusion of more licit affections.

For hours after the shepherd had been suppressed only the sun moved in our view. As it climbed we shifted our cloaks to filter its harshness, and basked in luxurious warmth. The restful hill-top gave me back something of the sense-interests which I had lost since I had been ill. I was able to note once more the typical hill scenery, with its hard stone crests, its sides of bare rock, and lower slopes of loose sliding screes, packed, as the base was approached, solidly with a thin dry soil. The stone itself was glistening, yellow, sunburned stuff; metallic in ring, and brittle; splitting red or green or brown as the case might be. From every soft place sprouted thorn-bushes; and there was frequent grass, usually growing from one root in a dozen stout blades, knee-high and straw-coloured: the heads were empty ears between many-feathered arrows of silvery down. With these, and with a shorter grass, whose bottle-brush heads of pearly grey reached only to the ankle, the hill-sides were furred white and bowed themselves lowly towards us with each puff of the casual wind.

Verdure it was not, but excellent pasturage; and in the valleys were bigger tufts of grass, coarse, waist-high and bright green when fresh though they soon faded to the burned yellow of ordinary life. They grew thickly in all the beds of water-ribbed sand and shingle, between the occasional thorn trees, some of which stood forty feet in height. The sidr trees, with their dry, sugary fruit, were rare. But bushes of browned tamarisk, tall broom, other varieties of coarse grass, some flowers, and everything which had thorns, flourished about our camp, and made it a rich sample of the vegetation of the Hejaz highlands. Only one of the plants profited ourselves, and that was the hemeid: a sorrel with fleshy heart-shaped leaves, whose pleasant acidity stayed our thirst.

At dusk we climbed down again with the goat-herd prisoner, and what we could gather of his flock. Our main body would come this night, so that Fauzan and I wandered out across the darkling plain till we found a pleasant gun-position in some low ridges not two thousand yards from the station. On our return, very tired, fires were burning among the trees. Shakir had just arrived, and his men and ours were roasting goat-flesh contentedly. The shepherd was tied up behind my sleeping place, because he had gone frantic when his charges were unlawfully slaughtered. He refused to taste the supper; and we only forced bread and rice into him by the threat of dire punishment if he insulted our hospitality. They tried to convince him that we should take the station next day and kill his masters; but he would not be comforted, and afterwards, for fear lest he escape, had to be lashed to his tree again.

After supper Shakir told me that he had brought only three hundred men instead of the agreed eight or nine hundred. However, it was his war, and therefore his tune, so we hastily modified the plans. We would not take the station; we would frighten it by a frontal artillery attack, while we mined the railway to the north and south, in the hope of trapping that halted train. Accordingly we chose a party of Garland-trained dynamiters who should blow up something north of the bridge at dawn, to seal that direction; while I went off with high explosive and a machine-gun with its crew to lay a mine to the south of the station, the probable direction from which the Turks would seek or send help, in their emergency.

Mohammed el Khadi guided us to a deserted bit of line just before midnight. I dismounted and fingered its thrilling rails for the first time during the war. Then, in an hour's busy work, we laid the mine, which was a trigger action to fire into twenty pounds of blasting gelatine when the weight of the locomotive overhead deflected the metals. Afterwards we posted the machine-gunners in a little bush-screened watercourse, four hundred yards from and fully commanding the spot where we hoped the train would be derailed. They were to hide there; while we went on to cut the telegraph, that isolation might persuade Aba el Naam to send their train for reinforcements, as our main attack developed.

So we rode another half-hour, and then turned in to the line, and again were fortunate to strike an unoccupied place. Unhappily the four remaining Juheina proved unable to climb a telegraph pole, and I had to struggle up it myself. It was all I could do, after my illness; and when the third wire was cut the flimsy pole shook so that I lost grip, and came slipping down the sixteen feet upon the stout shoulders of Mohammed, who ran in to break my fall, and nearly got broken himself. We took a few minutes to breathe, but afterwards were able to regain our camels. Eventually we arrived in camp just as the others had saddled up to go forward.

Our mine-laying had taken four hours longer than we had planned and the delay put us in the dilemma either of getting no rest, or of letting the main body march without us. Finally by Shakir's will we let them go, and fell down under our trees for an hour's sleep, without which I felt I should collapse utterly. The time was just before day-break, an hour when the uneasiness of the air affected trees and animals, and made even men-sleepers turn over sighingly. Mohammed, who wanted to see the fight, awoke. To get me up he came over and cried the morning prayer-call in my ear, the raucous voice sounding battle, murder, and sudden death across my dreams. I sat up and rubbed the sand out of red-rimmed aching eyes, as we disputed vehemently of prayer and sleep. He pleaded that there was not a battle every day, and showed the cuts and bruises sustained during the night in helping me. By my blackness and blueness I could feel for him, and we rode off to catch the army, after loosing the still unhappy shepherd boy, with advice to wait for our return.

A band of trodden untidiness in a sweep of gleaming water-rounded sand showed us the way, and we arrived just as the guns opened fire. They did excellently, and crashed in all the top of one building, damaged the second, hit the pump-room, and holed the water-tank. One lucky shell caught the front waggon of the train in the siding, and it took fire furiously. This alarmed the locomotive, which uncoupled and went off southward. We watched her hungrily as she approached our mine, and when she was on it there came a soft cloud of dust and a report and she stood still. The damage was to the front part, as she was reversed and the charge had exploded late; but, while the drivers got out, and jacked up the front wheels and tinkered at them, we waited and waited in vain for the machine-gun to open fire. Later we learned that the gunners, afraid of their loneliness, had packed up and marched to join us when we began shooting. Half an hour after, the repaired engine went away towards Jebel Antar, going at a foot pace and clanking loudly; but going none the less.

Our Arabs worked in towards the station, under cover of the bombardment, while we gnashed our teeth at the machine-gunners. Smoke clouds from the fired trucks screened the Arab advance which wiped out one enemy outpost, and captured another. The Turks withdrew their surviving detachments to the main position, and waited rigorously in their trenches for the assault, which they were in no better spirit to repel than we were to deliver. With our advantages in ground the place would have been a gift to us, if only we had had some of Feisal's men to charge home.

Meanwhile the wood, tents and trucks in the station were burning, and the smoke was too thick for us to shoot, so we broke off the action. We had taken thirty prisoners, a mare, two camels and some more sheep; and had killed and wounded seventy of the garrison, at a cost to ourselves of one man slightly hurt. Traffic was held up for three days of repair and investigation. So we did not wholly fail.

CHAPTER XXXV

WE left two parties in the neighbourhood to damage the line on the next day and the next, while we rode to Abdullah's camp on April the first. Shakir, splendid in habit, held a grand parade on entry, and had thousands of joy-shots fired in honour of his partial victory. The easy-going camp made carnival.

In the evening I went wandering in the thorn-grove behind the tents, till I began to see through the thick branches a wild light, from bursts of raw flame; and across the flame and smoke came the rhythm of drums, in tune with hand-clapping, and the deep roar of a tribal chorus. I crept up quietly, and saw an immense fire, ringed by hundreds of Ataiba sitting on the ground one by the other, gazing intently on Shakir, who, upright and alone in their midst, performed the dance of their song. He had put off his cloak, and wore only his white head-veil and white robes: the powerful firelight was reflected by these and by his pale, ravaged face. As he sang he threw back his head, and at the close of each phrase raised his hands, to let the full sleeves run back upon his shoulders, while he waved his bare arms weirdly. The tribe around him beat time with their hands, or bayed out the refrains at his nod. The grove of trees where I stood outside the circle of light was thronged with Arabs of stranger tribes, whispering, and watching the Atban.

In the morning we determined on another visit to the line, for fuller trial of the automatic mine-action which had half-failed at Aba el Naam. Old Dakhil-Allah said that he would come with me himself on this trip, the project of looting a train had tempted him. With us went some forty of the Juheina, who seemed to me stouter men than the high-bred Ateiba. However, one of the chiefs of the Ataiba, Sultan el Abbud, a boon friend of Abdulla and Shakir, refused to be left behind. This good-tempered but hare-brained fellow, sheikh of a poor section of the tribe, had had more horses killed under him in battle than any other Ateibi warrior. He was about twenty-six and a great rider; full of quips and fond of practical jokes, very noisy: tall and strong, with a big, square head, wrinkled forehead, and deep-set bright eyes. A young moustache and beard hid his ruthless jaw and the wide, straight mouth, with white teeth gleaming and locked like a wolf's.

We took a machine-gun and its soldier crew of thirteen with us, to settle our train when caught. Shakir, with his grave courtesy to the Emir's guest, set us on our road for the first half-hour. This time we kept to the Wadi Ais almost to its junction with Hamdh, finding it very green and full of grazing, since it had flooded twice already in this winter. At last we bore off to the right over a ditch on to a flat, and there slept in the sand, rather distressed by a shower of rain which sent little rills over the ground about midnight: but the next morning was bright and hot, and we rode into the huge plain where the three great valleys, Tubja, Ais and Jizil, flowed into and became one with Hamdh. The course of the main stream was overgrown by asla wood, just as at Abu Zereibat, with the same leprous bed of hummocky sand-blisters: but the thicket was only two hundred yards broad, and beyond it the plain with its grained intricacy of shallow torrent-beds stretched for yet further miles. At noon we halted by a place like a wilderness garden, waist deep in juicy grass and flowers, upon which our happy camels gorged themselves for an hour and then sat down, full and astonished.

The day seemed to be hotter and hotter: the sun drew close, and scorched us without intervening air. The clean, sandy soil was so baked that my bare feet could not endure it, and I had to walk in sandals, to the amusement of the Juheina, whose thick soles were proof even against slow fire. As the afternoon passed on the light became dim, but the heat steadily increased with an oppression and sultriness which took me by surprise. I kept turning my head to see if some mass was not just behind me, shutting off the air.

There had been long rolls of thunder all morning in the hills, and the two peaks, Serd and Jasim, were wrapped in folds of dark blue and yellow vapour, which looked motionless and substantial. At last I saw that part of the yellow cloud off Serd was coming slowly against the wind in our direction raising scores of dust devils before its feet.

The cloud was nearly as high as the hill. While it approached, two dust-spouts, tight and symmetrical chimneys, advanced, one on the right and one on the left of its front. Dakhil-Allah responsibly looked ahead and to each side for shelter, but saw none. He warned me that the storm would be heavy.

When it got near, the wind, which had been scorching our faces with its hot breathlessness, changed suddenly; and, after waiting a moment, blew bitter cold and damp upon our backs. It also increased greatly in violence, and at the same time the sun disappeared, blotted out by thick rags of yellow air over our heads. We stood in a horrible light, ochreous and fitful. The brown wall of cloud from the hills was now very near, rushing changelessly upon us with a loud grinding sound. Three minutes later it struck, wrapping about us a blanket of dust and stinging grains of sand, twisting and turning in violent eddies, and yet advancing eastward at the speed of a strong gale.

We had put our camels' backs to the storm, to march before it: but these internal whirling winds tore our tightly-held cloaks from our hands, filled our eyes, and robbed us of all sense of direction by turning our camels right or left from their course. Sometimes they were blown completely round: once we clashed helplessly together in a vortex, while large bushes, tufts of grass, and even a small tree were torn up by the roots in dense waves of soil about them, and driven against us, or blown over our heads with dangerous force. We never were blinded — it was always possible to see for seven or eight feet to each side — but it was risky to look out, as, in addition to the certain sand-blast, we never knew if we should not meet a flying tree, a rush of pebbles, or a spout of grass-laden dust.

This storm lasted for eighteen minutes, and then leaped forward from us as suddenly as it had come. Our party was scattered over a square mile or more, and before we could rally, while we, our clothes and our camels were yet smothered in dust, yellow and heavy with it from head to foot, down burst torrents of thick rain and muddied us to the skin. The valley began to run in plashes of water, and Dakhil-Allah urged us across it quickly. The wind chopped once more, this time to the north, and the rain came driving before it in harsh sheets of spray. It beat through our woollen cloaks in a moment, and moulded them and our shirts to our bodies, and chilled us to the bone.

We reached the hill-barrier in mid-afternoon, but found the valley bare and shelterless, colder than ever. After riding up it for three or four miles we halted, and climbed a great crag to see the railway which, they said, lay just beyond. On the height the wind was so terrible that we could not cling to the wet slippery rocks against the slapping and bellying of our cloaks and skirts. I took mine off, and climbed the rest of the way half-naked, more easily, and hardly colder than before. But the effort proved useless, the air being too thick for observation. So I worked down, cut and bruised, to the others; and dressed numbly. On our way back we suffered the only casualty of this trip. Sultan had insisted on coming with us, and his Ateibi servant, who must follow him though he had no head for heights, slipped in one bad place with a fall of forty feet to the stones, and plunged down headlong.

When we got back my hands and feet were too broken to serve me longer, and I lay down and shivered for an hour or so while the others buried the dead man in a side valley. On their return they met suddenly an unknown rider on a camel, crossing their track. He fired at them. They fired back, snap-shooting through the rain, and the evening swallowed him. This was disquieting, for surprise was our main ally, and we could only hope that he would not return to warn the Turks that there were raiders in the neighbourhood.

After the heavy camels with the explosives caught us, we mounted again to get closer to the line; but we had no more than started when brazenly down the visible wind in the misted valley came the food-call of Turkish bugles. Dakhil-Allah thrust his ear forward in the direction of the sound, and understood that over there lay Madahrij, the small station below which we meant to operate. So we steered on the hateful noise, hateful because it spoke of supper and of tents, whereas we were shelterless, and on such a night could not hope to make ourselves a fire and bake bread from the flour and water in our saddle-bags, and consequently must go hungry.

We did not reach the railway till after ten o'clock at night, in conditions of invisibility which made it futile to choose a machine-gun position. At random I pitched upon kilometre 1,121 from Damascus for the mine. It was a complicated mine, with a central trigger to fire simultaneous charges thirty yards apart: and we hoped in this way to get the locomotive whether it was going north or south. Burying the mine took four hours, for the rain had caked the surface and rotted it. Our feet made huge tracks on the flat and on the bank, as though a school of elephants had been dancing there. To hide these marks was out of the question, so we did the other thing, trampling about for hundreds of yards, even bringing up our camels to help, until it looked as though half an army had crossed the valley, and the mine-place was no better and no worse than the rest. Then we went back a safe distance behind some miserable mounds, and cowered down in the open, waiting for day. The cold was intense. Our teeth chattered, and we trembled and hissed involuntarily, while our hands drew in like claws.

At dawn the clouds had disappeared, and a red sun promised, over the very fine broken hills beyond the railway. Old Dakhil-Allah, our active guide and leader in the night, now took general charge, and sent us out singly and in pairs to all the approaches of our hiding-place. He himself crawled up the ridge before us to watch events upon the railway through his glasses. I was praying that there might be no events till the sun had gained power and warmed me, for the shivering fit still jerked me about. However, soon the sun was up and unveiled, and things improved. My clothes were drying. By noon it was nearly as hot as the day before, and we were gasping for shade, and thicker clothes, against the sun.

First of all, though, at six in the morning, Dakhil-Allah reported a trolley, which came from the south, and passed over the mine harmlessly — to our satisfaction, for we had not laid a beautiful compound charge for just four men and a sergeant. Then sixty men sallied out from Madahrij. This disturbed us till we saw that they were to replace five telegraph poles blown down by the storm of the afternoon before. Then at seven-thirty a patrol of eleven men went down the line: two inspecting each rail minutely, three marching each side of the bank looking for cross-tracks, and one, presumably the N.C.O., walking grandly along the metals with nothing to do.

However, to-day they did find something, when they crossed our footprints about kilometre 1,121. They concentrated there upon the permanent way, stared at it, stamped, wandered up and down, scratched the ballast; and thought exhaustively. The time of their search passed slowly for us: but the mine was well hidden, so that eventually they wandered on contentedly towards the south, where they met the Hedia patrol, and both parties sat together in the cool shade of a bridge-arch, and rested after their labours. Meanwhile the train, a heavy train, came along from the south. Nine of its laden trucks held women and children from Medina, civil refugees being deported to Syria, with their household stuff. It ran over the charges without explosion. As artist I was furious; as commander deeply relieved: women and children were not proper spoil.

The Juheina raced to the crest where Dakhil-Allah and myself lay hidden, when they heard the train coming, to see it blown in pieces. Our stone headwork had been built for two, so that the hill-top, a bald cone conspicuously opposite the working party, became suddenly and visibly populous. This was too much for the nerves of the Turks, who fled back into Madahrij, and thence, at about five thousand yards, opened a brisk rifle fire. They must also have telephoned to Hedia, which soon came to life: but since the nearest outpost on that side was about six miles off, its garrisons held their fire, and contented themselves with selections on the bugle, played all day. The distance made it grave and beautiful.

Even the rifle shooting did us no harm; but the disclosure of ourselves was unfortunate. At Madahrij were two hundred men, and at Hedia eleven hundred, and our retreat was by the plain of Hamdh on which Hedia stood. Their mounted troops might sally out and cut our rear. The Juheina had good camels, and so were safe; but the machine-gun was a captured German sledge-Maxim: a heavy load for its tiny mule. The servers were on foot, or on other mules: their top speed would be only six miles an hour, and their fighting value, with a single gun, not high. So after a council of war we rode back with them half-way through the hills, and there dismissed them, with fifteen Juheina, towards Wadi Ais.

This made us mobile, and Dakhil-Allah, Sultan, Mohammed and I rode back with the rest of our party for another look at the line. The sunlight was now terrific, with faint gusts of scorching heat blowing up at us out of the south. We took refuge about ten o'clock under some spacious trees, where we baked bread and lunched, in nice view of the line, and shaded from the worst of the sun. About us, over the gravel, circles of pale shadow from the crisping leaves ran to and fro, like grey, indeterminate bugs, as the slender branches dipped reluctantly in the wind. Our picnic annoyed the Turks, who shot or trumpeted at us incessantly through the middle day and till evening, while we slept in turn.

About five they grew quiet, and we mounted and rode slowly across the open valley towards the railway. Madahrij revived in a paroxysm of fire, and all the trumpets of Hedia blared again. The monkey-pleasure of pulling large and impressive legs was upon us. So when we reached the line we made our camels kneel down beside it, and, led by Dakhil-Allah as Imam, performed a sunset prayer quietly between the rails. It was probably the first prayer of the Juheina for a year or so, and I was a novice, but from a distance we passed muster, and the Turks stopped shooting in bewilderment. This was the first and last time I ever prayed in Arabia as a Moslem.

After the prayer it was still much too light to hide our actions: so we sat round on the embankment smoking, till dusk, when I tried to go off by myself and dig up the mine, to learn, for service on the next occasion, why it had failed. However, the Juheina were as interested in that as I. Along they came in a swarm and clustered over the metals during the search. They brought my heart into my throat, for it took me an hour to find just where the mine was hidden. Laying a Garland mine was shaky work, but scrabbling in pitch darkness up and down a hundred yards of railway, feeling for a hair-trigger buried in the ballast, seemed, at the time, an almost uninsurable occupation. The two charges connected with it were so powerful that they would have rooted out seventy yards of track, and I saw visions of suddenly blowing up, not only myself, but my whole force, every moment. To be sure, such a feat would have properly completed the bewilderment of the Turks!

At last I found it, and ascertained by touch that the lock had sunk one sixteenth of an inch, due to bad setting by myself or because the ground had subsided after the rain. I firmed it into its place. Then, to explain ourselves plausibly to the enemy, we began blowing up things to the north of the mine. We found a little four-arched bridge and put it into the air. Afterwards we turned to rails and cut about two hundred: and while the men were laying and lighting charges I taught Mohammed to climb a splintery pole; together we cut the wires, and with their purchase dragged down other poles. All was done at speed, for we feared lest Turks come after us: and when our explosive work was finished we ran back like hares to our camels, mounted them, and trotted without interruption down the windy valley once more to the plain of Hamdh.

There we were in safety, but old Dakhil-Allah was too pleased with the mess we had made of the line to go soberly. When we were on the sandy flat he beat up his camel into a canter, and we pounded madly after him through the colourless moonlight. The going was perfect, and we never drew rein for three hours, till we over-rode our machine-gun and its escort camping on the road home. The soldiers heard our rout yelling through the night, thought us enemies of sorts, and let fly at us with their Maxim: but it jammed after half a belt, and they, being tailors from Mecca, were unhandy with it. So no one was hurt, and we captured them mirthfully.

In the morning we slept lazily long, and breakfasted at Rubiaan, the first well in Wadi Ais. Afterwards we were smoking and talking, about to bring in the camels, when suddenly we felt the distant shock of a great explosion behind us on the railway. We wondered if the mine had been discovered or had done its duty. Two scouts had been left to report, and we rode slowly; for them, and because the rain two days ago had brought down Wadi Ais once more in flood, and its bed was all flecked over with shallow pools of soft, grey water, between banks of silvery mud, which the current had rippled into fish-scales. The warmth of the sun made the surface like fine glue, on which our helpless camels sprawled comically, or went down with a force and complete-ness surprising in such dignified beasts. Their tempers were roughened each time by our fit of mirth.

The sunlight, the easy march and the expectation of the scouts' news made everything gay, and we developed social virtues: but our limbs, stiff from the exertions of yesterday, and our abundant food, deter-mined us to fall short of Abu Markha for the night. So, near sunset, we chose a dry terrace in the valley to sleep upon. I rode up it first and turned and looked at the men reined in below me in a group, upon their bay camels like copper statues in the fierce light of the setting sun: they seemed to be burning with an inward flame.

Before bread was baked the scouts arrived, to tell us that at dawn the Turks had been busy round our damages; and a little later a locomotive with trucks of rails, and a crowded labour gang on top, had come up from Hedia, and had exploded the mine fore and aft of its wheels. This was everything we had hoped, and we rode back to Abdulla's camp on a morning of perfect springtime, in a singing company. We had proved that a well-laid mine would fire; and that a well-laid mine was difficult even for its maker to discover. These points were of importance; for Newcombe, Garland and Hornby were now out upon the railway, harrying it: and mines were the best weapon yet discovered to make the regular working of their trains costly and uncertain for our Turkish enemy.

CHAPTER XXXVI

DESPITE his kindness and charm, I could not like Abdullah or his camp: perhaps because I was not sociable, and these people had no personal solitude: perhaps because their good humour showed me the futility of my more than Palomides' pains, not merely to seem better than myself, but to make others better. Whereas nothing was futile in the atmosphere of higher thinking and responsibility which ruled at Feisal's. Abdulla passed his merry day in the big cool tent accessible only to friends, limiting suppliants or new adherents or the hearing of disputes to one public session in the afternoon. For the rest he read the papers, ate carefully, slept. Especially he played games, either chess with his staff or practical jokes with Mohammed Hassan. Mohammed, nominally Muedhdhin, was really court fool. A tiresome old fool I found him, as my illness left me less even than usual in jesting mood.

Abdulla and his friends, Shakir, Fauzan, and the two sons of Hamza among the Sherifs, with Sultan el Abbud and Hoshan, from the Ateiba, and ibn Mesfer, the guest-master, would spend much of the day and all the evening hours tormenting Mohammed Hassan. They stabbed him with thorns, stoned him, dropped sun-heated pebbles down his back, set him on fire. Sometimes the jest would be elaborate, as when they laid a powder trail under the rugs, and lured Mohammed Hassan to sit on its end. Once Abdulla shot a coffee-pot off his head thrice from twenty yards, and then rewarded his long-suffering servility with three months' pay.

Abdulla would sometimes ride a little, or shoot a little, and return exhausted to his tent for massage; and afterwards reciters would be introduced to soothe his aching head. He was fond of Arabic verses and exceptionally well read. The local poets found him a profitable audience. He was also interested in history and letters, and would have grammatical disputations in his tent and adjudge money prizes.

He affected to have no care for the Hejaz situation, regarding the autonomy of the Arabs as assured by the promises of Great Britain to

his father, and leaning at ease against this prop. I longed to tell him
that the half-witted old man had obtained from us no concrete or
unqualified undertaking of any sort, and that their ship might founder
on the bar of his political stupidity; but that would have been to give
away my English masters, and the mental tug of war between honesty
and loyalty, after swaying a while, settled again expediently into
deadlock.

Abdulla professed great interest in the war in Europe, and studied it
closely in the Press. He was also acquainted with Western politics, and
had learned by rote the courts and ministries of Europe, even to the
name of the Swiss President. I remarked again how much the comfortable circumstance that we still had a King made for the reputation of
England in this world of Asia. Ancient and artificial societies like this
of the Sherifs and feudal chieftains of Arabia found a sense of honourable security when dealing with us in such proof that the highest place
in our state was not a prize for merit or ambition.

Time slowly depressed my first, favourable, opinion of Abdulla's
character. His constant ailments, which once aroused compassion,
became fitter for contempt when their causes were apparent in laziness
and self-indulgence, and when he was seen to cherish them as occupa-
tions of his too-great leisure. His casual attractive fits of arbitrariness
now seemed feeble tyranny disguised as whims; his friendliness became
caprice; his good humour love of pleasure. The leaven of insincerity
worked through all the fibres of his being. Even his simplicity appeared
false upon experience; and inherited religious prejudice was allowed
rule over the keenness of his mind because it was less trouble to him
than unchartered thought. His brain often betrayed its intricate pattern,
disclosing idea twisted tightly over idea into a strong cord of design;
and thus his indolence marred his scheming, too. The webs were
constantly unravelling through his carelessness in leaving them unfinished. Yet they never separated into straight desires, or grew into
effective desires. Always he watched out of the corner of his bland
and open eye our returns to his innocent-sounding questions, reading
an insect-subtlety of significant meaning into every hesitation or
uncertainty or honest mistake.

One day I entered to find him sitting upright and wide-eyed with a spot of red in either cheek. Sergeant Prost, his old tutor, had just come from Colonel Bremond, innocent bearer of a letter which pointed out how the British were wrapping up the Arabs on all sides — at Aden, at Gaza, at Bagdad — and hoped that Abdulla realized his situation. He asked hotly what I thought of it. In answer, I fell back on artifice, and replied in a pretty phrase that I hoped he would suspect our honesty when he found us backbiting our allies in private letters. The delicately poisoned Arabic pleased him, and he paid us the edged compliment of saying that he knew we were sincere, since otherwise we would not be represented at Jeddah by Colonel Wilson. There, characteristically, his subtlety hanged itself, not perceiving the double subtlety which negatived him. He did not understand that honesty might be the best-paying cat's paw of rogues, and Wilson, too, downright readily or quickly to suspect evil in the dignitaries above him.

Wilson never told even a half-truth. If instructed to inform the King diplomatically that the subsidy of the month could not at present be increased, he would ring up Mecca and say 'Lord, Lord, there is no more money'. As for lying, he was not merely incapable of it, but also shrewd enough to know that it was the worst gambit against players whose whole life had passed in a mist of deceits, and whose perceptions were of the finest. The Arab leaders showed a completeness of instinct, a reliance upon intuition, the unperceived foreknown, which left our centrifugal minds gasping. Like women, they understood and judged quickly, effortlessly, unreasonably. It almost seemed as though the Oriental exclusion of woman from politics had conferred her particular gifts upon the men. Some of the speed and secrecy of our victory, and its regularity, might perhaps be ascribed to this double endowment's offsetting and emphasizing the rare feature that from end to end of it there was nothing female in the Arab movement, but the camels.

The outstanding figure of Abdulla's entourage was Sherif Shakir, a man of twenty-nine, and companion since boyhood of the four Emirs. His mother was Circassian, as had been his grandmother. From them he obtained his fair complexion; but the flesh of his face was torn away by smallpox. From its white ruin two restless eyes looked out, very bright and big; for the faintness of his eyelashes and eyebrows made his stare directly disconcerting. His figure was tall, slim, almost boyish from the continual athletic activity of the man. His sharp, decided, but pleasant voice frayed out if he shouted. His manner while delightfully frank, was abrupt, indeed imperious; with a humour as cracked as his cackling laugh.

This bursting freedom of speech seemed to respect nothing on earth except King Hussein: towards himself he exacted deference, more so than did Abdulla, who was always playing tricks with his companions, the bevy of silk-clad fellows who came about him when he would be easy. Shakir joined wildly in the sport, but would smartingly punish a liberty. He dressed simply, but very cleanly, and, like Abdulla, spent public hours with toothpick and toothstick. He took no interest in books and never wearied his head with meditation, but was intelligent and interesting in talk. He was devout, but hated Mecca, and played backgammon while Abdulla read the Koran. Yet by fits he would pray interminably.

In war he was the man at arms. His feats made him the darling of the tribes. He, in turn, described himself as a Bedawi, and an Ateibi, and imitated them. He wore his black hair in plaits down each side of his face, and kept it glossy with butter, and strong by frequent washing in camel urine. He encouraged nits, in deference to the Beduin proverb that a deserted head showed an ungenerous mind: and wore the *brîm*, a plaited girdle of thin leathern thongs wrapped three or four times round the loins to confine and support the belly. He owned splendid horses and camels: was considered the finest rider in Arabia: ready for a match with anyone.

Shakir gave me the sense that he preferred a fit of energy to sustained effort: but there was balance and shrewdness behind his mad manner. Sherif Hussein had used him on embassies to Cairo before the war, to arrange private business with the Khedive of Egypt. The Beduin figure must have looked strange in the stucco splendour of the Abdin. Abdulla had unlimited admiration for Shakir and tried to see the world with his eyes of gay carelessness. Between them they seriously complicated my mission to Wadi Ais.

CHAPTER XXXVII

OF the tactical situation, Abdulla made very little, pretending pettishly that it was Feisal's business. He had come to Wadi Ais to please his younger brother, and there he would stay. He would not go on raids himself, and hardly encouraged those who did. I detected jealousy of Feisal in this, as if he wished ostentatiously to neglect military operations to prevent unbecoming comparison with his brother's performance. Had Shakir not helped me in the first instance, I might have had delay and difficulty in getting started, though Abdulla would have ceded in time and graciously permitted anything not calling directly upon his own energies. However, there were now two parties on the railway, with reliefs enough to do a demolition of some sort every day or so. Much less interference than this would suffice to wreck the working of trains, and by making the maintenance of the Turkish garrison at Medina just a shade less difficult than its evacuation would serve the interests of British and Arab alike. So I judged my work in Wadi Ais sufficiently done, and well done.

I longed to get north again quit of this relaxing camp. Abdulla might let me do all I wanted, but would do nothing of his own: whereas for me the best value of the revolt lay in the things which the Arabs attempted without our aid. Feisal was the working enthusiast with the one idea of making his ancient race justify its renown by winning freedom with its own hands. His lieutenants Nasir or Sharraf or Ali ibn el Hussein seconded his plans with head and heart, so that my part became only synthetic. I combined their loose showers of sparks into a firm flame: transformed their series of unrelated incidents into a conscious operation.

We left on the morning of April the tenth, after pleasant farewells from Abdulla. My three Ageyl were again with me; and Arslan, the little Syrian Punch-figure, very conscious of Arab dress, and of the droll outlook and manners of all Bedouins. He rode disgracefully and endured sorrow the whole way at the uneasy steps of his camels: but he salved his self-respect by pointing out that in Damascus no decent man would ride a camel, and his humour by showing that in Arabia no one but a Damascene would ride so bad a camel as his. Mohammed el Kadhi was our guide, with six Juheina.

We marched up Wadi Tleih as we had come, but branched off to the right, avoiding the lava. We had brought no food, so stopped at some tents for hospitality of their rice and milk. This spring-time in the hills was the time of plenty for the Arabs, whose tents were full of sheep-milk and goat-milk and camel-milk, with everyone well fed and well looking. Afterwards we rode, in weather like a summer's day in England, for five hours down a narrow, flood-swept valley, Wadi Osman, which turned and twisted in the hills but gave an easy road. The last part of the march was after dark, and when we stopped, Arslan was missing. We fired volleys and lit fires hoping he would come upon us; but till dawn there was no sign, and the Juheina ran back and forward in doubting search. However, he was only a mile behind, fast asleep under a tree.

A short hour later we stopped at the tents of a wife of Dakhil-Allah, for a meal. Mohammed allowed himself a bath, a fresh braiding of his luxuriant hair, and clean clothes. They took very long about the food, and it was not till near noon that at last it came; a great bowl of saffron-rice, with a broken lamb littered over it. Mohammed, who felt it his duty in my honour to be dainty in service, arrested the main dish, and took from it the fill of a small copper basin for him and me. Then he waved the rest of the camp on to the large supply. Mohammed's mother knew herself old enough to be curious about me. She questioned me about the woman of the tribe of Christians and their way of life, marvelling at my white skin, and the horrible blue eyes which looked, she said, like the sky shining through the eye-sockets of an empty skull.

Wadi Osman to-day was less irregular in course, and broadened slowly. After two hours and a half it twisted suddenly to the right through a gap, and we found ourselves in Hamdh, in a narrow, cliff-walled gorge. As usual, the edges of the bed of hard sand were bare; and the middle bristled with hamdh-asla trees, in grey, salty, bulging scabs. Before us were flood-pools of sweet water, the largest of them nearly three hundred feet long, and sharply deep. Its narrow bed was cut into the light impervious clay. Mohammed said its water would remain till the year's end, but would soon turn salt and useless.

After drinks we bathed in it, and found it full of little silver fish like sardines: all ravenous. We loitered after bathing, prolonging our bodily pleasure; and remounting in the dark, rode for six miles, till sleepy. Then we turned away to higher ground for the night's camp. Wadi Hamdh differed from the other wild valleys of Hejaz, in its chill air. This was, of course, most obvious at night, when a white mist, glazing the valley with a salt sweat, lifted itself some feet up and stood over it motionless. But even by day, and in sunshine the Hamdh felt damp and raw and unnatural.

Next morning we started early and passed large pools in the valley; but only a few were fit to drink: the rest had gone green and brackish with the little white fish floating, dead and pickled, in them. Afterwards we crossed the bed, and struck northward over the plain of Ugila, where Ross, our flight commander from Wejh, had lately made an aerodrome. Arab guards were sitting by his petrol, and we breakfasted from them, and afterwards went along Wadi Methar to a shady tree, where we slept four hours.

In the afternoon everyone was fresh, and the Juheina began to match their camels against one another. At first it was two and two, but the others joined, till they were six abreast. The road was bad, and finally one lad cantered his animal into a heap of stones. She slipped, so that he crashed off and broke an arm. It was a misfortune: but Mohammed coolly tied him up with rags and camel-girths, and left him at ease under a tree to rest a little before riding back to Ugila for the night. The Arabs were casual about broken bones. In a tent at Wadi Ais I had seen a youth whose forearm had set crookedly; realizing this, he had dug into himself with a dagger till he had bared the bone, re-broken it, and set it straight; and there he lay, philosophically enduring the flies, with his left forearm huge under healing mosses and clay, waiting for it to be well.

In the morning we pushed on to Khauthila, a well, where we watered the camels. The water was impure and purged them. We rode again in the evening for another eight miles, intending to race straight through to Wejh in a long last day. So we got up soon after midnight, and before daylight were coming down the long slope from Raal into the plain, which extended across the mouths of Hamdh into the sea. The ground was scarred with motor tracks, exciting a lively ambition in the Juheina to hurry on and see the new wonders of Feisal's army. Fired by this, we did a straight march of eight hours, unusually long for these Hejaz Bedouin.

We were then reasonably tired, both men and camels, since we had had no food after breakfast the day before. Therefore it seemed fit to the boy Mohammed to run races. He jumped from his camel, took off his clothes, and challenged us to race to the clump of thorns up the slope in front, for a pound English. Everybody took the offer, and the camels set off in a mob. The distance, about three-quarters of a mile, uphill, over heavy sand, proved probably more than Mohammed had bargained for. However, he showed surprising strength and won, though by inches: then he promptly collapsed, bleeding from mouth and nose. Some of our camels were good, and they went their fastest when pitted against one another.

The air here was very hot and heavy for natives of the hills, and I feared there might be consequences of Mohammed's exhaustion: but after we had rested an hour and made him a cup of coffee he got going again and did the six remaining hours into Wejh as cheerfully as ever; continuing to play the little pranks which had brightened our long march from Abu Markha. If one man rode quietly behind another's camel, poked his stick suddenly up its rump, and screeched, it mistook him for an excited male, and plunged off at a mad gallop, very disconcerting to the rider. A second good game was to cannon one galloping camel with another, and crash it into a near tree. Either the tree went down (valley trees in the light Hejaz soil were notably unstable things) or the rider was scratched and torn; or, best of all, he was swept quite out of his saddle, and left impaled on a thorny branch, if not dropped violently to the ground. This counted as a bull, and was very popular with everyone but him.

The Bedu were odd people. For an Englishman, sojourning with them was unsatisfactory unless he had patience wide and deep as the sea. They were absolute slaves of their appetite, with no stamina of mind, drunkards for coffee, milk or water, gluttons for stewed meat, shameless beggars of tobacco. They dreamed for weeks before and after their rare sexual exercises, and spent the intervening days titillating themselves and their hearers with bawdy tales. Had the circumstances of their lives given them opportunity they would have been sheer sensualists. Their strength was the strength of men geographically beyond temptation: the poverty of Arabia made them simple, continent, enduring. If forced into civilized life they would have succumbed like any savage race to its diseases, meanness, luxury, cruelty, crooked dealing, artifice; and, like savages, they would have suffered them exaggeratedly for lack of inoculation.

If they suspected that we wanted to drive them either they were mulish or they went away. If we comprehended them, and gave time and trouble to make things tempting to them, then they would go to great pains for our pleasure. Whether the results achieved were worth the effort, no man could tell. Englishmen, accustomed to greater returns, would not, and, indeed, could not, have spent the time, thought and tact lavished every day by sheikhs and emirs for such meagre ends. Arab processes were clear, Arab minds moved logically as our own, with nothing radically incomprehensible or different, except the premiss: there was no excuse or reason, except our laziness and ignorance, whereby we could call them inscrutable or Oriental, or leave them misunderstood.

They would follow us, if we endured with them, and played the game according to their rules. The pity was, that we often began to do so, and broke down with exasperation and threw them over, blaming them for what was a fault in our own selves. Such strictures like a general's complaint of bad troops, were in reality a confession of our faulty foresight, often made falsely out of mock modesty to show that, though mistaken, we had at least the wit to know our fault.

CHAPTER XXXVIII

CLEANLINESS made me stop outside Wejh and change my filthy clothes. Feisal, when I reported, led me into the inner tent to talk. It seemed that everything was well. More cars had arrived from Egypt: Yenbo was emptied of its last soldiers and stores: and Sharraf himself had come up, with an unexpected unit, a new machine-gun company of amusing origin. We had thirty sick and wounded men in Yenbo when we marched away; also heaps of broken weapons, with two British armourer-sergeants repairing them. The sergeants, who found time hang heavily, had taken mended maxims and patients and combined them into a machine-gun company so thoroughly trained by dumb show that they were as good as the best we had.

Rabegh also was being abandoned. The aeroplanes from it had flown up here and were established. Their Egyptian troops had been shipped after them, with Joyce and Goslett and the Rabegh staff, who were now in charge of things at Wejh. Newcombe and Hornby were up country tearing at the railway day and night, almost with their own hands for lack of helpers. The tribal propaganda was marching forward: all was for the best, and I was about to take my leave when Suleiman, the guest-master, hurried in and whispered to Feisal, who turned to me with shining eyes, trying to be calm, and said, 'Auda is here'. I shouted, 'Auda abu Tayi', and at that moment the tent-flap was drawn back, before a deep voice which boomed salutations to Our Lord, the Commander of the Faithful. There entered a tall, strong figure, with a haggard face, passionate and tragic. This was Auda, and after him followed Mohammed, his son, a child in looks, and only eleven years old in truth.

Feisal had sprung to his feet. Auda caught his hand and kissed it, and they drew aside a pace or two and looked at each other — a splendidly unlike pair, typical of much that was best in Arabia, Feisal the prophet, and Auda the warrior, each filling his part to perfection, and immediately understanding and liking the other. They sat down. Feisal introduced

A COSTLY DINNER 229

us one by one, and Auda with a measured word seemed to register each person.

We had heard much of Auda, and were banking to open Akaba with his help; and after a moment I knew, from the force and directness of the man, that we would attain our end. He had come down to us like a knight-errant, chafing at our delay in Wejh, anxious only to be acquiring merit for Arab freedom in his own lands. If his performance was one-half his desire, we should be prosperous and fortunate. The weight was off all minds before we went to supper.

We were a cheerful party; Nasib, Faiz, Mohammed el Dheilan Auda's politic cousin, Zaal his nephew, and Sherif Nasir, resting in Wejh for a few days between expeditions. I told Feisal odd stories of Abdulla's camp, and the joy of breaking railways. Suddenly Auda scrambled to his feet with a loud 'God forbid', and flung from the tent. We stared at one another, and there came a noise of hammering outside. I went to learn what it meant, and there was Auda bent over a rock pounding his false teeth to fragments with a stone. 'I had forgotten,' he explained, 'Jemal Pasha gave me these. I was eating my Lord's bread with Turkish teeth!' Unfortunately he had few teeth of his own, so that henceforward eating the meat he loved was difficulty and after-pain, and he went about half-nourished till we had taken Akaba, and Sir Reginald Wingate sent him a dentist from Egypt to make an Allied set.

Auda was very simply dressed, northern fashion, in white cotton with a red Mosul head-cloth. He might be over fifty, and his black hair was streaked with white; but he was still strong and straight, loosely built, spare, and as active as a much younger man. His face was magnificent in its lines and hollows. On it was written how truly the death in battle of Annad, his favourite son, cast sorrow over all his life when it ended his dream of handing on to future generations the greatness of the name of Abu Tayi. He had large eloquent eyes, like black velvet in richness. His forehead was low and broad, his nose very high and sharp, powerfully hooked: his mouth rather large and mobile: his beard and moustaches had been trimmed to a point in Howeitat style, with the lower jaw shaven underneath.

Centuries ago the Howeitat came from Hejaz, and their nomad clans

prided themselves on being true Bedu. Auda was their master type.
His hospitality was sweeping; except to very hungry souls, inconvenient. His generosity kept him always poor, despite the profits of a
hundred raids. He had married twenty-eight times, had been wounded
thirteen times; while the battles he provoked had seen all his tribesmen
hurt and most of his relations killed. He himself had slain seventy-five
men, Arabs, with his own hand in battle: and never a man except in
battle. Of the number of dead Turks he could give no account: they
did not enter the register. His Toweiha under him had become the first
fighters of the desert, with a tradition of desperate courage, a sense of
superiority which never left them while there was life and work to do:
but which had reduced them from twelve hundred men to less than
five hundred, in thirty years, as the standard of nomadic fighting rose.

Auda raided as often as he had opportunity, and as widely as he could.
He had seen Aleppo, Basra, Wejh, and Wadi Dawasir on his expeditions: and was careful to be at enmity with nearly all tribes in the desert,
that he might have proper scope for raids. After his robber-fashion, he
was as hard-headed as he was hot-headed, and in his maddest exploits
there would be a cold factor of possibility to lead him through. His
patience in action was extreme: and he received and ignored advice,
criticism, or abuse, with a smile as constant as it was very charming. If he
got angry his face worked uncontrollably, and he burst into a fit of
shaking passion, only to be assuaged after he had killed: at such times he
was a wild beast, and men escaped his presence. Nothing on earth would
make him change his mind or obey an order to do the least thing he
disapproved; and he took no heed of men's feelings when his face
was set.

He saw life as a saga. All the events in it were significant: all person-
ages in contact with him heroic. His mind was stored with poems of
old raids and epic tales of fights, and he overflowed with them on the
nearest listener. If he lacked listeners, he would very likely sing them
to himself in his tremendous voice, deep and resonant and loud. He
had no control over his lips, and was therefore terrible to his own
interests and hurt his friends continually. He spoke of himself in the
third person, and was so sure of his fame that he loved to shout out
stories against himself. At times he seemed taken by a demon of

mischief, and in public assembly would invent and utter on oath appalling tales of the private life of his hosts or guests: and yet with all this he was modest, as simple as a child, direct, honest, kind-hearted, and warmly loved even by those to whom he was most embarrassing — his friends.

Joyce lived near the beach, beside the spread lines of the Egyptian troops, in an imposing array of large tents and small tents, and we talked over things done or to do. Every effort was still directed against the railway. Newcombe and Garland were near Muadhdham with Sherif Sharraf and Maulud. They had many Billi, the mule-mounted infantry, and guns and machine-guns, and hoped to take the fort and railway station there. Newcombe meant then to move all Feisal's men forward very close to Medain Salih, and, by taking and holding a part of the line, to cut off Medina and compel its early surrender. Wilson was coming up to help in this operation, and Davenport would take as many of the Egyptian army as he could transport, to reinforce the Arab attack.

All this programme was what I had believed necessary for the further progress of the Arab Revolt when we took Wejh. I had planned and arranged some of it myself. But now, since that happy fever and dysentery in Abdulla's camp had given me leisure to meditate upon the strategy and tactics of irregular war, it seemed that not merely the details but the essence of this plan were wrong. It therefore became my business to explain my changed ideas, and if possible to persuade my chiefs to follow me into the new theory.

So I began with three propositions. Firstly, that irregulars would not attack places, and so remained incapable of forcing a decision. Secondly, that they were as unable to defend a line or point as they were to attack it. Thirdly, that their virtue lay in depth, not in face.

The Arab war was geographical, and the Turkish Army an accident. Our aim was to seek the enemy's weakest material link and bear only on that till time made their whole length fail. Our largest resources, the Beduin on whom our war must be built, were unused to formal operations, but had assets of mobility, toughness, self-assurance, knowledge of the country, intelligent courage. With them dispersal was strength. Consequently we must extend our front to its maximum, to impose on the Turks the longest possible passive defence, since that was, materially, their most costly form of war.

Our duty was to attain our end with the greatest economy of life, since life was more precious to us than money or time. If we were patient and superhuman-skilled, we could follow the direction of Saxe and reach victory without battle, by pressing our advantages mathematical and psychological. Fortunately our physical weakness was not such as to demand this. We were richer than the Turks in transport, machine-guns, cars, high explosive. We could develop a highly mobile, highly equipped striking force of the smallest size, and use it successively at distributed points of the Turkish line, to make them strengthen their posts beyond the defensive minimum of twenty men. This would be a short cut to success.

We must not take Medina. The Turk was harmless there. In prison in Egypt he would cost us food and guards. We wanted him to stay at Medina, and every other distant place, in the largest numbers. Our ideal was to keep his railway just working, but only just, with the maximum of loss and discomfort. The factor of food would confine him to the railways, but he was welcome to the Hejaz Railway, and the Trans-Jordan railway, and the Palestine and Syrian railways for the duration of the war, so long as he gave us the other nine hundred and ninety-nine thousandths of the Arab world. If he tended to evacuate too soon, as a step to concentrating in the small area which his numbers could dominate effectually, then we should have to restore his confidence by reducing our enterprises against him. His stupidity would be our ally, for he would like to hold, or to think he held, as much of his old provinces as possible. This pride in his imperial heritage would keep him in his present absurd position — all flanks and no front.

In detail I criticized the ruling scheme. To hold a middle point of the railway would be expensive, for the holding force might be threatened from each side. The mixture of Egyptian troops with tribesmen was a moral weakness. If there were professional soldiers present, the Beduin would stand aside and watch them work, glad to be excused the leading part. Jealousy, superadded to inefficiency, would be the outcome. Further, the Billi country was very dry, and the maintenance of a large force up by the line technically difficult.

Neither my general reasoning, however, nor my particular objections had much weight. The plans were made, and the preparations advanced. Everyone was too busy with his own work to give me specific authority to launch out on mine. All I gained was a hearing, and a qualified admission that my counter-offensive might be a useful diversion. I was working out with Auda abu Tayi a march to the Howeitat in their spring pastures of the Syrian desert. From them we might raise a mobile camel force, and rush Akaba from the eastward without guns or machine-guns.

The eastern was the unguarded side, the line of least resistance, the easiest for us. Our march would be an extreme example of a turning movement, since it involved a desert journey of six hundred miles to capture a trench within gunfire of our ships: but there was no practicable alternative, and it was so entirely in the spirit of my sick-bed ruminations that its issue might well be fortunate, and would surely be instructive. Auda thought all things possible with dynamite and money, and that the smaller clans about Akaba would join us. Feisal, who was already in touch with them, also believed that they would help if we won a preliminary success up by Maan and then moved in force against the port. The Navy raided it while we were thinking, and their captured Turks gave us such useful information that I became eager to go off at once.

The desert route to Akaba was so long and so difficult that we could take neither guns nor machine-guns, nor stores nor regular soldiers. Accordingly the element I would withdraw from the railway scheme was only my single self; and, in the circumstances, this amount was negligible, since I felt so strongly against it that my help there would have been half-hearted. So I decided to go my own way, with or without orders. I wrote a letter full of apologies to Clayton, telling him that my intentions were of the best: and went.

BOOK IV

EXTENDING TO AKABA

Chapters XXXIX to LIV

THE *port of Akaba was naturally so strong that it could be taken only by surprise from inland: but the opportune adherence to Feisal of Auda abu Tayi made us hope to enrol enough tribesmen in the eastern desert for such a descent upon the coast.*

Nasir, Auda, and I set off together on the long ride. Hitherto Feisal had been the public leader: but his remaining in Wejh threw the ungrateful load of this northern expedition upon myself. I accepted it and its dishonest implication as our only means of victory. We tricked the Turks and entered Akaba with good fortune.

CHAPTER XXXIX

By May the ninth all things were ready, and in the glare of mid-afternoon we left Feisal's tent, his good wishes sounding after us from the hill-top as we marched away. Sherif Nasir led us: his lucent goodness, which provoked answering devotion even from the depraved, made him the only leader (and a benediction) for forlorn hopes. When we broke our wishes to him he had sighed a little, for he was body-weary after months of vanguard-service, and mind-weary too, with the passing of youth's careless years. He feared his maturity as it grew upon him, with its ripe thought, its skill, its finished art; yet which lacked the poetry of boyhood to make living a full end of life. Physically, he was young yet; but his changeful and mortal soul was ageing quicker than his body — going to die before it, like most of ours.

Our short stage was to the fort of Sebeil, inland Wejh, where the Egyptian pilgrims used to water. We camped by their great brick tank, in shade of the fort's curtain wall, or of the palms, and put to rights the deficiencies which this first march had shown. Auda and his kinsmen were with us; also Nesib el Bekri, the politic Damascene, to represent Feisal to the villagers of Syria. Nesib had brains and position, and the character of a previous successful desert-journey: his cheerful endurance of adventure, rare among Syrians, marked him out as our fellow, as much as his political mind, his ability, his persuasive good-humoured eloquence, and the patriotism which often overcame his native passion for the indirect. Nesib chose Zeki, a Syrian officer, as his companion. For escort we had thirty-five Ageyl under ibn Dgheithir, a man walled into his own temperament: remote, abstracted, self-sufficient. Feisal made up a purse of twenty-thousand pounds in gold — all he could afford and more than we asked for — to pay the wages of the new men we hoped to enrol, and to make such advances as should stimulate the Howeitat to swiftness.

This inconvenient load of four hundredweight of gold we shared out between us, against the chance of accident upon the road. Sheikh Yusuf, now back in charge of supply, gave us each a half-bag of flour, whose forty-five pounds were reckoned a man's pinched ration for six weeks. This went slung on the riding-saddle, and Nasir took enough on baggage camels to distribute a further fourteen pounds per man when we had marched the first fortnight, and had eaten room for it in our bags.

We had a little spare ammunition and some spare rifles as presents; and loaded six camels with light packs of blasting gelatine for rails or trains or bridges in the north. Nasir, a great Emir in his own place, also carried a good tent in which to receive visitors, and a camel load of rice for their entertainment: but the last we ate between us with huge comfort, as the unrelieved dietary of water-bread and water, week after week, grew uninspiring. Being beginners in this style of travelling, we did not know that dry flour, the lightest food, was therefore the best for a long journey. Six months later neither Nasir nor myself wasted transport and trouble on the rice-luxury.

My Ageyl — Mukheymer, Merjan, Ali — had been supplemented by Mohammed, blowsy obedient peasant boy from some village in Hauran, and by Gasim, of Maan, a fanged and yellow-faced outlaw, who fled into the desert to the Howeitat, after killing a Turkish official in a dispute over cattle tax. Crimes against tax-gatherers had a sympathetic aspect for all of us, and this gave Gasim a specious rumour of geniality, which actually was far from truth.

We seemed a small party to win a new province, and so apparently others thought; for presently Lamotte, Bremond's representative with Feisal, rode up to take a farewell photograph of us. A little later Yusuf arrived, with the good doctor, and Shefik, and Nesib's brothers, to wish us success on our march. We joined in a spacious evening meal, whose materials the prudent Yusuf had brought with him. His not-slender heart perhaps misgave him at the notion of a bread supper: or was it the beautiful desire to give us a last feast before we were lost in the wilderness of pain and evil refreshment?

After they had gone we loaded up, and started before midnight on another stage of our journey to the oasis of Kurr. Nasir, our guide, had grown to know this country nearly as well as he did his own.

While we rode through the moonlit and starry night, his memory was dwelling very intimately about his home. He told me of their stone-paved house whose sunk halls had vaulted roofs against the summer heat, and of the gardens planted with every kind of fruit tree, in shady paths about which they could walk at ease, mindless of the sun. He told me of the wheel over the well, with its machinery of leathern trip-buckets, raised by oxen upon an inclined path of hard-trodden earth; and of how the water from its reservoir slid in concrete channels by the borders of the paths; of worked fountains in the court beside the great vine-trellised swimming tank, lined with shining cement, within whose green depth he and his brother's household used to plunge at midday.

Nasir, though usually merry, had a quick vein of suffering in him, and to-night he was wondering why he, an Emir of Medina, rich and powerful and at rest in that garden-palace, had thrown up all to become the weak leader of desperate adventures in the desert. For two years he had been outcast, always fighting beyond the front line of Feisal's armies, chosen for every particular hazard, the pioneer in each advance; and, meanwhile, the Turks were in his house, wasting his fruit trees and chopping down his palms. Even, he said, the great well, which had sounded with the creak of the bullock wheels for six hundred years, had fallen silent; the garden, cracked with heat, was becoming waste as the blind hills over which we rode.

After four hours' march we slept for two, and rose with the sun. The baggage camels, weak with the cursed mange of Wejh, moved slowly, grazing all day as they went. We riders, light-mounted, might have passed them easily; but Auda, who was regulating our marches, forbade, because of the difficulties in front, for which our animals would need all the fitness we could conserve in them. So we plodded soberly on for six hours in great heat. The summer sun in this country of white sand behind Wejh, could dazzle the eyes cruelly, and the bare rocks each side our path threw off waves of heat which made our heads ache and swim. Consequently, by eleven of the forenoon we were mutinous against Auda's wish still to hold on. So we halted and lay under trees till half-past two, each of us trying to make a solid, though shifting shadow for himself by means of a doubled blanket caught across the thorns of overhanging boughs.

We rode again, after this break, for three gentle hours over level bottoms, approaching the walls of a great valley; and found the green garden of El Kurr lying just in front of us. White tents peeped from among the palms. While we dismounted, Rasim and Abdulla, Mahmud, the doctor, and even old Maulud, the cavalryman, came out to welcome us. They told us that Sherif Sharraf, whom we wished to meet at Abu Raga, our next stopping place, was away raiding for a few days. This meant that there was no hurry, so we made holiday at El Kurr for two nights.

It contented me: for the trouble of boils and fever which had shackled me in Wadi Ais had come afresh, more strongly, making each journey a pain, and each rest a blessed relaxation of my will strung to go on — a chance to add patience to a scant reserve. So I lay still, and received into my mind the sense of peace, the greenness and the presence of water which made this garden in the desert beautiful and haunting, as though pre-visited. Or was it merely that long ago we had seen fresh grass growing in the spring?

The inhabitant of Kurr, the only sedentary Belluwi, hoary Dhaif-Allah, laboured day and night with his daughters in the little terraced plot which he had received from his ancestors. It was built out of the south edge of the valley in a bay defended against flood by a massive wall of unhewn stone. In its midst opened the well of clear cold water, above which stood a balance-cantilever of mud and rude poles. By this Dhaif-Allah, morning and evening when the sun was low, drew up great bowls of water and spilled them into clay runnels contrived through his garden among the tree roots. He grew low palms, for their spreading leaves shaded his plants from the sun which otherwise might in that stark valley wither them, and raised young tobacco (his most profitable crop); with smaller plots of beans and melons, cucumbers and egg-plants, in due season.

The old man lived with his women in a brushwood hut beside the well, and was scornful of our politics, demanding what more to eat or drink these sore efforts and bloody sacrifices would bring. We gently teased him with notions of liberty; with freedom of the Arab countries for the Arabs. 'This Garden, Dhaif-Allah, should it not be your very own?' However, he would not understand, but stood up to strike himself proudly on the chest, crying, 'I — I am Kurr'.

He was free and wanted nothing for others; and only his garden for himself. Nor did he see why others should not become rich in a like frugality. His felt skull-cap, greased with sweat to the colour and consistence of lead, he boasted had been his grandfather's, bought when Ibrahim Pasha was in Wejh a century before: his other necessary garment was a shirt, and annually, with his tobacco, he would buy the shirt of the new year for himself; one for each of his daughters, and one for the old woman — his wife.

Still we were grateful to him, for, besides that he showed an example of contentment to us slaves of unnecessary appetite, he sold vegetables; and on them, and on the tinned bounty of Rasim and Abdulla and Mahmud, we lived richly. Each evening round the fires they had music, not the monotonous open-throated roaring of the tribes, nor the exciting harmony of the Ageyl, but the falsetto quarter tones and trills of urban Syria. Maulud had musicians in his unit; and bashful soldiers were brought up each evening to play guitars and sing café songs of Damascus or the love verses of their villages. In Abdulla's tent, where I was lodged, distance, the ripple of the fragrant out-pouring water, and the tree-leaves softened the music, so that it became dully pleasant to the ear.

Often, too, Nesib el Bekri would take out his manuscript of the songs of Selim el Jezairi, that fierce unscrupulous revolutionary who, in his leisure moments between campaigns, the Staff College, and the bloody missions he fulfilled for the Young Turks, his masters, had made up verses in the common speech of the people about the freedom which was coming to his race. Nesib and his friends had a swaying rhythm in which they would chant these songs, putting all hope and passion into the words, their pale Damascus faces moon-large in the firelight, sweating. The soldier camp would grow dead silent till the stanza ended, and then from every man would come a sighing, longing echo of the last note. Only old Dhaif-Allah went on splashing out his water, sure that after we had finished with our silliness someone would yet need and buy his greenstuff.

CHAPTER XL

To townsmen this garden was a memory of the world before we went mad with war and drove ourselves into the desert: to Auda there was an indecency of exhibition in the plant-richness, and he longed for an empty view. So we cut short our second night in paradise, and at two in the morning went on up the valley. It was pitch dark, the very stars in the sky being unable to cast light into the depths where we were wandering. To-night Auda was guide, and to make us sure of him he lifted up his voice in an interminable 'ho, ho, ho' song of the Howeitat; an epic chanted on three bass notes, up and down, back and forward, in so round a voice that the words were indistinguishable. After a little we thanked him for the singing, since the path went away to the left, and our long line followed his turn by the echoes of his voice rolling about the torn black cliffs in the moonlight.

On this long journey Sherif Nasir and Auda's sour-smiling cousin, Mohammed el Dheilan, took pains with my Arabic, giving me by turn lessons in the classical Medina tongue, and in the vivid desert language. At the beginning my Arabic had been a halting command of the tribal dialects of the Middle Euphrates (a not impure form), but now it became a fluent mingling of Hejaz slang and north-tribal poetry with household words and phrases from the limpid Nejdi, and book forms from Syria. The fluency had a lack of grammar, which made my talk a perpetual adventure for my hearers. Newcomers imagined I must be the native of some unknown illiterate district; a shot-rubbish ground of disjected Arabic parts of speech.

However, as yet I understood not three words of Auda's, and after half an hour his chant tired me, while the old moon climbed slowly up the sky, sailed over the topmost hills and threw a deceitful light, less sure than darkness, into our valley. We marched until the early sun, very trying to those who had ridden all night, opposed us.

Breakfast was off our own flour, thus lightening at last, after days of hospitality, our poor camels' food-load. Sharraf being not yet in Abu Raga, we made no more of haste than water-difficulties compelled;

and, after food, again put up our blanket roofs and lay till afternoon, fretfully dodging after their unstable shadow, getting moist with heat and the constant pricking of flies.

At last Nasir gave the marching signal, and we went on up the defile, with slightly pompous hills each side, for four hours; when we agreed to camp again in the valley bed. There was abundant brushwood for fuel; and up the cliff on our right were rock-pools of fresh water, which gave us a delicious drink. Nasir was wrought up; he commanded rice for supper, and the friends to feed with us.

Our rule of march was odd and elaborate. Nasir, Auda, and Nesib were so many separate, punctilious houses, admitting the supremacy of Nasir only because I lived with him as a guest and furnished them with the example of respect. Each required to be consulted on the details of our going, and where and when we should halt. This was inevitable with Auda, a child of battle who had never known a master, since, as a tiny boy, he had first ridden his own camel. It was advisable with Nesib, a Syrian of the queasy Syrian race; jealous; hostile to merit, or to its acknowledgement.

Such people demanded a war-cry and banner from outside to combine them, and a stranger to lead them, one whose supremacy should be based on an idea: illogical, undeniable, discriminant: which instinct might accept and reason find no rational basis to reject or approve. For this army of Feisal's the conceit was that an Emir of Mecca, a descendant of the prophet, a Sherif, was an other-worldly dignitary whom sons of Adam might reverence without shame. This was the binding assumption of the Arab movement; it was this which gave it an effective, if imbecile unanimity.

In the morning we rode at five. Our valley pinched together, and we went round a sharp spur, ascending steeply. The track became a bad goat-path, zigzagging up a hill-side too precipitous to climb except on all fours. We dropped off our camels and led them by the head-stalls. Soon we had to help each other, a man urging the camels from behind, another pulling them from the front, encouraging them over the worst places, adjusting their loads to ease them.

Parts of the track were dangerous, where rocks bulged out and narrowed it, so that the near half of the load grazed and forced the animal to the cliff-edge. We had to re-pack the food and explosives; and, in spite of all our care, lost two of our feeble camels in the pass. The Howeitat killed them where they lay broken, stabbing a keen dagger into the throat-artery near the chest, while the neck was strained tight by pulling the head round to the saddle. They were at once cut up and shared out as meat.

The head of the pass we were glad to find not a range but a spacious plateau which sloped slowly before us to the east. The first yards were rough and rocky, overgrown with low mats of thorns like ling; but afterwards we came to a valley of white shingle, in whose bed a Beduin woman was filling her water-skin with a copper cup, ladling milky water, quite pure and sweet, from a little hole a foot wide, scraped elbow deep in the pebbles. This was Abu Saad, and for its name's sake and for its water, and the joints of red meat bumping on our saddles, we settled we would stay here one night, filling up yet more of the time which must be filled before Sharraf came back from his expedition against the railway.

So we rode on four more miles, to camp under spreading trees, in close-grown thickets of thorn-scrub, hollow underneath like booths. By day these made tent-ribs for our blankets stretched against the masterful sun. At night they were bowers for our sleeping-places. We had learned to sleep with nothing overhead but moon and stars, and nothing either side to keep distant the winds and noises of the night; and by contrast it was strange, but quieting, to rest within walls, with a roof above; even though walls and roof were only interlacing twigs making a darker mesh against the star-scattered sky.

For myself, I was ill again; a fever increasing upon me, and my body very sore with boils and the rubbing of my sweaty saddle. When Nasir, without my prompting, had halted at the half-stage, I turned and thanked him warmly, to his astonishment. We were now on the lime-stone of the Shefa crest. Before us lay a great dark lava-field, and short of it a range of red and black banded sandstone cliffs with conical tops. The air on the high tableland was not so warm; and morning and evening there blew across us a free current which was refreshing after the suspended stillness of the valleys.

We breakfasted on our camel meat, and started more gaily the next

morning down a gently-falling plateau of red sandstone. Then we came
to the first break of surface, a sharp passage to the bottom of a shrub-
grown, sandy valley, on each side of which sandstone precipices and
pinnacles, gradually growing in height as we went down, detached
themselves sharply against the morning sky. It was shadowed in the
bottom, and the air tasted wet and decayed, as though sap was drying
out into it. The edges of the cliffs about us were clipped strangely, like
fantastic parapets. We wound on, ever deeper into the earth until, half
an hour later, by a sharp corner we entered Wadi Jizil, the main gutter
of these sandstone regions, whose end we had seen near Hedia.

Jizil was a deep gorge some two hundred yards in width, full of
tamarisk sprouting from the bed of drifted sand, as well as from the
soft twenty-foot banks, heaped up wherever an eddy in flood or wind
had laid the heavier dust under the returns of cliffs. The walls each side
were of regular bands of sandstone, streaked red in many shades. The
union of dark cliffs, pink floors, and pale green shrubbery was beautiful
to eyes sated with months of sunlight and sooty shadow. When evening
came, the declining sun crimsoned one side of the valley with its glow,
leaving the other in purple gloom.

Our camp was on some swelling dunes of weedy sand in an elbow
of the valley, where a narrow cleft had set up a back-wash and scooped
out a basin in which a brackish remnant of last winter's flood was
caught. We sent a man for news up the valley to an oleander thicket
where we saw the white peaks of Sharraf's tents. They expected him
next day; so we passed two nights in this strange-coloured, echoing
place. The brackish pool was fit for our camels, and in it we bathed at
noon. Then we ate and slept generously, and wandered in the nearer
valleys to see the horizontal stripes of pink and brown and cream and
red which made up the general redness of the cliffs, delighting in the
varied patterns of thin pencillings of lighter or darker tint which were
drawn over the plain body of rock. One afternoon I spent behind some
shepherd's fold of sandstone blocks in warm soft air and sunlight, with
a low burden of the wind plucking at the rough wall-top above my
head. The valley was instinct with peace, and the wind's continuing
noise made even it seem patient.

My eyes were shut and I was dreaming, when a youthful voice made me see an anxious Ageyli, a stranger, Daud, squatting by me. He appealed for my compassion. His friend Farraj had burned their tent in a frolic, and Saad, captain of Sharraf's Ageyl, was going to beat him in punishment. At my intercession he would be released. Saad happened, just then, to visit me, and I put it to him, while Daud sat watching us, his mouth slightly, eagerly, open; his eyelids narrowed over large, dark eyes, and his straight brows furrowed with anxiety. Daud's pupils, set a little in from the centre of the eyeball, gave him an air of acute readiness.

Saad's reply was not comforting. The pair were always in trouble, and of late so outrageous in their tricks that Sharraf, the severe, had ordered an example to be made of them. All he could do for my sake was to let Daud share the ordained sentence. Daud leaped at the chance, kissed my hand and Saad's, and ran off up the valley; while Saad, laughing, told me stories of the famous pair. They were an instance of the eastern boy and boy affection which the segregation of women made inevitable. Such friendships often led to manly loves of a depth and force beyond our flesh-steeped conceit. When innocent they were hot and unashamed. If sexuality entered, they passed into a give and take, unspiritual relation, like marriage.

Next day Sharraf did not come. Our morning passed with Auda talking of the march in front, while Nasir with forefinger and thumb flicked sputtering matches from the box across his tent at us. In the midst of our merriment two bent figures, with pain in their eyes, but crooked smiles upon their lips, hobbled up and saluted. These were Daud the hasty and his love-fellow, Farraj; a beautiful, soft-framed, girlish creature, with innocent, smooth face and swimming eyes. They said they were for my service. I had no need of them; and objected that after their beating they could not ride. They replied they had now come bare-backed. I said I was a simple man who disliked servants about him. Daud turned away, defeated and angry; but Farraj pleaded that we must have men, and they would follow me for company and out of gratitude. While the harder Daud revolted, he went over to Nasir and knelt in appeal, all the woman of him evident in his longing. At the end, on Nasir's advice, I took them both, mainly because they looked so young and clean.

CHAPTER XLI

SHARRAF delayed to come until the third morning, but then we heard him loudly, for the Arabs of his raiding force fired slow volleys of shots into the air, and the echoes were thrown about the windings of the valley till even the barren hills seemed to join in the salute. We dressed in our cleanest to go and call on him. Auda wore the splendours he had bought at Wejh: a mouse-coloured greatcoat of broadcloth with velvet collar, and yellow elastic-sided boots: these below his streaming hair and ruined face of a tired tragedian! Sharraf was kind to us, for he had captured prisoners on the line and blown up rails and a culvert. One piece of his news was that in Wadi Diraa, on our road, were pools of rain-water, new fallen and sweet. This would shorten our waterless march to Fejr by fifty miles, and remove its danger of thirst; a great benefit, for our total water carriage came to about twenty gallons, for fifty men; too slender a margin of safety.

Next day we left Abu Raga near mid-afternoon, not sorry, for this beautiful place had been unhealthy for us and fever had bothered us during our three days in its confined bed. Auda led us up a tributary valley which soon widened into the plain of the Shegg — a sand flat. About it, in scattered confusion, sat small islands and pinnacles of red sandstone, grouped like seracs, wind-eroded at the bases till they looked very fit to fall and block the road; which wound in and out between them, through narrows seeming to give no passage, but always opening into another bay of blind alleys. Through this maze Auda led unhesitatingly; digging along on his camel, elbows out, hands poised swaying in the air by his shoulders.

There were no footmarks on the ground, for each wind swept like a great brush over the sand surface, stippling the traces of the last travellers till the surface was again a pattern of innumerable tiny virgin waves. Only the dried camel droppings, which were lighter than the sand and rounded like walnuts, escaped over its ripples.

They rolled about, to be heaped in corners by the skirling winds. It was perhaps by them, as much as by his unrivalled road-sense, that

245

Auda knew the way. For us, the rock shapes were constant speculation and astonishment; their granular surfaces and red colour and the curved chiselling of the sand-blast upon them softened the sunlight, to give our streaming eyes relief.

In the mid-march we perceived five or six riders coming from the railway. I was in front with Auda, and we had that delicious thrill 'Friend or enemy?' of meeting strangers in the desert, whilst we circumspectly drew across to the vantage side which kept the rifle-arm free for a snap shot; but when they came nearer we saw they were of the Arab forces. The first, riding loosely on a hulking camel, with the unwieldy Manchester-made timber saddle of the British Camel Corps, was a fair-haired, shaggy-bearded Englishman in tattered uniform. This we guessed must be Hornby, Newcombe's pupil, the wild engineer who vied with him in smashing the railway. After we had exchanged greetings, on this our first meeting, he told me that Newcombe had lately gone to Wejh to talk over his difficulties with Feisal and make fresh plans to meet them.

Newcombe had constant difficulties owing to excess of zeal, and his habit of doing four times more than any other Englishman would do: ten times what the Arabs thought needful or wise. Hornby spoke little Arabic; and Newcombe not enough to persuade, though enough to give orders; but orders were not in place inland. The persistent pair would cling for weeks to the railway edge, almost without helpers, often without food, till they had exhausted either explosives or camels and had to return for more. The barrenness of the hills made their trips hungry for camels, and they wore out Feisal's best animals in turn. In this Newcombe was chief sinner, for his journeys were done at the trot; also, as a surveyor, he could not resist a look from each high hill over the country he crossed, to the exasperation of his escort who must either leave him to his own courses (a lasting disgrace to abandon a companion of the road) or founder their own precious and irreplaceable camels in keeping pace with him. 'Newcombe is like fire,' they used to complain; 'he burns friend and enemy'; and they admired his amazing energy with nervous shrinking lest they should be his next friendly victims.

Arabs told me Newcombe would not sleep except head on rails, and that Hornby would worry the metals with his teeth when gun-cotton failed. These were legends, but behind them lay a sense of their joint insatiate savagery in destroying till there was no more to destroy. Four Turkish labour battalions they kept busy, patching culverts, relaying sleepers, jointing new rails; and gun-cotton had to come in increasing tons to Wejh to meet their appetites. They were wonderful, but their too-great excellence discouraged our feeble teams, making them ashamed to exhibit their inferior talent: so Newcombe and Hornby remained as individualists, barren of the seven-fold fruits of imitation.

At sunset we reached the northern limit of the ruined sandstone land, and rode up a new level, sixty feet higher than the old, blue-black and volcanic, with a scattered covering of worn basalt-blocks, small as a man's hand, neatly bedded like cobble paving over a floor of fine, hard, black cinder-debris of themselves. The rain in its long pelting seemed to have been the agent of these stony surfaces by washing away the lighter dust from above and between, till the stones, set closely side by side and as level as a carpet, covered all the face of the plain and shielded from direct contact with weather the salty mud which filled the interstices of the lava flow beneath. It grew easier going, and Auda ventured to carry on after the light had failed, marching upon the Polar Star.

It was very dark; a pure night enough, but the black stone underfoot swallowed the light of the stars, and at seven o'clock, when at last we halted, only four of our party were with us. We had reached a gentle valley, with a yet damp, soft, sandy bed, full of thorny brush-wood, unhappily useless as camel food. We ran about tearing up these bitter bushes by the roots and heaping them in a great pyre, which Auda lit. When the fire grew hot a long black snake wormed slowly out into our group; we must have gathered it, torpid, with the twigs. The flames went shining across the dark flat, a beacon to the heavy camels which had lagged so much to-day that it was two hours before the last group arrived, the men singing their loudest, partly to encourage themselves and their hungry animals over the ghostly plain, partly so that we might know them friends. We wished their slowness slower, because of our warm fire.

In the night some of our camels strayed and our people had to go looking for them so long, that it was nearly eight o'clock, and we had baked bread and eaten, before again we started. Our track lay across more lava-field, but to our morning strength the stones seemed rarer, and waves or hard surfaces of laid sand often drowned them smoothly with a covering as good to march on as a tennis court. We rode fast over this for six or seven miles, and then turned west of a low cinder-crater across the flat, dark, stony watershed which divided Jizil from the basin in which the railway ran. These great water systems up here at their springing were shallow sandy beds, scoring involved yellow lines across the blue-black plain. From our height the lie of the land was patent for miles, with the main features coloured in layers, like a map.

We marched steadily till noon, and then sat out on the bare ground till three; an uneasy halt made necessary by our fear that the dejected camels, so long accustomed only to the sandy tracks of the coastal plain, might have their soft feet scorched by the sun-baked stones, and go lame with us on the road. After we mounted, the going became worse, and we had continually to avoid large fields of piled basalt, or deep yellow watercourses which cut through the crust into the soft stone beneath. After a while red sandstone again cropped out in crazy chimneys, from which the harder layers projected knife-sharp in level shelves beyond the soft crumbling rock. At last these sandstone ruins became plentiful, in the manner of yesterday, and stood grouped about our road in similar chequered yards of light and shade. Again we marvelled at the sureness with which Auda guided our little party through the mazy rocks.

They passed, and we re-entered volcanic ground. Little pimply craters stood about, often two or three together, and from them spines of high, broken basalt led down like disordered causeways across the barren ridges; but these craters looked old, not sharp and well-kept like those of Ras Gara, near Wadi Ais, but worn and degraded, some-times nearly to surface level, by a great bay broken into their central hollow. The basalt which ran out from them was a coarse bubbled rock like Syrian dolerite. The sand-laden winds had ground its exposed surfaces to a pitted smoothness like orange-rind, and the sunlight had faded out its blue to a hopeless grey.

Between craters the basalt was strewn in small tetrahedra, with angles rubbed and rounded, stone tight to stone like tesseræ upon a bed of pink-yellow mud. The ways worn across such flats by the constant passage of camels were very evident, since the slouching tread had pushed the blocks to each side of the path, and the thin mud of wet weather had run into these hollows and now inlaid them palely against the blue. Less-used roads for hundreds of yards were like narrow ladders across the stone-fields, for the tread of each foot was filled in with clean yellow mud, and ridges or bars of the blue-grey stone remained between each stepping place. After a stretch of such stone-laying would be a field of jet-black basalt cinders, firm as concrete in the sun-baked mud, and afterwards a valley of soft, black sand, with more crags of weathered sandstone rising from the blackness, or from waves of the wind-blown red and yellow grains of their own decay.

Nothing in the march was normal or reassuring. We felt we were in an ominous land, incapable of life, hostile even to the passing of life, except painfully along such sparse roads as time had laid across its face. We were forced into a single file of weary camels, picking a hesitant way step by step through the boulders for hour after hour. At last Auda pointed ahead to a fifty-foot ridge of large twisted blocks, lying coursed one upon the other as they had writhed and shrunk in their cooling. There was the limit of lava; and he and I rode on together and saw in front of us an open rolling plain (Wadi Aish) of fine scrub and golden sand, with green bushes scattered here and there. It held a very little water in holes which someone had scooped after the rainstorm of three weeks ago. We camped by them and drove our unladen camels out till sunset, to graze for the first adequate time since Abu Raga.

While they were scattered over the land, mounted men appeared on the horizon to the east, making towards the water. They came on too quickly to be honest, and fired at our herdsmen, but the rest of us ran at once upon the scattered reefs and knolls, shooting or shouting. Hearing us so many they drew off as fast as their camels would go; and from the ridge in the dusk we saw them, a bare dozen in all, scampering away towards the line. We were glad to see them avoid us so thoroughly. Auda though they were a Shammar patrol.

At dawn we saddled up for the short stage to Diraa, the water pools of which Sharraf had told us. The first miles were through the grateful sand and scrub of Wadi Aish, and afterwards we crossed a simple lava flat. Then came a shallow valley, more full of sandstone pillars and mushrooms and pinnacles than anywhere yesterday. It was a mad country, of nine-pins from ten to sixty feet in height. The sand-paths between them were wide enough for one only, and our long column wound blindly through, seldom a dozen of us having common sight at once. This ragged thicket of stone was perhaps a third of a mile in width, and stretched like a red copse to right and left across our path.

Beyond it a graded path over black ledges of rotten stone led us to a plateau strewn with small loose, blue-black basalt shards. After a while we entered Wadi Diraa and marched down its bed for an hour or more, sometimes over loose grey stone, sometimes along a sandy bottom between low lips of rock. A deserted camp with empty sardine tins gave proof of Newcombe and Hornby. Behind were the limpid pools, and we halted there till afternoon; for we were now quite near the railway, and had to drink our stomachs full and fill our few water-skins, ready for the long dash to Fejr.

In the halt Auda came down to see Farraj and Daud dress my camel with butter for relief against the intolerable itch of mange which had broken out recently on its face. The dry pasturage of the Billi country and the infected ground of Wejh had played havoc with our beasts. In all Feisal's stud of riding-camels there was not one healthy; in our little expedition every camel was weakening daily. Nasir was full of anxiety lest many break down in the forced march before us and leave their riders stranded in the desert.

We had no medicines for mange and could do little for it in spite of our need. However, the rubbing and anointing did make my animal more comfortable, and we repeated it as often as Farraj or Daud could find butter in our party. These two boys were giving me great satisfaction. They were brave and cheerful beyond the average of Arab servant-kind. As their aches and pains wore off they showed themselves active, good riders, and willing workmen. I liked their freedom towards myself and admired their instinctive understanding with one another against the demands of the world.

CHAPTER XLII

BY a quarter to four we were in the saddle, going down Wadi Diraa, into steep and high ridges of shifting sand, sometimes with a cap of harsh red rock jutting from them. After a while, three or four of us, in advance of the main body, climbed a sand-peak on hands and knees to spy out the railway. There was no air, and the exercise was more than we required; but our reward was immediate, for the line showed itself quiet and deserted-looking, on a green flat at the mouth of the deep valley down which the rest of the company was marching circumspectly with ready weapons.

We checked the men at the bottom of their narrow sand-fold, whilst we studied the railway. Everything was indeed peaceful and empty, even to the abandoned blockhouse in a rich patch of rank grass and weeds between us and the line. We ran to the edge of the rock-shelf, leaped out from it into the fine dry sand, and rolled down in a magnificent slide till we came to an abrupt and rather bruising halt in the level ground beside the column. We mounted, to hurry our camels out to the grazing, and leaving them there ran over to the railway and shouted the others on.

This unmolested crossing was blessed, for Sharraf had warned us seriously against the enemy patrols of mule-riding infantry and camel corps, reinforced from the entrenched posts by infantry on trolleys mounting machine-guns. Our riding beasts we chased into the grass to feed for a few minutes, while the heavy camels marched over the valley, the line, and the farther flat, till sheltered in the sand and rock mouths of the country beyond the railway. Meanwhile the Ageyl amused us by fixing gun-cotton or gelatine charges about our crossing-place to as many of the rails as we had time to reach, and when our munching camels had been dragged away into safety on the far side of the line, we began in proper order to light the fuses, filling the hollow valley with the echoes of repeated bursts.

Auda had not before known dynamite, and, with a child's first pleasure was moved to a rush of hasty poetry on its powerful glory.

We cut three telegraph wires, and fastened the free ends to the saddles of six riding-camels of the Howeitat. The astonished team struggled far into the eastern valleys with the growing weight of twanging, tangling wire and the bursting poles dragging after them. At last they could no longer move. So we cut them loose and rode laughing after the caravan.

For five miles we proceeded in the growing dusk, between ridges which seemed to run down like fingers from some knuckle in front of us. At last their rise and fall became too sharp to be crossed with safety by our weak animals in the dark, and we halted. The baggage and the bulk of our riders were still ahead of us, keeping the advantage they had gained while we played with the railway. In the night we could not find them, for the Turks were shouting hard and shooting at shadows from their stations on the line behind us; and we judged it prudent to keep quiet ourselves, not lighting fires nor sending up signals to attract attention.

However, ibn Dgheithir, in charge of the main body, had left a connecting file behind, and so before we had fallen asleep, two men came in to us, and reported that the rest were securely camped in the hidden fold of a steep sand-bank a little further on. We threw our saddle-bags again across our camels, and plodded after our guides in the murky dark (to-night was almost the last night of the moon) till we reached their hushed picket on the ridge, and bedded ourselves down beside them without words.

In the morning Auda had us afoot before four, going uphill, till at last we climbed a ridge, and plunged over, down a sand slope. Into it our camels sank knee-deep, held upright despite themselves by its clinging. They were able to make forward only by casting themselves on and down its loose face, breaking their legs out of it by their bodies' weight. At the bottom we found ourselves in the head-courses of a valley, which trended towards the railway. Another half-hour took us to the springing of this, and we breasted the low edge of the plateau which was the watershed between Hejaz and Sirhan. Ten yards more, and we were beyond the Red Sea slope of Arabia, fairly embarked upon the mystery of its central drainage.

Seemingly it was a plain, with an illimitable view downhill to the east, where one gentle level after another slowly modulated into a distance only to be called distance because it was a softer blue, and more hazy. The rising sun flooded this falling plain with a perfect level of light, throwing up long shadows of almost imperceptible ridges, and the whole life and play of a complicated ground-system — but a transient one; for, as we looked at it, the shadows drew in towards the dawn, quivered a last moment behind their mother-banks, and went out as though at a common signal. Full morning had begun: the river of sunlight, sickeningly in the full-face of us moving creatures, poured impartially on every stone of the desert over which we had to go.

Auda struck out north-eastward, aiming for a little saddle which joined the low ridge of Ugula to a lofty hill on the divide, to our left or north about three miles away. We crossed the saddle after four miles, and found beneath our feet little shallow runnels of watercourses in the ground. Auda pointed to them, saying that they ran to Nebk in Sirhan, and that we would follow their swelling bed northward and eastward to the Howeitat in their summer camp.

A little later we were marching over a low ridge of slivers of sand-stone with the nature of slate, sometimes quite small, but other times great slabs ten feet each way and, perhaps, four inches thick. Auda ranged up beside my camel, and pointing with his riding-stick told me to write down on my map the names and nature of the land. The valleys on our left were the Seyal Abu Arad, rising in Selhub, and fed by many successors from the great divide, as it prolonged itself north-ward to Jebel Rufeiya by Tebuk. The valleys on our right were the Siyul el Kelb, from Ugula, Agidat el Jemelein, Lebda and the other ridges which bent round us in a strung bow eastward and north-east-ward carrying the great divide as it were in a foray out across the plain. These two water systems united fifty miles before us in Fejr, which was a tribe, its well, and the valley of its well. I cried Auda mercy of his names, swearing I was no writer-down of unspoiled countries, or pandar to geographical curiosity; and the old man, much pleased, began to tell me personal notes and news of the chiefs with us, and in front upon our line of march. His prudent talk whiled away the slow passage of abominable desolation.

The Fejr Bedouin, whose property it was, called our plain El Houl because it was desolate; and to-day we rode in it without seeing signs of life; no tracks of gazelle, no lizards, no burrowing of rats, not even any birds. We, ourselves, felt tiny in it, and our urgent progress across its immensity was a stillness or immobility of futile effort. The only sounds were the hollow echoes, like the shutting down of pavements over vaulted places, of rotten stone slab on stone slab when they tilted under our camels' feet, and the low but piercing rustle of the sand, as it crept slowly westward before the hot wind along the worn sandstone, under the harder overhanging caps which gave each reef its eroded, rind-like shape.

It was a breathless wind, with the furnace taste sometimes known in Egypt when a khamsin came; and, as the day went on and the sun rose in the sky it grew stronger, more filled with the dust of the Nefudh, the great sand desert of Northern Arabia, close by us over there, but invisible through the haze. By noon it blew a half-gale, so dry that our shrivelled lips cracked open, and the skin of our faces chapped; while our eyelids, gone granular, seemed to creep back and bare our shrinking eyes. The Arabs drew their head-clothes tightly across their noses, and pulled the brow-folds forward like vizors with only a narrow, loose-flapping slit of vision.

At this stifling price they kept their flesh unbroken, for they feared the sand particles which would wear open the chaps into a painful wound: but, for my own part, I always rather liked a khamsin, since its torment seemed to fight against mankind with ordered conscious malevolence, and it was pleasant to outface it so directly, challenging its strength, and conquering its extremity. There was pleasure also in the salt sweat-drops which ran singly down the long hair over my fore-head, and dripped like ice-water on my cheek. At first, I played at catching them in my mouth; but, as we rode further into the desert and the hours passed, the wind became stronger, thicker in dust, more terrible in heat. All semblance of friendly contest passed. My camel's pace became sufficient increase to the irritation of the choking waves, whose dryness broke my skin and made my throat so painful that for three days afterwards I could eat little of our stodgy bread. When evening at last came to us I was content that my burned face still felt the other and milder air of darkness.

We plodded on all the day (even without the wind forbidding us there could have been no more luxury halts under the shadow of blankets if we would arrive unbroken men with strong camels at el Fejr), and nothing made us widen an eye or think a thought till after three in the afternoon. Then, above two natural tumuli, we came to a cross-ridge swelling at last into a hill. Auda huskily spat extra names at me.

Beyond it a long slope, slow degrees of a washed gravel surface with stripings of an occasional torrent-bed, went down westward. Auda and I trotted ahead together for relief against the intolerable slowness of the caravan. This side the sunset glow a modest wall of hills barred our way to the north. Shortly afterwards the Seil abu Arad, turning east, swept along our front in a bed a fair mile wide; it was inches deep with scrub as dry as dead wood, which crackled and split with little spurts of dust when we began to gather it for a fire to show the others where we had made the halt. We gathered and gathered vigorously, till we had a great cock ready for lighting. Then we found that neither of us had a match.

The mass did not arrive for an hour or more, when the wind had altogether died away, and the evening, calm and black and full of stars, had come down on us. Auda set a watch through the night, for this district was in the line of raiding parties, and in the hours of darkness there were no friends in Arabia. We had covered about fifty miles this day; all we could at a stretch, and enough according to our programme. So we halted the night hours; partly because our camels were weak and ill, and grazing meant much to them, and partly because the Howeitat were not intimate with this country, and feared to lose their way if they should ride too boldly without seeing.

CHAPTER XLIII

BEFORE dawn the following day we started down the bed of Seil Abu Arad till the white sun came up over the Zibliyat hills ahead of us. We turned more north to cut off an angle of the valley, and halted for half an hour till we saw the main body coming. Then Auda, Nasir and myself, unable longer to endure passively the hammer strokes of the sun upon our bowed heads, pushed forward at a jerky trot. Almost at once we lost sight of the others in the lymph-like heat-vapour throbbing across the flat: but the road was evident, down the scrubby bed of Wadi Fejr.

At the height of noon we reached the well of our desire. It was about thirty feet deep, stone-steyned, seemingly ancient. The water was abundant, slightly brackish, but not ill-tasting when drunk fresh: though it soon grew foul in a skin. The valley had flooded in some burst of rain the year before, and therefore contained much dry and thirsty pasturage: to this we loosed our camels. The rest came up, and drew water and baked bread. We let the camels crop industriously till nightfall, then watered them again, and pounded them under the bank a half mile from the water, for the night: thus leaving the well unmolested in case raiders should need it in the dark hours. Yet our sentries heard no one.

As usual we were off before dawn, though we had an easy march before us; but the heated glare of the desert became so painful that we designed to pass the midday in some shelter. After two miles the valley spread out, and later we came to a low, broken cliff on the east bank opposite the mouth of Seil Raugha. Here the country looked more green, and we asked Auda to fetch us game. He sent Zaal one way and rode westward himself across the open plain which stretched beyond view, while we turned in to the cliffs and found beneath their fallen crags and undercut ledges abundant shady nooks, cool against the sun and restful for our unaccustomed eyes.

The hunters returned before noon, each with a good gazelle. We had filled our water-skins at Fejr, and could use them up, for the water

of Abu Ajaj was near: so there was feasting on bread and meat in our
stone dens. These indulgences, amid the slow fatigue of long unbroken
marches, were grateful to the delicate townsfolk among us: to myself,
and to Zeki, and Nesib's Syrian servants, and in a lesser degree to Nesib
himself. Nasir's courtesy as host, and his fount of native kindliness,
made him exquisite in attention to us whenever the road allowed. To
his patient teaching I owed most of my later competence to accompany
tribal Arabs on the march without ruining their range and speed.

We rested till two in the afternoon, and reached our stage, Khabr
Ajaj, just before sunset, after a dull ride over a duller plain which prolonged Wadi Fejr to the eastward for many miles. The pool was of this
year's rain, already turned thick; and brackish; but good for camels and
just possible for men to drink. It lay in a shallow double depression by
Wadi Fejr, whose flood had filled it two feet deep over an area two
hundred yards across. At its north end was a low sandstone tump. We
had thought to find Howeitat here; but the ground was grazed bare
and the water fouled by their animals, while they themselves were gone.
Auda searched for their tracks, but could find none: the wind-storms
had swept the sand-face into clean new ripples. However, since they
had come down here from Tubaik, they must have gone on and out
into Sirhan: so, if we went away northward, we should find them.

The following day, despite the interminable lapse of time, was only
our fourteenth from Wejh; and its sun rose upon us again marching.
In the afternoon we at last left Wadi Fejr to steer for Arfaja in Sirhan, a
point rather east of north. Accordingly, we inclined right, over flats
of limestone and sand, and saw a distant corner of the Great Nefudh,
the famous belts of sand-dune which cut off Jebel Shammar from the
Syrian Desert. Palgrave, the Blunts, and Gertrude Bell amongst the
storied travellers had crossed it, and I begged Auda to bear off a little and
let us enter it, and their company: but he growled that men went to the
Nefudh only of necessity, when raiding, and that the son of his father
did not raid on a tottering, mangy camel. Our business was to reach
Arfaja alive.

So we wisely marched on, over monotonous, glittering sand; and
over those worse stretches, 'Giaan', of polished mud, nearly as white
and smooth as laid paper, and often whole miles square. They blazed

back the sun into our faces with glassy vigour, so we rode with its light raining direct arrows upon our heads, and its reflection glancing up from the ground through our inadequate eyelids. It was not a steady pressure, but a pain ebbing and flowing; at one time piling itself up and up till we nearly swooned; and then falling away coolly, in a moment of false shadow like a black web crossing the retina: these gave us a moment's breathing space to store new capacity for suffering, like the struggles to the surface of a drowning man.

We grew short-answered to one another; but relief came toward six o'clock, when we halted for supper, and baked ourselves fresh bread. I gave my camel what was left of my share, for the poor animal went tired and hungry in these bad marches. She was the pedigree camel given by Ibn Saud of Nejd to King Hussein and by him to Feisal; a splendid beast; rough, but sure-footed on hills, and great-hearted. Arabs of means rode none but she-camels, since they went smoother under the saddle than males, and were better tempered and less noisy: also, they were patient and would endure to march long after they were worn out, indeed until they tottered with exhaustion and fell in their tracks and died: whereas the coarser males grew angry, flung themselves down when tired, and from sheer rage would die there unnecessarily.

After dark we crawled for three hours, reaching the top of a sand-ridge. There we slept thankfully, after a bad day of burning wind, dust blizzards, and drifting sand which stung our inflamed faces, and at times, in the greater gusts, wrapped the sight of our road from us and drove our complaining camels up and down. But Auda was anxious about the morrow, for another hot head-wind would delay us a third day in the desert, and we had no water left: so he called us early in the night, and we marched down into the plain of the Bisaita (so called in derision, for its huge size and flatness), before day broke. Its fine surface-litter of sun-browned flints was restfully dark after sunrise for our streaming eyes, but hot and hard going for our camels, some of which were already limping with sore feet.

Camels brought up on the sandy plains of the Arabian coast had delicate pads to their feet; and if such animals were taken suddenly inland for long marches over flints or other heat-retaining ground, their soles would burn, and at last crack in a blister; leaving quick flesh, two inches or more across, in the centre of the pad. In this state they could march as ever over sand; but if, by chance, the foot came down on a pebble, they would stumble, or flinch as though they had stepped on fire, and in a long march might break down altogether unless they were very brave. So we rode carefully, picking the softest way, Auda and myself in front.

As we went, some little puffs of dust scurried into the eye of the wind. Auda said they were ostriches. A man ran up to us with two great ivory eggs. We settled to breakfast on this bounty of the Biseita, and looked for fuel; but in twenty minutes found only a wisp of grass. The barren desert was defeating us. The baggage train passed, and my eye fell on the loads of blasting gelatine. We broached a packet, shredding it carefully into a fire beneath the egg propped on stones, till the cookery was pronounced complete. Nasir and Nesib, really interested, dismounted to scoff at us. Auda drew his silver-hilted dagger and chipped the top of the first egg. A stink like a pestilence went across our party. We fled to a clean spot, rolling the second egg hot before us with gentle kicks. It was fresh enough, and hard as a stone. We dug out its contents with the dagger on to the flint flakes which were our platters, and ate it piecemeal; persuading even Nasir, who in his life before had never fallen so low as egg-meat, to take his share. The general verdict was: tough and strong, but good in the Biseita.

Zaal saw an oryx; stalked it on foot, and killed it. The better joints were tied upon the baggage camels for the next halt, and our march continued. Afterwards the greedy Howeitat saw more oryx in the distance and went after the beasts, who foolishly ran a little; then stood still and stared till the men were near, and, too late, ran away again. Their white shining bellies betrayed them; for, by the magnification of the mirage, they winked each move to us from afar.

CHAPTER XLIV

I WAS too weary, and too little sporting, to go out of the straight way for all the rare beasts in the world; so I rode after the caravan, which my camel overhauled quickly with her longer stride. At the tail of it were my men, walking. They feared that some of their animals would be dead before evening, if the wind blew stronger, but were leading them by hand in hope of getting them in. I admired the contrast between Mohammed the lusty, heavy-footed peasant, and the lithe Ageyl, with Farraj and Daud dancing along, barefooted, delicate as thoroughbreds. Only Gasim was not there: they thought him among the Howeitat, for his surliness offended the laughing soldiery and kept him commonly with the Beduin, who were more of his kidney.

There was no one behind, so I rode forward wishing to see how his camel was: and at last found it, riderless, being led by one of the Howeitat. His saddle-bags were on it, and his rifle and his food, but he himself nowhere; gradually it dawned on us that the miserable man was lost. This was a dreadful business, for in the haze and mirage the caravan could not be seen two miles, and on the iron ground it made no tracks: afoot he would never overtake us.

Everyone had marched on, thinking him elsewhere in our loose line; but much time had passed and it was nearly midday, so he must be miles back. His loaded camel was proof that he had not been forgotten asleep at our night halt. The Ageyl ventured that perhaps he had dozed in the saddle and fallen, stunning or killing himself: or perhaps someone of the party had borne him a grudge. Anyway they did not know. He was an ill-natured stranger, no charge on any of them, and they did not greatly care.

True: but it was true also that Mohammed, his countryman and fellow, who was technically his road-companion, knew nothing of the desert, had a foundered camel, and could not turn back for him.

If I sent him, it would be murder. That shifted the difficulty to my shoulders. The Howeitat, who would have helped, were away in the mirage out of sight, hunting or scouting. Ibn Dgheithir's Ageyl were so clannish that they would not put themselves about except for one another. Besides Gasim was my man: and upon me lay the responsibility of him.

I looked weakly at my trudging men, and wondered for a moment if I could change with one, sending him back on my camel to the rescue. My shirking the duty would be understood, because I was a foreigner: but that was precisely the plea I did not dare set up, while I yet presumed to help these Arabs in their own revolt. It was hard, anyway, for a stranger to influence another people's national movement, and doubly hard for a Christian and a sedentary person to sway Moslem nomads. I should make it impossible for myself if I claimed, simultaneously, the privileges of both societies.

So, without saying anything, I turned my unwilling camel round, and forced her, grunting and moaning for her camel friends, back past the long line of men, and past the baggage into the emptiness behind. My temper was very unheroic, for I was furious with my other servants, with my own play-acting as a Beduin, and most of all with Gasim, a gap-toothed, grumbling fellow, skrimshank in all our marches, bad-tempered, suspicious, brutal, a man whose engagement I regretted, and of whom I had promised to rid myself as soon as we reached a discharging-place. It seemed absurd that I should peril my weight in the Arab adventure for a single worthless man.

My camel seemed to feel it also, by her deep grumbling; but that was a constant recourse of ill-treated camels. From calfhood they were accustomed to live in droves, and some grew too conventional to march alone: while none would leave their habitual party without loud grief and unwillingness, such as mine was showing. She turned her head back on her long neck, lowing to the rest, and walked very slowly, and bouncingly. It needed careful guidance to hold her on the road, and a tap from my stick at every pace to keep her moving. However, after a mile or two, she felt better, and began to go forward less constrainedly, but still slowly. I had been noting our direction all these days with my oil compass, and hoped, by its aid, to return nearly to our starting place, seventeen miles away.

Before twenty minutes, the caravan was out of sight, and it was borne in on me how really barren the Bisaita was. Its only marks were the old sanded samh pits, across all possible of which I rode, because my camel tracks would show in them, and be so many blazes of the way back. This samh was the wild flour of the Sherarat; who, poor in all but camel-stocks, made it a boast to find the desert sufficient for their every need. When mixed with dates and loosened with butter, it was good food.

The pits, little threshing floors, were made by pushing aside the flints over a circle of ten feet across. The flints, heaped up round the rim of the pit, made it inches deep, and in this hollow place the women collected and beat out the small red seed. The constant winds, sweeping since over them, could not indeed put back the flint surface (that would perhaps be done by the rain in thousands of winters), but had levelled them up with pale blown sand, so that the pits were grey eyes in the black stony surface.

I had ridden about an hour and a half, easily, for the following breeze had let me wipe the crust from my red eyes and look forward almost without pain: when I saw a figure, or large bush, or at least something black ahead of me. The shifting mirage disguised height or distance; but this thing seemed moving, a little east of our course. On chance I turned my camel's head that way, and in a few minutes saw that it was Gasim. When I called he stood confusedly; I rode up and saw that he was nearly blinded and silly, standing there with his arms held out to me, and his black mouth gaping open. The Ageyl had put our last water in my skin, and this he spilled madly over his face and breast, in haste to drink. He stopped babbling, and began to wail out his sorrows. I sat him, pillion, on the camel's rump; then stirred her up and mounted.

At our turn the beast seemed relieved, and moved forward freely. I set an exact compass course, so exact that often I found our old tracks, as little spurts of paler sand scattered over the brown-black flint. In spite of our double weight the camel began to stride out, and at times she even put her head down and for a few paces developed that fast and most comfortable shuffle to which the best animals, while young, were broken by skilled riders. This proof of reserve spirit in her rejoiced me, as did the little time lost in search.

Gasim was moaning impressively about the pain and terror of his thirst: I told him to stop; but he went on, and began to sit loosely; until at each step of the camel he bumped down on her hinder quarters with a crash, which, like his crying, spurred her to greater pace. There was danger in this, for we might easily founder her so. Again I told him to stop, and when he only screamed louder, hit him and swore that for another sound I would throw him off. The threat, to which my general rage gave colour, worked. After it he clung on grimly without sound.

Not four miles had passed when again I saw a black bubble, lunging and swaying in the mirage ahead. It split into three, and swelled. I wondered if they were enemy. A minute later the haze unrolled with the disconcerting suddenness of illusion; and it was Auda with two of Nasir's men come back to look for me. I yelled jests and scoffs at them for abandoning a friend in the desert. Auda pulled his beard and grumbled that had he been present I would never have gone back. Gasim was transferred with insults to a better rider's saddle-pad, and we ambled forward together.

Auda pointed to the wretched hunched-up figure and denounced me. 'For that thing, not worth a camel's price . . .' I interrupted him with 'Not worth a half-crown, Auda', and he, delighted in his simple mind, rode near Gasim, and struck him sharply, trying to make him repeat, like a parrot, his price. Gasim bared his broken teeth in a grin of rage and afterwards sulked on. In another hour we were on the heels of the baggage camels, and as we passed up the inquisitive line of our caravan, Auda repeated my joke to each pair, perhaps forty times in all, till I had seen to the full its feebleness.

Gasim explained that he had dismounted to ease nature, and had missed the party afterwards in the dark: but, obviously, he had gone to sleep, where he dismounted, with the fatigue of our slow, hot journeying. We rejoined Nasir and Nesib in the van. Nesib was vexed with me, for perilling the lives of Auda and myself on a whim. It was clear to him that I reckoned they would come back for me. Nasir was shocked at his ungenerous outlook, and Auda was glad to rub into a townsman the paradox of tribe and city; the collective responsibility and group-brotherhood of the desert, contrasted with the isolation and competitive living of the crowded districts.

Over this little affair hours had passed, and the rest of the day seemed not so long; though the heat became worse, and the sand-blast stiffened in our faces till the air could be seen and heard, whistling past our camels like smoke. The ground was flat and featureless till five o'clock, when we saw low mounds ahead, and a little later found ourselves in comparative peace, amid sand-hills coated slenderly with tamarisk. These were the Kaseim of Sirhan. The bushes and the dunes broke the wind, it was sunset, and the evening mellowed and reddened on us from the west. So I wrote in my diary that Sirhan was beautiful.

Palestine became a land of milk and honey to those who had spent forty years in Sinai: Damascus had the name of an earthly paradise to the tribes which could enter it only after weeks and weeks of painful marching across the flint-stones of this northern desert: and likewise the Kaseim of Arfaja in which we spent that night, after five days across the blazing Houl in the teeth of a sand-storm, looked fresh and countryfied. They were raised only a few feet above the Biseita, and from them valleys seemed to run down towards the east into a huge depression where lay the well we wanted: but now that we had crossed the desert and reached the Sirhan safely, the terror of thirst had passed and we knew fatigue to be our chief ill. So we agreed to camp for the night where we were, and to make beacon fires for the slave of Nuri Shaalan, who, like Gasim, had disappeared from our caravan to-day.

We were not greatly perturbed about him. He knew the country and his camel was under him. It might be that he had intentionally taken the direct way to Jauf, Nuri's capital, to earn the reward of first news that we came with gifts. However it was, he did not come that night, nor next day; and when, months after, I asked Nuri of him, he replied that his dried body had lately been found, lying beside his un-plundered camel far out in the wilderness. He must have lost himself in the sand-haze and wandered till his camel broke down; and there died of thirst and heat. Not a long death — even for the very strongest a second day in summer was all — but very painful; for thirst was an active malady; a fear and panic which tore at the brain and reduced the bravest man to a stumbling babbling maniac in an hour or two: and then the sun killed him.

CHAPTER XLV

HAVING not a mouthful of water we of course ate nothing: which made it a continent night. Yet the certainty of drink on the morrow let us sleep easily, lying on our bellies to prevent the inflation of foodlessness. Arab habit was to fill themselves to vomiting point at each well, and either to go dry to the next; or, if they carried water, to use it lavishly at the first halt, drinking and bread-making. As my ambition was to avoid comment upon my difference, I copied them, trusting with reason that their physical superiority was not great enough to trap me into serious harm. Actually I only once went ill with thirst.

Next morning we rode down slopes, over a first ridge, and a second, and a third; each three miles from the other; till at eight o'clock we dismounted by the wells of Arfaja, the sweet-smelling bush so called being fragrant all about us. We found the Sirhan not a valley but a long fault draining the country on each side of it and collecting the waters into the successive depressions of its bed. The ground surface was of flinty gravel, alternating with soft sand; and the aimless valleys seemed hardly able to trace their slow and involved levels between the loose sand-dunes, over which blew the feathery tamarisk; its whipcord roots binding the slopes together.

The unlined wells were dug about eighteen feet, to water creamy to the touch with a powerful smell and brackish taste. We found it delicious, and since there was greenstuff about, good for camel food, decided to stay here the day while we searched for the Howeitat by sending to Maigua, the southernmost well of Sirhan. So we should establish whether they were behind us; and if they were not, could march towards the north with confidence that we were on their track.

Hardly, however, had our messenger ridden off when one of the Howeitat saw riders hiding in the scrub to the northward of us.

Instantly they called to arms. Mohammed el Dheilan, first into the saddle, with other Toweiha galloped out against the supposed enemy;

Nasir and I mustered the Ageyl (whose virtue lay not in fighting Beduin-fashion with Beduins) and placed them in sets about the dunes so as reasonably to defend the baggage. However, the enemy got off. Mohammed returned after half an hour to say that he had not made relentless pursuit for pity of the condition of his camel. He had seen only three tracks and supposed that the men had been scouts of a Shammar raiding party in the neighbourhood, Arfaja being commonly infested by them.

Auda called up Zaal, his nephew, the keenest eye of all the Howeitat, and told him to go out and discover the enemy's number and intention. Zaal was a lithe metallic man, with a bold appraising look, cruel lips, and a thin laugh, full of the brutality which these nomad Howeitat had caught from the peasantry. He went off and searched; but found the thicket of brushwood about us full of tracks; while the tamarisk kept the wind off the sandy floor, and made it impossible to distinguish particularly the footprints of to-day.

The afternoon passed peacefully, and we lulled ourselves, though we kept a sentry on the head of the great dune behind the water-holes. At sunset I went down and washed myself in the smarting brine; and on my way back halted at the Ageyl fire to take coffee with them, while listening to their Nejdi Arabic. They began to tell me long stories of Captain Shakespear, who had been received by ibn Saud in Riyadh as a personal friend, and had crossed Arabia from the Persian Gulf to Egypt; and been at last killed in battle by the Shammar in a set-back which the champions of Nejd had suffered during one of their periodic wars.

Many of the Ageyl of ibn Dgheithir had travelled with him, as escort or followers, and had tales of his magnificence and of the strange seclusion in which he kept himself day and night. The Arabs, who usually lived in heaps, suspected some ulterior reason for any too careful privacy. To remember this, and to foreswear all selfish peace and quiet while wandering with them, was one of the least pleasant lessons of the desert war: and humiliating, too, for it was a part of pride with Englishmen to hug solitude; ourselves finding ourselves to be remarkable, when there was no competition present.

While we talked the roasted coffee was dropped with three grains of cardamom into the mortar. Abdulla brayed it; with the dring-drang, dring-drang pestle strokes of village Nejd, two equal pairs of *legato* beats. Mohammed el Dheilan heard, came silently across the sand and sank down, slowly, groaningly, camel-like, on the ground by me. Mohammed was a companionable fellow; a powerful, thinking man with much wry humour, and an affection of sour craft, sometimes justified by his acts, but generally disclosing a friendly cynical nature. In build he was unusually strong and well-grown, not much under six feet in height; a man of perhaps thirty-eight, determined and active, with a high-coloured face ruggedly lined, and very baffling eyes.

He was second man of the Abu Tayi; richer and having more followers than Auda, and with more taste for the luscious. He had a little house in Maan, landed property (and it was whispered, 'cattle') near Tafileh. Under his influence the war parties of the Abu Tayi rode out delicately, with sunshades to defend them from the fierce rays of the sun and with bottles of mineral water in their saddle-bags, as refreshment upon the journey. He was the brain of the tribal councils and directed their politics. His sore-headed critical spirit pleased me; and often I used his intelligence and greed to convert him to my party before broaching a new idea.

The long ride in company had made companions of our minds and bodies. The hazardous goal was in our thoughts, day and night; consciously and unconsciously we were training ourselves; reducing our wills to the single purpose which oftenest engrossed these odd moments of talk about an evening fire. And we were so musing while the coffee-maker boiled up his coffee, tapped it down again, made a palm-fibre mat to strain it before he poured (grounds in the cup were evil manners), when there came a volley from the shadowy dunes east of us and one of the Ageyl toppled forward into the centre of the firelit circle with a screech.

Mohammed with his massive foot thrust a wave of sand over the fire and in the quick blinding darkness we rolled behind banks of tamarisk and scattered to get rifles, while our outlying pickets began to return the fire, aiming hurriedly towards the flashes. We had unlimited ammunition in our hand, and did not stint to show it.

Gradually the enemy slackened, astonished perhaps at our prepared-ness. Finally his fire stopped, and we held our own, listening for a rush or for attack from a new quarter. For half an hour we lay still; and silent, but for the groans, and at last the death struggle of the man hit with the first volley. Then we were impatient of waiting longer. Zaal went out to report what was happening to the enemy. After another half-hour he called to us that no one was left within reach. They had ridden away: about twenty of them, in his trained opinion.

Despite Zaal's assurances, we passed a restless night, and in the morning before dawn we buried Assaf, our first casualty, and moved off northward, keeping the bottom of the hollow, with the sand-hills mostly on our left. We rode for five hours and then halted for break-fast on the south bank of a great spill of torrent-beds running down into the Sirhan from the south-west. Auda told me these were the mouths of Seil Fejr, the valley whose head we had seen at Selhub and whose bed we had followed right across the Houl.

The grazing was better than at Arfaja, and we allowed our camels the four hours of noon to fill themselves — a poor proceeding, for the midday grazing was not profitable to them, though we enjoyed ourselves in the shadow of our blankets, sleeping out the sleep we had missed the night before. Here in the open, away from all possibility of hidden approach, was no fear of disturbance, and our displayed strength and confidence might dissuade the invisible enemy. Our desire was to fight Turks, and this inter-Arab business was sheer waste. In the afternoon we rode on twelve miles to a sharp group of firm sand-hills, enclosing an open space big enough for us, and commanding the country round about. We halted there, in anticipation of another night attack.

Next morning we did a fast march of five hours (our camels being full of life after their ease of yesterday) to an oasis-hollow of stunted palm-trees, with tamarisk clumps here and there, and plentiful water, about seven feet underground, tasting sweeter than the water of Arfaja. Yet this also upon experience proved 'Sirhan water', the first drink of which was tolerable, but which refused a lather to soap, and developed (after two days in closed vessels) a foul smell and a taste destructive to the intended flavour of coffee, tea, or bread.

Verily we were tiring of Wadi Sirhan, though Nesib and Zeki still designed works of plantation and reclamation here for the Arab Government when by them established. Such vaulting imagination was typical of Syrians, who easily persuaded themselves of possibilities, and as quickly reached forward to lay their present responsibilities on others. 'Zeki,' said I one day, 'your camel is full of mange.' 'Alas, and alack,' agreed he mournfully, 'in the evening, very quickly, when the sun is low, we shall dress her skin with ointment.'

During our next ride I mentioned mange once again. 'Aha,' said Zeki, 'it has given me a full idea. Conceive the establishment of a Veterinary Department of State, for Syria, when Damascus is ours. We shall have a staff of skilled surgeons, with a school of probationers and students, in a central hospital, or rather central hospitals, for camels and for horses, and for donkeys and cattle, even (why not?) for sheep and goats. There must be scientific and bacteriological branches to make researches into universal cures for animal disease. And what about a library of foreign books? . . . and district hospitals to feed the central, and travelling inspectors . . .' With Nesib's eager collaboration he carved Syria into four inspectorates general, and many sub-inspectorates.

Again on the morrow there was mention of mange. They had slept on their labour, and the scheme was rounding out. 'Yet, my dear, it is imperfect; and our nature stops not short of perfection. We grieve to see you thus satisfied to snatch the merely opportune. It is an English fault.' I dropped into their vein. 'O Nesib,' said I, 'and O Zeki, will not perfection, even in the least of things, entail the ending of this world? Are we ripe for that? When I am angry I pray God to swing our globe into the fiery sun, and prevent the sorrows of the not-yet-born: but when I am content, I want to lie for ever in the shade, till I become a shade myself.' Uneasily they shifted the talk to stud farms, and on the sixth day the poor camel died. Very truly, 'Because', as Zeki pointed out, 'you did not dress her'. Auda, Nasir, and the rest of us kept our beasts going by constant care. We could, perhaps, just stave the mange off till we should reach the camp of some well-provided tribe, and be able to procure medicines, with which to combat the disease whole-heartedly.

A mounted man came bearing down upon us. Tension there was, for a moment; but then the Howeitat hailed him. He was one of their herdsmen, and greetings were exchanged in an unhurried voice, as was proper in the desert, where noise was a low-bred business at the best, and urban at its worst.

He told us the Howeitat were camped in front, from Isawiya to Nebk, anxiously waiting our news. All was well with their tents. Auda's anxiety passed and his eagerness kindled. We rode fast for an hour to Isawiya and the tents of Ali abu Fitna, chief of one of Auda's clans. Old Ali, rheumy-eyed, red and unkempt, into whose jutting beard a long nose perpetually dripped, greeted us warmly and urged us to the hospitality of his tent. We excused ourselves as too many, and camped near by under some thorns, while he and the other tent-holders made estimate of our numbers, and prepared feasts for us in the evening, to each group of tents its little batch of visitors. The meal took hours to produce, and it was long after dark when they called us to it. I woke and stumbled across, ate, made my way back to our couched camels and slept again.

Our march was prosperously over. We had found the Howeitat: our men were in excellent fettle: we had our gold and our explosives still intact. So we drew happily together in the morning to a solemn council on action. There was agreement that first we should present six thousand pounds to Nuri Shaalan, by whose sufferance we were in Sirhan. We wanted from him liberty to stay while enrolling and preparing our fighting men; and when we moved off we wanted him to look after their families and tents and herds.

These were great matters. It was determined that Auda himself should ride to Nuri on embassy, because they were friends. Nuri's was too near and too big a tribe for Auda to fight, however lordly his delight in war. Self-interest, accordingly, had prompted the two great men to an alliance: and acquaintance had bred a whimsical regard, by virtue of which each suffered the other's oddities with patience. Auda would explain to Nuri what we hoped to do, and Feisal's desire that he make a public demonstration of adherence to Turkey. Only so could he cover us, while still pleasing the Turks.

CHAPTER XLVI

M EANWHILE we would stay with Ali abu Fitna, moving gently northward with him towards Nebk, where Auda would tell all the Abu Tayi to collect. He would be back from Nuri before they were united. This was the business, and we laded six bags of gold into Auda's saddle-bags, and off he went. Afterwards the chiefs of the Fitenna waited on us, and said they were honoured to feast us twice a day, forenoon and sunset, so long as we remained with them; and they meant what they said. Howeitat hospitality was unlimited — no three-day niggardliness for them of the nominal desert law — and importunate, and left us no honourable escape from the entirety of the nomad's dream of well-being.

Each morning, between eight and ten, a little group of blood mares under an assortment of imperfect saddlery would come to our camping place, and on them Nasir, Nesib, Zeki and I would mount, and with perhaps a dozen of our men on foot would move solemnly across the valley by the sandy paths between the bushes. Our horses were led by our servants, since it would be immodest to ride free or fast. So eventually we would reach the tent which was to be our feast-hall for that time; each family claiming us in turn, and bitterly offended if Zaal, the adjudicator, preferred one out of just order.

As we arrived, the dogs would rush out at us, and be driven off by onlookers — always a crowd had collected round the chosen tent — and we stepped in under the ropes to its guest half, made very large for the occasion and carefully dressed with its wall-curtain on the sunny side to give us the shade. The bashful host would murmur and vanish again out of sight. The tribal rugs, lurid red things from Beyrout, were ready for us, arranged down the partition curtain, along the back wall and across the dropped end, so that we sat down on three sides of an open dusty space. We might be fifty men in all.

The host would reappear, standing by the pole; our local fellow-guests, el Dheilan, Zaal and other sheikhs, reluctantly let themselves be placed on the rugs between us, sharing our elbow-room on the pack-saddles, padded with folded felt rugs, over which we leaned. The front of the tent was cleared, and the dogs were frequently chased away by excited children, who ran across the empty space pulling yet smaller children after them. Their clothes were less as their years were less, and their pot-bodies rounder. The smallest infants of all, out of their fly-black eyes, would stare at the company, gravely balanced on spread legs, stark-naked, sucking their thumbs and pushing out expectant bellies towards us.

Then would follow an awkward pause, which our friends would try to cover, by showing us on its perch the household hawk (when possible a sea-bird taken young on the Red Sea coast) or their watch-cockerel, or their greyhound. Once a tame ibex was dragged in for our admiration: another time an oryx. When these interests were exhausted they would try and find a small talk to distract us from the household noises, and from noticing the urgent whispered cookery-directions wafted through the dividing curtain with a powerful smell of boiled fat and drifts of tasty meat-smoke.

After a silence the host or a deputy would come forward and whisper, 'Black or white?' an invitation for us to choose coffee or tea. Nasir would always answer 'Black', and the slave would be beckoned forward with the beaked coffee-pot in one hand, and three or four clinking cups of white ware in the other. He would dash a few drops of coffee into the uppermost cup, and proffer it to Nasir; then pour the second for me, and the third for Nesib; and pause while we turned the cups about in our hands, and sucked them carefully, to get appreciatively from them the last richest drop.

As soon as they were empty his hand was stretched to clap them noisily one above the other, and toss them out with a lesser flourish for the next guest in order, and so on round the assembly till all had drunk. Then back to Nasir again. This second cup would be tastier than the first, partly because the pot was yielding deeper from the brew, partly because of the heel-taps of so many previous drinkers present in the cups; whilst the third and fourth rounds, if the serving of the meat delayed so long, would be of surprising flavour.

However, at last, two men came staggering through the thrilled crowd, carrying the rice and meat on a tinned copper tray or shallow bath, five feet across, set like a great brazier on a foot. In the tribe there was only this one food-bowl of the size, and an incised inscription ran round it in florid Arabic characters: 'To the glory of God, and in trust of mercy at the last, the property of His poor suppliant, Auda abu Tayi'. It was borrowed by the host who was to entertain us for the time; and, since my urgent brain and body made me wakeful, from my blankets in the first light I would see the dish going across country, and by marking down its goal would know where we were to feed that day.

The bowl was now brim-full, ringed round its edge by white rice in an embankment a foot wide and six inches deep, filled with legs and ribs of mutton till they toppled over. It needed two or three victims to make in the centre a dressed pyramid of meat such as honour pre-scribed. The centre-pieces were the boiled, upturned heads, propped on their severed stumps of necks, so that the ears, brown like old leaves, flapped out on the rice surface. The jaws gaped emptily upward, pulled open to show the hollow throat with the tongue, still pink, clinging to the lower teeth; and the long incisors whitely crowned the pile, very prominent above the nostrils' pricking hair and the lips which sneered away blackly from them.

This load was set down on the soil of the cleared space between us, where it steamed hotly, while a procession of minor helpers bore small cauldrons and copper vats in which the cooking had been done. From them, with much-bruised bowls of enamelled iron, they ladled out over the main dish all the inside and outside of the sheep; little bits of yellow intestine, the white tail-cushion of fat, brown muscles and meat and bristly skin, all swimming in the liquid butter and grease of the seething. The bystanders watched anxiously, muttering satisfactions when a very juicy scrap plopped out.

The fat was scalding. Every now and then a man would drop his baler with an exclamation, and plunge his burnt fingers, not re-luctantly, in his mouth to cool them: but they persevered till at last their scooping rang loudly on the bottoms of the pots; and, with a gesture of triumph, they fished out the intact livers from their hiding place in the gravy and topped the yawning jaws with them.

Two raised each smaller cauldron and tilted it, letting the liquid splash down upon the meat till the rice-crater was full, and the loose grains at the edge swam in the abundance: and yet they poured, till, amid cries of astonishment from us, it was running over, and a little pool congealing in the dust. That was the final touch of splendour, and the host called us to come and eat.

We feigned a deafness, as manners demanded: at last we heard him, and looked surprised at one another, each urging his fellow to move first; till Nasir rose coyly, and after him we all came forward to sink on one knee round the tray, wedging in and cuddling up till the twenty-two for whom there was barely space were grouped around the food. We turned back our right sleeves to the elbow, and, taking lead from Nasir with a low 'In the name of God the merciful, the loving-kind', we dipped together.

The first dip, for me, at least, was always cautious, since the liquid fat was so hot that my unaccustomed fingers could seldom bear it: and so I would toy with an exposed and cooling lump of meat till others' excavations had drained my rice-segment. We would knead between the fingers (not soiling the palm), neat balls of rice and fat and liver and meat cemented by gentle pressure, and project them by leverage of the thumb from the crooked fore-finger into the mouth. With the right trick and the right construction the little lump held together and came clean off the hand; but when surplus butter and odd fragments clung, cooling, to the fingers, they had to be licked carefully to make the next effort slip easier away.

As the meat pile wore down (nobody really cared about rice: flesh was the luxury) one of the chief Howeitat eating with us would draw his dagger, silver hilted, set with turquoise, a signed masterpiece of Mohammed ibn Zari, of Jauf,* and would cut criss-cross from the larger bones long diamonds of meat easily torn up between the fingers; for it was necessarily boiled very tender, since all had to be disposed of with the right hand which alone was honourable.

Our host stood by the circle, encouraging the appetite with pious

* The most famous sword-smith of my time was ibn Bani, a craftsman of the Ibn Rashid dynasty of Hail. He rode once on foray with the Shammar against the Rualla, and was captured. When Nuri recognized him, he shut up with him in prison ibn Zari, his own sword-smith, swearing they should not come out till their work was indistinguishable. So ibn Zari improved greatly in the skill of his craft, while remaining in design the better artist.

ejaculations. At top speed we twisted, tore, cut and stuffed: never speaking, since conversation would insult a meal's quality, though it was proper to smile thanks when an intimate guest passed a select fragment, or when Mohammed el Dheilan gravely handed over a huge barren bone with a blessing. On such occasions I would return the compliment with some hideous impossible lump of guts, a flippancy which rejoiced the Howeitat, but which the gracious, aristocratic Nasir saw with disapproval.

At length some of us were nearly filled, and began to play and pick; glancing sideways at the rest till they too grew slow, and at last ceased eating, elbow on knee, the hand hanging down from the wrist over the tray edge to drip, while the fat, butter and scattered grains of rice cooled into a stiff white grease which gummed the fingers together. When all had stopped, Nasir meaningly cleared his throat, and we rose up together in haste with an explosive 'God requite it you, O host', to group ourselves outside among the tent-ropes while the next twenty guests inherited our leaving.

Those of us who were nice would go to the end of the tent where the flap of the roof-cloth, beyond the last poles, dropped down as an end curtain; and on this clan handkerchief (whose coarse goat-hair mesh was pliant and glossy with much use) would scrape the thickest of the fat from the hands. Then we would make back to our seats, and re-take them sighingly; while the slaves, leaving aside their portion, the skulls of the sheep, would come round our rank with a wooden bowl of water, and a coffee-cup as dipper, to splash over our fingers, while we rubbed them with the tribal soap-cake.

Meantime the second and third sittings by the dish were having their turn, and there would be one more cup of coffee, or a glass of syrup-like tea; and at last the horses would be brought and we would slip out to them, and mount, with a quiet blessing to the hosts as we passed by. When our backs were turned the children would run in disorder upon the ravaged dish, tear our gnawed bones from one another, and escape into the open with valuable fragments to be devoured in security behind some distant bush: while the watchdogs of all the camp prowled round snapping, and the master of the tent fed the choicest offal to his greyhound.

CHAPTER XLVII

WE feasted on the first day once, on the second twice, on the third twice; at Isawiya: and then, on May the thirtieth, we saddled and rode easily for three hours, past an old sanded lava-field to a valley in which seven-foot wells of the usual brackish water lay all about us. The Abu Tayi struck camp when we struck, and journeyed at our side, and camped around us: so to-day for the first time I was spectator from the midst of an Arab tribe, and actor in the routine of its march.

It was strangely unlike the usual desert-constancy. All day the grey-green expanse of stones and bushes quivered like a mirage with the movement of men on foot; and horsemen; men on camels; camels bearing the hunched black loads which were the goat-hair tent-cloths; camels swaying curiously, like butterflies, under the winged and fringed howdahs of the women; camels tusked like mammoths or tailed like birds with the cocked or dragging tent-poles of silvery poplar. There was no order nor control nor routine of march, other than the wide front, the self-contained parties, the simultaneous start, which the insecurity of countless generations had made instinctive. The difference was that the desert, whose daily sparseness gave value to every man, to-day seemed with their numbers suddenly to come alive.

The pace was easy; and we, who had been guarding our own lives for weeks, found it a relaxation beyond feeling to know ourselves so escorted as to share the light liability of danger with a host. Even our most solemn riders let themselves go a little, and the wilder ones became licentious. First amongst these, of course, were Farraj and Daud, my two imps, whose spirits not all the privations of our road had quelled for a moment. About their riding places in our line of march centred two constant swirls of activity or of accident, according as their quenchless mischief found a further expression.

On my dry patience they grated a little, because the plague of snakes which had been with us since our first entry into Sirhan to-day rose to memorable height, and became a terror. In ordinary times, so the Arabs said, snakes were little worse here than elsewhere by water in the desert: but this year the valley seemed creeping with horned vipers and puff-adders, cobras and black snakes. By night movement was dangerous: and at last we found it necessary to walk with sticks, beating the bushes each side while we stepped warily through on bare feet.

We could not lightly draw water after dark, for there were snakes swimming in the pools or clustering in knots around their brinks. Twice puff-adders came twisting into the alert ring of our debating coffee-circle. Three of our men died of bites; four recovered after great fear and pain, and a swelling of the poisoned limb. Howeitat treatment was to bind up the part with snake-skin plaster, and read chapters of the Koran to the sufferer until he died. They also pulled thick Damascene ankle-boots, red, with blue tassels and horse-shoe heels, over their horny feet when they went late abroad.

A strange thing was the snakes' habit, at night, of lying beside us, probably for warmth, under or on the blanket. When we learned this our rising was with infinite care, and the first up would search round his fellows with a stick till he could pronounce them unencumbered. Our party of fifty men killed perhaps twenty snakes daily; at last they got so on our nerves that the boldest of us feared to touch ground; while those who, like myself, had a shuddering horror of all reptiles longed that our stay in Sirhan might end.

Not so Farraj and Daud. To them, this was a new and splendid game. They troubled us continually with alarms, and furious beatings upon the head of every harmless twig or root which caught their fancy. At last, in our noon-halt, I charged them strictly not to let the cry of snake again pass their lips aloud; and then, sitting by our traps upon the sand, we had peace. To live on the floor, whence it was so far to arise and walk, disposed to inaction, and there was much to think about so that it may have been an hour afterwards before I noticed the offending pair smiling and nudging one another. My eyes idly followed their eyes to the neighbouring bush under which a brown snake lay coiled, glittering at me.

Quickly I moved myself, and cried to Ali, who jumped in with his riding-cane and settled it. I told him to give the two boys a swinging half-dozen each, to teach them not again to be literal at my expense. Nasir, slumbering behind me, heard and with joy shouted to add six from himself. Nesib copied him, and then Zeki, and then ibn Dgheithir, till half the men were clamouring for revenge. The culprits were abashed when they saw that all the hides and all the sticks in the party would hardly expiate their account: however, I saved them the weight of it, and instead we proclaimed them moral bankrupts, and set them under the women to gather wood and draw water for the tents.

So they laboured shamefully for the two days we spent at Abu Tarfeiyat; where on the first day we feasted twice and on the second day twice. Then Nesib broke down, and on plea of illness took refuge inside Nasir's tent, and ate dry bread thankfully. Zeki had been ailing on the road, and his first effort at the Howeitat sodden meat and greasy rice had prostrated him. He also lay within the tent, breathing disgust and dysentery against us. Nasir's stomach had had long experience of tribal ways and stood the test grandly. It was incumbent on him, for the honour of our guesting, to answer every call; and for greater honour, he constrained me always to go with him. So we two leaders represented the camp each day, with a decent proportion of the hungering Ageyl.

Of course it was monotonous; but the crystal happiness in our hosts was a return satisfaction for our eyes, and to have shattered it a crime. Oxford or Medina had tried to cure Nasir and me of superstitious prejudice; and had complicated us to the point of regaining simplicity. These people were achieving in our cause the height of nomadic ambition, a continued orgy of seethed mutton. My heaven might have been a lonely, soft arm-chair, a book-rest, and the complete poets, set in Caslon, printed on tough paper: but I had been for twenty-eight years well-fed, and if Arab imagination ran on food-bowls, so much the more attainable their joy. They had been provident expressly on our account. A few days before we came, a drover had guested with them; and, by Auda's order, they had bought his fifty sheep to entertain us worthily. In fifteen meals (a week) we had consumed them all, and the hospitality guttered out.

Digestion returned, and with it our power of movement. We were very weary of Sirhan. The landscape was of a hopelessness and sadness deeper than all the open deserts we had crossed. Sand, or flint, or a desert of bare rocks was exciting sometimes, and in certain lights had the monstrous beauty of sterile desolation: but there was something sinister, something actively evil in this snake-devoted Sirhan, proliferant of salt water, barren palms, and bushes which served neither for grazing nor for firewood.

Accordingly we marched one day, and another, beyond Ghutti, whose weak well was nearly sweet. When we got near Ageila, we saw that it was held by many tents, and presently a troop came out to meet us. They were Auda abu Tayi, safely back from Nuri Shaalan, with the one-eyed Durzi ibn Dughmi, our old guest at Wejh. His presence proved Nuri's favour, as did their strong escort of Rualla horse; who, bareheaded and yelling, welcomed us to Nuri's empty house with a great show of spears and wild firing of rifles and revolvers at full gallop through the dust.

This modest manor had some fruitful palms, enclosed, and they had pitched beside the garden a Mesopotamian tent of white canvas. Here, also, stood Auda's tent, a huge hall seven poles long and three wide; and Zaal's tent was near it, and many others; and through the afternoon we received fusillades of honour, deputations, and gifts of ostrich eggs, or Damascus dainties, or camels, or scraggy horses, while the air was loud about us with the cries of Auda's volunteers demanding service, immediate service, against the Turks.

Affairs looked well, and we set three men to make coffee for the visitors, who came into Nasir one by one or group by group, swearing allegiance to Feisal and to the Arab Movement, in the Wejh formula; and promising to obey Nasir, and to follow after him with their contingents. Besides their formal presents, each new party deposited on our carpet their privy, accidental gift of lice; and long before sunset Nasir and I were in a fever, with relay after relay of irritation. Auda had a stiff arm, the effect of an old wound in the elbow joint, and so could not scratch all of himself; but experience had taught him a way of thrusting a cross-headed camel-stick up his left sleeve and turning it round and round inside against his ribs, which method seemed to relieve his itch more than our claws did ours.

CHAPTER XLVIII

NEBK, to be our next halt, had plentiful water, with some grazing. Auda had appointed it our rallying place, because of the convenient nearness of the Blaidat, or 'salt hamlets'. In it he and Sherif Nasir sat down for days, to consider enrolling the men, and to prepare the road along which we would march, by approaching the tribes and the sheikhs who lived near. Leisure remained for Nasib, Zeki and myself. As usual, the unstable Syrian judgement, not able to consist in the narrow point of virtue, staggered to the circumference. In the heady atmosphere of first enthusiasm they ignored Akaba and despised the plain purpose which had led us here. Nesib knew the Shaalans and the Druses. His mind enrolled them, not the Howeitat; struck at Deraa, not Maan: occupied Damascus, not Akaba. He pointed out that the Turks were all unready: that we were sure to gain our first objective, by sheer surprise: that therefore our objective should be the highest. Damascus was indicated by the finger of inevitable fate.

I pointed him in vain to Feisal yet in Wejh: to the British yet the wrong side of Gaza: to the new Turkish army massing in Aleppo to recover Mesopotamia. I showed how we in Damascus would be unsupported: without resources or organization: without a base: without even a line of communication with our friends. But Nesib was towering above geography, and beyond tactics, and only sordid means would bring him down. So I went to Auda, and said that with the new objective cash and credit would go to Nuri Shaalan, and not to him: I went to Nasir, and used influence and our liking for one another to keep him on my plan, fanning high the too easily-lit jealousy between a Sherif and a Damascene; between an authentic Shia descendant of Ali and the martyred Hussein, and a very doubtfully reputed descendant of the 'successor' Abu Bekr.

For our movement, the point was life and death. I was sure that if we took Damascus we should not hold it six weeks, for Murray could not instantly attack the Turks, nor would sea-transport be available at the moment's notice to land a British army at Beyrout: and in losing

Damascus we should lose our supporters (only their first flush was profitable: a rebellion which stood still or went back was lost) without having gained Akaba, which was the last base in safe water; and in my judgement the only door, except the Middle Euphrates, which we could unlock for an assuredly successful entry into Syria.

Akaba's special value to the Turks was that, when they pleased, it might be constituted a threat to the right flank of the British Army. At the end of 1914 their higher command had thought to make it their main route to the Canal: but they found the food and water difficulties great, and adopted the Beersheba route. Now, however, the British had left the Canal positions and had thrust forward to Gaza and Beersheba. This made the feeding of the Turkish army easier by shortening its line. Consequently, the Turks had surplus transport. Akaba was also of greater geographical value than of old, since it now lay behind the British right, and a small force operating from it would threaten either El Arish or Suez effectively.

The Arabs needed Akaba; firstly, to extend their front, which was their tactical principle; and, secondly, to link up with the British. If they took it the act gave them Sinai, and made positive junction between them and Sir Archibald Murray. Thus having become really useful, they would obtain material help. The human frailty of Murray's Staff was such that nothing but physical contact with our success could persuade them of our importance. Murray was friendly: but if we became his right wing he would equip us properly, almost without the asking. Accordingly, for the Arabs, Akaba spelt plenty in food, money, guns, advisers. I wanted contact with the British; to act as the right wing of the Allies in the conquest of Palestine and Syria; and to assert the Arabic-speaking peoples' desire or desert of freedom and self-government. In my view, if the revolt did not reach the main battle-field against Turkey it would have to confess failure, and remain a side-show of a side-show. I had preached to Feisal, from our first meeting, that freedom was taken, not given.

Both Nasir and Auda fortunately answered to my whispers; and, after recriminations, Nesib left us, and rode with Zeki to the Druse Mountain, there to do the preliminary work necessary to the launching of his great Damascus scheme. I knew his incapacity to create; but it was not in my mind to permit even a half-baked rising there, to spoil our future material. So I was careful to draw his teeth before he started, by taking from him most of the money Feisal had shared out to him. The fool made this easy for me, as he knew he had not enough for all he wanted; and, measuring the morality of England by his own pettiness, came to me for the promise of more if he raised a Syrian movement independent of Feisal, under his own leadership. I had no fear of so untoward a miracle; and, instead of calling him rat, gave my ready promise for future help, if he would for the present give me his balance, to get us to Akaba, where I would make funds available for the general need. He yielded to my condition with a bad grace; and Nasir was delighted to get two bags of money unexpectedly.

Yet the optimism of Nesib had its effect upon me; while I still saw the liberation of Syria happening in steps, of which Akaba was the indispensable first, I now saw these steps coming close together; and as soon as Nesib was out of the way planned to go off myself, rather in his fashion, on a long tour of the north country. I felt that one more sight of Syria would put straight the strategic ideas given me by the Crusaders and the first Arab conquest, and adjust them to the two new factors — the railways, and Murray in Sinai.

Also a rash adventure suited my abandoned mood. It should have been happiness, this lying out free as air, with the visible life striving its utmost along my own path; but the knowledge of the axe I was secretly grinding destroyed all my assurance.

The Arab Revolt had begun on false pretences. To gain the Sherif's help our Cabinet had offered, through Sir Henry McMahon, to support the establishment of native governments in parts of Syria and Mesopotamia, 'saving the interests of our ally, France'. The last modest clause concealed a treaty (kept secret, till too late, from McMahon, and therefore from the Sherif) by which France, England and Russia agreed to annex some of these promised areas, and to establish their respective spheres of influence over all the rest.

Rumours of the fraud reached Arab ears, from Turkey. In the East persons were more trusted than institutions. So the Arabs, having tested my friendliness and sincerity under fire, asked me, as a free agent, to endorse the promises of the British Government. I had had no previous or inner knowledge of the McMahon pledges and the Sykes-Picot treaty, which were both framed by war-time branches of the Foreign Office. But, not being a perfect fool, I could see that if we won the war the promises to the Arabs were dead paper. Had I been an honourable adviser I would have sent my men home, and not let them risk their lives for such stuff. Yet the Arab inspiration was our main tool in winning the Eastern war. So I assured them that England kept her word in letter and spirit. In this comfort they performed their fine things: but, of course, instead of being proud of what we did together, I was continually and bitterly ashamed.

Clear sight of my position came to me one night, when old Nuri Shaalan in his aisled tent brought out a file of documents and asked which British pledge was to be believed. In his mood, upon my answer, lay the success or failure of Feisal. My advice, uttered with some agony of mind, was to trust the latest in date of the contradictions. This disingenuous answer promoted me, in six months, to be chief confidence-man. In Hejaz the Sherifs were everything, and I had allayed my conscience by telling Feisal how hollow his basis was. In Syria England was mighty and the Sherif very low. So I became the principal.

In revenge I vowed to make the Arab Revolt the engine of its own success, as well as handmaid to our Egyptian campaign: and vowed to lead it so madly in the final victory that expediency should counsel to the Powers a fair settlement of the Arabs' moral claims. This presumed my surviving the war, to win the later battle of the Council Chamber — immodest presumptions, which still balance in fulfilment.* Yet the issue of the fraud was beside the point.

Clearly I had no shadow of leave to engage the Arabs, unknowing, in a gamble of life and death. Inevitably and justly we should reap bitterness, a sorry fruit of heroic endeavour. So in resentment at my false place (did ever second lieutenant so lie abroad for his betters?) I

* 1919: but two years later Mr. Winston Churchill was entrusted by our harassed Cabinet with the settlement of the Middle East; and in a few weeks, at his conference in Cairo, he made straight all the tangle, finding solutions fulfilling (I think) our promises in letter and spirit (where humanly possible) without sacrificing any interest of our Empire or any interest of the peoples concerned. So we were quit of the war-time Eastern adventure, with clean hands, but three years too late to earn the gratitude which peoples, if not states, can pay.

undertook this long, dangerous ride, in which to see the more important of Feisal's secret friends, and to study key-positions of our future campaigns: but the results were incommensurate with the risks, and the act artistically unjustifiable, like the motive. I had whispered to myself 'Let me chance it, now, before we begin', seeing truly that this was the last chance, and that after a successful capture of Akaba I would never again possess myself freely, without association, in the security lurking for the obscure in their protective shadow.

Before me lay a vista of responsibility and command, which disgusted my thought-riddled nature. I felt mean, to fill the place of a man of action; for my standards of value were a wilful reaction against theirs, and I despised their happiness. Always my soul hungered for less than it had, since my senses, sluggish beyond the senses of most men, needed the immediacy of contact to achieve perception; they distinguished kinds only, not degrees.

When I returned it was June the sixteenth, and Nasir was still labouring in his tent. He and Auda had been seeing too much of one another for their good, and lately there had been a breach; but this was easily healed, and after a day the old chief was as much with us as ever, and as kind and difficult. We stood up always when he entered; not for his sheikhhood, for sitting we received sheikhs of much older rank: but because he was Auda, and Auda was such a splendid thing to be. The old man loved it, and however much we might wrangle, everyone knew that really we were his friends.

We were now five weeks out from Wejh: we had spent nearly all the money we had brought with us: we had eaten all the Howeitat sheep: we had rested or replaced all our old camels: nothing hindered the start. The freshness of the adventure in hand consoled us for everything; and Auda, importing more mutton, gave a farewell feast, the greatest of the whole series, in his huge tent the eve before we started. Hundreds were present, and five fills of the great tray were eaten up in relay as fast as they were cooked and carried in.

Sunset came down, delightfully red, and after the feast the whole party lay round the outside coffee-hearth lingering under the stars, while Auda and others told us stories. In a pause I remarked casually that I had looked for Mohammed el Dheilan in his tent that afternoon, to thank him for the milch camel he had given me, but had not found him. Auda shouted for joy, till everybody looked at him; and then, in the silence which fell that they might learn the joke, he pointed to Mohammed sitting dismally beside the coffee mortar, and said in his huge voice:—

'Ho! Shall I tell why Mohammed for fifteen days has not slept in his tent?' Everybody chuckled with delight, and conversation stopped; all the crowd stretched out on the ground, chins in hands, prepared to take the good points of the story which they had heard perhaps twenty times. The women, Auda's three wives, Zaal's wife, and some of Mohammed's, who had been cooking, came across, straddling their bellies in the billowy walk which came of carrying burdens on their heads, till they were near the partition-curtain; and there they listened like the rest while Auda told at length how Mohammed had bought publicly in the bazaar at Wejh a costly string of pearls, and had not given it to any of his wives, and so they were all at odds, except in their common rejection of him.

The story was, of course, a pure invention — Auda's elvish humour heightened by the stimulus of Revolt — and the luckless Mohammed, who had dragged through the fortnight guesting casually with one or other of the tribesmen, called upon God for mercy, and upon me for witness that Auda lied. I cleared my throat solemnly. Auda asked for silence, and begged me to confirm his words.

I began with the introducing phrase of a formal tale: 'In the name of God the merciful, the loving-kind. We were six in Wejh. There were Auda, and Mohammed, and Zaal, Gasim el Shimt, Mufaddhi and the poor man (myself); and one night just before dawn, Auda said, "Let us make a raid against the market". And we said, "in the name of God". And we went; Auda in a white robe and a red head-cloth, and Kasim sandals of pieced leather; Mohammed in a silken tunic of "seven kings" and barefoot; Zaal . . . I forget Zaal. Gasim wore cotton, and Mufaddhi was in silk of blue stripes with an embroidered head-cloth. Your servant was as your servant.'

My pause was still with astonishment. This was a close parody of Auda's epic style; and I mimicked also his wave of the hand, his round voice, and the rising and dropping tone which emphasized the points, or what he thought were points, of his pointless stories. The Howeitat sat silent as death, twisting their full bodies inside their sweat-stiffened shirts for joy, and staring hungrily at Auda; for they all recognized the original, and parody was a new art to them and to him. The coffee man, Mufaddhi, a Shammar refugee from the guilt of blood, himself a character, forgot to pile fresh thorns on his fire for fixity of listening to the tale.

I told how we left the tents, with a list of the tents, and how we walked down towards the village, describing every camel and horse we saw, and all the passers-by, and the ridges, 'all bare of grazing, for by God that country was barren. And we marched: and after we had marched the time of a smoked cigarette, we heard something, and Auda stopped and said, "Lads, I hear something". And Mohammed stopped and said, "Lads, I hear something". And Zaal, "By God, you are right". And we stopped to listen, and there was nothing, and the poor man said, "By God, I hear nothing". And Zaal said, "By God, I hear nothing". And Mohammed said, "By God, I hear nothing." And Auda said, "By God, you are right".

'And we marched and we marched, and the land was barren, and we heard nothing. And on our right hand came a man, a negro, on a donkey. The donkey was grey, with black ears, and one black foot, and on its shoulder was a brand like this' (a scrabble in the air), 'and its tail moved and its legs: Auda saw it, and said, "By God, a donkey". And Mohammed said, "By the very God, a donkey and a slave". And we marched. And there was a ridge, not a great ridge, but a ridge as great as from the here to the what-do-you-call-it (*lil biliyeh el hok*) that is yonder: and we marched to the ridge and it was barren. That land is barren: barren: barren.

'And we marched: and beyond the what-do-you-call-it there was a what-there-is as far as hereby from hence, and thereafter a ridge: and we came to that ridge, and went up that ridge: it was barren, all that land was barren: and as we came up that ridge, and were by the head of that ridge, and came to the end of the head of that ridge, by God, by my God, by very God, the sun rose upon us.'

It ended the session. Everyone had heard that sunrise twenty times, in its immense bathos; an agony piled up of linked phrases, repeated and repeated with breathless excitement by Auda to carry over for hours the thrill of a raiding story in which nothing happened; and the trivial rest of it was exaggerated the degree which made it like one of Auda's tales; and yet, also, the history of the walk to market at Wejh which many of us had taken. The tribe was in waves of laughter on the ground.

Auda laughed the loudest and longest, for he loved a jest upon himself; and the fatuousness of my epic had shown him his own sure mastery of descriptive action. He embraced Mohammed, and confessed the invention of the necklace. In gratitude Mohammed invited the camp to breakfast with him in his regained tent on the morrow, an hour before we started for the swoop on Akaba. We should have a sucking camel-calf boiled in sour milk by his wives: famous cooks, and a legendary dish!

Afterwards we sat by the wall of Nuri's manor, and saw the women take down the great tent, greater than Auda's, eight-bayed of twenty-four poles in all, longer and broader and loftier than any other in the tribe, and new, like the rest of Mohammed's goods. The Abu Tayi were rearranging their camp, for security when their fighting men marched away. Throughout the afternoon tents were coming in and being pitched by us. The oblong cloth was stretched flat upon the ground; the ropes at the end, in the sides, by the pole-gussets, strained out and tied to pegs. Then the housewife would insert the light poles one by one, under the cloth, and lever it up by them, until the whole was in place, pitched single-handed by the one weak woman, however rough the wind.

If it rained one row of poles was drawn in at the foot, so slanting the roof-cloth obliquely to the shower, and making it reasonably waterproof. In summer the Arab tent was less hot than our canvas tents, for the sun-heat was not absorbed in this loose woven fabric of hair and wool, with the air spaces and currents between its threads.

CHAPTER XLIX

WE started an hour before noon. Nasir led us, riding his Ghazala — a camel vaulted and huge-ribbed as an antique ship; towering a good foot above the next of our animals, and yet perfectly proportioned, with a stride like an ostrich's — a lyrical beast, noblest and best bred of the Howeitat camels, a female of nine remembered dams. Auda was beside him, and I skirmished about their gravities on Naama, 'the hen-ostrich', a racing camel and my last purchase. Behind me rode my Ageyl, with Mohammed, the clumsy. Mohammed was now companioned by Ahmed, another peasant, who had been for six years living among the Howeitat by force of his thews and wits — a knowing eager ruffian.

Sixty feet of a rise took us out of Sirhan to the first terrace of the Ard el Suwan — a country of black flints upon marly limestone; not very solid, but hard enough in the tracks which the feet of passing centuries of camels had worn an inch or two into the surface. Our aim was Bair, a historic group of Ghassanid wells and ruins in the desert thirty or forty miles east of the Hejaz Railway. It lay some sixty miles ahead, and there we would camp a few days, while our scouts brought us flour from the hill villages above the Dead Sea. Our food from Wejh was nearly finished (except that Nasir still had some of the precious rice for great occasions), and we could not yet certainly forecast the date of our arrival in Akaba.

Our present party totalled more than five hundred strong; and the sight of this jolly mob of hardy, confident northerners chasing gazelle wildly over the face of the desert, took from us momentarily all sorry apprehension as to the issue of our enterprise. We felt it was a rice-night, and the chiefs of the Abu Tayi came to sup with us. Afterwards, with the embers of our coffee-fire pleasantly red between us against the cool of this upland north-country, we sat about on the carpets chatting discursively of this remote thing and that.

Nasir rolled over on his back, with my glasses, and began to study the stars, counting aloud first one group and then another; crying out with surprise at discovering little lights not noticed by his unaided eye. Auda sent us on to talk of telescopes — of the great ones — and of how man in three hundred years had so far advanced from his first essay that now he built glasses as long as a tent, through which he counted thousands of unknown stars. 'And the stars — what are they?' We slipped into talk of suns beyond suns, sizes and distance beyond wit. 'What will now happen with this knowledge?' asked Mohammed. 'We shall set to, and many learned and some clever men together will make glasses as more powerful than ours, as ours than Galileo's; and yet more hundreds of astronomers will distinguish and reckon yet more thousands of now unseen stars, mapping them, and giving each one its name. When we see them all, there will be no night in heaven.'

'Why are the Westerners always wanting all?' provokingly said Auda. 'Behind our few stars we can see God, who is not behind your millions.' 'We want the world's end, Auda.' 'But that is God's,' complained Zaal, half angry. Mohammed would not have his subject turned. 'Are there men on these greater worlds?' he asked. 'God knows.' 'And has each the Prophet and heaven and hell?' Auda broke in on him. 'Lads, we know our districts, our camels, our women. The excess and the glory are to God. If the end of wisdom is to add star to star our foolishness is pleasing.' And then he spoke of money, and distracted their minds till they all buzzed at once. Afterwards he whispered to me that I must get him a worthy gift from Feisal when he won Akaba.

We marched at dawn, and in an hour topped the Wagf, the watershed, and rode down its far side. The ridge was only a bank of chalk, flint-capped, a couple of hundred feet high. We were now in the hollow between the Snainirat on the south and, on the north, the three white heads of the Thlaithukhwat, a cluster of conical hills which shone brilliant as snow in the sunshine. Soon we entered Wadi Bair, and marched up and across it for hours. There had been a flood there in the spring, producing a rich growth of grasses between the scrubby bushes. It was green and pleasant to the eye and to our camels' hungry palates after the long hostility of the Sirhan.

Presently Auda told me he was riding ahead to Bair, and would I come? We went fast, and in two hours came upon the place suddenly, under a knoll. Auda had hurried on to visit the tomb of his son Annad, who had been waylaid by five of his Motalga cousins in revenge for Abtan, their champion, slain by Annad in single combat. Auda told me how Annad had ridden at them, one against five, and had died as he should; but it left only little Mohammed between him and childlessness. He had brought me along to hear him greatly lament his dead.

However, as we rode down towards the graves, we were astonished to see smoke wreathing from the ground about the wells. We changed direction sharply, and warily approached the ruins. It seemed there was no one there; but the thick dung-cake round the well-brink was charred, and the well itself shattered at the top. The ground was torn and blackened as if by an explosion; and when we looked down the shaft we saw its steyning stripped and split, and many blocks thrown down the bore half choking it and the water in the bottom. I sniffed the air and thought the smell was dynamite.

Auda ran to the next well, in the bed of the valley below the graves; and that, too, was ragged about the head and choked with fallen stones. 'This,' said he, 'is Jazi work.' We walked across the valley to the third — the Beni Sakhr — well. It was only a crater of chalk. Zaal arrived, grave at sight of the disaster. We explored the ruined khan, in which were night-old traces of perhaps a hundred horse. There was a fourth well, north of the ruins in the open flat, and to it we went hopelessly, wondering what would become of us if Bair were all destroyed. To our joy it was uninjured.

This was a Jazi well, and its immunity gave strong colour to Auda's theory. We were disconcerted to find the Turks so ready, and began to fear that perhaps they had also raided El Jefer, east of Maan, the wells at which we planned to concentrate before we attacked. Their blocking would be a real embarrassment. Meanwhile, thanks to the fourth well, our situation, though uncomfortable, was not dangerous. Yet its water facilities were altogether insufficient for five hundred camels; so it became imperative to open the least damaged of the other wells — that in the ruins, about whose lip the turf smouldered. Auda and I went off with Nasir to look again at it.

An Ageyli brought us an empty case of Nobel's gelignite, evidently the explosive which the Turks had used. From scars in the ground it was clear that several charges had been fired simultaneously round the well-head, and in the shaft. Staring down it till our eyes were adjusted to its dark, we suddenly saw many niches cut in the shaft less than twenty feet below. Some were still tamped, and had wires hanging down.

Evidently there was a second series of charges, either inefficiently wired, or with a very long time-fuse. Hurriedly we unrolled our bucket-ropes, twined them together, and hung them freely down the middle of the well from a stout cross-pole, the sides being so tottery that the scrape of a rope might have dislodged their blocks. I then found that the charges were small, not above three pounds each, and had been wired in series with field telephone cable. But something had gone wrong. Either the Turks had scamped their job or their scouts had seen us coming before they had had time to re-connect.

So we soon had two fit wells, and a clear profit of thirty pounds of enemy gelignite. We determined to stay a week in this fortunate Bair. A third object — to discover the condition of the Jefer wells — was now added to our needs for food, and for news of the state of mind of the tribes between Maan and Akaba. We sent a man to Jefer. We prepared a little caravan of pack-camels with Howeitat brands and sent them across the line to Tafileh with three or four obscure clansmen — people who would never be suspected of association with us. They would buy all the flour they could and bring it back to us in five or six days' time.

As for the tribes about the Akaba road, we wanted their active help against the Turks to carry out the provisional plan we had made at Wejh. Our idea was to advance suddenly from El Jefer, to cross the railway line and to crown the great pass—Nagb el Shtar—down which the road dipped from the Maan plateau to the red Guweira plain. To hold this pass we should have to capture Aba el Lissan, the large spring at its head, about sixteen miles from Maan; but the garrison was small, and we hoped to overrun it with a rush. We would then be astride the road, whose posts at the end of the week should fall from hunger; though probably before that the hill tribes, hearing of our successful beginning, would join us to wipe them out.

Crux of our plan was the attack on Aba el Lissan, lest the force in

Maan have time to sally out, relieve it, and drive us off the head of Shtar. If, as at present, they were only a battalion, they would hardly dare move; and should they let it fall while waiting for reinforcements to arrive, Akaba would surrender to us, and we should be based on the sea and have the advantageous gorge of Itm between us and the enemy. So our insurance for success was to keep Maan careless and weak, not suspecting our malevolent presence in the neighbourhood.

It was never easy for us to keep our movements secret, as we lived by preaching to the local people, and the unconvinced would tell the Turks. Our long march into Wadi Sirhan was known to the enemy, and the most civilian owl could not fail to see that the only fit objective was Akaba. The demolition of Bair (and Jefer, too, for we had it confirmed that the seven wells of Jefer were destroyed) showed that the Turks were to that extent on the alert.

However, there was no measuring the stupidity of the Turkish Army; a point which helped us now and again, and harmed us constantly, for we could not avoid despising them for it (Arabs being a race gifted with uncommon quickness of mind, and over-valuing it) and an army suffered when unable to yield honour to the enemy. For the moment the stupidity might be made use of; and so we had undertaken a prolonged campaign of deception, to convince them that our objective lay nearer to Damascus.

They were susceptible to pressure in that neighbourhood, for the railway from Damascus, north to Deraa and south to Amman, was the communication, not merely of Hejaz, but of Palestine; and if we attacked it we should do double damage. So, in my long trip round the north country, I had dropped hints of our near arrival in Jebel Druse; and I had been glad to let the notorious Nesib go up there, noisily, but with small resources. Nuri Shaalan had warned the Turks for us in the same sense; and Newcombe, down near Wejh, had contrived to lose official papers, including a plan (in which we were advance guard) for marching from Wejh, by Jefer and the Sirhan, to Tadmor, to attack Damascus and Aleppo. The Turks took the documents very seriously, and chained up an unfortunate garrison in Tadmor till the end of the war, much to our advantage.

CHAPTER L

IT seemed wise to make some concrete effort in the same direction during the week that we must spend in Bair, and Auda decided that Zaal should ride with me in command of a party to attack the line near Deraa. Zaal chose one hundred and ten men, individually, and we rode hard, in six-hour spells with one- or two-hour intervals, day and night. For me it was an eventful trip, for those reasons which made it dull to the Arabs; namely, that we were an ordinary tribal raiding party, riding on conventional lines, in the formation and after the pattern which generations of practice had proved efficient.

In the second afternoon we reached the railway just above Zerga, the Circassian village north of Amman. The hot sun and fast riding had tried our camels, and Zaal decided to water them at a ruined Roman village, the underground cisterns of which had been filled by the late rains. It lay within a mile of the railway, and we had to be circumspect, for the Circassians hated the Arabs, and would have been hostile had they seen us. Also there was a military post of two tents on a tall bridge just down the line. The Turks seemed active. Later we heard that a general's inspection was pending.

After the watering we rode another six miles, and in the early dark turned to Dhuleil bridge, which Zaal reported as a big one, good to destroy. The men and camels stayed on the high ground east of the railway to cover our retreat if anything untoward happened, while Zaal and I went down to the bridge to look it over. There were Turks two hundred yards beyond it, with many tents and cooking fires. We were puzzled to explain their strength, until we reached the bridge and found it being rebuilt; the spring flood had washed away four of its arches, and the line was temporarily laid on a deviation. One of the new arches was finished, another had the vault just turned, and the timber centring was set ready for a third.

Useless, of course, it was, bothering to destroy a bridge in such a state; so we drew off quietly (not to alarm the workmen), walking over loose stones which turned under our bare feet in a way imposing care if we would avoid risk of sprain. Once I put my foot on something moving, soft and cold; and stepped heavily, on chance it was a snake; but no harm followed. The brilliant stars cast about us a false light, not illumination, but rather a transparency of air lengthening slightly the shadow below each stone, and making a difficult greyness of the ground.

We decided to go further north, towards Minifir, where Zaal thought the land propitious for mining a train. A train would be better than a bridge, for our need was political, to make the Turks think that our main body was at Azrak in Sirhan, fifty miles away to the east. We came out on a flat plain, crossed by a very occasional shallow bed of fine shingle. Over this we were going easily when we heard a long rumble. We pricked ears, wondering: and there came out of the north a dancing plume of flame bent low by the wind of its speed. It seemed to light us, extending its fire-tagged curtain of smoke over our heads, so near were we to the railway; and we shrank back while the train rushed on. Two minutes' warning and I would have blown its locomotive into scrap.

Afterwards our march was quiet till the dawn, when we found ourselves riding up a narrow valley. At its head was a sharp turn to the left, into an amphitheatre of rock where the hill went up by step after step of broken cliff to a crest on which stood a massive cairn. Zaal said the railway was visible thence, and if this were true the place was an ideal ambush, for the camels could be herded without any guardians into the pit of excellent pasture.

I climbed at once to the cairn, the ruin of an Arab watch-tower of the Christian period, commanding a most gracious view of rich pastoral uplands beyond the line, which ran round the foot of our slope in a lazy curve, open to sight for perhaps five miles. Below on our left was the square box of the 'coffee-house', a railway halt, about which a few little soldiers were slouching peacefully. We lay alternately watching and sleeping, for many hours, during which a train ground slowly past up the stiff gradient. We made plans to descend upon the line that night, wherever seemed best for mining.

However, in mid-morning a dark mass approached from the northward. Eventually we made it out to be a force of perhaps one hundred and fifty mounted men, riding straight for our hill. It looked as though we had been reported; a quite possible thing, since all this area was grazed over by the sheep of the Belga tribes, whose shepherds, when they saw our stealthiness, would have taken us for robber-enemies and alarmed their tents.

Our position, admirable against the railway, was a death-trap in which to be caught by superior mobile forces; so we sent down the alarm, mounted and slipped across the valley of our entry, and over its eastern ridge into a small plain, where we could canter our animals. We made speed to low mounds on its further side, and got behind them before the enemy were in a position to see us.

There the terrain better suited our tactics and we waited for them; but they were at least imperfectly informed, for they rode past our old hiding-place and quickly away towards the south, leaving us puzzled. There were no Arabs among them — all were regulars — so we had not to fear being tracked, but here again it seemed as though the Turks were on the alert. This was according to my wish, and I was glad, but Zaal, on whom fell the military responsibility, was disquieted. He held a council with those others who knew the country, and eventually we remounted, and jogged off to another hill, rather north of our old one, but satisfactory enough. Particularly it happened to be free of tribal complications.

This was Minifir proper, a round-headed, grass-grown hill of two shoulders. The high neck between provided us, on its eastern face, a broad track perfectly covered from the north and south and west which afforded a safe retreat into the desert. At the top the neck was cupped, so that collected rain had made the soil rich, and the grazing sumptuous; but loosed camels required constant care, for if they wandered two hundred paces forward they became visible from the railway, a further four hundred yards down the western face of the hill.

On each side the shoulders pushed forward in spurs which the line passed in shallow cuttings. The excavated material had been thrown across the hollow in an embankment; through the centre of which a lofty culvert let the drainage of the little zigzag gully from the neck run down into a larger transverse valley bed beyond.

Northward the line curved away, hard uphill, to the wide level of the southern Hauran, spread out like a grey sky, and flecked with small dark clouds which were the dead basalt towns of Byzantine Syria. Southward was a cairn from which we could look down the railway for six miles or more.

The high land facing us to the west, the Belga, was spotted with black tent-villages of peasants in summer quarters. They could see us too, in our hill-cup, so we sent word who we were. Whereupon they kept silent till we had gone, and then were fervid and eloquent in proving that we fled eastward, to Azrak. When our messengers came back we had bread to eat — a luxury; since the dearth in Bair had reduced us to parched corn which, for lack of cooking-opportunity the men had been chewing raw. The trial was too steep for my teeth, so that I rode fasting.

Zaal and I buried that night on the culvert a great Garland mine, automatic-compound, to explode three charges in parallel by instantaneous fuse; and then lay down to sleep, sure that we would hear noises if a train came along in the dark and fired it. However, nothing happened, and at dawn I removed the detonators which (additional to the trigger action) had been laid on the metals. Afterwards we waited all day, fed and comfortable, cooled by a high wind which hissed like surf as it ruffled up the stiff-grassed hill.

For hours nothing came along: but at last there was a flutter among the Arabs, and Zaal, with the Hubsi and some of the more active men, dashed down towards the line. We heard two shots under us in the dead ground, and after half an hour the party reappeared, leading two ragged Turkish deserters from the mounted column of the day before. One had been badly wounded, while attempting to escape up the line; and in the afternoon he died, most miserable about himself and his fate. Exceptionally: for when death became certain most men felt the quietness of the grave waiting for them, and went to it not unwillingly. The other man was hurt also, a clean gunshot in the foot; but he was very feeble and collapsed when the wound grew painful with the cold. His thin body was so covered with bruises, tokens of army service and cause of his desertion, that he dared lie only on his face. We offered him the last of our bread and water and did what else we could for him: which was little.

Late in the afternoon came a thrill when the mule-mounted infantry reappeared, heading up-line towards us. They would pass below our ambush, and Zaal and the men were urgent to attack them on the sudden. We were one hundred, they little over two hundred. We had the upper ground, could hope to empty some of their saddles by our first volley, and then would camel-charge upon them. Camels, especially down a gentle slope, would overtake mules in a few strides, and their moving bulk would send spinning the lighter animals and their riders. Zaal gave me his word that no regular cavalry, let alone mere mounted infantry, could cope with tribal camels in a running fight. We should take not only the men, but their precious animals.

I asked him how many casualties we might incur. He guessed five or six, and then I decided to do nothing, to let them pass. We had one objective only, the capture of Akaba, and had come up here solely to make that easier by leading the Turks off on the false scent of thinking that we were at Azrak. To lose five or six men in such a demonstration, however profitable it proved financially, would be fatuous, or worse, because we might want our last rifle to take Akaba, the possession of which was vital to us. After Akaba had fallen we might waste men, if we felt callous; but not before.

I told Zaal, who was not content; while the furious Howeitat threatened to run off downhill at the Turks, willy-nilly. They wanted a booty of mules; and I, particularly, did not, for it would have diverted us. Commonly, tribes went to war to gain honour and wealth. The three noble spoils were arms, riding-animals, and clothes. If we took these two hundred mules, the proud men would throw up Akaba and drive them home by way of Azrak to their tents, to triumph before the women. As for prisoners, Nasir would not be grateful for two hundred useless mouths; so we should have to kill them; or let them go, revealing our numbers to the enemy.

We sat and gnashed our teeth at them and let them pass: a severe ordeal, from which we only just emerged with honour. Zaal did it. He was on his best behaviour, expecting tangible gratitude from me later; and glad, meanwhile, to show me his authority over the Beduin. They respected him as Auda's deputy, and as a famous fighter, and in one or two little mutinies he had shown a self-conscious mastery.

Now he was tested to the utmost. The Hubsi, Auda's cousin, a spirited youth, while the Turks were defiling innocently not three hundred yards from our itching rifle-muzzles, sprang to his feet and ran forward shouting to attract them, and compel a battle; but Zaal caught him in ten strides, threw him down and bludgeoned him savagely time and again till we feared lest the lad's now very different cries fulfil his former purpose.

It was sad to see a sound and pleasant little victory pass voluntarily out of our hands, and we were gloomy till evening came down and confirmed our sense that once more there would be no train. This was the final occasion, for thirst was hanging over us, and on the morrow the camels must be watered. So after nightfall we returned to the line, laid thirty charges of gelignite against the most-curved rails and fired them leisurely. The curved rails were chosen since the Turks would have to bring down new ones from Damascus. Actually, this took them three days; and then their construction train stepped on our mine (which we had left as hook behind the demolition's bait) and hurt its locomotive. Traffic ceased for three days while the line was picked over for traps.

For the moment of course, we could anticipate none of these good things. We did the destruction, returned sorrowfully to our camels, and were off soon after midnight. The prisoner was left behind on his hill-top, for he could neither walk nor ride, and we had no carriage for him. We feared he would starve to death where he lay: and, indeed, already he was very ill: so on a telegraph pole, felled across the rails by the damaged stretch, we put a letter in French and German, to give news of where he was, and that we had captured him wounded after a hard fight.

We hoped this might save him the penalties which the Turks inflicted on red-handed deserters, or from being shot if they thought he had been in collusion with us: but when we came back to Minifir six months later the picked bones of the two bodies were lying scattered on our old camping ground. We felt sorry always for the men of the Turkish Army. The officers, volunteer and professional, had caused the war by their ambition — almost by their existence — and we wished they could receive not merely their proportionate deserts, but all that the conscripts had to suffer through their fault.

CHAPTER LI

IN the night we lost our way among the stony ridges and valleys of Dhuleil, but kept moving until dawn, so that half an hour after sunrise, while the shadows were yet long across the green hollows, we had reached our former watering-place, Khau, whose ruins broke from the hill-top against Zerga like a scab. We were working hard at the two cisterns, watering our camels for the return march to Bair, when a young Circassian came in sight, driving three cows towards the rich green pasture of the ruins.

This would not do, so Zaal sent off his too-energetic offenders of the day previous to show their proper mettle by stalking him: and they brought him in, unharmed, but greatly frightened. Circassians were swaggering fellows, inordinate bullies in a clear road; but if firmly met they cracked; and so this lad was in a head-and-tail flux of terror, offending our sense of respect. We drenched him with water till he recovered, and then in disposal set him to fight at daggers with a young Sherari, caught stealing on the march; but after a scratch the prisoner threw himself down weeping.

Now he was a nuisance, for if we left him he would give the alarm, and send the horsemen of his village out against us. If we tied him up in this remote place he would die of hunger or thirst; and, besides, we had not rope to spare. To kill him seemed unimaginative: not worthy of a hundred men. At last the Sherari boy said if we gave him scope he would settle his account and leave him living.

He looped his wrist to the saddle and trotted him off with us for the first hour, till he was dragging breathlessly. We were still near the railway, but four or five miles from Zerga. There he was stripped of presentable clothes, which fell, by point of honour, to his owner. The Sherari threw him on his face, picked up his feet, drew a dagger, and chopped him with it deeply across the soles. The Circassian howled with pain and terror, as if he thought he was being killed.

Odd as was the performance, it seemed effective, and more merciful than death. The cuts would make him travel to the railway on hands and knees, a journey of an hour; and his nakedness would keep him in the shadow of the rocks, till the sun was low. His gratitude was not coherent; but we rode away, across undulations very rich in grazing. The camels, with their heads down snatching plants and grass, moved uncomfortably for us cocked over the chute of their sloped necks; yet we must let them eat, since we were marching eighty miles a day, with halts to breathe only in the brief gloamings of dawn and sunset.

Soon after daylight we turned west, and dismounted, short of the railway among broken reefs of limestone, to creep carefully forward until Atwi station lay beneath us. Its two stone houses (the first only one hundred yards away) were in line, one obscuring the other. Men were singing in them without disquietude. Their day was beginning, and from the guard-room thin blue smoke curled into the air, while a soldier drove out a flock of young sheep to crop the rich meadow between the station and the valley.

This flock sealed the business, for after our horse-diet of dry corn we craved meat. The Arabs' teeth gritted as they counted ten, fifteen, twenty-five, twenty-seven. Zaal dropped into the valley bed where the line crossed a bridge, and, with a party in file behind him, crept along till he faced the station across the meadow.

From our ridge we covered the station yard. We saw Zaal lean his rifle on the bank, shielding his head with infinite precaution behind grasses on the brink. He took slow aim at the coffee-sipping officers and officials in shaded chairs, outside the ticket office. As he pressed the trigger, the report overtook the crash of the bullet against the stone wall, while the fattest man bowed slowly in his chair and sank to the ground under the frozen stare of his fellows.

An instant later Zaal's men poured in their volleys, broke from the valley, and rushed forward: but the door of the northern house clanged to, and rifles began to speak from behind its steel window shutters. We replied, but soon saw our impotence, and ceased fire, as did the enemy. The Sherarat drove the guilty sheep eastward into the hills, where were the camels; everyone else ran down to join Zaal, who was busy about the nearer and undefended building.

Near the height of plundering came a pause and panic. The Arabs were such accustomed scouts that almost they felt danger before it came, sense taking precautions before mind was persuaded. Swinging down the line from the south was a trolley with four men, to whose ears the grinding wheels had deadened our shots. The Rualla section crept under a culvert three hundred yards up, while the rest of us crowded silently by the bridge.

The trolley rolled unsuspectingly over the ambush, who came out to line the bank behind, while we filed solemnly across the green in front. The Turks slowed in horror, jumped off, and ran into the rough: but our rifles cracked once more and they were dead. The trolley brought to our feet its load of copper wire and telegraph tools, with which we put 'earths' in the long-distance wire. Zaal fired our half of the station, whose petrol-splashed woodwork caught freely. The planks and cloth hangings twisted and jerked convulsively as the flames licked them up. Meanwhile the Ageyl were measuring out gelatine, and soon we lit their charges and destroyed a culvert, many rails, and furlongs of telegraph. With the roar of the first explosion our hundred knee-haltered camels rose smartly to their feet, and at each following burst hopped more madly on three legs till they shook off the rope-hitch about the fourth, and drove out every way like scattered starlings into the void. Chasing them and chasing the sheep took us three hours, for which graciously the Turks gave law, or some of us would have had to walk home.

We put a few miles between us and the railway before we sat down to our feast of mutton. We were short of knives, and, after killing the sheep in relay, had recourse to stray flints to cut them up. As men unaccustomed to such expedients, we used them in the eolithic spirit; and it came to me that if iron had been constantly rare we should have chipped our daily tools skilfully as palæoliths: whilst had we had no metal whatever, our art would have been lavished on perfect and polished stones. Our one hundred and ten men ate the best parts of twenty-four sheep at the sitting, while the camels browsed about, or ate what we left over; for the best riding-camels were taught to like cooked meat. When it was finished we mounted, and rode through the night towards Bair: which we entered without casualty, successful, well-fed, and enriched, at dawn.

CHAPTER LII

N ASIR had done great work. A week's flour for us had come from Tafileh, to restore our freedom of movement. We might well take Akaba before we starved again. He had good letters from the Dhumaniyeh, the Darausha, and the Dhiabat, three Howeitat clans on Nagb el Shtar, the first difficult pass of the Maan-Akaba road. They were willing to help us, and if they struck soon and strongly at Aba el Lissan the great factor of surprise would probably mean success to their effort.

My hopefulness misled me into another mad ride, which miscarried. Yet the Turks did not take alarm. As my party rode in there came a messenger post-haste from Nuri Shaalan. He brought greetings, and Nuri's news that the Turks had called upon his son Nawaf, as guide hostage, to take four hundred cavalry from Deraa down the Sirhan in search of us. Nuri had sent his better-spared nephew Trad, who was conducting them by devious routes in which men and horses were suffering terribly from thirst. They were near Nebk, our old camping ground. The Turkish Government would believe us still in the Wadi till their cavalry returned. For Maan especially they had no anxiety since the engineers who had blown up Bair reported every source of water utterly destroyed, while the wells of Jefer had been dealt with a few days earlier.

It might be that Jefer really was denied to us; but we were not without hope that there, too, we should find the technical work of demolition ill-done by these pitiful Turks. Dhaif-Allah, a leading man of the Jazi Howeitat, one who came down to Wejh and swore allegiance, had been present in Jefer when the King's Well was fired by dynamite placed about its lip; and sent us secret word from Maan that he had heard the upper stones clap together and key over the mouth of the well. His conviction was that the shaft was intact, and the clearing of it a few hours' work. We hoped so; and rode away from Bair all in order, on June the twenty-eighth, to find out.

Quickly we crossed the weird plain of Jefer. Next day by noon we were at the wells. They seemed most thoroughly destroyed; and the fear grew that we might find in them the first check to our scheme of operations, a scheme so much too elaborate that a check might be far reaching.

However, we went to the well — Auda's family property — of which Dhaif-Allah had told us the tale, and began to sound about it. The ground rang hollow under our mallet, and we called for volunteers able to dig and build. Some of the Ageyl came forward, led by the Mirzugi, a capable camel boy of Nasir's. They started with the few tools we had. The rest of us formed a ring round the well-depression and watched them work, singing to them and promising rewards of gold when they had found the water.

It was a hot task in the full glare of the summer sun; for the Jefer plain was of hard mud, flat as the hand, blinding white with salt, and twenty miles across; but time pressed, because if we failed, we might have to ride fifty miles in the night to the next well. So we pushed the work by relays at speed through the midday heat, turning into labourers all our amenable fellows. It made easy digging, for the explosion which shifted the stones had loosened the soil.

As they dug and threw out the earth, the core of the well rose up like a tower of rough stones in the centre of the pit. Very carefully we began to take away the ruined head of the pile: difficult work, for the stones had become interlocked in their fall; but this was the better sign, and our spirits rose. Before sunset the workers shouted that there was no more packing-soil, that the interstices between the blocks were clear, and they heard the mud fragments which slipped through splashing many feet below.

Half an hour later came a rush and rumble of stones in the mouth, followed by a heavy splash and yells. We hurried down, and by the Mirzugi's torch saw the well yawning open, no longer a tube, but a deep bottle-shouldered pit, twenty feet across at the bottom, which was black with water and white in the middle with spray where the Ageyli who had been clearing when the key slipped was striking out lustily in the effort not to drown. Everybody laughed down the well at him, till at last Abdulla lowered him a noose of rope, and we drew him up, very wet and angry, but in no way damaged by his fall.

We rewarded the diggers, and feasted them on a weak camel, which had failed in the march to-day; and then all night we watered, while a squad of Ageyl, with a long chorus, steyned up to ground level an eight-foot throat of mud and stones. At dawn the earth was stamped in round this, and the well stood complete, as fit in appearance as ever. Only the water was not very much. We worked it the twenty-four hours without rest, and ran it to a cream; and still some of our camels were not satisfied.

From Jefer we took action. Riders went forward into the Dhumaniyeh tents to lead their promised attack against Fuweilah, the blockhouse which covered the head of the pass of Aba el Lissan. Our attack was planned for two days before the weekly caravan which, from Maan, replenished the client garrisons. Starvation would make reduction of these distant places easier, by impressing on them how hopelessly they were cut off from their friends.

We sat in Jefer meanwhile, waiting to hear the fortune of the attack. On its success or failure would depend the direction of our next march. The halt was not unpleasant, for our position had its comic side. We were within sight of Maan, during those minutes of the day in which the mirage did not make eyes and glasses useless; and yet we strolled about admiring our new well-lip in complete security, because the Turkish garrison believed water impossible here or at Bair, and were hugging the pleasant idea that we were now desperately engaged with their cavalry in Sirhan.

I hid under some bushes near the well for hours, against the heat, very lazy, pretending to be asleep, the wide silk sleeve of my pillow-arm drawn over my face as veil against the flies. Auda sat up and talked like a river, telling his best stories in great form. At last I reproved him with a smile, for talking too much and doing too little. He sucked his lips with pleasure of the work to come.

In the following dawn a tired horseman rode into our camp with news that the Dhumaniyeh had fired on the Fuweilah post the afternoon before as soon as our men had reached them. The surprise had not been quite complete; the Turks manned their dry stone breastworks and drove them off. The crestfallen Arabs drew back into cover, and the enemy believing it only an ordinary tribal affray, had made a mounted sortie upon the nearest encampment.

One old man, six women and seven children were its only occupants. In their anger at finding nothing actively hostile or able-bodied, the troopers smashed up the camp and cut the throats of its helpless ones. The Dhumaniyeh on the hill-tops heard and saw nothing till it was too late; but then, in their fury, they dashed down across the return road of the murderers and cut them off almost to the last man. To complete their vengeance they assaulted the now weakly-garrisoned fort, carried it in the first fierceness of their rush, and took no prisoners.

We were ready saddled; and within ten minutes had loaded and marched for Ghadir el Haj, the first railway station south of Maan, on our direct road for Aba el Lissan. Simultaneously, we detached a small party to cross the railway just above Maan and create a diversion on that side. Especially they were to threaten the great herds of sick camels, casualties of the Palestine front, which the Turks pastured in the Shobek plains till once more fit for service.

We calculated that the news of their Fuweilah disaster would not have reached Maan till the morning, and that they could not drive in these camels (supposing our northern party missed them) and fit out a relief expedition, before nightfall; and if we were then attacking the line at Ghadir el Haj, they would probably divert the relief thither, and so let us move on Akaba unmolested.

With this hope we rode steadily through the flowing mirage till afternoon, when we descended on the line; and, having delivered a long stretch of it from guards and patrols, began on the many bridges of the captured section. The little garrison of Ghadir el Haj sallied out with the valour of ignorance against us, but the heat-haze blinded them, and we drove them off with loss.

They were on the telegraph, and would notify Maan, which beside, could not fail to hear the repeated thuds of our explosion. It was our aim to bring the enemy down upon us in the night; or rather down here, where they would find no people but many broken bridges, for we worked fast and did great damage. The drainage holes in the spandrils held from three to five pounds of gelatine each. We, firing our mines by short fuses, brought down the arch, shattered the pier, and stripped the side walls, in no more than six minutes' work. So we ruined ten bridges and many rails, and finished our explosive.

After dusk, when our departure could not be seen, we rode five miles westward of the line, to cover. There we made fires and baked bread. Our meal, however, was not cooked before three horsemen cantered up to report that a long column of new troops — infantry and guns — had just appeared at Aba el Lissan from Maan. The Dhumani-yeh, disorganized with victory, had had to abandon their ground without fighting. They were at Bara waiting for us. We had lost Aba el Lissan, the blockhouse, the pass, the command of the Akaba road: without a shot being fired.

We learned afterwards that this unwelcome and unwonted vigour on the part of the Turks was accident. A relief battalion had reached Maan that very day. The news of an Arab demonstration against Fuweilah arrived simultaneously; and the battalion, which happened to be formed up ready with its transport in the station yard, to march to barracks, was hurriedly strengthened by a section of pack artillery and some mounted men, and moved straight out as a punitive column to rescue the supposedly beseiged post.

They had left Maan in mid-morning and marched gently along the motor road, the men sweating in the heat of this south country after their native Caucasian snows, and drinking thirstily of every spring. From Aba el Lissan they climbed uphill towards the old blockhouse, which was deserted except for the silent vultures flying above its walls in slow uneasy rings. The battalion commander feared lest the sight be too much for his young troops, and led them back to the roadside spring of Aba el Lissan, in its serpentine narrow valley, where they camped all night in peace about the water.

CHAPTER LIII

SUCH news shook us into quick life. We threw our baggage across our camels on the instant and set out over the rolling downs of this end of the tableland of Syria. Our hot bread was in our hands, and, as we ate, there mingled with it the taste of the dust of our large force crossing the valley bottoms, and some taint of the strange keen smell of the wormwood which overgrew the slopes. In the breathless air of these evenings in the hills, after the long days of summer, everything struck very acutely on the senses: and when marching in a great column, as we were, the front camels kicked up the aromatic dust-laden branches of the shrubs, whose scent-particles rose into the air and hung in a long mist, making fragrant the road of those behind.

The slopes were clean with the sharpness of wormwood, and the hollows oppressive with the richness of their stronger, more luxuriant growths. Our night-passage might have been through a planted garden, and these varieties part of the unseen beauty of successive banks of flowers. The noises too were very clear. Auda broke out singing, away in front, and the men joined in from time to time, with the greatness, the catch at heart, of an army moving into battle.

We rode all night, and when dawn came were dismounting on the crest of the hills between Batra and Aba el Lissan, with a wonderful view westwards over the green and gold Guweira plain, and beyond it to the ruddy mountains hiding Akaba and the sea. Gasim abu Dumeik, head of the Dhumaniyeh, was waiting anxiously for us, surrounded by his hard-bitten tribesmen, their grey strained faces flecked with the blood of the fighting yesterday. There was a deep greeting for Auda and Nasir. We made hurried plans, and scattered to the work, knowing we could not go forward to Akaba with this battalion in possession of the pass. Unless we dislodged it, our two months' hazard and effort would fail before yielding even first-fruits.

Fortunately the poor handling of the enemy gave us an unearned advantage. They slept on, in the valley, while we crowned the hills in wide circle about them unobserved. We began to snipe them steadily in their positions under the slopes and rock-faces by the water, hoping to provoke them out and up the hill in a charge against us. Meanwhile, Zaal rode away with our horsemen and cut the Maan telegraph and telephone in the plain.

This went on all day. It was terribly hot — hotter than ever before I had felt it in Arabia — and the anxiety and constant moving made it hard for us. Some even of the tough tribesmen broke down under the cruelty of the sun, and crawled or had to be thrown under rocks to recover in their shade. We ran up and down to supply our lack of numbers by mobility, ever looking over the long ranges of hill for a new spot from which to counter this or that Turkish effort. The hill-sides were steep, and exhausted our breath, and the grasses twined like little hands about our ankles as we ran, and plucked us back. The sharp reefs of limestone which cropped out over the ridges tore our feet, and long before evening the more energetic men were leaving a rusty print upon the ground with every stride.

Our rifles grew so hot with sun and shooting that they seared our hands; and we had to be grudging of our rounds, considering every shot and spending great pains to make it sure. The rocks on which we flung ourselves for aim were burning, so that they scorched our breasts and arms, from which later the skin drew off in ragged sheets. The present smart made us thirst. Yet even water was rare with us; we could not afford men to fetch enough from Batra, and if all could not drink, it was better that none should.

We consoled ourselves with knowledge that the enemy's enclosed valley would be hotter than our open hills: also that they were Turks, men of white meat, little apt for warm weather. So we clung to them, and did not let them move or mass or sortie out against us cheaply. They could do nothing valid in return. We were no targets for their rifles, since we moved with speed, eccentrically. Also we were able to laugh at the little mountain guns which they fired up at us. The shells passed over our heads, to burst behind us in the air; and yet, of course, for all that they could see from their hollow place, fairly amongst us above the hostile summits of the hill.

Just after noon I had a heat-stroke, or so pretended, for I was dead weary of it all, and cared no longer how it went. So I crept into a hollow where there was a trickle of thick water in a muddy cup of the hills, to suck some moisture off its dirt through the filter of my sleeve. Nasir joined me, panting like a winded animal, with his cracked and bleeding lips shrunk apart in his distress: and old Auda appeared, striding powerfully, his eyes bloodshot and staring, his knotty face working with excitement.

He grinned with malice when he saw us lying there, spread out to find coolness under the bank, and croaked at me harshly, 'Well, how is it with the Howeitat? All talk and no work?' 'By God, indeed,' spat I back again, for I was angry with everyone and with myself, 'they shoot a lot and hit a little.' Auda, almost pale with rage, and trembling, tore his head-cloth off and threw it on the ground beside me. Then he ran back up the hill like a madman, shouting to the men in his dreadful strained and rustling voice.

They came together to him, and after a moment scattered away downhill. I feared things were going wrong, and struggled to where he stood alone on the hill-top, glaring at the enemy: but all he would say to me was, 'Get your camel if you want to see the old man's work'. Nasir called for his camel and we mounted.

The Arabs passed before us into a little sunken place, which rose to a low crest; and we knew that the hill beyond went down in a facile slope to the main valley of Aba el Lissan, somewhat below the spring. All our four hundred camel men were here tightly collected, just out of sight of the enemy. We rode to their head, and asked the Shimt what it was and where the horsemen had gone.

He pointed over the ridge to the next valley above us, and said, 'With Auda there': and as he spoke yells and shots poured up in a sudden torrent from beyond the crest. We kicked our camels furiously to the edge, to see our fifty horsemen coming down the last slope into the main valley like a run-away, at full gallop, shooting from the saddle. As we watched, two or three went down, but the rest thundered forward at marvellous speed, and the Turkish infantry, huddled together under the cliff ready to cut their desperate way out towards Maan, in the first dusk began to sway in and out, and finally broke before the rush, adding their flight to Auda's charge.

Nasir screamed at me, 'Come on', with his bloody mouth; and we plunged our camels madly over the hill, and down towards the head of the fleeing enemy. The slope was not too steep for a camel-gallop, but steep enough to make their pace terrific, and their course uncontrollable: yet the Arabs were able to extend to right and left and to shoot into the Turkish brown. The Turks had been too bound up in the terror of Auda's furious charge against their rear to notice us as we came over the eastward slope: so we also took them by surprise and in the flank; and a charge of ridden camels going nearly thirty miles an hour was irresistible.

My camel, the Sherari racer, Naama, stretched herself out, and hurled downhill with such might that we soon out-distanced the others. The Turks fired a few shots, but mostly only shrieked and turned to run: the bullets they did send at us were not very harmful, for it took much to bring a charging camel down in a dead heap.

I had got among the first of them, and was shooting, with a pistol of course, for only an expert could use a rifle from such plunging beasts; when suddenly my camel tripped and went down emptily upon her face, as though pole-axed. I was torn completely from the saddle, sailed grandly through the air for a great distance, and landed with a crash which seemed to drive all the power and feeling out of me. I lay there, passively waiting for the Turks to kill me, continuing to hum over the verses of a half-forgotten poem, whose rhythm something, perhaps the prolonged stride of the camel, had brought back to my memory as we leaped down the hill-side:

For Lord I was free of all Thy flowers, but I chose the world's sad roses,
And that is why my feet are torn and mine eyes are blind with sweat.

While another part of my mind thought what a squashed thing I should look when all that cataract of men and camels had poured over.

After a long time I finished my poem, and no Turks came, and no camel trod on me: a curtain seemed taken from my ears: there was a great noise in front. I sat up and saw the battle over, and our men driving together and cutting down the last remnants of the enemy. My camel's body had laid behind me like a rock and divided the charge into two streams: and in the back of its skull was the heavy bullet of the fifth shot I fired.

Mohammed brought Obeyd, my spare camel, and Nasir came back leading the Turkish commander, whom he had rescued, wounded, from Mohammed el Dheilan's wrath. The silly man had refused to surrender, and was trying to restore the day for his side with a pocket pistol. The Howeitat were very fierce, for the slaughter of their women on the day before had been a new and horrible side of warfare suddenly revealed to them. So there were only a hundred and sixty prisoners, many of them wounded; and three hundred dead and dying were scattered over the open valleys.

A few of the enemy got away, the gunners on their teams, and some mounted men and officers with their Jazi guides. Mohammed el Dheilan chased them for three miles into Mreigha, hurling insults as he rode, that they might know him and keep out of his way. The feud of Auda and his cousins had never applied to Mohammed, the political-minded, who showed friendship to all men of his tribe when he was alone to do so. Among the fugitives was Dhaif-Allah, who had done us the good turn about the King's Well at Jefer.

Auda came swinging up on foot, his eyes glazed over with the rapture of battle, and the words bubbling with incoherent speed from his mouth. 'Work, work, where are words, work, bullets, Abu Tayi' ... and he held up his shattered field-glasses, his pierced pistol-holster, and his leather sword-scabbard cut to ribbons. He had been the target of a volley which had killed his mare under him, but the six bullets through his clothes had left him scatheless.

He told me later, in strict confidence, that thirteen years before he had bought an amulet Koran for one hundred and twenty pounds and had not since been wounded. Indeed, Death had avoided his face, and gone scurvily about killing brothers, sons and followers. The book was a Glasgow reproduction, costing eighteen pence; but Auda's deadliness did not let people laugh at his superstition.

He was wildly pleased with the fight, most of all because he had confounded me and shown what his tribe could do. Mohammed was wroth with us for a pair of fools, calling me worse than Auda, since I had insulted him by words like flung stones to provoke the folly which had nearly killed us all: though it had killed only two of us, one Rueili and one Sherari.

It was, of course, a pity to lose any one of our men, but time was of importance to us, and so imperative was the need of dominating Maan, to shock the little Turkish garrisons between us and the sea into surrender, that I would have willingly lost much more than two. On occasions like this Death justified himself and was cheap.

I questioned the prisoners about themselves, and the troops in Maan; but the nerve crisis had been too severe for them. Some gaped at me and some gabbled, while others, with helpless weepings, embraced my knees, protesting at every word from us that they were fellow Moslems and my brothers in the faith.

Finally I got angry and took one of them aside and was rough to him, shocking him by new pain into a half-understanding, when he answered well enough, and reassuringly, that their battalion was the only reinforcement, and it merely a reserve battalion; the two companies in Maan would not suffice to defend its perimeter.

This meant we could take it easily, and the Howeitat clamoured to be led there, lured by the dream of unmeasured loot, though what we had taken here was a rich prize. However, Nasir, and afterwards Auda, helped me stay them. We had no supports, no regulars, no guns, no base nearer than Wejh, no communications, no money even, for our gold was exhausted, and we were issuing our own notes, promises to pay 'when Akaba is taken', for daily expenses. Besides, a strategic scheme was not changed to follow up a tactical success. We must push to the coast, and re-open sea-contact with Suez.

Yet it would be good to alarm Maan further: so we sent mounted men to Mreigha and took it; and to Waheida and took it. News of this advance, of the loss of the camels on the Shobek road, of the demolition of El Haj, and of the massacre of their relieving battalion all came to Maan together, and caused a very proper panic. The military headquarters wired for help, the civil authorities loaded their official archive into trucks, and left, hot-speed, for Damascus.

CHAPTER LIV

MEANWHILE our Arabs had plundered the Turks, their baggage train, and their camp; and soon after moonrise, Auda came to us and said that we must move. It angered Nasir and myself. To-night there was a dewy west wind blowing, and at Aba el Lissan's four thousand feet, after the heat and burning passion of the day, its damp chill struck very sharply on our wounds and bruises. The spring itself was a thread of silvery water in a runnel of pebbles across delightful turf, green and soft, on which we lay, wrapped in our cloaks, wondering if something to eat were worth preparing: for we were subject at the moment to the physical shame of success, a reaction of victory, when it became clear that nothing was worth doing, and that nothing worthy had been done.

Auda insisted. Partly it was superstition — he feared the newly-dead around us; partly lest the Turks return in force; partly lest other clans of the Howeitat take us, lying there broken and asleep. Some were his blood enemies; others might say they came to help our battle, and in the darkness thought we were Turks and fired blindly. So we roused ourselves, and jogged the sorry prisoners into line.

Most had to walk. Some twenty camels were dead or dying from wounds which they had got in the charge, and others were over-weak to take a double burden. The rest were loaded with an Arab and a Turk; but some of the Turkish wounded were too hurt to hold themselves on pillion. In the end we had to leave about twenty on the thick grass beside the rivulet, where at least they would not die of thirst, though there was little hope of life or rescue for them.

Nasir set himself to beg blankets for these abandoned men, who were half-naked; and while the Arabs packed, I went off down the valley where the fight had been, to see if the dead had any clothing they could spare. But the Beduin had been beforehand with me, and had stripped them to the skin. Such was their point of honour.

To an Arab an essential part of the triumph of victory was to wear the clothes of an enemy: and next day we saw our force transformed (as to the upper half) into a Turkish force, each man in a soldier's tunic: for this was a battalion straight from home, very well found and dressed in new uniforms.

The dead men looked wonderfully beautiful. The night was shining gently down, softening them into new ivory. Turks were white-skinned on their clothed parts, much whiter than the Arabs; and these soldiers had been very young. Close round them lapped the dark wormwood, now heavy with dew, in which the ends of the moon-beams sparkled like sea-spray. The corpses seemed flung so pitifully on the ground, huddled anyhow in low heaps. Surely if straightened they would be comfortable at last. So I put them all in order, one by one, very wearied myself, and longing to be of these quiet ones, not of the restless, noisy, aching mob up the valley, quarrelling over the plunder, boasting of their speed and strength to endure God knew how many toils and pains of this sort; with death, whether we won or lost, waiting to end the history.

In the end our little army was ready, and wound slowly up the height and beyond into a hollow sheltered from the wind; and there, while the tired men slept, we dictated letters to the Sheikhs of the coastal Howeitat, telling them of the victory, that they might invest their nearest Turks, and hold them till we came. We had been kind to one of the captured officers, a policeman despised by his regular col-leagues, and him we persuaded to be our Turkish scribe to the com-mandants of Guweira, Kethera, and Hadra, the three posts between us and Akaba, telling them that if our blood was not hot we took prisoners, and that prompt surrender would ensure their good treat-ment and safe delivery to Egypt.

This lasted till dawn, and then Auda marshalled us for the road, and led us up the last mile of soft heath-clad valley between the rounded hills. It was intimate and homelike till the last green bank; when suddenly we realized it was the last, and beyond lay nothing but clear air. The lovely change this time checked me with amazement; and afterwards, however often we came, there was always a catch of eager-ness in the mind, a pricking forward of the camel and straightening up to see again over the crest into openness.

Shtar hill-side swooped away below us for hundreds and hundreds of feet, in curves like bastions, against which summer-morning clouds were breaking: and from its foot opened the new earth of the Guweira plain. Aba el Lissan's rounded limestone breasts were covered with soil and heath, green, well watered. Guweira was a map of pink sand, brushed over with streaks of watercourses, in a mantle of scrub: and, out of this, and bounding this, towered islands and cliffs of glowing sandstone, wind-scarped and rain-furrowed, tinted celestially by the early sun.

After days of travel on the plateau in prison valleys, to meet this brink of freedom was a rewarding vision, like a window in the wall of life. We walked down the whole zigzag pass of Shtar, to feel its excellence, for on our camels we rocked too much with sleep to dare see anything. At the bottom the animals found a matted thorn which gave their jaws pleasure; we in front made a halt, rolled on to sand soft as a couch, and incontinently slept.

Auda came. We pleaded that it was for mercy upon our broken prisoners. He replied that they alone would die of exhaustion if we rode, but if we dallied, both parties might die: for truly there was now little water and no food. However, we could not help it, and stopped that night short of Guweira, after only fifteen miles. At Guweira lay Sheikh ibn Jad, balancing his policy to come down with the stronger: and to-day we were the stronger, and the old fox was ours. He met us with honeyed speeches. The hundred and twenty Turks of the garrison were his prisoners; we agreed with him to carry them at his leisure and their ease to Akaba.

Today was the fourth of July. Time pressed us, for we were hungry, and Akaba was still far ahead behind two defences. The nearer post, Kethira, stubbornly refused parley with our flags. Their cliff commanded the valley — a strong place which it might be costly to take. We assigned the honour, in irony, to ibn Jad and his unwearied men, advising him to try it after dark. He shrank, made difficulties, pleaded the full moon: but we cut hardly into this excuse, promising that to-night for a while there should be no moon. By my diary there was an eclipse. Duly it came, and the Arabs forced the post without loss, while the superstitious soldiers were firing rifles and clanging copper pots to rescue the threatened satellite.

Reassured we set out across the strandlike plain. Niazi Bey, the Turkish battalion commander, was Nasir's guest, to spare him the humiliation of Beduin contempt. Now he sidled up by me, and, his swollen eyelids and long nose betraying the moroseness of the man, began to complain that an Arab had insulted him with a gross Turkish word. I apologized, pointing out that it must have been learnt from the mouth of one of his Turkish fellow-governors. The Arab was repaying Cæsar.

Cæsar, not satisfied, pulled from his pocket a wizened hunch of bread to ask if it was fit breakfast for a Turkish officer. My heavenly twins, foraging in Guweira, had bought, found, or stolen a Turkish soldier's ration loaf; and we had quartered it. I said it was not breakfast, but lunch and dinner, and perhaps to-morrow's meals as well. I, a staff officer of the British Army (not less well fed than the Turkish), had eaten mine with the relish of victory. It was defeat, not bread, which stuck in his gullet, and I begged him not to blame me for the issue of a battle imposed on both our honours.

The narrows of Wadi Itm increased in intricate ruggedness as we penetrated deeper. Below Kethira we found Turkish post after Turkish post, empty. Their men had been drawn in to Khadra, the entrenched position (at the mouth of Itm), which covered Akaba so well against a landing from the sea. Unfortunately for them the enemy had never imagined attack from the interior, and of all their great works not one trench or post faced inland. Our advance from so new a direction threw them into panic.

In the afternoon we were in contact with this main position, and heard from the local Arabs that the subsidiary posts about Akaba had been called in or reduced, so that only a last three hundred men barred us from the sea. We dismounted for a council, to hear that the enemy were resisting firmly, in bomb-proof trenches with a new artesian well. Only it was rumoured that they had little food.

No more had we. It was a deadlock. Our council swayed this way and that. Arguments bickered between the prudent and the bold. Tempers were short and bodies restless in the incandescent gorge whose granite peaks radiated the sun in a myriad shimmering points of light, and into the depths of whose tortuous bed no wind could come to relieve the slow saturation of the air with heat.

Our numbers had swollen double. So thickly did the men crowd in the narrow space, and press about us, that we broke up our council twice or thrice, partly because it was not good that they should overhear us wrangling, partly because in the sweltering confinement our unwashed smells offended us. Through our heads the heavy pulses throbbed like clocks.

We sent the Turks summonses, first by white flag, and then by Turkish prisoners, but they shot at both. This inflamed our Beduin, and while we were yet deliberating a sudden wave of them burst up on to the rocks and sent a hail of bullets spattering against the enemy. Nasir ran out barefoot, to stop them, but after ten steps on the burning ground screeched for sandals; while I crouched in my atom of shadow, too wearied of these men (whose minds all wore my livery) to care who regulated their febrile impulses.

However, Nasir prevailed easily. Farraj and Daud had been ring-leaders. For correction they were set on scorching rocks till they should beg pardon. Daud yielded immediately; but Farraj, who, for all his soft form, was of whipcord and much the master-spirit of the two, laughed from his first rock, sat out the second sullenly, and gave way with a bad grace only when ordered to a third.

His stubbornness should have been stringently visited: but the only punishment possible to our hands in this vagrant life was corporal, which had been tried upon the pair so often and so uselessly that I was sick of it. If confined this side of cruelty the surface pain seemed only to irritate their muscles into activities wilder than those for which they had been condemned. Their sins were elvish gaiety, the thought-lessness of unbalanced youth, the being happy when we were not; and for such follies to hurt them mercilessly like criminals till their self-control melted and their manhood was lost under the animal distress of their bodies, seemed to me degrading, almost an impiety towards two sunlit beings, on whom the shadow of the world had not yet fallen — the most gallant, the most enviable, I knew.

We had a third try to communicate with the Turks, by means of a little conscript, who said that he understood how to do it. He undressed and went down the valley in little more than boots. An hour later he proudly brought us a reply, very polite, saying that in two days, if help did not come from Maan, they would surrender.

Such folly (for we could not hold our men indefinitely) might mean the massacre of every Turk. I held no great brief for them, but it was better they be not killed, if only to spare us the pain of seeing it. Besides we might have suffered loss. Night operations in the staring moon would be nearly as exposed as day. Nor was this, like Aba el Lissan, an imperative battle.

We gave our little man a sovereign as earnest of reward, walked down close to the trenches with him, and sent in for an officer to speak with us. After some hesitation this was achieved, and we explained the situation on the road behind us; our growing forces; and our short control over their tempers. The upshot was that they promised to surrender at daylight. So we had another sleep (an event rare enough to chronicle) in spite of our thirst.

Next day at dawn fighting broke out on all sides, for hundreds more hill-men, again doubling our number, had come in the night; and, not knowing the arrangement, began shooting at the Turks, who defended themselves. Nasir went out, with ibn Dgheithir and his Ageyl marching in fours, down the open bed of the valley. Our men ceased fire. The Turks then stopped, for their rank and file had no more fight in them and no more food, and thought we were well supplied. So the surrender went off quietly after all.

As the Arabs rushed in to plunder I noticed an engineer in grey uniform, with red beard and puzzled blue eyes; and spoke to him in German. He was the well-borer, and knew no Turkish. Recent doings had amazed him, and he begged me to explain what we meant. I said that we were a rebellion of the Arabs against the Turks. This, it took him time to appreciate. He wanted to know who was our leader. I said the Sherif of Mecca. He supposed he would be sent to Mecca. I said rather to Egypt. He inquired the price of sugar, and when I replied, 'cheap and plentiful', he was glad.

The loss of his belongings he took philosophically, but was sorry for the well, which a little work would have finished as his monument. He showed me where it was, with the pump only half-built. By pulling on the sludge bucket we drew enough delicious clear water to quench our thirsts. Then we raced through a driving sand-storm down to Akaba, four miles further, and splashed into the sea on July the sixth, just two months after our setting out from Wejh.

BOOK V

MARKING TIME

Chapters LV to LXVIII

OUR *capture of Akaba closed the Hejaz war, and gave us the task of helping the British invade Syria. The Arabs working from Akaba became virtual right wing of Allenby's army in Sinai.*

To mark the changed relation Feisal, with his Army, was transferred to Allenby's command. Allenby now became responsible for his operations and equipment. Meanwhile we organized the Akaba area as an unassailable base, from which to hinder the Hejaz Railway.

CHAPTER LV

THROUGH the whirling dust we perceived that Akaba was all a
ruin. Repeated bombardments by French and English warships
had degraded the place to its original rubbish. The poor houses
stood about in a litter, dirty and contemptible, lacking entirely that
dignity which the durability of their time-challenging bones conferred
on ancient remains.

We wandered into the shadowed grove of palms, at the very break
of the splashing waves, and there sat down to watch our men streaming
past as lines of flushed vacant faces without message for us. For months
Akaba had been the horizon of our minds, the goal: we had had no
thought, we had refused thought, of anything beside. Now, in achievement, we were a little despising the entities which had spent their
extremest effort on an object whose attainment changed nothing
radical either in mind or body.

In the blank light of victory we could scarcely identify ourselves.
We spoke with surprise, sat emptily, fingered upon our white skirts;
doubtful if we could understand or learn who we were. Others'
noise was a dreamlike unreality, a singing in ears drowned deep in
water. Against the astonishment of this unasked-for continued life
we did not know how to turn our gift to account. Especially for me
was it hard, because though my sight was sharp, I never saw men's
features: always I peered beyond, imagining for myself a spirit-reality
of this or that: and to-day each man owned his desire so utterly that he
was fulfilled in it, and became meaningless.

Hunger called us out of our trance. We had now seven hundred
prisoners in addition to our own five hundred men and two thousand
expectant allies. We had not any money (or, indeed, a market); and
the last meal had been two days ago. In our riding-camels we possessed
meat enough for six weeks, but it was poor diet, and a dear one,
indulgence in which would bring future immobility upon us.

Green dates loaded the palms overhead. Their taste, raw, was
nearly as nasty as the want they were to allay. Cooking left them still

deplorable; so we and our prisoners sadly faced a dilemma of constant hunger, or of violent diurnal pains more proper to gluttony than to our expedient eating. The assiduous food-habit of a lifetime had trained the English body to the pitch of producing a punctual nervous excitation in the upper belly at the fixed hour of each meal: and we sometimes gave the honoured name of hunger to this sign that our gut had cubic space for more stuff. Arab hunger was the cry of a long-empty labouring body fainting with weakness. They lived on a fraction of our bulk-food, and their systems made exhaustive use of what they got. A nomad army did not dung the earth richly with by-products.

Our forty-two officer prisoners were an intolerable nuisance. They were disgusted when they found how ill-provided we were: indeed they refused to believe it was not a fraud to annoy them, and plagued us for delicacies, as though Cairo lay hidden in our saddle-bags. To escape them Nasir and I slept. Always we tried to signalize each accomplished stage by this little extra peace; for in the desert we were only left alone by men and flies when lying on our backs, with a cloak to shield our faces, asleep or feigning sleep.

In the evening, our first reaction against success having passed off, we began to think how we should keep Akaba, having gained it. We settled that Auda should return to Guweira. He would there be covered by the descent of Shtar, and the Guweira sands. In fact, as safe as need be. But we would make him safer yet, in excess of precaution. We would put an outpost twenty miles to his north, in the impregnable rock-ruins of Nabathean Petra, and link them to him by a post at Delagha. Auda should also send men to Batra so that his Howeitat lie in a semi-circle of four positions round the edge of the Maan highlands, covering every way towards Akaba.

These four positions existed independently. The enemy had swallowed Goltz' impertinent generalities about the interdependence of strong-posts. We looked to their delivering a spirited drive against one, and sitting afterwards in it dazed for an uncomfortable month, unable to advance for the threat of the remaining three, scratching their heads and wondering why the others did not fall.

Supper taught us the urgent need to send news over the one hundred and fifty miles to the British at Suez for a relief-ship. I decided to go across myself with a party of eight, mostly Howeitat, on the best camels in the force — one even was the famous Jedhah, the seven-year-old for whom the Nowasera had fought the beni Sakhr. As we rode round the bay we discussed the manner of our journey. If we went gently, sparing the animals, they might fail with hunger. If we rode hard they might break down with exhaustion or sore feet in mid-desert.

Finally we agreed to keep at a walk, however tempting the surface, for so many hours of the twenty-four as our endurance would allow. On such time-tests the man, especially if he were a foreigner, usually collapsed before the beast: in particular, I had ridden fifty miles a day for the last month, and was near my limit of strength. If I held out, we should reach Suez in fifty hours of a march; and, to preclude cooking-halts upon the road, we carried lumps of boiled camel and broiled dates in a rag behind our saddles.

We rode up the Sinai scarp by the pilgrims' granite-hewn road with its gradient of one in three and a half. The climb was severe, because hasty, and when we reached the crest before sunset both men and camels were trembling with fatigue. One camel we thence sent back as unfit for the trip: with the others we pushed out across the plain to some thorn-scrub, where they cropped for an hour.

Near midnight we reached Themed, the only wells on our route, in a clean valley-sweep below the deserted guard-house of the Sinai police. We let the camels breathe, gave them water and drank ourselves. Then forward again, plodding through a silence of night so intense that continually we turned round in the saddles at fancied noises away there by the cloak of stars. But the activity lay in ourselves, in the crackling of our passage through the undergrowth perfumed like ghost-flowers about us.

We marched into the very slow dawn. At sun-up we were far out in the plain through which sheaves of watercourses gathered towards Arish: and we stopped to give our camels a few minutes' mockery of pasture. Then again in the saddle till noon, and past noon, when behind the mirage rose the lonely ruins of Nekhl. These we left on our right. At sunset we halted for an hour.

Camels were sluggish, and ourselves utterly wearied; but Motlog, the one-eyed owner of Jedhah, called us to action. We remounted, and at a mechanical walk climbed the Mitla Hills. The moon came out and their tops, contoured in form-lines of limestone strata, shone as though crystalline with snow.

In the dawn we passed a melon field, sown by some adventurous Arab in this no-man's-land between the armies. We halted another of our precious hours, loosing the disgusted camels to search the sand-valleys for food while we cracked the unripe melons and cooled our chapped lips on their pithy flesh. Then again forward, in the heat of the new day; though the canal valley, constantly refreshed by breezes from the Gulf of Suez, was never too oppressive.

By midday we were through the dunes, after a happy switchback ride up and down their waves, and out on the flatter plain. Suez was to be guessed at, as the frise of indeterminate points mowing and bobbing in the mirage of the canal-hollow far in front.

We reached great trench-lines, with forts and barbed wire, roads and railways, falling to decay. We passed them without challenge. Our aim was the Shatt, a post opposite Suez on the Asiatic bank of the Canal, and we gained it at last near three in the afternoon, forty-nine hours out of Akaba. For a tribal raid this would have been fair time, and we were tired men before ever we started.

Shatt was in unusual disorder, without even a sentry to stop us, plague having appeared there two or three days before. So the old camps had been hurriedly cleared, left standing, while the troops bivouacked out in the clean desert. Of course we knew nothing of this, but hunted in the empty offices till we found a telephone. I rang up Suez headquarters and said I wanted to come across.

They regretted that it was not their business. The Inland Water Transport managed transit across the Canal, after their own methods. There was a sniff of implication that these methods were not those of the General Staff. Undaunted, for I was never a partisan of my nominal branch of the service, I rang up the office of the Water Board, and explained that I had just arrived in Shatt from the desert with urgent news for Headquarters. They were sorry, but had no free boats just then. They would be sure to send first thing in the morning, to carry me to the Quarantine Department: and rang off.

CHAPTER LVI

Now I had been four months in Arabia continually on the move. In the last four weeks I had ridden fourteen hundred miles by camel, not sparing myself anything to advance the war; but I refused to spend a single superfluous night with my familiar vermin. I wanted a bath, and something with ice in it to drink: to change these clothes, all sticking to my saddle sores in filthiness: to eat something more tractable than green date and camel sinew. I got through again to the Inland Water Transport and talked like Chrysostom. It had no effect, so I became vivid. Then, once more, they cut me off. I was growing very vivid, when friendly northern accents from the military exchange floated down the line: 'It's no bluidy good, sir, talking to them fookin water boogers.'

This expressed the apparent truth; and the broad-spoken operator worked me through to the Embarkation Office. Here, Lyttleton, a major of the busiest, had added to his innumerable labours that of catching Red Sea warships one by one as they entered Suez roads and persuading them (how some loved it!) to pile high their decks with stores for Wejh or Yenbo. In this way he ran our thousands of bales and men, free, as a by-play in his routine; and found time as well to smile at the curious games of us curious folk.

He never failed us. As soon as he heard who and where I was, and what was not happening in the Inland Water Transport, the difficulty was over. His launch was ready: would be at the Shatt in half an hour. I was to come straight to his office: and not explain (till perhaps now after the war) that a common harbour launch had entered the sacred canal without permission of the Water Directorate. All fell out as he said. I sent my men and camels north to Kubri; where, by telephone from Suez, I would prepare them rations and shelter in the animal camp on the Asiatic shore. Later, of course, came their reward of hectic and astonishing days in Cairo.

Lyttleton saw my weariness and let me go at once to the hotel. Long ago it had seemed poor, but now was become splendid; and, after

conquering its first hostile impression of me and my dress, it produced
the hot baths and the cold drinks (six of them) and the dinner and bed
of my dreams. A most willing intelligence officer, warned by spies of a
disguised European in the Sinai Hotel, charged himself with the care
of my men at Kubri and provided tickets and passes for me to Cairo
next day.

The strenuous 'control' of civilian movement in the canal zone
entertained a dull journey. A mixed body of Egyptian and British
military police came round the train, interrogating us and scrutinizing
our passes. It was proper to make war on permit-men, so I replied
crisply in fluent English, 'Sherif of Mecca — Staff', to their Arabic
inquiries. They were astonished. The sergeant begged my pardon: he
had not expected to hear. I repeated that I was in the Staff uniform of
the Sherif of Mecca. They looked at my bare feet, white silk robes and
gold head-rope and dagger. Impossible! 'What army, sir?' 'Meccan.'
'Never heard of it: don't know the uniform.' 'Would you recognize a
Montenegrin dragoon?'

This was a home-thrust. Any Allied troops in uniform might travel
without pass. The police did not know all the allies, much less their
uniforms. Mine might really be some rare army. They fell back into
the corridor and watched me while they wired up the line. Just before
Ismailia, a perspiring intelligence officer in wet khaki boarded the train
to check my statements. As we had almost arrived I showed him the
special pass with which the forethought of Suez had twice-armed my
innocence. He was not pleased.

At Ismailia passengers for Cairo changed, to wait until the express
from Port Said was due. In the other train shone an opulent saloon,
from which descended Admiral Wemyss and Burmester and Neville,
with a very large and superior general. A terrible tension grew along
the platform as the party marched up and down it in weighty talk.
Officers saluted once: twice: still they marched up and down. Three
times was too much. Some withdrew to the fence and stood permanently to attention. These were the mean souls. Some fled: these
were the contemptibles. Some turned to the bookstall and studied
book-backs avidly: these were shy. Only one was blatant.

Burmester's eye caught my staring. He wondered who it was, for I was burned crimson and very haggard with travel. (Later I found my weight to be less than seven stone.) However, he answered; and I explained the history of our unannounced raid on Akaba. It excited him. I asked that the admiral send a storeship there at once. Burmester said the *Dufferin*, which came in that day, should load all the food in Suez, go straight to Akaba, and bring back the prisoners. (Splendid!) He would order it himself, not to interrupt the Admiral and Allenby.

'Allenby! What's he doing here?' cried I. 'Oh, he's in command now.' 'And Murray?' 'Gone home.' This was news of the biggest, importantly concerning me: and I climbed back and fell to wondering if this heavy, rubicund man was like ordinary generals, and if we should have trouble for six months teaching him. Murray and Belinda had begun so tiresomely that our thought those first days had been, not to defeat the enemy, but to make our own chiefs let us live. Only by time and performance had we converted Sir Archibald and his Chief of Staff, who, in their last months, wrote to the War Office commending the Arab venture, and especially Feisal in it. This was generous of them

and our secret triumph, for they were an odd pair in one chariot — Murray all brains and claws, nervous, elastic, changeable; Lynden Bell so solidly built up of layers of professional opinion, glued together after Government testing and approval, and later trimmed and polished to standard pitch.

At Cairo my sandalled feet slip-slapped up the quiet Savoy corridors to Clayton, who habitually cut the lunch hour to cope with his thronging work. As I entered he glanced up from his desk with a muttered 'Mush fadi' (Anglo-Egyptian for 'engaged') but I spoke and got a surprised welcome. In Suez the night before I had scribbled a short report; so we had to talk only of what needed doing. Before the hour ended, the Admiral rang up to say that the *Dufferin* was loading flour for her emergency trip.

Clayton drew sixteen thousand pounds in gold and got an escort to take it to Suez by the three o'clock train. This was urgent, that Nasir might be able to meet his debts. The notes we had issued at Bair, Jefer and Guweira were pencilled promises, on army telegraph forms, to pay so much to bearer in Akaba. It was a great system, but no one had dared issue notes before in Arabia, because the Beduins had neither pockets in their shirts nor strong-rooms in their tents, and notes could not be buried for safety. So there was an unconquerable prejudice against them, and for our good name it was essential that they be early redeemed.

Afterwards, in the hotel, I tried to find clothes less publicly exciting than my Arab get-up; but the moths had corrupted all my former store, and it was three days before I became normally ill-dressed.

Meanwhile I heard of Allenby's excellence, and of the last tragedy of Murray, that second attack on Gaza, which London forced on one too weak or too politic to resist; and how we went into it, everybody, general and staff-officers, even soldiers, convinced that we should lose; while Murray, in headquarters, worked for a perfectly safe defeat, costing enough men to prove he had tried, but not enough to be disastrous.

. Five thousand eight hundred was the casualty bill. They said Allenby was getting armies of fresh men, and hundreds of guns, and all would be different.

Before I was clothed the Commander-in-Chief sent for me, curiously. In my report, thinking of Saladin and Abu Obeida, I had stressed the strategic importance of the eastern tribes of Syria, and their proper use as a threat to the communications of Jerusalem. This jumped with his ambitions, and he wanted to weigh me.

It was a comic interview, for Allenby was physically large and confident, and morally so great that the comprehension of our littleness came slow to him. He sat in his chair looking at me — not straight, as his custom was, but sideways, puzzled. He was newly from France, where for years he had been a tooth of the great machine grinding the enemy. He was full of Western ideas of gun power and weight — the worst training for our war — but, as a cavalryman, was already half persuaded to throw up the new school, in this different world of Asia, and accompany Dawnay and Chetwode along the worn road of manœuvre and movement; yet he was hardly prepared for anything so odd as myself — a little bare-footed silk-skirted man offering to hobble the enemy by his preaching if given stores and arms and a fund of two hundred thousand sovereigns to convince and control his converts.

Allenby could not make out how much was genuine performer and how much charlatan. The problem was working behind his eyes, and I left him unhelped to solve it. He did not ask many questions, nor talk much, but studied the map and listened to my unfolding of Eastern Syria and its inhabitants. At the end he put up his chin and said quite directly, 'Well, I will do for you what I can', and that ended it. I was not sure how far I had caught him; but we learned gradually that he meant exactly what he said; and that what General Allenby could do was enough for his very greediest servant.

CHAPTER LVII

UPON Clayton I opened myself completely. Akaba had been taken on my plan by my effort. The cost of it had fallen on my brains and nerves. There was much more I felt inclined to do, and capable of doing — if he thought I had earned the right to be my own master. The Arabs said that each man believed his ticks to be gazelles: I did, fervently.

Clayton agreed they were spirited and profitable ticks; but objected that actual command could not be given to an officer junior to the rest. He suggested Joyce as commanding officer at Akaba: a notion which suited me perfectly. Joyce was a man in whom one could rest against the world: a serene, unchanging, comfortable spirit. His mind, like a pastoral landscape, had four corners to its view: cared-for, friendly, limited, displayed.

He had won golden opinion at Rabegh and Wejh, practising that very labour of building up an army and a base, which would be necessary at Akaba. Clayton-like, he was a good cartilage to set between opposing joints, but he had more laughter than Clayton, being broad and Irish and much over six feet in height. His nature was to be devoted to the nearest job without straining on his toes after longer horizons. Also, he was more patient than any recorded archangel, and only smiled that jolly smile of his whenever I came in with revolutionary schemes, and threw new ribbons of fancy about the neck of the wild thing he was slowly rearing.

The rest was easy. For supply officer we would have Goslett, the London business man who had made chaotic Wejh so prim. The aeroplanes could not yet be moved; but the armoured cars might come straight away, and a guard-ship if the Admiral was generous. We rang up Sir Rosslyn Wemyss, who was very generous: his flagship, the *Euryalus*, should sit there for the first few weeks.

Genius, this was, for in Arabia ships were esteemed by number of funnels, and the *Euryalus*, with four, was exceptional in ships. Her great reputation assured the mountains that we were indeed the winning side: and her huge crew, by the prompting of Everard Feilding, for fun built us a good pier.

On the Arab side, I asked that the expensive and difficult Wejh be closed down, and Feisal come to Akaba with his full army. A sudden demand, it seemed to Cairo. So I went further, pointing out that the Yenbo-Medina sector also became a back-number; and advised the transfer to Akaba of the stores, money, and officers now devoted to Ali and Abdulla. This was ruled to be impossible. But my wish regarding Wejh was granted me in compromise.

Then I showed that Akaba was Allenby's right flank, only one hundred miles from his centre, but eight hundred miles from Mecca. As the Arabs prospered their work would be done more and more in the Palestine sphere. So it was logical that Feisal be transferred from the area of King Hussein to become an army commander of the Allied expedition of Egypt under Allenby.

This idea held difficulties. 'Would Feisal accept?' I had talked it over with him in Wejh months ago. 'The High Commissioner?' Feisal's army had been the largest and most distinguished of the Hejaz units: its future would not be dull. General Wingate had assumed full responsibility for the Arab Movement in its darkest moment, at great risk in reputation: dare we ask him to relinquish its advance-guard now on the very threshold of success?

Clayton, knowing Wingate very well, was not afraid to broach the idea to him: and Wingate replied promptly that if Allenby could make direct and large use of Feisal, it would be both his duty and his pleasure to give him up for the good of the show.

A third difficulty of the transfer might be King Hussein: an obstinate, narrow-minded, suspicious character, little likely to sacrifice a pet vanity for unity of control. His opposition would endanger the scheme: and I offered to go down to talk him over, calling on the way to get from Feisal such recommendations of the change as should fortify the powerful letters which Wingate was writing to the King. This was accepted. The *Dufferin*, on returning from Akaba, was detailed to take me to Jidda for the new mission.

She took two days to reach Wejh. Feisal, with Joyce, Newcombe, and all the army, was at Jeida, one hundred miles inland. Stent, who had succeeded Ross in command of the Arabian flight, sent me up by air; so we crossed comfortably at sixty miles an hour the hills learned toilsomely on camel-back.

Feisal was eager to hear the details of Akaba, and laughed at our prentice wars. We sat and made plans the whole night. He wrote to his father; ordered his camel corps to march upon Akaba forthwith; and made first arrangements towards getting Jaafar Pasha and his army ferried up in the long-suffering *Hardinge*.

At dawn they flew me back to Wejh, and, an hour after, the *Dufferin* was making for Jidda, where things became easy for me with Wilson's powerful help. To render Akaba, our most promising sector, strong, he sent up a shipload of reserve stores and ammunition, and offered us any of his officers. Wilson was of the Wingate school.

The King came down from Mecca and talked discursively. Wilson was the royal touchstone, by which to try doubtful courses. Thanks to him, the proposed transfer of Feisal to Allenby was accepted at once, King Hussein taking the opportunity to stress his complete loyalty to our alliance. Then, changing his subject, as usual without obvious coherence, he began to expose his religious position, neither strong Shia nor strong Sunni, aiming rather at a simple pre-schism interpretation of the faith. In foreign politics he betrayed a mind as narrow as it had been broad in unworldly things; with much of that destructive tendency of little men to deny the honesty of opponents. I grasped something of the fixed jealousy which made the modern Feisal suspect in his father's court; and realized how easily mischief-makers could corrode the King.

While we played so interestingly at Jidda, two abrupt telegrams from Egypt shattered our peace. The first reported that the Howeitat were in treasonable correspondence with Maan. The second connected Auda with the plot. This dismayed us. Wilson had travelled with Auda, and formed the inevitable judgement of his perfect sincerity: yet Mohammed el Dheilan was capable of double play, and ibn Jad and his friends were still uncertain. We prepared to leave at once for Akaba. Treachery had not been taken into account when Nasir and I had built our plan for the town's defence.

Fortunately the *Hardinge* was in harbour for us. On the third afternoon we were in Akaba, where Nasir had no notion that anything was wrong. I told him only of my wish to greet Auda: he lent me a swift camel and a guide; and at dawn we found Auda and Mohammed and Zaal all in a tent at Guweira. They were confused when I dropped in on them, unheralded; but protested that all was well. We fed together as friends.

Others of the Howeitat came in, and there was gay talk about the war. I distributed the King's presents; and told them, to their laughter, that Nasir had got his month's leave to Mecca. The King, an enthusiast for the revolt, believed that his servants should work as manfully. So he would not allow visits to Mecca, and the poor men found continual military service heavy banishment from their wives. We had jested a hundred times that, if he took Akaba, Nasir would deserve a holiday; but he had not really believed in its coming until I gave him Hussein's letter the evening before. In gratitude he sold me Ghazala, the regal camel he won from the Howeitat. As her owner I became of new interest to the Abu Tayi.

After lunch, by pretence of sleep, I got rid of the visitors; and then abruptly asked Auda and Mohammed to walk with me to see the ruined fort and reservoir. When we were alone I touched on their present correspondence with the Turks. Auda began to laugh; Mohammed to look disgusted. At last they explained elaborately that Mohammed had taken Auda's seal and written to the Governor of Maan, offering to desert the Sherif's cause. The Turk had replied gladly, promising great rewards. Mohammed asked for something on account. Auda then heard of it, waited till the messenger with presents was on his way, caught him, robbed him to the skin: and was denying Mohammed a share of the spoils. A farcical story, and we laughed rightly over it: but there was more behind.

They were angry that no guns or troops had yet come to their support; and that no rewards had been given them for taking Akaba. They were anxious to know how I had learnt of their secret dealings, and how much more I knew. We were on a slippery ledge. I played on their fear by my unnecessary amusement, quoting in careless laughter, as if they were my own words, actual phrases of the letters they had exchanged. This created the impression desired.

Parenthetically I told them Feisal's entire army was coming up; and how Allenby was sending rifles, guns, high explosive, food and money to Akaba. Finally I suggested that Auda's present expenses in hospitality must be great; would it help if I advanced something of the great gift Feisal would make him, personally, when he arrived? Auda saw that the immediate moment would not be unprofitable: that Feisal would be highly profitable: and that the Turks would be always with him if other resources failed. So he agreed, in a very good temper, to accept my advance; and with it to keep the Howeitat well-fed and cheerful.

It was near sunset. Zaal had killed a sheep and we ate again in real amity. Afterwards I remounted, with Mufaddih (to draw Auda's allowance), and Abd el Rahman, a servant of Mohammed's who, so he whispered me, would receive any little thing I wished to send him separately. We rode all night towards Akaba, where I roused Nasir from sleep, to run over our last business. Then I paddled out in a derelict canoe from 'Euryalus jetty' to the *Hardinge* just as the first dawn crept down the western peaks.

I went below, bathed, and slept till mid-morning. When I came on deck the ship was rushing grandly down the narrow gulf under full steam for Egypt. My appearance caused a sensation, for they had not dreamed I could reach Guweira, assure myself, and get back in less than six or seven days, to catch a later steamer.

We rang up Cairo and announced that the situation at Guweira was thoroughly good, and no treachery abroad. This may have been hardly true; but since Egypt kept us alive by stinting herself, we must reduce impolitic truth to keep her confident and ourselves a legend. The crowd wanted book-heroes, and would not understand how more human old Auda was because, after battle and murder, his heart yearned towards the defeated enemy now subject, at his free choice, to be spared or killed; and therefore never so lovely.

CHAPTER LVIII

AGAIN there fell a pause in my work and again my thoughts built themselves up. Till Feisal and Jaafar and Joyce and the army came we could do little but think: yet that, for our own credit, was the essential process. So far our war had had but the one studied operation — the march on Akaba. Such haphazard playing with the men and movements of which we had assumed the leadership disgraced our minds. I vowed to know henceforward, before I moved, where I was going and by what roads.

At Wejh the Hejaz war was won: after Akaba it was ended. Feisal's army had cleared off its Arabian liabilities and now, under General Allenby the joint Commander-in-Chief, its role was to take part in the military deliverance of Syria.

The difference between Hejaz and Syria was the difference between the desert and the sown. The problem which faced us was one of character — the learning to become civil. Wadi Musa village was our first peasant recruit. Unless we became peasants too, the independence movement would get no further.

It was good for the Arab Revolt that so early in its growth this change imposed itself. We had been hopelessly labouring to plough waste lands; to make nationality grow in a place full of the certainty of God, that upas certainty which forbade all hope. Among the tribes our creed could be only like the desert grass — a beautiful swift seeming of spring; which, after a day's heat, fell dusty. Aims and ideas must be translated into tangibility by material expression. The desert men were too detached to express the one; too poor in goods, too remote from complexity, to carry the other. If we would prolong our life, we must win into the ornamented lands; to the villages where roofs or fields held men's eyes downward and near; and begin our campaign as we had begun that in Wadi Ais, by a study of the map, and a recollection of the nature of this our battleground of Syria.

Our feet were upon its southern boundary. To the east stretched the nomadic desert. To the west Syria was limited by the Mediterranean,

T. E. Lawrence

I

(a) The wells at Wejh

(b) Ghadir Osman, on the return journey from Ais to Wejh

(a) Yenbo, with T. E. Lawrence's house on the right

(b) Sgt Perry, A.V.C., Captain Hornby, and Lt Wade, with Colonel
Lawrence's Ghazala and foal

3

Emir Sherif Feisal, by James McBey

4

(a) Tribesmen. From left to right: An unknown tribesman, Mohamed el Dheilan, Auda abu Tayi, an unknown with a moustache, Auda's young son Mohamed, aged eleven, two unknown tribesmen

(b) Feisal and Ageyl bodyguard

(b) Lawrence in Arab dress

(a) Lt-Col S. F. Newcombe, March 1917

6

(a) General Sir Edmund Allenby, K.C.B., by James McBey

(b) Sir Ronald Storrs

7

(a) Remains of Lt Junor's B.E.12 aeroplane

(b) Rolls-Royce tender at Akaba, with Colonel Joyce in
front seat and Corporal Lowe at the bonnet

8

from Gaza to Alexandretta. On the north the Turkish populations of Anatolia gave it an end. Within these limits the land was much parcelled up by natural divisions. Of them the first and greatest was longitudinal; the rugged spine of mountains which, from north to south, divided a coast strip from a wide inland plain. These areas had climatic differences so marked that they made two countries, two races almost, with their respective populations. The shore Syrians lived in different houses, fed and worked differently, used an Arabic differing by inflection and in tone from that of the inlanders. They spoke of the interior unwillingly, as of a wild land of blood and terror.

The inland plain was sub-divided geographically into strips by rivers. These valleys were the most stable and prosperous tillages of the country. Their inhabitants reflected them: contrasting, on the desert side, with the strange, shifting populations of the borderland, wavering eastward or westward with the season, living by their wits, wasted by drought and locusts, by Beduin raids; or, if these failed them, by their own incurable blood feuds.

Nature had so divided the country into zones. Men, elaborating nature, had given to her compartments an additional complexity. Each of these main north-and-south strip divisions was crossed and walled off artificially into communitites at odds. We had to gather them into our hands for offensive action against the Turks. Feisal's opportunities and difficulties lay in these political complications of Syria which we mentally arranged in order, like a social map.

In the very north, furthest from us, the language-boundary followed, not inaptly, the coach road from Alexandretta to Aleppo, until it met the Baghdad Railway, up which it went to the Euphrates valley; but enclaves of Turkish speech lay to the south of this general line in the Turkoman villages north and south of Antioch, and in the Armenians who were sifted in among them.

Otherwise, a main component of the coast population was the community of Ansariya, those disciples of a cult of fertility, sheer pagan, anti-foreign, distrustful of Islam, drawn at moments towards Christians by common persecution. The sect, vital in itself, was clannish in feeling and politics. One Nosairi would not betray another, and would hardly not betray an unbeliever. Their villages lay in patchets down the main hills to the Tripoli gap. They spoke Arabic, but had lived there since the beginning of Greek letters in Syria. Usually they stood aside from affairs, and left the Turkish Government alone in hope of reciprocity.

Mixed among the Ansariyeh were colonies of Syrian Christians; and in the bend of the Orontes had been some firm blocks of Armenians, inimical to Turkey. Inland, near Harim were Druses, Arabic in origin; and some Circassians from the Caucasus. These had their hand against all. North-east of them were Kurds, settlers of some generations back, who were marrying Arabs and adopting their politics. They hated native Christians most: and, after them, they hated Turks and Europeans.

Just beyond the Kurds existed a few Yezidis, Arabic-speaking, but in thought affected by the dualism of Iran, and prone to placate the spirit of evil. Christians, Mohammedans, and Jews, peoples who placed revelation before reason, united to spit upon Yezid. Inland of them stood Aleppo, a town of two hundred thousand people, an epitome of all Turkey's races and religions. Eastward of Aleppo, for sixty miles, were settled Arabs whose colour and manner became more and more tribal as they neared the fringe of cultivation where the semi-nomad ended and the Bedawi began.

A section across Syria from sea to desert, a degree further south, began in colonies of Moslem Circassians near the coast. In the new generation they spoke Arabic and were an ingenious race, but quarrelsome, much opposed by their Arab neighbours. Inland of them were Ismailiya. These Persian immigrants had turned Arab in the course of centuries, but revered among themselves one Mohammed, who, in the flesh, was the Agha Khan. They believed him to be a great and wonderful sovereign, honouring the English with his friendship. They shunned Moslems, but feebly hid their beastly opinions under a veneer of orthodoxy.

Beyond them were the strange sights of villages of Christian tribal Arabs, under sheikhs. They seemed very sturdy Christians, quite unlike their snivelling brethren in the hills. They lived as the Sunni about them, dressed like them, and were on the best terms with them. East of the Christians lay semi-pastoral Moslem communities; and on the last edge of cultivation, some villages of Ismailia outcasts, in search of the peace men would not grant. Beyond were Beduin.

A third section through Syria, another degree lower, fell between Tripoli and Beyrout. First, near the coast, were Lebanon Christians; for the most part Maronites or Greeks. It was hard to disentangle the politics of the two Churches. Superficially, one should have been French and one Russian; but a part of the population, to earn a living, had been in the United States, and there developed an Anglo-Saxon vein, not the less vigorous for being spurious. The Greek Church prided itself on being Old Syrian, autochthonous, of an intense localism which might ally it with Turkey rather than endure irretrievable domination by a Roman power.

The adherents of the two sects were at one in unmeasured slander, when they dared, of Mohammedans. Such verbal scorn seemed to salve their consciousness of inbred inferiority. Families of Moslems lived among them, identical in race and habit, except for a less mincing dialect, and less parade of emigration and its results.

On the higher slopes of the hills clustered settlements of Metawala, Shia Mohammedans from Persia generations ago. They were dirty, ignorant, surly and fanatical, refusing to eat or drink with infidels; holding the Sunni as bad as Christians; following only their own priests and notables. Strength of character was their virtue: a rare one in garrulous Syria. Over the hill-crest lay villages of Christian yeomen living in free peace with their Moslem neighbours as though they had never heard the grumbles of Lebanon. East of them were semi-nomad Arab peasantry; and then the open desert.

A fourth section, a degree southward, would have fallen near Acre, where the inhabitants, from the seashore, were first Sunni Arabs, then Druses, then Metawala. On the banks of the Jordan valley lived bitterly-suspicious colonies of Algerian refugees, facing villages of Jews. The Jews were of varied sorts. Some, Hebrew scholars of the traditionalist pattern, had developed a standard and style of living befitting the country: while the later comers, many of whom were German-inspired, had introduced strange manners, and strange crops, and European houses (erected out of charitable funds) into this land of Palestine, which seemed too small and too poor to repay in kind their efforts: but the land tolerated them. Galilee did not show the deep-seated antipathy to its Jewish colonists which was an unlovely feature of the neighbouring Judea.

Across the eastern plains (thick with Arabs) lay a labyrinth of crackled lava, the Leja, where the loose and broken men of Syria had forgathered for unnumbered generations. Their descendants lived there in lawless villages, secure from Turk and Beduin, and worked out their internecine feuds at leisure. South and south-west of them opened the Hauran, a huge fertile land; populous with warlike, self-reliant and prosperous Arab peasantry.

East of them were the Druses, heterodox Moslem followers of a mad and dead Sultan of Egypt. They hated Maronites with a bitter hatred; which, when encouraged by the Government and the fanatics of Damascus, found expression in great periodic killings. None the less the Druses were disliked by the Moslem Arabs and despised them in return. They were at feud with the Beduins, and preserved in their mountain a show of the chivalrous semi-feudalism of Lebanon in the days of their autonomous Emirs.

A fifth section in the latitude of Jerusalem would have begun with Germans and with German Jews, speaking German or German-Yiddish, more intractable even than the Jews of the Roman era, unable to endure contact with others not of their race, some of them farmers, most of them shopkeepers, the most foreign, uncharitable part of the whole population of Syria. Around them glowered their enemies, the sullen Palestine peasants, more stupid than the yeomen of North Syria, material as the Egyptians, and bankrupt.

East of them lay the Jordan depth, inhabited by charred serfs; and across it group upon group of self-respecting village Christians who were, after their agricultural co-religionists of the Orontes valley, the least timid examples of our original faith in the country. Among them and east of them were tens of thousands of semi-nomad Arabs, holding the creed of the desert, living on the fear and bounty of their Christian neighbours. Down this debatable land the Ottoman Government had planted a line of Circassian immigrants from the Russian Caucasus. These held their ground only by the sword and the favour of the Turks, to whom they were, of necessity, devoted.

CHAPTER LIX

THE tale of Syria was not ended in this count of odd races and religions. Apart from the country-folk, the six great towns — Jerusalem, Beyrout, Damascus, Homs, Hama, and Aleppo — were entities, each with its character, direction, and opinion. The southernmost, Jerusalem, was a squalid town, which every Semitic religion had made holy. Christians and Mohammedans came there on pilgrimage to the shrines of its past, and some Jews looked to it for the political future of their race. These united forces of the past and the future were so strong that the city almost failed to have a present. Its people, with rare exceptions, were characterless as hotel servants, living on the crowd of visitors passing through. Ideals of Arab nationality were far from them, though familiarity with the differences of Christians at their moment of most poignant sentience had led the classes of Jerusalem to despise us all.

Beyrout was altogether new. It would have been bastard French in feeling as in language but for its Greek harbour and American college. Public opinion in it was that of the Christian merchants, fat men living by exchange; for Beyrout itself produced nothing. The next strongest component was the class of returned emigrants, happy on invested savings in the town of Syria which most resembled that Washington Avenue where they had made good. Beyrout was the door of Syria, a chromatic Levantine screen through which cheap or shop-soiled foreign influences entered: it represented Syria as much as Soho the Home Counties.

Yet Beyrout, because of its geographical position, because of its schools, and the freedom engendered by intercourse with foreigners, had contained before the war a nucleus of people, talking, writing, thinking like the doctrinaire Cyclopædists who paved the way for revolution in France. For their sake, and for its wealth, and its exceeding loud and ready voice, Beyrout was to be reckoned with.

Damascus, Homs, Hama and Aleppo were the four ancient cities in which native Syria took pride. They stretched like a chain along the fertile valleys between the desert and the hills. Because of their setting they turned their backs upon the sea and looked eastward. They were Arab, and knew themselves such. Of them, and of Syria, Damascus was the inevitable head; the seat of lay government; and the religious centre. Its sheikhs were leaders of opinion, more 'Meccan' than others elsewhere. Its fresh and turbulent citizens, always willing to strike, were as extreme in thought and word as in pleasure. The city boasted to move before any part of Syria. The Turks made it military head-quarters, just as certainly as the Arab Opposition, and Oppenheim, and Sheikh Shawish there established themselves. Damascus was a lode-star to which Arabs were naturally drawn: a capital which would not smoothly be subservient to any alien race.

Homs and Hama were twins disliking one another. All in them manufactured things: in Homs often cotton and wool, in Hama brocaded silks. Their industries were prosperous and increasing, their merchants quick to find new outlets, or to meet new tastes, in North Africa, the Balkans, Asia Minor, Arabia, Mesopotamia. They demonstrated the productive ability of Syria, unguided by foreigners, as Beyrout proved its skill in distribution. Yet while the prosperity of Beyrout made it Levantine, the prosperity of Homs and Hama reinforced their localism; made them more firmly native, more jealously native. Almost it seemed as though familiarity with plant and power taught people that their fathers' manners were best.

Aleppo was a great city in Syria, but not of it, nor of Anatolia, nor of Mesopotamia. There the races, creeds, and tongues of the Ottoman Empire met and knew one another in a spirit of compromise. The clash of characteristics, which made its streets a kaleidoscope, imbued the Aleppine with a lewd thoughtfulness which corrected in him what was blatant in the Damascene. Aleppo had shared in all the civilizations which turned about it: the result seemed to be a lack of zest in its people's belief. Even so, they surpassed the rest of Syria. They fought and traded more; were more fanatical and vicious; and made most beautiful things: but all with a dearth of conviction which rendered barren their multitudinous strength.

It was typical of Aleppo that in it, while yet Mohammedan feeling ran high, more fellowship should rule between Christian and Mohammedan, Armenian, Arab, Turk, Kurd, and Jew, than in perhaps any other great city of the Ottoman Empire, and that more friendliness, though little licence, should have been accorded to Europeans. Politically, the town stood aside altogether, save in Arab quarters which, like overgrown half-nomad villages scattered over with priceless mediæval mosques, extended east and south of the mural crown of its great citadel. The intensity of their self-sown patriotism tinged the bulk of the citizens outside them with a colour of local consciousness which was by so much less vivid than the Beyrout-acquired unanimity of Damascus.

All these people of Syria were open to us by the master-key of their common Arabic language. Their distinctions were political and religious: morally they differed only in the steady gradation from neurotic sensibility on the sea coast to reserve inland. They were quick-minded; admirers, but not seekers of truth; self-satisfied; not (like the Egyptians) helpless before abstract ideas, but unpractical; and so lazy in mind as to be habitually superficial. Their ideal was ease in which to busy themselves with others' affairs.

From childhood they were lawless, obeying their fathers only from physical fear; and their government later for much the same reason: yet few races had the respect of the upland Syrian for customary law. All of them wanted something new, for with their superficiality and lawlessness went a passion for politics, a science fatally easy for the Syrian to smatter, but too difficult for him to master. They were discontented always with what government they had; such being their intellectual pride; but few of them honestly thought out a working alternative, and fewer still agreed upon one.

In settled Syria there was no indigenous political entity larger than the village, in patriarchal Syria nothing more complex than the clan; and these units were informal and voluntary, devoid of sanction, with heads indicated from the entitled families only by the slow cementing of public opinion. All higher constitution was the imported bureau-system of the Turk, in practice either fairly good or very bad according to the frailty of the human instruments (generally gendarmes) through which, in the last resort, it worked.

The people, even the best-taught, showed a curious blindness to the unimportance of their country, and a misconception of the selfishness of great powers whose normal course was to consider their own interests before those of unarmed races. Some cried aloud for an Arab kingdom. These were usually Moslems; and the Catholic Christians would counter them by demanding European protection of a thelemic order, conferring privileges without obligation. Both proposals were, of course, far from the hearts of the national groups, who cried for autonomy for Syria, having a knowledge of what autonomy was, but not knowing Syria; for in Arabic there was no such name, nor any name for all the country any of them meant. The verbal poverty of their Rome-borrowed name indicated a political disintegration. Between town and town, village and village, family and family, creed and creed, existed intimate jealousies sedulously fostered by the Turks.

Time seemed to have proclaimed the impossibility of autonomous union for such a land. In history, Syria had been a corridor between sea and desert, joining Africa to Asia, Arabia to Europe. It had been a prize-ring, a vassal, of Anatolia, of Greece, of Rome, of Egypt, of Arabia, of Persia, of Mesopotamia. When given a momentary independence by the weakness of neighbours it had fiercely resolved into discordant northern, southern, eastern and western 'kingdoms' with the area at best of Yorkshire, at worst of Rutland; for if Syria was by nature a vassal country it was also by habit a country of tireless agitation and incessant revolt.

The master-key of opinion lay in the common language: where also, lay the key of imagination. Moslems whose mother tongue was Arabic looked upon themselves for that reason as a chosen people. Their heritage of the Koran and classical literature held the Arabic-speaking peoples together. Patriotism, ordinarily of soil or race, was warped to a language.

A second buttress of a polity of Arab motive was the dim glory of the early Khalifate, whose memory endured among the people through centuries of Turkish misgovernment. The accident that these traditions savoured rather of the Arabian Nights than of sheer history maintained the Arab rank and file in their conviction that their past was more splendid than the present of the Ottoman Turk.

Yet we knew that these were dreams. Arab Government in Syria, though buttressed on Arabic prejudices, would be as much 'imposed' as the Turkish Government, or a foreign protectorate, or the historic Caliphate. Syria remained a vividly coloured racial and religious mosaic. Any wide attempt after unity would make a patched and parcelled thing, ungrateful to a people whose instincts ever returned towards parochial home rule.

Our excuse for over-running expediency was War. Syria, ripe for spasmodic local revolt, might be seethed up into insurrection, if a new factor, offering to realize that centripetal nationalism of the Beyrout Cyclopædists, arose to restrain the jarring sects and classes. Novel the factor must be, to avoid raising a jealousy of itself: not foreign, since the conceit of Syria forbade.

Within our sight the only independent factor with acceptable groundwork and fighting adherents was a Sunni prince, like Feisal, pretending to revive the glories of Ommayad or Ayubid. He might momentarily combine the inland men until success came with its need to transfer their debauched enthusiasm to the service of ordered government. Then would come reaction; but only after victory; and for victory everything material and moral might be pawned.

There remained the technique and direction of the new revolts: but the direction a blind man could see. The critical centre of Syria in all ages had been the Yarmuk Valley, Hauran, and Deraa. When Hauran joined us our campaign would be well ended. The process should be to set up another ladder of tribes, comparable to that from Wejh to Akaba: only this time our ladder would be made of steps of Howeitat, Beni Sakhr, Sherarat, Rualla, and Serahin, to raise us three hundred miles to Azrak, the oasis nearest Hauran and Jebel Druse.

In character our operations of development for the final stroke should be like naval war, in mobility, ubiquity, independence of bases and communications, ignoring of ground features, of strategic areas, of fixed directions, of fixed points. 'He who commands the sea is at great liberty, and may take as much or as little of the war as he will.' And we commanded the desert. Camel raiding parties, self-contained like ships, might cruise confidently along the enemy's cultivation-frontier, sure of an unhindered retreat into their desert-element which the Turks could not explore.

Discrimination of what point of the enemy organism to disarrange would come to us with war practice. Our tactics should be tip and run: not pushes, but strokes. We should never try to improve an advantage. We should use the smallest force in the quickest time at the farthest place.

The necessary speed and range for distant war we would attain through the frugality of the desert men, and their efficiency on camels. The camel, that intricate, prodigious piece of nature, in expert hands yielded a remarkable return. On them we were independent of supply for six weeks, if each man had a half-bag of flour, forty-five pounds in weight, slung on his riding-saddle.

Of water we would not want to carry more than a pint each. The camels must drink, and there was no gain in making ourselves richer than our mounts. Some of us never drank between wells, but those were hardy men: most drank fully at each well, and carried a drink for an intermediate dry day. In summer the camels would do about two hundred and fifty miles after a watering; a three days' vigorous march. An easy stage was fifty miles: eighty was good: in an emergency we might do one hundred and ten miles in the twenty-four hours: twice the Ghazala, our greatest camel, did one hundred and forty-three alone with me. Wells were seldom a hundred miles apart, so the pint reserve was latitude enough.

Our six weeks' food gave us capacity for a thousand miles out and home. The endurance of our camels made it possible for us (for me, the camel-novice in the army, 'painful' would be the fitter word) to ride fifteen hundred miles in thirty days, without fear of starvation; because, even if we exceeded in time, each of us sat on two hundred pounds of potential meat, and the man made camel-less could double-bank another, riding two-up, in emergency.

The equipment of the raiding parties should aim at simplicity; with, nevertheless, a technical superiority over the Turks in the critical department. I sent to Egypt demands for great quantities of light automatic guns, Hotchkiss or Lewis, to be used as snipers' tools. The men we trained to them were kept deliberately ignorant of the mechanism, not to waste speed in action upon efforts at repair. Ours were battles of minutes, fought at eighteen miles an hour. If a gun jammed, the gunner must throw it aside and go in with his rifle.

Another distinguishing feature might be high explosives. We evolved special dynamite methods, and by the end of the war could demolish any quantity of track and bridges with economy and safety. Allenby was generous with explosive. It was only guns we never got until the last month — and the pity of it! In manœuvre war one long-range gun outweighed ninety-nine short.

The distribution of the raiding parties was unorthodox. We could not mix or combine tribes, because of their distrusts: nor could we use one in the territory of another. In compensation we aimed at the widest dissipation of force; and we added fluidity to speed by using one district on Monday, another on Tuesday, a third on Wednesday. Thus natural mobility was reinforced. In pursuit, our ranks refilled with fresh men at each new tribe, and maintained the pristine energy. In a real sense maximum disorder was our equilibrium.

The internal economy of our raiding parties achieved irregularity and extreme articulation. Our circumstances were not twice similar, so no system could fit them twice: and our diversity threw the enemy intelligence off the track. By identical battalions and divisions information built itself up, until a corps could be inferred on corpses from three companies. Our strengths depended upon whim.

We were serving a common ideal, without tribal emulation, and so could not hope for *esprit de corps*. Ordinary soldiers were made a caste either by great rewards in pay, dress and privilege: or by being cut off from life by contempt. We could not so knit man to man, for our tribesmen were in arms willingly. Many armies had been voluntarily enlisted: few served voluntarily. Any of our Arabs could go home without penalty whenever the conviction failed him: the only contract was honour.

Consequently we had no discipline in the sense in which it was restrictive, submergent of individuality, the Lowest Common Denominator of men. In peace-armies discipline meant the hunt, not of an average but of an absolute; the hundred per cent standard in which the ninety-nine were played down to the level of the weakest man on parade. The aim was to render the unit a unit, the man a type; in order that their effort might be calculable, and the collective output even in grain and bulk. The deeper the discipline, the lower was the individual excellence; also the more sure the performance.

By this substitution of a sure job for a possible masterpiece, military science made a deliberate sacrifice of capacity in order to reduce the uncertain element, the bionomic factor, in enlisted humanity. Discipline's necessary accompaniment was compound or social war — that form in which the fighting man was the product of the multiplied exertions of a long hierarchy, from workshop to supply unit, which kept him active in the field.

The Arab war should react against this, and be simple and individual. Every enrolled man should serve in the line of battle and be self-contained there. The efficiency of our forces was the personal efficiency of the single man. It seemed to me that, on our articulated war, the sum yielded by single men would at least equal the product of a compound system of the same strength.

In practice we should not employ in the firing line the great numbers which a simple system put theoretically at our disposal, lest our attack (as contrasted with our threat) become too extended. The moral strain of isolated fighting made 'simple' war very hard upon the soldier, exacting from him special initiative, endurance, enthusiasm. Irregular war was far more intellectual than a bayonet charge, far more exhausting than service in the comfortable imitative obedience of an ordered army. Guerillas must be allowed liberal work room: in irregular war, of two men together, one was being wasted. Our ideal should be to make our battle a series of single combats, our ranks a happy alliance of agile commanders-in-chief.

CHAPTER LX

VESSELS steamed up the Gulf of Akaba. Feisal landed, and with him Jaafar, his staff, and Joyce, the fairy godmother. There came the armoured cars, Goslett, Egyptian labourers and thousands of troops. To repair the six weeks' peace, Falkenhayn had been down to advise the Turks, and his fine intelligence made them worthier our opposition. Maan was a special command, under Behjet, the old G.O.C. Sinai. He had six thousand infantry, a regiment of cavalry and mounted infantry, and had entrenched Maan till it was impregnable according to the standard of manœuvre war. A flight of aeroplanes operated daily thence. Great supply dumps had been collected.

By now the Turkish preparations were complete; they began to move, disclosing that their objective was Guweira, the best road for Akaba. Two thousand infantry pushed out to Aba el Lissan, and fortified it. Cavalry kept the outskirts, to contain a possible Arab counter-stroke from the Wadi Musa side.

This nervousness was our cue. We would play with them and provoke them to go for us in Wadi Musa, where the natural obstacles were so tremendous that the human defending factor might behave as badly as it liked, and yet hold the place against attack.

To bait the hook, the men of neighbouring Delagha were set busy. The Turks, full of spirit, put in a counter-stroke, and suffered sharply. We rubbed into the peasantry of Wadi Musa the rich booty now enjoyed by their rivals of Delagha. Maulud, the old war-horse, went up with his mule-mounted regiment, and quartered himself among the famous ruins of Petra. The encouraged Liathena, under their one-eyed sheikh, Khalil, began to foray out across the plateau, and to snap up by twos and threes Turkish riding or transport animals, together with the rifles of their occasional guards. This went on for weeks, while the irritated Turks grew hotter and hotter.

We could also prick the Turks into discomfort by asking General Salmond for his promised long-distance air raid on Maan. As it was difficult, Salmond had chosen Stent, with other tried pilots of Rabegh or Wejh, and told them to do their best. They had experience of forced landing on desert surfaces and could pick out an unknown destination across unmapped hills: Stent spoke Arabic perfectly. The flight had to be air-contained, but its commander was full of resource and display, like other bundles of nerves, who, to punish themselves, did outrageous things. On this occasion he ordered low flying, to make sure the aim; and profited by reaching Maan, and dropping thirty-two bombs in and about the unprepared station. Two bombs into the barracks killed thirty-five men and wounded fifty. Eight struck the engine-shed, heavily damaging the plant and stock. A bomb in the General's kitchen finished his cook and his breakfast. Four fell on the aerodrome. Despite the shrapnel our pilots and engines returned safely to their temporary landing ground at Kuntilla above Akaba.

That afternoon they patched the machines, and after dark slept under their wings. In the following dawn they were off once more, three of them this time, to Aba el Lissan, where the sight of the great camp had made Stent's mouth water. They bombed the horselines and stampeded the animals, visited the tents and scattered the Turks. As on the day before, they flew low and were much hit, but not fatally. Long before noon they were back in Kuntilla.

Stent looked over the remaining petrol and bombs, and decided they were enough for one more effort. So he gave directions to everyone to look for the battery which had troubled them in the morning. They started in the midday heat. Their loads were so heavy they could get no height, and therefore came blundering over the crest behind Aba el Lissan, and down the valley at about three hundred feet. The Turks always somnolent at noon, were taken completely by surprise. Thirty bombs were dropped: one silenced the battery, the others killed dozens of men and animals. Then the lightened machines soared up and home to El Arish. The Arabs rejoiced: the Turks were seriously alarmed. Behjet Pasha set his men to digging shelters, and when his aeroplanes had been repaired, he disposed them innocuously about the plateau for camp defence.

By air we had perturbed the Turks: by irritative raids we were luring them towards a wrong objective. Our third resource to ruin their offensive was to hinder the railway, whose need would make them split up the striking force on defensive duties. Accordingly we arranged many demolitions for mid-September.

I decided also to revive the old idea of mining a train. Something more vigorous and certain than automatic mines was indicated, and I had imagined a direct firing, by electricity, of a charge under the locomotive. The British sappers encouraged me to try, especially General Wright, the chief engineer in Egypt, whose experience took a sporting interest in my irregularities. He sent me the recommended tools: an exploder and some insulated cable. With them I went on board H.M.S. *Humber*, our new guard-ship, and introduced myself to Captain Snagge, in command.

Snagge was fortunate in his ship, which had been built for Brazil, and was much more comfortably furnished than British monitors; and we were doubly fortunate in him and in this, for he was the spirit of hospitality. His inquiring nature took interest in the shore, and saw the comic side even of our petty disasters. To tell him the story of a failure was to laugh at it, and always for a good story he gave me a hot bath, and tea with civilized trappings, free from every suspicion of blown sand. His kindness and help served us in lieu of visits to Egypt for repairs, and enabled us to hammer on against the Turks through month after month of feckless disappointment.

The exploder was in a formidable locked white box, very heavy. We split it open, found a ratchet handle, and pushed it down without harming the ship. The wire was heavy rubber-insulated cable. We cut it in half, fastened the ends to screw terminals on the box, and transmitted shocks to one another convincingly. It worked.

I fetched detonators. We stuffed the free ends of the cable into one and pumped the handle: nothing followed. We tried again and again ineffectually, grieving over it. At last Snagge rang his bell for the gunner warrant officer who knew all about circuits. He suggested special electric detonators. The ship carried six, and gave me three of them. We joined one up with our box, and when the handle was crashed down it popped off beautifully. So I felt that I knew all about it and turned to arrange the details of the raid.

Of targets, the most promising and easiest-reached seemed Mudowwara, a water station eighty miles south of Maan. A smashed train there would embarrass the enemy. For men, I would have the tried Howeitat; and, at the same time, the expedition would test the three Haurani peasants whom I had added to my personal followers. In view of the new importance of the Hauran, there was need for us to learn its dialect, the construction and jealousies of its clan-framework, and its names and roads. These three fellows, Rahail, Assaf and Hemeid, would teach me their home-affairs imperceptibly, as we rode on business, chatting.

To make sure of the arrested train required guns and machine-guns. For the first, why not trench-mortars? For the second, Lewis guns? Accordingly, Egypt chose two forceful sergeant-instructors from the Army School at Zeitun, to teach squads of Arabs in Akaba how to use such things. Snagge gave them quarters in his ship, since we had, as yet, no convenient English camp ashore.

Their names may have been Yells and Brooke, but became Lewis and Stokes after their jealously-loved tools. Lewis was an Australian, long, thin and sinuous, his supple body lounging in unmilitary curves. His hard face, arched eyebrows, and predatory nose set off the peculiarly Australian air of reckless willingness and capacity to do something very soon. Stokes was a stocky English yeoman, workmanlike and silent; always watching for an order to obey.

Lewis, full of suggestion, emerged bursting with delight at what had been well done whenever a thing happened. Stokes never offered opinion until after action, when he would stir his cap reflectively, and painstakingly recount the mistakes he must next time avoid. Both were admirable men. In a month, without common language or interpreter, they got on terms with their classes and taught them their empirical habit appeared to agree with the spirit of our haphazard raids better than complete scientific knowledge.

As we worked at the organization of the raid, our appetites rose. Mudowwara station sounded vulnerable. Three hundred men might rush it suddenly. That would be an achievement, for its deep well was the only one in the dry sector below Maan. Without its water, the train service across the gap would become uneconomic in load.

CHAPTER LXI

Lewis, the Australian, at such an ambitious moment, said that he and Stokes would like to be of my party. A new, attractive idea. With them we should feel sure of our technical detachments, whilst attacking a garrisoned place. Also, the sergeants wanted to go very much, and their good work deserved reward. They were warned that their experiences might not at the moment seem altogether joyful. There were no rules; and there could be no mitigation of the marching, feeding, and fighting, inland. If they went they would lose their British Army comfort and privilege, to share and share with the Arabs (except in booty!) and suffer exactly their hap in food and discipline. If anything went wrong with me, they, not speaking Arabic, would be in a tender position.

Lewis replied that he was looking for just this strangeness of life. Stokes supposed that if we did it, he could. So they were lent two of my best camels (their saddle-bags tight with bully-beef and biscuits) and on September the seventh we went together up Wadi Itm, to collect our Howeitat from Auda in Guweira.

For the sergeants' sake, to harden them gently, things were made better than my word. We marched very easily for to-day, while we were our own masters. Neither had been on a camel before, and there was risk that the fearful heat of the naked granite walls of Itm might knock them out before the trip had properly begun. September was a bad month. A few days before, in the shade of the palm-gardens of Akaba beach, the thermometer had shown a hundred and twenty degrees. So we halted for midday under a cliff, and in the evening rode only ten miles to camp for the night.

We were comfortable with cans of hot tea, and rice and meat; and it was covertly enjoyable to watch the percussion of their surroundings on the two men. Each reacted to the type expected.

The Australian from the first seemed at home, and behaved freely towards the Arabs. When they fell into his spirit, and returned the fellowship, he was astonished: almost resentful: having never imagined

353

that they would be misled by his kindness to forget the difference between a white man and a brown.

It added humour to the situation that he was browner by far than my new followers, of whom the youngest interested me most. He, Rahail, was quite a lad: a free-built, sturdy fellow, too fleshy for the life we were to lead, but for that the more tolerant of pains. His face was high-coloured; his cheeks a little full and low-pouched, almost pendent. The mouth was budded and small, the chin very pointed. This, added to the high, strong brows and antimony-enlarged eyes, gave him a mixed air of artifice and petulance, with weary patience self-imposed upon a base of pride. He was blowsy-spoken (mouthing his Arabic); vulgar in dialect; forward and impudent in speech; always thrusting, flaunting, restless and nervous. His spirit was not as strong as his body, but mercurial. When exhausted or cross he broke into miserable tears easily chased away by any interference; and after, was fit for more endurance. My followers, Mohammed and Ahmed, with Rashid and Assaf, the probationers, gave Rahail much licence of behaviour; partly because of his animal attractiveness, and of his tendency to advertise his person. He had to be checked once or twice for taking liberties with the sergeants.

Stokes, the Englishman, was driven by the Arab strangeness to become more himself, more insular. His shy correctness reminded my men in every movement that he was unlike them, and English. Such consideration elicited a return of respect. To them he was 'the sergeant', while Lewis was 'the long one'.

These were points of character, which all showed in their degree. It was humiliating to find that our book-experience of all countries and ages still left us prejudiced like washerwomen, but without their verbal ability to get on terms with strangers. The Englishmen in the Middle East divided into two classes. Class one, subtle and insinuating, caught the characteristics of the people about him, their speech, their conventions of thought, almost their manner. He directed men secretly, guiding them as he would. In such frictionless habit of influence his own nature lay hid, unnoticed.

Class two, the John Bull of the books, became the more rampantly English the longer he was away from England. He invented an Old

Country for himself, a home of all remembered virtues, so splendid in the distance that, on return, he often found reality a sad falling off and withdrew his muddle-headed self into fractious advocacy of the good old times. Abroad, through his armoured certainty, he was a rounded sample of our traits. He showed the complete Englishman. There was friction in his track, and his direction was less smooth than that of the intellectual type: yet his stout example cut wider swathe.

Both sorts took the same direction in example, one vociferously, the other by implication. Each assumed the Englishman a chosen being, inimitable, and the copying him blasphemous or impertinent. In this conceit they urged on people the next best thing. God had not given it them to be English; a duty remained to be good of their type. Consequently we admired native custom; studied the language; wrote books about its architecture, folklore, and dying industries. Then one day, we woke up to find this chthonic spirit turned political, and shook our heads with sorrow over its ungrateful nationalism — truly the fine flower of our innocent efforts.

The French, though they started with a similar doctrine of the Frenchman as the perfection of mankind (dogma amongst them, not secret instinct), went on, contrarily, to encourage their subjects to imitate them; since, even if they could never attain the true level, yet their virtue would be greater as they approached it. We looked upon imitation as a parody; they as a compliment.

Next day, in the early heat, we were near Guweira, comfortably crossing the sanded plain of restful pink with its grey-green undergrowth, when there came a droning through the air. Quickly we drove the camels off the open road into the bush-speckled ground, where their irregular colouring would not be marked by the enemy airmen; for the loads of blasting gelatine, my favourite and most powerful explosive, and the many ammonal-filled shells of the Stokes' gun would be ill neighbours in a bombing raid. We waited there, soberly, in the saddle while our camels grazed the little which was worth eating in the scrub, until the aeroplane had circled twice about the rock of Guweira in front of us, and planted three loud bombs.

We collected our caravan again on the path and paced gently into camp. Guweira was thronged with life, and a mart for the Howeitat of both hills and highlands. As far as the eye reached the plain was softly moving with herded camels, whose multitude drained the near water-holes each morning before dawn, so that late risers must travel many miles to drink.

This was little matter, for the Arabs had nothing to do but wait for the morning aeroplane; and after its passing, nothing but talk to kill time till night was full enough for sleep. The talk and leisure were too plentiful and had revived old jealousies. Auda was ambitious to take advantage of our dependence on his help to assort the tribes. He drew the bulk-wages for the Howeitat; and, by the money, sought to compel the smaller free-sections to his leadership.

They resented it, and were threatening either to retire into their hills or to re-open touch with the Turks. Feisal sent up Sherif Mastur as mediator. The thousands of Howeitat, in hundreds of sections, were uncompromising, hard-headed, greedy land-lawyers. To hold them content without angering Auda was task delicate enough for the most fastidious mind. Also, it was one hundred and ten degrees in the shade, and the shade was a surge of flies.

The three southern clans on whom we had been counting for our raid were among the dissidents. Mastur spoke to them, the chiefs of the Abu Tayi spoke, we all spoke, without effect. It seemed as though our plans were to break down at the start.

One day, going along before noon under the rock, Mastur met me with news that the southerners were mounting to desert our camp and movement. Full of vexation, I swung round into Auda's tent. He sat on its sand-floor, feeding on boiled bread with his latest wife, a jolly girl, whose brown skin was blue with the indigo dye from her new smock. When I suddenly burst in, the little woman whisked away through the back-flap like a rabbit. To gain ground with him, I began to jeer at the old man for being so old and yet so foolish like the rest of his race, who regarded our comic reproductive processes not as an unhygienic pleasure, but as a main business of life.

Auda retorted with his desire for heirs. I asked if he had found life good enough to thank his haphazard parents for bringing him into it? or selfishly to confer the doubtful gift upon an unborn spirit?

He maintained himself. 'Indeed, I am Auda,' said he, firmly, 'and you know Auda. My father (to whom God be merciful) was master, greater than Auda; and he would praise my grandfather. The world is greater as we go back.' 'But, Auda, we say honour our sons and daughters, the heirs of our accumulated worth, fulfillers of our broken wisdom. With each generation the earth is older, mankind more removed from its childhood . . .'

The old thing, not to-day to be teased, looked at me through his narrowed eyes with a benign humour, and pointed to Abu Tayi, his son, out on the plain before us trying a new camel, banging it on the neck with his stick in vain effort to make it pace like a thoroughbred. 'O world's imp,' said he, 'if God please he has inherited my worth, but thank God not yet my strength; and if I find fault with him I will redden his tail. No doubt you are very wise.' The upshot of our talk was that I should go off to a clean spot, to wait events. We hired twenty camels to carry the explosives; and the morrow, two hours after the aeroplane, was fixed for our start.

The aeroplane was the quaint regulator of public business in the Guweira camp. The Arabs, up as ever before dawn, waited for it: Mastur set a slave on the crag's peak to sound the first warning. When its constant hour drew near the Arabs would saunter, chatting in parade of carelessness, towards the rock. Arrived beneath it, each man climbed to the ledge he favoured. After Mastur would climb the bevy of his slaves, with his coffee on the brazier, and his carpet. In a shaded nook he and Auda would sit and talk till the little shiver of excitement tightened up and down the crowded ledges when first was heard the song of the engine over the pass of Shtar.

Everyone pressed back against the wall and waited stilly while the enemy circled vainly above the strange spectacle of this crimson rock banded with thousands of gaily-dressed Arabs, nesting like ibises in every cranny of its face. The aeroplane dropped three bombs, or four bombs, or five bombs, according to the day of the week. Their bursts of dense smoke sat on the sage-green plain compactly like cream-puffs; writhing for minutes in the windless air before they slowly spread and faded. Though we knew there was no menace in it, yet we could not but catch our breath when the sharp-growing cry of the falling bombs came through the loud engine overhead.

CHAPTER LXII

GLADLY we left the noise and heart-burning of Guweira. So soon as we had lost our escort of flies we halted: indeed there was no need of haste, and the two unfortunate fellows with me were tasting of such heat as they had never known; for the stifling air was like a metal mask over our faces. It was admirable to see them struggle not to speak of it, that they might keep the spirit of the Akaba undertaking to endure as firmly as the Arabs; but by this silence the sergeants went far past their bond. It was ignorance of Arabic which made them so superfluously brave, for the Arabs themselves were loud against the tyrannous sun and the breathlessness; but the test-effect was wholesome; and, for effect, I played about, seeming to enjoy myself.

In the late afternoon we marched further and stopped for the night under a thick screen of tamarisk-trees. The camp was very beautiful, for behind us rose a cliff, perhaps four hundred feet in height, a deep red in the level sunset. Under our feet was spread a floor of buff-coloured mud, as hard and muffled as wood-paving, flat like a lake for half a mile each way: and on a low ridge to one side of it stood the grove of tamarisk-stems of brown wood, edged with a sparse and dusty fringe of green, which had been faded by drought and sunshine till it was nearly of the silvered grey below the olive-leaves about Les Baux when a wind from the river-mouth rustled up the valley-grass and made the trees turn pale.

We were riding for Rumm, the northern water of the Beni Atiyeh: a place which stirred my thought, as even the unsentimental Howeitat had told me it was lovely. The morrow would be new with our entry to it: but very early while the stars were yet shining, I was roused by Aid, the humble Harithi Sherif accompanying us. He crept to me, and said in a chilled voice, 'Lord, I am gone blind.' I made him lie down, and felt that he shivered as if cold; but all he could tell me was that in the night, waking up, there had been no sight, only pain in his eyes. The sun-blink had burned them out.

Day was still young as we rode between two great pikes of sandstone to the foot of a long, soft slope poured down from the domed hills in front of us. It was tamarisk-covered: the beginning of the Valley of Rumm, they said. We looked up on the left to a long wall of rock, sheering in like a thousand-foot wave towards the middle of the valley; whose other arc, to the right, was an opposing line of steep, red broken hills. We rode up the slope, crashing our way through the brittle undergrowth.

As we went, the brushwood grouped itself into thickets whose massed leaves took on a stronger tint of green the purer for their contrasted setting in plots of open sand of a cheerful delicate pink. The ascent became gentle, till the valley was a confined tilted plain. The hills on the right grew taller and sharper, a fair counterpart of the other side which straightened itself to one massive rampart of redness. They drew together until only two miles divided them: and then, towering gradually till their parallel parapets must have been a thousand feet above us, ran forward in an avenue for miles.

They were not unbroken walls of rock, but were built sectionally, in crags like gigantic buildings, along the two sides of their street. Deep alleys, fifty feet across, divided the crags, whose plans were smoothed by the weather into huge apses and bays, and enriched with surface fretting and fracture, like design. Caverns high up on the precipice were round like windows: others near the foot gaped like doors. Dark stains ran down the shadowed front for hundreds of feet, like accidents of use. The cliffs were striated vertically, in their granular rock; whose main order stood on two hundred feet of broken stone deeper in colour and harder in texture. This plinth did not, like the sandstone, hang in folds like cloth; but chipped itself into loose courses of scree, horizontal as the footings of a wall.

The crags were capped in nests of domes, less hotly red than the body of the hill; rather grey and shallow. They gave the finishing semblance of Byzantine architecture to this irresistible place: this processional way greater than imagination. The Arab armies would have been lost in the length and breadth of it, and within the walls a squadron of aeroplanes could have wheeled in formation. Our little caravan grew self-conscious, and fell dead quiet, afraid and ashamed to flaunt its smallness in the presence of the stupendous hills.

Landscapes, in childhood's dream, were so vast and silent. We looked backward through our memory for the prototype up which all men had walked between such walls toward such an open square as that in front where this road seemed to end. Later, when we were often riding inland, my mind used to turn me from the direct road, to clear my senses by a night in Rumm and by the ride down its dawn-lit valley towards the shining plains, or up its valley in the sunset towards that glowing square which my timid anticipation never let me reach. I would say, 'Shall I ride on this time, beyond the Khazail, and know it all?' But in truth I liked Rumm too much.

To-day we rode for hours while the perspectives grew greater and more magnificent in ordered design, till a gap in the cliff-face opened on our right to a new wonder. The gap, perhaps three hundred yards across, was a crevice in such a wall; and led to an amphitheatre, oval in shape, shallow in front, and long-lobed right and left. The walls were precipices, like all the walls of Rumm; but appeared greater, for the pit lay in the very heart of a ruling hill, and its smallness made the besetting heights seem overpowering.

The sun had sunk behind the western wall, leaving the pit in shadow; but its dying glare flooded with startling red the wings each side of the entry, and the fiery bulk of the further wall across the great valley. The pit-floor was of damp sand, darkly wooded with shrubs; while about the feet of all the cliffs lay boulders greater than houses, sometimes, indeed, like fortresses which had crashed down from the heights above. In front of us a path, pale with use, zigzagged up the cliff-plinth to the point from which the main face rose, and there it turned precariously southward along a shallow ledge outlined by occasional leafy trees. From between these trees, in hidden crannies of the rock, issued strange cries; the echoes, turned into music, of the voices of the Arabs watering camels at the springs which there flowed out three hundred feet above ground.

The rains, falling on the grey domes of the hill-top, seemed to have soaked slowly into the porous rock; and my mind followed them, filtering inch by inch downward through those mountains of sandstone till they came against the impervious horizontal layer of the plinth, and ran along its top under pressure, in jets which burst out on the cliff-face at the junction of the two rocky layers.

Mohammed turned into the amphitheatre's left hand lobe. At its far end Arab ingenuity had cleared a space under an overhanging rock: there we unloaded and settled down. The dark came upon us quickly in this high prisoned place; and we felt the water-laden air cold against our sunburnt skin. The Howeitat, who had looked after the loads of explosive collected their camel drove, and led them with echo-testing shouts up the hill-path to water against their early return to Guweira. We lit fires and cooked rice to add to the sergeants' bully-beef, while my coffee men prepared for the visitors who would come to us.

The Arabs in the tents outside the hollow of the springs had seen us enter, and were not slow to learn our news. In an hour we had the head men of the Darausha, Zelebani, Zuweida and Togatga clans about us; and there mounted great talk, none too happy. Aid, the Sherif, was too cast down in heart by his blindness to lift the burden of entertainment from my shoulders; and a work of such special requirements was not to be well done by me. These smaller clans, angry with the Abu Tayi, suspected us of abetting Auda in his ambition to win a predominance over them. They were unwilling to serve the Sherif till assured of his support of their extremest claims.

Gasim abu Dumeik, the fine horseman who had led the highland men on the day of Aba el Lissan, seemed particularly vicious. He was a dark man with an arrogant face and thin-lipped smile; good enough at heart, but crusted. To-day, he flamed with jealousy of the Toweiha. Alone, I could never win him, so to make patent his hostility I took him as adversary and fought him fiercely with my tongue till he was silenced. In shame his audience deserted him and rallied ever so little to my side. Their flickering judgements began to murmur at the chiefs, and to advocate marching off with me. I took the chance to say that Zaal would be here in the morning, and that he and I would accept the help of all except the Dhumaniyeh; who, made impossible by Gasim's words, would be erased from Feisal's book and forfeit their earned goodwill and rewards. Gasim, swearing he would join the Turks at once, withdrew from the fireside in great anger, while cautious friends tried vainly to stop his mouth.

CHAPTER LXIII

NEXT morning there he was, with his men, ready to join or oppose us, as the whim went. While he hesitated Zaal arrived. Gasim's dourness soon clashed upon Zaal's metallic cruelty, and the pair had high words. We got between them before a fight could start, but enough passed to overthrow the weak arrangement of the night. The other clans, disgusted at Gasim's fierceness, came to us quietly in twos and threes, as volunteers; but begged me to make their loyalty known to Feisal before we started.

Their doubts determined me to communicate at once with him, partly that this trouble might be composed, and partly to raise camels for carrying the explosives. To hire Dhumaniyeh camels would not be fitting; and there were no others here. The best way was to go myself; because while Gasim might stop a messenger, he would not dare hinder me. The two sergeants were commended to Zaal, who swore to answer for their lives; and off went Ahmed and myself on stripped camels, meaning to hurry to Akaba and back.

We knew only the very long way by Wadi Itm. A short cut existed, but we could find no guide to it. Vainly we searched up and down the valley; and were in despair when a boy blurted out that we should go along the next valley to our right. By it, after an hour, we were on a watershed from which valleys trended away westward. They could lead only into Wadi Itm, for there was no other drainage hereabouts through the hills to the sea; and we raced down them, ever and again cutting at a venture across ridges on our right into parallel tributaries, to shorten the assumed line.

In the beginning it was clean sandstone country, of pleasant rock-shapes: but as we went spines of granite, the material of the shore, rose up in front of us, and after thirty miles of good trotting gradient we passed, by the southern Itm, into the main valley, just above the well of the surrender of Akaba. The journey took us only six hours.

In Akaba we rode straight to Feisal's house. My sudden return scared him, but a word explained the little drama which was being played at Rumm. After we had fed we took the necessary steps. The twenty baggage camels should start up in two days with enough of Feisal's camel-men to transport the explosives, and a few of his personal slaves to guard them. He would lend me Sherif Abdulla el Feir, the best of his henchmen now in camp, as mediator. The families of the men who rode with me to the railway should draw provisions from his stores on my certificate.

Abdulla and I went off before dawn, and in the afternoon, after a friendly ride, reached Rumm to find all safe: so anxiety was lifted. Sherif Abdulla at once got to work. Having collected the Arabs, including the recalcitrant Gasim, he began to smooth over their griefs with that ready persuasiveness which was the birthmark of an Arab leader, and which all his experience served to whet.

In the idleness forced on him by our absence, Lewis had explored the cliff, and reported the springs very good for washing in; so, to get rid of the dust and strain after my long rides, I went straight up the gully into the face of the hill, along the ruined wall of the conduit by which a spout of water had once run down the ledges to a Nabataean well-house on the valley floor. It was a climb of fifteen minutes to a tired person, and not difficult. At the top, the waterfall, el Shellala as the Arabs named it, was only a few yards away.

Its rushing noise came from my left, by a jutting bastion of cliff over whose crimson face trailed long falling runners of green leaves. The path skirted it in an undercut ledge. On the rock-bulge above were clear-cut Nabathaean inscriptions, and a sunk panel incised with a monogram or symbol. Around and about were Arab scratches, including tribe-marks, some of which were witnesses of forgotten migrations: but my attention was only for the splashing of water in a crevice under the shadow of the overhanging rock.

From this rock a silver runlet issued into the sunlight. I looked in to see the spout, a little thinner than my wrist, jetting out firmly from a fissure in the roof, and falling with that clean sound into a shallow, frothing pool, behind the step which served as entrance. The walls and roof of the crevice dripped with moisture. Thick ferns and grasses of the finest green made it a paradise just five feet square.

Upon the water-cleansed and fragrant ledge I undressed my soiled body, and stepped into the little basin, to taste at last a freshness of moving air and water against my tired skin. It was deliciously cool. I lay there quietly, letting the clear, dark red water run over me in a ribbly stream, and rub the travel-dirt away. While I was so happy, a grey-bearded, ragged man, with a hewn face of great power and weariness, came slowly along the path till opposite the spring; and there he let himself down with a sigh upon my clothes spread out over a rock beside the path, for the sun-heat to chase out their thronging vermin.

He heard me and leaned forward, peering with rheumy eyes at this white thing splashing in the hollow beyond the veil of sun-mist. After a long stare he seemed content, and closed his eyes, groaning, 'The love is from God; and of God; and towards God.'

His low-spoken words were caught by some trick distinctly in my water pool. They stopped me suddenly. I had believed Semites unable to use love as a link between themselves and God, indeed, unable to conceive such a relation except with the intellectuality of Spinoza, who loved so rationally and sexlessly, and transcendently that he did not seek, or rather had not permitted, a return. Christianity had seemed to me the first creed to proclaim love in this upper world, from which the desert and the Semite (from Moses to Zeno) had shut it out: and Christianity was a hybrid, except in its first root not essentially Semitic.

Its birth in Galilee had saved it from being just one more of the innumerable revelations of the Semite. Galilee was Syria's non-Semitic province, contact with which was almost uncleanness for the perfect Jew. Like Whitechapel to London, it lay alien to Jerusalem. Christ by choice passed his ministry in its intellectual freedom; not among the mud-huts of a Syrian village, but in polished streets among fora and pillared houses and rococo baths, products of an intense if very exotic provincial and corrupt Greek civilization.

The people of this stranger-colony were not Greek — at least not in the majority — but Levantines of sorts, aping a Greek culture; and in revenge producing, not the correct banal Hellenism of the exhausted homeland, but a tropical rankness of idea, in which the rhythmical balance of Greek art and Greek ideality blossomed into novel shapes tawdry with the larded passionate colours of the East.

Gadarene poets, stuttering their verses in the prevailing excitement, held a mirror to the sensuality and disillusioned fatalism, passing into disordered lust, of their age and place; from whose earthiness the ascetic Semite religiosity perhaps caught the tang of humanity and real love that made the distinction of Christ's music, and fitted it to sweep across the hearts of Europe in a fashion which Judaism and Islam could not achieve.

And then Christianity had had the fortune of later architects of genius; and in its passage through time and clime had suffered sea-changes incomparably greater than the unchanging Jewry, from the abstraction of Alexandrian bookishness into Latin prose, for the mainland of Europe: and last and most terrible passing of all, when it became Teuton, with a formal synthesis to suit our chilly disputatious north. So remote was the Presbyterian creed from the Orthodox faith of its first or second embodiment that, before the war, we were able to send missionaries to persuade these softer Oriental Christians to our presentation of a logical God.

Islam, too, had inevitably changed from continent to continent. It had avoided metaphysics, except in the introspective mysticism of Iranian devotees: but in Africa it had taken on colours of fetishism (to express in a loose word the varied animalities of the dark continent), and in India, it had to stoop to the legality and literalism of its converts' minds. In Arabia, however, it had kept a Semitic character, or rather the Semitic character had endured through the phase of Islam (as through all the phases of the creeds with which the town-dwellers continually vested the simplicity of faith), expressing the monotheism of open spaces, the pass-through-infinity of pantheism and its everyday usefulness of an all-pervading, household God.

By contrast with this fixity, or with my reading of it, the old man of Rumm loomed portentous in his brief, single sentence, and seemed to overturn my theories of the Arab nature. In fear of a revelation, I put an end to my bath, and advanced to recover my clothes. He shut his eyes with his hands and groaned heavily. Tenderly I persuaded him to rise up and let me dress, and then to come with me along the crazy path which the camels had made in their climbing to and from the other water-springs. He sat down by our coffee-place, where Mohammed blew up the fire, while I sought to make him utter doctrine.

When the evening meal was ready we fed him, so checking for some minutes his undercurrent of groans and broken words. Late at night, he rose painfully to his feet and tottered deafly into the night, taking his beliefs, if any, with him. The Howeitat told me that life-long he had wandered among them moaning strange things, not knowing day or night, not troubling himself for food or work or shelter. He was given bounty of them all, as an afflicted man: but never replied a word, or talked aloud, except when abroad by himself or alone among the sheep and goats.

CHAPTER LXIV

ABDULLA made progress with his settlement. Gasim, no longer defiant, but sulky, would not give public counsel: so about a hundred men of the smaller clans dared defy him by promising to ride with us. We talked it over with Zaal, and decided to try our fortune to the utmost of this power. By longer delay we risked adherents whom we now had, with little hope of getting others in the present temper of the tribes.

It was a tiny party, only a third of what had been hoped. Our weakness would modify our plans regrettably: also we lacked an assured leader. Zaal, as ever, showed himself capable of being chief, prescient and active in all concrete preparations. He was a man of great mettle, but too close to Auda to suit the others; and his sharp tongue and the sneer hovering on his blue, wet lips fanned distrust and made men reluctant to obey even his good advice.

Next day the baggage camels came from Feisal, twenty of them in charge of ten freedmen, and guarded by four of his body-slaves. These were the trustiest attendants in the army, with a quite particular reading of the duties of personal service. They would have died to save their master hurt, or have died with him if he were hurt. We attached two to each sergeant, so that whatever happened to me their safe return would be assured. The loads needed for the reduced raid were sorted out and all made ready for an early start.

Accordingly at dawn on September the sixteenth we rode out from Rumm. Aid, the blind Sherif, insisted on coming, despite his lost sight; saying he could ride, if he could not shoot, and that if God prospered us he would take leave from Feisal in the flush of the success, and go home, not too sorry, to the blank life which would be left. Zaal led his twenty-five Nowasera, a clan of Auda's Arabs who called themselves my men, and were famous the desert over for their saddle-camels. My hard riding tempted them to my company.

Old Motlog el Awar, owner of el Jedha, the finest she-camel in North Arabia, rode her in our van. We looked at her with proud or greedy eyes, according to our relationship with him. My Ghazala was taller and more grand, with a faster trot, but too old to be galloped. However, she was the only other animal in the party, or, indeed, in this desert, to be matched with the Jedha, and my honour was increased by her dignity.

The rest of our party strayed like a broken necklace. There were groups of Zuweida, Darausha, Togatga, and Zelebani; and it was on this ride that the virtue of Hammad el Tugtagi was first brought to my mind. Half an hour after we started there rode out from a side-valley some shame-faced men of the Dhumaniyeh, unable to endure others raiding while they idled with the women.

No one group would ride or speak with another, and I passed back and forth all day like a shuttle, talking first to one lowering sheikh, and then to another, striving to draw them together, so that before a cry to action came there might be solidarity. As yet they agreed only in not hearing any word from Zaal as to the order of our march; though he was admitted the most intelligent warrior, and the most experienced. For my private part he was the only one to be trusted further than eye-sight. Of the others, it seemed to me that neither their words nor their counsels, perhaps not their rifles, were sure.

Poor Sherif Aid's uselessness, even as nominal leader, forced me to assume the direction myself, against both principle and judgement; since the special arts of tribal raiding and the details of food-halts and pasturage, road-direction, pay, disputes, division of spoils, feuds and march order were much outside the syllabus of the Oxford School of Modern History. The need to vamp these matters kept me too busied to see the country, and prevented my worrying out how we must assault Mudowwara, and the best surprise uses of explosive.

We put our midday halt in a fertile place, where the late spring rain, falling on a sandy talus, had brought up a thick tufting of silvery grass which our camels loved. The weather was mild, perfect as an August in England, and we lingered in great content, recovered at last from the bickering appetites of the days before the start, and from that slight rending of nerve inevitable when leaving even a temporary settlement. Man, in our circumstances, took root so soon.

Late in the day we rode again, winding downhill in a narrow valley between moderate sandstone walls: till before sunset we were out on another flat of laid yellow mud, like that which had been so wonderful a prelude to Rumm's glory. By its edge we camped. My care had borne fruit, for we settled in only three parties, by bright fires of crackling, flaring tamarisk. At one supped my men; at the second Zaal; at the third the other Howeitat; and late at night, when all the chiefs had been well adjusted with gazelle meat and hot bread, it became possible to bring them to my neutral fire, and discuss sensibly our course for the morrow.

It seemed that about sunset we should water at Mudowwara well, two or three miles this side of the station, in a covered valley. Then, in the early night, we might go forward to examine the station and see if, in our weakness, we might yet attempt some stroke against it. I held strongly to this (against the common taste) for it was by so much the most critical point of the line. The Arabs could not see it, since their minds did not hold a picture of the long, linked Turkish front with its necessitous demands. However, we had reached internal harmony, and scattered confidently to sleep.

In the morning we delayed to eat again, having only six hours of march before us; and then pushed across the mud-flat to a plain of firm limestone rag, carpeted with brown, weather-blunted flint. This was succeeded by low hills, with occasional soft beds of sand, under the steeper slopes where eddying winds had dropped their dust. Through these we rode up shallow valleys to a crest; and then by like valleys down the far side, whence we issued abruptly, from dark, tossed stone-heaps into the sun-steeped wideness of a plain. Across it an occasional low dune stretched a drifting line.

We had made our noon halt at the first entering of the broken country; and, rightly, in the late afternoon came to the well. It was an open pool, a few yards square, in a hollow valley of large stone-slabs and flint and sand. The stagnant water looked uninviting. Over its face lay a thick mantle of green slime, from which swelled curious bladder-islands of floating fatty pink. The Arabs explained that the Turks had thrown dead camels into the pool to make the water foul; but that time had passed and the effect was grown faint. It would have been fainter had the criterion of their effort been my taste.

Yet it was all the drink we should get up here unless we took Mudowwara, so we set to and filled our water-skins. One of the Howeitat, while helping in this, slipped off the wet edge into the water. Its green carpet closed oilily over his head and hid him for an instant: then he came up, gasping vigorously, and scrambled out amid our laughter; leaving behind him a black hole in the scum from which a stench of old meat rose like a visible pillar, and hung about us and him and the valley, disconcertingly.

At dusk, Zaal and I, with the sergeants and others, crept forward quietly. In half an hour we were at the last crest, in a place where the Turks had dug trenches and stoned up an elaborate outpost of engrailed sangars which on this black new-moon night of our raid were empty. In front and below lay the station, its doors and windows sharply marked by the yellow cooking fires and lights of the garrison. It seemed close under our observation; but the Stokes gun would carry only three hundred yards. Accordingly we went nearer, hearing the enemy noises, and attentively afraid lest their barking dogs uncover us. Sergeant Stokes made casts out to left and right, in search of gun-positions, but found nothing that was satisfactory.

Meanwhile, Zaal and I crawled across the last flat, till we could count the unlighted tents and hear the men talking. One came out a few steps in our direction, then hesitated. He struck a match to light a cigarette, and the bold light flooded his face, so that we saw him plainly, a young, hollow-faced sickly officer. He squatted, busy for a moment, and returned to his men, who hushed as he passed.

We moved back to our hill and consulted in whispers. The station was very long, of stone buildings, so solid that they might be proof against our time-fused shell. The garrison seemed about two hundred. We were one hundred and sixteen rifles and not a happy family. Surprise was the only benefit we could be sure of.

So, in the end, I voted that we leave it, unalarmed, for a future occasion, which might be soon. But, actually, one accident after another saved Mudowwara; and it was not until August, 1918, that Buxton's Camel Corps at last measured to it the fate so long overdue.

CHAPTER LXV

QUIETLY we regained our camels and slept. Next morning we returned on our tracks to let a fold of the plain hide us from the railway, and then marched south across the sandy flat; seeing tracks of gazelle, oryx and ostrich; with, in one spot, stale padmarks of leopard. We were making for the low hills bounding the far side, intending to blow up a train; for Zaal said that where these touched the railway was such a curve as we needed for mine-laying, and that the spurs commanding it would give us ambush and field of fire for our machine-guns.

So we turned east in the southern ridges till within half a mile of the line. There the party halted in a thirty-foot valley, while a few of us walked down to the line, which bent a little eastward to avoid the point of higher ground under our feet. The point ended in a flat table fifty feet above the track facing north across the valley.

The metals crossed the hollow on a high bank, pierced by a two-arched bridge for the passage of rain-water. This seemed an ideal spot to lay the charge. It was our first try at electric mining and we had no idea what would happen; but it stood to our reason that the job would be more sure with an arch under the explosive because, whatever the effect on the locomotive, the bridge would go, and the succeeding coaches be inevitably derailed.

The ledge would make an admirable position for Stokes. For the automatics, it was rather high; but the enfilade would be masterful whether the train was going up or down the line. So we determined to put up with the disadvantages of plunging fire. It was good to have my two British responsibilities in one place, safe from surprise and with an independent retreat into the rough: for to-day Stokes was in pain with dysentery. Probably the Mudowwara water had upset his stomach. So few Englishmen seemed to have been endowed by their upbringing with any organic resistance to disease.

Back with our camels, we dumped the loads, and sent the animals to safe pasture near some undercut rocks from which the Arabs scraped salt. The freedmen carried down the Stokes gun with its shells; the Lewis guns; and the gelatine with its insulated wire, magneto and tools to the chosen place. The sergeants set up their toys on a terrace, while we went down to the bridge to dig a bed between the ends of two steel sleepers, wherein to hide my fifty pounds of gelatine. We had stripped off the paper wrapping of the individual explosive plugs and kneaded them together by help of the sun-heat into a shaking jelly in a sand-bag.

The burying of it was not easy. The embankment was steep, and in the sheltered pocket between it and the hill-side was a wind-laid bank of sand. No one crossed this but myself, stepping carefully; yet I left unavoidable great prints over its smoothness. The ballast dug out from the track I had to gather in my cloak for carriage in repeated journeys to the culvert, whence it could be tipped naturally over the shingle bed of the watercourse.

It took me nearly two hours to dig in and cover the charge: then came the difficult job of unrolling the heavy wires from the detonator to the hills whence we would fire the mine. The top sand was crusted and had to be broken through in burying the wires. They were stiff wires, which scarred the wind-rippled surface with long lines like the belly marks of preposterously narrow and heavy snakes. When pressed down in one place they rose into the air in another. At last they had to be weighted down with rocks which, in turn, had to be buried at the cost of great disturbance of the ground.

Afterwards it was necessary, with a sand-bag, to stipple the marks into a wavy surface; and, finally, with a bellows and long fanning sweeps of my cloak, to simulate the smooth laying of the wind. The whole job took five hours to finish; but then it was well finished: neither myself nor any of us could see where the charge lay, or that double wires led out underground from it to the firing point two hundred yards off, behind the ridge marked for our riflemen.

The wires were just long enough to cross from this ridge into a depression. There we brought up the two ends and connected them with the electric exploder. It was an ideal place both for it and the man who fired it, except that the bridge was not visible thence.

However, this only meant that someone would have to press the handle at a signal from a point fifty yards ahead, commanding the bridge and the ends of the wire alike. Salem, Feisal's best slave, asked for this task of honour, and was yielded it by acclamation. The end of the afternoon was spent in showing him (on the disconnected exploder) what to do, till he was act-perfect and banged down the ratchet precisely as I raised my hand with an imaginary engine on the bridge.

We walked back to camp, leaving one man on watch by the line. Our baggage was deserted, and we stared about in a puzzle for the rest, till we saw them suddenly sitting against the golden light of sunset along a high ridge. We yelled to them to lie down or come down, but they persisted up there on their perch like a school of hooded crows, in full view of north and south.

At last we ran up and threw them off the skyline, too late. The Turks in a little hill-post by Hallat Ammar, four miles south of us, had seen them, and opened fire in their alarm upon the long shadows which the declining sun was pushing gradually up the slopes towards the post. Beduin were past masters in the art of using country, but in their abiding contempt for the stupidity of the Turks they would take no care to fight them. This ridge was visible at once from Mudowwara and Hallat Ammar, and they had frightened both places by their sudden ominous expectant watch.

However, the dark closed on us, and we knew we must sleep away the night patiently in hope of the morrow. Perhaps the Turks would reckon us gone if our place looked deserted in the morning. So we lit fires in a deep hollow, baked bread and were comfortable. The common tasks had made us one party, and the hill-top folly shamed everyone into agreement that Zaal should be our leader.

Day broke quietly, and for hours we watched the empty railway with its peaceful camps. The constant care of Zaal and of his lame cousin Howeimil, kept us hidden, though with difficulty, because of the insatiate restlessness of the Beduin, who would never sit down for ten minutes, but must fidget and do or say something. This defect made them very inferior to the stolid English for the long, tedious strain of a waiting war. Also it partly accounted for their uncertain stomachs in defence. To-day they made us very angry.

Perhaps, after all, the Turks saw us, for at nine o'clock some forty men came out of the tents on the hill-top by Hallat Ammar to the south and advanced in open order. If we left them alone, they would turn us off our mine in an hour; if we opposed them with our superior strength and drove them back, the railway would take notice, and traffic be held up. It was a quandary, which eventually we tried to solve by sending thirty men to check the enemy patrol gradually; and, if possible, to draw them lightly aside into the broken hills. This might hide our main position and reassure them as to our insignificant strength and purpose.

For some hours it worked as we had hoped; the firing grew desultory and distant. A permanent patrol came confidently up from the south and walked past our hill, over our mine and on towards Mudowwara without noticing us. There were eight soldiers and a stout corporal, who mopped his brow against the heat, for it was now after eleven o'clock and really warm. When he had passed us by a mile or two the fatigue of the tramp became too much for him. He marched his party into the shade of a long culvert, under whose arches a cool draught from the east was gently flowing, and there in comfort they lay on the soft sand, drank water from their bottles, smoked, and at last slept. We presumed that this was the noon-day rest which every solid Turk in the hot summer of Arabia took as a matter of principle, and that their allowing themselves the pause showed that we were disproved or ignored. However, we were in error.

CHAPTER LXVI

NOON brought fresh care. Through my powerful glasses we saw a hundred Turkish soldiers issue from Mudowwara Station and make straight across the sandy plain towards our place. They were coming very slowly, and no doubt unwillingly, for sorrow at losing their beloved midday sleep: but at their very worst marching and temper they could hardly take more than two hours before they reached us.

We began to pack up, preparatory to moving off, having decided to leave the mine and its leads in place on chance that the Turks might not find them, and we be able to return and take advantage of all the careful work. We sent a messenger to our covering party on the south, that they should meet us farther up, near those scarred rocks which served as screen for our pasturing camels.

Just as he had gone, the watchman cried out that smoke in clouds was rising from Hallat Ammar. Zaal and I rushed uphill and saw by its shape and volume that indeed there must be a train waiting in that station. As we were trying to see it over the hill, suddenly it moved out in our direction. We yelled to the Arabs to get into position as quick as possible, and there came a wild scramble over sand and rock. Stokes and Lewis, being booted, could not win the race; but they came well up, their pains and dysentery forgotten.

The men with rifles posted themselves in a long line behind the spur running from the guns past the exploder to the mouth of the valley. From it they would fire directly into the derailed carriages at less than one hundred and fifty yards, whereas the ranges for the Stokes and Lewis guns were about three hundred yards. An Arab stood up on high behind the guns and shouted to us what the train was doing — a necessary precaution, for if it carried troops and detrained them behind our ridge we should have to face about like a flash and retire fighting up the valley for our lives. Fortunately it held on at all the speed the two locomotives could make on wood fuel.

It drew near where we had been reported, and opened random fire into the desert. I could hear the racket coming, as I sat on my hillock by the bridge to give the signal to Salem, who danced round the exploder on his knees, crying with excitement, and calling urgently on God to make him fruitful. The Turkish fire sounded heavy, and I wondered with how many men we were going to have affair, and if the mine would be advantage enough for our eighty fellows to equal them. It would have been better if the first electrical experiment had been simpler.

However, at that moment the engines, looking very big, rocked with screaming whistles into view around the bend. Behind them followed ten box-waggons, crowded with rifle-muzzles at the windows and doors; and in little sand-bag nests on the roofs Turks precariously held on, to shoot at us. I had not thought of two engines, and on the moment decided to fire the charge under the second, so that however little the mine's effect, the uninjured engine should not be able to uncouple and drag the carriages away.

Accordingly, when the front 'driver' of the second engine was on the bridge, I raised my hand to Salem. There followed a terrific roar, and the line vanished from sight behind a spouting column of black dust and smoke a hundred feet high and wide. Out of the darkness came shattering crashes and long, loud metallic clangings of ripped steel, with many lumps of iron and plate; while one entire wheel of a loco-motive whirled up suddenly black out of the cloud against the sky, and sailed musically over our heads to fall slowly and heavily into the desert behind. Except for the flight of these, there succeeded a deathly silence, with no cry of men or rifle-shot, as the now grey mist of the explosion drifted from the line towards us, and over our ridge until it was lost in the hills.

In the lull, I ran southward to join the sergeants. Salem picked up his rifle and charged out into the murk. Before I had climbed to the guns the hollow was alive with shots, and with the brown figures of the Beduin leaping forward to grips with the enemy. I looked round to see what was happening so quickly, and saw the train stationary and dismembered along the track, with its waggon sides jumping under the bullets which riddled them, while Turks were falling out from the far doors to gain the shelter of the railway embankment.

As I watched, our machine-guns chattered out over my head, and the long rows of Turks on the carriage roofs rolled over, and were swept off the top like bales of cotton before the furious shower of bullets which stormed along the roofs and splashed clouds of yellow chips from the planking. The dominant position of the guns had been an advantage to us so far.

When I reached Stokes and Lewis the engagement had taken another turn. The remaining Turks had got behind the bank, here about eleven feet high, and from cover of the wheels were firing point-blank at the Beduin twenty yards away across the sand-filled dip. The enemy in the crescent of the curving line were secure from the machine-guns; but Stokes slipped in his first shell, and after a few seconds there came a crash as it burst beyond the train in the desert.

He touched the elevating screw, and his second shot fell just by the trucks in the deep hollow below the bridge where the Turks were taking refuge. It made a shambles of the place. The survivors of the group broke out in a panic across the desert, throwing away their rifles and equipment as they ran. This was the opportunity of the Lewis gunners. The sergeant grimly traversed with drum after drum, till the open sand was littered with bodies. Mushagraf, the Sherari boy behind the second gun, saw the battle over, threw aside his weapon with a yell, and dashed down at speed with his rifle to join the others who were beginning, like wild beasts, to tear open the carriages and fall to plunder. It had taken nearly ten minutes.

I looked up-line through my glasses and saw the Mudowwara patrol breaking back uncertainly towards the railway to meet the train-fugitives running their fastest northward. I looked south, to see our thirty men cantering their camels neck and neck in our direction to share the spoils. The Turks there, seeing them go, began to move after them with infinite precaution, firing volleys. Evidently we had a half hour respite, and then a double threat against us.

I ran down to the ruins to see what the mine had done. The bridge was gone; and into its gap was fallen the front waggon, which had been filled with sick. The smash had killed all but three or four and had rolled dead and dying into a bleeding heap against the splintered end. One of those yet alive deliriously cried out the word typhus. So I wedged shut the door, and left them there, alone.

Succeeding waggons were derailed and smashed: some had frames irreparably buckled. The second engine was a blanched pile of smoking iron. Its driving wheels had been blown upward, taking away the side of the fire-box. Cab and tender were twisted into strips, among the piled stones of the bridge abutment. It would never run again. The front engine had got off better: though heavily derailed and lying half-over, with the cab burst, yet its steam was at pressure, and driving-gear intact.

Our greatest object was to destroy locomotives, and I had kept in my arms a box of gun-cotton with fuse and detonator ready fixed, to make sure such a case. I now put them in position on the outside cylinder. On the boiler would have been better, but the sizzling steam made me fear a general explosion which would sweep across my men (swarming like ants over the booty) with a blast of jagged fragments. Yet they would not finish their looting before the Turks came. So I lit the fuse, and in the half-minute of its burning drove the plunderers a little back, with difficulty. Then the charge burst, blowing the cylinder to smithers, and the axle too. At the moment I was distressed with uncertainty whether the damage were enough; but the Turks, later, found the engine beyond use and broke it up.

The valley was a weird sight. The Arabs, gone raving mad, were rushing about at top speed bareheaded and half-naked, screaming, shooting into the air, clawing one another nail and fist, while they burst open trucks and staggered back and forward with immense bales, which they ripped by the rail-side, and tossed through, smashing what they did not want. The train had been packed with refugees and sick men, volunteers for boat-service on the Euphrates, and families of Turkish officers returning to Damascus.

There were scores of carpets spread about; dozens of mattresses and flowered quilts, blankets in heaps, clothes for men and women in full variety; clocks, cooking-pots, food, ornaments and weapons. To one side stood thirty or forty hysterical women, unveiled, tearing their clothes and hair; shrieking themselves distracted. The Arabs without regard to them went on wrecking the household goods; looting their absolute fill. Camels had become common property. Each man frantically loaded the nearest with what it could carry and shooed it westward into the void, while he turned to his next fancy.

Seeing me tolerably unemployed, the women rushed, and caught at me with howls for mercy. I assured them that all was going well: but they would not get away till some husbands delivered me. These knocked their wives off and seized my feet in a very agony of terror of instant death. A Turk so broken down was a nasty spectacle: I kicked them off as well as I could with bare feet, and finally broke free.

Next a group of Austrians, officers and non-commissioned officers, appealed to me quietly in Turkish for quarter. I replied with my halting German; whereupon one, in English, begged for a doctor for his wounds. We had none: not that it mattered, for he was mortally hurt and dying. I told them the Turks would return in an hour and care for them. But he was dead before that, as were most of the others (instructors in the new Skoda mountain howitzers supplied to Turkey for the Hejaz war), because some dispute broke out between them and my own bodyguard, and one of them fired a pistol shot at young Rahail. My infuriated men cut them down, all but two or three, before I could return to interfere.

So far as could be seen in the excitement, our side had suffered no loss. Among the ninety military prisoners were five Egyptian soldiers, in their underclothes. They knew me, and explained that in a night raid of Davenport's, near Wadi Ais, they had been cut off by the Turks and captured. They told me something of Davenport's work: of his continual pegging away in Abdulla's sector, which was kept alive by him for month after month, without any of the encouragement lent to us by success and local enthusiasm. His best helpers were such stolid infantrymen as these, whom I made lead the prisoners away to our appointed rallying place at the salt rocks.

CHAPTER LXVII

LEWIS and Stokes had come down to help me. I was a little anxious about them; for the Arabs, having lost their wits, were as ready to assault friend as foe. Three times I had had to defend myself when they pretended not to know me and snatched at my things. However, the sergeants' war-stained khaki presented few attractions. Lewis went out east of the railway to count the thirty men he had slain; and incidentally, to find Turkish gold and trophies in their haversacks. Stokes strolled through the wrecked bridge, saw there the bodies of twenty Turks torn to pieces by his second shell, and retired hurriedly.

Ahmed came up to me with his arms full of booty and shouted (no Arab could speak normally in the thrill of victory) that an old woman in the last waggon but one wished to see me. I sent him at once, empty-handed, for my camel and some baggage camels to remove the guns; for the enemy's fire was now plainly audible, and the Arabs, sated with spoils, were escaping one by one towards the hills, driving tottering camels before them into safety. It was bad tactics to leave the guns until the end: but the confusion of a first, overwhelmingly successful, experiment had dulled our judgement.

In the end of the waggon sat an ancient and very tremulous Arab dame, who asked me what it was all about. I explained. She said that though an old friend and hostess of Feisal, she was too infirm to travel and must wait her death there. I replied that she would not be harmed. The Turks were almost arrived and would recover what remained of the train. She accepted this, and begged me to find her old negress, to bring her water. The slave woman filled a cup from the spouting tender of the first engine (delicious water, from which Lewis was slaking his thirst), and then I led her to her grateful mistress. Months after there came to me secretly from Damascus a letter and a pleasant little Baluchi carpet from the lady Ayesha, daughter of Jellal el Lel, of Medina, in memory of an odd meeting.

Ahmed never brought the camels. My men, possessed by greed, had dispersed over the land with the Beduins. The sergeants and I were alone by the wreck, which had a strange silence now. We began to fear that we must abandon the guns and run for it, but just then saw two camels dashing back. Zaal and Howeimil had missed me and had returned in search.

We were rolling up the insulated cable, our only piece. Zaal dropped from his camel and would have me mount and ride; but, instead, we loaded it with the wire and the exploder. Zaal found time to laugh at our quaint booty, after all the gold and silver in the train. Howeimil was dead lame from an old wound in the knee and could not walk, but we made him couch his camel, and hoisted the Lewis guns, tied butt to butt like scissors, behind his saddle. There remained the trench mortars; but Stokes reappeared, unskilfully leading by the nose a baggage camel he had found straying. We packed the mortars in haste; put Stokes (who was still weak with his dysentery) on Zaal's saddle, with the Lewis guns, and sent off the three camels in charge of Howeimil, at their best pace.

Meanwhile, Lewis and Zaal, in a sheltered and invisible hollow behind the old-gun position, made a fire of cartridge boxes, petrol and waste, banked round it the Lewis drums and the spare small-arms ammunition; and, gingerly, on the top, laid some loose Stokes' shells. Then we ran. As the flames reached the cordite and ammonal there was a colossal and continuing noise. The thousands of cartridges exploded in series like massed machine-guns, and the shells roared off in thick columns of dust and smoke. The outflanking Turks, impressed by the tremendous defence, felt that we were in strength and strongly posted. They halted their rush, took cover, and began carefully to surround our position and reconnoitre it according to rule, while we sped panting into concealment among the ridges.

It seemed a happy ending to the affair, and we were glad to get off with no more loss than my camels and baggage; though this included the sergeants' cherished kits. However, there was food at Rumm, and Zaal thought perhaps we should find our property with the others, who were waiting ahead. We did. My men were loaded with booty, and had with them all our camels whose saddles were being suddenly delivered of spoils to look ready for our mounting.

Softly I explained what I thought of the two men who had been ordered to bring up the camels when the firing ceased. They pleaded that the explosion had scattered everyone in fright, and afterwards the Arabs had appropriated each man any animal he saw. This was probably true; but my men also were able-bodied and might have helped themselves. We asked if anyone were hurt, and a voice said that the Shimt's boy — a very dashing fellow — had been killed in the first rush forward at the train. This rush was a mistake, made without instructions, as the Lewis and Stokes guns were sure to end the business if the mine worked properly. So I felt that his loss was not directly my reproach.

Three men had been slightly wounded. Then one of Feisal's slaves vouchsafed that Salem was missing. We called everyone together and questioned them. At last an Arab said that he had seen him lying hit, just beyond the engine. This reminded Lewis, who, ignorant that he was one of us, had seen a negro on the ground there, badly hurt. I had not been told and was angry, for half the Howeitat must have known of it, and that Salem was in my charge. By their default now, for the second time, I had left a friend behind.

I asked for volunteers to come back and find him. After a little Zaal agreed, and then twelve of the Nowasera. We trotted fast across the plain towards the line. As we topped the last ridge but one we saw the train-wreck with Turks swarming over it. There must have been one hundred and fifty of them, and our attempt was hopeless. Salem would have been dead, for the Turks did not take Arab prisoners. Indeed, they used to kill them horribly; so, in mercy, we were finishing those of our badly wounded who would have to be left helpless on abandoned ground.

We must give up Salem; but, to make some profit out of our return, I suggested to Zaal that we slip up-valley and recover the sergeants' kits. He was willing, and we rode till the Turks' shooting drove us to cover behind a bank. Our camp had been in the next hollow, across a hundred yards of flat. So, watching the time, one or two of the quicker youths nipped across to drag back the saddle-bags. The Turks were distant, and Turkish long-range fire was always bad; but for our third trip they got up a machine-gun, and the dusty splashes of the bullets on the dark flints let them group well about us.

I sent the running boys away, picked out what was light and best of the remaining baggage, and rejoined the party. We pounded down the slope and across. In the open the Turks could clearly count our fewness. They grew bold and ran forward on both flanks to cut us off. Zaal threw himself from his camel, climbed with five men to the peak of the ridge we had just crossed, and fired back at them. He was a marvellous shot, whom I had seen to bring down a running gazelle from the saddle with his second bullet at three hundred yards, and his fire checked them.

He called to us laden men to hurry across the next hollow and hold it while he fell back on us, and in this fashion we retired from ridge to ridge, putting up a good delay action and hitting thirteen or fourteen Turks at a cost of four camels wounded. At last, when we were only two ridges from our supports, and were feeling sure that we should do it easily, a solitary rider appeared, coming up. It was Lewis, with a Lewis gun held efficiently across his thighs. He had heard the rapid fire, and thought to see if we needed nelp.

He changed our strength very much, and my mind, for I was angry with the Turks, who had got Salem and had chased us breathless so far in dust and heat and streaming sweat. Therefore we took place to give our pursuers a knock; but either they suspected our silence, or they feared the distance they had come; anyway, we saw no more of them. After a few minutes we became cool, and wise-headed enough to ride off after the others.

They had marched very heavy-laden. Of our ninety prisoners, ten were friendly Medina women electing to go to Mecca by way of Feisal. There had been twenty-two riderless camels. The women had climbed on to five pack-saddles, and the wounded were in pairs on the residue. It was late in the afternoon. We were exhausted, the prisoners had drunk all our water. We must re-fill from the old well at Mudow-wara that night to sustain ourselves so far as Rumm.

As the well was close to the station, it was highly desirable that we get to it and away, lest the Turks divine our course and find us there defenceless. We broke up into little parties and struggled north. Victory always undid an Arab force, so we were no longer a raiding party, but a stumbling baggage caravan, loaded to breaking point with enough household goods to make rich an Arab tribe for years.

My sergeants asked me for a sword each, as souvenir of their first private battle. As I went down the column to look out something, suddenly I met Feisal's freedmen; and to my astonishment on the crupper behind one of them, strapped to him, soaked with blood, unconscious, was the missing Salem.

I trotted up to Ferhan and asked wherever he had found him. He told me that when the Stokes gun fired its first shell, Salem rushed past the locomotive, and one of the Turks shot him in the back. The bullet had come out near his spine, without, in their judgment, hurting him mortally. After the train was taken, the Howeitat had stripped him of cloak, dagger, rifle and head-gear. Mijbil, one of the freedmen, had found him, lifted him straight to his camel, and trekked off homeward without telling us. Ferhan, overtaking him on the road, had relieved him of Salem; who, when he recovered, as later he did, perfectly, bore me always a little grudge for having left him behind, when he was of my company and wounded. I had failed in staunchness. My habit of hiding behind a Sherif was to avoid measuring myself against the pitiless Arab standard, with its no-mercy for foreigners who wore its clothes, and aped its manners. Not often was I caught with so poor a shield as blind Sherif Aid.

We reached the well in three hours and watered without mishap. Afterwards we moved off another ten miles or so, beyond fear of pursuit. There we lay down and slept, and in the morning found ourselves happily tired. Stokes had had his dysentery heavy upon him the night before, but sleep and the ending of anxiety made him well. He and I and Lewis, the only unburdened ones, went on in front across one huge mud-flat after another till just before sunset we were at the bottom of Wadi Rumm.

This new route was important for our armoured cars, because its twenty miles of hard mud might enable them to reach Mudowwara easily. If so, we should be able to hold up the circulation of trains when we pleased. Thinking of this, we wheeled into the avenue of Rumm, still gorgeous in sunset colour; the cliffs as red as the clouds in the west, like them in scale and in the level bar they raised against the sky. Again we felt how Rumm inhibited excitement by its serene beauty. Such whelming greatness dwarfed us, stripped off the cloak of laughter in which we had ridden over the jocund flats.

Night came down, and the valley became a mind-landscape. The invisible cliffs boded as presences; imagination tried to piece out the plan of their battlements by tracing the dark pattern they cut in the canopy of stars. The blackness in the depth was very real — it was a night to despair of movement. We felt only our camels' labour, as hour after hour monotonously and smoothly they shouldered their puny way along the unfenced level, with the wall in front no nearer and the wall behind no further than at first.

About nine at night we were before the pit in which lay the water and our old camp. We knew its place because the deep darkness there grew humidly darker. We turned our camels to the right and advanced towards the rock, which reared its crested domes so high over us that the ropes of our head-cloths slipped back round our necks as we stared up. Surely if we stretched out even our camel-sticks in front of us we should touch the facing walls; yet for many paces more we crept in under their horns.

At last we were in the tall bushes: then we shouted. An Arab shouted back. The echoes of my voice rolling down from the cliff met his rising cry, and the sounds wrapped themselves together and wrestled among the crags. A flame flickered palely on the left, and we found Musa our watchman there. He lit a fire of powerfully scented wood, and by its light we broke open bully-beef and fed ravenously; gulping down, through our food, bowl after bowl of the delicious water, ice-cold, and heady after the foul drink of Mudowwara; which, for days, had seared our throats.

We slept through the coming of the rest. Two days later we were at Akaba; entering in glory, laden with precious things, and boasting that the trains were at our mercy. From Akaba the two sergeants took hurried ship to Egypt. Cairo had remembered them and gone peevish because of their non-return. However, they could pay the penalty of this cheerfully. They had won a battle single-handed; had had dysentery; lived on camel-milk; and learned to ride a camel fifty miles a day without pain. Also Allenby gave them a medal each.

CHAPTER LXVIII

DAYS passed, talking politics, organization and strategy with Feisal, while preparations for a new operation went forward. Our luck had quickened the camp; and the mining of trains promised to become popular, if we were able to train in the technique of the work enough men for several parties. Captain Pisani was first volunteer. He was the experienced commander of the French at Akaba, an active soldier who burned for distinction — and distinctions. Feisal found me three young Damascenes of family, who were ambitious to lead tribal raids. We went to Rumm and announced that this raid was specially for Gasim's clan. Such coals of fire scorched them; but greed would not let them refuse. Everyone for days around flocked to join. Most were denied: nevertheless, we started out with one hundred and fifty men and a huge train of empty pack-camels for the spoils.

For variety we determined to work by Maan. So we rode up to Batra, climbing out of heat into cold, out of Arabia into Syria, from tamarisk to wormwood. As we topped the pass and saw the blood-red stain on the hills above the leech-infested wells, there met us a first breath of the northern desert; that air too fine to describe, which told of perfect loneliness, dried grass, and the sun on burning flints.

The guides said that Kilometre 475 would be good for mining: but we found it beset by blockhouses, and had to creep shyly away. We marched down the line till it crossed a valley on a high bank, pierced by bridges on each side and in the middle. There, after midnight, we laid an automatic mine of a new and very powerful lyddite type. The burying took hours, and dawn caught us as we worked. There was no perceptible lightening, and when we stared round to know where the dark was yielding, we could see no special onset of the day. Long minutes afterwards the sun disclosed itself, high above the earth's rim, over a vignetted bank of edgeless mist.

We retired a thousand yards up the valley's scrubby bed to ambush for the intolerable day. As the hours passed the sun increased, and shone so closely upon our radiant trench that we felt crowded by its rays. The men were a mad lot, sharpened to distraction by hope of success. They would listen to no word but mine, and brought me their troubles for judgement. In the six days' raid there came to a head, and were settled, twelve cases of assault with weapons, four camel-liftings, one marriage, two thefts, a divorce, fourteen feuds, two evil eyes, and a bewitchment.

These decisions were arrived at despite my imperfect knowledge of Arabic. The fraudulence of my business stung me. Here were more fruits, bitter fruits, of my decision, in front of Akaba, to become a principal of the Revolt. I was raising the Arabs on false pretences, and exercising a false authority over my dupes, on little more evidence than their faces, as visible to my eyes weakly watering and stinging after a year's exposure to the throb, throb of sunlight.

We waited that day, and night. At sunset a scorpion scuttled out of the bush by which I had lain down to make note of the day's weariness, and fastening on my left hand struck me, it seemed repeatedly. The pain of my swollen arm kept me awake until the second dawn: to the relief of my overburdened mind, for its body became clamant enough to interrupt my self-questioning when the fire of some such surface injury swept the sluggish nerves.

Yet pain of this quality never endured long enough really to cure mind-sickness. After a night it would give way to that unattractive, and not honourable, internal ache which in itself provoked thought and left its victim yet weaker to endure. In such conditions the war seemed as great a folly as my sham leadership a crime; and, sending for our sheikhs, I was about to resign myself and my pretensions into their puzzled hands, when the fugleman announced a train.

It came down from Maan, a water-train, and passed over the mine without accident. The Arabs thanked me, for a booty of water was not their dream. The mine-action had failed; so at noon, with my pupils, I went down to lay an electric mine over the lyddite, that the detonation of one might fire the other. For concealment we trusted to the mirage and midday drowsiness of the Turks; justifiably, for there was no alarm in the hour we spent burying the charge.

From the southern bridge we brought the electric leads to the middle bridge, whose arch would conceal the exploder from a train overhead.

The Lewis guns we put under the northern bridge, to rake the far side of the train when the mine went off. The Arabs would line the bushes of a cross-channel of the valley three hundred yards our side of the railway. We waited afterwards throughout a day of sunlight and flies. Enemy patrols marched actively along the line, morning, afternoon and evening.

On the second day, about eight in the morning, a pillar of smoke left Maan. At the same time the first patrol approached. They were only half a dozen men, but their warning would deter the train; and we watched strainingly, in wonder which would win the race. The train was very slow, and sometimes the patrol halted.

We calculated they might be two or three hundred yards short of us when the train came. So we ordered everybody to stations. With twelve loaded wagons the engine panted on the up grade. However, it held on steadily. I sat by a bush in the stream-bed, a hundred yards from the mine; in view of it and of the exploder-party and of the machine-guns. When Faiz and Bedri heard the engine over their arch, they danced a war-dance round their little electric box. The Arabs in the ditch were hissing softly to me that it was time to fire: but not until the engine was exactly over the arch did I jump up and wave my cloak. Faiz instantly pressed his handle, and the great noise and dust and blackness burst up, as at Mudowwara a week before, and enveloped me where I sat, while the green-yellow sickly smoke of lyddite hung sluggishly about the wreck. The Lewis guns rattled out suddenly, three or four short bursts: there was a yell from the Arabs, and, headed by Pisani sounding the women's vibrant battle-cry, they rushed in a wild torrent for the train.

A Turk appeared on the buffers of the fourth truck from the end, loosed the couplings, and let the tail of the train slip back down the gradient. I made a languid effort to get behind the wheel with a stone, but scarcely cared enough to do it well. It seemed fair and witty that this much of the booty should escape. A Turkish colonel from the window fired at me with a Mauser pistol, cutting the flesh of my hip. I laughed at his too-great energy, which thought, like a regular officer, to promote the war by the killing of an individual.

Our mine had taken out the near arch of the bridge. Of the loco-motive, the fire-box was torn open, and many tubes burst. The cab was cleared out, a cylinder gone, the frame buckled, two driving wheels and their journals shattered. The tender and first waggon had telescoped. About twenty Turks were dead, and others prisoners, including four officers, who stood by the line weeping for the life which the Arabs had no mind to take.

The contents of the trucks were food-stuffs, some seventy tons of them; 'urgently needed', according to the way-bill, in Medain Salih. We sent one way-bill to Feisal, as detailed report of our success, and left the other receipted in the van. We also kicked northward some dozen civilians, who had thought they were going to Medina.

Pisani superintended the carrying off or destruction of the booty. As before, the Arabs were now merely camel-drivers, walking behind laden pack-animals. Farraj held my camel, while Salem and Dheilan helped with the exploder and the too-heavy wire. Rescue parties of Turks were four hundred yards away when we had finished, but we rode off without a man killed or wounded.

My pupils practised the art of mining afterwards by themselves, and taught others. Rumours of their fortune rolled about the tribes in a growing wave: not always intelligently. 'Send us a lurens and we will blow up trains with it', wrote the Beni Atiyeh to Feisal. He lent them Saad, a cut-and-thrust Ageyli, by whose help they got an important train carrying Suleiman Rifada, our old nuisance of Wejh, with twenty thousand pounds in gold, and precious trophies. Saad repeated history by saving only the wire for his share.

In the next four months our experts from Akaba destroyed seventeen locomotives. Travelling became an uncertain terror for the enemy. At Damascus people scrambled for the back seats in trains, even paid extra for them. The engine-drivers struck. Civilian traffic nearly ceased; and we extended our threat to Aleppo by the mere posting a notice one night on Damascus Town Hall, that good Arabs would henceforward travel by the Syrian railway at their own risk. The loss of the engines was sore upon the Turks. Since the rolling stock was pooled for Palestine and Hejaz, our destructions not merely made the mass evacuation of Medina impossible, but began to pinch the army about Jerusalem, just as the British threat grew formidable.

Meanwhile Egypt had wired for me. An aeroplane carried me to

G.H.Q., where Allenby by splendour of will was re-creating the broken British Army. He asked what our railway efforts meant; or rather if they meant anything beyond the melodramatic advertisement they gave Feisal's cause.

I explained my hope to leave the line just working, but only just, to Medina; where Fakhri's corps fed itself at less cost than if in prison at Cairo. The surest way to limit the line without killing it was by attacking trains. The Arabs put into mining a zest absent from their pure demolitions. We could not yet break the line, since railhead was the strongest point of a railway, and we preferred weakness in the nearest enemy neighbour till our regular army was trained and equipped and numerous enough to invest Maan.

He asked about Wadi Musa, because Turkish messages showed their intention to assault it at once. I explained that we had tried to provoke the Turks to attack Wadi Musa, and were about to be rewarded by their falling, foxed and fogged, into our trap. We went about in parties, not in stiff formation, and their aeroplanes failed to estimate us. No spies could count us, either, since even ourselves had not the smallest idea of our strength at any given moment.

On the other hand, we knew them exactly; each single unit, and every man they moved. They treated us as regulars, and before venturing a move against us calculated the total force we could meet them with. We, less orthodox, knew exactly what they would meet us with. This was our balance. For these years the Arab Movement lived on the exhilarating but slippery tableland between 'could' and 'would'. We allowed no margin for accident: indeed 'no margins' was the Akaba motto, continuously in the mouths of all.

When at last it came, Jemal's great attack on Wadi Musa made no noise. Maulud presided beautifully. He opened his centre, and with the greatest of humour let in the Turks until they broke their faces against the vertical cliffs of the Arab refuge. Then, while they were still puzzled and hurt, he came down simultaneously on both flanks. They never again attacked a prepared Arab position. Their losses had been heavy, but the loss of nerve at finding us invisible and yet full of back-lash cost them more than the casualties. Thanks to Maulud, Akaba became quit of all concern for its own present safety.

BOOK VI

THE RAID UPON THE BRIDGES

Chapters LXIX to LXXXI

BY *November, 1917, Allenby was ready to open a general attack against the Turks along his whole front. The Arabs should have done the same in their sector: but I was afraid to put everything on a throw, and designed instead the specious operation of cutting the Yarmuk Valley Railway, to throw into disorder the expected Turkish retreat. This half-measure met with the failure it deserved.*

CHAPTER LXIX

OCTOBER, accordingly, was a month of anticipation for us, in the knowledge that Allenby, with Bols and Dawnay, was planning to attack the Gaza-Beersheba line; while the Turks, a quite small army strongly entrenched, with excellent lateral communications, had been puffed up by successive victories to imagine that all British generals were incompetent to keep what their troops had won for them by dint of sheer hard fighting.

They deceived themselves. Allenby's coming had re-made the English. His breadth of personality swept away the mist of private or departmental jealousies behind which Murray and his men had worked. General Lynden Bell made way for General Bols, Allenby's chief of staff in France, a little, quick, brave, pleasant man; a tactical soldier, perhaps, but principally an admirable and effaced foil to Allenby, who used to relax himself on Bols. Unfortunately, neither of them had the power of choosing men; but Chetwode's judgement completed them with Guy Dawnay as third member of the staff.

Bols had never an opinion, nor any knowledge. Dawnay was mainly intellect. He lacked the eagerness of Bols, and the calm drive and human understanding of Allenby, who was the man the men worked for, the image we worshipped. Dawnay's cold, shy mind gazed upon our efforts with bleak eye, always thinking, thinking. Beneath this mathematical surface he hid passionate many-sided convictions, a reasoned scholarship in higher warfare, and the brilliant bitterness of a judgement disappointed with us, and with life.

He was the least professional of soldiers, a banker who read Greek history, a strategist unashamed, and a burning poet with strength over daily things. During the war he had had the grief of planning the attack at Suvla (spoiled by incompetent tacticians) and the battle for Gaza. As each work of his was ruined he withdrew further into the hardnesses of frosted pride, for he was of the stuff of fanatics.

Allenby, by not seeing his dissatisfaction, broke into him; and Dawnay replied by giving for the Jerusalem advance all the talent which he abundantly possessed. A cordial union of two such men made the Turks' position hopeless from the outset.

Their divergent characters were mirrored in the intricate plan. Gaza had been entrenched on a European scale with line after line of defences in reserve. It was so obviously the enemy's strongest point, that the British higher command had twice chosen it for frontal attack. Allenby, fresh from France, insisted that any further assault must be delivered by overwhelming numbers of men and guns, and their thrust maintained by enormous quantities of all kinds of transport. Bols nodded his assent. Dawnay was not the man to fight a straight battle. He sought to destroy the enemy's strength with the least fuss. Like a master politician he used the bluff Chief as a cloak for the last depth of justifiable slimness. He advised a drive at the far end of the Turkish line, near Beersheba. To make his victory cheap he wanted the enemy main force behind Gaza, which would be best secured if the British concentration was hidden so that the Turks would believe the flank attack to be a shallow feint. Bols nodded his assent.

Consequently the movements were made in great secrecy; but Dawnay found an ally in his intelligence staff who advised him to go beyond negative precautions, and to give the enemy specific (and speciously wrong) information of the plans he matured.

This ally was Meinertzhagen, a student of migrating birds drifted into soldiering, whose hot immoral hatred of the enemy expressed itself as readily in trickery as in violence. He persuaded Dawnay: Allenby reluctantly agreed: Bols assented, and the work began.

Meinertzhagen knew no half measures. He was logical, an idealist of the deepest, and so possessed by his convictions that he was willing to harness evil to the chariot of good. He was a strategist, a geographer, and a silent laughing masterful man; who took as blithe a pleasure in deceiving his enemy (or his friend) by some unscrupulous jest, as in spattering the brains of a cornered mob of Germans one by one with his African knob-kerri. His instincts were abetted by an immensely powerful body and a savage brain, which chose the best way to its purpose, unhampered by doubt or habit. Meiner thought out false Army papers, elaborate and confidential, which to a trained staff officer would indicate wrong positions for Allenby's main formation, a wrong direction of the coming attack, and a date some days too late. This information was led up to by careful hints given in code wireless messages. When he knew the enemy had picked these up, Meinertz-hagen rode out with his note books, on reconnaissance. He pushed forward until the enemy saw him. In the ensuing gallop he lost all his loose equipment and very nearly himself, but was rewarded by seeing the enemy reserves held behind Gaza and their whole preparations swung towards the coast and made less urgent. Simultaneously, an Army order by Ali Fuad Pasha cautioned his staff against carrying documents into the line.

We on the Arab front were very intimate with the enemy. Our Arab officers had been Turkish officers, and knew every leader on the other side personally. They had suffered the same training, thought the same, took the same point of view. By practising modes of approach upon the Arabs we could explore the Turks: understand, almost get inside, their minds. Relation between us and them was universal, for the civil population of the enemy area was wholly ours without pay or persuasion. In consequence our intelligence service was the widest, fullest and most certain imaginable.

We knew, better than Allenby, the enemy hollowness, and the magnitude of the British resources. We under-estimated the crippling effect of Allenby's too plentiful artillery, and the cumbrous intricacy of his infantry and cavalry, which moved only with rheumatic slow-ness. We hoped Allenby would be given a month's fine weather; and, in that case, expected to see him take, not merely Jerusalem, but Haifa too, sweeping the Turks in ruin through the hills.

Such would be our moment, and we needed to be ready for it in the spot where our weight and tactics would be least expected and most damaging. For my eyes the centre of attraction was Deraa, the junction of the Jerusalem-Haifa-Damascus-Medina railways, the navel of the Turkish Armies in Syria, the common point of all their fronts; and, by chance, an area in which lay great untouched reserves of Arab fighting men, educated and armed by Feisal from Akaba. We could there use Rualla, Serahin, Serdiyeh, Khoreisha; and, far stronger than tribes, the settled peoples of Hauran and Jebel Druse.

I pondered for a while whether we should not call up all these adherents and tackle the Turkish communications in force. We were certain, with any management, of twelve thousand men: enough to rush Deraa, to smash all the railway lines, even to take Damascus by surprise. Any one of these things would make the position of the Beersheba army critical: and my temptation to stake our capital instantly upon the issue was very sore.

Not for the first or last time service to two masters irked me. I was one of Allenby's officers, and in his confidence: in return, he expected me to do the best I could for him. I was Feisal's adviser, and Feisal relied upon the honesty and competence of my advice so far as often to take it without argument. Yet I could not explain to Allenby the whole Arab situation, nor disclose the full British plan to Feisal.

The local people were imploring us to come. Sheikh Talal el Hareidhin, leader of the hollow country about Deraa, sent in repeated messages that, with a few of our riders as proof of Arab support, he would give us Deraa. Such an exploit would have done the Allenby business, but was not one which Feisal could scrupulously afford unless he had a fair hope of then establishing himself there. Deraa's sudden capture, followed by a retreat, would have involved the massacre, or the ruin of all the splendid peasantry of the district.

They could only rise once, and their effort on that occasion must be decisive. To call them out now was to risk the best asset Feisal held for eventual success, on the speculation that Allenby's first attack would sweep the enemy before it, and that the month of November would be rainless, favourable to a rapid advance.

I weighed the English army in my mind, and could not honestly assure myself of them. The men were often gallant fighters, but their generals as often gave away in stupidity what they had gained in ignorance. Allenby was quite untried, sent to us with a not-blameless record from France, and his troops had broken down in and been broken by the Murray period. Of course, we were fighting for an Allied victory, and since the English were the leading partners, the Arabs would have, in the last resort, to be sacrificed for them. But was it the last resort? The war generally was going neither well nor very ill, and it seemed as though there might be time for another try next year. So I decided to postpone the hazard for the Arabs' sake.

CHAPTER LXX

HOWEVER the Arab Movement lived on Allenby's good pleasure, so it was needful to undertake some operation, less than a general revolt, in the enemy rear: an operation which could be achieved by a raiding party without involving the settled peoples; and yet one which would please him by being of material help to the British pursuit of the enemy. These conditions and qualifications pointed, upon consideration, to an attempted cutting of one of the great bridges in the Yarmuk valley.

It was by the narrow and precipitous gorge of the River Yarmuk that the railway from Palestine climbed to Hauran, on its way to Damascus. The depth of the Jordan depression, and the abruptness of the eastern plateau-face made this section of the line most difficult to build. The engineers had to lay it in the very course of the winding river-valley: and to gain its development the line had to cross and recross the stream continually by a series of bridges, the farthest west and the farthest east of which were hardest to replace.

To cut either of these bridges would isolate the Turkish army in Palestine, for one fortnight, from its base in Damascus, and destroy its power of escaping from Allenby's advance. To reach the Yarmuk we should need to ride from Akaba, by way of Azrak, some four hundred and twenty miles. The Turks thought the danger from us so remote that they guarded the bridges insufficiently.

Accordingly we suggested the scheme to Allenby, who asked that it be done on November the fifth, or one of the three following days. If it succeeded, and the weather held up afterwards for a fortnight, the odds were that no coherent unit of von Kress's army would survive its retreat to Damascus. The Arabs would then have their opportunity to carry their wave forward into the great capital, taking up at the halfway point from the British, whose original impulse would then be nearly exhausted, with the exhaustion of their transport.

For such an eventuality we needed at Azrak an authority to lead the potential local adherents. Nasir, our usual pioneer, was absent: but out with the Beni Sakhr was Ali ibn el Hussein, the youthful and attractive Harith Sherif, who had distinguished himself in Feisal's early desperate days about Medina, and later had out-newcombed New-combe about el Ula.

Ali, having been Jemal's guest in Damascus, had learned something of Syria: so I begged a loan of him from Feisal. His courage, his resource, and his energy were proven. There had never been any adventure, since our beginning, too dangerous for Ali to attempt, nor a disaster too deep for him to face with his high yell of a laugh.

He was physically splendid: not tall nor heavy, but so strong that he would kneel down, resting his forearms palm-up on the ground, and rise to his feet with a man on each hand. In addition, Ali could outstrip a trotting camel on his bare feet, keep his speed over half a mile and then leap into the saddle. He was impertinent, headstrong, conceited; as reckless in word as in deed; impressive (if he pleased) on public occasions, and fairly educated for a person whose native ambition was to excel the nomads of the desert in war and sport.

Ali would bring us the Beni Sakhr. We had good hopes of the Serahin, the tribe at Azrak. I was in touch with the Beni Hassan. The Rualla, of course, at this season were away at their winter quarters, so that our greatest card in the Hauran could not be played. Faiz el Ghusein had gone into the Lejah to prepare for action against the Hauran Railway if the signal came. Explosives were stored in desirable places. Our friends in Damascus were warned; and Ali Riza Pasha Rikabi, the city's military governor for the innocent Turks, and at the same time chief agent and conspirator for the Sherif, took quiet steps to retain control if the emergency arose.

My detailed plan was to rush from Azrak, under guidance of Rafa (that most gallant sheikh who had convoyed me in June), to Um Keis, in one or two huge marches with a handful of, perhaps, fifty men. Um Keis was Gadara, very precious with its memories of Menippus and of Meleager, the immoral Greek-Syrian whose self-expression marked the highest point of Syrian letters. It stood just over the westernmost of the Yarmuk bridges, a steel masterpiece whose destruction would fairly enrol me in the Gadarene school. Only half a dozen sentries were stationed actually on the girders and abutments. Reliefs for them were supplied from a garrison of sixty, in the station buildings of Hemme, where the hot springs of Gadara yet gushed out to the advantage of local sick. My hope was to persuade some of the Abu Tayi under Zaal to come with me. These men-wolves would make certain the actual storming of the bridge. To prevent enemy reinforcements coming up we would sweep the approaches with machine-guns, handled by Captain Bray's Indian volunteers from the cavalry division in France, under Jemadar Hassan Shah, a firm and experienced man. They had been months up country, rail-cutting, from Wejh, and might fairly be assumed to have become experts on camel-back, fit for the forced marches in prospect.

The demolition of great underslung girders with limited weights of explosive was a precise operation, and demanded a necklace of blasting gelatine, fired electrically. The *Humber* made us canvas straps and buckles, to simplify the fixing. None the less, the job remained a difficult one to do under fire. For fear of a casualty, Wood, the base engineer at Akaba, the only sapper available, was invited to come along and double me. He immediately agreed, though knowing he had been condemned medically for active service as the result of a bullet through the head in France. George Lloyd, who was spending a last few days in Akaba before going to Versailles on a regretted inter-allied Commission, said that he would ride up with us to Jefer: as he was one of the best fellows and least obtrusive travellers alive, his coming added greatly to our forlorn anticipation.

We were making our last preparations when an unexpected ally arrived in Emir Abd el Kader el Jezairi, grandson of the chivalrous defender of Algiers against the French. The exiled family had lived in Damascus for a generation. One of them, Omar, had been hanged by Jemal for treason disclosed in the Picot papers. The others had been deported, and Abd el Kader told us a long story of his escape from Brusa, and his journey, with a thousand adventures, across Anatolia to Damascus. In reality, he had been enlarged by the Turks upon request of the Khedive Abbas Hilmi, and sent down by him on private business to Mecca. He went there, saw King Hussein, and came back with a crimson banner, and noble gifts, his crazy mind half persuaded of our right, and glowing jerkily with excitement.

To Feisal he offered the bodies and souls of his villagers, sturdy, hard-smiting Algerian exiles living compactly along the north bank of the Yarmuk. We seized at the chance this would give us to control for a little time the middle section of the Valley railway, including two or three main bridges, without the disability of raising the country-side; since the Algerians were hated strangers and the Arab peasantry would not join them. Accordingly, we put off calling Rafa to meet us at Azrak, and said not a word to Zaal, concentrating our thoughts instead on Wadi Khalid and its bridges.

While we were in this train of mind arrived a telegram from Colonel Bremond, warning us that Abd el Kader was a spy in pay of the Turks. It was disconcerting. We watched him narrowly, but found no proof of the charge, which was not to be accepted blindly, as from Bremond, who was more a liability than our colleague; his military temper might have carried away his judgement when he heard Abd el Kader's outspoken public and private denunciations of France. The French conception of their country as a fair woman lent to them a national spitefulness against those who scorned her charms.

Feisal told Abd el Kader to ride with Ali and myself, and said to me, 'I know he is mad. I think he is honest. Guard your heads and use him.' We carried on, showing him our complete confidence, on the principle that a crook would not credit our honesty, and that an honest man was made a crook soonest by suspicion. As a matter of fact, he was an Islamic fanatic, half-insane with religious enthusiasm and a most violent belief in himself. His Moslem susceptibilities were outraged by my undisguised Christianity. His pride was hurt by our companionship; for the tribes greeted Ali as greater, and treated me as better, than himself. His bullet-headed stupidity broke down Ali's self-control twice or thrice into painful scenes: while his final effort was to leave us in the lurch at a desperate moment, after hindering our march and upsetting ourselves and our plans as far as he could.

CHAPTER LXXI

TARTING was as difficult as ever. For my bodyguard I took six recruits. Of these Mahmud was a native of the Yarmuk. He was an alert and hot-tempered lad of nineteen, with the petulance often accompanying curly hair. Another, Aziz, of Tafas, an older fellow, had spent three years with the Beduin in avoidance of military service. Though capable with camels, he was a shallow spirit, almost rabbit-mouthed, but proud. A third was Mustafa, a gentle boy from Deraa, very honest, who went about sadly by himself because he was deaf, and ashamed of his infirmity. One day on the beach, in a short word he had begged admittance to my bodyguard. So evidently did he expect to be refused that I took him; and it was a good choice for the others, since he was a mild peasant, whom they could bully into all the menial tasks. Yet he, too, was happy, for he was among desperate fellows, and the world would think him desperate. To balance his inefficiency on the march I enrolled Showak and Salem, two Sherari camel-herds, and Abd el Rahman, a runaway slave from Riyadth.

Of the old bodyguard I gave Mohammed and Ali a rest. They were tired after train-wrecking adventures; and, like their camels, needed to pasture quietly awhile. This left Ahmed the inevitable head man. His ruthless energy deserved promotion, but the obvious choice as ever failed. He misused his power and became oppressive; so it was his last march with me. I took Kreim for the camels; and Rahail, the lusty, conceited Haurani lad, for whom overwork was the grace which kept him continent. Matar, a parasite fellow of the Beni Hassan, attached himself to us. His fat peasant's buttocks filled his camel-saddle, and took nearly as large a share in the lewd or lurid jokes which, on march, helped pass my guards' leisure. We might enter Beni Hassan territory, where he had some influence. His unblushing greed made us sure of him, till his expectations failed.

My service was now profitable, for I knew my worth to the movement, and spent freely to keep myself safe. Rumour, for once in a helpful mood, gilded my open hand. Farraj and Daud, with Khidr and Mijbil, two Biasha, completed the party.

Farraj and Daud were capable and merry on the road, which they loved as all the lithe Ageyl loved it; but in camp their excess of spirit led them continually into dear affairs. This time they surpassed themselves by disappearing on the morning of our departure. At noon came a message from Sheikh Yusuf that they were in his prison, and would I talk to him about it? I went up to the house and found his bulk shaking between laughter and rage. He had just bought a cream-coloured riding-camel of purest blood. The beast had strayed in the evening into the palm-garden where my Ageyl were camped. They never suspected she belonged to the Governor, but laboured till dawn dyeing her head bright red with henna, and her legs blue with indigo, before turning her loose.

Akaba bubbled immediately in an uproar about this circus beast. Yusuf recognized her with difficulty and hurled all his police abroad to find the criminals. The two friends were dragged before the judgement seat, stained to the elbows with dye, and loudly protesting their entire innocence. Circumstances, however, were too strong; and Yusuf after doing his best with a palm-rib to hurt their feelings, put them in irons for a slow week's meditation. My concern made good his damage by the loan of a camel till his own should be respectable. Then I explained our instant need of the sinners, and promised another dose of his treatment for them when their skins were fit: so he ordered their release. They were delighted to escape the verminous prison on any terms, and rejoined us singing.

This business had delayed us. So we had an immense final meal in the luxury of camp, and started in the evening. For four hours we marched slowly: a first march was always slow, and both camels and men hated setting out on a new hazard. Loads slipped, saddles had to be re-girthed, and riders changed. In addition to my own camels (Ghazala, the old grandmother, now far gone in foal, and Rima, a full-pointed Sherari camel which the Sukhur had stolen from the Rualla) and those of the bodyguard, I had mounted the Indians, and lent one to Wood (who was delicate in the saddle and rode a fresh animal nearly every day), and one to Thorne, Lloyd's yeomanry trooper, who sat his saddle like an Arab and looked workmanlike in a head-cloth, with a striped cloak over his khaki. Lloyd himself was on a thoroughbred Dheraiyeh which Feisul had lent him: a fine, fast-looking animal, but clipped after mange and thin.

Our party straggled. Wood fell behind, and my men, being fresh, and having much work to keep the Indians together, lost touch with him. So he found himself alone with Thorne, and missed our turn to the east, in the blackness which always filled the depths of the Itm gorge by night, except when the moon was directly overhead. They went on up the main track towards Guweira, riding for hours; but at last decided to wait for day in a side valley. Both were new to the country, and not sure of the Arabs, so they took turns to keep watch. We guessed what had happened when they failed to appear at our midnight halt, and before dawn Ahmed, Aziz and Abd el Rahman went back, with orders to scatter up the three or four practicable roads and bring the missing pair to Rumm.

I stayed with Lloyd and the main body as their guide across the curved slopes of pink sandstone and tamarisk-green valleys to Rumm. Air and light were so wonderful that we wandered without thinking in the least of to-morrow. Indeed, had I not Lloyd to talk to? The world became very good. A faint shower last evening had brought earth and sky together in the mellow day. The colours in cliffs and trees and soil were so pure, so vivid, that we ached for real contact with them, and at our tethered inability to carry anything of them away. We were full of leisure. The Indians proved bad camel-masters, while Farraj and Daud pleaded a new form of saddle-soreness, called 'Yusufiyeh', which made them walk mile after mile.

We entered Rumm at last, while the crimson sunset burned on its stupendous cliffs and slanted ladders of hazy fire down the walled avenue. Wood and Thorne were there already, in the sandstone amphitheatre of the springs. Wood was ill, and lying on the platform of my old camp. Abd el Rahman had caught them before noon, and persuaded them to follow him after a good deal of misunderstanding, for their few words of Egyptian did not help much with his clipped Aridh dialect or the Howeiti slang with which he eked it out. He had cut across the hills by a difficult path to their great discomfort.

Wood had been hungry and hot and worried, angry to the point of refusing the native mess which Abd el Rahman contrived them in a way-side tent. He had begun to believe that he would never see us again, and was ungrateful when we proved too overcome with the awe that Rumm compelled on her visitors to sympathize deeply with his sufferings. In fact, we stared and said 'Yes', and left him lying there while we wandered whispering about the wonder of the place. Fortunately Ahmed and Thorne thought more of food: and with supper friendly relations were restored.

Next day, while we were saddling, Ali and Abd el Kader appeared. Lloyd and I had a second lunch with them, for they were quarrelling, and to have guests held them in check. Lloyd was the rare sort of traveller who could eat anything with anybody, anyhow and at any time. Then, making pace, we pushed after our party down the giant valley, whose hills fell short of architecture only in design.

At the bottom we crossed the flat Gaa, matching our camels in a burst over its velvet surface, until we overtook the main body, and scattered them with the excitement of our gallop. The Indians' soberly laden camels danced like ironmongery till they had shed their burdens. Then we calmed ourselves, and plodded together gently up Wadi Hafira, a gash like a sword-cut into the plateau. At its head lay a stiff pass to the height of Batra; but to-day we fell short of this, and out of laziness and craving for comfort stopped in the sheltered bottom of the valley. We lit great fires, which were cheerful in the cool evening. Farraj prepared rice in his manner for me as usual. Lloyd and Wood and Thorne had brought with them bully beef in tins and British army biscuits. So we joined ranks and feasted.

Next day we climbed the zigzag broken pass, the grassy street of Hafira below us framing a cone-hill in its centre, with, as background, the fantastic grey domes and glowing pyramids of the mountains of Rumm, prolonged to-day into wider fantasies by the cloud-masses brooding over them. We watched our long train wind upwards, till before noon the camels, Arabs, Indians and baggage had reached the top without accident. Contentedly we plumped ourselves down in the first green valley over the crest, sheltered from the wind, and warmed by the faint sunshine which tempered the autumn chill of this high tableland. Someone began to talk again about food.

CHAPTER LXXII

I WENT away north, scouting with Awad, a Sherari camel boy, engaged in Rumm without investigation. There were so many baggage camels in our party, and the Indians proved such novices at loading and leading them, that my bodyguard were being diverted from their proper duty of riding with me. So when Showakh introduced his cousin, a Khayal Sherari who would serve with me on any conditions, I accepted him at the glance: and now set out to measure his worth in a predicament.

We circled round Aba el Lissan to make sure that the Turks were in seemly idleness, for they had a habit of rushing a mounted patrol over the Batra sites at sudden notice, and I had no mind to put our party into unnecessary action yet. Awad was a ragged brown-skinned lad of perhaps eighteen, splendidly built, with the muscles and sinews of an athlete, active as a cat, alive in the saddle (he rode magnificently) and not ill-looking, though with something of the base appearance of the Sherarat, and in his savage eye an air of constant and rather suspicious expectancy, as though he looked any moment for something new from life, and that something not of his seeking or ordering, nor wholly grateful.

These Sherarat helots were an enigma of the desert. Other men might have hopes or illusions. Sherarat knew that nothing better than physical existence was willingly permitted them by mankind in this world or another. Such extreme degradation was a positive base on which to build a trust. I treated them exactly like the others in my bodyguard. This they found astonishing; and yet pleasant, when they had learned that my protection was active and sufficient. While they served me they became wholly my property, and good slaves they were, for nothing practicable in the desert was beneath their dignity, or beyond their tempered strength and experience.

Awad before me showed himself confused and self-conscious, though with his fellows he could be merry and full of japes. His engagement was a sudden fortune beyond dreams, and he was pitifully determined

to suit my mind. For the moment this was to wander across the Maan
high road in order to draw the Turks' notice. When we had succeeded,
and they trotted out in chase, we returned back, doubled again, and so
tricked their mule-riders away northward out of the direction of danger.
Awad took gleeful concern in the game and handled his new rifle well.

Afterwards I climbed with him to the top of a hill overlooking Batra,
and the valleys which sloped to Aba el Lissan, and we lay there lazily
till afternoon, watching the Turks riding in a vain direction, and our
fellows asleep, and their pasturing camels, and the shadows of the low
clouds seeming like gentle hollows as they chased over the grass in the
pale sunlight. It was peaceful, chilly, and very far from the fretting
world. The austerity of height shamed back the vulgar baggage of our
cares. In the place of consequence it set freedom, power to be alone, to
slip the escort of our manufactured selves; a rest and forgetfulness of
the chains of being.

But Awad could not forget his appetite and the new sensation of
power in my caravan to satisfy it regularly each day: so he fidgeted
about the ground on his belly chewing innumerable stalks of grass, and
talking to me of his animal joys in jerky phrases with averted face, till
we saw Ali's cavalcade beginning to lip over the head of the pass. Then
we ran down the slopes to meet them, and heard how he had lost four
camels on the pass, two broken by falls, two failing through weakness
as they mounted the rocky ledges. Also, he had fallen out again with
Abd el Kader, from whose deafness and conceit and boorish manners
he prayed God to deliver him. The Emir moved so cumbrously,
having no sense of the road: and flatly refused to join with Lloyd and
myself into one caravan, for safety.

We left them to follow us after dark, and as they had no guide, I
loaned them Awad. We would meet again in Auda's tents. Then we
moved forward over shallow valleys and cross-ridges till the sun set
behind the last high bank, from whose top we saw the square box of the
station at Ghadir el Haj breaking artificially out of the level, miles and
miles away. Behind us in the valley were broom bushes, so we called
a halt, and made our supper-fires. This evening Hassan Shah devised a
pleasant notion (later to become a habit) of winding up our meal by an
offering of his Indian tea. We were too greedy and grateful to refuse,

and shamelessly exhausted his tea and sugar before fresh rations could be sent him from the base.

Lloyd and I marked the bearing of the railway where we purposed to cross just below Shedia. As the stars rose we agreed that we must march upon Orion. So we started and marched on Orion for hour after hour, with effect that Orion seemed no nearer, and there were no signs of anything between us and him. We had debouched from the ridges upon the plain, and the plain was never-ending, and monotonously striped by shallow wadi-beds, with low, flat, straight banks, which in the milky star-light looked always like the earthwork of the expected railway. The going underfoot was firm, and the cool air of the desert in our faces made the camels swing out freely.

Lloyd and I went in front to spy out the line, that the main body might not be involved if chance put us against a Turkish blockhouse or night-patrol. Our fine camels, lightly ridden, set too long a stride; so that, without knowing, we drew more and more ahead of the laden Indians. Hassan Shah the Jemadar threw out a man to keep us in sight, and then another, and after that a third, till his party was a hurrying string of connecting files. Then he sent up an urgent whisper to go slowly, but the message which reached us after its passage through three languages was unintelligible.

We halted and so knew that the quiet night was full of sounds, while the scents of withering grass ebbed and flowed about us with the dying wind. Afterwards we marched again more slowly, as it seemed for hours, and the plain was still barred with deceitful dykes, which kept our attention at unprofitable stretch. We felt the stars were shifting and that we were steering wrong. Lloyd had a compass somewhere. We halted and groped in his deep saddle-bags. Thorne rode up and found it. We stood around calculating on its luminous arrow-head, and deserted Orion for a more auspicious northern star. Then again interminably forward till as we climbed a larger bank Lloyd reined up with a gasp and pointed. Fair in our track on the horizon were two cubes blacker than the sky, and by them a pointed roof. We were bearing straight for Shedia station, nearly into it.

We swung to the right, and jogged hastily across an open space, a little nervous lest some of the caravan strung out behind us should miss the abrupt change of course: but all was well, and a few minutes later in the next hollow we exchanged our thrill in English and Turkish, Arabic and Urdu. Behind us broke out a faint pulse-quickening clamour of dogs in the Turkish camp.

We now knew our place, and took a fresh bearing to avoid the first blockhouse below Shedia. We led off confidently, expecting in a little to cross the line. Yet again time dragged and nothing showed itself. It was midnight, we had marched for six hours, and Lloyd began to speak bitterly of reaching Bagdad in the morning. There could be no railway here. Thorne saw a row of trees, and saw them move; the bolts of our rifles clicked, but they were only trees.

We gave up hope, and rode carelessly, nodding in our saddles, letting our tired eyes lid themselves. My Rima lost her temper suddenly. With a squeal she plunged sideways, nearly unseating me, pranced wildly over two banks and a ditch and flung herself flat in a dusty place. I hit her over the head, and she rose and paced forward nervously. Again the Indians lagged far behind our hasty selves; but after an hour the last bank of to-night loomed differently in front of us. It took straight shape, and over its length grew darker patches which might be the shadowed mouths of culverts. We spurred our minds to a fresh interest, and drove our animals swiftly and silently forward. When we were nearer it, the bank put up a fencing of sharp spikes along its edge. These were the telegraph poles. A white-headed figure checked us for a moment, but he never stirred, and so we judged him a kilometre post.

Quickly we halted our party and rode to one side and then straight in, to challenge what lay behind the quiet of the place, expecting the darkness to spout fire at us suddenly, and the silence to volley out in rifle shots. But there was no alarm. We reached the bank and found it deserted. We dismounted and ran up and down each way two hundred yards: nobody. There was room for our passage.

We ordered the others immediately over into the empty, friendly desert on the east, and sat ourselves on the metals under the singing wires, while the long line of shadowy bulks wavered up out of the dark, shuffled a little on the bank and its ballast, and passed down behind us into the dark in that strained noiselessness which was a night march of camels. The last one crossed. Our little group collected about a telegraph post. Out of a short scuffle Thorne rose slowly up the pole to catch the lowest wire and swing himself to its insulator-bracket. He reached for the top, and a moment later there was a loud metallic twang and shaking of the post as the cut wire leaped back each way into the air, and slapped itself free from six or more poles on either side. The second and third wires followed it, twisting noisily along the stony ground, and yet no answering sound came out of the night, showing that we had passed rightly in the empty distance of two blockhouses. Thorne, with splintery hands, slid down the tottering pole. We walked to our kneeling camels, and trotted after the company. Another hour, and we ordered a rest till dawn; but before then were roused by a brief flurry of rifle fire and the tapping of a machine-gun far away to the north. Little Ali and Abd el Kadir were not making so clean a crossing of the line.

Next morning, in a cheerful sunshine, we marched up parallel with the line to salute the first train from Maan, and then struck inland over the strange Jefer plain. The day was close, and the sun's power increased, making mirages on all the heated flats. Riding apart from our straggling party, we saw some of them drowned in the silver flood, others swimming high over its changing surface, which stretched and shrank with each swaying of the camel, or inequality of ground.

Early in the afternoon we found Auda camped unobtrusively in the broken, bushy expanse south-west of the wells. He received us with constraint. His large tents, with the women, had been sent away beyond reach of the Turkish aeroplanes. There were few Toweiha present: and those in violent dispute over the distribution of tribal wages. The old man was sad we should find him in such weakness.

I did my best tactfully to smooth the troubles by giving their minds a new direction and countervailing interests. Successfully too, for they smiled, which with Arabs was often half the battle. Enough advantage for the time; we adjourned to eat with Mohammed el Dheilan. He was a better diplomat, because less open than Auda; and would have looked cheerful if he thought proper, whatever the truth. So we were made very welcome to his platter of rice and meat and dried tomatoes. Mohammed, a villager at heart, fed too well.

After the meal, as we were wandering back over the grey dry

ditches, like mammoth-wallows, which floods had hacked deeply into the fibrous mud, I broached to Zaal my plans for an expedition to the Yarmuk bridges. He disliked the idea very much. Zaal in October was not the Zaal of August. Success was changing the hard-riding gallant of spring into a prudent man, whose new wealth made life precious to him. In the spring he would have led me anywhere; but the last raid had tried his nerve, and now he said he would mount only if I made a personal point of it.

I asked what party we could make up; and he named three of the men in the camp as good fellows for so desperate a hope. The rest of the tribe were away, dissatisfied. To take three Toweiha would be worse than useless, for their just conceit would inflame the other men, while they themselves were too few to suffice alone: so I said I would try elsewhere. Zaal showed his relief.

While we were still discussing what we ought to do (for I needed the advice of Zaal, one of the finest raiders alive, and most competent to judge my half-formed scheme), a scared lad rushed to our coffee-hearth and blurted that riders in a dust-cloud were coming up fast from the side of Maan. The Turks there had a mule-regiment and a cavalry regiment, and were always boasting that they would some day visit the Abu Tayi. So we jumped up to receive them.

Auda had fifteen men, of whom five were able-bodied, and the rest greybeards or boys, but we were thirty strong, and I pondered the hard luck of the Turkish commander who had chosen for his surprise the day on which there happened to be guesting with the Howeitat a section of Indian machine-gunners who knew their business. We couched and knee-haltered the camels in the deeper water-cuts, and placed the Vickers and Lewis in others of these natural trenches, admirably screened with alkali bushes, and commanding a flat field eight hundred yards each way. Auda dropped his tents, and threw out his riflemen to supplement our fire; and then we waited easily till the first horseman rode up the bank on to our level, and we saw they were Ali ibn el Hussein and Abd el Kadir, coming to Jefer from the enemy direction. We forgathered merrily, while Mohammed produced a second edition of tomato-rice for Ali's comfort. They had lost two men and a mare in the shooting on the railway in the night.

CHAPTER LXXIII

LLOYD was to go back from here to Versailles, and we asked Auda for a guide to take him across the line. About the man there was no difficulty, but great difficulty in mounting him; for the Howeitat camels were at pasture: and the nearest pasture lay a full day's journey south-east of these barren wells. I cut this difficulty by providing a mount for the new guide from my own beasts. Choice fell on my ancient Ghazala, whose pregnancy had proved more heavy than we thought. Before our long expedition ended she would be unfit for fast work. So, in honour of his good seat and cheerful spirit, Thorne was transferred to her, while the Howeitat stared open-mouthed. They esteemed Ghazala above all the camels of their desert and would have paid much for the honour of riding her, and here she was given to a soldier, whose pink face and eyes swollen with ophthalmia made him look feminine and tearful; a little, said Lloyd, like an abducted nun. It was a sorry thing to see Lloyd go. He was understanding, helped wisely, and wished our cause well. Also he was the only fully-taught man with us in Arabia, and in these few days together our minds had ranged abroad, discussing any book or thing in heaven or earth which crossed our fancy. When he left we were given over again to war and tribes and camels without end.

The night began with a surfeit of such work. The matter of the Howeitat must be put right. After dark we gathered round Auda's hearth, and for hours I was reaching out to this circle of fire-lit faces, playing on them with all the tortuous arts I knew, now catching one, now another (it was easy to see the flash in their eyes when a word got home); or again, taking a false line, and wasting minutes of precious time without response. The Abu Tayi were as hard-minded as they were hard-bodied, and the heat of conviction had burned out of them long since in stress of work.

Gradually I won my points, but the argument was yet marching near midnight when Auda held up his stick and called silence. We listened, wondering what the danger was, and after a while we felt a creeping reverberation, a cadence of blows too dull, too wide, too slow easily to find response in our ears. It was like the mutter of a distant, very lowly thunderstorm. Auda raised his haggard eyes towards the west, and said, 'The English guns'. Allenby was leading off in preparation, and his helpful sounds closed my case for me beyond dispute.

Next morning the atmosphere of the camp was serene and cordial. Old Auda, his difficulties over for this time, embraced me warmly, invoking peace upon us. At the last, whilst I was standing with my hand on my couched camel, he ran out, took me in his arms again, and strained me to him. I felt his harsh beard brush my ear as he whispered to me windily, 'Beware of Abd el Kader.' There were too many about us to say more.

We pushed on over the unending but weirdly beautiful Jefer flats, till night fell on us at the foot of a flint scarp, like a cliff above the plain. We camped there, in a snake-infested pocket of underwood. Our marches were short and very leisurely. The Indians had proved novices on the road. They had been for weeks inland from Wejh, and I had rashly understood that they were riders; but now, on good animals, and trying their best, they could average only thirty-five miles a day, a holiday for the rest of the party.

So for us each day was an easy movement, without effort, quite free from bodily strain. A golden weather of misty dawns, mild sunlight, and an evening chill added a strange peacefulness of nature to the peacefulness of our march. This week was a St. Martin's summer, which passed like a remembered dream. I felt only that it was very gentle, very comfortable, that the air was happy, and my friends content. Conditions so perfect must needs presage the ending of our time; but this certainty, because of its being unchallenged by any rebellious hope, served only to deepen the quiet of the autumnal present. There was no thought or care at all. My mind was as near stilled those days as ever in my life.

We camped for lunch and for a midday rest – the soldiers had to have three meals a day. Suddenly there was an alarm. Men on horses and camels appeared from the west and north and closed quickly on us. We snatched our rifles. The Indians, getting used to short notices, now carried their Vickers and Lewis mounted for action. After thirty seconds we were in complete posture of defence, though in this shallow country our position held little of advantage. To the front on each flank were my bodyguards in their brilliant clothes, lying spread out between the grey tufts of weed, with their rifles lovingly against their cheeks. By them the four neat groups of khaki Indians crouched about their guns. Behind them lay Sherif Ali's men, himself in their midst, bareheaded and keen, leaning easily upon his rifle. In the background the camel men were driving in our grazing animals to be under cover of our fire.

It was a picture that the party made. I was admiring ourselves and Sherif Ali was exhorting us to hold our fire till the attack became real, when Awad, with a merry laugh sprang up and ran out towards the enemy, waving his full sleeve over his head in sign of friendliness. They fired at, or over him, ineffectually. He lay down and shot back, one shot, aimed just above the head of the foremost rider. That, and our ready silence perplexed them. They pulled off in a hesitant group, and after a minute's discussion, flagged back their cloaks in half-hearted reply to our signal.

One of them rode towards us at a foot's pace. Awad, protected by our rifles, went two hundred yards to meet him, and saw that he was a Sukhurri, who, when he heard our names, feigned shock. We walked together to Sherif Ali, followed at a distance by the rest of the newcomers, after they had seen our peaceful greeting. They were a raiding party from the Zebn Sukhur, who were camped, as we had expected, in front at Bair.

Ali, furious with them, for their treacherous attack on us, threatened all sorts of pains. They accepted his tirade sullenly, saying that it was a Beni Sakhr manner to shoot over strangers. Ali accepted this as their habit, and a good habit in the desert, but protested that their unheralded appearance against us from three sides showed a premeditated ambush. The Beni Sakhr were a dangerous gang, not pure enough nomads to hold the nomadic code of honour or to obey the desert law in spirit, and not villagers enough to have abjured the business of rapine and raid.

Our late assailants went into Bair to report our coming. Mifleh, chief of their clan, thought it best to efface the ill-reception by a public show in which all men and horses in the place turned out to welcome us with wild cheers and gallopings and curvettings, and much firing of shots and shouting. They whirled round and round us in desperate chase, clattering over rocks with reckless horsemanship and small regard for our staidness, as they broke in and out of the ranks and let off their rifles under our camels' necks continually. Clouds of parching chalk dust arose, so that men's voices croaked.

Eventually the parade eased off, but then Abd el Kader, thinking the opinion even of fools desirable, felt it upon him to assert his virtue. They were shouting to Ali ibn el Hussein 'God give victory to our Sherif' and were reining back on their haunches beside me with 'Welcome, Aurans, harbinger of action.' So he climbed up his mare, into her high Moorish saddle, and with his seven Algerian servants behind him in stiff file, began to prance delicately in slow curves, crying out 'Houp, Houp', in his throaty voice, and firing a pistol unsteadily in the air.

The Bedu, astonished at this performance, gaped silently, till Mifleh came to us, and said, in his wheedling way, 'Lords pray call off your servant, for he can neither shoot nor ride, and if he hits someone he will destroy our good fortune of to-day'. Mifleh did not know the family precedent for his nervousness. Abd el Kader's brother held what might well be a world's record for three successive fatal accidents with automatic pistols in the circle of his Damascus friends. Ali Riza Pasha, chief local gladiator, had said 'Three things are notably impossible: one, that Turkey win this war; one, that the Mediterranean become champagne; one that I be found in the same place with Mohammed Said, and he armed'.

We off-loaded by the ruins. Beyond us the black tents of the Beni Sakhr were like a herd of goats spotting the valley. A messenger bade us to Mifleh's tent. First, however, Ali had an inquiry to make. At the request of the Beni Sakhr, Feisal had sent a party of Bisha masons and well-sinkers to reline the blasted well from which Nasir and I had picked the gelignite on our way to Akaba. They had been for months in Bair and yet reported that the work was not nearly finished. Feisal had deputed us to inquire into the reasons for the costly delay. Ali found that the Bisha men had been living at ease and forcing the Arabs to provide them with meat and flour. He charged them with it. They prevaricated, vainly, for Sherifs had a trained judicial instinct, and Mifleh was preparing a great supper for us. My men whispered excitedly that sheep had been seen to die behind his tent high on the knoll above the graves. So Ali's justice moved on wings before the food-bowls could be carried up. He heard and condemned the blacks all in a moment, and had judgement inflicted on them by his slaves inside the ruins. They returned a little self-conscious, kissed hands in sign of amenity and forgiveness, and a reconciled party knelt together to meat.

Howeitat feasts had been wet with butter; the Beni Sakhr were overflowing. Our clothes were splashed, our mouths running over, the tips of our fingers scalded with its heat. As the sharpness of hunger was appeased the hands dipped more slowly; but the meal was still far from its just end when Abd el Kader grunted, rose suddenly to his feet, wiped his hands on a handkerchief, and sat back on the carpets by the tent wall. We hesitated, but Ali muttered 'The fellah' and the work continued until all the men of our sitting were full, and the more frugal of us had begun to lick the stiff fat from our smarting fingers.

Ali cleared his throat, and we returned to our carpets while the second and third relays round the pans were satisfied. One little thing, of five or six, in a filthy smock, sat there stuffing solemnly with both hands from first to last, and, at the end, with swollen belly and face glistening with grease, staggered off speechlessly hugging a huge unpicked rib in triumph to its breast.

In front of the tent the dogs cracked the dry bones loudly, and Mifleh's slave in the corner split the sheep's skull and sucked out the brains. Meanwhile, Abd el Kader sat spitting and belching and picking his teeth. Finally, he sent one of his servants for his medicine chest, and poured himself out a draught, grumbling that tough meat was bad for his digestion. He had meant by such unmannerliness to make himself a reputation for grandeur. His own villagers could no doubt be brow-beaten so, but the Zebn were too near the desert to be measured by a purely peasant-measure. Also to-day they had before their eyes the contrary example of Sherif Ali ibn el Hussein, a born desert-lord.

His fashion of rising all at once from the food was of the central deserts. On fringes of cultivation, among the semi-nomadic, each guest slipped aside as he was full. The Anazeh of the extreme north set the stranger by himself, and in the dark, that he be not ashamed of his appetite. All these were modes; but among the considerable clans the manner of the Sherifs was generally praised. So poor Abd el Kader was not understood.

He took himself off, and we sat in the tent-mouth, above the dark hollow, now set out in little constellations of tent-fires, seeming to mimic or reflect the sky above. It was a calm night, except when the dogs provoked one another to choral howlings, and as these grew rarer we heard again the quiet, steady thudding of the heavy guns preparing assault in Palestine.

To this artillery accompaniment we told Mifleh that we were about to raid the Deraa district, and would be glad to have him and some fifteen of his tribesmen with us, all on camels. After our failure with the Howeitat, we had decided not to announce our plain object, lest its forlorn character dissuade our partisans. However, Mifleh agreed at once, apparently with haste and pleasure, promising to bring with him the fifteen best men in the tribe and his own son. This lad, Turki by name, was an old love of Ali ibn el Hussein; the animal in each called to the other, and they wandered about inseparably, taking pleasure in a touch and silence. He was a fair, open-faced boy of perhaps seventeen; not tall, but broad and powerful, with a round freckled face, upturned nose, and very short upper lip, showing his strong teeth, but giving his full mouth rather a sulky look, belied by the happy eyes.

We found him plucky and faithful on two critical occasions. His good temper atoned for his having caught a little of the begging habit of his father, whose face was eaten up with greed. Turki's great anxiety was to be sure that he was reckoned a man among the men, and he was always looking to do something bold and wonderful which would let him flaunt his courage before the girls of his tribe. He rejoiced exceedingly in a new silk robe which I gave him at dinner, and walked, to display it, twice through the tent-village without his cloak, railing at those who seemed laggard from our meet.

CHAPTER LXXIV

DARK had fallen long before our caravan left Bair, after watering. We chiefs waited longer still while the Zebn got ready. Mifleh's preparations included a visit to Essad, the supposed ancestor of the clan, in his bedecked tomb near Annad's grave. The Beni Sakhr were already settled enough to have dressed themselves in the Semitic village-superstitions of sacred places, holy trees, and funerary shrines. Sheikh Mifleh thought the occasion warranted his adding another head-cord to the ragged collection looped round Essad's headstone, and characteristically asked us to provide the offering. I handed over one of my rich red-and-silk-silver Mecca ornaments, remarking that the virtue lay with the donor. The thrifty Mifleh pressed upon me one halfpenny in exchange, that he might plead purchase; and when I came past a few weeks later and saw that the gaud was gone, he cursed loudly in my hearing the sacrilege of some godless Sherari, who had robbed his ancestor. Turki would have told me more.

A steep old pathway took us out of Wadi Bair. Near the crest of a ridge we found the others camped for the night round a fire, but there passed no talk or coffee-making for this time. We lay close together, hushed and straining the ears to catch the throbbing of Allenby's guns. They spoke eloquently: and sheet lightning in the west made gun-flashes for them.

Next day we passed to the left of the Thlaithukhwat, the 'Three Sisters' whose clean white peaks were landmarks on their lofty water-shed for a day's journey all about; and went down the soft rolling slopes beyond them. The exquisite November morning had a softness in it like an English summer; but its beauty had to be fought off. I was spending the halts, and riding the stages, in the ranks of the Beni Sakhr teaching my ear their dialect, and storing in my memory the tribal, family or personal notes they let drop.

In the little-peopled desert every worshipful man knew every other; and instead of books they studied their generation. To have fallen short in such knowledge would have meant being branded either as ill-bred, or as a stranger; and strangers were not admitted to familiar intercourse or councils, or confidences. There was nothing so wearing, yet nothing so important for the success of my purpose, as this constant mental gymnastic of apparent omniscience at each time of meeting a new tribe.

At nightfall we camped in an affluent of Wadi Jesha, by some bushes of faint grey-green foliage, which pleased our camels and gave us fire-wood. That night the guns were very clear and loud, perhaps because the intervening hollow of the Dead Sea drummed the echoes up and over our high plateau. The Arabs whispered 'They are nearer; the English are advancing; God deliver the men under that rain'. They were thinking compassionately of the passing Turks, so long their weak oppressors; whom, for their weakness, though oppressors, they loved more than the strong foreigner with his blind indiscriminate justice.

The Arab respected force a little: he respected craft more, and often had it in enviable degree: but most of all he respected blunt sincerity of utterance, nearly the sole weapon God had excluded from his arma-ment. The Turk was all things by turn, and so commended himself to the Arabs for such while as he was not corporately feared. Much lay in this distinction of the corporate and the personal. There were Englishmen whom, individually, the Arabs preferred to any Turk, or foreigner; but, on the strength of this, to have generalized and called the Arabs pro-English, would have been a folly. Each stranger made his own poor bed among them.

We were up early, meaning to push the long way to Ammari by sunset. We crossed ridge after carpeted ridge of sun-burned flints, grown over with a tiny saffron plant so bright and close that all the view was gold. Safra el Jesha, the Sukhur called it. The valleys were only inches deep, their beds grained like morocco leather, in an intricate curving mesh, by innumerable rills of water after the last rain. The swell of every curve was a grey breast of sand set hard with mud, sometimes glistening with salt-crystals, and sometimes rough with the projecting brush of half-buried twigs which had caused it. These tailings of valleys running into Sirhan were always rich in grazing. When there was water in their hollows the tribes collected, and peopled them with tent-villages. The Beni Sakhr with us had so camped; and,

as we crossed the monotonous downs they pointed first to one in-
distinctive hollow with hearth and straight gutter-trenches and then to
another saying, 'There was my tent and there lay Hamdan el Saih.
Look at the dry stones for my bed-place, and for Tarfa's next it. God
have mercy upon her, she died the year of samh, in the Snainirat, of a
puff-adder.'

About noon a party of trotting camels appeared over the ridge,
moving fast, and openly towards us. Little Turki cantered out on his
old she-camel, with cocked carbine across his thighs, to find what they
meant. 'Ha,' cried Mifleh to me while they were still a mile off, 'that
is Fahad, on his Shaara, in the front. These are our kinsmen', and sure
enough they were. Fahad and Adhub, chief war-leaders of the Zebn,
had been camped west of the railway by Ziza, when a Gomani came in
with news of our march. They had saddled at once, and by hard riding
caught us only half-way on the road. Fahad, in courteous fashion,
chided me gently for presuming to ride their district on an adventure
while his father's sons lay in their tent.

Fahad was a melancholy, soft-voiced, little-spoken man of perhaps
thirty, with a white face, trim beard and tragic eyes. His young brother
Adhub was taller and stronger, yet not above middle height. Unlike
Fahad, he was active, noisy, uncouth-looking; with a snub nose, hairless
boy's face and gleaming green eyes flickering hungrily from object to
object. His commonness was pointed by his dishevelled hair and dirty
clothes. Fahad was neater, but still very plainly dressed, and the pair,
on their shaggy home-bred camels, looked as little like sheikhs of their
reputation as can be conceived. However, they were famous fighters.

At Ammari a high cold night wind was stirring the ashen dust of the
salt-ground about the wells into a haze, which gritted in our teeth like
the stale breath of an eruption; and we were ungrateful for the water.
It was on the surface, like so much of Sirhan, but most of the pools
were too bitter to drink. One notable one, however, called Bir el
Emir was thought very good by contrast. It lay in a little floor of bare
limestone among sand-hummocks.

The water (opaque and tasting of mixed brine and ammonia) was
just below the level of the rock-slab, in a stone bath with ragged undercut lips. Its depth Daud proved, by hurling Farraj fully-dressed into it.

He sank out of view in its yellowness, and afterwards rose quietly to the surface under the rock-edge where he could not be seen in the dusk. Daud waited a strained minute; but when his victim did not appear tore off his cloak and plunged after — to find him smiling under the over-hanging ledge. Pearl-diving in the gulf had made them like fishes in the water.

They were dragged out, and then had a wild struggle in the sand beside the water-hole. Each sustained hurt, and they returned to my fire dripping wet, in rags, bleeding, with their hair and faces, legs, arms and bodies covered with mud and thorns, more like the devils of a whirlwind than their usual suave delicate presences. They said they had been dancing, and had tripped over a bush; it would be like my generosity to make them a gift of new clothes. I blasted their hopes, and sent them off to repair damages.

My bodyguard, more especially the Ageyl in it, were by nature foppish, and spent their wages on dress or ornaments, and much time in braiding their plaits of shining hair. Butter gave it the polish; and to keep down the vermin they frequently dragged the scalp with a fine-toothed comb, and sprinkled it with camel-staling. A German doctor at Beersheba, in their Turkish days (these were the men who one misty dawn rushed our Yeomanry in Sinai and wiped out a post) had taught them to be clean by prisoning the lousy ones in army latrines until they had swallowed their lice.

The wind became faint at dawn, and we moved forward for Azrak, half a march ahead. Hardly, however, were we clear of the drifts beside the wells when there was an alarm. Mounted men had been seen in the brushwood. This country was a tom-tiddler's ground of raiding parties. We drew together in the best place and halted. The Indian section chose a tiny ridge hacked about with narrow ruts of water-channels. They couched camels in the hollow behind, and had their guns mounted in due order in a moment. Ali and Abd el Kader threw out their great crimson banners in the intermittent breeze. Our skirmishers headed by Ahmed and Awad, ran out to right and left, and long shots were exchanged. All of it ended suddenly. The enemy broke cover and marched in line towards us, waving their cloaks and sleeves in the air and chanting their war-march of welcome. They were the fighting men of the Serhan tribe on their way to swear allegiance to Feisal. When they heard our news they turned back with us, rejoicing to be spared the road, for this tribe was not ordinarily warlike or nomadic. They made some little pomp over our joint entry to their tents at Ain el Beidha, a few miles east of Azrak, where the whole tribe was gathered; and our reception was loud, because there had been fear and lamentation among the women that morning when they saw their men march away on the hazard of rebellion.

However, here they were returning the same day, with a Sherif of their own, and Arab banners, and machine-guns, marching a ragged hundred men abreast, and singing as merrily as when they started out. My eyes were upon a notable red camel, perhaps a seven-year-old, under a Sirhani in the second line. The tall beast would not be put upon, but with a long, swinging pace, of which there was no equal in the crowd of us, forged to the front, and kept there. Ahmed slipped off to get acquainted with her owner.

In the camp the chief men distributed our party among their tents for the privilege of entertainment. Ali, Abd el Kader, Wood and myself were taken in by Mteir, the paramount sheikh of the tribe, an old, toothless, friendly thing, whose loose jaw sagged in his supporting hand all the while he talked. He gave us a fussy greeting and abundant hospitality of seethed sheep and bread. Wood and Abd el Kader were, perhaps, a little squeamish, for the Serahin seemed primitive in food-discipline, and at the common bowl there was more splashing and spluttering than was proper in the best tents. Afterwards, by constraint of Mteir's urgency, we lay on his rugs for the one night. Round our fresh bodies, for the change of food, collected all such local ticks, fleas and lice as were sick of a diet of unmitigated Serhan. Their delight made them so ravenous that with the best will in the world I could not go on feasting them. Nor apparently could Ali; for he, too, sat up and said that he felt wakeful. So we roused Sheikh Mteir, and sent for Mifleh ibn Bani, a young, active man, accustomed to command their battles. To them we explained Feisal's needs, and our plan to relieve him.

Gravely they heard us. The western bridge, they said, was quite impossible. The Turks had just filled its country with hundreds of military wood-cutters. No hostile party could slip through undetected. They professed great suspicion of the Moorish villages, and of Abd el Kader. Nothing would persuade them to visit the one under the guidance of the other. For Tell el Shehab, the nearest bridge, they feared lest the villagers, their inveterate enemies, attack them in the rear. Also if it rained the camels would be unable to trot back across the muddy plains by Remthe, and the whole party would be cut off and killed.

We were now in deep trouble. The Serahin were our last resource, and if they refused to come with us we should be unable to carry out Allenby's project by the appointed time. Accordingly Ali collected about our little fire more of the better men of the tribe, and fortified the part of courage by bringing in Fahad, and Mifleh, and Adhub. Before them we began to combat in words this crude prudence of the Serahin, which seemed all the more shameful to us after our long sojourn in the clarifying wilderness.

We put it to them, not abstractedly, but concretely, for their case, how life in mass was sensual only, to be lived and loved in its extremity. There could be no rest-houses for revolt, no dividend of joy paid out. Its spirit was accretive, to endure as far as the senses would endure, and to use each such advance as base for further adventure, deeper privation, sharper pain. Sense could not reach back or forward. A felt emotion was a conquered emotion, an experience gone dead, which we buried by expressing it.

To be of the desert was, as they knew, a doom to wage unending battle with an enemy who was not of the world, nor life, nor anything, but hope itself; and failure seemed God's freedom to mankind. We might only exercise this our freedom by not doing what it lay within our power to do, for then life would belong to us, and we should have mastered it by holding it cheap. Death would seem best of all our works, the last free loyalty within our grasp, our final leisure: and of these two poles, death and life, or, less finally, leisure and subsistence, we should shun subsistence (which was the stuff of life) in all save its faintest degree, and cling close to leisure. Thereby we would serve to promote the not-doing rather than the doing. Some men, there might be, uncreative; whose leisure was barren; but the activity of these would have been material only. To bring forth immaterial things, things creative, partaking of spirit, not of flesh, we must be jealous of spending time or trouble upon physical demands, since in most men the soul grew aged long before the body. Mankind had been no gainer by its drudges.

There could be no honour in a sure success, but much might be wrested from a sure defeat. Omnipotence and the Infinite were our two worthiest foemen, indeed the only ones for a full man to meet, they being monsters of his own spirit's making; and the stoutest enemies were always of the household. In fighting Omnipotence, honour was proudly to throw away the poor resources that we had, and dare Him empty-handed; to be beaten, not merely by more mind, but by its advantage of better tools. To the clear-sighted, failure was the only goal. We must believe, through and through, that there was no victory, except to go down into death fighting and crying for failure itself, calling in excess of despair to Omnipotence to strike harder, that by His very striking He might temper our tortured selves into the weapon of His own ruin.

This was a halting, half-coherent speech, struck out desperately, moment by moment, in our extreme need, upon the anvil of those white minds round the dying fire; and hardly its sense remained with me afterwards; for once my picture-making memory forgot its trade and only felt the slow humbling of the Serahin, the night-quiet in which their worldliness faded, and at last their flashing eagerness to ride with us whatever the bourne. Before daylight we called old Abd el Kader, and, taking him aside among the sandy thickets, screamed into his dense ear that the Serahin would start with us, under his auspices, for Wadi Khalid, after sunrise. He grunted that it was well: and we said to one another that never, if life and opportunity were prolonged for us, would we take a deaf man for a conspirator again.

CHAPTER LXXV

EXHAUSTED, we lay down a moment, but were astir again very early to review the camel-men of the Sirhan. They made a wild and ragged show, dashing past, but we thought them loose riders, and they blustered too much to be quite convincing. It was a pity they had no real leader. Mteir was too old for service, and ibn Bani was an indistinct man, ambitious rather as a politician than as a fighter. However, they were the force we had, so there was an end to it, and at three in the afternoon we mounted for Azrak, since another night in the tent would have left us picked to dry bones. Abd el Kader and his servants mounted their mares, as sign that the fighting line was near. They rode just behind us.

It was to be Ali's first view of Azrak, and we hurried up the stony ridge in high excitement, talking of the wars and songs and passions of the early shepherd kings, with names like music, who had loved this place; and of the Roman legionaries who languished here as garrison in yet earlier times. Then the blue fort on its rock above the rustling palms, with the fresh meadows and shining springs of water, broke on our sight. Of Azrak, as of Rumm, one said *'Numen inest'*. Both were magically haunted: but whereas Rumm was vast and echoing and God-like, Azrak's unfathomable silence was steeped in knowledge of wandering poets, champions, lost kingdoms, all the crime and chivalry and dead magnificence of Hira and Ghassan. Each stone or blade of it was radiant with half-memory of the luminous silky Eden, which had passed so long ago.

At last Ali shook his rein, and his camel picked her careful way down the lava flow to the rich turf behind the springs. Our puckered eyes opened wide with relief that the bitterness of many weeks was gone out of the reflected sunlight. Ali screamed 'Grass', and flung himself off the saddle to the ground on hands and feet, his face bowed down among the harsh stems which seemed so kindly in the desert. He leaped up, flushed, with his Harith war-cry, tore his head-cloth off, and raced along the marsh, bounding over the red channels where water clotted among the reeds. His white feet flashed beneath the tossed folds of his cash-mere robes. We in the West seldom experienced that added beauty when the body was seen lightly poised on bare feet; when the rhythm and grace of movement became visible, with the play of muscle and sinew pointing the mechanism of each stride and the balance of repose.

When we turned again to business there was no Abd el Kader. We looked for him in the castle, in the palm-garden, over by the spring. Eventually we sent our men away to search, and they came back with Arabs, who told us that from just after the start he had ridden off north-ward through the flaky hillocks, towards Jebel Druse. The rank and file did not know our plans, hated him, and had been glad to see him go: but it was bad news for us.

Of our three alternatives, Um Keis had been abandoned: without Abd el Kader, Wadi Khalid was impossible: this meant that we must necessarily attempt the bridge at Tell el Shehab. To reach it we had to cross the open land between Remthe and Deraa. Abd el Kader was gone up to the enemy, with information of our plans and strength. The Turks, if they took the most reasonable precautions, would trap us at the bridge. We took council with Fahad and decided to push on none the less, trusting to the usual incompetence of our enemy. It was not a confident decision. While we took it the sunshine seemed less lambent, and Azrak not so aloof from fear.

Next morning we wound pensively along a flinty valley and over a ridge into Wadi el Harith, whose green course had a sickening likeness to some lands at home. Ali rejoiced to see a rich pasture-valley bearing his family name, and was as glad as our camels when we found limpid pools of last week's rain-water in hollows among the bushes. We stopped and used the discovery for lunch, making a long halt. Adhub went off with Ahmed and Awad to look for gazelle. He came back with three. So we stopped yet longer and made a second lunch, like a feast, of meat gobbets roasted on ramrods till the outside was black as coal, while the heart remained juicily sweet. Sojourners in the desert loved its accidental bounty; also on this trip a reluctance weighed down our daily marching, to make us glad of each delay.

Unhappily my rest time was spoiled by a bed of justice. The feud between Ahmed and Awad broke out during this gazelle chase into a duel. Awad shot off Ahmed's head-rope; Ahmed holed Awad's cloak. I disarmed them and gave loud order that the right thumb and fore-finger of each be cut off. The terror of this drove them into an instant, violent and public kissing of peace. A little later all my men went capital bail that the trouble had ended. I referred the case to Ali ibn el Hussein, who set them at liberty on probation, after sealing their promise with the ancient and curious nomad penance of striking the head sharply with the edge of a weighty dagger again and again till the issuing blood had run down to the waist belt. It caused painful but not dangerous scalp wounds, whose ache at first and whose scars later were supposed to remind the would-be defaulter of the bond he had given.

We pushed on again for miles over perfect going, through rich country for the camels, till at Abu Sawana we found a flinty hollow, brim-full of deliciously clear rain-water in a narrow channel two feet deep, and perhaps ten feet wide, but half a mile long. This would serve as starting point for our bridge-raid. To be sure of its safety, we rode a few yards further, to the top of a stony knoll; and there found ourselves looking down upon a retreating party of Circassian horse-men, sent out by the Turks to report if the waters were occupied. They had missed us, to our mutual benefit, by five minutes.

Next morning we filled our water-skins, since we should find nothing to drink between here and the bridge; and then marched leisurely until the desert ended in a three-foot depression at the edge of a clean plain, which extended flatly to the metals of the railway some miles off. We halted for dusk to make its crossing possible. Our plan was to slip over secretly, and hide in the further foothills, below Deraa. In the spring these hills were full of grazing sheep, for the rain cloaked their low sides in new grass and flowers. With the coming of summer they dried, and became deserted save for chance travellers on obscure errands. We might fairly calculate on lying in their folds for a day undisturbed.

We made our halt another opportunity of food, for we were reck-lessly eating all we could as often as we had the chance. It lightened our stores, and kept us from thinking: but even with this help the day was very long. At last sunset came. The plain shivered once, as the darkness, which for an hour had been gathering among the facing hills,

flowed slowly out and drowned it. We mounted. Two hours later
after a quick march over gravel, Fahad and myself, out scouting ahead,
came to the railway; and without difficulty found a stony place where
our caravan would make no signs of passage. The Turkish rail-guards
were clearly at their ease, which meant that Abd el Kader had not yet
caused a panic by what news he brought.

We rode the other side of the line for half an hour, and then dipped
into a very slight rocky depression full of succulent plants. This was
Ghadir el Abyadh, recommended by Mifleh as our ambush. We took
his surprising word that we were in cover, and lay down among or
alongside our loaded beasts for a short sleep. Dawn would show us
how far we were safe and hidden.

As day was breaking, Fahad led me to the edge of our pit, some fifteen
feet above, and from it we looked straight across a slowly-dropping
meadow to the railway, which seemed nearly within shot. It was most
inconveniently close, but the Sukhur knew no better place. We had to
stand-to all the day. Each time something was reported, our men ran
to look at it, and the low bank would grow a serried frieze of human
heads. Also, the grazing camels required many guards to keep them
from straying into view. Whenever a patrol passed we had to be very
gentle in controlling the beasts, since if one of them had roared or
ruckled it would have drawn the enemy. Yesterday had been long:
to-day was longer: we could not feed, as our water had to be husbanded
with jealous care against the scarcity of to-morrow. The very knowledge made us thirsty.

Ali and I worked at the last arrangements for our ride. We were
penned here until sunset; and must reach Tell el Shehab, blow up the
bridge, and get back east of the railway by dawn. This meant a ride
of at least eighty miles in the thirteen hours of darkness, with an
elaborate demolition thrown in. Such a performance was beyond the
capacity of most of the Indians. They were not good riders, and had
broken up their camels in the march from Akaba. An Arab by saving
his beast, could bring it home in fair condition after hard work. The
Indians had done their best; but the discipline of their cavalry training
had tired out them and the animals in our easy stages.

So we picked out the six best riders and put them on the six best camels, with Hassan Shab, their officer and greatest-hearted man, to lead them. He decided that this little party would be fittest armed with just one Vickers gun. It was a very serious reduction of our offensive power. The more I looked at it, the less fortunate seemed the development of this Yarmuk plan of ours.

The Beni Sakhr were fighting men; but we distrusted the Serahin. So Ali and I decided to make the Beni Sakhr, under Fahad, our storming party. We would leave some Serahin to guard the camels while the others carried the blasting gelatine in our dismounted charge upon the bridge. To suit the hurried carriage down steep hill-sides in the dark we changed the explosive loads into thirty-pound lumps, which were put, for visibility, each lump into its own white bag. Wood undertook to repack the gelatine, and shared the rare headache all got from handling it. This helped pass the time.

My bodyguard had to be carefully distributed. One good rider was told off to each of the less expert local men, whose virtue was that they knew the country: the pairs so made were attached to one or other of my foreign liabilities, with instructions to keep close to him all night. Ali ibn el Hussein took six of his servants, and the party was completed by twenty Beni Sakhr and forty Serahin. We left the lame and weak camels behind at Abyadh in charge of the balance of our men, with instructions to get back to Abu Sawana before dawn to-morrow and wait there for our news. Two of my men developed sudden illnesses, which made them feel unable to ride with us. I excused them for the night, and afterward from all duties whatsoever.

CHAPTER LXXVI

J UST at sunset we said good-bye to them, and went off up our valley, feeling miserably disinclined to go on at all. Darkness gathered as we rode over the first ridge and turned west, for the abandoned pilgrim road, whose ruts would be our best guide. We were stumbling down the irregular hill-side, when the men in front suddenly dashed forward. We followed and found them surrounding a terrified pedlar, with two wives and two donkeys laden with raisins, flour and cloaks. They had been going to Mafrak, the station just behind us. This was awkward; and in the end we told them to camp, and left a Sirhani to see they did not stir: he was to release them at dawn, and escape over the line to Abu Sawana.

We went plodding across country in the now absolute dark till we saw the gleam of the white furrows of the pilgrim road. It was the same road along which the Arabs had ridden with me on my first night in Arabia out by Rabegh. Since then in twelve months we had fought up it for some twelve hundred kilometres, past Medina and Hedia, Dizad, Mudowwara and Maan. There remained little to its head in Damascus where our armed pilgrimage should end.

But we were apprehensive of to-night: our nerves had been shaken by the flight of Abd el Kader, the solitary traitor of our experience. Had we calculated fairly we should have known that we had a chance in spite of him: yet a dispassionate judgement lay not in our mood, and we thought half-despairingly how the Arab Revolt would never perform its last stage, but would remain one more example of the caravans which started out ardently for a cloud-goal, and died man by man in the wilderness without the tarnish of achievement.

Some shepherd or other scattered these thoughts by firing his rifle at our caravan, seen by him approaching silently and indistinctly in the dark. He missed widely, but began to cry out in extremity of terror and, as he fled, to pour shot after shot into the brown of us.

Mifleh el Gomaan, who was guiding, swerved violently, and in a blind trot carried our plunging line down a slope, over a breakneck bottom, and round the shoulder of a hill. There we had peaceful unbroken night once more, and swung forward in fair order under the stars. The next alarm was a barking dog on the left, and then a camel unexpectedly loomed up in our track. It was, however, a stray, and riderless. We moved on again.

Mifleh made me ride with him, calling me 'Arab' that my known name might not betray me to strangers in the blackness. We were coming down into a very thick hollow when we smelt ashes, and the dusky figure of a woman leaped from a bush beside the track and rushed shrieking out of sight. She may have been a gipsy, for nothing followed. We came to a hill. At the top was a village which blazed at us while we were yet distant. Mifleh bore off to the right over a broad stretch of plough; we climbed it slowly, with creaking saddles. At the edge of the crest we halted.

Away to the north below our level were some brilliant clusters of lights. Those were the flares of Deraa station, lit for army traffic: and we felt something reassuring perhaps, but also a little blatant in this Turkish disregard for us. [It was our revenge to make it their last illumination: Deraa was obscured from the morrow for a whole year until it fell.] In a close group we rode to the left along the summit and down a long valley into the plain of Remthe, from which village an occasional red spark glowed out, in the darkness to the north-west. The going became flat; but it was land half-ploughed, and very soft with a labyrinth of cony-burrows, so that our plunging camels sank fetlock-in and laboured. None the less, we had to put on speed, for the incidents and roughness of the way had made us late. Mifleh urged his reluctant camel into a trot.

I was better mounted than most, on the red camel which had led our procession into Beidha. She was a long, raking beast, with a huge piston-stride very hard to suffer: pounding, yet not fully mechanical, because there was courage in the persistent effort which carried her sailing to the head of the line. There, all competitors out-stripped, her ambition died into a solid step, longer than normal by some inches, but like any other animal's, except that it gave a confident feeling of immense reserve in strength and endurance. I rode back down the ranks and told them to press forward faster. The Indians, riding wooden, like horsemen, did their best, as did most of our number; but the ground was so bad that the greatest efforts were not very fruitful, and as hours went on first one and then another rider dropped behind. Thereupon I chose the rear position, with Ali ibn el Hussein who was riding a rare old racing camel. She may have been fourteen years old but never flagged nor jogged the whole night. With her head low she shuffled along in the quick, hang-kneed Nejd pace which was so easy for the rider. Our speed and camel-sticks made life miserable for the last men and camels.

Soon after nine o'clock we left the plough. The going should have improved: but it began to drizzle, and the rich surface of the land grew slippery. A Sirhani camel fell. Its rider had it up in a moment and trotted forward. One of the Beni Sakhr came down. He also was unhurt, and remounted hastily. Then we found one of Ali's servants standing by his halted camel. Ali hissed him on, and when the fellow mumbled an excuse cut him savagely across the head with his cane. The terrified camel plunged forward, and the slave, snatching at the hinder girth, was able to swing himself into the saddle. Ali pursued him with a rain of blows. Mustafa, my man, an inexperienced rider, fell off twice. Awad, his rank-man, each time caught his halter, and had helped him up before we overtook them.

The rain stopped, and we went faster. Downhill, now. Suddenly Mifleh, rising in his saddle, slashed at the air overhead. A sharp metallic contact from the night showed we were under the telegraph line to Mezerib. Then the grey horizon before us went more distant. We seemed to be riding on the camber of an arc of land, with a growing darkness at each side and in front. There came to our ears a faint sighing like wind among trees very far away, but continuous and slowly increasing. This must be from the great waterfall below Tell el Shehab, and we pressed forward confidently.

A few minutes later Mifleh pulled up his camel and beat her neck very gently till she sank silently on her knees. He threw himself off, while we reined up beside him on this grassy platform by a tumbled cairn. Before us from a lip of blackness rose very loudly the rushing of the river which had been long dinning our ears. It was the edge of the Yarmuk gorge, and the bridge lay just under us to the right.

We helped down the Indians from their burdened camels, that no sound betray us to listening ears; then mustered, whispering, on the clammy grass. The moon was not yet over Hermon, but the night was only half-dark in the promise of its dawn, with wild rags of tattered clouds driving across a livid sky. I served out the explosives to the fifteen porters, and we started. The Beni Sakhr under Adhub sank into the dark slopes before us to scout the way. The rainstorm had made the steep hill treacherous, and only by driving our bare toes sharply into the soil could we keep a sure foothold. Two or three men fell heavily.

When we were in the stiffest part, where rocks cropped out brokenly from the face, a new noise was added to the roaring water as a train clanked slowly up from Galilee, the flanges of its wheels screaming on the curves and the steam of its engine panting out of the hidden depths of the ravine in white ghostly breaths. The Serahin hung back. Wood drove them after us. Fahad and I leaped to the right, and in the light of the furnace-flame saw open trucks in which were men in khaki, perhaps prisoners going up to Asia Minor.

A little farther; and at last, below our feet, we saw a something blacker in the precipitous blackness of the valley, and at its other end a speck of flickering light. We halted to examine it with glasses. It was the bridge, seen from this height in plan, with a guard-tent pitched under the shadowy village-crested wall of the opposite bank. Everything was quiet, except the river; everything was motionless, except the dancing flame outside the tent.

Wood, who was only to come down if I were hit, got the Indians ready to spray the guard-tent if affairs became general; while Ali, Fahad, Mifleh and the rest of us, with Beni Sakhr and explosive porters, crept on till we found the old construction path to the near abutment. We stole along this in single file, our brown cloaks and soiled clothes blending perfectly with the limestone above us, and the depths below, until we reached the metals just before they curved to the bridge. There the crowd halted, and I crawled on with Fahad.

We reached the naked abutment, and drew ourselves forward on our faces in the shadow of its rails till we could nearly touch the grey skeleton of underhung girders, and see the single sentry leaning against the other abutment, sixty yards across the gulf. Whilst we watched, he began to move slowly up and down, up and down, before his fire, without ever setting foot on the dizzy bridge. I lay staring at him fascinated, as if planless and helpless, while Fahad shuffled back by the abutment wall where it sprang clear of the hill-side.

This was no good, for I wanted to attack the girders themselves; so I crept away to bring the gelatine bearers. Before I reached them there was the loud clatter of a dropped rifle and a scrambling fall from up the bank. The sentry started and stared up at the noise. He saw, high up, in the zone of light with which the rising moon slowly made beautiful the gorge, the machine-gunners climbing down to a new position in the receding shadow. He challenged loudly, then lifted his rifle and fired, while yelling the guard out.

Instantly all was complete confusion. The invisible Beni Sakhr, crouched along the narrow path above our heads, blazed back at random. The guard rushed into trenches, and opened rapid fire at our flashes. The Indians, caught moving, could not get their Vickers in action to riddle the tent before it was empty. Firing became general. The volleys of the Turkish rifles, echoing in the narrow place, were doubled by the impact of their bullets against the rocks behind our party. The Serahin porters had learned from my bodyguard that gelatine would go off if hit. So when the shots spattered about them they dumped the sacks over the edge and fled. Ali leaped down to Fahad and me, where we stood on the obscure abutment unperceived, but with empty hands, and told us that the explosives were now somewhere in the deep bed of the ravine.

It was hopeless to think of recovering them, with such hell let loose, so we scampered, without accident, up the hill-path through the Turkish fire, breathlessly to the top. There we met the disgusted Wood and the Indians, and told them it was all over. We hastened back to the cairn where the Serahin were scrambling on their camels. We copied them as soon as might be, and trotted off at a speed, while the Turks were yet rattling away in the bottom of the valley. Turra, the nearest village, heard the clamour and joined in. Other villages awoke, and lights began to sparkle everywhere across the plain.

Our rush overran a party of peasants returning from Deraa. The Serahin, sore at the part they had played (or at what I said in the heat of running away) were looking for trouble, and robbed them bare.

The victims dashed off through the moonlight with their women, raising the ear-piercing Arab call for help. Remthe heard them. Its massed shrieks alarmed every sleeper in the neighbourhood. Their mounted men turned out to charge our flank, while settlements for miles about manned their roofs and fired volleys.

We left the Serahin offenders with their encumbering loot, and drove on in grim silence, keeping together in what order we could, while my trained men did marvellous service helping those who fell, or mounting behind them those whose camels got up too hurt to canter on. The ground was still muddy, and the ploughed strips more laborious than ever; but behind us was the riot, spurring us and our camels to exertion, like a pack hunting us into the refuge of the hills. At length we entered these, and cut through by a better road towards peace, yet riding our jaded animals as hard as we could, for dawn was near. Gradually the noise behind us died away, and the last stragglers fell into place, driven together, as on the advance, by the flail of Ali ibn el Hussein and myself in the rear.

The day broke just as we rode down to the railway, and Wood, Ali and the chiefs, now in front to test the passage, were amused by cutting the telegraph in many places while the procession marched over. We had crossed the line the night before to blow up the bridge at Tell el Shehab, and so cut Palestine off from Damascus, and we were actually cutting the telegraph to Medina after all our pains and risks! Allenby's guns, still shaking the air away there on our right, were bitter recorders of the failure we had been.

The grey dawn drew on with gentleness in it, foreboding the grey drizzle of rain which followed, a drizzle so soft and hopeless that it seemed to mock our broken-footed plodding towards Abu Sawana. At sunset we reached the long water-pool; and there the rejects of our party were curious after the detail of our mistakes. We were fools, all of us equal fools, and so our rage was aimless. Ahmed and Awad had another fight; young Mustafa refused to cook rice; Farraj and Daud knocked him about until he cried; Ali had two of his servants beaten: and none of us or of them cared a little bit. Our minds were sick with failure, and our bodies tired after nearly a hundred strained miles over bad country in bad conditions, between sunset and sunset, without halt or food.

CHAPTER LXXVII

Food was going to be our next preoccupation, and we held a council in the cold driving rain to consider what we might do. For lightness' sake we had carried from Azrak three days' rations, which made us complete until to-night; but we could not go back empty-handed. The Beni Sakhr wanted honour, and the Serahin were too lately disgraced not to clamour for more adventure. We had still a reserve bag of thirty pounds of gelatine, and Ali ibn el Hussein who had heard of the performances below Maan, and was as Arab as any Arab, said, 'Let's blow up a train'. The word was hailed with universal joy, and they looked at me: but I was not able to share their hopes, all at once.

Blowing up trains was an exact science when done deliberately, by a sufficient party, with machine-guns in position. If scrambled at it might become dangerous. The difficulty this time was that the available gunners were Indians; who, though good men fed, were only half-men in cold and hunger. I did not propose to drag them off without rations on an adventure which might take a week. There was no cruelty in starving Arabs; they would not die of a few days' fasting, and would fight as well as ever on empty stomachs; while, if things got too difficult, there were the riding-camels to kill and eat: but the Indians, though Moslems, refused camel-flesh on principle.

I explained these delicacies of diet. Ali at once said that it would be enough for me to blow up the train, leaving him and the Arabs with him to do their best to carry its wreck without machine-gun support. As, in this unsuspecting district, we might well happen on a supply train, with civilians or only a small guard of reservists aboard, I agreed to risk it. The decision having been applauded, we sat down in a cloaked circle, to finish our remaining food in a very late and cold supper (the rain had sodden the fuel and made fire not possible) our hearts somewhat comforted by chance of another effort.

At dawn, with the unfit of the Arabs, the Indians moved away for Azrak, miserably. They had started up country with me in hope of a

434

really military enterprise, and first had seen the muddled bridge, and now were losing this prospective train. It was hard on them; and to soften the blow with honour I asked Wood to accompany them. He agreed, after argument, for their sakes; but it proved a wise move for himself, as a sickness which had been troubling him began to show the early signs of pneumonia.

The balance of us, some sixty men, turned back towards the railway. None of them knew the country, so I led them to Minifir, where, with Zaal, we had made havoc in the spring. The re-curved hill-top was an excellent observation post, camp, grazing ground and way of retreat, and we sat there in our old place till sunset, shivering and staring out over the immense plain which stretched map-like to the clouded peaks of Jebel Druse, with Um el Jemal and her sister-villages like ink-smudges on it through the rain.

In the first dusk we walked down to lay the mine. The rebuilt culvert of kilometre 172 seemed still the fittest place. While we stood by it there came a rumbling, and through the gathering darkness and mist a train suddenly appeared round the northern curve, only two hundred yards away. We scurried under the long arch and heard it roll over-head. This was annoying; but when the course was clear again we fell to burying the charge. The evening was bitterly cold, with drifts of rain blowing down the valley.

The arch was solid masonry, of four metres span, and stood over a shingle water-bed which took its rise on our hill-top. The winter rains had cut this into a channel four feet deep, narrow and winding, which served us as an admirable approach till within three hundred yards of the line. There the gully widened out and ran straight towards the culvert, open to the sight of anyone upon the rails.

We hid the explosive carefully on the crown of the arch, deeper than usual, beneath a tie, so that the patrols would not feel its jelly softness under their feet. The wires were taken down the bank into the shingle bed of the watercourse, where concealment was quick; and up it as far as they would reach. Unfortunately, this was only sixty yards, for there had been difficulty in Egypt over insulated cable and no more had been available when our expedition started. Sixty yards was plenty for the bridge, but little for a train: however, the ends happened to coincide with a little bush about ten inches high, on the edge of the watercourse, and we buried them beside this very convenient mark. It was impossible to leave them joined up to the exploder in the proper way, since the spot was evident to the permanent-way patrols as they made their rounds.

Owing to the mud the job took longer than usual, and it was very nearly dawn before we finished. I waited under the draughty arch till day broke, wet and dismal, and then I went over the whole area of disturbance, spending another half-hour in effacing its every mark, scattering leaves and dead grass over it, and watering down the broken mud from a shallow rain-pool near. Then they waved to me that the first patrol was coming, and I went up to join the others.

Before I had reached them they came tearing down into their prearranged places, lining the watercourse and spurs each side. A train was coming from the north. Hamud, Feisal's long slave, had the exploder; but before he reached me a short train of closed box-waggons rushed by at speed. The rainstorms on the plain and the thick morning had hidden it from the eyes of our watchman until too late. This second failure saddened us further and Ali began to say that nothing would come right this trip. Such a statement held risk as prelude of the discovery of an evil eye present; so, to divert attention, I suggested new watching posts be sent far out, one to the ruins on the north, one to the great cairn of the southern crest.

The rest, having no breakfast, were to pretend not to be hungry. They all enjoyed doing this, and for a while we sat cheerfully in the rain, huddling against one another for warmth behind a breastwork of our streaming camels. The moisture made the animals' hair curl up like a fleece, so that they looked queerly dishevelled. When the rain paused, which it did frequently, a cold moaning wind searched out the unprotected parts of us very thoroughly. After a time we found our wetted shirts clammy and comfortless things. We had nothing to eat, nothing to do and nowhere to sit except on wet rock, wet grass or mud. However, this persistent weather kept reminding me that it would delay Allenby's advance on Jerusalem, and rob him of his great possibility. So large a misfortune to our lion was a half-encouragement for the mice. We would be partners into next year.

In the best circumstances, waiting for action was hard. To-day it was beastly. Even enemy patrols stumbled along without care, perfunctorily, against the rain. At last, near noon, in a snatch of fine weather, the watchmen on the south peak flagged their cloaks wildly in signal of a train. We reached our positions in an instant, for we had squatted the late hours on our heels in a streaming ditch near the line, so as not to miss another chance. The Arabs took cover properly. I looked back at their ambush from my firing point, and saw nothing but the grey hill-sides.

I could not hear the train coming, but trusted, and knelt ready for perhaps half an hour, when the suspense became intolerable, and I signalled to know what was up. They sent down to say it was coming very slowly, and was an enormously long train. Our appetites stiffened. The longer it was the more would be the loot. Then came word that it had stopped. It moved again.

Finally, near one o'clock, I heard it panting. The locomotive was evidently defective (all these wood-fired trains were bad), and the heavy load on the up-gradient was proving too much for its capacity. I crouched behind my bush, while it crawled slowly into view past the south cutting, and along the bank above my head towards the culvert. The first ten trucks were open trucks, crowded with troops. However, once again it was too late to choose, so when the engine was squarely over the mine I pushed down the handle of the exploder. Nothing happened. I sawed it up and down four times.

Still nothing happened; and I realized that it had gone out of order, and that I was kneeling on a naked bank, with a Turkish troop train crawling past fifty yards away. The bush, which had seemed a foot high, shrank smaller than a fig-leaf; and I felt myself the most distinct object in the country-side. Behind me was an open valley for two hundred yards to the cover where my Arabs were waiting and wondering what I was at. It was impossible to make a bolt for it, or the Turks would step off the train and finish us. If I sat still, there might be just a hope of my being ignored as a casual Bedouin.

So there I sat, counting for sheer life, while eighteen open trucks, three box-waggons, and three officers' coaches dragged by. The engine panted slower and slower, and I thought every moment that it would break down. The troops took no great notice of me, but the officers were interested, and came out to the little platforms at the ends of their carriages, pointing and staring. I waved back at them, grinning nervously, and feeling an improbable shepherd in my Meccan dress, with its twisted golden circlet about my head. Perhaps the mud-stains, the wet and their ignorance made me accepted. The end of the brake van slowly disappeared into the cutting on the north.

As it went, I jumped up, buried my wires, snatched hold of the wretched exploder, and went like a rabbit uphill into safety. There I took breath and looked back to see that the train had finally stuck. It waited, about five hundred yards beyond the mine, for nearly an hour to get up a head of steam, while an officers' patrol came back and searched, very carefully, the ground where I had been sitting. However the wires were properly hidden: they found nothing: the engine plucked up heart again, and away they went.

CHAPTER LXXVIII

MIFLEH was past tears, thinking I had intentionally let the train through; and when the Serahin had been told the real cause they said 'Bad luck is with us'. Historically they were right; but they meant it for a prophecy, so I made sarcastic reference to their courage at the bridge the week before, hinting that it might be a tribal preference to sit on camel-guard. At once there was uproar, the Serahin attacking me furiously, the Beni Sakhr defending. Ali heard the trouble, and came running.

When we had made it up the original despondency was half forgotten. Ali backed me nobly, though the wretched boy was blue with cold and shivering in an attack of fever. He gasped that their ancestor the Prophet had given to Sherifs the faculty of 'sight', and by it he knew that our luck was turning. This was comfort for them: my first instalment of good fortune came when in the wet, without other tool than my dagger, I got the box of the exploder open and persuaded its electrical gear to work properly once more.

We returned to our vigil by the wires, but nothing happened, and evening drew down with more squalls and beastliness, everybody full of grumbles. There was no train; it was too wet to light a cooking fire; our only potential food was camel. Raw meat did not tempt anyone that night; and so our beasts survived to the morrow.

Ali lay down on his belly, which position lessened the hunger-ache, trying to sleep off his fever. Khazen, Ali's servant, lent him his cloak for extra covering. For a spell I took Khazen under mine, but soon found it becoming crowded. So I left it to him and went downhill to connect up the exploder. Afterwards I spent the night there alone by the singing telegraph wires, hardly wishing to sleep, so painful was the cold. Nothing came all the long hours, and dawn, which broke wet, looked even uglier than usual. We were sick to death of Minifir, of railways, of train watching and wrecking, by now. I climbed up to the main body while the early patrol searched the railway. Then the day cleared a little. Ali awoke, much refreshed, and his new spirit cheered

439

us. Hamud, the slave, produced some sticks which he had kept under his clothes by his skin all night. They were nearly dry. We shaved down some blasting gelatine, and with its hot flame got a fire going, while the Sukhur hurriedly killed a mangy camel, the best spared of our riding-beasts, and began with entrenching tools to hack it into handy joints.

Just at that moment the watchman on the north cried a train. We left the fire and made a breathless race of the six hundred yards down hill to our old position. Round the bend, whistling its loudest, came the train, a splendid two-engined thing of twelve passenger coaches, travelling at top speed on the favouring grade. I touched off under the first driving wheel of the first locomotive, and the explosion was terrific. The ground spouted blackly into my face, and I was sent spinning, to sit up with the shirt torn to my shoulder and the blood dripping from long ragged scratches on my left arm. Between my knees lay the exploder, crushed under a twisted sheet of sooty iron. In front of me was the scalded and smoking upper half of a man. When I peered through the dust and steam of the explosion the whole boiler of the first engine seemed to be missing.

I dully felt that it was time to get away to support; but when I moved, learnt that there was a great pain in my right foot, because of which I could only limp along, with my head swinging from the shock. Movement began to clear away this confusion, as I hobbled towards the upper valley, whence the Arabs were now shooting fast into the crowded coaches. Dizzily I cheered myself by repeating aloud in English 'Oh, I wish this hadn't happened'.

When the enemy began to return our fire, I found myself much between the two. Ali saw me fall, and thinking that I was hard hit, ran out, with Turki and about twenty men of his servants and the Beni Sakhr, to help me. The Turks found their range and got seven of them in a few seconds. The others, in a rush, were about me — fit models, after their activity, for a sculptor. Their full white cotton drawers drawn in, bell-like, round their slender waists and ankles, their hairless brown bodies; and the love-locks plaited tightly over each temple in long horns, made them look like Russian dancers.

We scrambled back into cover together, and there, secretly, I felt myself over, to find I had not once been really hurt; though besides the bruises and cuts of the boiler-plate and a broken toe, I had five different bullet-grazes on me (some of them uncomfortably deep) and my clothes ripped to pieces.

From the watercourse we could look about. The explosion had destroyed the arched head of the culvert, and the frame of the first engine was lying beyond it, at the near foot of the embankment down which it had rolled. The second locomotive had toppled into the gap, and was lying across the ruined tender of the first. Its bed was twisted. I judged them both beyond repair. The second tender had disappeared over the further side; and the first three waggons had telescoped and were smashed in pieces.

The rest of the train was badly derailed, with the listing coaches butted end to end at all angles, zigzagged along the track. One of them was a saloon, decorated with flags. In it had been Mehmed Jemal Pasha, commanding the Eighth Army Corps, hurrying down to defend Jerusalem against Allenby. His chargers had been in the first waggon; his motor-car was on the end of the train, and we shot it up. Of his staff we noticed a fat ecclesiastic, whom we thought to be Assad Shukair, Imam to Ahmed Jemal Pasha, and a notorious pro-Turk pimp. So we blazed at him till he dropped.

It was all long bowls. We could see that our chances of carrying the wreck were slight. There had been some four hundred men on board, and the survivors, now recovered from the shock, were under shelter and shooting hard at us. At the first moment our party on the north spur had closed, and nearly won the game. Mifleh on his mare chased the officers from the saloon into the lower ditch. He was too excited to stop and shoot, and so they got away scatheless. The Arabs following him had turned to pick up some of the rifles and medals littering the ground, and then to drag bags and boxes from the train. If we had had a machine gun posted to cover the far side, according to my mining practice, not a Turk would have escaped.

Mifleh and Adhub rejoined us on the hill, and asked after Fahad. One of the Serahin told how he had led the first rush, while I lay knocked out beside the exploder, and had been killed near it. They showed his belt and rifle as proof that he was dead and that they had tried to save him. Adhub said not a word, but leaped out of the gully, and raced downhill. We caught our breaths till our lungs hurt us, watching him; but the Turks seemed not to see. A minute later he was dragging a body behind the left-hand bank.

Mifleh went back to his mare, mounted, and took her down behind a spur. Together they lifted the inert figure on to the pommel, and returned. A bullet had passed through Fahad's face, knocking out four teeth, and gashing the tongue. He had fallen unconscious, but had revived just before Adhub reached him, and was trying on hands and knees, blinded with blood, to crawl away. He now recovered poise enough to cling to a saddle. So they changed him to the first camel they found and led him off at once.

The Turks, seeing us so quiet, began to advance up the slope. We let them come half-way, and then poured in volleys which killed some twenty and drove the others back. The ground about the train was strewn with dead, and the broken coaches had been crowded: but they were fighting under eye of their Corps Commander, and undaunted began to work round the spurs to outflank us.

We were now only about forty left, and obviously could do no good against them. So we ran in batches up the little stream-bed, turning at each sheltered angle to delay them by pot-shots. Little Turki much distinguished himself by quick coolness, though his straight-stocked Turkish cavalry carbine made him so expose his head that he got four bullets through his head-cloth. Ali was angry with me for retiring slowly. In reality my raw hurts crippled me, but to hide from him this real reason I pretended to be easy, interested in and studying the Turks. Such successive rests while I gained courage for a new run kept him and Turki far behind the rest.

At last we reached the hill-top. Each man there jumped on the nearest camel, and made away at full speed eastward into the desert, for an hour. Then in safety we sorted our animals. The excellent Rahail, despite the ruling excitement, had brought off with him, tied to his saddle-girth, a huge haunch of the camel slaughtered just as the train arrived. He gave us the motive for a proper halt, five miles farther on, as a little party of four camels appeared marching in the same direction. It was our companion, Matar, coming back from his home village to Azrak with loads of raisins and peasant delicacies.

So we stopped at once, under a large rock in Wadi Dhuleil, where was a barren fig-tree, and cooked our first meal for three days. There, also, we bandaged up Fahad, who was sleepy with the lassitude of his severe hurt. Adhub, seeing this, took one of Matar's new carpets, and doubling it across the camel-saddle, stitched the ends into great pockets. In one they laid Fahad, while Adhub crawled into the other as make-weight: and the camel was led off southward towards their tribal tents.

The other wounded men were seen to at the same time. Mifleh brought up the youngest lads of the party, and had them spray the wounds with their piss, as a rude antiseptic. Meanwhile we whole ones refreshed ourselves. I bought another mangy camel for extra meat, paid rewards, compensated the relatives of the killed, and gave prize-money, for the sixty or seventy rifles we had taken. It was small booty, but not to be despised. Some Serahin, who had gone into the action without rifles, able only to throw unavailing stones, had now two guns apiece. Next day we moved into Azrak, having a great welcome, and boasting – God forgive us – that we were victors.

CHAPTER LXXIX

RAIN had set in steadily, and the country was sodden wet. Allenby had failed in his weather, and there could be no great advance this year. Nevertheless, for progress' sake we determined to hold to Azrak. Partly it would be a preaching base, from which to spread our movement in the North: partly it would be a centre of intelligence: partly it would cut off Nuri Shaalan from the Turks. He hesitated to declare himself only because of his wealth in Syria, and the possible hurt to his tribesmen if they were deprived of their natural market. We, by living in one of his main manors, would keep him ashamed to go in to the enemy. Azrak lay favourably for us, and the old fort would be convenient headquarters if we made it habitable, no matter how severe the winter.

So I established myself in its southern gate-tower, and set my six Haurani boys (for whom manual labour was not disgraceful) to cover with brushwood, palm-branches, and clay the ancient split stone rafters, which stood open to the sky. Ali took up his quarters in the south-east corner tower, and made that roof tight. The Indians weather-proofed their own north-west rooms. We arranged the stores on the ground floor of the western tower, by the little gate, for it was the soundest, driest place. The Biasha chose to live under me in the south gate. So we blocked that entry and made a hall of it. Then we opened a great arch from the court to the palm-garden, and made a ramp, that our camels might come inside each evening.

Hassan Shah we appointed seneschal. As a good Moslem his first care was for the little mosque in the square. It had been half unroofed and the Arabs had penned sheep within the walls. He set his twenty men to dig out the filth, and wash the pavement clean. The mosque then became a most attractive house of prayer. What had been a place shut off, dedicated to God alone, Time had broken open to the Evanescent with its ministering winds and rain and sunlight; these entering into the worship taught worshippers how the two were one.

Our prudent Jemadar's next labour was to make positions for

machine-guns in the upper towers, from whose tops the approaches lay at mercy. Then he placed a formal sentry (a portent and cause of wonder in Arabia) whose main duty was the shutting of the postern gate at sundown. The door was a poised slab of dressed basalt, a foot thick, turning on pivots of itself, socketed into threshold and lintel. It took a great effort to start swinging, and at the end went shut with a clang and crash which made tremble the west wall of the old castle.

Meanwhile, we were studying to provision ourselves. Akaba was far off, and in winter the roads thither would be rigorous: so we prepared a caravan to go up to Jebel Druse, the neutral land, only a day off. Matar went in charge of this for us, with a long train of camels to carry back varieties of food for our motley party. Besides my bodyguard, who were taught to live on what they got, we had the Indians, for whom pepperless food was no food at all. Ali ibn el Hussein wanted sheep and butter and parched wheat for his men and the Biasha. Then there were the guests and refugees whom we might expect so soon as the news of our establishment was rumoured in Damascus. Till they came we should have a few days' repose, and we sat down to enjoy these dregs of autumn — the alternate days of rain and shine. We had sheep and flour, milk and fuel. Life in the fort, but for the ill-omened mud, went well enough.

Yet the peacefulness ended sooner than we thought. Wood, who had been ailing for some time, went down with a sharp attack of dysentery. This was nothing by itself, but the consequent weakness might have endangered him when winter set in earnestly. Besides, he was their base engineer at Akaba; and, except for the comfort of his companionship, I had no justification in keeping him longer. So we made up a party to go down with him to the coast, choosing as the escort, Ahmed, Abd el Rahman, Mahmoud, and Aziz. These were to return to Azrak forthwith from Akaba with a new caravan of stores, particularly comprising Indian rations. The rest of my men would stay in chilly idleness watching the situation develop.

Then began our flood of visitors. All day and every day they came, now in the running column of shots, raucous shoutings and rush of camel-feet which meant a Bedouin parade, it might be of Rualla, or Sherarat, or Serahin, Serdiyeh, or Beni Sakhr, chiefs of great name like ibn Zuhair, ibn Kaebir, Rafa el Khoreisha, or some little father of a family demonstrating his greedy goodwill before the fair eyes of Ali ibn el Hussein. Then it would be a wild gallop of horse: Druses, or the ruffling warlike peasants of the Arab plain. Sometimes it was a cautious, slow-led caravan of ridden camels, from which stiffly dismounted Syrian politicians or traders not accustomed to the road. One day arrived a hundred miserable Armenians, fleeing starvation and the suspended terror of the Turks. Again would come a spick and span group of mounted officers, Arab deserters from the Turkish armies, followed, often as not, by a compact company of Arab rank and file. Always they came, day after day, till the desert, which had been trackless when we came, was starred out with grey roads.

Ali appointed first one, then two, and at last three, guest-masters, who received the rising tide of these newcomers, sorted worshipful from curious, and marshalled them in due time before him or me. All wanted to know about the Sherif, the Arab army and the English. Merchants from Damascus brought presents: sweetmeats, sesame, caramel, apricot paste, nuts, silk clothes for ourselves, brocade cloaks, head-cloths, sheepskins, felt rugs with coloured strands beaten into them in arabesques, Persian carpets. We returned them coffee and sugar, rice, and rolls of white cotton sheeting; necessities of which they had been deprived by war. Everybody learned that in Akaba there was plenty, coming across the open sea from all the markets of the world; and so the Arab cause which was theirs by sentiment, and instinct and inclination, became theirs by interest also. Slowly our example and teaching converted them: very slowly, by our own choice, that they might be ours more surely.

The greatest asset of Feisal's cause in this work up North was Sherif Ali ibn el Hussein. The lunatic competitor of the wilder tribesmen in their wildest feats was now turning all his force to greater ends. The mixed natures in him made of his face and body powerful pleadings, carnal, perhaps, except in so far as they were transfused by character. No one could see him without the desire to see him again; especially when he smiled, as he did rarely, with both mouth and eyes at once. His beauty was a conscious weapon. He dressed spotlessly, all in black or all in white; and he studied gesture.

Fortune had added physical perfection and unusual grace, but these qualities were only the just expression of his powers. They made obvious the pluck which never yielded, which would have let him be cut to pieces, holding on. His pride broke out in his war-cry, 'I am of the Harith', the two-thousand-year-old clan of freebooters; while the huge eyes, white with large black pupils slowly turning in them, emphasized the frozen dignity which was his ideal carriage, and to which he was always striving to still himself. But as ever the bubbling laugh would shriek out of him unawares; and the youth, boyish or girlish, of him, the fire and deviltry would break through his night like a sunrise.

Yet, despite this richness, there was a constant depression with him, the unknown longing of simple, restless people for abstract thought beyond their minds' supply. His bodily strength grew day by day, and hatefully fleshed over this humble something which he wanted more. His wild mirth was only one sign of the vain wearing-out of his desire. These besetting strangers underlined his detachment, his unwilling detachment, from his fellows. Despite his great instinct for confession and company, he could find no intimates. Yet he could not be alone. If he had no guests, Khazen, the servant, must serve his meals, while Ali and his slaves ate together.

In these slow nights we were secure against the world. For one thing, it was winter, and in the rain and the dark few men would venture either over the labyrinth of lava or through the marsh — the two approaches to our fortress; and, further, we had ghostly guardians. The first evening we were sitting with the Serahin, Hassan Shah had made the rounds, and the coffee was being pounded by the hearth, when there rose a strange, long wailing round the towers outside. Ibn Bani seized me by the arm and held to me, shuddering. I whispered to him, 'What is it?' and he gasped that the dogs of the Beni Hillal, the mythical builders of the fort, quested the six towers each night for their dead masters.

We strained to listen. Through Ali's black basalt window-frame crept a rustling, which was the stirring of the night-wind in the withered palms, an intermittent rustling, like English rain on yet-crisp fallen leaves. Then the cries came again and again and again, rising slowly in power, till they sobbed round the walls in deep waves to die away choked and miserable. At such times our men pounded the coffee harder while the Arabs broke into sudden song to occupy their ears against the misfortune. No Bedouin would lie outside in wait for the mystery, and from our windows we saw nothing but the motes of water in the dank air which drove through the radiance of our firelight. So it remained a legend: but wolves or jackals, hyænas, or hunting dogs, their ghost-watch kept our ward more closely than arms could have done.

In the evening, when we had shut-to the gate, all guests would assemble, either in my room or in Ali's, and coffee and stories would go round until the last meal, and after it, till sleep came. On stormy nights we brought in brushwood and dung and lit a great fire in the middle of the floor. About it would be drawn the carpets and the saddle-sheep-skins, and in its light we would tell over our own battles, or hear the visitors' traditions. The leaping flames chased our smoke-ruffled shadows strangely about the rough stone wall behind us, distorting them over the hollows and projections of its broken face. When these stories came to a period, our tight circle would shift over, uneasily, to the other knee or elbow; while coffee-cups went clinking round, and a servant fanned the blue reek of the fire towards the loophole with his cloak, making the glowing ash swirl and sparkle with his draught. Till the voice of the story-teller took up again, we would hear the rain-spots hissing briefly as they dripped from the stone-beamed roof into the fire's heart.

At last the sky turned solidly to rain, and no man could approach us. In loneliness we learned the full disadvantages of imprisonment within such gloomy ancient unmortared places. The rains guttered down within the walls' thickness and spouted into the rooms from their chinks. We set rafts of palm-branches to bear us clear of the streaming floor, covered them with felt mats, and huddled down on them under sheepskins, with another mat over us like a shield to throw off the water. It was icy cold, as we hid there, motionless, from the murky daylight until dark, our minds seeming suspended within these massive walls, through whose every shot-window the piercing mist streamed like a white pennant. Past and future flowed over us like an uneddying river. We dreamed ourselves into the spirit of the place; sieges and feasting, raids, murders, love-singing in the night.

This escape of our wits from the fettered body was an indulgence against whose enervation only change of scene could avail. Very painfully I drew myself again into the present, and forced my mind to say that it must use this wintry weather to explore the country lying round about Deraa.

As I was thinking how I would ride, there came to us, unheralded, one morning in the rain, Talal el Hareidhin, sheikh of Tafas. He was a famous outlaw with a price upon his head; but so great that he rode about as he pleased. In two wild years he had killed, according to report, some twenty-three of the Turks. His six followers were splendidly mounted, and himself the most dashing figure of a man in the height of Hauran fashion. His sheepskin coat was finest Angora covered in green broadcloth, with silk patches and designs in braid. His other clothes were silk; and his high boots, his silver saddle, his sword, dagger, and rifle matched his reputation.

He swaggered to our coffee-hearth, as a man sure of his welcome, greeting Ali boisterously (after our long sojourn with the tribes all peasants sounded boisterous), laughing broad-mouthed at the weather and our old fort and the enemy. He looked about thirty-five, was short and strong, with a full face, trimmed beard and long, pointed mou-staches. His round eyes were made rounder, larger and darker by the antimony loaded on in villager style. He was ardently ours, and we rejoiced, since his name was one to conjure with in Hauran. When a day had made me sure of him, I took him secretly to the palm-garden, and told him my ambition to see his neighbourhood. The idea delighted him, and he companioned me for the march as thoroughly and cheerfully as only a Syrian on a good horse could. Halim and Faris, men specially engaged, rode with me as guards.

We went past Umtaiye, looking at tracks, well and lava-fields, crossed the line to Sheikh Saad, and turned south to Tafas, where Talal was at home. Next day we went on to Tell Arar, a splendid position closing the Damascus railway and commanding Deraa. Afterwards we rode through tricky rolling country to Mezerib on the Palestine railway; planning, here also, for the next time; when with men, money and guns we should start the general rising to win inevitable victory. Perhaps the coming spring might see Allenby leap forward.

CHAPTER LXXX

PROPERLY to round off this spying of the hollow land of Hauran, it was necessary to visit Deraa, its chief town. We could cut it off on north and west and south, by destroying the three railways; but it would be more tidy to rush the junction first and work outwards. Talal, however, could not venture in with me since he was too well known in the place. So we parted from him with many thanks on both sides, and rode southward along the line until near Deraa. There we dismounted. The boy, Halim, took the ponies, and set off for Nisib, south of Deraa. My plan was to walk round the railway station and town with Faris, and reach Nisib after sunset. Faris was my best companion for the trip, because he was an insignificant peasant, old enough to be my father, and respectable.

The respectability seemed comparative as we tramped off in the watery sunlight, which was taking the place of the rain last night. The ground was muddy, we were barefoot, and our draggled clothes showed the stains of the foul weather to which we had been exposed. I was in Halim's wet things, with a torn Hurani jacket, and was yet limping from the broken foot acquired when we blew up Jemal's train. The slippery track made walking difficult, unless we spread out our toes widely and took hold of the ground with them: and doing this for mile after mile was exquisitely painful to me. Because pain hurt me so, I would not lay weight always on my pains in our revolt: yet hardly one day in Arabia passed without a physical ache to increase the corroding sense of my accessory deceitfulness towards the Arabs, and the legitimate fatigue of responsible command.

We mounted the curving bank of the Palestine Railway, and from its vantage surveyed Deraa Station: but the ground was too open to admit of surprise attack. We decided to walk down the east front of the defences: so we plodded on, noting German stores, barbed wire here and there, rudiments of trenches. Turkish troops were passing incuriously between the tents and their latrines dug out on our side.

At the corner of the aerodrome by the south end of the station we struck over towards the town. There were old Albatros machines in the sheds, and men lounging about. One of these, a Syrian soldier, began to question us about our villages, and if there was much 'government' where we lived. He was probably an intending deserter, fishing for a refuge. We shook him off at last and turned away. Someone called out in Turkish. We walked on deafly; but a sergeant came after, and took me roughly by the arm, saying 'The Bey wants you'. There were too many witnesses for fight or flight, so I went readily. He took no notice of Faris.

I was marched through the tall fence into a compound set about with many huts and a few buildings. We passed to a mud room, outside which was an earth platform, whereon sat a fleshy Turkish officer, one leg tucked under him. He hardly glanced at me when the sergeant brought me up and made a long report in Turkish. He asked my name: I told him Ahmed ibn Bagr, a Circassian from Kuneitra. 'A deserter?' 'But we Circassians have no military service'. He turned, stared at me, and said very slowly 'You are a liar. Enrol him in your section, Hassan Chowish, and do what is necessary till the Bey sends for him'.

They led me into a guard-room, mostly taken up by large wooden cribs, on which lay or sat a dozen men in untidy uniforms. They took away my belt, and my knife, made me wash myself carefully, and fed me. I passed the long day there. They would not let me go on any terms, but tried to reassure me. A soldier's life was not all bad. To-morrow, perhaps, leave would be permitted, if I fulfilled the Bey's pleasure this evening. The Bey seemed to be Nahi, the Governor. If he was angry, they said, I would be drafted for infantry training to the depot in Baalbek. I tried to look as though, to my mind, there was nothing worse in the world than that.

Soon after dark three men came for me. It had seemed a chance to get away, but one held me all the time. I cursed my littleness. Our march crossed the railway, where were six tracks, besides the sidings of the engine-shop. We went through a side gate, down a street, past a square, to a detached, two-storied house. There was a sentry outside, and a glimpse of others lolling in the dark entry. They took me up-stairs to the Bey's room; or to his bedroom, rather. He was another bulky man, a Circassian himself, perhaps, and sat on the bed in a night-gown, trembling and sweating as though with fever. When I was pushed in he kept his head down, and waved the guard out. In a breathless voice he told me to sit on the floor in front of him, and after that was dumb; while I gazed at the top of his great head, on which the bristling hair stood up, no longer than the dark stubble on his cheeks and chin. At last he looked me over, and told me to stand up: then to turn round. I obeyed; he flung himself back on the bed, and dragged me down with him in his arms. When I saw what he wanted I twisted round and up again, glad to find myself equal to him, at any rate in wrestling.

He began to fawn on me, saying how white and fresh I was, how fine my hands and feet, and how he would let me off drills and duties, make me his orderly, even pay me wages, if I would love him.

I was obdurate, so he changed his tone, and sharply ordered me to take off my drawers. When I hesitated, he snatched at me; and I pushed him back. He clapped his hands for the sentry, who hurried in and pinioned me. The Bey cursed me with horrible threats: and made the man holding me tear my clothes away, bit by bit. His eyes rounded at the half-healed places where the bullets had flicked through my skin a little while ago. Finally he lumbered to his feet, with a glitter in his look, and began to paw me over. I bore it for a little, till he got too beastly; and then jerked my knee into him.

He staggered to his bed, squeezing himself together and groaning with pain, while the soldier shouted for the corporal and the other three men to grip me hand and foot. As soon as I was helpless the Governor regained courage, and spat at me, swearing he would make me ask pardon. He took off his slipper, and hit me repeatedly with it in the face, while the corporal braced my head back by the hair to receive the blows. He leaned forward, fixed his teeth in my neck and bit till the blood came. Then he kissed me. Afterwards he drew one of the men's bayonets. I thought he was going to kill me, and was sorry: but he only pulled up a fold of the flesh over my ribs, worked the point through, after considerable trouble, and gave the blade a half-turn. This hurt, and I winced, while the blood wavered down my side and dripped to the front of my thigh. He looked pleased and dabbled it over my stomach with his finger-tips.

In my despair I spoke. His face changed and he stood still, then controlled his voice with an effort, to say significantly, 'You must understand that I know: and it will be easier if you do as I wish.' I was dumbfounded, and we stared silently at one another, while the men who felt an inner meaning beyond their experience, shifted uncomfortably. But it was evidently a chance shot, by which he himself did not, or would not, mean what I feared. I could not again trust my twitching mouth, which faltered always in emergencies, so at last threw up my chin, which was the sign for 'No' in the East; then he sat down, and half-whispered to the corporal to take me out and teach me everything.

They kicked me to the head of the stairs, and stretched me over a guard-bench, pommelling me. Two knelt on my ankles, bearing down on the back of my knees, while two more twisted my wrists till they cracked, and then crushed them and my neck against the wood. The corporal had run downstairs; and now came back with a whip of the Circassian sort, a thong of supple black hide, rounded, and tapering from the thickness of a thumb at the grip (which was wrapped in silver) down to a hard point finer than a pencil.

He saw me shivering, partly I think, with cold, and made it whistle over my ear, taunting me that before his tenth cut I would howl for mercy, and at the twentieth beg for the caresses of the Bey; and then he began to lash me madly across and across with all his might, while I locked my teeth to endure this thing which lapped itself like flaming wire about my body.

To keep my mind in control I numbered the blows, but after twenty lost count, and could feel only the shapeless weight of pain, not tearing claws, for which I had prepared, but a gradual cracking apart of my whole being by some too-great force whose waves rolled up my spine till they were pent within my brain, to clash terribly together. Somewhere in the place a cheap clock ticked loudly, and it distressed me that their beating was not in its time. I writhed and twisted, but was held so tightly that my struggles were useless. After the corporal ceased, the men took up, very deliberately, giving me so many, and then an interval during which they would squabble for the next turn, ease themselves, and play unspeakably with me. This was repeated often, for what may have been no more than ten minutes. Always for the first of every new series, my head would be pulled round, to see how a hard white ridge, like a railway, darkening slowly into crimson, leaped over my skin at the instant of each stroke, with a bead of blood where two ridges crossed. As the punishment proceeded the whip fell more and more upon existing weals, biting blacker or more wet, till my flesh quivered with accumulated pain, and with terror of the next blow coming. They soon conquered my determination not to cry, but while my will ruled my lips I used only Arabic, and before the end a merciful sickness choked my utterance.

At last when I was completely broken they seemed satisfied. Somehow I found myself off the bench, lying on my back on the dirty floor, where I snuggled down, dazed, panting for breath, but vaguely comfortable. I had strung myself to learn all pain until I died, and no longer actor, but spectator, thought not to care how my body jerked and squealed. Yet I knew or imagined what passed about me.

I remembered the corporal kicking with his nailed boot to get me up; and this was true, for the next day my right side was dark and lacerated, and a damaged rib made each breath stab me sharply. I remembered smiling idly at him, for a delicious warmth, probably sexual, was swelling through me: and then that he flung up his arm and hacked with the full length of his whip into my groin. This doubled me half-over, screaming, or, rather, trying impotently to scream, only shuddering through my open mouth. One giggled with amusement. A voice cried, 'Shame, you've killed him.' Another slash followed. A roaring, and my eyes went black: while within me the core of life seemed to heave slowly up through the rending nerves, expelled from its body by this last indescribable pang.

By the bruises perhaps they beat me further: but I next knew that I was being dragged about by two men, each disputing over a leg as though to split me apart: while a third man rode me astride. It was momently better than more flogging. Then Nahi called. They splashed water in my face, wiped off some of the filth, and lifted me between them retching and sobbing for mercy, to where he lay: but he now rejected me in haste, as a thing too torn and bloody for his bed, blaming their excess of zeal which had spoilt me: whereas no doubt they had laid into me much as usual, and the fault rested mainly upon my indoor skin, which gave way more than an Arab's.

So the crestfallen corporal, as the youngest and best-looking of the guard, had to stay behind, while the others carried me down the narrow stair into the street. The coolness of the night on my burning flesh, and the unmoved shining of the stars after the horror of the past hour, made me cry again. The soldiers, now free to speak, warned me that men must suffer their officer's wishes or pay for it, as I had just done, with greater suffering.

They took me over an open space, deserted and dark, and behind the Government house to a lean-to wooden room, in which were many dusty quilts. An Armenian dresser appeared to wash and bandage me in sleepy haste. Then all went away, the last soldier delaying by my side a moment to whisper in his Druse accent that the door into the next room was not locked.

I lay there in a sick stupor, with my head aching very much, and growing slowly numb with cold, till the dawn light came shining through the cracks of the shed, and a locomotive whistled in the station. These and a draining thirst brought me to life, and I found I was in no pain. Pain of the slightest had been my obsession and secret terror, from a boy. Had I now been drugged with it, to bewilderment? Yet the first movement was anguish: in which I struggled nakedly to my feet, and rocked moaning in wonder that it was not a dream, and myself back five years ago, a timid recruit at Khalfati, where something, less staining, of the sort had happened.

The next room was a dispensary. On its door hung a suit of shoddy clothes. I put them on slowly and unhandily, because of my swollen wrists: and from the drugs chose corrosive sublimate, as safeguard against recapture. The window looked on a long blank wall. Stiffly I climbed out, and went shaking down the road towards the village, past the few people already astir. They took no notice; indeed there was nothing peculiar in my dark broadcloth, red fez and slippers: but it was only by the full urge of my tongue silently to myself that I refrained from being foolish out of sheer fright. Deraa felt inhuman with vice and cruelty, and it shocked me like cold water when a soldier laughed behind me in the street.

By the bridge were the wells, with men and women about them. A side trough was free. From its end I scooped up a little water in my hands, and rubbed it over my face; then drank, which was precious to me; and afterwards wandered along the bottom of the valley, towards the south, unobtrusively retreating out of sight. This valley provided the hidden road by which our projected raid could attain Deraa town secretly, and surprise the Turks. So, in escaping I solved, too late, the problem which had brought me to Deraa.

Further on, a Serdi, on his camel, overtook me hobbling up the road towards Nisib. I explained that I had business there, and was already footsore. He had pity and mounted me behind him on his bony animal, to which I clung the rest of the way, learning the feelings of my adopted name-saint on his gridiron. The tribe's tents were just in front of the village, where I found Faris and Halim anxious about me, and curious to learn how I had fared. Halim had been up to Deraa in the night, and knew by the lack of rumour that the truth had not been discovered. I told them a merry tale of bribery and trickery, which they promised to keep to themselves, laughing aloud at the simplicity of the Turks.

During the night I managed to see the great stone bridge by Nisib. Not that my maimed will now cared a hoot about the Arab Revolt (or about anything but mending itself); yet, since the war had been a hobby of mine, for custom's sake I would force myself to push it through. Afterwards we took horse, and rode gently and carefully towards Azrak, without incident, except that a raiding party of Wuld Ali let us and our horses go unplundered when they heard who we were. This was an unexpected generosity, the Wuld Ali being not yet of our fellowship. Their consideration (rendered at once, as if we had deserved men's homage) momently stayed me to carry the burden, whose certainty the passing days confirmed: how in Deraa that night the citadel of my integrity had been irrevocably lost.

CHAPTER LXXXI

XURY, the Druse Emir of Salkhad, reached our old castle just before me on his first visit to Sherif Ali. He told us the rest of the history of the Emir Abd el Kader, the Algerian. After stealing away from us he had ridden straight to their village, and entered in triumph, the Arab flag displayed, and his seven horsemen cantering about him, firing joy-shots. The people were astonished, and the Turkish Governor protested that such doings were an insult to him. He was introduced to Abd el Kader, who, sitting in pomp on the divan, made a bombastic speech, stating that the Sherif now took over Jebel Druse through his agency, and all existing officials were confirmed in their appointments.

Next morning he made a second progress through the district. The suffering Governor complained again. Emir Abd el Kader drew his gold-mounted Meccan sword, and swore that with it he would cut off Jemal Pasha's head. The Druses reproved him, vowing that such things should not be said in their house before his Excellency the Governor. Abd el Kader called them whoresons, ingle's accidents, sons of a bitch, profiteering cuckolds and pimps, jetting his insults broadcast to the roomful. The Druses got angry. Abd el Kader flung raging out of the house and mounted, shouting that when he stamped his foot all Jebel Druse would rise on his side.

With his seven servants, he spurred down the road to Deraa Station, which he entered as he had entered Salkhad. The Turks, who knew his madness of old, left him to play. They disbelieved even his yarn that Ali and I would try the Yarmuk bridge that night. When, however, we did, they took a graver view, and sent him under custody to Damascus. Jemal's brutal humour was amused, and he enlarged him as a butt. Abd el Kader gradually became amenable. The Turks began to use him once more as *agent provocateur* and dissipator of the energy generated by their local Syrian nationalists.

The weather was now dreadful, with sleet and snow and storms continually; it was obvious that at Azrak there would be nothing but teaching and preaching in the next months. For this I was not eager. When necessary, I had done my share of proselytizing fatigues, converting as best I could; conscious all the time of my strangeness, and of the incongruity of an alien's advocating national liberty. The war for me held a struggle to side-track thought, to get into the people's attitude of accepting the revolt naturally and trustingly. I had to persuade myself that the British Government could really keep the spirit of its promises. Especially was this difficult when I was tired and ill, when the delirious activity of my brain tore to shreds my patience. And then, after the blunt Beduin, who would thrust in, hailing me '*Ya Aurans*', and put their need without compliments, these smooth townspeople were maddening as they crawled for the favour of an audience with their Prince and Bey and Lord and Deliverer. Such imputed dignities, like body armour in a duel, were no doubt useful; but uncomfortable, and mean, too.

I had never been a lofty person; on the contrary I had tried to be accessible to everyone, even if it continually felt as though most of them came and saw me every day. I had striven as eloquently as I could by my own example to keep plain the standard of existence. I had had no tents, no cooks, no body-servants: just my guards, who were fighting men, not servile: and behold these Byzantine shopkeepers endeavouring to corrupt our simplicity! So I flung away from them in a rage, determined to go south and see if anything active could be done, in the cold weather, about the Dead Sea, which the enemy held as a trench dividing us from Palestine.

My remaining money was handed over to Sherif Ali, for his maintenance till the spring; and the Indians were commended to his care. Particularly we bought them fresh riding-camels, in case the need to move came suddenly upon them in the winter; though the daily news of a threat by the Turks against Azrak was scornfully discounted by young Ali. He and I took affectionate leave of one another. Ali gave me half his wardrobe: shirts, head-cloths, belts, tunics. I gave him an equivalent half of mine, and we kissed like David and Jonathan, each wearing the other's clothes. Afterwards, with Rahail only, on my two best camels, I struck away southward.

We left Azrak one evening, riding into a glowing west, while over our heads schools of cranes flew into the sunset like the out-drawn barbs of arrows. It was toilsome from the start. Night was deep by Wadi Butum, where the conditions became even worse. All the plain was wet, and our poor camels slithered and fell time and again. We fell as often as they did, but at least our part of sitting still, between falls, was easier than their part of movement. By midnight we had crossed the Ghadaf and the quag felt too awful for further progress. Also the mishandling at Deraa had left me curiously faint; my muscles seemed at once pappy and inflamed, and all effort frightened me in anticipation. So we halted.

We slept where we were, in the mud; rose up plated with it at dawn; and smiled crackily at one another. The wind blew, and the ground began to dry. It was important, for I wanted to reach Akaba before Wood's men had left it with the return caravan, and their eight days' start called for speed. My body's reluctance to ride hard was another (and perverse) reason for forcing the march. Until noon we made poor travelling, for the camels still broke through the loose crust of flints, and foundered in the red under-clay. After noon, on the higher ground, we did better, and began rapidly to close the white sky-tents which were the Thlaithakhwat peaks.

Suddenly shots rang out at close range, and four mouthing men dashed down the slope towards us. I stopped my camel peaceably. Seeing this they jumped off, and ran to us brandishing their arms. They asked who I was: volunteering that they were Jazi Howeitat. This was an open lie, because their camel-brands were Faiz. They covered us with rifles at four yards, and told us to dismount. I laughed at them, which was good tactics with Beduin at a crisis. They were puzzled. I asked the loudest if he knew his name. He stared at me, thinking I was mad. He came nearer, with his finger on the trigger, and I bent down to him and whispered that it must be '*Teras*' since no other tradesman could be so rude. As I spoke, I covered him with a pistol hidden under my cloak.

It was a shooting insult, but he was so astonished that anyone should provoke an armed man, as to give up for the moment his thought of murdering us. He took a step back, and looked around, fearful that there was a reserve somewhere, to give us confidence. At once I rode off slowly, with a creepy feeling in my back, calling Rahail to follow.

They let him go too, unhurt. When we were a hundred yards away, they repented themselves, and began to shoot, but we dashed over the watershed into the next depression, and across it cantered more confidently into safe ground.

From the ridge at sunset we looked back for an instant upon the northern plain, as it sank away from us greyly, save that here and there glowed specks or great splashes of crimson fire, the reflection of the dying sun in shallow pools of rain-water on the flats. These eyes of a dripping bloody redness were so much more visible than the plain that they carried our sight miles into the haze, and seemed to hang detached in the distant sky, tilted up, like mirage.

We passed Bair long after dark, when only its latest tent-fires still shone. As we went we saw the stars mirrored in a valley bottom, and were able to water our breathless camels in a pool of yesterday's rain. After their drink, we eased them for half an hour. This night-journeying was hard on both men and animals. By day the camels saw the irregularities of their path, and undulated over them; and the rider could swing his body to miss the jerk of a long or short stride: but by night everything was blinded, and the march racked with shocks. I had a heavy bout of fever on me, which made me angry, so that I paid no attention to Rahail's appeals for rest. That young man had maddened all of us for months by his abundant vigour, and by laughing at our weaknesses; so this time I was determined to ride him out, showing no mercy. Before dawn he was blubbering with self-pity; but softly, lest I hear him.

Dawn in Jefer came imperceptibly through the mist like a ghost of sunlight, which left the earth untouched, and demonstrated itself as a glittering blink against the eyes alone. Things at their heads stood matt against the pearl-grey horizon, and at their feet melted softly into the ground. Our shadows had no edge: we doubted if that faint stain upon the soil below was cast by us or not. In the forenoon we reached Auda's camp; and stopped for a greeting, and a few Jauf dates. Auda could not provide us a relay of camels. We mounted again to get over the railway in the early night. Rahail was past protest now. He rode beside me white-faced, bleak and silent, wrought up only to outstay me, beginning to take a half pride in his pains.

Even had we started fair, he had the advantage anyhow over me in strength, and now I was nearly finished. Step by step I was yielding myself to a slow ache which conspired with my abating fever and the numb monotony of riding to close up the gate of my senses. I seemed at last approaching the insensibility which had always been beyond my reach: but a delectable land: for one born so slug-tissued that nothing this side fainting would let his spirit free. Now I found myself dividing into parts. There was one which went on riding wisely, sparing or helping every pace of the wearied camel. Another hovering above and to the right bent down curiously, and asked what the flesh was doing. The flesh gave no answer, for, indeed, it was conscious only of a ruling impulse to keep on and on; but a third garrulous one talked and wondered, critical of the body's self-inflicted labour, and contemptuous of the reason for effort.

The night passed in these mutual conversations. My unseeing eyes saw the dawn-goal in front; the head of the pass, below which that other world of Rumm lay out like a sunlit map, and my parts debated that the struggle might be worthy, but the end foolishness and a re-birth of trouble. The spent body toiled on doggedly and took no heed, quite rightly, for the divided selves said nothing which I was not capable of thinking in cold blood; they were all my natives. Telesius, taught by some such experience, split up the soul. Had he gone on, to the furthest limit of exhaustion, he would have seen his conceived regiment of thoughts and acts and feelings ranked around him as separate creatures; eyeing, like vultures, the passing in their midst of the common thing which gave them life.

Rahail collected me out of my death-sleep by jerking my head-stall and striking me, while he shouted that we had lost our direction, and were wandering towards the Turkish lines at Aba el Lissan. He was right, and we had to make a long cut back to reach Batra safely. We walked down the steeper portions of the pass, and then stumbled along Wadi Hafira. In its midst a gallant little Howeiti, aged perhaps fourteen, darted out against us, finger on trigger, and told us to stand and explain; which we did, laughing. The lad blushed, and pleaded that his father's camels kept him always in the field so that he had not known us either by sight or by description. He begged that we would not do him shame by betraying his error. The incident broke the tension between Rahail and myself; and, chatting, we rode out upon the Gaa. There under the tamarisk we passed the middle hour of the day in sleep, since by our slowness in the march over Batra we had lost the possibility of reaching Akaba within the three days from Azrak. The breaking of our intention we took quietly. Rumm's glory would not let a man waste himself in feverish regrets.

We rode up its valley in the early afternoon; easier now and exchanging jests with one another, as the long winter evening crept down. When we got past the Khazail in the ascent we found the sun veiled behind the level banks of low clouds in the west, and enjoyed a rich twilight of the English sort. In Itm the mist steamed up gently from the soil, and collected into wool-white masses in each hollow. We reached Akaba at midnight, and slept outside the camp till breakfast, when I called on Joyce, and found the caravan not yet ready to start: indeed Wood was only a few days returned.

Later came urgent orders for me to go up at once to Palestine by air. Croil flew me to Suez. Thence I went up to Allenby's headquarters beyond Gaza. He was so full of victories that my short statement that we had failed to carry a Yarmuk bridge was sufficient, and the miserable details of failure could remain concealed.

While I was still with him, word came from Chetwode that Jerusalem had fallen; and Allenby made ready to enter in the official manner which the catholic imagination of Mark Sykes had devised. He was good enough, although I had done nothing for the success, to let Clayton take me along as his staff officer for the day. The personal Staff tricked me out in their spare clothes till I looked like a major in the British Army. Dalmeny lent me red tabs, Evans his brass hat; so that I had the gauds of my appointment in the ceremony of the Jaffa gate, which for me was the supreme moment of the war.

BOOK VII

THE DEAD SEA CAMPAIGN

Chapters LXXXII to XCI

AFTER *the capture of Jerusalem, Allenby, to relieve his right, assigned us a limited objective. We began well; but when we reached the Dead Sea, bad weather, bad temper and division of purpose blunted our offensive spirit and broke up our force.*

I had a misunderstanding with Zeid, threw in my hand, and returned to Palestine reporting that we had failed, and asking the favour of other employment. Allenby was in the hopeful midst of a great scheme for the coming spring. He sent me back at once to Feisal with new powers and duties.

CHAPTER LXXXII

SHAMEFACED with triumph — which was not so much a triumph as homage by Allenby to the mastering spirit of the place — we drove back to Shea's headquarters. The aides pushed about, and from great baskets drew a lunch, varied, elaborate and succulent. On us fell a short space of quiet, to be shattered by Monsieur Picot, the French political representative permitted by Allenby to march beside Clayton in the entry, who said in his fluting voice: 'And to-morrow, my dear general, I will take the necessary steps to set up civil government in this town.'

It was the bravest word on record; a silence followed, as when they opened the seventh seal in heaven. Salad, chicken mayonnaise and foie gras sandwiches hung in our wet mouths unmunched, while we turned to Allenby and gaped. Even he seemed for the moment at a loss. We began to fear that the idol might betray a frailty. But his face grew red: he swallowed, his chin coming forward (in the way we loved), whilst he said, grimly, 'In the military zone the only authority is that of the Commander-in-Chief — myself.' 'But Sir Grey, Sir Edward Grey' ... stammered M. Picot. He was cut short. 'Sir Edward Grey referred to the civil government which will be established when I judge that the military situation permits.' And by car again, through the sunshine of a great thankfulness, we sped down the saluting mountain-side into our camp.

There Allenby and Dawnay told me the British were marched and fought nearly to a standstill, in the ledged and precipitous hills, shell-torn and bullet-spattered, amid which they wrestled with the Turks along a line from Ramleh to Jerusalem. So they would ask us in the lull to come north towards the Dead Sea until, if possible, we linked right up to its southern end, and renewed the continuous front. Fortunately, this had already been discussed with Feisal, who was preparing the convergent move on Tafileh, its necessary first step.

It was the moment to ask Allenby what he would do next. He thought he was immobilized till the middle of February, when he would push down to Jericho. Much enemy food was being lightered up the Dead Sea, and he asked me to note this traffic as a second objective if the effort to Tafileh prevailed.

I, hoping to improve on this, replied that, should the Turks be continually shaken, we might join him at the north end of the Dead Sea. If he could put Feisal's fifty tons a day of supplies, stores and ammunition into Jericho, we would abandon Akaba and transfer our headquarters to the Jordan Valley. The Arab regulars, now some three thousand strong, would suffice to make our retention of the river's eastern bank reasonably secure.

This idea commended itself to Allenby and Dawnay. They could almost promise us such facilities when the railway reached Jerusalem some time towards the end of the coming January. We might be able to move our base two months after the line was through.

This talk left us a clear course of operations. The Arabs were to reach the Dead Sea as soon as possible; to stop the transport of food up it to Jericho before the middle of February; and to arrive at the Jordan before the end of March. Since the first movement would take a month to start, and all preliminaries were in hand, I could take a holiday. So I went down to Cairo, and stayed there a week experimenting with insulated cable and explosives.

After the week it seemed best to return to Akaba, where we arrived on Christmas Day; to find Snagge, as senior officer in Akaba, entertaining the British Community to dinner. He had screened-in the after deck and built tables, which took the hosts and the twenty-odd guests easily. Snagge stood godfather to the land, in hospitality, in the loan of his ship's doctor and workshop, and in cheerfulness.

In the early days of the revolt it had been the *Hardinge* which played his role of providence to us. Once, at Yenbo, Feisal had ridden in from the hills on a streaming day of winter, cold, wet, miserable and tired. Captain Linberry sent a launch ashore and invited him to the ship, where he found, waiting for him, a warm cabin, a peaceful meal, and a bountiful bath. Afterwards he lay back in an arm-chair, smoking one of his constant cigarettes, and remarked dreamily to me that now he knew what the furnishings of heaven would be.

Joyce told me that things were well. The situation had sensibly changed since Maulud's victory. The Turks had concentrated in Aba

el Lissan. We were distracting them by raids against the line south of
Maan. Abdulla and Ali were doing the same near Medina; and the
Turks, being pinched to guard the railway, had to draw men from
Aba el Lissan to strengthen weak sections.

Maulud boldly threw our posts to places on the plateau, and began to
harry the supply caravans from Maan. He was hampered by the intense
cold, the rain and snow on the heights. Some of his ill-clad men
actually died of exposure. But the Turks lost equally in men and much
more in transport, since their mangy camels died off rapidly in the
storms and mud. The loss straitened them in food-carrying and
involved further withdrawals from Aba el Lissan.

At last they were too weak to hold the wide position, and, early in
January, Maulud was able to force them out towards Mreigha. The
Beduin caught the Turks moving, and cut up the hindmost battalion.
This threw the Turks back precipitately, to Uheida, only six miles from
Maan, and when we pressed after menacingly, they withdrew to
Semna, the outpost line of Maan, three miles out. So by January the
seventh Maulud was containing Maan directly.

Prosperity gave us ten days' leisure; and as Joyce and myself
were rarely at liberty together we decided to celebrate the occasion by
taking a car-trip down the mud-flats towards Mudowwara.

The cars were now at Guweira, in permanent camp. Gilman and
Dowsett, with their crews and fifty Egyptian soldiers, had spent
months in Wadi Itm, building, like engineers, a motor road through
the gorge. It had been a great work, and was now in order to Guweira.
So we took the Rolls tenders, filled them with spare tyres, petrol, and
food for four days, and set off on our exploring trip.

The mud-flats were bone-dry and afforded perfect going. Our tyres
left only a faint white scar across their velvet surface, as we twisted
about the spacious smoothness at speed, skirting clumps of tamarisk
and roaring along under the great sandstone crags. The drivers rejoiced
for the first time in nine months, and flung forward abreast in a mad
race. Their speedometers touched sixty-five; not bad for cars which
had been months ploughing the desert with only such running repairs
as the drivers had time and tools to give them.

Across the sandy neck from the first flat to the second we built a corduroy road of brushwood. When this was ready, the cars came steaming and hissing along it, dangerously fast to avoid getting stuck, rocking over hummocks in a style which looked fatal for springs. However, we knew it was nearly impossible to break a Rolls-Royce, and so were sorrier for the drivers, Thomas, Rolls and Sanderson. The jolts tore the steering-wheel from their grip, and left them breathless with bleeding hands after the crossing.

We lunched and rested, and then had another burst of speed, with a wild diversion in the middle when a gazelle was sighted over the flat and two of the great cars lurched aside in unavailing chase.

At the end of this second flat, the Gaa of Disi, we had a rough mile to the third flat of Abu Sawana, across which we had a final glorious sprint of fifteen miles, over the mud and over the equally firm flint plains beyond. We slept there that chilly night, happy with bully beef and tea and biscuit, with English talk and laughter round the fire, golden with its shower of sparks from the fierce brushwood. When these things tired, there was soft sand beneath our bodies and two blankets to wrap ourselves in. For me it was a holiday, with not an Arab near, before whom I must play out my tedious part.

In the morning we ran on nearly to Mudowwara, finding the ground surface excellent to the watershed. So our reconnaissance had been a quick and easy success. At once we turned back, to fetch the armoured cars and undertake an immediate operation, with the help of the mountain gun section on Talbots.

This section was an oddment, which General Clayton had seen in Egypt, and had sent down to us in an inspired moment. Its six Talbots, specially geared for heavy work, carried two ten-pounders with British gunners. It was wicked to give good men such rotten tools; yet their spirit seemed hardly affected by the inferior weapons. Their commander, Brodie, was a silent Scotsman, never very buoyant and never too anxious; a man who found difficulties shameful to notice, and who stamped himself on his fellows. However hard the duty given them, they always attacked it with such untroubled determination that their will prevailed. On every occasion and in every crisis they would be surely in place at their moment, perspiring but imperturbable, with never a word in explanation or complaint.

Eight imposing cars drove off from Guweira next day, and reached our old stopping-place behind Mudowwara by sundown. This was excellent; and we camped, intending to find a road to the railway in the morning. Accordingly we set off early in a Rolls tender and searched through the very nasty low hills till evening, when we were in place behind the last ridge, above Tell Shahm, the second station northward from Mudowwara.

We had talked vaguely of mining a train, but the country was too open, and enemy blockhouses numerous. Instead we determined to attack a little entrenched work exactly opposite our hiding-place. So late in new year's morning, a day as cool as a good summer's day in England, after a pleasant breakfast we rolled gently over a stony plain to a hillock which overlooked the Turkish post. Joyce and I got out of our cars and climbed its summit, to look on.

Joyce was in charge, and for the first time I was at a fight as spectator. The novelty was most enjoyable. Armoured car work seemed fighting de luxe, for our troops, being steel-covered, could come to no hurt. Accordingly we made a field-day of it like the best regular generals, sitting in laconic conference on our hill-top and watching the battle intently through binoculars.

The Talbot battery opened the affair, coming spiritedly into action just below our point; while the three armoured cars crawled about the flanks of the Turkish earthwork like great dogs nosing out a trail. The enemy soldiers popped up their heads to gaze, and everything was very friendly and curious, till the cars slewed round their Vickers and began to spray the trenches. Then the Turks, realizing that it was an attack, got down behind their parapets and fired at the cars raggedly. It was about as deadly as trying to warm a rhinoceros with bird-shot: after a while they turned their attention to Brodie's guns and peppered the earth about them with bullets.

Obviously they did not mean to surrender, and obviously we had no means at disposal to compel them. So we drew off, contented with having prowled up and down the line, and proved the surface hard enough for car-operations at deliberate speed. However, the men looked for more, and to humour them we drove southward till opposite Shahm. There Brodie chose a gun-position at two thousand yards and began to throw shell after shell neatly into the station area.

Hating this, the Turks trickled off to a blockhouse, while the cars put leisurely bullets through the station doors and windows. They might have entered it safely, had there been point in doing so. As it was we called everybody off again, and returned into our hiding-hills. Our anxiety and forethought had been all to reach the railway through the manifold difficulties of the plains and hills. When we did reach it, we were entirely unready for action, with not a conception of what (ur tactics or methods should be: yet we learned much from this very indecision.

The certainty that in a day from Guweira we could be operating along the railway, meant that traffic lay at our mercy. All the Turks in Arabia could not fight a single armoured car in open country. Thereby the situation of Medina, already bad, became hopeless. The German Staff saw it, and after Falkenhayn's visit to Maan, they repeatedly urged abandonment of everything south of that point; but the old Turk party valued Medina as the last remnant of their sovereignty in the Holy Places, their surviving claim upon the Caliphate. Sentiment swung them to the decision, against military expediency.

The British seemed curiously dense about Medina. They insisted that it must be captured, and lavished money and explosives on the operations which Ali and Abdulla continually undertook from their Yenbo base. When I pleaded to the contrary, they treated my view as a witty paradox. Accordingly, to excuse our deliberate inactivity in the north, we had to make a show of impotence, which gave them to understand that the Arabs were too poltroon to cut the line near Maan and keep it cut. This reason gratified their sense of fitness, for soldiers, always ready to believe ill of native action, took its inferiority as a compliment. So we battened on our ill reputation, which was an ungenerous stratagem, but the easiest. The staff knew so much more of war than I did that they refused to learn from me of the strange conditions in which Arab irregulars had to act; and I could not be bothered to set up a kindergarten of the imagination for their benefit.

CHAPTER LXXXIII

ON our return to Akaba domestic affairs engaged the remaining free days. My part mostly concerned the bodyguard which I formed for private protection, as rumour gradually magnified my importance. On our first going up country from Rabegh and Yenbo, the Turks had been curious: afterwards they were annoyed; to the point of ascribing to the English the direction and motive force of the Arab Revolt, much as we used to flatter ourselves by attributing the Turkish efficiency to German influence.

However, the Turks said it often enough to make it an article of faith, and began to offer a reward of one hundred pounds for a British officer alive or dead. As time went on they not only increased the general figure, but made a special bid for me. After the capture of Akaba the price became respectable; while after we blew up Jemal Pasha they put Ali and me at the head of their list; worth twenty thousand pounds alive or ten thousand dead.

Of course, the offer was rhetorical; with no certainty whether in gold or paper, or that the money would be paid at all. Still, perhaps, it might justify some care. I began to increase my people to a troop, adding such lawless men as I found, fellows whose dash had got them into trouble elsewhere. I needed hard riders and hard livers; men proud of themselves, and without family. By good fortune three or four of this sort joined me at the first, setting a tone and standard.

One afternoon, I was quietly reading in Marshall's tent at Akaba (I lodged with Marshall, our Scottish doctor, as often as I was in camp) when there entered over the noiseless sand an Ageyly, thin, dark, and short, but most gorgeously dressed. He carried on his shoulder the richest Hasa saddle-bag I had ever seen. Its woollen tapestry of green and scarlet, white, orange and blue, had tassels woven over its sides in five rows, and from the middle and bottom hung five-foot streamers of geometric pattern, tasselled and fringed.

Respectfully greeting me, the young man threw the saddle-bag on my carpet, saying 'Yours' and disappeared suddenly, as he had come. Next day, he returned with a camel-saddle of equal beauty, the long brass horns of its cantles adorned with exquisite old Yemeni engraving. On the third day he reappeared empty-handed, in a poor cotton shirt, and sank down in a heap before me, saying he wished to enter my service. He looked odd without his silk robes; for his face, shrivelled and torn with smallpox, and hairless, might have been of any age; while he had a lad's supple body, and something of a lad's recklessness in his carriage.

His long black hair was carefully braided into three shining plaits down each cheek. His eyes were weak, closed up to slits. His mouth was sensual, loose, wet; and gave him a good-humoured, half cynical expression. I asked him his name; he replied Abdulla, surnamed el Nahabi, or the Robber; the nickname, he said was an inheritance from his respected father. His own adventures had been unprofitable. He was born in Boreida, and while young had suffered from the civil power for his impiety. When half-grown, a misfortune in a married woman's house had made him leave his native town, in a hurry, and take service with ibn Saud, Emir of Nejd.

In this service his hard swearing earned lashes and imprisonment. Consequently he deserted to Kuweit, where again he had been amorous. On his release he had moved to Hail, and enrolled himself among the retainers of ibn Rashid, the Emir. Unfortunately there he had disliked his officer to the point of striking him in public with a camel-stick. Return was made in kind; and, after a slow recovery in prison, he had once more been thrust friendless on the world.

The Hejaz Railway was being built, and to its works he had come in search of fortune; but a contractor docked his wages for sleeping at noonday. He retorted by docking the contractor of his head. The Turkish Government interfered, and he found life very hard in the prison at Medina. However, through a window, he came to Mecca, and for his proved integrity and camel-manship was made post-carrier between Mecca and Jidda. To this employ he settled down, laying aside his young extravagances, bringing to Mecca his father and mother and setting them up in a shop to work for him, with the capital provided by commission from merchants and robbers.

After a year's prosperity he was waylaid, losing his camel and its consignment. They seized his shop in compensation. From the wreck he saved enough to fit himself out as a man at arms, in the Sherifian camel-police. Merit made him a petty officer, but too much attention was drawn to his section by a habit of fighting with daggers, and by his foul mouth; a maw of depravity which had eaten filth in the stews of every capital in Arabia. Once too often his lips trembled with humour, sardonic, salacious, lying; and when reduced, he charged his downfall to a jealous Ateibi, whom he stabbed in Court before the eyes of the outraged Sherif Sharraf.

Sharraf's stern sense of public decency punished Abdulla, by the severest of his chastisements, from which he very nearly died. When well enough, he entered Sharraf's service. On the outbreak of war he became orderly to ibn Dakhil, captain of the Ageyl with Feisal. His reputation grew: but the mutiny at Wejh turned ibn Dakhil into an ambassador. Adbulla missed the comradeship of the ranks, and ibn Dakhil had given him a written character to enter my service.

The letter said that for two years he had been faithful, but disrespectful; the wont of sons of shame. He was the most experienced Ageyli, having served every Arabian prince and having been dismissed each employment, after stripes and prison, for offences of too great individuality. Ibn Dakhil said that the Nahabi rode second to himself, was a master-judge of camels, and as brave as any son of Adam; easily since he was too blind-eyed to see danger. In fact, he was the perfect retainer and I engaged him instantly.

In my service only once did he taste cells. That was at Allenby's headquarters, when a despairing provost-marshal rang up to say that a wild man, with weapons, found sitting on the Commander-in-Chief's doorstep, had been led without riot to the guard-room, where he was eating oranges as though for a wager, and proclaiming himself my son, one of Feisal's dogs. Oranges were running short.

So Abdulla experienced his first telephone conversation. He told the A.P.M. that such a fitting would be a comfort in all prisons, and took a ceremonious leave. He scouted absolutely the notion that he might walk about Ramleh unarmed, and was given a pass to make lawful his sword, dagger, pistol, and rifle. His first use of this pass was to re-visit the guard-room with cigarettes for the military police.

He examined the applicants for my service, and, thanks to him and to the Zaagi, my other commander (a stiff man of normal officer cut), a wonderful gang of experts grew about me. The British at Akaba called them cut-throats; but they cut throats only to my order. Perhaps in others' eyes it was a fault that they would recognize no authority but mine. Yet when I was away they were kind to Major Marshall, and would hold him in incomprehensible talk about points of camels, their breeds and ailments, from dawn till night time. Marshall was very patient; and two or three of them would sit attentive by his bedside, from the first daylight, waiting to continue his education as soon as he became conscious.

A good half (nearly fifty of the ninety) were Ageyl, the nervous limber Nejdi villagers who made the colour and the parade in Feisal's army, and whose care for their riding camels was such a feature of their service. They would call them by name, from a hundred yards away, and leave them in charge of the kit when they dismounted. The Ageyl, being mercenaries, would not do well unless well paid, and for lack of that condition had fallen into disrepute: yet the bravest single effort of the Arab war belonged to that one of them who twice swam down the subterranean water-conduit into Medina, and returned with a full report of the invested town.

I paid my men six pounds a month, the standard army wage for a man and camel, but mounted them on my own animals, so that the money was clear income: this made the service enviable, and put the eager spirits of the camp at my disposal. For my time-table's sake, since I was more busy than most, my rides were long, hard and sudden. The ordinary Arab, whose camel represented half his wealth, could not afford to founder it by travelling my speed: also such riding was painful for the man.

Consequently, I had to have with me picked riders, on my own beasts. We bought at long prices the fastest and strongest camels to be obtained. We chose them for speed and power, no matter how hard and exhausting they might be under the saddle: indeed, often we chose the hard-paced as the more enduring. They were changed or rested in our own camel-hospital when they became thin: and their riders were treated likewise. The Zaagi held each man bodily responsible for his mount's condition, and for the fitness of his saddlery.

Fellows were very proud of being in my bodyguard, which developed a professionalism almost flamboyant. They dressed like a bed of tulips, in every colour but white; for that was my constant wear, and they did not wish to seem to presume. In half an hour they would make ready for a ride of six weeks, that being the limit for which food could be carried at the saddle-bow. Baggage camels they shrank from as a disgrace. They would travel day and night at my whim, and made it a point of honour never to mention fatigue. If a new man grumbled, the others would silence him, or change the current of his complaint, brutally.

They fought like devils, when I wanted, and sometimes when I did not, especially with Turks or with outsiders. For one guardsman to strike another was the last offence. They expected extravagant reward and extravagant punishment. They made boast throughout the army of their pains and gains. By this unreason in each degree they were kept apt for any effort, any risk.

Abdulla and the Zaagi ruled them, under my authority, with a savagery palliated only by the power of each man to quit the service if he wished. Yet we had but one resignation. The others, though adolescents full of carnal passion, tempted by this irregular life, well-fed, exercised, rich, seemed to sanctify their risk, to be fascinated by their suffering. Servitude, like other conduct, was profoundly modified to Eastern minds by their obsession with the antithesis between flesh and spirit. These lads took pleasure in subordination; in degrading the body: so as to throw into greater relief their freedom in equality of mind: almost they preferred servitude as richer in experience than authority, and less binding in daily care.

Consequently the relation of master and man in Arabia was at once more free and more subject than I had experienced elsewhere. Servants were afraid of the sword of justice and of the steward's whip, not because the one might put an arbitrary term to their existence, and the other print red rivers of pain about their sides, but because these were the symbols and the means to which their obedience was vowed. They had a gladness of abasement, a freedom of consent to yield to their master the last service and degree of their flesh and blood, because their spirits were equal with his and the contract voluntary. Such boundless engagement precluded humiliation, repining and regret.

In this pledging of their endurance, it disgraced men if, from weakness of nerve or insufficiency of courage, they fell short of the call. Pain was to them a solvent, a cathartic, almost a decoration, to be fairly worn while they survived it. Fear, the strongest motive in slothful man, broke down with us, since love for a cause — or for a person — was aroused. For such an object, penalties were discounted, and loyalty became open-eyed, not obedient. To it men dedicated their being, and in its possession they had no room for virtue or vice. Cheerfully they nourished it upon what they were; gave it their lives; and, greater than that, the lives of their fellowship: it being many times harder to offer than to endure sacrifice.

To our strained eyes, the ideal, held in common, seemed to transcend the personal, which before had been our normal measure of the world. Did this instinct point to our happily accepting final absorption in some pattern wherein the discordant selves might find reasonable, inevitable purpose? Yet this very transcending of individual frailty made the ideal transient. Its principle became Activity, the primal quality, external to our atomic structure, which we could simulate only by unrest of mind and soul and body, beyond holding point. So always the ideality of the ideal vanished, leaving its worshippers exhausted: holding for false what they had once pursued.

However, for the time the Arabs were possessed, and cruelty of governance answered their need. Besides, they were blood enemies of thirty tribes, and only for my hand over them would have murdered in the ranks each day. Their feuds prevented them combining against me; while their unlikeness gave me sponsors and spies wherever I went or sent, between Akaba and Damascus, between Beersheba and Bagdad. In my service nearly sixty of them died.

With quaint justice, events forced me to live up to my bodyguard, to become as hard, as sudden, as heedless. The odds against me were heavy, and the climate cogged the die. In the short winter I outdid them, with my allies of the frost and snow: in the heat they outdid me. In endurance there was less disparity. For years before the war I had made myself trim by constant carelessness. I had learned to eat much one time; then to go two, three, or four days without food; and after to overeat. I made it a rule to avoid rules in food; and by a course of exceptions accustomed myself to no custom at all.

So, organically, I was efficient in the desert, felt neither hunger nor surfeit, and was not distracted by thought of food. On the march I could go dry between wells, and, like the Arabs, could drink greatly to-day for the thirst of yesterday and of to-morrow.

In the same way, though sleep remained for me the richest pleasure in the world, I supplied its place by the uneasy swaying in the saddle of a night-march, or failed of it for night after laborious night without undue fatigue. Such liberties came from years of control (contempt of use might well be the lesson of our manhood), and they fitted me peculiarly for our work: but, of course, in me they came half by training, half by trying, out of mixed choice and poverty, not effortlessly, as with the Arabs. Yet in compensation stood my energy of motive. Their less taut wills flagged before mine flagged, and by comparison made me seem tough and active.

Into the sources of my energy of will I dared not probe. The conception of antithetical mind and matter, which was basic in the Arab self-surrender, helped me not at all. I achieved surrender (so far as I did achieve it) by the very opposite road, through my notion that mental and physical were inseparably one: that our bodies, the universe, our thoughts and tactilities were conceived in and of the molecular sludge of matter, the universal element through which form drifted as clots and patterns of varying density. It seemed to me unthinkable that assemblages of atoms should cogitate except in atomic terms. My perverse sense of values constrained me to assume that abstract and concrete, as badges, did not denote oppositions more serious than Liberal and Conservative.

The practice of our revolt fortified the nihilist attitude in me. During it, we often saw men push themselves or be driven to a cruel extreme of endurance: yet never was there an intimation of physical break. Collapse rose always from a moral weakness eating into the body, which of itself, without traitors from within, had no power over the will. While we rode we were disbodied, unconscious of flesh or feeling: and when at an interval this excitement faded and we did see our bodies, it was with some hostility, with a contemptuous sense that they reached their highest purpose, not as vehicles of the spirit, but when, dissolved, their elements served to manure a field.

CHAPTER LXXXIV

REMOTE from the fighting line, in Akaba, during this pause, we saw the reverse of the shield, the corruption of our enthusiasm, which made the moral condition of the base unsatisfactory. We rejoiced when at last we were able to escape into the clean, fresh hills about Guweira. The early winter gave us days hot and sunny, or days overcast, with clouds massed about the head of the plateau nine miles away, where Maulud was keeping his watch in the mist and rain. The evenings held just enough of chill to add delightful value to a thick cloak and a fire.

We waited in Guweira for news of the opening of our operation against Tafileh, the knot of villages commanding the south end of the Dead Sea. We planned to tackle it from west, south, and east, at once; the east opening the ball by attacking Jurf, its nearest station on the Hejaz line. Conduct of this attack had been trusted to Sherif Nasir, the Fortunate. With him went Nuri Said, Jaafar's chief of staff, commanding some regulars, a gun, and some machine-guns. They were working from Jefer. After three days their post came in. As usual Nasir had directed his raid with skill and deliberation. Jurf, the objective, was a strong station of three stone buildings with outer-works and trenches. Behind the station was a low mound, trenched and walled, on which the Turks had set two machine-guns and a mountain gun. Beyond the mount lay a high, sharp ridge, the last spur of the hills which divided Jefer from Bair.

The weakness of the defence lay in this ridge, for the Turks were too few to hold both it and the knoll or station, and its crest overlooked the railway. Nasir one night occupied the whole top of the hill without alarm, and then cut the line above and below the station. A few minutes later, when it was light enough to see, Nuri Said brought his mountain gun to the edge of the ridge; and, with a third lucky shot, a direct hit, silenced the Turkish gun beneath his view.

Nasir grew greatly excited: the Beni Sakhr mounted their camels, swearing they would charge in forthwith. Nuri thought it madness while Turkish machine-guns were still in action from trenches: but his words had no effect upon the Bedu. In desperation he opened a rattling fire with all he had against the Turkish position, and the Beni Sakhr swept round the foot of the main ridge and up over the knoll in a flash. When they saw this camel-horde racing at them, the Turks flung away their rifles and fled into the station. Only two Arabs were fatally hurt.

Nuri ran down to the knoll. The Turkish gun was undamaged. He slewed it round and discharged it point blank into the ticket office. The Beni Sakhr mob yelled with joy to see the wood and stones flying, jumped again on their camels and loped into the station just as the enemy surrendered. Nearly two hundred Turks, including seven officers, survived as our prisoners.

The Bedu became rich: besides the weapons, there were twenty-five mules, and in the siding seven trucks of delicacies for the officers' messes of Medina. There were things the tribesmen had only heard of, and things they had never heard of: they were supremely happy. Even the unfortunate regulars got a share, and were able once more to enjoy olives, sesame paste, dried apricot, and other sweet or pickled products of their native, half-forgotten, Syria.

Nuri Said had artificial tastes, and rescued tinned meats and liquors from the wilder men. There was one whole truck of tobacco. As the Howeitat did not smoke, it was divided between the Beni Sakhr and the regulars. By its loss the Medina garrison became tobacco-less: their sad plight later so worked on Feisal, a confirmed smoker, that he loaded some pack-camels with cheap cigarettes and drove them into Tebuk with his compliments.

After the looting, the engineers fired charges under the two engines, against the water-tower, in the pump, and between the points of the sidings. They burned the captured trucks and damaged a bridge; but perfunctorily, for, as usual after victory, everyone was too loaded and too hot to care for altruistic labour. They camped behind the station, and about midnight had an alarm, when the noise and lights of a train came from the south and halted, clearly with foreknowledge, by the break of the evening before. Auda sent scouts to report.

Before they had returned a solitary sergeant walked into Nasir's camp as a volunteer for the Sherif's army. He had been sent out by the Turks to explore the station. His story was that there were only sixty men and a mountain gun on the relief train, which, if he went back with smooth news, might be surprised without a shot fired. Nasir called Auda, who called the Howeitat, and they went off silently to lay the trap: but just before they got there our scouts decided to do their unaided best, and opened fire against the coaches. In fear, the engine reversed and rolled the train back, unhurt, to Maan. It was the only sorrow of Jurf.

After this raid the weather once more broke. For three successive days came falls of snow. Nasir's force with difficulty regained the tents at Jefer. This plateau about Maan lay between three and five thousand feet above sea level, open to all winds from north and east. They blew from Central Asia, or from Caucasus, terribly over the great desert to these low hills of Edom, against which their first fury broke. The surplus bitterness lipped the crest and made a winter, quite severe of its degree, below in Judæa and Sinai.

Outside Beersheba and Jerusalem the British found it cold; but our Arabs fled there to get warm. Unhappily the British supply staff realized too late that we were fighting in a little Alp. They would not give us tents for one-quarter of our troops, nor serge clothing, nor boots, nor blankets enough to issue two to each man of the mountain garrisons. Our soldiers, if they neither deserted nor died, existed in an aching misery which froze the hope out of them.

According to our plan the good news of Jurf was to send the Arabs of Petra, under Sherif Abd el Mayin, at once up their hills into the forest towards Shobek. It was an uncanny march in the hoar mist, that of these frozen-footed peasants in their sheepskins, up and down sharp valleys and dangerous hill-sides, out of whose snow-drifts the heavy trunks of junipers, grudging in leaves, jutted like castings in grey iron. The ice and frost broke down the animals, and many of the men; yet these hardy highlanders, used to being too cold throughout their winter, persisted in the advance.

The Turks heard of them as they struggled slowly nearer, and fled from the caves and shelters among the trees to the branch railhead, littering the roads of their panic with cast baggage and equipment.

Railhead of the forest railway, with its temporary sheds, was commanded from low ridges by the Arab gun-fire, and no better than a trap. The tribesmen, in a pack, tore the enemy to pieces as they ran out from their burning and falling walls. One disciplined company of proper troops, under an Albanian officer, fought their way to the main line; but the Arabs killed or took the others, and also the stores in Shobek, the old Crusader fort of Monreale, poised high on a chalk cone above its winding valley. Abd el Mayein put his headquarters there, and sent word to Nasir. Mastur, too, was told. He drew his Motalga horse and foot from the comfort of their tents in the sunny depths of Arabia and with them climbed the hill-pass eastward towards Tafileh.

However, the advantage lay with Nasir, who leaped in one day from Jefer, and after a whirlwind night appeared at dawn on the rocky brink of the ravine in which Tafileh hid, and summoned it to surrender on pain of bombardment: an idle threat, for Nuri Said with the guns had gone back to Guweira. There were only one hundred and eighty Turks in the village, but they had supporters in the Muhaisin, a clan of the peasantry; not for love so much as because Dhiab, the vulgar headman of another faction, had declared for Feisal. So they shot up at Nasir a stream of ill-directed bullets.

The Howeitat spread out along the cliffs to return the peasants' fire. This manner of going displeased Auda, the old lion, who raged that a mercenary village folk should dare to resist their secular masters, the Abu Tayi. So he jerked his halter, cantered his mare down the path, and rode out plain to view beneath the easternmost houses of the village. There he reined in, and shook a hand at them, booming in his wonderful voice: 'Dogs, do you not know Auda?' When they realized it was that implacable son of war their hearts failed them, and an hour later Sherif Nasir in the town-house was sipping tea with his guest the Turkish Governor, trying to console him for the sudden change of fortune.

At dark Mastur rode in. His Motalga looked blackly at their blood enemies the Abu Tayi, lolling in the best houses. The two Sherifs divided up the place, to keep their unruly followers apart. They had little authority to mediate, for by passage of time Nasir was nearly adopted into the Abu Tayi, and Mastur into the Jazi.

When morning came the factions were bickering; and the day passed anxiously; for besides these blood enemies, the Muhaisin were fighting for authority among the villagers, and further complications developed in two stranger elements: one a colony of freebooting Senussi from North Africa, who had been intruded by the Turks into some rich, but half-derelict plough-land; the other a plaintive and active suburb of a thousand Armenians, survivors of an infamous deportation by the Young Turks in 1915.

The people of Tafileh went in deadly fear of the future. We were, as usual, short of food and short of transport, and they would remedy neither ill. They had wheat or barley in their bins; but hid it. They had pack-animals, asses and mules in abundance; but drove them away for safety. They could have driven us away too, but were, fortunately for us, short of the sticking point. Incuriousness was the most potent ally of our imposed order; for Eastern government rested not so much on consent or force, as on the common supinity, hebetude, lack-a-daisiness, which gave a minority undue effect.

Feisal had delegated command of this push towards the Dead Sea to his young half-brother Zeid. It was Zeid's first office in the north, and he set out eager with hope. As adviser he had Jaafar Pasha, our general. His infantry, gunners and machine-gunners stuck, for lack of food, at Petra; but Zeid himself and Jaafar rode on to Tafileh.

Things were almost at a break. Auda affected a magnanimity very galling to the Motalga boys, Metaab and Annad, sons of Abtan, whom Auda's son had killed. They, lithe, definite, self-conscious figures, began to talk big about revenge — tom-tits threatening a hawk. Auda declared he would whip them in the market-place if they were rude. This was very well, but their followers were two to every man of his, and we should have the village in a blaze. The young fellows, with Rahail, my ruffler, went flaunting in every street.

Zeid thanked and paid Auda and sent him back to his desert. The enlightened heads of the Muhaisin had to go as forced guests to Feisal's tent. Dhiab, their enemy, was our friend: we remembered regretfully the adage that the best allies of a violently-successful new regime were not its partisans, but its opponents. By Zeid's plenty of gold the economic situation improved. We appointed an officer-governor and organized our five villages for further attack.

CHAPTER LXXXV

NOTWITHSTANDING, these plans quickly went adrift. Before they had been agreed upon we were astonished by a sudden try of the Turks to dislodge us. We had never dreamed of this, for it seemed out of the question that they should hope to keep Tafileh, or want to keep it. Allenby was just in Jerusalem, and for the Turks the issue of the war might depend on their successful defence of the Jordan against him. Unless Jericho fell, or until it fell, Tafileh was an obscure village of no interest. Nor did we value it as a possession; our desire was to get past it towards the enemy. For men so critically placed as the Turks to waste one single casualty on its recapture appeared the rankest folly.

Hamid Fakhri Pasha, commanding the 48th Division and the Amman sector, thought otherwise, or had his orders. He collected about nine hundred infantry, made up of three battalions (in January 1918 a Turkish battalion was a poor thing) with a hundred cavalry, two mountain howitzers, and twenty-seven machine-guns, and sent them by rail and road to Kerak. There he impressed all the local transport, drew a complete set of civil officials to staff his new administration in Tafileh, and marched southward to surprise us.

Surprise us he did. We first heard of him when his cavalry feelers fell on our pickets in Wadi Hesa, the gorge of great width and depth and difficulty which cut off Kerak from Tafileh, Moab from Edom. By dusk he had driven them back, and was upon us.

Jaafar Pasha had sketched a defence position on the south bank of the great ravine of Tafileh; proposing, if the Turks attacked, to give them the village, and defend the heights which overhung it, behind. This seemed to me doubly unsound. The slopes were dead, and their defence as difficult as their attack. They could be turned from the east; and by quitting the village we threw away the local people, whose votes and hands would be for the occupiers of their houses.

However, it was the ruling idea — all Zeid had — and so about midnight he gave the order, and servants and retainers loaded up their stuff. The men-at-arms proceeded to the southern crest, while the baggage train was sent off by the lower road to safety. This move created panic in the town. The peasants thought we were running away (I think we were) and rushed to save their goods and lives. It was freezing hard, and the ground was crusted with noisy ice. In the blustering dark the confusion and crying through the narrow streets were terrible.

Dhiab the Sheikh had told us harrowing tales of the disaffection of the townspeople, to increase the splendour of his own loyalty; but my impression was that they were stout fellows of great potential use. To prove it I sat out on my roof, or walked in the dark up and down the steep alleys, cloaked against recognition, with my guards unobtrusively about me within call. So we heard what passed. The people were in a very passion of fear, nearly dangerous, abusing everybody and everything: but there was nothing pro-Turkish abroad. They were in horror of the Turks returning, ready to do all in their physical capacity to support against them a leader with fighting intention. This was satisfactory, for it chimed with my hankering to stand where we were and fight stiffly.

Finally, I met the young Jazi sheikhs Metaab and Annad, beautiful in silks and gleaming silver arms, and sent them to find their uncle, Hamd el Arar. Him I asked to ride away north of the ravine, to tell the peasantry, who, by the noise, were still fighting the Turks, that we were on our way up to help them. Hamd, a melancholy, courtly, gallant cavalier, galloped off at once with twenty of his relations, all that he could gather in the distracted moment.

Their passage at speed through the streets added the last touch required to perfect the terror. The housewives bundled their goods pell-mell out of doors and windows, though no men were waiting to receive them. Children were trampled on, and yelled, while their mothers were yelling anyhow. The Motalga during their gallop fired shot after shot into the air to encourage themselves, and, as though to answer them, the flashes of the enemy rifles became visible, outlining the northern cliffs in that last blackness of sky before the dawn. I walked up the opposite heights to consult with Sherif Zeid.

Zeid sat gravely on a rock, sweeping the country with field-glasses for the enemy. As crises deepened, Zeid drew detached, nonchalant. I was in a furious rage. The Turks should never, by the rules of sane generalship, have ventured back to Tafileh at all. It was simple greed, a dog-in-the-manger attitude unworthy of a serious enemy, just the sort of hopeless thing a Turk would do. How could they expect a proper war when they gave us no chance to honour them? Our morale was continually being ruined by their follies, for neither could our men respect their courage, nor our officers respect their brains. Also, it was an icy morning, and I had been up all night and was Teutonic enough to decide that they should pay for my changed mind and plan.

They must be few in number, judging by their speed of advance. We had every advantage, of time, of terrain, of number, of weather, and could checkmate them easily: but to my wrath that was not enough. We would play their kind of game on our pigmy scale; deliver them a pitched battle such as they wanted; kill them all. I would rake up my memory of the half-forgotten maxims of the orthodox army text-book, and parody them in action.

This was villainous, for with arithmetic and geography for allies we might have spared the suffering factor of humanity; and to make a conscious joke of victory was wanton. We could have won by refusing battle, foxed them by manœuvring our centre as on twenty such occasions before and since; yet bad temper and conceit united for this time to make me not content to know my power, but determined to give public advertisement of it to the enemy and to everyone. Zeid, now convinced of the inconvenience of the defence-line, was very ready to listen to the voice of the tempter.

First I suggested that Abdulla go forward with two Hotchkiss guns to test the strength and disposition of the enemy. Then we talked of what next; very usefully, for Zeid was a cool and gallant little fighter, with the temperament of a professional officer. We saw Abdulla climb the other bank. The shooting became intense for a time, and then faded into distance. His coming had stimulated the Motalga horsemen and the villagers, who fell on the Turkish cavalry and drove them over a first ridge, across a plain two miles wide, and over a ridge beyond it down the first step of the great Hesa depression.

Behind this lay the Turkish main body, just getting on the road again after a severe night which had stiffened them in their places. They came properly into action, and Abdulla was checked at once. We heard the distant rolling of machine-gun fire, growing up in huge bursts, laced by a desultory shelling. Our ears told us what was happening as well as if we saw it, and the news was excellent. I wanted Zeid to come forward at once on that authority: but his caution stepped in and he insisted that we wait exact word from his advance-guard, Abdulla.

This was not necessary, according to book, but they knew I was a sham soldier, and took licence to hesitate over my advice when it came peremptorily. However, I held a hand worth two of that and went off myself for the front to prejudice their decision. On the way I saw my bodyguard, turning over the goods exposed for removal in the streets, and finding much of interest to themselves. I told them to recover our camels and to bring their Hotchkiss automatic to the north bank of the gorge in a hurry,

The road dipped into a grove of fig-trees, knots of blue snaky boughs; bare, as they would be long after the rest of nature was grown green. Thence it turned eastward, to wind lengthily in the valley to the crest. I left it, climbing straight up the cliffs. An advantage of going barefoot was a new and incredible sureness upon rock when the soles had got hard by painful insistence, or were too chilled to feel jags and scrapes. The new way, while warming me, also shortened my time appreciably, and very soon, at the top, I found a level bit, and then a last ridge overlooking the plateau.

This last straight bank, with Byzantine foundations in it, seemed very proper for a reserve or ultimate line of defence for Tafileh. To be sure, we had no reserve as yet — no one had the least notion who or what we would have anywhere — but, if we did have anybody, here was their place: and at that precise moment Zeid's personal Ageyl became visible, hiding coyly in a hollow. To make them move required words of a strength to unravel their plaited hair: but at last I had them sitting along the skyline of Reserve Ridge. They were about twenty, and from a distance looked beautiful, like 'points' of a considerable army. I gave them my signet as a token, with orders to collect there all newcomers, especially my fellows with their gun.

As I walked northward towards the fighting, Abdulla met me, on his way to Zeid with news. He had finished his ammunition, lost five men from shell-fire, and had one automatic gun destroyed. Two guns, he thought the Turks had. His idea was to get up Zeid with all his men and fight: so nothing remained for me to add to his message; and there was no subtlety in leaving alone my happy masters to cross and dot their own right decision.

He gave me leisure in which to study the coming battlefield. The tiny plain was about two miles across, bounded by low green ridges, and roughly triangular, with my reserve ridge as base. Through it ran the road to Kerak, dipping into the Hesa valley. The Turks were fighting their way up this road. Abdulla's charge had taken the western or left-hand ridge, which was now our firing-line.

Shells were falling in the plain as I walked across it, with harsh stalks of wormwood stabbing into my wounded feet. The enemy fusing was too long, so that the shells grazed the ridge and burst away behind. One fell near me, and I learned its calibre from the hot cap. As I went they began to shorten range, and by the time I got to the ridge it was being freely sprinkled with shrapnel. Obviously the Turks had got observation somehow, and looking round I saw them climbing along the eastern side beyond the gap of the Kerak road. They would soon outflank us at our end of the western ridge.

CHAPTER LXXXVI

'U s' proved to be about sixty men, clustered behind the ridge in two bunches, one near the bottom, one by the top. The lower was made up of peasants, on foot, blown, miserable, and yet the only warm things I had seen that day. They said their ammunition was finished, and it was all over. I assured them it was just beginning and pointed to my populous reserve ridge, saying that all arms were there in support. I told them to hurry back, refill their belts and hold on to it for good. Meanwhile we would cover their retreat by sticking here for the few minutes yet possible.

They ran off, cheered, and I walked about among the upper group quoting how one should not quit firing from one position till ready to fire from the next. In command was young Metaab, stripped to his skimp riding-drawers for hard work, with his black love-curls awry, his face stained and haggard. He was beating his hands together and crying hoarsely with baffled vexation, for he had meant to do so well in this, his first fight for us.

My presence at the last moment, when the Turks were breaking through, was bitter; and he got angrier when I said that I only wanted to study the landscape. He thought it flippancy, and screamed something about a Christian going into battle unarmed. I retorted with a quip from Clausewitz, about a rearguard effecting its purpose more by being than by doing: but he was past laughter, and perhaps with justice, for the little flinty bank behind which we sheltered was crackling with fire. The Turks, knowing we were there, had turned twenty machine-guns upon it. It was four feet high and fifty feet long, of bare flinty ribs, off which the bullets slapped deafeningly: while the air above so hummed or whistled with ricochets and chips that it felt like death to look over. Clearly we must leave very soon, and as I had no horse I went off first, with Metaab's promise that he would wait where he was if he dared, for another ten minutes.

The run warmed me. I counted my paces, to help in ranging the Turks when they ousted us; since there was only that one position for them, and it was poorly protected against the south. In losing this

Motalga ridge we would probably win the battle. The horsemen held on for almost their ten minutes, and then galloped off without hurt. Metaab lent me his stirrup to hurry me along, till we found ourselves breathless among the Ageyl. It was just noon, and we had leisure and quiet in which to think.

Our new ridge was about forty feet up, and a nice shape for defence. We had eighty men on it, and more were constantly arriving. My guards were in place with their gun; Lutfi, an engine-destroyer, rushed up hotly with his two, and after him came another hundred Ageyl. The thing was becoming a picnic, and by saying 'excellent' and looking overjoyed, we puzzled the men, and made them consider the position dispassionately. The automatics were put on the skyline, with orders to fire occasional shots, short, to disturb the Turks a little, but not too much, after the expedient of Massena in delaying enemy deployment. Otherwise a lull fell; I lay down in a sheltered place which caught a little sun, and no wind, and slept a blessed hour, while the Turks occupied the old ridge, extending over it like a school of geese, and about as wisely. Our men left them alone, being contented with a free exhibition of themselves.

In the middle of the afternoon Zeid arrived, with Mastur, Rasim and Abdulla. They brought our main body, comprising twenty mounted infantry on mules, thirty Motalga horsemen, two hundred villagers, five automatic rifles, four machine-guns and the Egyptian Army mountain gun which had fought about Medina, Petra and Jurf. This was magnificent, and I woke up to welcome them.

The Turks saw us crowding, and opened with shrapnel and machine-gun fire: but they had not the range and fumbled it. We reminded one another that movement was the law of strategy, and started moving. Rasim became a cavalry officer, and mounted with all our eighty riders of animals to make a circuit about the eastern ridge and envelop the enemy's left wing, since the books advised attack not upon a line, but upon a point, and by going far enough along any finite wing it would be found eventually reduced to a point of one single man. Rasim liked this, my conception of his target.

He promised, grinningly, to bring us that last man: but Hamd el Arar took the occasion more fittingly. Before riding off he devoted himself to the death for the Arab cause, drew his sword ceremoniously, and made to it, by name, a heroic speech. Rasim took five automatic guns with him; which was good.

We in the centre paraded about, so that their departure might be unseen of the enemy, who were bringing up an apparently endless procession of machine-guns and dressing them by the left at intervals along the ridge as though in a museum. It was lunatic tactics. The ridge was flint, without cover for a lizard. We had seen how, when a bullet struck the ground, it and the ground spattered up in a shower of deadly chips. Also we knew the range and elevated our Vickers guns carefully, blessing their long, old-fashioned sights; our mountain gun was propped into place ready to let go a sudden burst of shrapnel over the enemy when Rasim was at grips.

As we waited, a reinforcement was announced of one hundred men from Aima. They had fallen out with Zeid over war-wages the day previous, but had grandly decided to sink old scores in the crisis. Their arrival convinced us to abandon Marshal Foch and to attack from, at any rate, three sides at once. So we sent the Aima men, with three automatic guns, to outflank the right, or western wing. Then we opened against the Turks from our central position, and bothered their exposed lines with hits and ricochets.

The enemy felt the day no longer favourable. It was passing, and sunset often gave victory to defenders yet in place. Old General Hamid Fakhri collected his Staff and Headquarters, and told each man to take a rifle. 'I have been forty years a soldier, but never saw I rebels fight like these. Enter the ranks' . . . but he was too late. Rasim pushed forward an attack of his five automatic guns, each with its two-man crew. They went in rapidly, unseen till they were in position, and crumpled the Turkish left.

The Aima men, who knew every blade of grass on these, their own village pastures, crept, unharmed, within three hundred yards of the Turkish machine-guns. The enemy, held by our frontal threat, first knew of the Aima men when they, by a sudden burst of fire, wiped out the gun-teams and flung the right wing into disorder. We saw it, and cried advance to the camel men and levies about us.

Mohamed el Ghasib, comptroller of Zeid's household, led them on his camel, in shining wind-billowed robes, with the crimson banner of the Ageyl over his head. All who had remained in the centre with us, our servants, gunners and machine-gunners, rushed after him in a wide, vivid line.

The day had been too long for me, and I was now only shaking with desire to see the end: but Zeid beside me clapped his hands with joy at the beautiful order of our plan unrolling in the frosty redness of the setting sun. On the one hand Rasim's cavalry were sweeping a broken left wing into the pit beyond the ridge: on the other the men of Aima were bloodily cutting down fugitives. The enemy centre was pouring back in disorder through the gap, with our men after them on foot, on horse, on camel. The Armenians, crouching behind us all day anxiously, now drew their knives and howled to one another in Turkish as they leaped forward.

I thought of the depths between here and Kerak, the ravine of Hesa, with its broken, precipitous paths, the undergrowth, the narrows and defiles of the way. It was going to be a massacre and I should have been crying-sorry for the enemy; but after the angers and exertions of the battle my mind was too tired to care to go down into that awful place and spend the night saving them. By my decision to fight, I had killed twenty or thirty of our six hundred men, and the wounded would be perhaps three times as many. It was one-sixth of our force gone on a verbal triumph, for the destruction of this thousand poor Turks would not affect the issue of the war.

In the end we had taken their two mountain howitzers (Skoda guns, very useful to us), twenty-seven machine-guns, two hundred horses and mules, two hundred and fifty prisoners. Men said only fifty got back, exhausted fugitives, to the railway. The Arabs on their track rose against them and shot them ignobly as they ran. Our own men gave up the pursuit quickly, for they were tired and sore and hungry, and it was pitifully cold. A battle might be thrilling at the moment for generals, but usually their imagination played too vividly beforehand, and made the reality seem sham; so quiet and unimportant that they ranged about looking for its fancied core. This evening there was no glory left, but the terror of the broken flesh, which had been our own men, carried past us to their homes.

As we turned back it began to snow; and only very late, and by a last effort did we get our hurt men in. The Turkish wounded lay out, and were dead next day. It was indefensible, as was the whole theory of war: but no special reproach lay on us for it. We risked our lives in the blizzard (the chill of victory bowing us down) to save our own fellows; and if our rule was not to lose Arabs to kill even many Turks, still less might we lose them to save Turks.

Next day and the next it snowed yet harder. We were weather-bound, and as the days passed in monotony we lost the hope of doing. We should have pushed past Kerak on the heels of victory, frighting the Turks to Amman with our rumour: as it was, nothing came of all the loss and effort, except a report which I sent over to the British headquarters in Palestine for the Staff's consumption. It was meanly written for effect, full of quaint similes and mock simplicities; and made them think me a modest amateur, doing his best after the great models; not a clown, leering after them where they with Foch, band-master, at their head went drumming down the old road of effusion of blood into the house of Clausewitz. Like the battle, it was nearly-proof parody of regulation use. Headquarters loved it, and innocently, to crown the jest, offered me a decoration on the strength of it. We should have more bright breasts in the Army if each man was able without witnesses, to write out his own despatch.

CHAPTER LXXXVII

HESA'S sole profit lay, then, in its lesson to myself. Never again were we combative, whether in jest, or betting on a certainty. Indeed, only three days later, our honour was partially redeemed by a good and serious thing we arranged through Abdulla el Feir, who was camped beneath us in the paradise of the Dead Sea's southern shore, a plain gushing with brooks of sweet water, and rich in vegetation. We sent him news of victory, with a project to raid the lake-port of Kerak and destroy the Turks' flotilla.

He chose out some seventy horsemen, of the Beersheba Beduin. They rode in the night along the shelf of track between the hills of Moab and the Sea's brim as far as the Turkish post; and in the first greyness, when their eyes could reach far enough for a gallop, they burst out of their undergrowth upon motor launch and sailing lighters, harboured in the northern bight, with the unsuspecting crews sleeping on the beach or in the reed-huts near by.

They were from the Turkish Navy, not prepared for land fighting, still less for receiving cavalry: they were awakened only by the drumming of our horses' hooves in the headlong charge: and the engagement ended at the moment. The huts were burned, the stores looted, the shipping taken out to deep sea and scuttled. Then, without a casualty, and with their sixty prisoners, our men rode back praising themselves. January the twenty-eighth; and we had attained our second objective — the stopping of Dead Sea traffic — a fortnight sooner than we had promised Allenby.

The third objective had been the Jordan mouth by Jericho, before the end of March; and it would have been a fair prospect, but for the paralysis which weather and distaste for pain had brought upon us since the red day of Hesa. Conditions in Tafileh were mended. Feisal had sent us ammunition and food. Prices fell, as men grew to trust our strength. The tribes about Kerak, in daily touch with Zeid, purposed to join him in arms so soon as he moved forward.

Just this, however, we could not do. The winter's potency drove

493

leaders and men into the village and huddled them in a lack-lustre idleness against which counsels of movement availed little. Indeed, Reason, also, was within doors. Twice I ventured up to taste the snow-laden plateau, upon whose even face the Turkish dead, poor brown pats of stiffened clothes, were littered: but life there was not tolerable. In the day it thawed a little and in the night it froze. The wind cut open the skin: fingers lost power, and sense of feel: cheeks shivered like dead leaves till they could shiver no more, and then bound up their muscles in a witless ache.

To launch out across the snow on camels, beasts singularly inept on slippery ground, would be to put ourselves in the power of however few horsemen wished to oppose us; and, as the days dragged on, even this last possibility was withdrawn. Barley ran short in Tafileh, and our camels, already cut off by the weather from natural grazing, were now also cut off from artificial food. We had to drive them down into the happier Ghor, a day's journey from our vital garrison.

Though so far by the devious road, yet in direct distance the Ghor lay little more than six miles away, and in full sight, five thousand feet below. Salt was rubbed into our miseries by the spectacle of that near winter garden beneath us by the lake-side. We were penned in ver-minous houses of cold stone; lacking fuel, lacking food; storm-bound in streets like sewers, amid blizzards of sleet and an icy wind: while there in the valley was sunshine upon spring grass, deep with flowers, upon flocks in milk and air so warm that men went uncloaked.

My private party were more fortunate than most, as the Zaagi had found us an empty unfinished house, of two sound rooms and a court. My money provided fuel, and even grain for our camels, which we kept sheltered in a corner of the yard, where Abdulla, the animal lover, could curry them and teach every one by name to take a gift of bread, like a kiss, from his mouth, gently, with her loose lips, when he called her. Still, they were unhappy days, since to have a fire was to be stifled with green smoke, and in the window-spaces were only make-shift shutters of our own joinery. The mud roof dripped water all the day long, and the fleas on the stone floor sang together nightly, for praise of the new meats given them. We were twenty-eight in the two tiny rooms, which reeked with the sour smell of our crowd.

In my saddle-bags was a *Morte d'Arthur*. It relieved my disgust. The men had only physical resources; and in the confined misery their tempers roughened. Their oddnesses, which ordinary time packed with a saving film of distance, now jostled me angrily; while a grazed wound in my hip had frozen, and irritated me with painful throbbing. Day by day, the tension among us grew, as our state became more sordid, more animal.

At last Awad, the wild Sherari, quarrelled with little Mahmas; and in a moment their daggers clashed. The rest nipped the tragedy, so that there was only a slight wounding: but it broke the greatest law of the bodyguard, and as both example and guilt were blatant, the others went packing into the far room while their chiefs forthwith executed sentence. However, the Zaagi's shrill whip-strokes were too cruel for my taught imagination, and I stopped him before he was well warmed. Awad, who had lain through his punishment without complaint, at this release levered himself slowly to his knees and with bent legs and swaying head staggered away to his sleeping-place.

It was then the turn of the waiting Mahmas, a tight-lipped youth with pointed chin and pointed forehead, whose beady eyes dropped at the inner corners with an indescribable air of impatience. He was not properly of my guard, but a camel-driver; for his capacity fell far below his sense of it, and a constantly-hurt pride made him sudden and fatal in companionship. If worsted in argument, or laughed at, he would lean forward with his always handy little dagger and rip up his friend. Now he shrank into a corner showing his teeth, vowing, across his tears, to be through those who hurt him. Arabs did not dissect endurance, their crown of manhood, into material and moral, making allowance for nerves. So Mahmas' crying was called fear, and when loosed, he crept out disgraced into the night to hide.

I was sorry for Awad: his hardness put me to shame. Especially I was ashamed when, next dawn, I heard a limping step in the yard, and saw him attempting to do his proper duty by the camels. I called him in to give him an embroidered head-cloth as reward for faithful service. He came pitiably sullen, with a shrinking, mobile readiness for more punishment: my changed manner broke him down. By afternoon he was singing and shouting, happier than ever, as he had found a fool in Tafileh to pay him four pounds for my silken gift.

Such nervous sharpening ourselves on each other's faults was so revolting that I decided to scatter the party, and to go off myself in search of the extra money we should need when fine weather came. Zeid had spent the first part of the sum set aside for Tafileh and the Dead Sea; partly on wages, partly on supplies and in rewards to the victors of Seil Hesa. Wherever we next put our front line, we should have to enlist and pay fresh forces, for only local men knew the qualities of their ground instinctively; and they fought best, defending their homes and crops against the enemy.

Joyce might have arranged to send me money: but not easily in this season. It was surer to go down myself: and more virtuous than continued fœtor and promiscuity in Tafileh. So five of us started off on a day which promised to be a little more open than usual. We made good time to Reshidiya and as we climbed the saddle beyond, found ourselves momentarily above the clouds in a faint sunshine.

In the afternoon the weather drew down again and the wind hardened from the north and east, and made us sorry to be out on the bare plain. When we had forded the running river of Shobek, rain began to fall, first in wild gusts, but then more steadily, reeding down over our left shoulders and seeming to cloak us from the main bleakness of wind. Where the rain-streaks hit the ground they furred out whitely like a spray. We pushed on without halting and till long after sunset urged our trembling camels, with many slips, and falls across the greasy valleys. We made nearly two miles an hour, despite our difficulties; and progress was become so exciting and unexpected that its mere exercise kept us warm.

It had been my intention to ride all night: but, near Odroh, mist came down about us in a low ring curtain, over which the clouds, like tatters of a veil, spun and danced high up across the calmness of the sky. The perspective seemed to change, so that far hills looked small, and near hillocks great. We bore too much to the right.

This open country, though appearing hard, broke rottenly beneath their weight and let our camels in, four or five inches deep, at every stride. The poor beasts had been chilled all day, and had bumped down so often that they were stiff with bruises. Consequently, they made unwilling work of the new difficulties. They hurried for a few steps, stopped abruptly, looked round, or tried to dart off sideways.

We prevented their wishes, and drove them forward till our blind way met rocky valleys, with a broken skyline; dark to right and left, and in front apparent hills where no hills should be. It froze again, and the slabby stones of the valley became iced. To push farther, on the wrong road, through such a night was folly. We found a larger out-crop of rock. Behind it, where there should have been shelter, we couched our camels in a compact group, tails to wind: facing it, they might die of cold. We snuggled down beside them hoping for warmth and sleep.

The warmth I, at least, never got, and hardly the sleep. I dozed once only to wake with a start when slow fingers seemed to stroke my face. I stared out into a night livid with large, soft snowflakes. They lasted a minute or two; but then followed rain, and after it more frost, while I squatted in a tight ball, aching every way but too miserable to move, till dawn. It was a hesitant dawn, but enough: I rolled over in the mud to see my men, knotted in their cloaks, cowering abandoned against the beasts' flanks. On each man's face weighed the most dolorous expression of resigned despair.

They were four southerners, whom fear of the winter had turned ill at Tafileh, and who were going to rest in Guweira till it was warm again: but here in the mist they had made up their minds, like he-camels, that death was upon them: and, though they were too proud to grumble at it, they were not above showing me silently that this which they made for my sake was a sacrifice. They did not speak or move in reply to me. Under a flung camel it was best to light a slow fire, to raise it: but I took the smallest of these dummies by the head-curls, and proved to him that he was still capable of feeling. The others got to their feet, and we kicked up the stiff camels. Our only loss was a water-skin, frozen to the ground.

With daylight the horizon had grown very close, and we saw that our proper road was a quarter of a mile to our left. Along it we struggled afoot. The camels were too done to carry our weight (all but my own died later of this march) and it was so muddy in the clay bottoms that we ourselves slid and fell like them. However, the Deraa trick helped, of spreading wide the toes and hooking them downward into the mud at each stride: and by this means, in a group, clutching and holding one another, we maintained progress.

The air seemed cold enough to freeze anything, but did not: the wind, which had changed during the night, swept into us from the west in hindering blizzards. Our cloaks bellied out and dragged like sails, against us. At last we skinned them off, and went easier, our bare shirts wrapped tightly about us to restrain their slapping tails. The whirling direction of the squalls was shown to our eyes by the white mist they carried across hill and dale. Our hands were numbed into insensibility, so that we knew the cuts on them only by red stains in their plastered mud: but our bodies were not so chill, and for hours quivered under the hailstones of each storm. We twisted ourselves to get the sharpness on an unhurt side, and held our shirts free from the skin, to shield us momentarily.

By late afternoon we had covered the ten miles to Aba el Lissan. Maulud's men were gone to ground, and no one hailed us; which was well, for we were filthy and miserable; stringy like shaven cats. Afterwards the going was easier, the last two miles to the head of Shtar being frozen like iron. We remounted our camels, whose breath escaped whitely through their protesting nostrils, and raced up to the first wonderful glimpse of the Guweira plain, warm, red and comfortable, as seen through the cloud-gaps. The clouds had ceiled the hollow strangely, cutting the mid-sky in a flat layer of curds at the level of the hill-top on which we stood: we gazed on them contentedly for minutes. Every little while a wisp of their fleecy sea-foam stuff would be torn away and thrown at us. We on the wall of bluffs would feel it slash across our faces; and, turning, would see a white hem draw over the rough crest, tear to shreds and vanish in a powdering of hoar grains or a trickle of water across the peat soil.

After having wondered at the sky we slid and ran gaily down the pass to dry sand in a calm mild air. Yet the pleasure was not vivid, as we had hoped. The pain of the blood fraying its passage once more about our frozen limbs and faces was much faster than the pain of its driving out: and we grew sensible that our feet had been torn and bruised nearly to pulp among the stones. We had not felt them tender while in the icy mud; but this warm, salty sand scoured the cuts. In desperation we climbed up our sad camels, and beat them woodenly towards Guweira. However, the change had made them happier, and they brought us home there sedately, but with success.

CHAPTER LXXXVIII

LAZY nights, three of them, in the armoured car tents at Guweira were pleasant, with Alan Dawnay, Joyce, and others talking, and Tafileh to boast about. Yet these friends were a little grieved at my luck, for their great expedition with Feisal a fortnight ago to overwhelm Mudowwara had turned out unprofitably. Partly it was the ancient problem of the co-operation of regulars with irregulars; partly it was the fault of old Mohammed Ali el Beidawi, who, put over the Beni Atiyeh, had come with them to water, cried, 'Noon-halt!' and sat there for two months, pandering to that hedonistic streak among the Arabs which made them helpless slaves of carnal indulgence. In Arabia, where superfluities lacked, the temptation of necessary food lay always on men. Each morsel which passed their lips might, if they were not watchful, become a pleasure. Luxuries might be as plain as running water or a shady tree, whose rareness and misuse often turned them into lusts. Their story reminded me of Apollonius' 'Come off it, you men of Tarsus, sitting on your river like geese, drunken with its white water!'

Then thirty thousand pounds in gold came up from Akaba for me and my cream camel, Wodheiha, the best of my remaining stud. She was Ateiba-bred and had won many races for her old owner: also, she was in splendid condition, fat but not too fat, her pads hardened by much practice over the northern flints, and her coat thick and matted. She was not tall, and looked heavy, but was docile and smooth to ride, turning left or right if the saddle-horn were tapped on the required side. So I rode her without a stick, comfortably reading a book when the march permitted.

As my proper men were at Tafileh or Azrak, or out on mission, I asked Feisal for temporary followers. He lent me his two Ateiba horsemen, Serj and Rameid; and, to help carry my gold, added to the party Sheikh Motlog, whose worth we had discovered when our armoured cars explored the plains below Mudowwara for Tebuk.

Motlog had gone as sponsor, pointing out the country from a perch

high on the piled baggage of a box-Ford. They were dashing in and
out of sand-hills at speed, the Fords swaying like launches in a swell.
At one bad bend they skidded half-round on two wheels crazily.
Motlog was tossed out on his head. Marshall stopped the car and ran
back contrite, with ready excuses for the driving; but the Sheikh,
ruefully rubbing his head, said gently 'Don't be angry with me. I
have not learnt to ride these things'.

The gold was in thousand-pound bags. I gave two bags each to
fourteen of Motlog's twenty men, and took the last two myself. A bag
weighed twenty-two pounds, and in the awful road-conditions two
were weight enough for a camel, and swung fairly on either side in the
saddle-bags. We started at noon, hoping to make a good first stage
before getting into the trouble of the hills: but unfortunately it turned
wet after half an hour, and a steady rain soaked us through and through,
and made our camels' hair curl like a wet dog's.

Motlog at that precise stage saw a tent, Sherif Fahad's, in the corner
of a sandstone pike. Despite my urging, he voted to spend the night
there, and see what it looked like on the hills to-morrow. I knew this
would be a fatal course, wasting days in indecision: so I said farewell to
him and rode on with my two men, and with six Shobek-bound
Howeitat, who had joined our caravan.

The argument had delayed us, and consequently we only reached the
foot of the pass at dark. By the sad, soft rain we were made rather
sorry for our virtue; inclined to envy Motlog his hospitality with
Fahad, when suddenly a red spark to our left drew us across to find
Saleh ibn Shefia camped there in a tent and three caves, with a hundred
of his freed-men fighters from Yenbo. Saleh, the son of poor old
Mohammed, our jester, was the proper lad who had carried Wejh by
assault on Vickery's field-day.

'*Cheyf ent?*' ('How are you?') said I earnestly twice or thrice. His
eyes sparkled at the Juheina manner. He came near me and with bowed
head and intense voice poured out a string of twenty '*Cheyf ents*' before
drawing breath. I disliked being outdone, so replied with a dozen as
solemnly. He took me up with another of his long bursts, many more
than twenty this time. So I gave up trying to learn how many are the
possible repetitions of salutations in Wadi Yenbo.

He welcomed me, in spite of my drenched condition, to his own carpet in his tent and gave me a new garment of his mother's sewing, while waiting for the hot stew of meat and rice. Then we lay down and slept a full night of great satisfaction, hearing the patter of rain on the double canvas of his Meccan tent.

In the morning we were off at dawn, munching a handful of Saleh's bread. As we set foot on the ascent, Serj looked up and said, 'The mountain wears his skull-cap'. There was a white dome of snow on every crest; and the Ateiba pushed quickly and curiously up the pass to feel this new wonder with their hands. The camels, too, were ignorant, and stretched their slow necks down to sniff its whiteness twice or thrice in tired inquiry; but then drew their heads away and looked forward without life-interest, once more.

Our inactivity lasted only another moment; for, as we put our heads over the last ridge, a wind from the north-east took us in the teeth, with a cold so swift and biting that we gasped for breath and turned hurriedly back into shelter. It seemed as if it would be fatal to face it; but that we knew was silly: so we pulled ourselves together and rode hard through its first extreme to the half-shelter of the valley. Serj and Rameid, terrified by these new pains in their lungs, thought they were strangling; and to spare them the mental struggle of passing a friendly camp, I led our little party aside behind Maulud's hill, so that we saw nothing of his weather-beaten force.

These men of Maulud's had been camped in this place, four thousand feet above the sea, for two months without relief. They had to live in shallow dug-outs on the hill-side. They had no fuel except the sparse, wet wormwood, over which they were just able to bake their necessary bread every other day. They had no clothes but khaki drill uniform of the British summer sort. They slept in their rain-sodden verminous pits on empty or half-empty flour sacks, six or eight of them together in a knotted bunch, that enough of the worn blankets might be pooled for warmth.

Rather more than half of them died or were injured by the cold and wet; yet the others maintained their watch, exchanging shots daily with the Turkish outposts, and protected only by the inclement weather from crushing counter-attack. We owed much to them, and more to Maulud, whose fortitude stiffened them in their duty.

The old scarred warrior's history in the Turkish army was a cata-
logue of affairs provoked by his sturdy sense of Arab honour and
nationality, a creed for which three or four times he had sacrificed his
prospects. It must have been a strong creed which enabled him to
endure cheerfully three winter months in front of Maan and to share
out enough spirit among five hundred ordinary men to keep them
stout-heartedly about him.

We, for our one day, had a fill of hardship. Just on the ridge about
Aba el Lissan the ground was crusted with frost, and only the smart of
the wind in our eyes hindered us: but then our troubles began. The
camels came to a standstill in the slush at the bottom of a twenty-foot
bank of slippery mud, and lowed at it helplessly, as if to say that they
could not carry us up that. We jumped off to help them, and slid back
ourselves just as badly. At last we took off our new, cherished boots,
donned to armour us against the winter; and hauled the camels up the
glacis barefoot, as on the journey down.

That was the end of our comfort, and we must have been off twenty
times before sunset. Some of the dismounts were involuntary, when
our camels side-slipped under us, and came down with the jingle of
coin ringing through the hollow rumble of their cask-like bellies.
While they were strong this falling made them as angry as she-camels
could be: afterwards they grew plaintive, and finally afraid. We also
grew short with one another, for the foul wind gave us no rest.
Nothing in Arabia could be more cutting than a north wind at Maan,
and to-day's was of the sharpest and strongest. It blew through our
clothes as if we had none, fixed our fingers in claws not able to hold
either halter or riding-stick, and cramped our legs so that we had no
grip of the saddle-pin. Consequently, when thrown from our falling
beasts we pitched off, to crash stiffly on the ground, still frozen-brittle
in the cross-legged attitude of riding.

However, there was no rain, and the wind felt like a drying one, so
we held on steadily to the north. By evening we had almost made the
rivulet of Basta. This meant that we were travelling more than a mile
an hour; and for fear lest on the morrow we and our camels would both
be too tired to do so well, I pushed on in the dark across the little stream.

It was swollen, and the beasts jibbed at it, so that we had to lead the way on foot, through three feet of chilly water.

Over the high ground, beyond, the wind buffeted us like an enemy: at about nine o'clock the others flung themselves crying down on the ground and refused to go further. I, too, was very near crying; sustained, indeed, only by my annoyance with their open lamentations; and therefore reluctantly glad at heart to yield to their example. We built up the nine camels in a phalanx, and lay between them in fair comfort, listening to the driving wrack clashing about us as loud as the surges by night round a ship at sea. The visible stars were brilliant, seeming to change groups and places waywardly between the clouds which scudded over our heads. We had each two army blankets, and a packet of cooked bread; so we were armed against evil and could sleep securely in the mud and cold.

CHAPTER LXXXIX

AT dawn we went forward refreshed: but the weather had turned soft, with a greyness through which loomed the sad wormwood-covered hills. Upon their slopes the limestone ribs of this very old earth stood wearily exposed. In their hollows our difficulties increased with the mud. The misty valleys were sluggish streams of melting snow: and at last new thick showers of wet flakes began to fall. We reached the desolate ruins of Odroh in a midday like twilight: a wind was blowing and dying intermittently, and slow-moving banks of cloud and drizzle closed us about.

I bore right, to avoid the Beduin between us and Shobek: but our Howeitat companions led us straight upon their camp. We had ridden six miles in seven hours, and they were exhausted. The two Ateiba were not only exhausted, but demoralized, and swore mutinously that nothing in the world should keep us from the tribal tents. We wrangled by the roadside under the soft drift.

For myself I felt quite fresh and happy, averse from the delay of needless tribal hospitality. Zeid's penniless state was excellent pretext for a trial of strength with the Edomite winter. Shobek was only ten miles further, and daylight had yet five hours to run. So I decided to go on alone. It would be quite safe, for in such weather neither Turk nor Arab was abroad, and the roads were mine. I took their four thousand pounds from Serj and Rameid, and cursed them into the valley for cowards: which really they were not. Rameid was catching his breath in great sobs, and Serj's nervous pain marked each lurch of his camel with a running moan. They raved with miserable rage when I dismissed them and turned away.

The truth was that I had the best camel. The excellent Wodheiha struggled gamely forward under the weight of the extra gold. In flat places I rode her: at ascents and descents we used to slide together side by side with comic accidents, which she seemed rather to enjoy.

By sunset the snow-fall ceased; we were coming down to the river of Shobek, and could see a brown track straggling over the opposite hill towards the village. I tried a short cut, but the frozen crust of the mud-banks deceived me, and I crashed through the cat-ice (which was sharp, like knives) and bogged myself so deeply that I feared I was going to pass the night there, half in and half out of the sludge: or wholly in, which would be a tidier death.

Wodheiha, sensible beast, had refused to enter the morass: but she stood at a loss on the hard margin, and looked soberly at my mud-larking. However, I managed, with the still-held head-stall, to persuade her a little nearer. Then I flung my body suddenly backward against the squelching quag, and, grabbing wildly behind my head, laid hold of her fetlock. She was frightened, and started back: and her purchase dragged me clear. We crawled farther down the bed to a safe place, and there crossed: after I had hesitatingly sat in the stream and washed off the weight of stinking clay.

Shiveringly I mounted again. We went over the ridge and down to the base of the shapely cone, whose mural crown was the ring-wall of the old castle of Monreale, very noble against the night sky. The chalk was hard, and it was freezing; snow-drifts lay a foot deep each side of the spiral path which wound up the hill. The white ice crackled desolately under my naked feet as we neared the gate, where, to make a stage entry, I climbed up by Wodheiha's patient shoulder into the saddle. Then I repented, since only by throwing myself sideways along her neck did I avoid the voussoirs of the arch as she crashed underneath in half-terror of this strange place.

I knew that Sherif Abd el Main should be still at Shobek, so rode boldly up the silent street in the reeded starlight, which played with the white icicles and their underlying shadow among the walls and snowy roofs and ground. The camel stumbled doubtfully over steps hidden beneath a thick covering of snow: but I had no care of that, having reached my night's goal, and having so powdery a blanket to fall on. At the crossways I called out the salutation of a fair night: and after a minute, a husky voice protested to God through the thick sacking which stuffed a loophole of the mean house on my right. I asked for Abd el Mayein, and was told 'in the Government house' which lay at the further end of the old castle's enceinte.

Arrived there I called again. A door was flung open, and a cloud of smoky light streamed recklessly across, whirling with motes, through which black faces peered to know who I was. I hailed them friendly, by name, saying that I was come to eat a sheep with the master: upon which these slaves ran out, noisy with astonishment, and relieved me of Wodheiha, whom they led into the reeking stable where themselves lived. One lit me with a flaming spar up the stone outside stairs to the house door, and between more servants, down a winding passage dripping with water from the broken roof, into a tiny room. There lay Abd el Muein upon a carpet, face down, breathing the least smoky level of air.

My legs were shaky, so I dropped beside him, and gladly copied his position to avoid the choking fumes of a brass brazier of flaming wood which crackled in a recessed shot-window of the mighty outer wall. He searched out for me a waist-cloth, while I stripped off my things and hung them to steam before the fire, which became less smarting to the eyes and throat as it burned down into red coals. Meanwhile Abd el Mayin clapped his hands for supper to be hastened and served 'Fauzan' (tea in Harith slang, so named from his cousin, governor of their village) hot and spiced and often, till the mutton, boiled with raisins in butter, was carried in.

He explained, with his blessings on the dish, that next day they would starve or rob, since he had here two hundred men, and no food or money, and his messengers to Feisal were held up in the snow. Whereat I, too, clapped hands, commanding my saddle-bags, and presented him with five hundred pounds on account, till his subsidy came. This was good payment for the food, and we were very merry over my oddness of riding alone, in winter, with a hundredweight and more of gold for baggage. I repeated that Zeid, like himself, was straitened; and told of Serj and Rameid with the Arabs. The Sherif's eyes darkened and he made passes in the air with his riding-stick. I explained, in extenuation of their failure, that the cold did not trouble me, since the English climate was of this sort most of the year. 'God forbid it,' said Abd el Muyein.

After an hour he excused himself, because he had just married a Shobek wife. We talked of their marriage, whose end was the bearing of children: I withstood it, quoting old Dionysus of Tarsus.

At his sixty years without marriage they were shocked, holding procreation and evacuation alike as inevitable movements of the body; they repeated their half of the commandment to honour parents. I asked how they could look with pleasure on children, embodied proofs of their consummated lust? And invited them to picture the minds of the children, seeing crawl wormlike out of the mother that bloody, blinded thing which was themselves! It sounded to him a most excellent joke, and after it we rolled up in the rugs and slept warmly. The fleas were serried, but my nakedness, the Arab defence against a verminous bed, lessened their plague: and the bruises did not prevail because I was too tired.

In the morning I rose with a splitting headache, and said I must go on. Two men were found to ride with me, though all said we should not reach Tafileh that night. However, I thought it could not be worse than yesterday; so we skated timorously down the rapid path to the plain across which still stretched the Roman road with its groups of fallen milestones, inscribed by famous emperors.

From this plain the two faint-hearts with me slipped back to their fellows on the castle-hill. I proceeded, alternately on and off my camel, like the day before, though now the way was all too slippery, except on the ancient paving, the last footprint of Imperial Rome which had once, so much more preciously, played the Turk to the desert dwellers. On it I could ride: but I had to walk and wade the dips where the floods of fourteen centuries had washed the road's foundations out. Rain came on, and soaked me, and then it blew fine and freezing till I crackled in armour of white silk, like a theatre knight: or like a bridal cake, hard iced.

The camel and I were over the plain in three hours; wonderful going: but our troubles were not ended. The snow was indeed as my guides had said, and completely hid the path, which wound uphill between walls and ditches, and confused piles of stone. It cost me an infinity of pain to turn the first two corners. Wodheiha, tired of wading to her bony knees in useless white stuff, began perceptibly to flag. However, she got up one more steep bit, only to miss the edge of the path in a banked place. We fell together some eighteen feet down the hill-side into a yard-deep drift of frozen snow. After the fall she rose to her feet whimpering and stood still, in a tremble.

When he-camels so baulked, they would die on their spot, after days; and I feared that now I had found the limit of effort in she-camels. I plunged to my neck in front of her, and tried to tow her out, vainly. Then I spent a long time hitting her behind. I mounted, and she sat down. I jumped off, heaved her up, and wondered if, perhaps, it was that the drift was too thick. So I carved her a beautiful little road, a foot wide, three deep, and eighteen paces long, using my bare feet and hands as tools. The snow was so frozen on the surface that it took all my weight, first to break it down, and then to scoop it out. The crust was sharp, and cut my wrists and ankles till they bled freely, and the roadside became lined with pink crystals, looking like pale, very pale, water-melon flesh.

Afterwards I went back to Wodheiha, patiently standing there, and climbed into the saddle. She started easily. We went running at it, and such was her speed that the rush carried her right over the shallow stuff, back to the proper road. Up this we went cautiously, with me afoot, sounding the path in front with my stick, or digging new passes when the drifts were deep. In three hours we were on the summit, and found it wind-swept on the western side. So we left the track, and scrambled unsteadily along the very broken crest, looking down across the chess-board houses of Dana village, into sunny Arabah, fresh and green thousands of feet below.

When the ridge served no more we did further heavy work, and at last Wodheiha baulked again. It was getting serious, for the evening was near; suddenly I realized the loneliness, and that if the night found us yet beyond help on this hill-top, Wodheiha would die, and she was a very noble beast. There was also the solid weight of gold, and I felt not sure how far, even in Arabia, I could safely put six thousand sovereigns by the roadside with a signet as mark of ownership, and leave them for a night. So I took her back a hundred yards along our beaten track, mounted, and charged her at the bank. She responded. We burst through and over the northern lip which looked down on the Senussi village of Rasheidiya.

This face of the hill, sheltered from the wind and open to the sun all afternoon, had thawed. Underneath the superficial snow lay wet and muddy ground; and when Wodheiha ran upon this at speed her feet went from under her and she sprawled, with her four feet locked. So on her tail, with me yet in the saddle, we went sliding round and down a hundred feet. Perhaps it hurt the tail (there were stones under the snow) for on the level she sprang up unsteadily, grunting, and lashed it about like a scorpion's. Then she began to run at ten miles an hour down the greasy path towards Rasheidiya, sliding and plunging wildly: with me, in terror of a fall and broken bones, clinging to the horns of the saddle.

A crowd of Arabs, Zeid's men, weather-bound here on their way to Feysal, ran out when they heard her trumpeting approach, and shouted with joy at so distinguished an entry to the village. I asked them the news; they told me all was well. Then I remounted, for the last eight miles into Tafileh, where I gave Zeid his letters and some money, and went gladly to bed . . . flea-proof for another night.

CHAPTER XC

ORNING found me nearly snow-blind, but glad and vigorous. I cast about for something to fill the inactive days before the other gold arrived. The final judgement was to make a personal examination of the approaches to Kerak, and the ground over which we would later advance to Jordan. I asked Zeid to take from Motlog the coming twenty-four thousand pounds, and spend what was necessary for current expenses until my return.

Zeid told me there was another Englishman in Tafileh. The news astonished me, and I went off to meet Lieutenant Kirkbride, a young Arabic-speaking staff officer sent by Deedes to report intelligence possibilities on the Arab Front. It was the beginning of a connection profitable to us, and creditable to Kirkbride; a taciturn, enduring fellow, only a boy in years, but ruthless in action, who messed for eight months with the Arab officers, their silent companion.

The cold had passed off and movement, even on the heights, was practicable. We crossed Wadi Hesa, and rode as far as the edge of the Jordan Valley, whose depths were noisy with Allenby's advance. They said the Turks yet held Jericho. Thence we turned back to Tafileh, after a reconnaissance very assuring for our future. Each step of our road to join the British was possible: most of them easy. The weather was so fine that we might reasonably begin at once: and could hope to finish in a month.

Zeid heard me coldly. I saw Motlog next him, and greeted him sarcastically, asking what was his tally of the gold: then I began to repeat my programme of what we might fairly do. Zeid stopped me: 'But that will need a lot of money'. I said, 'Not at all': our funds in hand would cover it, and more. Zeid replied that he had nothing; and when I gaped at him, muttered rather shamefacedly that he had spent all I brought. I thought he was joking: but he went on to say that so much had been due to Dhiab, sheikh of Tafileh; so much to the villagers; so much to the Jazi Howeitat; so much to the Beni Sakhr.

Only for a defensive was such expenditure conceivable. The peoples named were elements centring in Tafileh, men whose blood feuds made them impossible for use north of Wadi Hesa. Admittedly, the Sherifs, as they advanced, enrolled all the men of every district at a monthly wage: but it was perfectly understood that the wage was fictitious, to be paid only if they had been called on for active service. Feysul had more than forty thousand on his Akaba books: while his whole subsidy from England would not pay seventeen thousand. The wages of the rest were nominally due and often asked for: but not a lawful liability. However, Zeid said that he had paid them.

I was aghast; for this meant the complete ruin of my plans and hopes, the collapse of our effort to keep faith with Allenby. Zeid stuck to his word that the money was all gone. Afterwards I went off to learn the truth from Nasir, who was in bed with fever. He despondently said that everything was wrong — Zeid too young and shy to counter his dishonest, cowardly counsellors.

All night I thought over what could be done, but found a blank; and when morning came could only send word to Zeid that, if he would not return the money, I must go away. He sent me back his supposed account of the spent money. While we were packing, Joyce and Marshall arrived. They had ridden from Guweira to give me a pleasant surprise. I told them why it had happened that I was going back to Allenby to put my further employment in his hands. Joyce made a vain appeal to Zeid, and promised to explain to Feisal.

He would close down my affairs and disperse my bodyguard. So I was able, with only four men, to set off, late that very afternoon, for Beersheba, the quickest way to British Headquarters. The coming of spring made the first part of the ride along the edge of the Araba scarp surpassingly beautiful, and my farewell mood showed me its beauties, keenly. The ravines were clothed below with trees: but near to us, by the top, their precipitous flanks, as seen from above, were a patchwork of close lawns, which tipped toward downright faces of bare rock of many colours. Some of the colours were mineral, in the rock itself: but others were accidental, due to water from the melting snow falling over the cliff-edge, either in drifts of dusty spray, or diamond-strings down hanging tresses of green fern.

At Buseira, the little village on a hull of rock over the abyss, they insisted that we halt to eat. I was willing, because if we fed our camels here with a little barley we might ride all night and reach Beersheba on the morrow: but to avoid delay I refused to enter their houses, and instead ate in the little cemetery, off a tomb, into whose joints were cemented plaits of hair, the sacrificed head-ornaments of mourners. Afterwards we went down the zigzags of the great pass into the hot bottom of Wadi Dhahal, over which the cliffs and the hills so drew together that hardly did the stars shine into its pitchy blackness. We halted a moment while our camels stilled the nervous trembling of their forelegs after the strain of the terrible descent. Then we plashed, fetlock deep, down the swift stream, under a long arch of rustling bamboos, which met so nearly over our heads that their fans brushed our faces. The strange echoes of the vaulted passage frightened our camels into a trot.

Soon we were out of it, and out of the horns of the valley, scouring across the open Araba. We reached the central bed, and found that we were off the track — not wonderful, for we were steering only on my three-year-old memories of Newcombe's map. A half-hour was wasted in finding a ramp for the camels, up the earth cliff.

At last we found one, and threaded the windings of the marly labyrinth beyond — a strange place, sterile with salt, like a rough sea suddenly stilled, with all its tossing waves transformed into hard, fibrous earth, very grey under to-night's half-moon. Afterwards we aimed westward till the tall branched tree of Husb outlined itself against the sky, and we heard the murmurings of the great spring which flowed out from the roots. Our camels drank a little. They had come down five thousand feet from the Tafileh hills, and had to climb up three thousand now to Palestine.

In the little foot-hills before Wadi Murra, suddenly, we saw a fire of large logs, freshly piled, and still at white heat. No one was visible, proof that the kindlers were a war party: yet it was not kindled in nomad fashion. The liveliness showed that they were still near it: the size that they were many: so prudence made us hurry on. Actually it was the camp-fire of a British section of Ford cars, under the two famous Macs, looking for a car-road from Sinai to Akaba. They were hidden in the shadows, covering us with their Lewis guns.

We climbed the pass as day broke. There was a little rain, balmy after the extreme of Tafileh. Rags of thinnest cloud stood unreasonably motionless in the hills, as we rode over the comfortable plain, to Beersheba, about noon: a good performance, down and up hills for nearly eighty miles.

They told us Jericho was just taken. I went through to Allenby's headquarters. Hogarth was there on the platform. To him I confessed that I had made a mess of things: and had come to beg Allenby to find me some smaller part elsewhere. I had put all myself into the Arab business, and had come to wreck because of my sick judgement; the occasion being Zeid, own brother to Feisal, and a little man I really liked. I now had no tricks left worth a meal in the Arab market-place, and wanted the security of custom: to be conveyed; to pillow myself on duty and obedience: irresponsibly.

I complained that since landing in Arabia I had had options and requests, never an order: that I was tired to death of free-will, and of many things beside free-will. For a year and a half I had been in motion, riding a thousand miles each month upon camels: with added nervous hours in crazy aeroplanes, or rushing across country in powerful cars. In my last five actions I had been hit, and my body so dreaded further pain that now I had to force myself under fire. Generally I had been hungry: lately always cold: and frost and dirt had poisoned my hurts into a festering mass of sores.

However, these worries would have taken their due petty place, in my despite of the body, and of my soiled body in particular, but for the rankling fraudulence which had to be my mind's habit: that pretence to lead the national uprising of another race, the daily posturing in alien dress, preaching in alien speech: with behind it a sense that the 'promises' on which the Arabs worked were worth what their armed strength would be when the moment of fulfilment came. We had deluded ourselves that perhaps peace might find the Arabs able, unhelped and untaught, to defend themselves with paper tools. Meanwhile we glozed our fraud by conducting their necessary war purely and cheaply. But now this gloss had gone from me. Chargeable against my conceit were the causeless, ineffectual deaths of Hesa. My will had gone and I feared to be alone, lest the winds of circumstance, or power, or lust, blow my empty soul away.

CHAPTER XCI

DIPLOMATICALLY, Hogarth replied not a word, but took me to breakfast with Clayton. There I gathered that Smuts had come from the War Cabinet to Palestine, with news which had changed our relative situation. For days they had been trying to get me to the Conferences, and finally had sent out aeroplanes to find Tafileh; but the pilots had dropped their messages near Shobek, among Arabs too weather-daunted to move.

Clayton said that in the new conditions there could be no question of letting me off. The East was only now going to begin. Allenby told me that the War Cabinet were leaning heavily on him to repair the stalemate of the West. He was to take at least Damascus; and, if possible, Aleppo, as soon as he could. Turkey was to be put out of the war once and for all. His difficulty lay with his eastern flank, the right, which to-day rested on Jordan. He had called me to consider if the Arabs could relieve him of its burden.

There was no escape for me. I must take up again my mantle of fraud in the East. With my certain contempt for half-measures I took it up quickly and wrapped myself in it completely. It might be fraud or it might be farce: no one should say that I could not play it. So I did not even mention the reasons which had brought me across; but pointed out that this was the Jordan scheme seen from the British angle. Allenby assented, and asked if we could still do it. I said: not at present, unless new factors were first discounted.

The first was Maan. We should have to take it before we could afford a second sphere. If more transport gave a longer range to the units of the Arab Regular Army, they could take position some miles north of Maan and cut the railway permanently, so forcing the Maan garrison to come out and fight them; and in the field the Arabs would easily defeat the Turks. We would require seven hundred baggage camels; more guns and machine-guns; and lastly, assurance against flank attack from Amman, while we dealt with Maan.

On this basis a scheme was worked out. Allenby ordered down to

Akaba two units of the Camel Transport Corps, an organization of Egyptians under British officers, which had proved highly successful in the Beersheba campaign. It was a great gift, for its carrying capacity ensured that we should now be able to keep our four thousand regulars eighty miles in advance of their base. The guns and machine-guns were also promised. As for shielding us against attack from Amman, Allenby said that was easily arranged. He intended, for his own flank's security, shortly to take Salt, beyond Jordan, and hold it with an Indian Brigade. A Corps Conference was due next day, and I was to stay for it.

At this Conference it was determined that the Arab Army move instantly to the Maan Plateau to take Maan. That the British cross the Jordan, occupy Salt, and destroy south of Amman as much of the railway as possible; especially the great tunnel. It was debated what share the Amman Arabs should take in the British operation. Bols thought we should join in the advance. I opposed this, since the later retirement to Salt would cause rumour and reaction, and it would be easier if we did not enter till this had spent itself.

Chetwode, who was to direct the advance, asked how his men were to distinguish friendly from hostile Arabs, since their tendency was a prejudice against all wearing skirts. I was sitting skirted in their midst and replied, naturally, that skirt-wearers disliked men in uniform. The laugh clinched the question, and it was agreed that we support the British retention of Salt only after they came to rest there. As soon as Maan fell, the Arab Regulars would move up and draw supplies from Jericho. The seven hundred camels would come along, still giving them eighty miles, radius of action. This would be enough to let them work above Amman in Allenby's grand attack along the line from the Mediterranean to the Dead Sea, the second phase of the operation, directed to the capture of Damascus.

My business was finished. I went to Cairo for two days, and then was flown to Akaba, to make my new terms with Feisal. I told him I thought they had treated me badly, in diverting without my knowledge money of the special account which, by agreement, I had drawn solely for the Dead Sea campaign. Consequently, I had left Zeid, it being impossible for a flouted adviser to carry on.

Allenby had sent me back. But my return did not mean that the damage was repaired. A great opportunity had been missed, and a valuable advance thrown away. The Turks would retake Tafileh in a week's time without difficulty.

Feisal was distressed lest the loss of Tafileh do his reputation harm; and shocked by my little interest in its fate. To comfort him, I pointed out that it now meant nothing to us. The two interests were the extremes of his area, Amman and Maan. Tafileh was not worth losing a man over; indeed, if the Turks moved there, they would weaken either Maan or Amman, and make our real work easier.

He was a little reconciled by this, but sent urgent warnings to Zeid of the coming danger: without avail, for six days later the Turks retook Tafileh. Meanwhile, Feisal re-arranged the basis of his army funds. I gave him the good news that Allenby, as thanks for the Dead Sea and Aba el Lissan, had put three hundred thousand pounds into my independent credit, and given us a train of seven hundred pack-camels complete with personnel and equipment.

This raised great joy in all the army, for the baggage columns would enable us to prove the value in the field of the Arab regular troops on whose training and organization Joyce, Jaafar, and so many Arab and English officers had worked for months. We arranged rough time-tables and schemes: then I shipped busily back to Egypt.

BOOK VIII

THE RUIN OF HIGH HOPE

Chapters XCII to XCVII

IN conjunction with Allenby we laid a triple plan
to join hands across Jordan, to capture Maan, and
to cut off Medina, in one operation. This was too
proud and neither of us fulfilled his part. So the
Arabs exchanged the care of the placid Medina Railway for the greater burden of investing, in Maan,
a Turk force as big as their available Regular Army.

To help in this duty Allenby increased our
transport, that we might have longer range and
more mobility. Maan was impregnable for us, so
we concentrated on cutting its northern railway
and diverting the Turkish effort to relieve its
garrison from the Amman side.

Clearly no decision lay in such tactics: but the
German advance in Flanders at this moment took
from Allenby his British units; and consequently
his advantage over the Turks. He notified us that
he was unable to attack.

A stalemate, as we were, throughout 1918 was an
intolerable prospect. We schemed to strengthen
the Arab Army for autumn operations near Deraa
and in the Beni Sakhr country. If this drew off
one division from the enemy in Palestine it would
make possible a British ancillary attack, one of
whose ends would be our junction in the lower
Jordan valley, by Jericho. After a month's
preparation this plan was dropped,
because of its risk, and because a
better offered.

CHAPTER XCII

IN Cairo, where I spent four days, our affairs were now far from haphazard. Allenby's smile had given us Staff. We had supply officers, a shipping expert, an ordnance expert, an intelligence branch: under Alan Dawnay, brother of the maker of the Beersheba plan, who had now gone to France. Dawnay was Allenby's greatest gift to us — greater than thousands of baggage camels. As a professional officer, he had the class-touch: so that even the reddest hearer recognized an authentic redness. His was an understanding mind, feeling instinctively the special qualities of rebellion: at the same time, his war-training enriched his treatment of this antithetic subject. He married war and rebellion in himself; as, of old in Yenbo, it had been my dream every regular officer would. Yet, in three years' practice, only Dawnay succeeded.

He could not take complete, direct command, because he did not know Arabic; and because of his Flanders-broken health. He had the gift, rare among Englishmen, of making the best of a good thing. He was exceptionally educated, for an Army officer, and imaginative. His perfect manner made him friends with all races and classes. From his teaching we began to learn the technique of fighting in matters we had been content to settle by rude and wasteful rules of thumb. His sense of fitness remodelled our standing.

The Arab Movement had lived as a wild-man show, with its means as small as its duties and prospects. Henceforward Allenby counted it as a sensible part of his scheme; and the responsibility upon us of doing better than he wished, knowing that forfeit of our failure would necessarily be part-paid in his soldiers' lives, removed it terrifyingly further from the sphere of joyous adventure.

With Joyce we laid our triple plan to support Allenby's first stroke. In our centre the Arab regulars, under Jaafar, would occupy the line a march north of Maan. Joyce with our armoured cars would slip down to Mudowwara, and destroy the railway — permanently this time, for now we were ready to cut off Medina. In the north, Merzuk, with myself, would join Allenby when he fell back to Salt about March the thirtieth. Such a date gave me leisure: and I settled to go to Shobek, with Zeid and Nasir.

It was springtime: very pleasant after the biting winter, whose excesses seemed dream-like, in the new freshness and strength of nature: for there was strength in this hill-top season, when a chill sharpness at sundown corrected the languid noons.

All life was alive with us: even the insects. In our first night I had laid my cashmere head-cloth on the ground under my head as pad: and at dawn, when I took it up again, twenty-eight lice were tangled in its snowy texture. Afterwards we slept on our saddle-covers, the tanned fleece hooked last of all over the saddle-load to make a slippy and sweat-proof seat for the rider. Even so, we were not left alone. The camel-ticks, which had drunk themselves (with blood from our tethered camels) into tight slaty-blue cushions, thumbnail wide, and thick, used to creep under us, hugging the leathern underside of the sheep-skins: and if we rolled on them in the night, our weight burst them to brown mats of blood and dust.

While we were in this comfortable air, with milk plentiful about us, news came from Azrak, of Ali ibn el Hussein and the Indians still on faithful watch. One Indian had died of cold, and also Daud, my Ageyli boy, the friend of Farraj. Farraj himself told us.

These two had been friends from childhood, in eternal gaiety: working together, sleeping together, sharing every scrape and profit with the openness and honesty of perfect love. So I was not astonished to see Farraj look dark and hard of face, leaden-eyed and old, when he came to tell me that his fellow was dead; and from that day till his service ended he made no more laughter for us. He took punctilious care, greater even than before, of my camel, of the coffee, of my clothes and saddles, and fell to praying his three regular prayings every day. The others offered themselves to comfort him, but instead he wandered restlessly, grey and silent, very much alone.

When looked at from this torrid East, our British conception of woman seemed to partake of the northern climate which had also contracted our faith. In the Mediterranean, woman's influence and supposed purpose were made cogent by an understanding in which she was accorded the physical world in simplicity, unchallenged, like the poor in spirit. Yet this same agreement, by denying equality of sex, made love, companionship and friendliness impossible between man and woman. Woman became a machine for muscular exercise, while man's psychic side could be slaked only amongst his peers. Whence arose these partnerships of man and man, to supply human nature with more than the contact of flesh with flesh.

We Westerners of this complex age, monks in our bodies' cells, who searched for something to fill us beyond speech and sense, were, by the mere effort of the search, shut from it for ever. Yet it came to children like these unthinking Ageyl, content to receive without return, even from one another. We racked ourselves with inherited remorse for the flesh-indulgence of our gross birth, striving to pay for it through a lifetime of misery; meeting happiness, life's overdraft, by a compensating hell, and striking a ledger-balance of good or evil against a day of judgement.

Meanwhile at Aba el Lissan things went not well with our scheme to destroy the Maan garrison by posting the Arab Army across the railway in the north, and forcing them to open battle, as Allenby attacked their base and supports at Amman. Feisal and Jaafar liked the scheme, but their officers clamoured for direct attack on Maan. Joyce pointed out their weakness in artillery and machine-guns, their untried men, the greater strategical wisdom of the railway scheme: it was of no effect. Maulud, hot for immediate assault, wrote memoranda to Feisal upon the danger of English interference with Arab liberty. At such a moment Joyce fell ill of pneumonia, and left for Suez. Dawnay came up to reason with the malcontents. He was our best card, with his proved military reputation, exquisite field-boots, and air of well-dressed science; but he came too late, for the Arab officers now felt their honour to be engaged.

We agreed that we must give them their heads on the point, though we were really all-powerful, with the money, the supplies, and now the transport, in our hands. However, if the people were slattern, why, then, they must have a slatternly government: and particularly must we go slow with that self-governing democracy, the Arab Army, in which service was as voluntary as enlistment. Between us we were familiar with the Turkish, the Egyptian and the British Armies: and championed our respective task-masters. Joyce alleged the parade-magnificence of his Egyptians — formal men, who loved mechanical movement and surpassed British troops in physique, in smartness, in perfection of drill. I maintained the frugality of the Turks, that shambling, ragged army of serfs. The British Army we all were acquainted with in a fashion; and as we contrasted services we found variety of obedience according to the degree of ordered force which served each as sanction.

In Egypt soldiers belonged to their service without check of public opinion. Consequently they had a peace-incentive to perfection of formal conduct. In Turkey the men were, in theory, equally the officers': body and soul: but their lot was mitigated by the possibility of escape. In England the voluntary recruit served as utterly as any Turk, except that the growth of civil decency had taken away from authority the resource of inflicting direct physical pain: but in practice, upon our less obtuse population, the effects of pack-drill or fatigues fell little short of an Oriental system.

In the regular Arab Army there was no power of punishment whatever: this vital difference showed itself in all our troops. They had no formality of discipline; there was no subordination. Service was active; attack always imminent: and, like the Army of Italy, men recognized the duty of defeating the enemy. For the rest they were not soldiers, but pilgrims, intent always to go the little farther.

I was not discontented with this state of things, for it had seemed to me that discipline, or at least formal discipline, was a virtue of peace: a character or stamp by which to mark off soldiers from complete men, and obliterate the humanity of the individual. It resolved itself easiest into the restrictive, the making men not do this or that: and so could be fostered by a rule severe enough to make them despair of disobedience. It was a process of the mass, an element of the impersonal crowd, inapplicable to one man, since it involved obedience, a duality of will. It was not to impress upon men that their will must actively second the officer's, for then there would have been, as in the Arab Army and among irregulars, that momentary pause for thought transmission, or digestion; for the nerves to resolve the relaying private will into active consequence. On the contrary, each regular Army sedulously rooted out this significant pause from its companies on parade. The drill-instructors tried to make obedience an instinct, a mental reflex, following as instantly on the command as though the motor power of the individual wills had been invested together in the system.

This was well, so far as it increased quickness: but it made no provision for casualties, beyond the weak assumption that each subordinate had his will-motor not atrophied, but reserved in perfect order, ready at the instant to take over his late superior's office; the efficiency of direction passing smoothly down the great hierarchy till vested in the senior of the two surviving privates.

It had the further weakness, seeing men's jealousy, of putting power in the hands of arbitrary old age, with its petulant activity: additionally corrupted by long habit of control, an indulgence which ruined its victim, by causing the death of his subjunctive mood. Also, it was an idiosyncrasy with me to distrust instinct, which had its roots in our animality. Reason seemed to give men something deliberately more precious than fear or pain: and this made me discount the value of peace smartness as a war-education.

For with war a subtle change happened to the soldier. Discipline was modified, supported, even swallowed by an eagerness of the man to fight. This eagerness it was which brought victory in the moral sense, and often in the physical sense, of the combat. War was made up of crises of intense effort. For psychological reasons commanders wished for the least duration of this maximum effort: not because the men would not try to give it — usually they would go on till they dropped — but because each such effort weakened their remaining force. Eagerness of the kind was nervous, and, when present in high power, it tore apart flesh and spirit.

To rouse the excitement of war for the creation of a military spirit in peace-time would be dangerous, like the too-early doping of an athlete. Consequently discipline, with its concomitant 'smartness' (a suspect word implying superficial restraint and pain), was invented to take its place. The Arab Army, born and brought up in the fighting line, had never known a peace-habit, and was not faced with problems of maintenance till armistice-time: then it failed signally.

CHAPTER XCIII

AFTER Joyce and Dawnay had gone, I rode off from Aba el Lissan, with Mirzuk. Our starting day promised to crown the spring-freshness of this lofty tableland. A week before there had been a furious blizzard, and some of the whiteness of the snow seemed to have passed into the light. The ground was vivid with new grass; and the sunlight, which slanted across us, pale like straw, mellowed the fluttering wind.

With us journeyed two thousand Sirhan camels, carrying our ammunition and food. For the convoy's sake we marched easily, to reach the railway after dark. A few of us rode forward, to search the line by daylight, and be sure of peace during the hours these scattered numbers would consume in crossing.

My bodyguard was with me, and Mirzuk had his Ageyl, with two famous racing camels. The gaiety of the air and season caught them. Soon they were challenging to races, threatening one another, or skirmishing. My imperfect camel-riding (and my mood) forbade me to thrust among the lads, who swung more to the north, while I worked on, ridding my mind of the lees of camp-clamour and intrigue. The abstraction of the desert landscape cleansed me, and rendered my mind vacant with its superfluous greatness; a greatness achieved not by the addition of thought to its emptiness, but by its subtraction. In the weakness of earth's life was mirrored the strength of heaven, so vast, so beautiful, so strong.

Near sunset the line became visible, curving spaciously across the disclosed land, among low tufts of grass and bushes. Seeing everything was peaceful I pushed on, meaning to halt beyond and watch the others over. There was always a little thrill in touching the rails which were the target of so many of our efforts.

As I rode up the bank my camel's feet scrambled in the loose ballast, and out of the long shadow of a culvert to my left, where, no doubt, he had slept all day, rose a Turkish soldier. He glanced wildly at me and at the pistol in my hand, and then with sadness at his rifle against the abutment, yards beyond. He was a young man; stout, but sulky-looking. I stared at him, and said softly, 'God is merciful.' He knew the sound and sense of the Arabic phrase, and raised his eyes like a flash to mine, while his heavy sleep-ridden face began slowly to change into incredulous joy.

However, he said not a word. I pressed my camel's hairy shoulder with my foot, she picked her delicate stride across the metals and down the further slope, and the little Turk was man enough not to shoot me in the back, as I rode away, feeling warm towards him, as ever towards a life one has saved. At a safe distance I glanced back. He put thumb to nose, and twinkled his fingers at me.

We lit a coffee-fire as beacon for the rest, and waited till their dark lines passed by. Next day we marched to Wadi el Jinz; to flood-pools, shallow eyes of water set in wrinkles of the clay, their rims lashed about with scrubby stems of brushwood. The water was grey, like the marly valley bed, but sweet. There we rested for the night, since the Zaagi had shot a bustard, and Xenophon did rightly call its white meat good. While we feasted the camels feasted. By the bounty of spring they were knee-deep in succulent green-stuff.

A fourth easy march took us to the Atara, our goal, where our allies, Mifleh, Fahad and Adhub, were camped. Fahad was still stricken, but Mifleh, with honeyed words, came out to welcome us, his face eaten up by greed, and his voice wheezy with it.

Our plan, thanks to Allenby's lion-share, promised simply. We would, when ready, cross the line to Themed, the main Beni Sakhr watering. Thence under cover of a screen of their cavalry we would move to Madeba, and fit it as our headquarters, while Allenby put the Jericho-Salt road in condition. We ought to link up with the British comfortably without firing a shot.

Meanwhile we had only to wait in the Atatir, which to our joy were really green, with every hollow a standing pool, and the valley beds of tall grass prinked with flowers. The chalky ridges, sterile with salt, framed the water-channels delightfully. From their tallest point we could look north and south, and see how the rain, running down, had painted the valleys across the white in broad stripes of green, sharp and firm like brush-strokes. Everything was growing, and daily the picture was fuller and brighter till the desert became like a rank water-meadow. Playful packs of winds came crossing and tumbling over one another, their wide, brief gusts surging through the grass, to lay it momentarily in swathes of dark and light satin, like young corn after the roller. On the hill we sat and shivered before these sweeping shadows, expecting a heavy blast — and there would come into our faces a warm and per-fumed breath, very gentle, which passed away behind us as a silver-grey light down the plain of green. Our fastidious camels grazed an hour or so, and then lay down to digest, bringing up stomach-load after stomach-load of butter-smelling green cud, and chewing weightily.

At last news came that the English had taken Amman. In half an hour we were making for Themed, across the deserted line. Later messages told us that the English were falling back, and though we had forewarned the Arabs of it, yet they were troubled. A further messen-ger reported how the English had just fled from Salt. This was plainly contrary to Allenby's intention, and I swore straight out that it was not true. A man galloped in to say that the English had broken only a few rails south of Amman, after two days of vain assaults against the town. I grew seriously disturbed in the conflict of rumour, and sent Adhub, who might be trusted not to lose his head, to Salt with a letter for Chetwode or Shea, asking for a note on the real situation. For the intervening hours we tramped restlessly over the fields of young barley, our minds working out plan after plan with feverish activity.

Very late at night Adhub's racing horse-hooves echoed across the valley and he came in to tell us that Jemal Pasha was now in Salt, victorious, hanging those local Arabs who had welcomed the English. The Turks were still chasing Allenby far down the Jordan Valley. It was thought that Jerusalem would be recovered. I knew enough of my countrymen to reject that possibility; but clearly things were very wrong. We slipped off, bemused, to the Atatir again.

This reverse, being unawares, hurt me the more. Allenby's plan had seemed modest, and that we should so fall down before the Arabs was deplorable. They had never trusted us to do the great things which I foretold; and now their independent thoughts set out to enjoy the springtide here. They were abetted by some gipsy families from the north with the materials of their tinkering trade on donkeys. The Zebn tribesmen greeted them with a humour I little understood — till I saw that, beside their legitimate profits of handicraft, the women were open to other advances.

Particularly they were easy to the Ageyl; and for a while they prospered exceedingly, since our men were eager and very generous. I also made use of them. It seemed a pity to be at a loose end so near to Amman, and not bother to look at it. So Farraj and I hired three of the merry little women, wrapped ourselves up like them, and strolled through the village. The visit was successful, though my final determination was that the place should be left alone. We had one evil moment, by the bridge, when we were returning. Some Turkish soldiers crossed our party, and taking us all five for what we looked, grew much too friendly. We showed a coyness, and good turn of speed for gipsy women, and escaped intact. For the future I decided to resume my habit of wearing ordinary British soldiers' rig in enemy camps. It was too brazen to be suspect.

After this I determined to order the Indians from Azrak back to Feisal, and to return myself. We started on one of those clean dawns which woke up the senses with the sun, while the intellect, tired after the thinking of the night, was yet abed. For an hour or two on such a morning the sounds, scents and colours of the world struck man individually and directly, not filtered through or made typical by thought; they seemed to exist sufficiently by themselves, and the lack of design and of carefulness in creation no longer irritated.

We marched southward along the railway, expecting to cross the slower-moving Indians from Azrak; our little party on prize camels swooping from one point of vantage to another, on the look-out. The still day encouraged us to speed over all the flint-strewn ridges, ignoring the multitude of desert paths which led only to the abandoned camps of last year, or of the last thousand or ten thousand years: for a road, once trodden into such flint and limestone, marked the face of the desert for so long as the desert lasted.

By Faraifra we saw a little patrol of eight Turks marching up the line. My men, fresh after the holiday in the Atatir, begged me to ride on them. I thought it too trifling, but when they chafed, agreed. The younger ones instantly rushed forward at a gallop. I ordered the rest across the line, to drive the enemy away from their shelter behind a culvert. The Zaagi, a hundred yards to my right, seeing what was wanted, swerved aside at once. Mohsin followed him a moment later, with his section; whilst Abdulla and I pushed forward steadily on our side, to take the enemy on both flanks together.

Farraj, riding in front of everyone, would not listen to our cries nor notice the warning shots fired past his head. He looked round at our manœuvre, but himself continued to canter madly towards the bridge, which he reached before the Zaagi and his party had crossed the line. The Turks held their fire, and we supposed them gone down the further side of the embankment into safety; but as Farraj drew rein beneath the archway, there was a shot, and he seemed to fall or leap out of the saddle, and disappeared. A while after, the Zaagi got into position on the bank and his party fired twenty or thirty ragged shots, as though the enemy was still there.

I was very anxious about Farraj. His camel stood unharmed by the bridge, alone. He might be hit, or might be following the enemy. I could not believe that he had deliberately ridden up to them in the open and halted; yet it looked like it. I sent Feheyd to the Zaagi and told him to rush along the far side as soon as possible, whilst we went at a fast trot straight in to the bridge.

We reached it together, and found there one dead Turk, and Farraj terribly wounded through the body, lying by the arch just as he had fallen from his camel. He looked unconscious; but, when we dismounted, greeted us, and then fell silent, sunken in that loneliness which came to hurt men who believed death near. We tore his clothes away and looked uselessly at the wound. The bullet had smashed right through him, and his spine seemed injured. The Arabs said at once that he had only a few hours to live.

We tried to move him, for he was helpless, though he showed no pain. We tried to stop the wide, slow bleeding, which made poppy-splashes in the grass; but it seemed impossible, and after a while he told us to let him alone, as he was dying, and happy to die, since he had no care of life. Indeed, for long he had been so, and men very tired and sorry often fell in love with death, with that triumphal weakness coming home after strength has been vanquished in a last battle.

While we fussed about him Abd el Latif shouted an alarm. He could see about fifty Turks working up the line towards us, and soon after a motor trolley was heard coming from the north. We were only sixteen men, and had an impossible position. I said we must retire at once, carrying Farraj with us. They tried to lift him, first in his cloak, afterwards in a blanket; but consciousness was coming back, and he screamed so pitifully that we had not the heart to hurt him more.

We could not leave him where he was, to the Turks, because we had seen them burn alive our hapless wounded. For this reason we were all agreed, before action, to finish off one another, if badly hurt: but I had never realized that it might fall to me to kill Farraj.

I knelt down beside him, holding my pistol near the ground by his head, so that he should not see my purpose; but he must have guessed it, for he opened his eyes, and clutched me with his harsh, scaly hand, the tiny hand of these unripe Nejd fellows. I waited a moment, and he said, 'Daud will be angry with you', the old smile coming back so strangely to this grey shrinking face. I replied, 'Salute him from me'. He returned the formal answer, 'God will give you peace', and at last wearily closed his eyes.

The Turkish trolley was now very close, swaying down the line towards us like a dung-beetle: and its machine-gun bullets stung the air about our heads as we fled back into the ridges. Mohsin led Farraj's camel, on which were his sheepskin and trappings, still with the shape of his body in them just as he had fallen by the bridge. Near dark we halted; and the Zaagi came whispering to me that all were wrangling as to who should ride the splendid animal next day. He wanted her for himself; but I was bitter that these perfected dead had again robbed my poverty: and to cheapen the great loss with a little one I shot the poor beast with my second bullet.

Then the sun set on us. Through the breathless noon in the valleys of Kerak the prisoned air had brooded stagnantly without relief, while the heat sucked the perfume from the flowers. With darkness the world moved once more, and a breath from the west crept out over the desert. We were miles from the grass and flowers, but suddenly we felt them all about us, as waves of this scented air drew past us with a sticky sweetness. However, quickly it faded, and the night-wind, damp and wholesome, followed. Abdulla brought me supper, rice and camel-meat (Farraj's camel). Afterwards we slept.

CHAPTER XCIV

IN the morning, near Wadi el Jinz, we met the Indians, halted by a solitary tree. It was like old times, like our gentle and memorable ride to the bridges the year before, to be going again across country with Hassan Shah, hearing the Vickers guns still clinking in the carriers, and helping the troopers re-tie their slipping loads, or saddles. They seemed just as unhandy with camels as at first; so not till dusk did we cross the railway.

There I left the Indians, because I felt restless, and movement fast in the night might cure my mind. So we pressed forward all the chill darkness, riding for Odroh. When we topped its rise we noticed gleams of fire to our left: bright flashes went up constantly, it might be from about Jerdun. We drew rein and heard the low boom of explosions: a steady flame appeared, grew greater and divided into two. Perhaps the station was burning. We rode quick, to ask Mastur.

However, his place was deserted, with only a jackal on the old camping-ground. I decided to push ahead to Feisal. We trotted our fastest, as the sun grew higher in the heavens. The road was bestial with locusts — though from a little distance they looked beautiful, silvering the air with the shimmer of their wings. Summer had come upon us unawares; my seventh consecutive summer in this East.

As we approached, we heard firing in front, on Semna, the crescent mound which covered Maan. Parties of troops walked gently up its face to halt below the crest. Evidently we had taken the Semna, so we rode towards the new position. On the flat, this side of it, we met a camel with litters. The man leading it said, 'Maulud Pasha', pointing to his load. I ran up, crying, 'Is Maulud hit?' for he was one of the best officers in the army, a man also most honest towards us; not, indeed that admiration could anyhow have been refused so sturdy and uncompromising a patriot. The old man replied out of his litter in a weak voice, saying, 'Yes, indeed, Lurens Bey, I am hurt: but, thanks be to God, it is nothing. We have taken Semna.' I replied that I was going there. Maulud craned himself feverishly over the edge of the litter, hardly able to see or speak (his thigh-bone was splintered above the knee), showing me point after point, for organizing the hill-side defensively.

We arrived as the Turks were beginning to throw half-hearted shells at it. Nuri Said was commanding in Maulud's place. He stood coolly on the hill-top. Most men talked faster under fire, and acted a betraying ease and joviality. Nuri grew calmer and Zeid bored.

I asked where Jaafar was. Nuri said that at midnight he was due to have attacked Jerdun. I told him of the night-flares, which must have marked his success. While we were glad together his messengers arrived reporting prisoners and machine-guns; also the station and three thousand rails destroyed. So splendid an effort would settle the northern line for weeks. Then Nuri told me that the preceding dawn he had rushed Ghadir el Haj station and wrecked it, with five bridges and a thousand rails. So the southern line was also settled.

Late in the afternoon it grew deadly quiet. Both sides stopped their aimless shelling. They said that Feisal had moved to Uheida. We crossed the little flooded stream, by a temporary hospital where Maulud lay. Mahmud, the red-bearded, defiant doctor, thought that he would recover without amputation. Feisal was on the hill-top, on the very edge, black against the sun, whose light threw a queer haze about his slender figure, and suffused his head with gold, through the floss-silk of his head-cloth. I made my camel kneel. Feisal stretched out his hands crying, 'Please God, good?' I replied, 'The praise and the victory be to God'. And he swept me into his tent that we might exchange the news.

Feisal had heard from Dawnay more than I knew of the British failure before Amman; of the bad weather and confusion, and how Allenby had telephoned to Shea, and made one of his lightning decisions to cut the loss; a wise decision, though it hurt us sorely. Joyce was in hospital, but mending well; and Dawnay lay ready at Guweira to start for Mudowwara with all the cars.

Feisal asked me about Semna and Jaafar, and I told him what I knew, and Nuri's opinion, and the prospect. Nuri had complained that the Abu Tayi had done nothing for him all day. Auda denied it; and I recalled the story of our first taking the plateau, and the gibe by which

I had shamed them into the charge at Aba el Lissan. The tale was new to Feisal. Its raking-up hurt old Auda deeply. He swore vehemently that he had done his best to-day, only conditions were not favourable for tribal work: and, when I withstood him further, he went out of the tent, very bitter.

Maynard and I spent the next days watching operations. The Abu Tayi captured two outposts east of the station, while Saleh ibn Shefia took a breastwork with a machine-gun and twenty prisoners. These gains gave us liberty of movement round Maan; and on the third day Jaafar massed his artillery on the southern ridge, while Nuri Said led a storming party into the sheds of the railway station. As he reached their cover the French guns ceased fire. We were wandering in a Ford car, trying to keep up with the successive advances, when Nuri, perfectly dressed and gloved, smoking his briar pipe, met us and sent us back to Captain Pisani, artillery commander, with an urgent appeal for support. We found Pisani wringing his hands in despair, every round expended. He said he had implored Nuri not to attack at this moment of his penury.

There was nothing to do, but see our men volleyed out of the railway station again. The road was littered with crumpled khaki figures, and the eyes of the wounded, gone rich with pain, stared accusingly at us. The control had gone from their broken bodies and their torn flesh shook them helplessly. We could see everything and think dispassionately, but it was soundless: our hearing had been taken away by the knowledge that we had failed.

Afterwards we understood that we had never expected such excellent spirit from our infantry, who fought cheerfully under machine-gun fire, and made clever use of ground. So little leading was required that only three officers were lost. Maan showed us that the Arabs were good enough without British stiffening. This made us more free to plan: so the failure was not unredeemed.

On the morning of April the eighteenth, Jaafar wisely decided that he could not afford more loss, and drew back to the Semna positions while the troops rested. Being an old college friend of the Turkish Commandant, he sent him a white-flagged letter, inviting surrender. The reply said that they would love it, but had orders to hold out to the

last cartridge. Jaafar offered a respite, in which they could fire off their
reserves: but the Turks hesitated till Jemal Pasha was able to collect
troops from Amman, re-occupy Jerdun, and pass a pack-convoy of
food and ammunition into the beleaguered town. The railway
remained broken for weeks.

Forthwith I took car to join Dawnay. I was uneasy at a regular
fighting his first guerilla battle with that most involved and intricate
weapon, the armoured car. Also Dawnay was no Arabist, and neither
Peake, his camel-expert, nor Marshall, his doctor, was fluent. His
troops were mixed, British, Egyptian and Bedouin. The last two were
antipathetic. So I drove into his camp above Tell Shahm after midnight, and offered myself, delicately, as an interpreter.

Fortunately he received me well, and took me round his lines. A
wonderful show. The cars were parked geometrically here; armoured
cars there; sentries and pickets were out, with machine-guns ready.
Even the Arabs were in a tactical place behind a hill, in support, but out
of sight and hearing; by some magic Sherif Hazaa and himself had kept
them where they were put. My tongue coiled into my cheek with the
wish to say that the only thing lacking was an enemy.

His conversation as he unfolded his plan deepened my admiration to
unplumbed depths. He had prepared operation orders; orthodox-
sounding things with zero times and a sequence of movements. Each
unit had its appointed duty. We would attack the 'plain post' at dawn
(armoured cars) from the vantage of the hillock on which Joyce and
myself had sat and laughed ruefully the last abortive time. The cars,
with closed cut-out, would 'take station' before daylight, and carry the
trenches by surprise. Tenders 1 and 3 would then demolish bridges
A and B on the operations' plan (scale 1/250,000) at zero 1.30 hours
while the cars moved to Rock Post, and with the support of Hazaa and
the Arabs rushed it (zero 2.15).

Hornby and the explosives, in Talbots No. 40531 and 41226,
would move after them, and demolish bridges D, E and F, while the
force lunched. After lunch, when the low sun permitted sight through
the mirage, at zero 8 hours to be exact, the united mass would attack
South Post; the Egyptians from the East, the Arabs from the North,
covered by long range machine-gun fire from the cars, and by Brodie's

ten-pounder guns, sited on Observation Hill. The post would fall and the force transport itself to the station of Tell Shahm, which would be shelled by Brodie from the North-West, bombed by aeroplanes flying from the mud-flats of Rum (at zero 10 hours) and approached by armoured cars from the west. The Arabs would follow the cars, while Peake with his Camel Corps descended from South Post. 'The station will be taken at zero 11.30' said the scheme, breaking into humour at the last. But there it failed, for the Turks, ignorantly and in haste, surrendered ten minutes too soon, and made the only blot on a bloodless day.

In a liquid voice I inquired if Hazaa understood. I was informed that as he had no watch to synchronize (by the way, would I please put mine right now?) he would make his first move when the cars turned northward and time his later actions by express order. I crept away and hid myself for an hour's sleep.

At dawn we saw the cars roll silently on top of the sleeping sandy trenches, and the astonished Turks walk out with their hands up. It was like picking a ripe peach. Hornby dashed up in his two Rolls tenders, put a hundredweight of gun-cotton under bridge A and blew it up convincingly. The roar nearly lifted Dawnay and myself out of our third tender, in which we sat grandly overseeing all: and we ran in, to show Hornby the cheaper way of the drainage holes as mine-chambers. Subsequent bridges came down for ten slabs apiece.

While we were at bridge B the cars concentrated their machine-guns on the parapet of 'Rock Post', a circle of thick stone walls (very visible from their long early shadows) on a knoll too steep for wheels. Hazaa was ready, willing and excited, and the Turks so frightened by the splashing and splattering of the four machine-guns that the Arabs took them almost in their stride. That was peach the second.

Then it was interval for the others, but activity for Hornby, and for myself, now assistant-engineer. We ran down the line in our Rolls-Royces, carrying two tons of gun-cotton; bridges and rails roared up wherever fancy dictated. The crews of the cars covered us; and sometimes covered themselves, under their cars, when fragments came sailing musically through the smoky air. One twenty-pound flint clanged plumb on a turret-head and made a harmless dint. At intervals everybody took photographs of the happy bursts. It was fighting de luxe, and demolition de luxe: we enjoyed ourselves. After the peripatetic lunch-hour we went off to see the fall of 'south post'. It fell to its minute, but not properly. Hazaa and his Amran were too wound up to advance soberly in alternate rushes like Peake and the Egyptians. Instead they thought it was a steeplechase, and did a camel-charge up the mound over breastwork and trenches. The war-weary Turks gave it up in disgust.

Then came the central act of the day, the assault upon the station. Peake drew down towards it from the north, moving his men by repeated exposure of himself; hardly, for they were not fierce for honour. Brodie opened on it with his usual nicety, while the aeroplanes circled round in their cold-blooded way, to drop whistling bombs into its trenches. The armoured cars went forward snuffling smoke, and through this haze a file of Turks waving white things rose out of their main trench in a dejected fashion.

We cranked up our Rolls tenders; the Arabs leaped on to their camels; Peake's now-bold men broke into a run, and the force converged wildly upon the station. Our car won; and I gained the station bell, a dignified piece of Damascus brass-work. The next man took the ticket punch and the third the office stamp, while the bewildered Turks stared at us, with a growing indignation that their importance should be merely secondary.

A minute later, with a howl, the Beduin were upon the maddest looting of their history. Two hundred rifles, eighty thousand rounds of ammunition, many bombs, much food and clothing were in the station, and everybody smashed and profited. An unlucky camel increased the confusion by firing one of the many Turkish trip-mines as it entered the yard. The explosion blew it arse over tip, and caused a panic. They thought Brodie was opening up again.

In the pause the Egyptian officer found an unbroken storehouse, and put a guard of soldiers over it, because they were short of food. Hazaa's wolves, not yet sated, did not recognize the Egyptians' right to share equally. Shooting began: but by mediation we obtained that the Egyptians pick first what rations they needed: afterwards there followed a general scramble, which burst the store-room walls.

The profit of Shahm was so great that eight out of every ten of the Arabs were contented with it. In the morning only Hazaa and a handful of men remained with us for further operations. Dawnay's programme said Ramleh station; but his orders were inchoate, since the position had not been examined. So we sent down Wade in his armoured car, with a second car in support. He drove on, cautiously, stage by stage, in dead silence. At last, without a shot fired, he entered the station yard, carefully, for fear of the mines, whose trip and trigger wires diapered the ground.

The station was closed up. He put half a belt through the door and shutters, and, getting no reply, slipped out of his car, searched the building, and found it empty of men, though full enough of desirable goods to make Hazaa and the faithful remnant prize their virtue aloud. We spent the day destroying miles more of the unoccupied line, till we judged that we had done damage to occupy the largest possible repair party for a fortnight.

The third day was to be Mudowwara, but we had no great hope or force left. The Arabs were gone, Peake's men too little warlike. However, Mudowwara might panic like Ramleh, so we slept the night by our latest capture. The unwearied Dawnay set out sentries, who, emulous of their smart commanding officer, did a Buckingham Palace stunt up and down beside our would-be sleeping heads, till I got up, and instructed them in the arts of desert-watching.

In the morning we set off to look at Mudowwara, driving like kings splendidly in our roaring cars over the smooth plains of sand and flint, with the low sun pale behind us in the east. The light hid us till we were close in and saw that a long train stood in the station. Reinforcement or evacuation? A moment afterwards they let fly at us with four guns, of which two were active and accurate little Austrian mountain howitzers. At seven thousand yards they did admirable shooting, while we made off in undignified haste to some distant hollows. Thence we made a wide circuit to where, with Zaal, we had mined our first train. We blew up the long bridge, under which the Turkish patrol had slept out that tense midday. Afterwards we returned to Ramleh, and persevered in destroying line and bridges, to make our break permanent, a demolition too serious for Fakhri ever to restore: while Feisal sent

Mohammed el Dheilan against the yet intact stations between our break and Maan. Dawnay joined up with them, geographically, below the escarpment, a day later; and so this eighty miles from Maan to Mudow-wara, with its seven stations, fell wholly into our hands. The active defence of Medina ended with this operation.

A new officer, Young, came from Mesopotamia to reinforce our staff. He was a regular of exceptional quality, with long and wide experience of war, and perfect fluency in Arabic. His intended role was to double mine, with the tribes, that our activity against the enemy might be broader, and better directed. To let him play himself in to our fresh conditions, I handed him over the possibility of combining Zeid, Nasir and Mirzuk into an eighty-mile long interruption of the railway from Maan northward, while I went down to Akaba, and took ship for Suez, to discuss futures with Allenby.

CHAPTER XCV

DAWNAY met me, and we talked over our brief before going up to Allenby's camp. There General Bols smiled happily at us, and said, 'Well, we're in Salt all right'. To our amazed stares he went on that the chiefs of the Beni Sakhr had come into Jericho one morning, to offer the immediate co-operation of their twenty thousand tribesmen at Themed; and in his bath next day he had thought out a scheme, and fixed it all right.

I asked who the chief of the Beni Sakhr was, and he said 'Fahad': triumphing in his efficient inroad into what had been my province. It sounded madder and madder. I knew that Fahad could not raise four hundred men; and, that at the moment there was not a tent on Themed: they had moved south, to Young.

We hurried to the office for the real story, and learned that it was, unfortunately, as Bols had said. The British cavalry had gone impromptu up the hills of Moab on some airy promise of the Zebn sheikhs; greedy fellows who had ridden into Jerusalem only to taste Allenby's bounty but had there been taken at their mouth-value.

In this season there was no third partner at G.H.Q. Guy Dawnay, brother of our gladiator, he who had made the Jerusalem plan, had gone to Haig's staff: Bartholomew, who was to work out the autumn drive upon Damascus, was still with Chetwode. So the executive of Allenby's work in these months was unequal to the conception.

For, of course, this raid miscarried, while I was still in Jerusalem, solacing myself against the inadequacy of Bols with Storrs, now the urbane and artful Governor of the place. The Beni Sakhr were supine in their tents or away with Young. General Chauvel, without the help of one of them, saw the Turks re-open the Jordan fords behind his back and seize the road by which he had advanced. We escaped heavy disaster only because Allenby's instinct for a situation showed him his danger just in time. Yet we suffered painfully. The check taught the British to be more patient with Feisal's difficulties; convinced the Turks that the Amman sector was their danger point; and made the Beni Sakhr feel that the English were past understanding: not great fighting men, perhaps, but ready on the spur of the moment to be odd. So, in part, it redeemed the Amman failure by its deliberate repetition of what had looked accidental. At the same time it ruined the hopes which Feisal had entertained of acting independently with the Beni Sakhr. This cautious and very wealthy tribe asked for dependable allies.

Our movement, clean-cut while alone with a simple enemy, was now bogged in its partner's contingencies. We had to take our tune from Allenby, and he was not happy. The German offensive in France was stripping him of troops. He would retain Jerusalem, but could not afford a casualty, much less an attack, for months. The War Office promised him Indian divisions from Mesopotamia, and Indian drafts. With these he would rebuild his army on the Indian model; perhaps, after the summer, he might be again in fighting trim: but for the moment we must both just hold on.

This he told me on May the fifth, the date chosen under the Smuts arrangement for the heave northward of the whole army as prelude to the fall of Damascus and Aleppo. As first phase of his arrangement we had undertaken the liability of Maan: and Allenby's pause stuck us with this siege of a superior force. In addition, the Turks from Amman might now have leisure to sweep us off Aba el Lissan, back to Akaba. In so nasty a situation the common habit of joint operations — cursing the other partner — weighed strongly upon me. However, Allenby's staunchness was aiming to relieve us. He was threatening the enemy by a vast bridge-head across Jordan, as if he were about to cross a third time. So he would keep Amman tender. To strengthen us on our plateau he offered what technical equipment we needed.

We took the opportunity to ask for repeated air-raids on the Hejaz Railway. General Salmond was called in, and proved as generous, in word and deed, as the Commander-in-Chief. The Royal Air Force kept up a dull, troublesome pressure on Amman from now till the fall of Turkey. Much of the inactivity of the enemy in our lean season was due to the disorganization of their railway by bombing. At tea-time Allenby mentioned the Imperial Camel Brigade in Sinai, regretting that in the new stringency he must abolish it and use its men as mounted reinforcements. I asked: 'What are you going to do with their camels?' He laughed, and said, 'Ask "Q".'

Obediently, I went across the dusty garden, broke in upon the Quartermaster-General, Sir Walter Campbell — very Scotch — and repeated my question. He answered firmly that they were earmarked as divisional transport for the second of the new Indian divisions. I explained that I wanted two thousand of them. His first reply was irrelevant: his second conveyed that I might go on wanting. I argued, but he seemed unable to see my side at all. Of course, it was of the nature of a 'Q' to be costive.

I returned to Allenby and said aloud, before his party, that there were for disposal two thousand, two hundred riding-camels, and thirteen hundred baggage camels. All were provisionally allotted to transport; but of course, riding-camels were riding-camels. The staff whistled, and looked wise; as though they, too, doubted whether riding-camels could carry baggage. A technicality, even a sham one, might be helpful. Every British officer understood animals, as a point of honour. So I was not astonished when Sir Walter Campbell was asked to dine with the Commander-in-Chief that night.

We sat on the right hand and on the left, and with the soup Allenby began to talk about camels. Sir Walter broke out that the providential dispersing of the camel brigade brought the transport of the ——th Division up to strength; a godsend, for the Orient had been vainly ransacked for camels. He over-acted. Allenby, a reader of Milton, had an acute sense of style: and the line was a weak one. He cared nothing for strengths, the fetish of administrative branches.

He looked at me with a twinkle, 'And what do you want them for?' I reply hotly, 'To put a thousand men into Deraa any day you please'. He smiled and shook his head at Sir Walter Campbell, saying sadly, 'Q, you lose'. The goat became giddy and the sheep sheepish. It was an immense, a regal gift; the gift of unlimited mobility. The Arabs could now win their war when and where they liked.

Next morning I was off to join Feisal in his cool eyrie at Aba el Lissan. We discussed histories, tribes, migration, sentiments, the spring rains, pasture, at length. Finally, I remarked that Allenby had given us two thousand camels. Feisal gasped and caught my knee saying 'How?'

I told him all the story. He leaped up and kissed me; then he clapped his hands loudly. Hejris' black shape appeared at the tent-door. 'Hurry', cried Feisal, 'call them.' Hejris asked whom. 'Oh, Fahad, Abdulla el Feir, Auda, Motlog, Zaal . . .' 'And not Mirzuk?' queried Hejris mildly. Feisal shouted at him for a fool, and the black ran off; while I said, 'It is nearly finished. Soon you can let me go'. He protested, saying that I must remain with them always, and not just till Damascus, as I had promised in Um Lejj. I, who wanted so to get away.

Feet came pattering to the tent-door, and paused, while the chiefs recovered their grave faces and set straight their head-cloths for the entry. One by one they sat down stilly on the rugs, each saying unconcernedly, 'Please God, good?' To each Feisal replied, 'Praise God!' and they stared in wonder at his dancing eyes.

When the last had rustled in, Feisal told them that God had sent the means of victory — two thousand riding-camels. Our war was to march unchecked to freedom, its triumphant end. They murmured in astonishment; doing their best, as great men, to be calm; eyeing me to guess my share in the event. I said, 'The bounty of Allenby . . .' Zaal cut in swiftly for them all, 'God keep his life and yours'. I replied, 'We have been made victorious', stood up, with a 'by your leave' to Feisal, and slipped away to tell Joyce. Behind my back they burst out into wild words of their coming wilder deeds: childish, perhaps, but it would be a pretty war in which each man did not feel that he was winning it.

Joyce also was gladdened and made smooth by the news of the two thousand camels. We dreamed of the stroke to which they should be put: of their march from Beersheba to Akaba: and where for two months we could find grazing for this vast multitude of animals; they must be broken from barley if they were to be of use to us.

These were not pressing thoughts. We had, meanwhile, the need to maintain ourselves all summer on the plateau, besieging Maan, and keeping the railways cut. The task was difficult.

First, about supply. I had just thrown the existing arrangements out of gear. The Egyptian Camel Transport companies had been carrying steadily between Akaba and Aba el Lissan, but carrying less and marching less than our least sanguine estimate. We urged them to increase weights and speeds, but found ourselves up against cast-iron corps regulations, framed to keep down the figures of animal wastage. By increasing them slightly, we could double the carrying capacity of the column; consequently, I had offered to take over the animals and send back the Egyptian camel-men.

The British, being short of labour, jumped at my idea; almost too quickly. We had a terrible scramble to improvise drivers upon the moment. Goslett, single-handed, had hitherto done supplies, transport, ordnance, paymaster, base commandant. The extra work was cruelty to him. So Dawnay found Scott, a perfect Irishman, for base commandant. He had good temper, capacity, spirit. Akaba breathed quietly. Ordnance we gave to Bright, sergeant or sergeant-major: and Young took over transport and quartermaster work.

Young had overstrained himself, riding furiously between Naimat, Hejaia and Beni Sakhr, between Nasir and Mirzuk and Feisal, striving to combine and move them in one piece. Incidentally he had furiously overstrained the Arabs. In transport duties his drive and ability would be better employed. Using his full power, he grappled with the chaos. He had no stores for his columns, no saddles, no clerks, no veterinaries, no drugs and few drivers, so that to run a harmonious and orderly train was impossible; but Young very nearly did it, in his curious ungrateful way. Thanks to him, the supply problem of the Arab regulars on the plateau was solved.

All this time the face of our Revolt was growing. Feisal, veiled in his tent, maintained incessantly the teaching and preaching of his Arab movement. Akaba boomed: even our field-work was going well. The Arab regulars had just had their third success against Jerdun, the battered station which they made it almost a habit to take and lose. Our armoured cars happened on a Turkish sortie from Maan and smashed it in such style that the opportunity never recurred. Zeid, in command of half the army posted north of Uheida, was showing great vigour. His gaiety of spirit appealed more to the professional officers than did Feisal's poetry and lean earnestness; so this happy association of the two brothers gave every sort of man a sympathy with one or other of the leaders of the revolt.

Yet there were clouds in the north. At Amman was a forcible

Turkish concentration of troops earmarked for Maan when supply conditions would let them move. This supply reserve was being put in by rail from Damascus, as well as the bombing attacks of the Royal Air Force from Palestine permitted.

To make head against them, Nasir, our best guerilla general, had been appointed, in advance of Zeid, to do something great against the railway. He had camped in Wadi Hesa, with Hornby, full of explosives and Peake's trained section of Egyptian Army Camel Corps to help in demol'tion. Time, till Allenby recovered, was what we had to fight for, and Nasir would very much help our desire if he secured us a month's breathing space by playing the intangible ghost at the Turkish Army. If he failed we must expect the relief of Maan and an onslaught of the reinvigorated enemy upon Aba el Lissan.

CHAPTER XCVI

NASIR attacked Hesa station in his old fashion, cutting the line to north and south the night before, and opening a sharp bombardment of the buildings when it was light enough to see. Rasim was the gunner and the gun our Krupp antiquity of Medina, Wejh and Tafileh. When the Turks weakened, the Arabs charged into the station, Beni Sakhr and Howeitat vying for the lead.

We had, of course, no killed; as was ever the way with such tactics. Hornby and Peake reduced the place to a heap of ruins. They blew in the well, the tanks, engines, pumps, buildings, three bridges, rolling stock, and about four miles of rail. Next day Nasir moved north, and destroyed Faraifra station. Peake and Hornby continued work that day and the day following. Altogether it sounded like our biggest demolition. I determined to go up and see for myself.

A dozen of my men marched with me. Below the Rasheidiya ridge we came to the lone tree, Shejerat el Tayar. My Hauranis drew rein under its thorny branches, on which were impaled many tatters of wayfarers' offered clothes. Mohammed said, 'Upon you, O Mustafa'. Reluctantly Mustafa let himself down from his saddle and piece by piece took off his clothes, till nearly naked, when he lay down arching himself over the tumbled cairn. The other men dismounted, picked each a thorn, and in solemn file drove them (hard and sharp as brass) deep into his flesh and left them standing there. The Ageyl stared open-mouthed at the ceremony, but before it ended swung themselves monkey-like down, grinning lewdly, and stabbed in their thorns where they would be most painful. Mustafa shivered quietly till he heard Mohammed say, 'Get up', using the feminine inflexion. He sadly pulled out the thorns, dressed, and remounted. Abdulla knew no reason for the punishment: and the Hauranis' manner showed that they did not wish me to ask them. We reached Hesa to find Nasir, with six hundred men, concealed under cliffs and bushes, afraid of enemy aircraft, which had killed many. One bomb had fallen into a pool while eleven camels had been drinking, and had thrown them all, dead, in a ring about the water-side among torn flowers of oleander. We wrote to Air-Vice-Marshal Salmond for a revengeful counter-stroke.

The railway was still in Nasir's hand, and whenever they had explosives Hornby and Peake went down to it. They had blown in a cutting, and were developing a new rail-demolition, turning over each section by main force, as it was cut. From Sultani in the north to Jurf in the south, the damage extended. Fourteen miles. Nasir fully understood the importance of maintaining his activity, and there seemed a fair hope of his lasting. He had found a comfortable and bomb-proof cave between two limestone reefs, which, articulated like teeth, broke out from the green hill-side. The heat and flies in the valley were not yet formidable. It was running with water: fertile with pasture. Behind lay Tafileh; and if Nasir were hard pressed he had only to send a message, and the mounted peasantry of the villages, on their rough ponies jangling with shrill bells, would come pouring over the range to his support.

The day of our arrival the Turks sent a force of camel corps, cavalry and infantry, down to re-occupy Faraifra as a first counter-stroke. Nasir at once was up and at them. While his machine-guns kept down the Turks' heads, the Abu Tayi charged up to within a hundred yards of the crumbling wall which was the only defence, and cut out all the camels and some horses. To expose riding-animals to the sight of Beduins was a sure way to lose them.

Afterwards I was down with Auda, near the fork of the valley, when there came the throbbing and moaning overhead of Mercedes engines. Nature stilled itself before the master noise; even the birds and insects hushed. We crawled between fallen boulders, and heard the first bomb drop lower in the valley where Peake's camp lay hidden in a twelve-foot oleander thicket. The machines were flying towards us, for the next bombs were nearer; and the last fell just in front, with a shattering, dusty roar, by our captured camels.

When the smoke cleared, two of them were kicking in agony on the ground. A faceless man, spraying blood from a fringe of red flesh about his neck, stumbled screaming towards our rocks. He crashed blindly over one and another, tripping and scrambling with arms outstretched, maddened by pain. In a moment he lay quiet, and we who had scattered from him ventured near: but he was dead.

I went back to Nasir, safe in his cave with Nawaf el Faiz, brother of Mithgal, head of the Beni Sakhr. Nawaf, a shifty man, was so full and careful of his pride that he would stoop to any private meanness to preserve it publicly: but then he was mad, like all the Faiz clan; uncertain like them; and voluble, with flickering eyes.

Our acquaintance of before the war had been renewed secretly a year before, when three of us crept in after sunset to their rich family tents near Ziza. Fawaz, the senior Faiz, was a notable Arab, a committeeman of the Damascus group, prominent in the party of independence. He received me with fair words and hospitality, fed us richly, and brought out, after we had talked, his richest bed-quilts.

I had slept an hour or two when a charged voice whispered through a smoke-smelling beard into my ear. It was Nawaf, the brother, to say that, behind the friendly seeming, Fawaz had sent horsemen to Ziza and soon the troops would be here to take me. We were certainly caught. My Arabs crouched in their place, meaning to fight like cornered animals, and kill at least some of the enemy before they themselves died. Such tactics displeased me. When combats came to the physical, bare hand against hand, I was finished. The disgust of being touched revolted me more than the thought of death and defeat: perhaps because one such terrible struggle in my youth had given me an enduring fear of contact: or because I so reverenced my wits and depised my body that I would not be beholden to the second for the life of the first.

I whispered to Nawaf for counsel. He crawled back through the tent-curtain; we followed dragging my few things in their light saddle-pouch. Behind the next tent, his own, sat the camels, knee-haltered and saddled. We mounted circumspectly. Nawaf led out his mare, and guided us, loaded rifle across his thigh, to the railway and beyond it into the desert. There he gave us the star-direction of our supposed goal in Bair. A few days later Sheikh Fawaz was dead.

CHAPTER XCVII

I EXPLAINED to Feisal that Nasir's cutting of the line would endure another month; and, after the Turks had got rid of him, it would be yet a third month before they attacked us in Aba el Lissan. By then our new camels should be fit for use in an offensive of our own. I suggested that we ask his father, King Hussein, to transfer to Akaba the regular units at present with Ali and Abdulla. Their reinforcement would raise us to ten thousand strong, in uniformed men.

We would divide them into three parts. The immobile would constitute a retaining force to hold Maan quiet. A thousand, on our new camels, would attack the Deraa-Damascus sector. The balance would form a second expedition, of two or three thousand infantry, to move into the Beni Sakhr country and connect with Allenby at Jericho. The long-distance mounted raid, by taking Deraa or Damascus would compel the Turks to withdraw from Palestine one division, or even two, to restore their communications. By so weakening the enemy, we would give Allenby the power to advance his line, at any rate to Nablus. The fall of Nablus would cut the lateral communication which made the Turks strong in Moab; and they would be compelled to fall back on Amman, yielding us quiet possession of the Jordan bottom. Practically I was proposing that we use up the Hauran Arabs to let us reach Jericho, half-way to our Damascus goal. Feisal fell in with the proposal, and gave me letters to his father advising it. Unhappily the old man was, nowadays, little inclined to take his advice, out of green-eyed hatred for his son who was doing too well and was being disproportionately helped by the British. For dealing with the King I relied on joint-action by Wingate and Allenby, his paymasters. I decided to go up to Egypt personally, to press them to write him letters of the necessary stiffness. In Cairo, Dawnay agreed both to the transfer of the southern regulars, and to the independent offensive. We went to Wingate, argued it, and convinced him that the ideas were good. He wrote letters to King Hussein strongly advising the reinforcement of Feisal. I pressed him to make clear to the King that the continuance of a war-subsidy would depend on his giving effect to our advice: but he refused to be stringent, and couched the letter in terms of politeness, which would be lost on the hard and suspicious old man in Mecca.

Yet the effort promised so much for us that we went up to Allenby, to beg his help with the King. At G.H.Q., we felt a remarkable difference in the air. The place was, as always, throbbing with energy and hope, but now logic and co-ordination were manifest in an uncommon degree. Allenby had a curious blindness of judgement in choosing men, due largely to his positive greatness, which made good qualities in his subordinates seem superfluous; but Chetwode, not content, had interposed again, setting up Bartholomew, his own Chief of Staff, in the third place of the hierarchy. Bartholomew, not made, like Dawnay, with many foreign sides to his imagination, was yet more intricate, yet more polished as a soldier, more careful and conscientious, and seemed a friendly team-leader.

We unrolled before him our scheme to start the ball rolling in the autumn, hoping by our pushes to make it possible for him to come in later vigorously to our support. He listened smiling, and said that we were three days too late. Their new army was arriving to time from Mesopotamia and India; prodigious advances in grouping and training were being made. On June the fifteenth it had been the considered opinion of a private conference that the army would be capable of a general and sustained offensive in September.

The sky was, indeed, opening over us; and we went in to Allenby, who said outright that late in September he would make a grand attack to fulfil the Smuts' plan even to Damascus and Aleppo. Our role would be as laid down in the spring; we must make the Deraa raid on the two thousand new camels. Times and details would be fixed as the weeks went on, and as Bartholomew's calculations took shape.

Our hope of victory had been too often dashed for me to take this as assured. So, for second string, I got Allenby's blessing upon the transfer of Ali's and Abdulla's khaki-clad contingents; and set off, fortified, to Jeddah, where I had no more success than I expected. The

King had got wind of my purpose and took refuge, on the pretext of Ramadhan, in Mecca, his inaccessible capital. We talked over the telephone, King Hussein sheltering himself behind the incompetence of the operators in the Mecca exchange, whenever the subject turned dangerous. My thronged mind was not in the mood for farce, so I rang off, put Feisal's, Wingate's and Allenby's letters back unopened into my bag and returned to Cairo in the next ship.

BOOK IX

BALANCING FOR A LAST EFFORT

Chapters XCVIII to CVI

ALLENBY, *in rapid embodiment of reliefs from India and Mesopotamia, so surpassed hope that he was able to plan an Autumn offensive. The near balance of the forces on each side meant that victory would depend on his subtly deceiving the Turks that their entire danger yet lay beyond the Jordan.*

We might help, by lying quiet for six weeks, feigning a feebleness which should tempt the Turks to attack.

The Arabs were then to lead off at the critical moment by cutting the railway communications of Palestine.

Such bluff within bluff called for most accurate timing, since the balance would have been wrecked either by a premature Turkish retreat in Palestine, or by their premature attack against the Arabs beyond Jordan. We borrowed from Allenby some Imperial Camel Corps to lend extra colour to our supposed critical situation; while preparations for Deraa went on with no more check than an untimely show of pique from King Hussein.

CHAPTER XCVIII

O<small>N</small> July the eleventh Dawnay and I were again talking to Allenby and Bartholomew, and, of their generosity and confidence, seeing the undress working of a general's mind. It was an experience: technical, reassuring, and very valuable to me, who was mildly a general, too, in my own odd show. Bols was on leave while the plans were working out. Sir Walter Campbell also was absent; Bartholomew and Evans, their deputies, plotted to re-arrange the army transport, regardless of formations, with such elasticity that any pursuit could be sustained.

Allenby's confidence was like a wall. Before the attack he went to see his troops massed in secrecy, waiting the signal, and told them he was sure, with their good help, of thirty thousand prisoners; this, when the whole game turned on a chance! Bartholomew was most anxious. He said it would be desperate work to have the whole army re-formed by September, and, even if they were ready (actually some brigades existed as such for the first time when they went over), we must not assume that the attack would follow as planned. It could be delivered only in the coastal sector, opposite Ramleh, the railhead, where only could a necessary reserve of stores be gathered. This seemed so obvious that he could not dream of the Turks staying blind, though momently their dispositions ignored it.

Allenby's plan was to collect the bulk of his infantry and all his cavalry under the orange and olive groves of Ramlegh just before September the nineteenth. Simultaneously he hoped to make in the Jordan Valley such demonstrations as should persuade the Turks of a concentration there in progress. The two raids to Salt had fixed the Turks' eyes exclusively beyond Jordan. Every move there, whether of British or Arabs, was accompanied by counter-precautions on the Turks' part, showing how fearful they were. In the coast sector, the area of real danger, the enemy had absurdly few men. Success hung on maintaining them in this fatal mis-appreciation.

After the Meinertzhagen success, deceptions, which for the ordinary general were just witty hors d'œuvres before battle, became for Allenby a main point of strategy. Bartholomew would accordingly erect (near Jericho) all condemned tents in Egypt; would transfer veterinary hospitals and sick lines there; would put dummy camps, dummy horses and dummy troops wherever there was plausible room; would throw more bridges across the river; would collect and open against enemy country all captured guns; and on the right days would ensure the movement of non-combatant bodies along the dusty roads, to give the impression of eleventh-hour concentrations for an assault. At the same time the Royal Air Force was going to fill the air with husbanded formations of the latest fighting machines. The preponderance of these would deprive the enemy for days of the advantage of air reconnaissance.

Bartholomew wished us to supplement his efforts with all vigour and ingenuity, from our side of Amman. Yet he warned us that, even with this, success would hang on a thread, since the Turks could save themselves and their army, and give us our concentration to do over again, by simply retiring their coast sector seven or eight miles. The British Army would then be like a fish flapping on dry land, with its railways, its heavy artillery, its dumps, its stores, its camps all misplaced; and without olive groves in which to hide its concentration next time. So, while he guaranteed that the British were doing their utmost, he implored us not to engage the Arabs, on his behalf, in a position from which they could not escape.

The noble prospect sent Dawnay and myself back to Cairo in great fettle and cogitation. News from Akaba had raised again the question of defending the plateau against the Turks, who had just turned Nasir out of Hesa and were contemplating a stroke against Aba el Lissan about the end of August, when our Deraa detachment should start. Unless we could delay the Turks another fortnight, their threat might cripple us. A new factor was urgently required.

At this juncture Dawnay was inspired to think of the surviving battalion of the Imperial Camel Corps. Perhaps G.H.Q. might lend it us to confuse the Turks' reckoning. We telephoned Bartholomew, who understood, and backed our request to Bols in Alexandria, and to Allenby. After an active telegraphing, we got our way. Colonel

Buxton, with three hundred men, was lent to us for a month on two conditions: first, that we should forthwith furnish their scheme of operations; second, that they should have no casualties. Bartholomew felt it necessary to apologize for the last magnificent, heart-warming condition, which he thought unsoldierly!

Dawnay and I sat down with a map and measured that Buxton should march from the Canal to Akaba; thence, by Rum, to carry Mudowwara by night-attack; thence by Bair, to destroy the bridge and tunnel near Amman; and back to Palestine on August the thirtieth. Their activity would give us a peaceful month, in which our two thousand new camels could learn to graze, while carrying the extra dumps of forage and food which Buxton's force would expect.

As we worked out these schemes, there came from Akaba one more elaborate, worked out graphically by Young for Joyce, on our June understanding for independent Arab operations in Hauran. They had figured out the food, ammunition, forage, and transport for two thousand men of all ranks, from Aba el Lissan to Deraa. They had taken into consideration all our resources and worked out schedules by which dumps would be completed and the attack begun in November.

Even had Allenby not pulled his army together this scheme would have broken down intrinsically. It depended on the immediate reinforcement of the Arab Army at Aba el Lissan, which King Hussein had refused; also November was too near to winter, with its muddy impassable roads in the Hauran.

Weather and strengths might be matters of opinion: but Allenby meant to attack on September the nineteenth, and wanted us to lead off not more than four nor less than two days before he did. His words to me were that three men and a boy with pistols in front of Deraa on September the sixteenth would fill his conception; would be better than thousands a week before or a week after. The truth was, he cared nothing for our fighting power, and did not reckon us part of his tactical strength. Our purpose, to him, was moral, psychological, diathetic; to keep the enemy command intent upon the trans-Jordan front. In my English capacity I shared this view, but on my Arab side both agitation and battle seemed equally important, the one to serve the joint success, the other to establish Arab self-respect, without which victory would not be wholesome.

So, unhesitatingly, we laid the Young scheme aside and turned to build up our own. To reach Deraa from Aba el Lissan would take a fortnight: the cutting of the three railways and withdrawal to reform in the desert, another week. Our raiders must carry their maintenance for three weeks. The picture of what this meant was in my head — we had been doing it for two years — and so at once I gave Dawnay my estimate that our two thousand camels, in a single journey, without advanced depots or supplementary supply columns, would suffice five hundred regular mounted infantry, the battery of French quick-firing .65 mountain guns, proportionate machine-guns, two armoured cars, sappers, camel-scouts, and two aeroplanes until we had fulfilled our mission. This seemed like a liberal reading of Allenby's three men and a boy. We told Bartholomew, and received G.H.Q. blessing.

Young and Joyce were not best pleased when I returned to say that the great schedule had been torn up. I did not call their plans top-heavy and too late: I threw the onus of change on Allenby's recovery. My new proposal — for which in advance I had pledged their perform-ance — was an intricate dovetailing in the next crowded month and a half, of a 'spoiling' raid by the British Camel Corps and the main raid to surprise the Turks by Deraa.

Joyce felt that I had made a mistake. To introduce foreigners would unman the Arabs; and to let them go a month later would be even worse. Young returned a stubborn, combative 'impossible' to my idea. The Camel Corps would engross the baggage camels, which otherwise might have enabled the Deraa force to reach its goal. By trying to do two greedy things I should end in doing neither. I argued my case and we had a battle.

In the first place I tackled Joyce concerning the Imperial Camel Corps. They would arrive one morning at Akaba — no Arab suspect-ing them — and would vanish equally suddenly towards Rumm. From Mudowwara to Kissir bridge they would march in the desert, far from the sight of the Arab Army, and from the hearing of the villages. In the resultant vagueness the enemy intelligence would conclude that the whole of the defunct camel brigade was now on Feisal's front. Such an accession of shock-strength to Feisal would make the Turks very tender of the safety of their railway: while Buxton's appearance at Kissir, apparently on preliminary reconnaissance, would put credence into the wildest tales of our intention shortly to attack Amman. Joyce, disarmed by these reasonings, now backed me with his favourable opinion.

For Young's transport troubles I had little sympathy. He, a newcomer, said my problems were insoluble: but I had done such things casually, without half his ability and concentration; and knew they were not even difficult. For the Camel Corps, we left him to grapple with weights and time-tables, since the British Army was his profession; and though he would not promise anything (except that it could not be done), done of course it was, and two or three days before the necessary time. The Deraa raid was a different proposition, and point by point I disputed his conception of its nature and equipment.

I crossed out forage, the heaviest item, after Bair. Young became ironic upon the patient endurance of camels: but this year the pasture was grand in the Azrak Deraa region. From the men's food I cut off provision for the second attack, and the return journey. Young supposed aloud that the men would fight well hungry. I explained that we would live on the country. Young thought it a poor country to live on. I called it very good.

He said that the ten days' march home after the attacks would be a long fast: but I had no intention of coming back to Akaba. Then might he ask if it was defeat or victory which was in my mind? I pointed out how each man had a camel under him, and if we killed only six camels a day the whole force would feed abundantly. Yet this did not solace him. I went on to cut down his petrol, cars, ammunition, and everything else to the exact point, without margin, which would meet what we planned. In riposte he became aggressively regular. I prosed forth on my hoary theorem that we lived by our raggedness and beat the Turk by our uncertainty. Young's scheme was faulty, because precise.

Instead, we would march a camel column of one thousand men to Azrak where their concentration must be complete on September the thirteenth. On the sixteenth we would envelop Deraa, and cut its railways. Two days later we would fall back east of the Hejaz Railway and wait events with Allenby. As reserve against accident we would purchase barley in Jebel Druse, and store it at Azrak.

Nuri Shaalan would accompany us with a contingent of Rualla: also the Serdiyeh; the Serahin; and Haurani peasants of the 'Hollow Land', under Talal el Hareidhin. Young thought it a deplorable adventure. Joyce, who had loved our dog-fight conference, was game to try, though doubting I was ambitious. However, it was sure that both would do their best, since the thing was already settled; and Dawnay had helped the organizing side by getting us from G.H.Q. the loan of Stirling, a skilled staff officer, tactful and wise. Stirling's passion for horses was a passport to intimacy with Feisal and the chiefs.

Among the Arab officers were distributed some British military decorations, tokens of their gallantry about Maan. These marks of Allenby's esteem heartened the Arab Army. Nuri Pasha Said offered to command the Deraa expedition, for which his courage, authority and coolness marked him as the ideal leader. He began to pick for it the best four hundred men in the army.

Pisani, the French commandant, fortified by a Military Cross, and in urgent pursuit of a D.S.O., took bodily possession of the four Schneider guns which Cousse had sent down to us after Bremond left; and spent agonized hours with Young, trying to put the scheduled ammunition, and mule-forage, with his men and his own private kitchen on to one-half the requisite camels. The camps buzzed with eagerness and preparations, and all promised well.

Our own family rifts were distressing, but inevitable. The Arab affair had now outgrown our rough and ready help-organization. But the next was probably the last act, and by a little patience we might make our present resources serve. The troubles were only between ourselves, and thanks to the magnificent unselfishness of Joyce, we preserved enough of team-spirit to prevent a complete breakdown, however high-handed I appeared: and I had a reserve of confidence to carry the whole thing, if need be, on my shoulders. They used to think me boastful when I said so: but my confidence was not so much ability to do a thing perfectly, as a preference for botching it somehow rather than letting it go altogether by default.

CHAPTER XCIX

IT was now the end of July, and by the end of August the Deraa expedition must be on the road. In the meantime Buxton's Camel Corps had to be guided through their programme, Nuri Shaalan warned, the armoured cars taught their road to Azrak, and landing-grounds found for aeroplanes. A busy month. Nuri Shaalan, the furthest, was tackled first. He was called to meet Feisal at Jefer about August the seventh. Buxton's force seemed the second need. I told Feisal, under seal, of their coming. To ensure their having no casualties, they must strike Mudowwara with absolute surprise. I would guide them myself to Rumm, in the first critical march through the fag-ends of Howeitat about Akaba.

Accordingly I went down to Akaba, where Buxton let me explain to each company their march, and the impatient nature of the Allies whom they, unasked, had come to help; begging them to turn the other cheek if there was a row; partly because they were better educated than the Arabs, and therefore less prejudiced; partly because they were very few. After such solemnities came the ride up the oppressive gorge of Itm, under the red cliffs of Nejed and over the breast-like curves of Imran — that slow preparation for Rumm's greatness — till we passed through the gap before the rock Khuzail, and into the inner shrine of the springs, with its worship-compelling coolness. There the landscape refused to be accessory, but took the skies, and we chattering humans became dust at its feet.

In Rumm the men had their first experience of watering in equality with Arabs, and found it troublesome. However, they were wonderfully mild, and Buxton was an old Sudan official, speaking Arabic, and understanding nomadic ways; very patient, good-humoured, sympathetic. Hazaa was helpful in admonishing the Arabs, and Stirling and Marshall, who accompanied the column, were familiars of the Beni Atiyeh. Thanks to their diplomacy, and to the care of the British rank and file, nothing untoward happened.

I stayed at Rumm for their first day, dumb at the unreality of these healthy-looking fellows, like stiff-bodied school boys in their shirt-sleeves and shorts, as they wandered, anonymous and irresponsible, about the cliffs which had been my private resort. Three years of Sinai had burned the colour from their tanned faces, in which the blue eyes flickered weakly against the dark possessed gaze of the Beduin. For the rest they were a broad-faced, low-browed people, blunt-featured beside the fine-drawn Arabs whom generations of in-breeding had sharpened to a radiance ages older than the primitive, blotched, honest Englishmen. Continental soldiers looked lumpish beside our lean-bred fellows: but against my supple Nejdis the British in their turn looked lumpish.

Later I rode for Akaba, through the high-walled Itm, alone now with six silent, unquestioning guards, who followed after me like shadows, harmonious and submerged in their natural sand and bush and hill; and a home-sickness came over me, stressing vividly my outcast life among these Arabs, while I exploited their highest ideals and made their love of freedom one more tool to help England win.

It was evening, and on the straight bar of Sinai ahead the low sun was falling, its globe extravagantly brilliant in my eyes, because I was dead-tired of my life, longing as seldom before for the moody skies of England. This sunset was fierce, stimulant, barbaric; reviving the colours of the desert like a draught — as indeed it did each evening, in a new miracle of strength and heat — while my longings were for weakness, chills and grey mistiness, that the world might not be so crystalline clear, so definitely right and wrong.

We English, who lived years abroad among strangers, went always dressed in the pride of our remembered country, that strange entity which had no part with the inhabitants, for those who loved England most, often liked Englishmen least. Here, in Arabia, in the war's need, I was trading my honesty for her sustenance, inevitably.

In Akaba the rest of my bodyguard were assembled, prepared for victory, for I had promised the Hauran men that they should pass this great feast in their freed villages: and its date was near. So for the last time we mustered on the windy beach by the sea's edge, the sun on its brilliant waves glinting in rivalry with my flashing and changing men.

They were sixty. Seldom had the Zaagi brought so many of his troop together, and as we rode into the brown hills for Guweira he was busy sorting them in Ageyl fashion, centre and wings, with poets and singers on the right and left. So our ride was musical. It hurt him I would not have a banner, like a prince.

I was on my Ghazala, the old grandmother camel, now again magnificently fit. Her foal had lately died, and Abdulla, who rode next me, had skinned the little carcase, and carried the dry pelt behind his saddle, like a crupper piece. We started well, thanks to the Zaagi's chanting, but after an hour Ghazala lifted her head high, and began to pace uneasily, picking up her feet like a sword-dancer.

I tried to urge her; but Abdulla dashed alongside me, swept his cloak about him, and sprang from his saddle, calf's skin in hand. He lighted with a splash of gravel in front of Ghazala, who had come to a standstill, gently moaning. On the ground before her he spread the little hide, and drew her head down to it. She stopped crying, shuffled its dryness thrice with her lips; then again lifted her head and, with a whimper, strode forward. Several times in the day this happened; but afterwards she seemed to forget.

At Guweira, Siddons had an aeroplane waiting. Nuri Shaalan and Feisal wanted me at once in Jefer. The air was thin and bumpy, so that we hardly scraped over the crest of Shtar. I sat wondering if we would crash, almost hoping it. I felt sure Nuri was about to claim fulfilment of our dishonourable half-bargain, whose execution seemed more impure than its thought. Death in the air would be a clean escape; yet I scarcely hoped it, not from fear, for I was too tired to be much afraid: nor from scruple, for our lives seemed to me absolutely our own, to keep or give away: but from habit, for lately I had risked myself only when it seemed profitable to our cause.

I was busy compartmenting-up my mind, finding instinct and reason as ever at strong war. Instinct said 'Die', but reason said that was only to cut the mind's tether, and loose it into freedom: better to seek some mental death, some slow wasting of the brain to sink it below these puzzlements. An accident was meaner than deliberate fault. If I did not hesitate to risk my life, why fuss to dirty it? Yet life and honour seemed in different categories, not able to be sold one for another: and for honour, had I not lost that a year ago when I assured the Arabs that England kept her plighted word?

Or was honour like the Sybil's leaves, the more that was lost the more precious the little left? Its part equal to the whole? My self-secrecy had left me no arbiter of responsibility. The debauch of physical work yet ended in a craving for more, while the everlasting doubt, the questioning, bound up my mind in a giddy spiral and left me never space for thought.

So we came at last, alive, to Jefer, where met us Feisal and Nuri in the smoothest spirits, with no mention of my price. It seemed incredible that this old man had freely joined our youth. For he was very old; livid, and worn, with a grey sorrow and remorse about him and a bitter smile the only mobility of his face. Upon his coarse eyelashes the eyelids sagged down in tired folds, through which, from the overhead sun, a red light glittered into his eye-sockets and made them look like fiery pits in which the man was slowly burning. Only the dead black of his dyed hair, only the dead skin of the face, with its net of lines, betrayed his seventy years.

There was ceremonial talk about this little-spoken leader, for with him were the head men of his tribe, famous sheikhs so bodied out with silks of their own wearing, or of Feisal's gift, that they rustled like women while moving in slow state like oxen. First of them was Faris: like Hamlet, not forgiving Nuri his murdered father, Sottam: a lean man with drooping moustache, and white, unnatural face, who met the hidden censure of the world with a soft manner and luscious deprecating voice. '*Yifham*' he squeaked of me in astonishment 'He understands our Arabic'. Trad and Sultan were there, round-eyed, grave, and direct-spoken; honourable figures of men, and great leaders of cavalry. Also Mijhem, the rebellious, had been brought in by Feisal and reconciled with his unwilling uncle, who seemed only half to tolerate his small-featured bleak presence beside him, though Mijhem's manner was eagerly friendly.

Mijhem was a great leader too, Trad's rival in the conduct of raids, but weak and cruel at heart. He sat next Khalid, Trad's brother, another healthy, cheerful rider, like Trad in face, but not so full a man. Durzi ibn Dughmi swelled in and welcomed me, reminding me ungratefully of his greediness at Nebk: a one-eyed, sinister, hook-nosed man; heavy, menacing and mean, but brave. There was the Khaffaji, the spoilt child of Nuri's age, who looked for equality of friendliness from me, because of his father, and not for any promise in himself: he was young enough to be glad of the looming adventure of war and proud of his new bristling weapons.

Bender, the laughing boy, fellow in years and play with the Khaffaji, tripped me before them all by begging for a place in my bodyguard. He had heard from my Rahail, his foster-brother, of their immoderate griefs and joys, and servitude called to him with its unwholesome glamour. I fenced, and when he pleaded further, turned it by muttering that I was not a King to have Shaalan servants. Nuri's sombre look met mine for a moment, in approval.

Beside me sat Rahail, peacocking his lusty self in strident clothes. Under cover of the conversation he whispered me the name of each chief. They had not to ask who I was, for my clothes and appearance were peculiar in the desert. It was notoriety to be the only cleanshaven one, and I doubled it by wearing always the suspect pure silk, of the whitest (at least outside), with a gold and crimson Meccan head-rope, and gold dagger. By so dressing I staked a claim which Feisal's public consideration of me confirmed.

Many times in such councils had Feisal won over and set aflame new tribes, many times had the work fallen to me; but never until to-day had we been actively together in one company, reinforcing and relaying one another, from our opposite poles: and the work went like child's play; the Rualla melted in our double heat. We could move them with a touch and a word. There was tenseness, a holding of breath, the glitter of belief in their thin eyes so fixed on us.

Feisal brought nationality to their minds in a phrase, which set them thinking of Arab history and language; then he dropped into silence for a moment: for with these illiterate masters of the tongue words were lively, and they liked to savour each, unmingled, on the palate. Another phrase showed them the spirit of Feisal, their fellow and leader, sacrificing everything for the national freedom; and then silence again, while they imagined him day and night in his tent, teaching, preaching, ordering and making friends: and they felt something of the idea behind this pictured man sitting there iconically, drained of desires, ambitions, weakness, faults; so rich a personality enslaved by an abstraction, made one-eyed, one armed, with the one sense and purpose, to live or die in its service.

Of course it was a picture-man; not flesh and blood, but nevertheless true, for his individuality had yielded its third dimension to the idea, had surrendered the world's wealth and artifices. Feisal was hidden in his tent, veiled to remain our leader: while in reality he was nationality's best servant, its tool, not its owner. Yet in the tented twilight nothing seemed more noble.

He went on to conjure up for them the trammelled enemy on the eternal defensive, whose best end was to have done no more than the necessary. While we abstinents swam calmly and coolly in the friendly silence of the desert, till pleased to come ashore.

Our conversation was cunningly directed to light trains of their buried thoughts; that the excitement might be their own and the conclusions native, not inserted by us. Soon we felt them kindle: we leaned back, watching them move and speak, and vivify each other with mutual heat, till the air was vibrant, and in stammered phrases they experienced the first heave and thrust of notions which ran up beyond their sight. They turned to hurry us, themselves the begetters, and we laggard strangers: strove to make us comprehend the full intensity of their belief; forgot us; flashed out the means and end of our desire. A new tribe was added to our comity: though Nuri's plain 'Yes' at the end carried more than all had said.

In our preaching there was nothing merely nervous. We did our best to exclude the senses, that our support might be slow, durable, unsentimental. We wanted no rice-converts. Persistently we did refuse to let our abundant and famous gold bring over those not spiritually convinced. The money was a confirmation; mortar, not building stone. To have bought men would have put our movement on the base of interest; whereas our followers must be ready to go all the way without other mixture in their motives than human frailty. Even I, the stranger, the godless fraud inspiring an alien nationality, felt a delivery from the hatred and eternal questioning of self in my imitation of their bondage to the idea; and this despite the lack of instinct in my own performance.

For naturally I could not long deceive myself; but my part was worked out so flippantly that none but Joyce, Nesib and Mohammed el Dheilan seemed to know I was acting. With man-instinctive, anything believed by two or three had a miraculous sanction to which individual ease and life might honestly be sacrificed. To man-rational, wars of nationality were as much a cheat as religious wars, and nothing was worth fighting for: nor could fighting, the act of fighting, hold any meed of intrinsic virtue. Life was so deliberately private that no circumstances could justify one man in laying violent hands upon another's: though a man's own death was his last free will, a saving grace and measure of intolerable pain.

We made the Arabs strain on tip-toe to reach our creed, for it led to works, a dangerous country where men might take the deed for the will. My fault, my blindness of leadership (eager to find a quick means to conversion) allowed them this finite image of our end, which properly existed only in unending effort towards unattainable imagined light. Our crowd seeking light in things were like pathetic dogs snuffling round the shank of a lamp-post. It was only myself who valeted the abstract, whose duty took him beyond the shrine.

The irony was in my loving objects before life or ideas; the incongruity in my answering the infectious call of action, which laid weight on the diversity of things. It was a hard task for me to straddle feeling and action. I had had one craving all my life — for the power of self-expression in some imaginative form — but had been too diffuse ever to acquire a technique. At last accident, with perverted humour, in casting me as a man of action had given me place in the Arab Revolt, a theme ready and epic to a direct eye and hand, thus offering me an outlet in literature, the technique-less art. Whereupon I became excited only over mechanism. The epic mode was alien to me, as to my generation. Memory gave me no clue to the heroic, so that I could not feel such men as Auda in myself. He seemed fantastic as the hills of Rumm, old as Mallory.

Among the Arabs I was the disillusioned, the sceptic, who envied their cheap belief. The unperceived sham looked so well-fitting and becoming a dress for shoddy man. The ignorant, the superficial, the deceived were the happy among us. By our swindle they were glorified. We paid for them our self-respect, and they gained the deepest feeling of their lives. The more we condemned and despised ourselves, the more we could cynically take pride in them, our creatures. It was so easy to overcredit others: so impossible to write down their motives to the level of our own uncharitable truth. They were our dupes, wholeheartedly fighting the enemy. They blew before our intentions like chaff, being not chaff, but the bravest, simplest and merriest of men. *Credo quia sum?* But did not the being believed by many make for a distorted righteousness? The mounting together of the devoted hopes of years from near-sighted multitudes, might endow even an unwilling idol with Godhead, and strengthen It whenever men prayed silently to Him.

CHAPTER C

UPON this text my mind went weaving across its dusty space, amid the sunbeam thoughts and their dancing motes of idea. Then I saw that this preferring the Unknown to the God was a scapegoat idea, which lulled only to a false peace. To endure by order, or because it was a duty — that was easy. The soldier suffered only involuntary knocks; whereas our will had to play the ganger till the workmen fainted, to keep in a safe place and thrust others into danger. It might have been heroic to have offered up my own life for a cause in which I could not believe: but it was a theft of souls to make others die in sincerity for my graven image. Because they accepted our message as truth, they were ready to be killed for it; a condition which made their acts more proper than glorious, a logical bastard fortitude, suitable to a profit and loss balance of conduct. To invent a message, and then with open eye to perish for its self-made image — that was greater.

The whole business of the movement seemed to be expressible only in terms of death and life. Generally we were conscious of our flesh because it hurt us. Joy came sharper from our long habitude of pain; but our resources in suffering seemed greater than our capacity for gladness. Lethargy played its part here. Both emotions were in our gift, for our pain was full of eddies, confusing its purity.

A reef on which many came to a shipwreck of estimation was the vanity that our endurance might win redemption, perhaps for all a race. Such false investiture bred a hot though transient satisfaction, in that we felt we had assumed another's pain or experience, his personality. It was triumph, and a mood of enlargement; we had avoided our sultry selves, conquered our geometrical completeness, snatched a momentary 'change of mind'.

Yet in reality we had borne the vicarious for our own sakes, or at least because it was pointed for our benefit: and could escape from this knowledge only by a make-belief in sense as well as in motive.

The self-immolated victim took for his own the rare gift of sacrifice;

and no pride and few pleasures in the world were so joyful, so rich as this choosing voluntarily another's evil to perfect the self. There was a hidden selfishness in it, as in all perfections. To each opportunity there could be only one vicar, and the snatching of it robbed the fellows of their due hurt. Their vicar rejoiced, while his brethren were wounded in their manhood. To accept humbly so rich a release was imperfection in them: their gladness at the saving of its cost was sinful in that it made them accessory, part-guilty of inflicting it upon their mediator. His purer part, for the mediator, might have been to stand among the crowd, to watch another win the cleanness of a redeemer's name. By the one road lay self-perfection, by the other self-immolation, and a making perfect of the neighbour. Hauptmann told us to take as generously as we gave: but rather we seemed like the cells of a bee-comb, of which one might change, or swell itself, only at the cost of all.

To endure for another in simplicity gave a sense of greatness. There was nothing loftier than a cross, from which to contemplate the world. The pride and exhilaration of it were beyond conceit. Yet each cross, occupied, robbed the late-comers of all but the poor part of copying: and the meanest of things were those done by example. The virtue of sacrifice lay within the victim's soul.

Honest redemption must have been free and child-minded. When the expiator was conscious of the under-motives and the after-glory of his act, both were wasted on him. So the introspective altruist appropriated a share worthless, indeed harmful, to himself, for had he remained passive, his cross might have been granted to an innocent. To rescue simple ones from such evil by paying for them his complicated self would be avaricious in the modern man. He, thought-riddled, could not share their belief in others' discharge through his agony, and they, looking on him without understanding, might feel the shame which was the manly disciple's lot: or might fail to feel it and incur the double punishment of ignorance.

Or was this shame, too, a self-abnegation, to be admitted and admired for its own sake? How was it right to let men die because they did not understand? Blindness and folly aping the way of right were punished more heavily than purposed evil, at least in the present consciousness and remorse of man alive. Complex men who knew how self-sacrifice uplifted the redeemer and cast down the bought, and who held back in this knowledge, might so let a foolish brother take the place of false nobility and its later awakened due of heavier sentence. There seemed no straight walking for us leaders in this crooked lane of conduct, ring within ring of unknown, shamefaced motives cancelling or double-charging their precedents.

Yet I cannot put down my acquiescence in the Arab fraud to weakness of character or native hypocrisy: though of course I must have had some tendency, some aptitude, for deceit, or I would not have deceived men so well, and persisted two years in bringing to success a deceit which others had framed and set afoot. I had had no concern with the Arab Revolt in the beginning. In the end I was responsible for its being an embarrassment to the inventors. Where exactly in the interim my guilt passed from accessory to principal, upon what headings I should be condemned, were not for me to say. Suffice it that since the march to Akaba I bitterly repented my entanglement in the movement, with a bitterness sufficient to corrode my inactive hours, but insufficient to make me cut myself clear of it. Hence the wobbling of my will, and endless, vapid complainings.

SIDDONS flew me back to Guweira that evening, and in the night at Akaba I told Dawnay, just arrived, that life was full, but slipping smoothly. Next morning we heard by aeroplane how Buxton's force had fared at Mudowwara. They decided to assault it before dawn mainly by means of bombers, in three parties, one to enter the station, the other two for the main redoubts.

Accordingly, before midnight white tapes were laid as guides to the zero point. The opening had been timed for a quarter to four but the way proved difficult to find, so that daylight was almost upon them before things began against the southern redoubt. After a number of bombs had burst in and about it, the men rushed up and took it easily — to find that the station party had achieved their end a moment before. These alarms roused the middle redoubt, but only for defeat. Its men surrendered twenty minutes later.

The northern redoubt, which had a gun, seemed better-hearted and splashed its shots freely into the station yard, and at our troops. Buxton, under cover of the southern redoubt, directed the fire of Brodie's guns which, with their usual deliberate accuracy, sent in shell after shell. Siddons came over in his machines and bombed it, while the Camel Corps from north and east and west subjected the breastworks to severe Lewis gun-fire. At seven in the morning the last of the enemy surrendered quietly. We had lost four killed and ten wounded. The Turks lost twenty-one killed, and one hundred and fifty prisoners, with two field-guns and three machine-guns.

Buxton at once set the Turks to getting steam on the pumping engine, so that he could water his camels, while men blew in the wells, and smashed the engine-pumps, with two thousand yards of rail. At dusk, charges at the foot of the great water-tower spattered it in single stones across the plain: Buxton a moment later called 'Walk-march!' to his men, and the four-hundred camels, rising like one and roaring like the day of judgment, started off for Jefer. Dawnay went up very brightly to Aba el Lissan, to greet Feisal. Allenby had sent him across to give Feisal a warning message. He was to beg him to do nothing rash, as the British push was a chance, and if it failed the Arabs would be on the wrong side of Jordan to be given help. Particularly, Allenby begged Feisal not to rush upon Damascus, but to hold his hand till events were surely favourable.

This very sound and proper caution had come on my account. Exasperated one night at G.H.Q., I had blurted out that to me 1918 seemed the last chance, and we would take Damascus, anyhow, whatever happened at Deraa or Ramleh; since it was better to have taken it and lost it, than never to have taken it at all.

Feisal smiled wisely at Dawnay's homily, and replied that he would try this autumn for Damascus though the heavens fell, and, if the British were not able to carry their share of the attack, he would save his own people by making separate peace with Turkey.

He had been long in touch with elements in Turkey, Jemal Pasha opening the correspondence. By instinct, when sober, Jemal was Islamic, and to him the revolt of Mecca was a judgement. He was ready to do almost anything to compose such a breach in the faith. His letters were, for this reason, illuminating. Feisal sent them to Mecca and Egypt, hoping that they would read into them what we did: but the points were taken literally, and we received injunction to reply that the sword was now our judge. This was magnificent; but in war so rich a diathetical opportunity could not be missed.

True, that accommodation with Jemal was not possible. He had lopped the tall heads of Syria, and we should deny our friends' blood if we admitted him to our peace: but by indicating this subtly in our reply we might widen the national-clerical rift in Turkey.

Our particular targets were the anti-German section of the General Staff, under Mustapha Kemal, who were too keen on the 'Turkishness' of their mission to deny the right of autonomy to the Arabic provinces of the Ottoman Empire. Accordingly, Feisal sent back tendencious answers; and the correspondence continued brilliantly. The Turkish soldiers began to complain of the pietists, who put relics before strategy. The Nationalists wrote that Feisal was only putting into premature and disastrous activity their own convictions upon the just, inevitable self-determination of Turkey.

Knowledge of the ferment affected Jemal's determination. At first we were offered autonomy for Hejaz. Then Syria was admitted to the benefit: then Mesopotamia. Feisal seemed still not content; so Jemal's deputy (while his master was in Constantinople) boldly added a Crown to the offered share of Hussein of Mecca. Lastly, they told us they saw logic in the claim of the Prophet's family to the spiritual leadership of Islam!

The comic side of the letters must not obscure their real help in dividing the Turkish Staff. Old-fashioned Moslems thought the Sherif an unpardonable sinner. Modernists thought him a sincere but impatient Nationalist misled by British promises. They had a desire to correct him rather by argument than by military defeat.

Their strongest card was the Sykes-Picot agreement, an old-style division of Turkey between England, France, and Russia, made public by the Soviets. Jemal read the more spiteful paragraphs at a banquet in Beyrout. For a while the disclosure hurt us; justly, for we and the French had thought to plaster over a split in policy by a formula vague enough for each to interpret in his divergent way.

Fortunately, I had early betrayed the treaty's existence to Feisal, and had convinced him that his escape was to help the British so much that after peace they would not be able, for shame, to shoot him down in its fulfilment; while, if the Arabs did as I intended, there would be no one-sided talk of shooting. I begged him to trust not in our promises, like his father, but in his own strong performance.

Conveniently, at this juncture the British Cabinet, in joyous style, gave with the left hand also. They promised to the Arabs, or rather to an unauthorized committee of seven Gothamites in Cairo, that the Arabs should keep, for their own, the territory they conquered from Turkey in the war. The glad news circulated over Syria.

To help the downcast Turks, and to show us that it could give as many promises as there were parties, the British finally countered document A to the Sherif, B to their Allies, C to the Arab Committee, by document D to Lord Rothschild, a new power, whose race was promised something equivocal in Palestine. Old Nuri Shaalam, wrinkling his wise nose, returned to me with his file of documents, asking in puzzlement which of them all he might believe. As before, I glibly repeated 'The last in date', and the Emir's sense of the honour of his word made him see the humour. Ever after he did his best for our joint cause, only warning me, when he failed in a promise, that it had been superseded by a later intention!

However, Jemal went on hoping, he being an obstinate and ruffianly man. After Allenby's defeat at Salt, he sent down to us the Emir Mohammed Said, brother of the egregious Abd el Kadir. Mohammed Said, a low-browed degenerate with a bad mouth, was as devious as his brother, but less brave. He was very modest as he stood before Feisal and offered him Jemal's peace.

Feisal told him that he was come at an opportune moment. He could offer Jemal the loyal behaviour of the Arab Army, if Turkey evacuated Amman, and handed over its province to Arab keeping. The seely Algerian, thinking he had scored a huge success, rushed back to Damascus: where Jemal nearly hanged him for his pains.

Mustafa Kemal, alarmed, begged Feisal not to play into Jemal's hands, promising that when the Arabs were installed in their capital, the disaffected in Turkey would rally to them, and use their territory as a base from which to attack Enver and his German allies in Anatolia. Mustafa hoped that the adhesion of all Turkish forces east of the Taurus would enable him to march direct on Constantinople.

Events at the end made abortive these complicated negotiations, which were not disclosed to Egypt or to Mecca, because of the disappointing issue of our first confidence. I feared that the British might be shaken at Feisal's thus entertaining separate relations. Yet in fairness to the fighting Arabs, we could not close all avenues of accommodation with Turkey. If the European war failed, it was their only way out: and I had always the lurking fear that Great Britain might forestall Feisal and conclude its own separate peace, not with the Nationalist, but with the Conservative Turks.

The British Government had gone very far in this direction, without informing her smallest ally. Our information of the precise steps, and of the proposals (which would have been fatal to so many of the Arabs in arms on our side), came, not officially, to me, but privately. It was only one of the twenty times in which friends helped me more than did our Government: whose action and silence were at once an example, a spur and a licence to me to do the like.

CHAPTER CII

AFTER the peace-talk we could set again to clean work. Joyce and myself decided upon another of our joint car excursions, this time to Azrak, to break trail so far towards Deraa. Therefore we ran out to Jefer to meet the victorious Camel Corps, who came gliding, in splendid trim and formal appearance, across the shining flat just before sunset, officers and men delighted at their Mudowwara success, and their freedom from orders and restraint in the desert. Buxton said they were fit to go anywhere.

They would rest two nights and draw four days' rations from their store, duly set out near Auda's tent by Young's care. Accordingly, on the morrow, early, Joyce and I got into our tender, with the resourceful Rolls to drive us, and ran easily into Wadi Bair, at whose wells lay Alwain, Auda's kinsman, a smooth-cheeked, oppressed silent man; hiding, to possess himself in peace far from Auda.

We stopped only the few minutes to arrange with him the safety of Buxton's men; and then drove out, with a young and very wild Sherari to help us find our way. His camel-training would not equip him to road-pick for a five-ton armoured car: but his knowing the track might serve other cars coming up by themselves later.

The plateau of Erha was good going, its flint openings interspersed with beds of hard mud; and we devoured the fast miles into the shallow heads of Wadi Jinz, well grown with pasture.

There, numbers of grazing camels were being driven anxiously together by their ragged herdsmen of the Abu Tayi, who, riding bareheaded, rifles in hand, were singing a war-chant. When they heard our roaring exhausts they rushed towards us, with urgent shouts of mounted men seen lurking in the low grounds ahead. We put the cars in the direction and after a little flushed five camel-riders, who made off northwards at their best. We ran them down in ten minutes. They couched their camels gracefully and came to meet us as friends — the only role left them, since naked men could not quarrel with swifter men in armour. They were Jazi Howeitat, undoubted robbers, but now all kindness, crying loudly at the pleasure of meeting me here suddenly. I was a little short, and ordered them back to their tents at once. They went off, crestfallen, westwards.

We followed Um Kharug's east bank, finding the way firm, but slow, for there were gutters of tributaries to cross; and we had to lay brushwood fascines where the old beds of the flood-water were soft or full of sand. Towards the end of the day the valleys grew thick with tufted grass, grazing for our prospective caravans.

In the morning the northern air and fresh wind of this desert were so cool to us that we made a hot breakfast before we cranked up the cars and purred over the meeting of Um Kharug and Dhirwa, over the broad basin of Dhirwa itself, and past its imperceptible water-parting into the Jesha. These were shallow systems running into Sirhan, by Ammari, which I meant to visit; for if evil came to us at Azrak, our next refuge should be Ammari, if accessible to cars. Such battalions of 'ifs' skirmished about every new plan continually.

The night's rest had refreshed Rolls and Sanderson, and they drove splendidly over the saffron ridge of the little Jesha into the great valley. In the afternoon we saw the chalk banks, and turned down their ashy slopes, into the Sirhan, just by the water-holes. This made our retreat always safe, for no enemy would be mobile enough to close both Azrak and Ammari at once to us.

So we refilled our radiators with the horrible water of the pool in which Farraj and Daud had played, and drew westward over the open ridges, until far enough from the wells to acquit raiding parties from the need to stumble on us in the dark. There Joyce and I sat down and watched a sunset, which grew from grey to pink, and to red; and then to a crimson so intolerably deep that we held our breath in trepidation for some stroke of flame or thunder to break its dizzy stillness. The men, meanwhile, cut open tinned meats, boiled tea, and laid them out with biscuits on a blanket for our supper table. Afterwards there were more blankets, in which we slept lusciously.

Next day we ran quickly across the delta of Ghadaf till we were out on the immense mud-flat which stretched for seven miles, southward and eastward, from the marshes by the old castle of Azrak.

To-day the mirage blotted its limits for us with blurs of steely blue, which were the tamarisk bounds raised high in the air and smoothed by heat-vapour. I wanted the Mejaber springs, down whose tree-grown bed we might creep unperceived: so Rolls made his car leap forward in a palpitant rush across the great width. The earth fell away in front of us, and a plume like a dust-devil waved along our track behind.

At the end the brakes sang protestingly as we slowed into a young plantation of tamarisk, tall on heaps of wind-collected sand. We twisted through them on the hard, intervening soil, till tamarisk ceased, and damp sand, speckled with close thorn-bushes, took its place. The cars stopped behind the hummock of Ain el Assad, under cover of this high-lipped cup of reeds, between whose vivid stems the transparent water dripped like jewels.

We went gently up the knoll of graves over the great pools, and saw that the watering places were empty. A mirage hung over the open spaces: but here, where the ground was bushed, no heat-waves could collect, and the strong sunlight showed us the valley as crystal clear as its running waters, and deserted except by wild birds, and these herds of gazelles, which, alarmed by the popple of our closed exhausts, were grouping timidly in preparation for flight.

Rolls drew his tender past the Roman fish-pond; we skirted the western lava-field, along the now hard, grass-grown swamp, to the blue walls of the silent fort, with its silken-sounding palms, behind whose stillness lay perhaps more fear than peace. I felt guilty at introducing the throbbing car, and its trim crew of khaki-clad northerners, into the remoteness of this most hidden legendary place: but my anticipation went astray, for it was the men who looked real and the background which became scene-painting. Their newness and certainty (the Definiteness of British troops in uniform) did Azrak greater honour than plain loneliness.

We stopped only a moment. Joyce and I climbed the western tower, and agreed upon the manifold advantages of Azrak as a working base; though, to my sorrow, there was no grazing here, so that we could not linger in it for the interval of our first and second raids. Then we crossed to the northern lobe of the mud-flat, a fit landing-ground for the aeroplanes which Siddons was adding to our flying column. Amongst other qualities was its visibility. Our machines flying two hundred miles to this, their new base, could not fail to see its electrum shield reflecting the sunlight.

We went back to Ain el Assad, where the armoured car was, and led it at a faster pace out to the open flint desert once again. It was mid-afternoon, and very hot, especially in the glowing metal of the steel-turreted car; but the broiling drivers kept at it, and before sunset we were on the dividing ridge between the Jesha valleys, to find a shorter and easier way than our coming.

Night caught us not far south of Ammari, and we camped on the top of the country, with a breeze, very precious after the blistering day, coming down to us scent-laden from the flowering slopes of Jebel Druse. It made us glad of the men's hot tea, and of the blankets with which we had softly padded the angles of the box-body.

The trip was one delight to me, since I had no responsibility but the road. Also there was the spice of the reflections of the Sherari boy, reflections naturally confided to me, since I alone wore his sort of clothes, and spoke his dialect. He, poor outcast, had never before been treated as a considerate thing, and was astonished at the manners of the English. Not once had he been struck or even threatened.

He said that each soldier carried himself apart like a family, and that he felt something of defence in their tight, insufficient clothes and laborious appearance. He was fluttering in skirts, head-cloth and cloak. They had only shirts and shorts, puttees and boots, and the breeze could take no hold on them. Indeed, they had worn these things so long day and night in heat and sweat, busied about the dusty oily cars, that the cloth had set to their bodies, like bark to a tree.

Then they were all clean-shaven, and all dressed alike; and his eye, which most often distinguished man from man by clothes, here was baffled by an outward uniformity. To know them apart he must learn their individual, as though naked, shapes. Their food took no cooking, their drink was hot, they hardly spoke to one another; but then a word sent them into fits of incomprehensible crackling laughter, unworthy and inhuman. His belief was that they were my slaves, and that there was little rest or satisfaction in their lives, though to a Sherari it would have been luxury so to travel like the wind, sitting down; and a privilege to eat meat, tinned meat, daily.

In the morning we hurried along our ridge, to reach Bair in the after-noon. Unfortunately there were tyre-troubles. The armoured car was too heavy for the flints, and always she sank in a little, making heavy going on third speed. This heated up the covers. We endured a vexatious series of bursts, of stoppings to jack up and change wheel or tyre. The day was hot and we were hurried, so that the repeated levering and pumping wore thin our tempers. At noon we reached the great spinal ridge to Ras Muheiwir. I promised the sulky drivers it would be splendid going.

And it was. We all took new heart, even the tyres stood better, while we rushed along the winding ridge, swinging in long curves from east to west and back again, looking now to the left over the shallow valleys trending towards Sirhan, now to the right as far as the Hejaz Railway. Gleaming specks in the haze of distance were its white stations lit by the pouring sun.

In late afternoon we reached the end of the ridge, dipped into the hollow and roared at forty miles an hour up the breast of Hadi. Dark-ness was near as we cut across the furrows of Ausaji to Bair wells, where the valley was alive with fires; Buxton, Marshall and the Camel Corps were pitching camp, after two easy marches from El Jefer.

There was heartburning among them, for Bair had still only two wells, and both were beset. At one the Howeitat and Beni Sakhr were drawing for six hundred of their camels, thirsty from the pastures a day's journey to the south-east, and at the other was a mob of a thousand Druses and Syrian refugees, Damascus merchants and Armenians, on their way to Akaba. These unhandy travellers cluttered up our access to the water with their noisy struggles.

We sat down with Buxton in a council of war. Young had duly sent to Bair fourteen days' rations for man and beast. Of this there remained eight days for the men, ten for the animals. The camel-drivers of the supply column, driven forward only by Young's strong will, had left Jefer half-mutinous with fear of the desert. They had lost, stolen or sold the rest of Buxton's stores upon their way.

I suspected the complaining Armenians, but nothing could be recovered from them, and we had to adjust the plan to its new con-ditions. Buxton purged his column of every inessential, while l cut down the two armoured cars to one, and changed the route.

CHAPTER CIII

LAZILY and mildly I helped the Camel Corps in their long watering at the forty-foot wells, and enjoyed the kindness of Buxton and his three hundred fellows. The valley seemed alive with them; and the Howeitat, who had never imagined there were so many English in the world, could not have their fill of staring. I was proud of my kind, for their dapper possession and the orderly busyness of their self-appointed labour. Beside them the Arabs looked strangers in Arabia; also Buxton's talk was a joy, as he was understanding, well read and bold; though mostly he was engaged in preparing for the long forced march.

Accordingly, I spent hours apart by myself, taking stock of where I stood, mentally, on this my thirtieth birthday. It came to me queerly how, four years ago, I had meant to be a general and knighted, when thirty. Such temporal dignities (if I survived the next four weeks) were now in my grasp—only that my sense of the falsity of the Arab position had cured me of crude ambition: while it left me my craving for good repute among men.

This craving made me profoundly suspect my truthfulness to myself. Only too good an actor could so impress his favourable opinion. Here were the Arabs believing me, Allenby and Clayton trusting me, my bodyguard dying for me: and I began to wonder if all established reputations were founded, like mine, on fraud.

The praise-wages of my acting had now to be accepted. Any protestation of the truth from me was called modesty, self depreciation; and charming — for men were always fond to believe a romantic tale. It irritated me, this silly confusion of shyness, which was conduct, with modesty, which was a point of view. I was not modest, but ashamed of my awkwardness, of my physical envelope, and of my solitary unlikeness which made me no companion, but an acquaintance, complete, angular, uncomfortable, as a crystal.

With men I had a sense always of being out of depth. This led to elaboration — the vice of amateurs tentative in their arts. As my war was overthought, because I was not a soldier, so my activity was over-wrought, because I was not a man of action. They were intensely conscious efforts, with my detached self always eyeing the performance from the wings in criticism.

To be added to this attitude were the cross-strains of hunger, fatigue, heat or cold, and the beastliness of living among the Arabs. These made for abnormality. Instead of facts and figures, my note-books were full of states of mind, the reveries and self-questioning induced or educed by our situations, expressed in abstract words to the dotted rhythm of the camels' marching.

On this birthday in Bair, to satisfy my sense of sincerity, I began to dissect my beliefs and motives, groping about in my own pitchy darkness. This self-distrusting shyness held a mask, often a mask of indifference or flippancy, before my face, and puzzled me. My thoughts clawed, wondering, at this apparent peace, knowing that it was only a mask; because, despite my trying never to dwell on what was interesting, there were moments too strong for control when my appetite burst out and frightened me.

I was very conscious of the bundled powers and entities within me; it was their character which hid. There was my craving to be liked — so strong and nervous that never could I open myself friendly to another. The terror of failure in an effort so important made me shrink from trying; besides, there was the standard; for intimacy seemed shameful unless the other could make the perfect reply, in the same language, after the same method, for the same reasons.

There was a craving to be famous; and a horror of being known to like being known. Contempt for my passion for distinction made me refuse every offered honour. I cherished my independence almost as did a Beduin, but my impotence of vision showed me my shape best in painted pictures, and the oblique overheard remarks of others best taught me my created impression. The eagerness to overhear and over-see myself was my assault upon my own inviolate citadel.

The lower creation I avoided, as a reflection upon our failure to attain real intellectuality. If they forced themselves on me I hated them. To put my hand on a living thing was defilement; and it made me tremble if they touched me or took too quick an interest in me. This was an atomic repulsion, like the intact course of a snowflake. The opposite would have been my choice if my head had not been tyrannous. I had a longing for the absolutism of women and animals, and lamented myself most when I saw a soldier with a girl, or a man fondling a dog, because my wish was to be as superficial, as perfected; and my jailer held me back.

Always feelings and illusion were at war within me, reason strong enough to win, but not strong enough to annihilate the vanquished, or refrain from liking them better; and perhaps the truest knowledge of love might be to love what self despised. Yet I could only wish to: could see happiness in the supremacy of the material, and could not surrender to it: could try to put my mind to sleep that suggestion might blow through me freely; and remained bitterly awake.

I liked the things underneath me and took my pleasures and adventures downward. There seemed a certainty in degradation, a final safety. Man could rise to any height, but there was an animal level beneath which he could not fall. It was a satisfaction on which to rest. The force of things, years and an artificial dignity, denied it me more and more; but there endured the after-taste of liberty from one youthful submerged fortnight in Port Said, coaling steamers by day with other outcasts of three continents and curling up by night to sleep on the breakwater by De Lesseps, where the sea surged past.

True there lurked always that Will uneasily waiting to burst out. My brain was sudden and silent as a wild cat, my senses like mud clogging its feet, and my self (conscious always of itself and its shyness) telling the beast it was bad form to spring and vulgar to feed upon the kill. So meshed in nerves and hesitation, it could not be a thing to be afraid of; yet it was a real beast, and this book its mangy skin, dried, stuffed and set up squarely for men to stare at.

I quickly outgrew ideas. So I distrusted experts, who were often intelligences confined within high walls, knowing indeed every paving-stone of their prison courts: while I might know from what quarry the stones were hewn and what wages the mason earned. I gainsaid them out of carelessness, for I had found materials always apt to serve a purpose, and Will a sure guide to some one of the many roads leading from purpose to achievement. There was no flesh.

Many things I had picked up, dallied with, regarded, and laid down; for the conviction of doing was not in me. Fiction seemed more solid than activity. Self-seeking ambitions visited me, but not to stay, since my critical self would make me fastidiously reject their fruits. Always I grew to dominate those things into which I had drifted, but in none of them did I voluntarily engage. Indeed, I saw myself a danger to ordinary men, with such capacity yawing rudderless at their disposal.

I followed and did not institute; indeed, had no desire even to follow. It was only weakness which delayed me from mind-suicide, some slow task to choke at length this furnace in my brain. I had developed ideas of other men, and helped them, but had never created a thing of my own, since I could not approve creation. When other men created, I would serve and patch to make it as good as might be; for, if it were sinful to create, it must be sin and shame added to have created one-eyed or halt.

Always in working I had tried to serve, for the scrutiny of leading was too prominent. Subjection to order achieved economy of thought, the painful, and was a cold-storage for character and Will, leading painlessly to the oblivion of activity. It was a part of my failure never to have found a chief to use me. All of them, through incapacity or timidity or liking, allowed me too free a hand; as if they could not see that voluntary slavery was the deep pride of a morbid spirit, and vicarious pain its gladdest decoration. Instead of this, they gave me licence, which I abused in insipid indulgence. Every orchard fit to rob must have a guardian, dogs, a high wall, barbed wire. Out upon joyless impunity!

Feisal was a brave, weak, ignorant spirit, trying to do work for which only a genius, a prophet or a great criminal, was fitted. I served him out of pity, a motive which degraded us both. Allenby came nearest to my longings for a master, but I had to avoid him, not daring to bow down for fear lest he show feet of clay with that friendly word which must shatter my allegiance. Yet, what an idol the man was to us, prismatic with the unmixed self-standing quality of greatness, instinct and compact with it.

There were qualities like courage which could not stand alone, but must be mixed with a good or bad medium to appear. Greatness in

Allenby showed itself other, in category: self-sufficient, a facet of character, not of intellect. It made superfluous in him ordinary qualities; intelligence, imagination, acuteness, industry, looked silly beside him. He was not to be judged by our standards, any more than the sharpness of bow of a liner was to be judged by the sharpness of razors. He dispensed with them by his inner power.

The hearing other people praised made me despair jealously of myself, for I took it at its face value; whereas, had they spoken ten times as well of me, I would have discounted it to nothing. I was a standing court martial on myself, inevitably, because to me the inner springs of action were bare with the knowledge of exploited chance. The creditable must have been thought out beforehand, foreseen, prepared, worked for. The self, knowing the detriment, was forced into depreciation by others' uncritical praise. It was a revenge of my trained historical faculty upon the evidence of public judgement, the lowest common denominator to those who knew, but from which there was no appeal because the world was wide.

When a thing was in my reach, I no longer wanted it; my delight lay in the desire. Everything which my mind could consistently wish for was attainable, as with all the ambitions of all sane men, and when a desire gained head, I used to strive until I had just to open my hand and take it. Then I would turn away, content that it had been within my strength. I sought only to assure myself, and cared not a jot to make the others know it.

There was a special attraction in beginnings, which drove me into everlasting endeavour to free my personality from accretions and project it on a fresh medium, that my curiosity to see its naked shadow might be fed. The invisible self appeared to be reflected clearest in the still water of another man's yet incurious mind. Considered judgements, which had in them of the past and the future, were worthless compared with the revealing first sight, the instinctive opening or closing of a man as he met the stranger.

Much of my doing was from this egoistic curiosity. When in fresh company, I would embark on little wanton problems of conduct, observing the impact of this or that approach on my hearers, treating fellow-men as so many targets for intellectual ingenuity: until I could hardly tell my own self where the leg-pulling began or ended. This pettiness helped to make me uncomfortable with other men, lest my whim drive me suddenly to collect them as trophies of marksmanship; also they were interested in so much which my self-consciousness rejected. They talked of food and illness, games and pleasures, with me, who felt that to recognize our possession of bodies was degradation enough, without enlarging upon their failings and attributes. I would feel shame for myself at seeing them wallow in the physical which could be only a glorification of man's cross. Indeed, the truth was I did not like the 'myself' I could see and hear.

CHAPTER CIV

I HAD reached this useful stage when there was a disturbance from the Toweiha tents. Shouting men ran towards me. I pulled myself together to appease a fight between the Arabs and the Camel Corps, but instead it was an appeal for help against a Shammar raid two hours since, away by the Snainirat. Eighty camels had been driven off. Not to seem wholly ungracious, I put on our spare camels the four or five of my men whose friends or relatives had suffered, and sent them off.

Buxton and his men started in the mid-afternoon while I delayed till evening, seeing my men load our six thousand pounds of gun-cotton on the thirty Egyptian pack-camels. My disgusted bodyguard were for this ride to lead or drive the explosives' train.

We had judged that Buxton would sleep just short of the Hadi, so we rode thither: but saw no camp-fire, nor was the track trodden. We looked over the crest of the ridge, into a bitter north wind coming off Hermon into our flustered faces. The slopes beyond were black and silent, and to us town-dwellers, accustomed to the reek of smoke, or sweat, or the ferment of soil freshly dug, there was something searching, disquieting, almost dangerous, in the steely desert wind. So we turned back a few paces, and hid under the lip of the ridge to sleep comfortably in its cloistered air.

In the morning we looked out across fifty miles of blank country, and wondered at this missing our companions: but Daher shouted suddenly from the Hadi side, seeing their column winding up from the south-east. They had early lost the track and camped till dawn. My men jested with humour against Sheikh Saleh, their guide, as one who could lose his road between the Thlaithukhwat and Bair: just like one might say between the Marble Arch and Oxford Circus.

However, it was a perfect morning, with the sun hot on our backs, and the wind fresh in our faces. The Camel Corps strode splendidly past the frosted tips of the three peaks into the green depths of Dhirwa. They looked different from the stiff, respectful companies which had reached Akaba, for Buxton's supple brain and friendly observation had taken in the experience of irregular fighting, and revised their training rules for the new needs.

He had changed their column formation, breaking its formal sub-division of two hard companies: he had changed the order of march, so that, instead of their old immaculate lines, they came clotted, in groups which split up or drew together without delay upon each variation of road or ground surface. He had reduced the loads and rehung them, thereby lengthening the camels' pace and daily mileage. He had cut into their infantry system of clockwork halts every so often (to let the camels stale!) and grooming was less honoured. In the old days, they had prinked their animals, cosseting them like Pekinese, and each halt had been lightened by a noisy flapping massage of the beasts' stripped humps with the saddle-blanket; whereas now the spare time was spent in grazing.

Consequently, our Imperial Camel Corps had become rapid, elastic, enduring, silent; except when they mounted by numbers, for then the three hundred he-camels would roar in concert, giving out a wave of sound audible miles across the night. Each march saw them more workmanlike, more at home on the animals, tougher, leaner, faster. They behaved like boys on holiday, and the easy mixing of officers and men made their atmosphere delightful.

My camels were brought up to walk in Arab fashion, that bent-kneed gait with much swinging of the fetlock, the stride a little longer and a little quicker than the normal. Buxton's camels strolled along at their native pace, unaffected by the men on their backs, who were kept from direct contact with them by iron-shod boots and by their wood and steel Manchester-made saddles.

Consequently, though I started each stage alongside Buxton in the van, I forged steadily in front with my five attendants; especially when I rode my Baha, the immensely tall, large-boned, upstanding beast, who got her name from the bleat-voice forced on her by a bullet through the chin. She was very finely bred, but bad-tempered, half a wild camel, and had never patience for an ordinary walk. Instead, with high nose and wind-stirred hair, she would jig along in an uneasy dance, hateful to my Ageyl for it strained their tender loins, but to me not un-amusing.

In this fashion we would gain three miles on the British, look for a plot of grass or juicy thorns, lie in the warm freshness of air, and let our beasts graze while we were overtaken; and a beautiful sight the Camel Corps would be as it came up.

Through the mirage of heat which flickered over the shining flint-stones of the ridge we would see, at first, only the knotted brown mass of the column, swaying in the haze. As it grew nearer the masses used to divide into little groups, which swung; parting and breaking into one another. At last, when close to us, we would distinguish the individual riders, like great water-birds breast-deep in the silver mirage, with Buxton's athletic, splendidly-mounted figure leading his sun-burnt, laughing, khaki men.

It was odd to see how diversely they rode. Some sat naturally, despite the clumsy saddle; some pushed out their hinder-parts, and leaned forward like Arab villagers; others lolled in the saddle as if they were Australians riding horses. My men, judging by the look, were inclined to scoff. I told them how from that three hundred I would pick forty fellows who would out-ride, out-fight and out-suffer any forty men in Feisal's army.

At noon, by Ras Muheiwer, we halted an hour or two, for though the heat to-day was less than in Egypt in August, Buxton did not wish to drive his men through it without a break. The camels were loosed out, while we lay and lunched and tried to sleep, defying the multitude of flies which had marched with us from Bair in colonies on our sweaty backs. Meanwhile, my bodyguard passed through, grumbling at their indignity of baggage driving, making believe never to have been so shamed before, and praying profanely that the world would not hear of my tyranny to them.

Their sorrow was doubled since the baggage animals were Somali camels, whose greatest speed was about three miles an hour. Buxton's force marched nearly four, myself more than five, so that the marches were for the Zaagi and his forty thieves a torment of slowness, modified only by baulking camels, or displaced loads.

We abused their clumsiness, calling them drovers and coolies, offering to buy their goods when they came to market; till perforce they laughed at their plight. After the first day they kept up with us by lengthening the march into the night (only a little, for these ophthalmia-stricken brutes were blind in the dark) and by stealing from the breakfast and midday halts. They brought their caravan through without losing one of all their charges; a fine performance for such gilded gentlemen; only possible because under their gilt they were the best camel-masters for hire in Arabia.

That night we slept in Ghadaf. The armoured car overtook us as we halted, its delighted Sherari guide grinning in triumph on the turret lid. An hour or two later the Zaagi arrived, reporting all up and well. He begged that Buxton should not kill, directly in the road, such camels as broke down on the march; for his men made each successive carcase excuse for a feast and a delay.

Abdulla was troubled to understand why the British shot their abandoned beasts. I pointed out how we Arabs shot one another if badly wounded in battle; but Abdulla retorted it was to save us from being so tortured that we might do ourselves shame. He believed there was hardly a man alive who would not choose a gradual death of weakness in the desert, rather than a sudden cutting off; indeed, in his judgement, the slowest death was the most merciful of all, since absence of hope would prevent the bitterness of a losing fight, and leave the man's nature untrammelled to compose itself and him into the mercy of God. Our English argument, that it was kinder to kill quickly anything except a man, he would not take seriously.

CHAPTER CV

Our morrow was like the day before, a steady grind of forty miles. Next day was the last before the bridge-effort. I took half of my men from the baggage train, and threw them forward on our line of march, to crown each hill-top. This was well done, but did not profit us, for in mid-morning, with Muaggar, our ambush in full sight, we were marching strongly and hopefully when a Turkish aeroplane came from the south, flew the length of our column, and went down, before us, into Amman.

We plodded heavily into Muaggar by noon, and hid in the substructures of the Roman temple-platform. Our watchers took post on the crest, looking out over the harvested plains to the Hejaz Railway. Over these hill-slopes, as we stared through our glasses, the grey stones seemed to line out like flocks of grazing sheep.

We sent my peasants into the villages below us, to get news, and warn the people to keep within doors. They returned to say that chance was fighting against us. Round the winnowed corn upon the threshing floors stood Turkish soldiers, for the tax-gatherers were measuring the heaps under guard of sections of mounted infantry. Three such troops, forty men, lay for this night in the three villages nearest the great bridge — villages through whose precincts we must necessarily go and come.

We held a hurried council. The aeroplane had or had not seen us. It would cause, at worst, the strengthening of the bridge-guard, but I had little fear of its effect. The Turks would believe we were the advance-guard of a third raid on Amman, and were more likely to concentrate than to detach troops. Buxton's men were great fighters, he had laid admirable plans. Success was certain.

The doubt was about the bridge's cost, or rather as to its value in British life, having regard to Bartholomew's prohibition of casualties.

The presence of these mule-riders meant that our retreat would not be unencumbered. The camel corps were to dismount nearly a mile from the bridge (their noisy camels!) and advance on foot. The noise of their assault, not to speak of the firing of three tons of gun-cotton against the bridge-piers, would wake up the district. The Turkish patrols in the villages might stumble on our camel-park — a disaster for us — or, at least, would hamper us in the broken ground, as we retired.

Buxton's men could not scatter like a swarm of birds, after the bridge explosion, to find their own way back to the Muaggar. In any night-fighting some would be cut off and lost. We should have to wait for them, possibly losing more in the business. The whole cost might be fifty men, and I put the worth of the bridge at less than five. Its destruction was so to frighten and disturb the Turks, that they would leave us alone till August the thirtieth when our long column set out for Azrak. To-day was the twentieth. The danger had seemed pressing in July, but was now nearly over.

Buxton agreed. We decided to cry off, and move back at once. At the moment more Turkish machines got up from Amman and quartered the rough hills northward from Muaggar, looking for us.

The men groaned in disappointment when they heard the change. They had set pride on this long raid, and were burning to tell incredulous Egypt that their programme had been literally fulfilled.

To gain what we could, I sent Saleh and the other chiefs down to spruce their people with tall rumours of our numbers, and our coming as the reconnaissance of Feisal's army, to carry Amman by assault in the new moon. This was the story the Turks feared to learn: the operation they imagined: the stroke they dreaded. They pushed cavalry cautiously into Muaggar, and found confirmation of the wild tales of the villagers, for the hill-top was littered with empty meat tins, and the valley slopes cut up by the deep tracks of enormous cars. Very many tracks there were! This alarm checked them, and, at a bloodless price for us, kept them hovering a week. The destruction of the bridge would have gained us a fortnight.

We waited till dusk was thick, and then rode off for Azrak, fifty miles away. We pretended that the raid was become a tour, and talked of Roman remains and of Ghassanide hunting-places. The Camel Corps had a practice, almost a habit, of night-journeys, so that their pace was as by day, and units never strayed nor lost touch. There was a brilliant moon and we marched till it was pale in the morning, passing

the lone palace of Kharaneh about midnight, too careless to turn aside
and see its strangeness. Part-blame for this lay on the moon, whose
whiteness made our minds as frozen and shadowless as itself, so that we
sat still in our saddles, just sitting still.

At first I feared lest we encounter Arab raiders, who might have
attacked the Camel Corps in ignorance; so I put forward with my men
some half-mile before the column. As we slipped on, gradually we
became aware of night-birds, flying up from under our feet in numbers,
black and large. They increased, till it seemed as though the earth was
carpeted in birds, so thickly did they start up, but in dead silence, and
dizzily, wheeling about us in circles, like feathers in a soundless whirl of
wind. The weaving curves of their mad flight spun into my brain.
Their number and quietness terrified my men, who unslung their
rifles, and lashed bullet after bullet into the flutter. After two miles the
night became empty again; and at last we lay down and slept in the
fragrant wormwood, till the sun roused us out.

In the afternoon, tired, we came to Kusair el Amra, the little hunting
lodge of Harith, the Shepherd King, a patron of poets; it stood
beautifully against its background of bosky rustling trees. Buxton put
headquarters in the cool dusk of its hall, and we lay there puzzling out
the worn frescoes of the wall, with more laughter than moral profit.
Of the men, some sheltered themselves in other rooms, most, with the
camels, stretched themselves beneath the trees, for a slumberous
afternoon and evening. The aeroplanes had not found us — could not
find us here. To-morrow there was Azrak, and fresh water to replace
this stuff of Bair which, with the passing days, was getting too tasty for
our liking.

Also Azrak was a famous place, queen of these oases, more beautiful
than Amruh, with its verdure and running springs. I had promised
everyone a bathe; the Englishmen, not washed since Akaba, were
longing towards it. Meanwhile, Amruh was wonderful. They asked
me with astonishment who were these Kings of Ghassan with the
unfamiliar halls and pictures. I could tell them vague tales of their
poetry, and cruel wars: but it seemed so distant and tinselled an age.

Next day we walked gently to Azrak. When we were over the last
ridge of lava-pebbles and saw the ring of the Mejabar graves, that most

592 TOURING ABOUT 22. viii. 18

beautifully put of cemeteries, I trotted forward with my men, to be sure against accident in the place, and to feel again its remoteness before the others came. These soldiers seemed so secure that I dreaded lest Azrak lose its rareness and be drawn back to the tide of life which had left it a thousand years ago.

However, both fears were silly. Azrak was empty of Arabs, beautiful as ever, and even more beautiful a little later when its shining pools were brilliant with the white bodies of our men swimming, and the slow drift of the wind through its reeds was pointed by their gay shouts and splashing echoed off the water. We made a great pit, and buried our tons of gun-cotton, for the Deraa expedition in September; and then roamed about collecting the scarlet sweet-water-berry of the Saa bushes. 'Sherari grapes' my followers, indulgent to our caprice, called them.

We rested there two days, the refreshment of the pools being so great. Buxton rode with me to the fort, to examine the altar of Diocletian and Maximian, meaning to add a word in favour of King George the Fifth; but our stay was poisoned by the grey flies, and then ruined by a tragic accident. An Arab, shooting fish in the fort pool, dropped his rifle, which exploded and killed instantly Lieutenant Rowan, of the Scottish Horse. We buried him in the little Mejaber graveyard, whose spotless quiet had long been my envy.

On the third day we marched past Ammari, across Jesha to near the Thlaithukhwat, the old country whose almost imperceptible variations I had come to know. By the Hadi we felt at home, and made a night-march, the men's strident yells of 'Are we well fed? No.' 'Do we see life? Yes', thundering up the long slopes after me. When they tired of telling the truth I could hear the rattle of their accoutrements hitched over the wooden saddles — eleven or fifteen hitchings they had, each time they loaded up, in place of the Arab's all-embracing saddle-bag thrown on in one movement.

I was so bound up in their dark body and tail behind me, that I, too, lost my way between the Hadi and Bair. However, till dawn we steered by the stars (the men's next meal was in Bair, for yesterday their iron ration was exhausted), and day broke on us in a wooded valley which was certainly Wadi Bair; but for my life I could not tell if we were above or below the wells. I confessed my fault to Buxton and Marshall and we tettered for a while, till, by chance, Sagr ibn Shaalan, one of our old allies of the distant days of Wejh, rode down the track, and put us on the road. An hour later the Camel Corps had new rations and their old tents by the wells, and found that Salama, the provident Egyptian doctor, calculating their return to-day, had already filled the drinking cisterns with enough water to slake the half of their thirsty beasts.

I determined to go into Aba el Lissan with the armoured cars, for Buxton was now on proved ground among friends, and could do without my help. So we drove fast down the scarp to the Jefer flat, and skipped across it at sixty miles an hour, ourselves the leading car. We threw up such a dust-cloud that we lost our sister, and when we reached the south edge of the flat she was nowhere visible. Probably tyre trouble, so we sat down to wait, gazing back into the dappled waves of mirage which streamed over the ground. Their dark vapour, below the pale sky (which got more and more blue as it went higher), shifted a dozen times in the hour, giving us a false alarm of our coming friends; but at last, through the greyness, came spinning a black spot wagging a long trail of sun-shining dust.

This was Greenhill tearing after, at speed through the shrivelling air, which eddied about his burning metal turret, making it so hot that its naked steel seared the bare arms and knees of the crew whenever the huge car lurched in the soft heat-powdered ground, whose carpeted dust lay waiting for the low autumn wind to sweep it across the open in a blinding choking storm.

Our car stood tyre-deep, and, while we waited, the men slopped petrol on a hillock of dust and boiled tea for us — Army tea, as full of leaves as flood water, and yellow with tinned milk, but good for parched throats. While we drank the others drew alongside, and reported two bursts of Beldam tubes in the heat of their swoop at a mile a minute across the scorching plain. We gave them of our boiled tea, and laughing they knocked the dust off their faces with oily hands. They looked aged, with its greyness in their bleached eyebrows and eyelashes and in the pores of their faces, except where the sweat had washed dark-edged furrows through to the red skin.

They drank hurriedly (for the sun was falling, and we had yet fifty miles to go), throwing out the last dregs on the ground, where the drops ran apart like quicksilver upon the dusty surface till they were clotted and sank in speckled shot-holes over its drifted greyness. Then we drove through the ruined railway to Aba el Lissan, where Joyce, Dawnay and Young reported all going marvellously. In fact, preparations were complete, and they were breaking up, Joyce for Cairo to see a dentist, Dawnay for G.H.Q., to tell Allenby we were prosperous and obedient.

CHAPTER CVI

JOYCE's ship had come up from Jidda, with the Meccan mail. Feisal opened his Kibla (King Hussein's Gazette) to find staring at him a Royal Proclamation, saying that fools were calling Jaafar Pasha the General Officer Commanding the Arab Northern Army, whereas there was no such rank, indeed no rank higher than captain in the Arab Army, wherein Sheikh Jaafar, like another, was doing his duty!

This had been published by King Hussein (after reading that Allenby had decorated Jaafar) without warning Feisal; to spite the northern town-Arabs, the Syrian and Mesopotamian officers, whom the King at once despised for their laxity and feared for their accomplishments. He knew that they were fighting, not to give him dominion, but to set free their own countries for their own governing, and the lust for power had grown uncontrollable in the old man.

Jaafar came in and proffered his resignation to Feisal. There followed him our divisional officers and their staffs, with the regimental and battalion commanders. I begged them to pay no heed to the humours of an old man of seventy, out of the world in Mecca, whose greatness they themselves had made; and Feisal refused to accept their resignations, pointing out that the commissions (since his father had not approved their service) were issued by himself, and he alone was discredited by the proclamation.

On this assumption he telegraphed to Mecca, and received a return telegram which called him traitor and outlaw. He replied laying down his command of the Akaba front. Hussein appointed Zeid to succeed him. Zeid promptly refused. Hussein's cipher messages became corrupt with rage, and the military life of Aba el Lissan came to a sudden stop. Dawnay, from Akaba, before the ship sailed, rang me up, and asked dolefully if all hope were over. I answered that things hung on chance, but perhaps we should get through.

Three courses lay before us. The first, to get pressure put on King Hussein to withdraw his statement. The second, to carry on, ignoring it. The third, to set up Feisal in formal independence of his father. There were advocates of each course, amongst the English, as amongst the Arabs. We wired to Allenby asking him to smooth out the incident. Hussein was obstinate and crafty, and it might take weeks to force him out of his obstacles to an apology. Normally, we could have afforded three weeks; but to-day we were in the unhappy position that after three days, if at all, our expedition to Deraa must start. We must find some means of carrying on the war, while Egypt sought for a solution.

My first duty was to send express to Nuri Shaalan that I could not meet him at the gathering of his tribes in Kaf, but would be in Azrak from the first day of the new moon, at his service. This was a sad expedient, for Nuri might take suspicion of my change and fail at the tryst; and without the Rualla half our efficiency and importance at Deraa on September the sixteenth would disappear. However, we had to risk this smaller loss, since without Feisal and the regulars and Pisani's guns there would be no expedition, and for the sake of reforming their tempers I must wait in Aba el Lissan.

My second duty was to start off the caravans for Azrak — the baggage, the food, the petrol, the ammunition. Young prepared these, rising, as ever, to any occasion not of his own seeking. He was his own first obstacle, but would have no man hinder him. Never could I forget the radiant face of Nuri Said, after a joint conference, encountering a group of Arab officers with the cheerful words, 'Never mind, you fellows; he talks to the English just as he does to us!' Now he saw that each echelon started — not, indeed, to time but only a day late — under its appointed officers, according to programme. It had been our principle to issue orders to the Arabs only through their own chiefs, so they had no precedent either for obedience or for disobedience: and off they went like lambs.

My third duty was to face a mutiny of the troops. They had heard false rumours about the crisis. Particularly, the gunners misunderstood, and one afternoon fell out with their officers, and rushed off to turn the guns on their tents. However, Rasim, the artillery commandant, had forestalled them by collecting the breech-blocks into a pyramid inside his tent. I took advantage of this comic moment to meet the men.

They were tense at first, but eventually out of curiosity they fell to talking with me, who to them had been only an eccentric name, as a half-Beduin Englishman.

I told them the coffee-cup storm which was raging among the high heads, and they laughed merrily. Their faces were turned towards Damascus, not Mecca, and they cared for nothing outside their army. Their fear was that Feisal had deserted, since for days he had not been out. I promised to bring him down instantly. When he, with Zeid, looking as usual, drove through the lines in the Vauxhall, which Bols had had painted specially green for him, their eyes convinced them of their error.

My fourth duty was to start off the troops for Azrak on the right day. To effect this, their confidence in the confidence of the officers had to be restored. Stirling's tact was called upon. Nuri Said was ambitious, as any soldier would have been, to make much of the opportunity before him, and readily agreed to move as far as Azrak, pending Hussein's apology. If this was unsatisfactory they could return, or throw off allegiance; if it was adequate, as I assured him it would be, the interim and unmerited services of the Northern Army should bring a blush to the old man's cheek.

The ranks responded to bluffer arguments. We made plain that such gross questions as food and pay depended entirely on the maintenance of organization. They yielded, and the separate columns, of mounted infantry, of machine-gunners, of Egyptian sappers, of Ghurkas, of Pisani's gunners, moved off in their courses, according to the routine of Stirling and Young, only two days late.

The last obligation was to restore Feisal's supremacy. To attempt anything serious between Deraa and Damascus without him would be vain. We could put in the attack on Deraa, which was what Allenby expected from us; but the capture of Damascus — which was what I expected from the Arabs, the reason why I had joined with them in the field, taken ten thousand pains, and spent my wit and strength — that depended on Feisal's being present with us in the fighting line, undistracted by military duties, but ready to take over and exploit the political value of what our bodies conquered for him. Eventually he offered to come up under my orders.

As for the apology from Mecca, Allenby and Wilson were doing their best, engrossing the cables. If they failed, my course would be to promise Feisal the direct support of the British Government, and drive him into Damascus as sovereign prince. It was possible: but I wanted to avoid it except as a last necessity. The Arabs hitherto in their revolt had made clean history, and I did not wish our adventure to come to the pitiable state of scission before the common victory and its peace.

King Hussein behaved truly to type, protesting fluently, with endless circumlocution, showing no understanding of the grave effect of his incursion into Northern Army affairs. To clear his mind we sent him plain statements, which drew abusive but involved returns. His telegrams came through Egypt and by wireless to our operators in Akaba, and were sent up to me by car, for delivery to Feisal. The Arabic ciphers were simple, and I had undesirable passages mutilated by rearranging their figures into nonsense, before handing them in code to Feisal. By this easy expedient the temper of his entourage was not needlessly complicated.

The play went on for several days, Mecca never repeating a message notified corrupt, but telegraphing in its place a fresh version toned down at each re-editing from the previous harshness. Finally, there came a long message, the first half a lame apology and withdrawal of the mischievous proclamation, the second half a repetition of the offence in a new form. I suppressed the tail, and took the head marked 'very urgent' to Feisal's tent, where he sat in the full circle of his staff officers.

His secretary worked out the despatch, and handed the decipher to Feisal. My hints had roused expectation, and all eyes were on him as he read it. He was astonished, and gazed wonderingly at me, for the meek words were unlike his father's querulous obstinacy. Then he pulled himself together, read the apology aloud, and at the end said thrillingly, 'The telegraph has saved all our honour'.

A chorus of delight burst out, during which he bent aside to whisper in my ear, 'I mean the honour of nearly all of us'. It was done so delightfully that I laughed, and said demurely, 'I cannot understand what you mean'. He replied, 'I offered to serve for this last march under your orders: why was that not enough?' 'Because it would not go with your honour.' He murmured, 'You prefer mine always before your own', and then sprang energetically to his feet, saying, 'Now, Sirs, praise God and work'.

In three hours we had settled time-tables, and arranged for our successors here in Aba el Lissan, with their spheres and duties. I took my leave. Joyce had just returned to us from Egypt, and Feisal promised that he would come, with him and Marshall, to Azrak to join me on the twelfth at latest. All the camp was happy as I got into a Rolls tender and set off northward, hoping yet to rally the Rualla under Nuri Shaalan in time for our attack on Deraa.

BOOK X

THE HOUSE IS PERFECTED

Chapters CVII to CXXII

OUR *mobile column of aeroplanes, armoured cars, Arab regulars and Beduin collected at Azrak, to cut the three railways out of Deraa. The southern line we cut near Mefrak; the northern at Arar; the western by Mezerib. We circumnavigated Deraa, and rallied, despite air raids, in the desert.*

Next day Allenby attacked, and in a few hours had scattered the Turkish armies beyond recovery.

I flew to Palestine for aeroplane help, and got orders for a second phase of the thrust northward.

We moved behind Deraa to hasten its abandonment. General Barrow joined us; in his company we advanced to Kiswe, and there met the Australian Mounted Corps. Our united forces entered Damascus unopposed. Some confusion manifested itself in the city. We strove to allay it; Allenby arrived and smoothed out all difficulties. Afterwards he let me go.

CHAPTER CVII

IT was an inexpressible pleasure to have left the mists behind. We caught at each other with thankfulness as we drove along, Winterton, Nasir and myself. Lord Winterton was our last-found recruit; an experienced officer from Buxton's Camel Corps. Sherif Nasir, who had been the spear-point of the Arab Army since the first days of Medina, had been chosen by us for the field work on this last occasion also. He deserved the honour of Damascus, for his had been the honours of Medina, of Wejh, of Akaba, and of Tafileh; and of many barren days beside.

A painstaking little Ford hung on in the dust, behind, as our splendid car drank up the familiar miles. Once I had been proud of riding from Azrak to Akaba in three days; but now we drove it in two, and slept well of nights after this mournful comfort of being borne at ease in Rolls-Royces, like the great ones of war.

We noted again how easy their lives were; the soft body and its unexhausted sinews helping the brain to concentrate upon an arm-chair work: whereas our brains and bodies lay down only for the stupor of an hour's sleep, in the flush of dawn and the flush of sunset, the two seasons of the day unwholesome for riding. Many a day we had been twenty-two out of the twenty-four hours in the saddle, each taking it in turn to lead through the darkness while the others let their heads nod forward over the pommel in nescience.

Not that it was more than a thin nescience: for even in the deepest of such sleep the foot went on pressing the camel's shoulder to keep it at the cross-country pace, and the rider woke if the balance were lost ever so little at a false stride or turn. Then we had had rain, snow or sun beating upon us; little food, little water, and no security against either Turks or Arabs. Yet those forced months with the tribes had let me plan in a surety which seemed lunatic rashness to new comers, but actually was an exact knowledge of my materials.

Now the desert was not normal: indeed, it was shamefully popular. We were never out of sight of men; of tenuous camel columns of troops and tribesmen and baggage moving slowly northward over the interminable Jefer flat. Past this activity (of good omen for our punctual concentration at Azrak) we roared, my excellent driver, Green, once achieving sixty-seven miles an hour. The half-stifled Nasir who sat in the box-body could only wave his hand across a furlong to each friend we overtook.

At Bair we heard from the alarmed Beni Sakhr that the Turks, on the preceding day, had launched suddenly westward from Hesa into Tafileh. Mifleh thought I was mad, or most untimely merry, when I laughed outright at the news which four days sooner would have held up the Azrak expedition: but, now we were started, the enemy might take Aba el Lissan, Guweira, Akaba itself — and welcome! Our formidable talk of advance by Amman had pulled their leg nearly out of socket, and the innocents were out to counter our feint. Each man they sent south was a man, or rather ten men, lost.

In Azrak we found a few servants of Nuri Shaalan, and the Crossley car with a flying officer, an airman, some spares, and a canvas hangar for the two machines protecting our concentration. We spent our first night on their aerodrome and suffered for it. A reckless armoured-plated camel-fly, biting like a hornet, occupied our exposed parts till sunset. Then came a blessed relief as the itch grew milder in the evening cool — but the wind changed and hot showers of blinding salty dust swept us for three hours. We lay down and drew covers over our heads, but could not sleep. Each half-hour we had to throw off the sand which threatened to bury us. At midnight the wind ceased. We issued from our sweaty nests and restfully prepared to sleep — when singing, a cloud of mosquitoes rolled over us: them we fought till dawn.

Consequently, at dawn we changed camp to the height of the Mejaber ridge, a mile west of the water and a hundred feet above the marshes, open to all winds that blew. We rested a while, then put up the hangar, and afterwards went off to bathe in the silver water. We undressed beside the sparkling pools whose pearl-white sides and floor reflected the sky with a moony radiance. 'Delicious!' I yelled as I splashed in and swam about. 'But why do you keep on bobbing under water?' asked Winterton a moment later. Then a camel-fly bit him behind, and he understood, and leapt in after me. We swam about desperately keeping our heads wet, to dissuade the grey swarms: but they were too bold with hunger to be afraid of water, and after five minutes we struggled out, and frantically into our clothes, the blood running from twenty of their dagger-bites.

Nasir stood and laughed at us: and later we journeyed together to the fort, to rest midday there. Ali ibn el Hussein's old corner tower, this only roof in the desert, was cool and peaceful. The wind stirred the palm-fronds outside to a frosty rustling: neglected palms, too northerly for their red-date-crop to be good; but the stems were thick with low branches, and threw a pleasant shade. Under them, on his carpet, sat Nasir in the quietness. The grey smoke of his thrown-away cigarette undulated out on the warm air, flickering and fading through the sun-spots which shone between the leaves. 'I am happy', said he. We were all happy.

In the afternoon an armoured car came up, completing our necessary defence, though the risk of enemy was minute. Three tribes covered the country between us and the railway. There were only forty horse-men in Deraa, none in Amman: also, as yet the Turks had no news of us. One of their aeroplanes flew over on the morning of the ninth, made a perfunctory circle, and went off, probably without seeing us. Our camp, on its airy summit, gave us splendid observation of the Deraa and Amman roads. By day we twelve English, with Nasir and his slave, lazed, roaming, bathing at sunset, sight-seeing, thinking; and slept comfortably at night: or rather I did: enjoying the precious interval between the conquered friends of Aba el Lissan and the enemy of next month.

The preciousness would seem to have been partly in myself, for on this march to Damascus (and such it was already in our imagination) my normal balance had changed. I could feel the taut power of Arab excitement behind me. The climax of the preaching of years had come, and a united country was straining towards its historic capital. In confidence that this weapon, tempered by myself, was enough for the utmost of my purpose, I seemed to forget the English companions who stood outside my idea in the shadow of ordinary war. I failed to make them partners of my certainty.

Long after, I heard that Winterton rose each dawn and examined the horizon, lest my carelessness subject us to surprise: and at Umtaiye and Sheikh Saad the British for days thought we were a forlorn hope. Actually I knew (and surely said?) that we were as safe as anyone in the world at war. Because of the pride they had, I never saw their doubt of my plans.

These plans were a feint against Amman and a real cutting of the Deraa railways: further than this we hardly went, for it was ever my habit, while studying alternatives, to keep the stages in solution.

The public often gave credit to Generals because it had seen only the orders and the result: even Foch said (before he commanded troops) that Generals won battles: but no General ever truly thought so. The Syrian campaign of September 1918 was perhaps the most scientifically perfect in English history, one in which force did least and brain most. All the world, and especially those who served them, gave the credit of the victory to Allenby and Bartholomew: but those two would never see it in our light, knowing how their inchoate ideas were discovered in application, and how their men, often not knowing, wrought them.

By our establishment at Azrak the first part of our plan, the feint, was accomplished. We had sent our 'horsemen of St. George', gold sovereigns, by the thousand to the Beni Sakhr, purchasing all the barley on their threshing floors: begging them not to mention it, but we would require it for our animals and for our British allies, in a fortnight. Dhiab of Tafileh — that jerky, incomplete hobbledehoy — gossiped the news instantly through to Kerak.

In addition, Feisal warned the Zebn to Bair, for service; and Hornby, now (perhaps a little prematurely) wearing Arab clothes, was active in preparations for a great assault on Madeba. His plan was to move about the nineteenth, when he heard that Allenby was started; his hope being to tie on to Jericho, so that if we failed by Deraa our force could return and reinforce his movement: which would then be, not a feint, but the old second string to our bow. However, the Turks knocked this rather crooked by their advance to Tafileh, and Hornby had to defend Shobek against them.

For our second part, the Deraa business, we had to plan an attack proper. As preliminary we determined to cut the line near Amman, thus preventing Amman's reinforcement of Deraa, and maintaining its conviction that our feint against it was real. It seemed to me that (with Egyptians to do the actual destruction) this preliminary could be undertaken by the Ghurkas, whose detachment would not distract our main body from the main purpose.

This main purpose was to cut the railways in the Hauran and keep them cut for at least a week; and there seemed to be three ways of doing it. The first was to march north of Deraa to the Damascus railway, as on my ride with Tallal in the winter, cut it; and then cross to the Yarmuk railway. The second was to march south of Deraa to the Yarmuk, as with Ali ibn el Hussein in November, 1917. The third was to rush straight at Deraa town.

The third scheme could be undertaken only if the Air Force would promise so heavy a daylight bombing of Deraa station that the effect would be tantamount to artillery bombardment, enabling us to risk an assault against it with our few men. Salmond hoped to do this; but it depended on how many heavy machines he received or assembled in time. Dawnay would fly over to us here with his last word on September the eleventh. Till then we would hold the schemes equal in our judgement.

Of our supports, my bodyguard were the first to arrive, prancing up Wadi Sirhan on September the ninth: happy, fatter than their fat camels, rested, and amused after their month of feasting with the Rualla. They reported Nuri nearly ready, and determined to join us. The contagion of the new tribe's first vigour had quickened in them a life and spirit which made us jolly.

On the tenth the two aeroplanes came through from Akaba. Murphy and Junor, the pilots, settled down to the horse-flies, which gambolled in the air about their juiciness. On the eleventh, the other armoured cars and Joyce drove in, with Stirling, but without Feisal. Marshall had remained to squire him up next day; and things were always safe to go well where Marshall, the capable soul, directed them with a cultivated humour, which was not so much riotous as persistent. Young, Peake, Scott-Higgins and the baggage arrived. Azrak became many-peopled and its lakes were again resonant with voices and the plunge of brown and lean, brown and strong, copper-coloured, or white bodies into the transparent water.

On the eleventh the aeroplane from Palestine arrived. Unfortunately, Dawnay was again ill, and the staff officer who took his place (being raw) had suffered severely from the roughness of the air; and had left behind the notes he was to bring us. His rather concrete assurance, that regard upon his world of the finished Englishman, gave way before these shocks, and the final shock of our naked carelessness out there in the desert, without pickets or watching posts, signallers, sentries or telephones, or any apparent reserves, defence-line, refuges and bases.

So he forgot his most important news, how on September the sixth Allenby, with a new inspiration, had said to Bartholomew, 'Why bother about Messudieh?' Let the cavalry go straight to Afuleh, and Nazareth': and so the whole plan had been changed, and an enormous indefinite advance substituted for the fixed objective. We got no notion of this; but by cross-questioning the pilot, whom Salmond had informed, we got a clear statement of the resources in bombing machines. They fell short of our minimum for Deraa; so we asked for just a hamper-bombing of it while we went round it by the north, to make sure of destroying the Damascus line.

The next day Feisal arrived with, behind him, the army of troops, Nuri Said the spick and span, Jemil the gunner, Pisani's coster-like Algerians, and the other items of our 'three men and a boy' effort. The grey flies had now two thousand camels to fatten upon, and in their weariness gave up Junor and his half-drained mechanics.

In the afternoon Nuri Shaalan appeared, with Trad and Khalid, Faris, Durzi, and the Khaffaji. Auda abu Tayi arrived, with Mohammed el Dheilan; also Fahad and Adhub, the Zebn leaders, with ibn Bani, the chief of the Serahin, and ibn Genj of the Serdiyeh. Majid ibn Sultan, of the Adwan near Salt, rode across to learn the truth of our attack on Amman. Later in the evening there was a rattle of rifle fire in the north, and Talal el Hareidhin, my old companion, came ruffling at the gallop, with forty or fifty mounted peasants behind him. His sanguine face beamed with joy at our long-hoped-for arrival. Druses and town-Syrians, Isawiyeh and Hawarneh swelled the company. Even the barley for our return if the venture failed (a possibility we seldom entertained) began to arrive in a steady file of loads. Everyone was stout and in health. Except myself. The crowd had destroyed my pleasure in Azrak, and I went off down the valley to our remote Ain el Essad and lay there all day in my old lair among the tamarisk, where the wind in the dusty green branches played with such sounds as it made in English trees. It told me I was tired to death of these Arabs; petty incarnate Semites who attained heights and depths beyond our reach, though not beyond our sight. They realized our absolute in their unrestrained capacity for good and evil; and for two years I had profitably shammed to be their companion!

To-day it came to me with finality that my patience as regards the false position I had been led into was finished. A week, two weeks, three, and I would insist upon relief. My nerve had broken; and I would be lucky if the ruin of it could be hidden so long.

Joyce meanwhile shouldered the responsibility which my defection endangered. By his orders Peake, with the Egyptian Camel Corps, now a sapper party, Scott-Higgins, with his fighting Ghurkas, and two armoured cars as insurance, went off to cut the railway by Ifdein.

The scheme was for Scott-Higgins to rush a blockhouse after dark with his nimble Indians — nimble on foot that was to say, for they were like sacks, on camels. Peake was then to demolish until dawn. The cars would cover their retreat eastward in the morning, over the plain, upon which we, the main body, would be marching north from Azrak for Umtaiye, a great pit of rain-water fifteen miles below Deraa, and our advanced base. We gave them Rualla guides and saw them off, hopefully, for this important preliminary.

CHAPTER CVIII

JUST at dawn our column marched. Of them one thousand were the Aba el Lissan contingent: three hundred were Nuri Shaalan's nomad horse. He had also two thousand Rualla camel-riders: these we asked him to keep in Wadi Sirhan. It seemed not wise, before the supreme day, to launch so many disturbing Beduin among the villages of Hauran. The horsemen were sheikhs, or sheikhs' servants, men of substance, under control.

Affairs with Nuri and Feisal held me the whole day in Azrak: but Joyce had left me a tender, the Blue Mist, by which on the following morning I overtook the army, and found them breakfasting among the grass-filled roughness of the Giaan el Khunna. The camels, joying to be out of the barren circle of Azrak, were packing their stomachs hastily with this best of food.

Joyce had bad news. Peake had rejoined, reporting failure to reach the line, because of trouble with Arab encampments in the neighbourhood of his proposed demolition. We had set store on breaking the Amman railway, and the check was an offence. I left the car, took a load of gun-cotton, and mounted my camel, to push in advance of the force. The others made a detour to avoid harsh tongues of lava which ran down westwards towards the railway; but we, Ageyl and others of the well-mounted, cut straight across by a thieves' path to the open plain about the ruined Um el Jemal.

I was thinking hard about the Amman demolition, puzzled as to what expedient would be quickest and best; and the puzzle of these ruins added to my care. There seemed evidence of bluntness of mind in these Roman frontier cities, Um el Jemal, Um el Surab, Umtaiye. Such incongruous buildings, in what was then and now a desert cockpit, accused their builders of insensitiveness; almost of a vulgar assertion of man's right (Roman right) to live unchanged in all his estate. Italianate buildings — only to be paid for by taxing more docile provinces — on these fringes of the world disclosed a prosaic blindness to the transience of politics. A house which so survived the purpose of its builder was a pride too trivial to confer honour upon the mind responsible for its conception.

Um el Jemal seemed aggressive and impudent, and the railway beyond it so tiresomely intact, that they blinded me to an air-battle between Murphy in our Bristol Fighter and an enemy two-seater. The Bristol was badly shot about before the Turk went down in flames. Our army were delighted spectators, but Murphy, finding the damage too great for his few materials at Azrak, went for repair to Palestine in the morning. So our tiny Air Force was reduced to the B.E. 12, a type so out of date that it was impossible for fighting, and little use for reconnaissance. This we discovered on the day: meanwhile we were as glad as the army at our man's win.

Umtaiye was reached, just before sunset. The troops were five or six miles behind, so as soon as our beasts had had a drink we struck off to the railway, four miles downhill to the westward, thinking to do a snatch-demolition. The dusk let us get close without alarm, and, to our joy, we found that the going was possible for armoured cars: while just before us were two good bridges.

These points decided me to return in the morning, with cars and more gun-cotton, to abolish the larger, four-arched bridge. Its destruction would give the Turks some days' hard mending, and set us free of Amman all the time of our first Deraa raid; thus the purpose of Peake's frustrated demolition would be filled. It was a happy discovery, and we rode back, quartering the ground while the darkness gathered, to pick the best car road.

As we climbed the last ridge, a high unbroken watershed which hid Umtaiye completely from the railway and its possible watchmen, the fresh north-east wind blew into our faces the warm smell and dust of ten thousand feet; and from the crest the ruins appeared so startlingly unlike themselves three hours before that we pulled up to gasp. The hollow ground was festively spangled with a galaxy of little evening fires, fresh-lighted, still twinkling with the flame reflections in their smoke. About them men were making bread or coffee, while others drove their noisy camels to and from the water.

I rode to the dark camp, the British one, and sat there with Joyce and Winterton and Young, telling them of what we must do first thing in

610 A SOUND SCHEME 15. ix. 18

the morning. Beside us lay and smoked the British soldiers, quietly
risking themselves on this expedition, because we ordered it. It was a
thing typical, as instinct with our national character as that babbling
laughing turmoil over there was Arab. In their crises the one race
drew in, the other spread.

In the morning, while the army breakfasted, and thawed the dawn-
chill from its muscles in the sun, we explained to the Arab leaders in
council the fitness of the line for a car-raid; and it was determined that
two armoured cars should run down to the bridge and attack it, while
the main body continued their march to Tell Arar on the Damascus
Railway, four miles north of Deraa. They would take post there,
possessing the line, at dawn to-morrow, September the seventeenth;
and we with the cars would have finished this bridge and rejoined
them before that.

About two in the afternoon, as we drove towards the railway, we
had the great sight of a swarm of our bombing planes droning steadily
up towards Deraa on their first raid. The place had hitherto been
carefully reserved from air attack; so the damage among the unaccustomed, unprotected, unarmed garrison was heavy. The morale
of the men suffered as much as the railway traffic: and till our onslaught
from the north forced them to see us, all their efforts went into digging
bomb-proof shelters.

We lurched across plots of grass, between bars and fields of rough
stone, in our two tenders and two armoured cars; but arrived all well
behind a last ridge, just this side of our target. On the rise south of the
bridge stood a stone blockhouse.

We settled to leave the tenders here, under cover. I transferred
myself, with one hundred and fifty pounds of gun-cotton, fused and
ready, to one armoured car; intending to drive passively down the
valley towards the bridge, till its arches, sheltering us from the fire of the
post, enabled me to lay and light the demolition charges. Meanwhile
the other, the active fighting car, would engage the blockhouse at
short range to cover my operation.

The two cars set out simultaneously. When they saw us the
astonished garrison of seven or eight Turks got out of their trenches,
and, rifles in hand, advanced upon us in open order: moved either by

panic, by misunderstanding, or by an inhuman unmixed courage.

In a few minutes the second car came into action against them: while four other Turks appeared beside the bridge and shot at us. Our machine-gunners ranged, and fired a short burst. One man fell, another was hit: the rest ran a little way, thought better of it, and returned, making friendly signs. We took their rifles, and sent them up valley to the tenders, whose drivers were watching us keenly from their ridge. The blockhouse surrendered at the same moment. We were very content to have taken the bridge, and its section of track, in five minutes without loss.

Joyce rushed down in his tender with more gun-cotton, and hastily we set about the bridge, a pleasant little work, eighty feet long and fifteen feet high, honoured with a shining slab of white marble, bearing the name and titles of Sultan Abd el Hamid. In the drainage holes of the spandrils six small charges were inserted zigzag, and with their explosion all the arches were scientifically shattered; the demolition being a fine example of that finest sort which left the skeleton of its bridge intact indeed, but tottering, so that the repairing enemy had a first labour to destroy the wreck, before they could attempt to rebuild.

When we had finished, enemy patrols were near enough to give us fair excuse for quitting. The few prisoners, whom we valued for Intelligence reasons, were given place on our loads; and we bumped off. Unfortunately we bumped too carelessly in our satisfaction, and at the first watercourse there was a crash beneath my tender. One side of its box-body tipped downward till the weight came on the tyre at the back wheel, and we stuck.

The front bracket of the near back spring had crystallized through by the chassis, in a sheer break which nothing but a workshop could mend. We gazed in despair, for we were only three hundred yards from the railway, and stood to lose the car, when the enemy came along in ten minutes. A Rolls in the desert was above rubies: and though we had been driving in these for eighteen months, not upon the polished roads of their makers' intention, but across country of the vilest, at speed, day or night, carrying a ton of goods and four or five men up, yet this was our first structural accident in the team of nine.

Rolls, the driver, our strongest and most resourceful man, the ready mechanic, whose skill and advice largely kept our cars in running order, was nearly in tears over the mishap. The knot of us, officers and men, English, Arabs and Turks, crowded round him and watched his face anxiously. As he realized that he, a private, commanded in this emergency, even the stubble on his jaw seemed to harden in sullen determination. At last he said there was just one chance. We might jack up the fallen end of the spring, and wedge it, by baulks upon the running board, in nearly its old position. With the help of ropes the thin angle-irons of the running boards might carry the additional weight.

We had on each car a length of scantling to place between the double tyres if ever the car stuck in sand or mud. Three blocks of this would make the needful height. We had no saw, but drove bullets through it cross-wise till we could snap it off. The Turks heard us firing, and halted cautiously. Joyce heard us and ran back to help. Into his car we piled our load, jacked up the spring and the chassis, lashed in the wooden baulks, let her down on them (they bore splendidly), cranked up, and drove off. Rolls eased her to walking speed at every stone and ditch, while we, prisoners and all, ran beside with cries of encouragement, clearing the track.

In camp we stitched the blocks with captured telegraph wire, and bound them together and to the chassis, and the spring to the chassis; till it looked as strong as possible, and we put back the load. So enduring was the running board that we did the ordinary work with the car for the next three weeks, and took her so into Damascus at the end. Great was Rolls, and great was Royce! They were worth hundreds of men to us in these deserts.

This darning the car delayed us for hours, and at its end we slept in Umtaiye, confident that, by starting before dawn, we should not be much late in meeting Nuri Said on the Damascus line to-morrow: and we could tell him that, for a week, the Amman line was sealed, by loss of a main bridge. This was the side of quickest reinforcement for Deraa, and its death made our rear safe. Even we had helped poor Zeid behind there in Aba el Lissan: for the Turks massed in Tafileh would hold up that attack till their communications were again open. Our last campaign was beginning auspiciously.

CHAPTER CIX

DULY, before dawn, we drove upon the track of Stirling's cars, eager to be with them before their fight. Unfortunately the going was not helpful. At first we had a bad descent, and then difficult flats of jagged dolerite, across which we crawled painfully. Later we ran over ploughed slopes. The soil was heavy for the cars, for with summer drought this red earth cracked a yard deep and two or three inches wide. The five-ton armoured cars were reduced to first speed, and nearly stuck.

We overtook the Arab Army about eight in the morning, on the crest of the slope to the railway, as it was deploying to attack the little bridge-guarding redoubt between us and the mount of Tell Arar whose head overlooked the country-side to Deraa.

Rualla horsemen, led by Trad, dashed down the long slope and over the liquorice-grown bed of the watercourse to the line. Young bounced after them in his Ford. From the ridge we thought the railway taken without a shot, but while we gazed, suddenly from the neglected Turkish post came a vicious spitting fire, and our braves, who had been standing in splendid attitudes on the coveted line (wondering privately what on earth to do next) disappeared.

Nuri Said moved down Pisani's guns and fired a few shots. Then the Rualla and troops rushed the redoubt easily, with only one killed. So the southern ten miles of the Damascus line was freely ours by nine in the morning. It was the only railway to Palestine and Hejaz and I could hardly realize our fortune; hardly believe that our word to Allenby was fulfilled so simply and so soon.

The Arabs streamed down from the ridge in rivers of men, and swarmed upon the round head of Tell Arar, to look over their plain, whose rimmed flatness the early sun speciously relieved, by yet throwing more shadow than light. Our soldiers could see Deraa, Mezerib and Ghazale, the three key-stations, with their naked eyes.

I was seeing further than this: northward to Damascus, the Turkish base, their only link with Constantinople and Germany, now cut off:

southward to Amman and Maan and Medina, all cut off: westward to Liman von Sandars isolated in Nazareth: to Nablus: to the Jordan Valley. To-day was September the seventeenth, the promised day, forty-eight hours before Allenby would throw forward his full power. In forty-eight hours the Turks might decide to change their dispositions to meet our new danger; but they could not change them before Allenby struck. Bartholomew had said, 'Tell me if he will be in his Auja line the day before we start, and I will tell you if we will win'. Well, he was; so we would win. The question was by how much.

I wanted the whole line destroyed in a moment: but things seemed to have stopped. The army had done its share: Nuri Said was posting machine-guns about the Arar mound to keep back any sortie from Deraa: but why was there no demolition going on? I rushed down, to find Peake's Egyptians making breakfast. It was Drake's game of bowls, and I fell dumb with admiration.

However, in an hour they were mustered for their rhythmic demolition by numbers; and already the French gunners, who also carried gun-cotton, had descended with intention upon the near bridge. They were not very good, but at the second try did it some hurt.

From the head of Tell Arar, before the mirage had begun to dance, we examined Deraa carefully through my strong glass, wanting to see what the Turks had in store for us this day. The first discovery was disturbing. Their aerodrome was alive with gangs pulling machine after machine into the open. I could count eight or nine lined up. Otherwise things were as we expected. Some few infantry were doubling out into the defence position, and their guns were being fired towards us: but we were four miles off. Locomotives were getting up steam: but the trains were unarmoured. Behind us, towards Damascus, the country lay still as a map. From Mezerib on our right, there was no movement. We held the initiative.

Our hope was to fire six hundred charges, tulip-fashion, putting out of commission six kilometres of rail. Tulips had been invented by Peake and myself for this occasion. Thirty ounces of gun-cotton were planted beneath the centre of the central sleeper of each ten-metre section of the track. The sleepers were steel, and their box-shape left an air-chamber which the gas expansion filled, to blow the middle of the sleeper upward. If the charge was properly laid, the metal did not snap, but humped itself, bud-like, two feet in the air. The lift of it pulled the rails three inches up: the drag of it pulled them six inches together; and, as the chairs gripped the bottom flanges, warped them inward seriously. The triple distortion put them beyond repair. Three or five sleepers would be likewise ruined, and a trench driven across the earthwork: all this with one charge, fired by a fuse, so short that the first, blowing off while the third was being lighted, cast its debris safely overhead.

Six hundred such charges would take the Turks a fair week to mend. This would be a generous reading of Allenby's 'three men and a boy with pistols'. I turned to go back to the troops, and at that moment two things happened. Peake fired his first charge, like a poplar-tree of black smoke, with a low following report; and the first Turkish machine got up and came for us. Nuri Said and I fitted admirably under an outcrop of rock, fissured into deep natural trenches, on the hill's southern face. There we waited coolly for the bomb: but it was only a reconnaissance machine, a Pfalz, which studied us, and returned to Deraa with its news.

Bad news it must have been, for three two-seaters, and four scouts and an old yellow-bellied Albatros got up in quick succession, and circled over us, dropping bombs, or diving at us with machine-gun fire. Nuri put his Hotchkiss gunners in the rock cracks, and rattled back at them. Pisani cocked up his four mountain guns, and let fly some optimistic shrapnel. This disturbed the enemy, who circled off, and came back much higher. Their aim became uncertain.

We scattered out the troops and camels, while the irregulars scattered themselves. To open into the thinnest target was our only hope of safety, as the plain had not overhead cover for a rabbit; and our hearts misgave us when we saw what thousands of men we had, dotted out below. It was strange to stand on the hill-top looking at these two rolling square miles, liberally spread with men and animals, and bursting out irregularly with lazy silent bulbs of smoke where bombs dropped (seemingly quite apart from their thunder) or with sprays of dust where machine-gun groups lashed down.

Things looked and sounded hot, but the Egyptians went on working as methodically as they had eaten. Four parties dug in tulips, while Peake and one of his officers lit each series as it was laid. The two slabs of gun-cotton in a tulip-charge were not enough to make a showy explosion, and the aeroplanes seemed not to see what was going on: at least they did not wash them particularly with bombs; and as the demolition proceeded, the party drew gradually out of the danger-area into the quiet landscape to the north. We traced their progress by the degradation of the telegraph. In virgin parts its poles stood trimly, drilled by the taut wire: but behind Peake they leaned and tottered anyhow, or fell.

Nuri Said, Joyce and myself met in council, and pondered how to get at the Yarmuk section of the Palestine line to top off our cutting of the Damascus and Hejaz Railways. In view of the reported opposition there we must take nearly all our men, which seemed hardly wise under such constant air observation. For one thing, the bombs might hurt us badly on the march across the open plain; and for another, Peake's demolition party would be at the mercy of Deraa if the Turks plucked up the courage to sally. For the moment they were fearful: but time might make them brave.

While we hesitated, things were marvellously solved. Junor, the pilot of the B.E. 12 machine, now alone at Azrak, had heard from the disabled Murphy of the enemy machines about Deraa, and in his own mind decided to take the Bristol Fighter's place, and carry out the air programme. So when things were at their thickest with us he suddenly sailed into the circus.

We watched with mixed feelings, for his hopelessly old-fashioned machine made him cold meat for any one of the enemy scouts or two-seaters: but at first he astonished them, as he rattled in with his two guns. They scattered for a careful look at this unexpected opponent. He flew westward across the line, and they went after in pursuit, with that amiable weakness of aircraft for a hostile machine, however important the ground target.

We were left in perfect peace. Nuri caught at the lull to collect three hundred and fifty regulars, with two of Pisani's guns; and hurried them over the saddle behind Tell Arar, on the first stage of their march to Mezerib. If the aeroplanes gave us a half-hour's law, they would probably notice neither the lessened numbers by the mound, nor the scattered groups making along every slope and hollow across the stubble westward. This cultivated land had a quilt-work appearance from the air: also the ground was tall with maize stalks, and thistles grew saddle-high about it in great fields.

We sent the peasantry after the soldiers, and half an hour later I was calling up my bodyguard that we might get to Mezerib before the others, when again we heard the drone of engines; and, to our astonishment, Junor reappeared, still alive, though attended on three sides by enemy machines, spitting bullets. He was twisting and slipping splendidly, firing back. Their very numbers hindered them but of course the affair could have only one ending.

In the faint hope that he might get down intact we rushed towards the railway where was a strip of ground, not too boulder-strewn. Everyone helped to clear it at speed, while Junor was being driven lower. He threw us a message to say his petrol was finished. We worked feverishly for five minutes, and then put out a landing-signal. He dived at it, but as he did so the wind flawed and blew across at a sharp angle. The cleared strip was too little in any case. He took ground beautifully, but the wind puffed across once more. His under-carriage went, and the plane turned over in the rough.

We rushed up to rescue, but Junor was out, with no more hurt than a cut on the chin. He took off his Lewis gun, and the Vickers, and the drums of tracer ammunition for them. We threw everything into Young's Ford, and fled, as one of the Turkish two-seaters dived viciously and dropped a bomb by the wreck.

Junor five minutes later was asking for another job. Joyce gave him a Ford for himself, and he ran boldly down the line till near Deraa, and blew a gap in the rails there, before the Turks saw him. They found such zeal excessive, and opened on him with their guns: but he rattled away again in his Ford, unhurt for the third time.

CHAPTER CX

My bodyguard waited in two long lines on the hill-side. Joyce was staying at Tell Arar as covering force, with a hundred of Nuri Said's men, the Rualla, the Ghurkas and the cars; while we slipped across to break the Palestine Railway. My party would look like Beduins, so I determined to move openly to Mezerib by the quickest course, for we were very late.

Unfortunately we drew enemy attention. An aeroplane crawled over us, dropping bombs: one, two, three, misses: the fourth into our midst. Two of my men went down. Their camels, in bleeding masses, struggled on the ground. The men had not a scratch, and leaped up behind two of their friends. Another machine floated past us, its engine cut off. Two more bombs, and a shock which spun my camel round, and knocked me half out of the saddle with a burning numbness in my right elbow. I felt I was hard hit, and began to cry for the pity of it: to be put out just when another day's control would have meant a vast success. The blood was running down my arm: perhaps if I did not look at it I might carry on as if I were unhurt.

My camel swung to a spatter of machine-gun bullets. I clutched at the pommel, and found my damaged arm there and efficient. I had judged it blown off. My left hand threw the cloak aside and explored for the wound — to feel only a very hot little splinter of metal too light to do real harm after driving through the massed folds of my cloak. The trifle showed how much my nerve was on edge. Curiously enough it was the first time I had been hit from the air.

We opened out and rode greatly, knowing the ground by heart; checking only to tell the young peasants we met that the work was now at Mezerib. The field-paths were full of these fellows, pouring out afoot from every village to help us. They were very willing: but our eyes had rested so long on the brown leanness of desert men that these gay village lads with their flushed faces, clustering hair, and plump pale arms and legs seemed like girls. They had kilted up their gowns above the knee for fast work: and the more active raced beside us through the fields, chaffing back my veterans.

As we reached Mezerib, Durzi ibn Dughmi met us, with news that Nuri Said's soldiers were only two miles back. We watered our camels, and drank deeply ourselves, for it had been a long, hot day, and was not ended. Then from behind the old fort we looked over the lake, and saw movement in the French railway station.

Some of the white-legged fellows told us that the Turks held it in force. However the approaches were too tempting. Abdulla led our charge, for my days of adventure were ended, with the sluggard excuse that my skin must be kept for a justifying emergency. Otherwise I wanted to enter Damascus. This job was too easy. Abdulla found grain: also flour; and some little booty of weapons, horses, ornaments. These excited my hangers-on. New adherents came running across the grass, like flies to honey. Tallal arrived at his constant gallop. We passed the stream, and walked together up the far bank knee-deep in weeds till we saw the Turkish station three hundred yards in front. We might capture this before attacking the great bridge below Tell el Shehab. Tallal advanced carelessly. Turks showed themselves to right and left: 'It's all right,' said he, 'I know the stationmaster': but when we were two hundred yards away, twenty rifles fired a shocking volley at us. We dropped unhurt into the weeds (nearly all of them thistles), and crawled gingerly back, Tallal swearing.

My men heard him, or the shots, and came streaming up from the river: but we returned them, fearing a machine-gun in the station buildings. Nuri Said was due. He arrived with Nasir, and we considered the business. Nuri pointed out that delay at Mezerib might lose us the bridge, a greater objective. I agreed, but thought this bird in hand might suffice, since Peake's main line demolition would stand for a week, and the week's end bring a new situation.

So Pisani unfolded his willing guns and smashed in a few rounds of point-blank high explosive. Under their cover, with our twenty machine-guns making a roof overhead, Nuri walked forward, gloved and sworded, to receive the surrender of the forty soldiers left alive.

Upon this most rich station hundreds of Haurani peasants hurled themselves in frenzy, plundering. Men, women and children fought like dogs over every object. Doors and windows, door-frames and window-frames, even steps of the stairs, were carried off. One hopeful blew in the safe and found postage stamps inside. Others smashed open the long range of waggons in the siding, to find all manner of goods. Tons were carried off. Yet more were strewn in wreckage on the ground.

Young and I cut the telegraph, here an important network of trunk and local lines, indeed the Palestine army's main link with their home-land. It was pleasant to imagine Liman von Sandars' fresh curse, in Nazareth, as each severed wire tanged back from the clippers. We did them slowly, with ceremony, to draw out the indignation. The Turks' hopeless lack of initiative made their army a 'directed' one, so that by destroying the telegraphs we went far towards turning them into a leaderless mob. After the telegraph we blew in the points, and planted tulips: not very many, but enough to annoy. While we worked a light engine came down the line from Deraa on patrol. The bang and dust-clouds of our tulips perturbed it. It withdrew discreetly. Later an aeroplane visited us.

Among the captured rolling stock, on platform trucks, were two lorries crammed with delicacies for some German canteen. The Arabs, distrusting tins and bottles, had spoiled nearly everything: but we got some soups and meat, and later Nuri Said gave us bottled asparagus. He had found an Arab prising open the case and had cried 'pigs' bones' at him in horror when the contents came to light. The peasant spat and dropped it, and Nuri quickly stuffed all he could into his saddle-bags.

The lorries had huge petrol tanks. Beyond them were some trucks of firewood. We set the whole afire at sunset, when the plundering was finished, and the troops and tribesmen had fallen back to the soft grass by the outlet from the lake.

The splendid blaze spreading along the line of waggons illuminated our evening meal. The wood burned with a solid glare, and the fiery tongues and bursts of the petrol went towering up, higher than the water-tanks. We let the men make bread and sup and rest, before a night-attempt on the Shehab bridge, which lay three miles to the westward. We had meant to attack at dark, but the wish for food stopped us, and then we had swarms of visitors, for our beacon-light advertised us over half Hauran.

Visitors were our eyes, and had to be welcomed. My business was to see every one with news, and let him talk himself out to me, afterwards arranging and combining the truth of these points into a complete picture in my mind. Complete, because it gave me certainty of judgement: but it was not conscious nor logical, for my informants were so many that they informed me to distraction, and my single mind bent under all its claims.

Men came pouring down from the north on horse, on camel, and on foot, hundreds and hundreds of them in a terrible grandeur of enthusiasm, thinking this was the final occupation of the country, and that Nasir would seal his victory by taking Deraa in the night. Even the magistrates of Deraa came to open us their town. By acceding we should hold the water supply of the railway station, which must inevitably yield: yet later, if the ruin of the Turkish army came but slowly, we might be forced out again, and lose the plainsmen between Deraa and Damascus, in whose hands our final victory lay. A nice calculation, if hardly a fresh one, but on the whole the arguments were still against taking Deraa. Again we had to put off our friends with excuses within their comprehension.

CHAPTER CXI

SLOW work; and when at last we were ready a new visitor appeared, the boy-chief of Tell el Shehab. His village was the key to the bridge. He described the position; the large guard; how it was placed. Obviously the problem was harder than we had believed, if his tale was true. We doubted it, for his just-dead father had been hostile, and the son sounded too suddenly devoted to our cause. However, he finished by suggesting that he return after an hour with the officer commanding the garrison, a friend of his. We sent him off to bring his Turk, telling our waiting men to lie down for another brief test.

Soon the boy was back with a captain, an Armenian, anxious to harm his government in any way he could. Also he was very nervous. We had hard work to assure him of our enlightenment. His subalterns, he said, were loyal Turks, and some of the non-commissioned officers. He proposed we move close to the village, and lie there secretly, while three or four of our lustiest men hid in his room. He would call his subordinates one by one to see him; and, as each entered, our ambush might pinion him.

This sounded in the proper descent from books of adventure, and we agreed enthusiastically. It was nine at night. At eleven precisely we would line up round the village and wait for the Sheikh to show our strong men to the Commandant's house. The two conspirators departed, content, while we woke up our army, asleep with the sleep of exhaustion beside their loaded camels. It was pitchy dark.

My bodyguard prepared bridge-cutting charges of gelatine. I filled my pockets with detonators. Nasir sent men to each section of the Camel Corps to tell them of the coming adventure, that they might work themselves up to the height of it: and to ensure their mounting quietly, without the disaster of a roaring camel. They played up. In a long double line our force crept down a winding path, beside an irrigation ditch, on the crest of the dividing ridge. If there was treachery before us, this bare road would be a death-trap, without issue to right or left, narrow, tortuous, and slippery with the ditch-water. So Nasir and I went first with our men, their trained ears attentive to every sound, their eyes keeping constant guard. In front of us was the waterfall, whose burdening roar had given its character to that unforgettable night with Ali ibn el Hussein when we had attempted this bridge from the other wall of the ravine. Only to-night we were nearer, so that the noise flooded up oppressively and filled our ears.

We crept very slowly and carefully now, soundless on our bare feet, while behind us the heavier soldiery snaked along, holding their breath. They also were soundless, for camels moved always stilly at night, and we had packed the equipment not to tap, the saddles not to creak. Their quietness made the dark darker, and deepened the menace of those whispering valleys either side. Waves of dank air from the river met us, chilly in our faces; and then Rahail came down swiftly from the left and caught my arm, pointing to a slow column of white smoke rising from the valley.

We ran to the edge of the descent, and peered over: but the depth was grey with mist risen off the water, and we saw only dimness and this pale vapour spiring from the level fog bank. Somewhere down there was the railway, and we stopped the march, afraid lest this be the suspected trap. Three of us went foot by foot down the slippery hill-side till we could hear voices. Then suddenly the smoke broke and shifted, with the panting of an opened throttle, and afterwards the squealing of brakes as an engine came again to a standstill. There must be a long train waiting beneath; reassured, we marched again to the very spur below the village.

We extended in line across its neck, and waited five minutes, ten minutes. They passed slowly. The murk night before moonrise was hushing in its solidity, and would have compelled patience on our restless fellows, without the added warnings of the dogs, and the intermittent ringing challenge of sentries about the bridge. At length we let the men slip quietly from their camels to the ground, and sat wondering at the delay, and the Turks' watchfulness, and the meaning of that silent train standing below us in the valley. Our woollen cloaks got stiff and heavy with the mist, and we shivered.

After a long while a lighter speck came through the dark. It was the boy sheikh, holding his brown cloak open to show us his white shirt like a flag. He whispered that his plan had failed. A train (this one in the ravine), had just arrived with a German colonel and the German and Turk reserves from Afuleh, sent up by Liman von Sandars, to rescue panic-stricken Deraa.

They had put the little Armenian under arrest for being absent from his post. There were machine-guns galore, and sentries patrolling the approaches with ceaseless energy. In fact, there was a strong picket on the path, not a hundred yards from where we sat: the oddity of our joint state made me laugh, though quietly.

Nuri Said offered to take the place by main force. We had bombs enough, and pistol flares; numbers and preparedness would be on our side. It was a fair chance: but I was at the game of reckoning the value of the objective in terms of life, and as usual finding it too dear. Of course, most things done in war were too dear, and we should have followed good example by going in and going through with it. But I was secretly and disclaimedly proud of the planning of our campaigns: so I told Nuri that I voted against it. We had to-day twice cut the Damascus-Palestine railway; and the bringing here of the Afuleh garrison was a third benefit to Allenby. Our bond had been most heavily honoured.

Nuri, after a moment's thought, agreed. We said good-night to the lad who had honestly tried to do so much for us. We passed down the lines, whispering to each man to lead back in silence. Then we sat in a group with our rifles (mine Enver's gold-inscribed Lee-Enfield trophy from the Dardanelles, given by him to Feisal years ago) waiting till our men should be beyond the danger zone.

Oddly enough this was the hardest moment of the night. Now the work was over we could scarcely resist the temptation to rouse the spoil-sport Germans out. It would have been so easy to have cracked off a Very light into their bivouac; and the solemn men would have turned out in ludicrous hurry, and shot hard into the bare, misty hillside silent at their feet. The identical notion came independently to Nasir, Nuri Said, and myself. We blurted it out together, and each promptly felt ashamed that the others had been as childish. By mutual cautions we managed to keep our respectability. At Mezerib, after midnight, we felt that something must be done to avenge the forfeited bridge. So two parties of my fellows, with guides of Tallal's men, went beyond Shehab, and cut the line twice behind it on deserted gradients. Their echoing explosions gave the German detachment a bad night. Flares were lit and the neighbourhood searched for some brewing attack.

We were glad to give them as tiresome a night as ours, for then they too would be languid in the morning. Our friends were still coming in every minute, to kiss our hands and swear eternal fealty. Their wiry ponies threaded our misted camp, between the hundreds of sleeping men, and the uneasy camels, whose great jaws were munching all night at the windy grass swallowed in the day hours.

Before dawn Pisani's other guns and the rest of Nuri Said's troops arrived from Tell Arar. We had written to Joyce that on the morrow we would return southward, by Nisib, to complete the circle of Deraa. I suggested that he move straight back to Umtaiye and there wait for us: for it, with its abundant water, splendid pasture, and equi-distance from Deraa and Jebel Druse and the Rualla Desert, seemed an ideal place in which we might rally and wait news of Allenby's fortune. By holding Umtaiye we as good as cut off the Turkish fourth army of beyond Jordan (our special bird) from Damascus: and were in place quickly to renew our main-line demolitions, whenever the enemy had nearly set them right.

CHAPTER CXII

RELUCTANTLY we pulled ourselves together for another day of effort, called up the army, and moved in a huge straggle through Mezerib station. Our fires had burned out, and the place stood dishevelled. Young and myself leisurely laid tulips, while the troops melted into broken ground towards Remthe, to be out of sight of both Deraa and Shehab. Turkish aeroplanes were humming overhead, looking for us, so we sent our peasants back through Mezerib for their villages. Consequently, the airmen reported that we were very numerous, possibly eight or nine thousand strong, and that our centrifugal movements seemed to be directed towards every direction at once.

To increase their wonderment, the French gunners' long-fused charge blew up the water-tower at Mezerib, loudly, hours after we had passed. The Germans were marching out of Shehab for Deraa, at the moment, and the inexplicable shock sent these humourless ones back there on guard till late afternoon.

Meanwhile we were far away, plodding steadily towards Nisib, whose hill-top we reached about four in the afternoon. We gave the mounted infantry a short rest, while we moved our gunners and machine-guns to the crest of the first ridge, from which the ground fell away hollowly to the railway station.

We posted the guns there in shelter, and asked them to open deliberately upon the station buildings at two thousand yards. Pisani's sections worked in emulation so that, before long, ragged holes appeared in the roofs and sheds. At the same time we pushed our machine-gunners forward on the left, to fire long bursts against the trenches, which returned a hot obstinate fire. However our troops had natural shelter and the advantage of the afternoon sun behind their backs. So we suffered no hurt. Nor did the enemy. Of course, all this was just a game, and the capture of the station not in our plan. Our real objective was the great bridge north of the village. The ridge below our feet curved out in a long horn to this work, serving as one bank of the valley which it was built to span. The village stood on the other

626

bank. The Turks held the bridge by means of a small redoubt, and maintained touch with it by riflemen posted in the village under cover of its walls.

We turned two of Pisani's guns and six machine-guns on the small but deeply-dug bridge-post, hoping to force its defenders out. Five machine-guns directed their fire on the village. In fifteen minutes its elders were out with us, very much perturbed. Nuri put, as the condition of cease-fire, their instant ejectment of the Turks from the houses. They promised. So station and bridge were divided.

We redoubled against these. The firing from the four wings became violent, thanks to our twenty-five machine-guns, the Turks also being plentifully supplied. At last we put all four of Pisani's guns against the redoubt; and, after a few salvoes, thought we saw its guard slipping from their battered trenches through the bridge into cover of the railway embankment.

This embankment was twenty feet high. If the bridge-guard chose to defend their bridge through its arches, they would be in a costly position. However, we reckoned that the attraction of their fellows in the station would draw them away. I told off the half of my bodyguard carrying explosives, to move along the machine-gun crest till within a stone's throw of the redoubt.

It was a noble evening, yellow, mild and indescribably peaceful; a foil to our incessant cannonade. The declining light shone down the angle of the ridges, its soft rays modelling them and their least contour in a delicate complexity of planes. Then the sun sank another second, and the surface became shadow, out of which for a moment there rose, starkly, the innumerable flints strewing it; each western (reflecting) facet tipped like a black diamond with flame.

A very unfit afternoon for dying, seemed to think my men: for the first time their nerves failed, and they refused to quit their shelter for the enemy's clattering bullets. They were tired, and their camels so marched out they could only walk: also they knew that one bullet in the blasting gelatine would send them sky-high.

A try to stir them by jest failed; at last I cast them off, choosing only Hemeid, the young and timid one amongst them, to come up with me on the hill-top. He shook like a man in a sick dream, but followed quietly. We rode down the ridge to its furthest edge, to have a close look at the bridge.

Nuri Said was there, sucking his briar pipe, and cheering the gunners, who were keeping a barrage over the darkening roads between the bridge, the village and the station. Nuri, being happy, propounded to me plans of attack and alternative assaults against this station, which we did not wish to assault. We argued theory for ten minutes on the skyline, with Hemeid wincing in his saddle as bullets, some of which were overs, spat past us, or ricochets hummed like slow, angry bees beside our ears. The few proper hits splashed loudly into the flints, kicking up a chalk-dust which hung transparently for a moment in the reflected light.

Nuri agreed to cover my movements to the bridge as well as he could. Then I turned Hemeid back with my camel, to tell the rest that I would hurt them worse than bullets if they did not follow him across the danger-zone to meet me: for I meant to walk round till I could be sure the bridge-post was empty.

While they hesitated, there came up Abdulla, the imperturbable, improvident, adventurous, who feared nothing; and the Zaagi. They, mad with fury that I had been let down, dashed at the shrinkers, who pounded over the shoulder with only six bullet-scratches. The redoubt was indeed abandoned: so we dismounted, and signalled Nuri to cease fire. In the silence we crept discreetly through the bridge-arches, and found them also evacuated.

Hurriedly we piled gun-cotton against the piers, which were about five feet thick and twenty-five feet high; a good bridge, my seventy-ninth, and strategically most critical, since we were going to live opposite it at Umtaiye until Allenby came forward and relieved us. So I had determined to leave not a stone of it in place.

Nuri meanwhile was hurrying the infantry, gunners and machine-gunners down in the thickening light, towards the line, with orders to get a mile beyond into the desert, form up into column and wait.

Yet the passing of so many camels over the track must take tediously long. We sat and chafed under the bridge, matches in hand, to light at once (despite the troops) if there was an alarm. Fortunately everything went well, and after an hour Nuri gave me my signal. Half a minute later (my preference for six-inch fuses!) just as I tumbled into the Turkish redoubt, the eight hundred pounds of stuff exploded in one burst, and the black air became sibilant with flying stones. The explosion was numbing from my twenty yards, and must have been heard half-way to Damascus.

Nuri, in great distress, sought me out. He had given the 'all clear' signal before learning that one company of mounted infantry was missing. Fortunately my guards were aching for redeeming service. Talal el Hareidhin took them with him up the hills, while Nuri and I stood by the yawning pit which had been the bridge, and flashed an electric torch, to give them a fixed point for their return.

Mahmud came back in half an hour triumphantly leading the lost unit. We fired shots to recall the other searchers, and then rode two or three miles into the open towards Umtaiye. The going became very broken, over moraines of slipping dolerite: so we gladly called a halt, and lay down in our ranks for an earned sleep.

CHAPTER CXIII

HOWEVER, it seemed that Nasir and I were to lose the habit of sleeping. Our noise at Nisib had proclaimed us as widely as the flames of Mezerib. Hardly were we still when visitors came streaming in from three sides to discuss the latest events. It was being rumoured that we were raiding, and not occupying; that later we would run away, as had the British from Salt, leaving our local friends to pay the bills.

The night, for hour after hour, was broken by these new-comers challenging round our bivouacs, crying their way to us like lost souls; and, peasant-fashion, slobbering over our hands with protestations that we were their highest lords and they our deepest servants. Perhaps the reception of them fell short of our usual standard; but, in revenge, they were applying the torture of keeping us awake, uneasily awake. We had been at strain for three days and nights; thinking, ordering and executing; and now, on our road to rest, it was bitter to play away this fourth night also, at the old lack-lustre, dubious game of making friends.

And their shaken morale impressed us worse and worse, till Nasir drew me aside and whispered that clearly there existed a focus of discontent in some centre near. I loosed out my peasant bodyguards to mix with the villagers and find the truth; and from their reports it seemed that the cause of distrust lay in the first settlement, at Taiyibe, which had been shaken by the return of Joyce's armoured cars yesterday, by some chance incidents, and by a just fear that they were the spot most exposed in our retreat.

I called Aziz, and we rode straight to Taiyibe, over rough stretches of lava, trackless, and piled across with walls of broken stone. In the head-man's hut sat the conclave which infected our visitors. They were debating whom to send to implore mercy from the Turks; when we walked in unannounced. Our single coming abashed them, in its assumption of supreme security. We talked irrelevantly an hour, of crops and farmyard prices, and drank some coffee: then rose to go. Behind us the babble broke out again; but now their inconstant spirits had veered to what seemed our stronger wind, and they sent no word to the enemy; though next day they were bombed and shelled for such stubborn complicity with us.

We got back before dawn, and stretched out to sleep: when there came a loud boom from the railway, and a shell shattered beyond our sleeping host. The Turks had sent down an armoured train mounting a field-gun. By myself I would have chanced its aim, for my sleep had been just long enough to make me rage for more: but the army had slept six hours and was moving.

We hurried across the horrible going. An aeroplane came over, and circled round to help the gunners. Shells began to keep accurate pace with our line of march. We doubled our speed, and broke into a ragged procession of very open order. The directing aeroplane faltered suddenly, swerved aside towards the line, and seemed to land. The gun put in one more lucky shot, which killed two camels; but for the rest it lost accuracy, and after about fifty shots we drew out of range. It began to punish Taiyibe.

Joyce, at Umtaiye, had been roused by the shooting, and came out to welcome us. Behind his tall figure the ruins were crested by a motley band, samples from every village and tribe in the Hauran, come to do homage and offer at least lip-service. To Nasir's tired disgust I left these to him, while I went off with Joyce and Winterton, telling them of the landed aeroplane, and suggesting that an armoured car beat it up at home. Just then two more enemy machines appeared and landed in about the same place.

However breakfast, our first for some while, was getting ready. So we sat down and Joyce related how the men of Taiyibe had fired at him as he passed by, presumably to show their opinion of strangers who stirred up a hornets' nest of Turks, and then hopped it!

Breakfast ended. We called for a volunteer car to investigate the enemy aerodrome. Everybody came forward with a silent goodwill and readiness which caught me by the throat. Finally Joyce chose two cars — one for Junor and one for me — and we drove for five miles to the valley in whose mouth the planes had seemed to land.

We silenced the cars and crept down its course. When about two thousand yards from the railway, it bent round into a flat meadow, by whose further side stood three machines. This was magnificent, and we leaped forward, to meet a deep ditch with straight banks of cracking earth, quite impassable.

We raced frantically along it, by a diagonal route, till we were within twelve hundred yards. As we stopped two of the aeroplanes started. We opened fire, searching the range by dust spurts, but already they had run their distance and were off, swaying and clattering up across the sky over our heads.

The third engine was sulky. Its pilot and observer savagely pulled the propeller round, while we ranged nearer. Finally they leaped into the railway ditch as we put bullet after bullet into the fuselage till it danced under the rain. We fired fifteen hundred bullets at our target (they burned it in the afternoon) and then turned home.

Unfortunately the two escaped machines had had time to go to Deraa, and return, feeling spiteful. One was not clever and dropped his four bombs from a height, missing us widely. The other swooped low, placing one bomb each time with the utmost care. We crept on defencelessly, slowly, among the stones, feeling like sardines in a doomed tin, as the bombs fell closer. One sent a shower of small stuff through the driving slit of the car, but only cut our knuckles. One tore off a front tyre and nearly lurched the car over.

Of all danger give me the solitary sort. However we reached Umtaiye well and reported success to Joyce. We had proved to the Turks that that aerodrome was not fit to use; and Deraa lay equally open to car attack. Later I lay in the shadow of a car and slept; all the Arabs in the desert, and the Turkish aeroplanes which came and bombed us, having no effect upon my peace. In the clash of events men became feverishly tireless: but to-day we had finished our first round, fortunately; and it was necessary that I rest, to clear my mind about our next moves. As usual when I lay down I dropped asleep, and slept till afternoon.

Strategically, our business was to hold on to Umtaiye, which gave us command at will of Deraa's three railways. If we held it another week we should strangle the Turkish armies, however little Allenby did. Yet tactically Umtaiye was a dangerous place. An inferior force composed exclusively of regulars, without a guerilla screen, could not safely hold it: yet to that we should shortly be reduced, if our air helplessness continued patent.

The Turks had at least nine machines. We were camped twelve miles from their aerodrome, in the open desert, about the only possible water-supply, with great herds of camels and many horses necessarily grazing round us. The Turks' beginning of bombing had been enough to disquiet the irregulars who were our eyes and ears. Soon they would break up and go home, and our usefulness be ended: Taiyibe, too, that first village which covered us from Deraa — it lay defenceless and quivering under repeated attack. If we were to remain in Umtaiye, Taiyibe must be content with us.

Clearly our first duty was to get air reinforcement from Allenby, who had arranged to send a news machine to Azrak on the day after to-morrow. I judged it would be profitable for me to go across and talk with him. I could be back on the twenty-second. Umtaiye would hold out so long, for we might always fox the aeroplanes a while by moving to Um el Surab, the next Roman village.

Whether at Umtaiye or Um el Surab, to be safe we must keep the initiative. The Deraa side was temporarily closed by the suspicion of the peasants: there remained the Hejaz line. The bridge at Kilometre 149 was nearly mended. We must smash it again, and smash another to the south, to deny the repair trains access to it. An effort by Winterton yesterday showed that the first was a matter for troops and guns. The second was objective for a raid. I went across to see if my bodyguard could do it with me on our way to Azrak.

Something was wrong. They were red-eyed, hesitant, trembling: at last I understood that while I was away in the morning the Zaagi, Abdulla and their other chiefs had gone mercilessly through the tally of those who flinched at Nisib. It was their right, for since Tafileh I had left its discipline to the company itself; but the effect for the moment was to make them useless for my purpose. Such punishment was preceded by fear: but the memory of its infliction provoked wilder lawlessness among the stronger victims, and a likelihood of crimes or violence among the witnesses. They would have been dangerous to me, to themselves, or to the enemy, as whim and opportunity provided, had we gone that night into action.

So, instead, I suggested to Joyce that the Egyptians and Ghurkas return to Akaba; proposing further that he lend me an armoured car to go down with them to the railway, their first stage, and do what could be done. We went up to Nasir and Nuri Said, and told them I would be back on the twenty-second with fighting machines, to deliver us from air-scouts and bombing. Meanwhile we would salve Taiyibe with money for the Turkish damage, and Joyce would make landing-grounds, here and at Um el Surab, against my return with our air reinforcements.

The demolition of that night was a fantastic muddle. We moved at sunset to an open valley, three easy miles from the railway. Trouble might threaten from Mafrak station. My armoured car, with Junor attendant in his Ford, would guard that side against hostile advance. The Egyptians would move direct to the line, and fire their charges.

My guiding fell through. We wandered for three hours in a maze of valleys, not able to find the railway, nor the Egyptians, nor our starting-point. At last we saw a light and drove for it, to find ourselves in front of Mafrak. We turned back to get into place, and heard the clank of an engine running northward out of the station. We chased its inter-mittent flame, hoping to catch it between us and the broken bridge: but before we overtook it there came flashes and explosions far up, as Peake fired his thirty charges.

Some mounted men galloped headlong past us, southward. We fired at them, and then the patrolling train returned, backing at its best speed from Peake's danger. We ran alongside, and opened on the tracks with our Vickers, while Junor sent a green shower of tracer bullets from his Lewis across the dark. Above our shooting and the noise of the engine we heard the Turks howling with terror of this luminous attack. They fired back raggedly, but as they did so the big car suddenly sneezed and stood still. A bullet had pierced the un-armoured end of the petrol tank, the only unarmoured spot of all our team of cars. It took us an hour to plug the leak.

Then we drove along the silent line to the twisted rails and gaping culverts, but could not find our friends. So we drew a mile back, and there at last I had my sleep out, three perfect hours of it before the dawn. I awoke fresh, and recognized our place. Probably it was only the fifth sleepless night which had made my wits woolly. We pushed forward, passing the Egyptians with the Ghurkas, and reached Azrak in the early afternoon. There were Feisal and Nuri Shaalan, eager to hear our news. We explained particularly; and then I went over to Marshall, in the temporary hospital. He had all our badly-wounded in his quiet care: but they were fewer than he had expected, so he was able to spare me a stretcher for my bed.

At dawn Joyce unexpectedly arrived. He had made up his mind that in this lull it was his duty to go down to Aba el Lissan to help Zeid and Jaafar before Maan, and to press forward Hornby among the Beni Sakhr. Then the plane from Palestine arrived, and we heard the amazing first chronicle of Allenby's victory. He had smashed and burst through and driven the Turks inconceivably. The face of our war was changed, and we gave hurried word of it to Feisal, with counsels of the general revolt to take profit of the situation. An hour later I was safely in Palestine.

From Ramleh the Air Force gave me a car up to Headquarters; and there I found the great man unmoved, except for the light in his eye as Bols bustled in every fifteen minutes, with news of some wider success. Allenby had been so sure, before he started, that to him the result was almost boredom: but no general, however scientific, could see his intricate plan carried out over an enormous field in every particular with complete success, and not know an inward gladness: especially when he felt it (as he must have felt it) a reward of the breadth and judgement which made him conceive such unorthodox movements; and break up the proper book of his administrative services to suit them; and support them by every moral and material asset, military or political, within his grasp.

He sketched to me his next intentions. Historic Palestine was his, and the broken Turks, in the hills, expected a slackening of the pursuit. Not at all! Bartholomew and Evans were prepared to provision three more thrusts: one across Jordan to Amman, to be done by Chaytor's New Zealanders; one across Jordan to Deraa, to be done by Barrow and his Indians; one across Jordan to Kuneitra, to be done by Chauvel's Australians. Chaytor would rest at Amman; Barrow and Chauvel on attaining the first objectives would converge on Damascus. We were to assist the three: and I was not to carry out my saucy threat to take Damascus, till we were all together.

I explained our prospects, and how everything was being wrecked by air-impotence. He pressed a bell and in a few minutes Salmond and Borton were conferring with us. Their machines had taken an indispensable part in Allenby's scheme: (the perfection of this man who could use infantry and cavalry, artillery and Air Force, Navy and armoured cars, deceptions and irregulars, each in its best fashion!): and had fulfilled it. There were no more Turks in the sky — except on our side, as I hurriedly interpolated. So much the better, said Salmond; they would send two Bristol fighters over to Umtaiye to sit with us while we needed them. Had we spares? Petrol? Not a drop? How was it to be got there? Only by air? An air-contained fighting unit? Unheard of!

However, Salmond and Borton were men avid of novelty. They worked out loads for D.H.9 and Handley-Page, while Allenby sat by, listening and smiling, sure it would be done. The co-operation of the air with his unfolding scheme had been so ready and elastic, the liaison so complete and informed and quick. It was the R.A.F., which had converted the Turkish retreat into rout, which had abolished their telephone and telegraph connections, had blocked their lorry columns, scattered their infantry units.

The Air chiefs turned on me and asked if our landing-grounds were good enough for a Handley-Page with full load. I had seen the big machine once in its shed, but unhesitatingly said 'Yes' though they had better send an expert over with me in the Bristols to-morrow and make sure. He might be back by noon, and the Handley come at three o'clock. Salmond got up: 'That's all right, Sir, we'll do the necessary.' I went out and breakfasted.

Allenby's headquarter was a perfect place: a cool, airy, whitewashed house, proofed against flies, and made musical by the moving of the wind in the trees outside. I felt immoral, enjoying white table-cloths, and coffee, and soldier servants, while our people at Umtaiye lay like lizards among the stones, eating unleavened bread, and waiting for the next plane to bomb them. I felt restless as the dusty sunlight which splashed a diaper over the paths, through chinks in the leaves; because, after a long spell of the restrained desert, flowers and grass seemed to fidget, and the everywhere-burgeoning green of tilth became vulgar, in its fecundity.

However, Clayton and Deedes and Dawnay were friendliness itself, and also the Air Force staff; while the good cheer and conscious strength of the Commander-in-Chief was a bath of comfort to a weary person after long strained days. Bartholomew moved maps about, explaining what they would do. I added to his knowledge of the enemy, for I was his best served intelligence officer: and in return his perspective showed me the victory sure, whatever happened to our strained little stop-block over there. Yet it seemed to me that in the Arab hands lay an option, whether to let this victory be just one more victory, or, by risking themselves once more, to make it final. Not that, so stated, it was a real option: but, when body and spirit were as wearily sick as mine, they almost instinctively sought a plausible avoidance of the way of danger.

CHAPTER CXIV

BEFORE dawn, on the Australian aerodrome, stood two Bristols and a D.H.9. In one was Ross Smith, my old pilot, who had been picked out to fly the new Handley-Page, the single machine of its class in Egypt, the apple of Salmond's eye. His lending it to fly over the enemy line on so low an errand as baggage carrying, was a measure of the goodwill toward us.

We reached Umtaiye in an hour, and saw that the army had gone: so I waved ourselves back to Um el Surab; and there they were, the defensive group of cars, and Arabs hiding from our suspect noise here, there and everywhere; the cute camels dispersed singly over the plain, filling themselves with the wonderful grazing. Young, when he saw our markings, put a landing-signal and smoke bombs on the turf which his care and Nuri Said's had swept clear of stones.

Ross Smith anxiously paced the length and breadth of the prepared space, and studied its imperfections: but rejoined us, where the drivers were making breakfast, with a clear face. The ground was O.K. for the Handley-Page. Young told us of repeated bombings yesterday and the day before, which had killed some regulars and some of Pisani's gunners and tired the life out of everyone, so that they moved in the night to Um el Surab. The idiot Turks were still bombing Umtaiye though men went to it only in the neutral noons and nights to draw water.

Also I heard of Winterton's last blowing up of the railway: an amusing night, in which he had met an unknown soldier and explained to him in broken Arabic how well they were getting on. The soldier had thanked God for His mercies, and disappeared in the dark; whence a moment later, machine-gun fire opened from left and right! Nevertheless, Winterton had fired all his charges, and withdrawn in good order without loss. Nasir came to us, and reported this man hurt, and that killed, this clan getting ready, those already joined, but others gone home — all the gossip of the country. The three shining aeroplanes had much restored the Arabs, who lauded the British, and their own bravery and endurance, while I told them the scarce-credible epic of

Allenby's success — Nablus taken, Afuleh taken, Beisan and Semakh and Haifa. My hearers' minds drew after me like flames. Tallal took fire, boasting; while the Rualla shouted for instant march upon Damascus. Even my bodyguard, still bearing witness of the Zaagi's severity in their muddy eyes and constrained faces, cheered up and began to preen a little before the crowd, with a dawn of happiness. A shiver of self-assertion and confidence ran across the camp. I determined to bring up Feisal and Nuri Shaalan for the final effort.

Meanwhile it was breakfast time with a smell of sausage in the air. We sat round, very ready: but the watcher on the broken tower yelled 'Aeroplane up', seeing one coming over from Deraa. Our Australians, scrambling wildly to their yet-hot machines, started them in a moment. Ross Smith, with his observer, leaped into one, and climbed like a cat up the sky. After him went Peters, while the third pilot stood beside the D.H.9 and looked hard at me.

I seemed not to understand him. Lewis guns, scarfe mountings, sights, rings which turned, vanes, knobs which rose and fell on swinging parallel bars; to shoot, one aimed with this side of the ring or with that, according to the varied speed and direction of oneself and the enemy. I had been told the theory, could repeat some of it: but it was in my head, and rules of action were only snares of action till they had run out of the empty head into the hands, by use. No: I was not going up to air-fight, no matter what caste I lost with the pilot. He was an Australian, of a race delighting in additional risks, not an Arab to whose gallery I must play.

He was too respectful to speak: only he looked reproach at me while we watched the battle in the air. There were one enemy two-seater and three scouts. Ross Smith fastened on the big one, and, after five minutes of sharp machine-gun rattle, the German dived suddenly towards the railway line. As it flashed behind the low ridge, there broke out a pennon of smoke, and from its falling place a soft, dark cloud. An 'Ah!' came from the Arabs about us. Five minutes later Ross Smith was back, and jumped gaily out of his machine, swearing that the Arab front was the place.

Our sausages were still hot; we ate them, and drank tea (our last English stores, broached for the visitors), but were hardly at the grapes from Jebel Druse when again the watchman tossed up his cloak and screamed, 'A plane!' This time Peters won the race, Ross Smith second, with Traill, disconsolate, in reserve: but the shy enemy turned back so soon that Peters did not catch them till near Arar: there he drove down his quarry, fighting. Later, when the wave of war rolled thither, we found the hopeless crash, and two charred German bodies.

Ross Smith wished he might stay for ever on this Arab front with an enemy every half-hour; and deeply envied Peters his coming days. However, he must go back for the Handley-Page with petrol, food and spares. The third plane was for Azrak, to get the observer marooned there yesterday; and I went in it so far, to see Feisal.

Time became spacious to those who flew: we were in Azrak thirty hours after leaving it. Ghurkas and Egyptians I turned back to rejoin the army, for new demolitions in the north. Then, with Feisal and Nuri Shaalan, I packed into the green Vauxhall, and off we went for Um el Surab to see the Handley-Page alight.

We ran at speed over the smooth flint or mud-flat, letting the strong car throb itself fully: but luck was hostile. A dispute was reported us, and we had to turn aside to a local Serahin camp. However, we made profit of our loss, by ordering their fighting men to Umtaiye: and we had them send word of victory across the railway, that the roads through the Ajlun hills might be closed to the broken Turkish armies, trying to escape into safety.

Then our car flashed northward again. Twenty miles short of Ul em Surab we perceived a single Bedawi, running southward all in a flutter, his grey hair and grey beard flying in the wind, and his shirt (tucked up in his belly-cord) puffing out behind him. He altered course to pass near us, and, raising his bony arms, yelled, 'The biggest aeroplane in the world', before he flapped on into the south, to spread his great news among the tents.

At Um el Surab the Handley stood majestic on the grass, with Bristols and 9.A like fledglings beneath its spread of wings. Round it admired the Arabs, saying, 'Indeed and at last they have sent us THE aeroplane, of which these things were foals.' Before night rumour of Feisal's resource went over Jebel Druse and the hollow of Hauran, telling people that the balance was weighted on our side.

Borton himself had come over in the machine, to concert help. We talked with him while our men drew from her bomb-racks and fuselage a ton of petrol; oil and spare parts for Bristol Fighters; tea and sugar and rations for our men; letters, Reuter telegrams and medicines for us. Then the great machine rose into the early dusk, for Ramleh, with an agreed programme of night-bombing against Deraa and Mafrak, to complete that ruin of the railway traffic which our gun-cotton had begun.

We, for our share, would keep up the gun-cotton pressure. Allenby had assigned us the Turkish Fourth Army, to harass and contain till Chaytor forced them out of Amman; and afterwards to cut up, on their retreat. This retreat was only an affair of days, and it was as certain as things could be in war that we should raise the plains between us and Damascus next week. So Feisal decided to add to our column Nuri Shaalan's Rualla camel men from Azrak. It would increase to us about four thousand strong, more than three-fourths irregular; but reliably so, for Nuri, the hard, silent, cynical old man, held the tribe between his fingers like a tool.

He was that rarity in the desert, a man without sense of argument. He would or would not, and there was no more to it. When others finished talking, he would announce his will in a few flat phrases, and wait calmly for obedience; which came, for he was feared. He was old and wise, which meant tired and disappointed: so old that it was my abiding wonder he should link himself to our enthusiasm.

I rested next day in Nasir's tent, among his peasant visitors; sorting out the too-abundant news furnished by their quick wit and goodwill. During my rest-day, Nuri Said, with Pisani and two guns, Stirling, Winterton, Young, their armoured cars, and a considerable force, went openly to the railway, cleared it by approved military means, destroyed a kilometre of rail, and burnt the tentative wooden structure with which the Turks were mending the bridge blown up by Joyce and myself before our first attack on Deraa. Nuri Shaalan, in black broadcloth cloak, personally led his Rualla horsemen, galloping with the best of them. Under his eye the tribe showed a valour which drew praise even from Nuri Said.

CHAPTER CXV

Nuri's operation of to-day was the Turks' final blow, after which they gave up trying to restore the line between Amman and Deraa. We did not know this, but still had its bogy set over us, and were urgent to put out of action a yet longer stretch. Accordingly, next dawn, Winterton, Jemil and I went out on cars to examine the line south of Mafrak station. We were received with machine-gun fire of a vigour, direction and intensity beyond any of our experience. Later we captured the experts and found they were a German machine-gun unit. For the moment we drew out, puzzled, and went further to a tempting bridge. My plan was to run under it in the car till the vault enabled us to lay the charge against the pier in shelter. So I transferred myself to an armoured car, put sixty pounds of gun-cotton on the back-board, and told the driver to push in under the arch.

Winterton and Jemil came behind in the supporting car. 'It's very hot', groaned Jemil. 'It's going to be still hotter where we're going', replied Winterton, as we drew in slowly over indifferent ground with aimless shells falling about. We were picking our way forward, about fifty yards from the bank, with enough machine-gun bullets for a week's fighting rattling off our armour, when someone from behind the line bowled a hand grenade at us.

This new condition made impossible my plan of getting under the bridge. For one thing, a hit on the back of the car would have set off our gun-cotton and blown us to blazes; for another, the car was helpless against a lobbed grenade. So we drew off, perplexed to understand this defence lavished on a bit of railway, and much interested, indeed amused, at worthy opposition after so long ease. In our imaginations, Check was a short, compact, furious man, darting glances every way from beneath tangled eyebrows, for an end to his troubles; beside him Victory seemed a lanky, white-skinned, rather languid woman. We must try again after dark. At Um el Surab we found that Nasir wished to fix camp once more at Umtaiye. It was a first stage of our journey to Damascus, so his wish delighted me, and we moved; winning thereby good excuse for doing nothing this night to the line. Instead, we sat and told stories of experience and waited for midnight, when the Handley-Page was to bomb Mafrak station. It came, and hundred-pound bomb after hundred-pound bomb crashed into the packed sidings till they caught fire, and the Turks' shooting stopped.

We slept, having given prize of the night to a tale of Enver Pasha, after the Turks re-took Sharkeui. He went to see it, in a penny steamer, with Prince Jemil and a gorgeous staff. The Bulgars, when they came, had massacred the Turks; as they retired the Bulgar peasants went too. So the Turks found hardly any one to kill. A greybeard was led on board for the Commander-in-Chief to bait. At last Enver tired of this. He signed to two of his bravo aides, and throwing open the furnace door, said, 'Push him in.' The old man screamed, but the officers were stronger and the door was slammed-to on his jerking body. 'We turned, feeling sick, to go away, but Enver, his head on one side, listening, halted us. So we listened, till there came a crash within the furnace. He smiled and nodded, saying, "Their heads always pop, like that".'

All night, and next day, the fire among the trucks burned greater and greater. It was proof of the breakdown of the Turks, which the Arabs had been rumouring since yesterday. They said the Fourth Army was streaming up from Amman in a loose mob. The Beni Hassan, who were cutting off stragglers and weak detachments, compared them to gipsies on the march.

We held a council. Our work against the Fourth Army was finished. Such remnants as avoided out of the hands of the Arabs would reach Deraa as unarmed stragglers. Our new endeavour should be to force the quick evacuation of Deraa, in order to prevent the Turks there reforming the fugitives into a rearguard. So I proposed that we march north, past Tell Arar, and over the railway at dawn to-morrow, into Sheikh Saad village. It lay in familiar country with abundant water, perfect observation, and a secure retreat west or north, or even southwest, if we were directly attacked. It cut off Deraa from Damascus and Mezerib also.

Tallal seconded me with fervour. Nuri Shaalan gave his nod: Nasir and Nuri Said. So we prepared to strike camp. The armoured cars could not come with us. They had better stay in Azrak, till Deraa fell and we wanted them to help us into Damascus. The Bristol Fighters, likewise, had done their work, clearing the air of Turkish aeroplanes. They might return to Palestine with news of our move to Sheikh Saad.

Off they circled. We, watching their line of flight, noticed a great cloud of dust added to the slow smoke from ruined Mafrak. One machine turned back and dropped a scribble that a large body of hostile cavalry were heading out from the railway towards us.

This was unwelcome news, for we were not in trim for a fight. The cars had gone, the aeroplanes had gone, one company of the mounted infantry had marched, Pisani's mules were packed and drawn up in column. I went off to Nuri Said, standing with Nasir on an ash heap at the head of the hill, and we wavered whether to run or stand. At last it seemed wiser to run, since Sheikh Saad was a more profitable stop-block. So we hurried the regulars away.

Yet things could hardly be left like that. Accordingly Nuri Shaalan and Tallal led the Rualla horse and the Hauran horse back to delay the pursuit. They had an unexpected ally, for our cars, on their way to Azrak, had seen the enemy. After all, the Turks were not cavalry coming to attack us, but deluded elements seeking a shorter way home. We took some hundreds of thirsty prisoners and much transport; causing such panic that the main rout in the plain cut the traces of their limbers and rode off on the bare horses. The infection of terror spread down the line, and troops miles from any Arab interference threw away all they had, even to their rifles, and made a mad rush towards supposed safety in Deraa.

However, this interruption delayed us; for we could hardly march a khaki-clad body of regular camel corps across Hauran at night without enough local cavalry to go bail to the suspicious villagers that we were not Turks. So late in the afternoon we halted for Tallal and Nasir and Nuri Shaalan to catch up.

This halt gave some people time to review the proceedings, and new questions arose as to the wisdom of crossing the railway again, to put ourselves in the dangerous position of Sheikh Saad, astride the retreat of the main Turkish forces. Finally, near midnight, Sabin appeared where I lay awake in the midst of the army on my carpet. He suggested that we had done enough. Allenby had appointed us watchmen of the Fourth Army. We had just seen its disordered flight. Our duty was completed; and we might honourably fall back to Bosra, twenty miles out of the way to the east, where the Druses were collecting under Nesib el Bekri to help us. We might wait with them for the British to take Deraa, and for our reward, in the victorious close of the campaign.

This attitude passed me by, since, if we withdrew to Jebel Druse, we ended our active service before the game was won, leaving the last brunt on Allenby. I was very jealous for the Arab honour, in whose service I would go forward at all costs. They had joined the war to win freedom, and the recovery of their old capital by force of their own arms was the sign they would best understand.

'Duty', like people who praised it, was a poor thing. Evidently, by thrusting behind Deraa into Sheikh Saad we put more pressure on the Turks than any British unit was in place to put. It would forbid the Turks fighting again this side of Damascus; for which gain our few lives would be cheap payment. Damascus meant the end of this war in the East, and, I believed, the end of the general war, too; because the Central Powers being inter-dependent, the breaking of their weakest link — Turkey — would swing the whole cluster loose. Therefore, for every sensible reason, strategical, tactical, political, even moral, we were going on.

Sabin's stubborn resistant mind was not to be convinced. He returned with Pisani and Winterton, and began to debate; speaking slowly because Nuri Said was lying on the next rug only half asleep, and he wanted to include him in the conference.

Accordingly he stressed the military aspect: our fulfilled purpose and the danger of the Hejaz Railway. This delay made us too late to cross to-night. To-morrow it would be madness to attempt the operation. The line would be guarded from end to end by tens of thousands of Turks pouring out of Deraa. If they let us over we would only be in still greater danger. Joyce, he said, had appointed him military adviser to the expedition; and it was his duty to point out, reluctantly, that as a regular officer he knew his business.

Had I been a regular officer I might have found Sabin's upsetting the others irregular. As it was I endured his complaints, patiently sighing whenever I thought it would irritate the protestant. At the end wanderingly I said I wanted to sleep, since we would have to be up early to cross the line, and it was my intention to go in front with my bodyguard among the Beduin, wherever they were, for it was odd that Nuri Shaalan and Tallal had not overtaken us. Anyway, I was going to sleep now.

Pisani, whose long military life had been all as subordinate, said with correctness that he took his orders and would follow. I liked him for that, and tried to soothe his honest doubts by reminding him that we had worked for eighteen months together without his ever finding cause to call me rash. He replied with a French laugh that he thought it all very rash, but was a soldier.

Winterton's instinct joined him to the weaker and more sporting side in any choice but fox-hunting. Nuri Said had lain silently through our talk, pretending to be asleep; but, when Sabin went away, he rolled over whispering, 'Is it true?' I replied that I saw no unusual risk in crossing the line in mid-afternoon, and with care we should avoid traps at Sheikh Saad. He lay back satisfied.

CHAPTER CXVI

NASIR, Nuri Shaalan and Talal had overshot us in the dark. Our joined forces marched, with a heady breeze in the teeth, northward across the ploughlands' fat, happy villages. Over the harvested fields, whose straw had been rather plucked than reaped, grew thistles, tall as a child, but now yellow and dried and dead. The wind snapped them off at the hollow root, and pitch-polled their branchy tops along the level ground, thistle blowing against thistle and interlocking spines, till in huge balls they careered like run-away haycocks across the fallow.

Arab women, out with their donkeys to fetch water, ran to us, crying that an aeroplane had landed a while since, near by. It bore the round rings of the Sherifian camel brand upon its body. Peake rode across, to find two Australians whose Bristol had been hit in the radiator over Deraa. They were glad, though astonished, to meet friends. After the leak had been plugged, we levied water from the women, to fill them up, and they flew home safely.

Men rode up every minute and joined us, while from each village the adventurous young ran out afoot to enter our ranks. As we moved on, so closely knit in the golden sunlight, we were able, in rare chance, to see ourselves as a whole: quickly we became a character, an organism, in whose pride each of us was uplifted. We cracked bawdy jokes to set off the encompassing beauty.

At noon we entered water-melon fields. The army ran upon them, while we spied out the line, which lay desertedly quivering in the sunlight ahead. As we watched a train passed down. Only last night had the railway been mended: and this was the third train. We moved without opposition upon the line in a horde two miles across, and began hastily to blow up things, anyone who had explosive using it as he fancied. Our hundreds of novices were full of zeal and the demolitions, albeit uninstructed, were wide.

Clearly our return had surprised the dazed enemy: we must extend and improve this chance. So we went to Nuri Shaalan, Auda, and

Talal, and asked what local effort each would undertake. Talal, the energetic, would attack Ezraa, the big grain depot to the north: Auda was for Khirbet el Ghazala, the corresponding station southward: Nuri would sweep his men down the main road, towards Deraa, on chance of Turkish parties.

These were three good ideas. The chiefs went to put them into being, while we, pulling our column to its shape again, pursued our road past the ruined colony of Sheikh Miskin, very gaunt in the moonlight. Its obstacle of water ditches muddled our thousands, so that we halted on the stubble plain beyond, for dawn. Some made fires against the penetrating mist of this clay Hauran: others slept as they were on the dew-slimy ground. Lost men went about calling their friends, in that sharp, full-throated wail of the Arab villager. The moon had set, and the world was black and very cold.

I roused my bodyguard, who rode so briskly that we entered Sheikh Saad with the dawn. As we passed between the rocks into the field behind the trees, the earth sprang to life again with the new sun. The morning airs flashed the olive-yards to silver, and men from a great goat-hair tent on the right called us to guest with them. We asked whose camp it was. 'Ibn Smeir's' they replied. This threatened complications. Rashid was an enemy of Nuri Shaalan's, unreconciled, chance-met. At once we sent a warning to Nasir. Fortunately Ibn Smeir was absent. So his family would be our temporary guests, and Nuri, as host, must observe the rules.

It was a relief, for already in our ranks we had hundreds of deadly enemies, their feuds barely suspended by Feisal's peace. The strain of keeping them in play, and employing their hot-heads in separate spheres, balancing opportunity and service that our direction might be esteemed as above jealousy — all that was evil enough. Conduct of the war in France would have been harder if each division, almost each brigade of our army had hated every other with a deadly hatred and fought when they met suddenly. However, we had kept them quiet for two years, and it would be only a few days now.

The parties of the night returned, full of spoil. Ezraa had been feebly held by Abd el Kader, the Algerian, with his retainers, some volunteers and troops. When Talal came the volunteers joined him, the troops fled, and the retainers were so few that Abd el Kader had to abandon the place without fighting. Our men were too heavy with their great booty to catch him.

Auda came, boasting. He had taken el Ghazale by storm, capturing a derelict train, guns and two hundred men, of whom some were Germans. Nuri Shaalan reported four hundred prisoners with mules and machine-guns. The rank and file of Turks had been farmed out to remote villages, to earn their keep.

An English aeroplane flew round and round, wondering if we were the Arab force. Young spread out ground signals, and to him they dropped a message that Bulgaria had surrendered to the Allies. We had not known there was an offensive in the Balkans, so the news came orphaned, and as it were insignificant to us. Undoubtedly the end, not only of the great war, but of our war, was near. A sharp effort, and our trial would be over and everyone loosed back to his affairs, forgetting the madness: since for most of us it was the first war, and we looked to its end as rest and peace.

The army had arrived. The groves became thronged as each detachment picked out the best vacant place and unsaddled, whether beside fig-trees, or under palms, or olives, from which the birds burst out in frightened clouds, with a multitudinous crying. Our men took their animals to the stream meandering through green bushes and flowers and cultivated fruits, things strange to us during the years of our wandering in the flinty desert.

The people of Sheikh Saad came shyly to look at Feisal's army, which had been a whispered legendary thing, and was now in their village, led by renowned or formidable names — Talal, Nasir, Nuri, Auda. We stared back, in secret envy of their peasant life.

While the men stretched the saddle-stiffness of riding from their legs, we went up, five or six of us, above the ruins, whence across the southern plain we should see the measure of security in store for us. To our astonishment we perceived, just over the walls, a thin company of regulars in uniform — Turks, Austrians, Germans — with eight machine-guns on pack-animals. They were toiling up from Galilee towards Damascus after their defeat by Allenby; hopeless, but care-free, marching at ease, thinking themselves fifty miles from any war.

We did not give an alarm, to spare our tired troops pains: just Durzi ibn Dughmi, with the Khaffaji and others of the family, mounted quietly and fell on them from a narrow lane. The officers showed fight and were instantly killed. The men threw down their arms, and in five minutes had been searched and robbed and were being shepherded in file along the water-paths between the gardens to an open pound which seemed fit for our prison. Sheikh Saad was paying soon and well.

Away to the east appeared three or four black knots of people, moving northward. We loosed the Howeitat on them, and after an hour they returned in laughter, each man leading a mule or pack-horse; poor, tired, galled brutes, showing all too clearly the straits of the beaten army. Their riders had been unarmed soldiers fleeing from the British. The Howeitat disdained to make such prisoners. 'We gave them to the boys and girls of the villages for servants,' sneered Zaal, with his thin-lipped smile.

News came to us from the west that small companies of Turks were retiring into the local villages from Chauvel's attacks. We sent against them armed parties of Naim, a peasant tribe which had joined us last night at Sheikh Miskin, as appointed by Nasir, to do what they could. The mass rising we had so long prepared was now in flood, rising higher as each success armed more rebels. In two days' time we might have sixty thousand armed men in movement.

We snapped up further trifles on the Damascus road; and then saw heavy smoke above the hill which hid Deraa. A man cantered in, to inform Tallal that the Germans had set fire to aeroplanes and store-houses, and stood ready to evacuate the town. A British plane dropped word that Barrow's troops were near Remtha, and that two Turkish columns, one of four thousand, one of two thousand, were retiring towards us from Deraa and Mezerib respectively.

It seemed to me that these six thousand men were all that remained of the Fourth Army, from Deraa, and of the Seventh Army, which had been disputing Barrow's advance. With their destruction would end our purpose here. Yet, till we knew, we must retain Sheikh Saad. So the larger column, the four thousand, we would let pass, only fastening to them Khalid and his Rualla, with some northern peasantry, to harry their flanks and rear.

CHAPTER CXVII

THE nearer two thousand seemed more our size. We would meet them with half our regulars, and two of Pisani's guns. Tallal was anxious, for their indicated route would bring them through Tafas, his own village. He determined us to make speed there and seize the ridge south of it. Unfortunately speed was only a relative term with men so tired. I rode with my troop to Tafas, hoping to occupy a shadow position beyond it and fight a retiring action till the rest came up. Half-way on the road, there met us mounted Arabs, herding a drove of stripped prisoners towards Sheikh Saad. They were driving them mercilessly, the bruises of their urging blue across the ivory backs; but I left them to it, for these were Turks of the police battalion of Deraa, beneath whose iniquities the peasant-faces of the neighbourhood had run with tears and blood, innumerable times.

The Arabs told us that the Turkish column — Jemal Pasha's lancer regiment — was already entering Tafas. When we got within sight, we found they had taken the village (from which sounded an occasional shot) and were halted about it. Small pyres of smoke were going up from between the houses. On the rising ground to this side, knee-deep in the thistles, stood a remnant of old men, women and children, telling terrible stories of what had happened when the Turks rushed in an hour before.

We lay on watch, and saw the enemy force march away from their assembly-ground behind the houses. They headed in good order towards Miskin, the lancers in front and rear, composite formations of infantry disposed in column with machine-gun support as flank guards, guns and a mass of transport in the centre. We opened fire on the head of their line when it showed itself beyond the houses. They turned two field-guns upon us, for reply. The shrapnel was as usual over-fused, and passed safely above our heads.

Nuri came with Pisani. Before their ranks rode Auda abu Tayi, expectant, and Tallal, nearly frantic with the tales his people poured out of the sufferings of the village. The last Turks were now quitting it.

We slipped down behind them to end Tallal's suspense, while our infantry took position and fired strongly with the Hotchkiss; Pisani advanced his half battery among them; so that the French high explosive threw the rearguard into confusion.

The village lay stilly under its slow wreaths of white smoke, as we rode near, on our guard. Some grey heaps seemed to hide in the long grass, embracing the ground in the close way of corpses. We looked away from these, knowing they were dead; but from one a little figure tottered off, as if to escape us. It was a child, three or four years old, whose dirty smock was stained red over one shoulder and side, with blood from a large half-fibrous wound, perhaps a lance thrust, just where neck and body joined.

The child ran a few steps, then stood and cried to us in a tone of astonishing strength (all else being very silent), 'Don't hit me, Baba'. Abd el Aziz, choking out something — this was his village, and she might be of his family — flung himself off his camel, and stumbled, kneeling, in the grass beside the child. His suddenness frightened her, for she threw up her arms and tried to scream; but, instead, dropped in a little heap, while the blood rushed out again over her clothes; then, I think, she died.

We rode past the other bodies of men and women and four more dead babies, looking very soiled in the daylight, towards the village; whose loneliness we now knew meant death and horror. By the outskirts were low mud walls, sheepfolds, and on one something red and white. I looked close and saw the body of a woman folded across it, bottom upwards, nailed there by a saw bayonet whose haft stuck hideously into the air from between her naked legs. She had been pregnant, and about her lay others, perhaps twenty in all, variously killed, but set out in accord with an obscene taste.

The Zaagi burst into wild peals of laughter, the more desolate for the warm sunshine and clear air of this upland afternoon. I said, 'The best of you brings me the most Turkish dead', and we turned after the fading enemy, on our way shooting down those who had fallen out by the roadside, and came imploring our pity. One wounded Turk, half naked, not able to stand, sat and wept to us. Abdulla turned away his camel's head, but the Zaagi, with curses, crossed his track and whipped three bullets from his automatic through the man's bare chest. The blood came out with his heart beats, throb, throb, throb, slower and slower.

Tallal had seen what we had seen. He gave one moan like a hurt animal; then rode to the upper ground and sat there awhile on his mare, shivering and looking fixedly after the Turks. I moved near to speak to him, but Auda caught my rein and stayed me. Very slowly Tallal drew his head-cloth about his face; and then he seemed suddenly to take hold of himself, for he dashed his stirrups into the mare's flanks and galloped headlong, bending low and swaying in the saddle, right at the main body of the enemy.

It was a long ride down a gentle slope and across a hollow. We sat there like stone while he rushed forward, the drumming of his hoofs unnaturally loud in our ears, for we had stopped shooting, and the Turks had stopped. Both armies waited for him; and he rocked on in the hushed evening till only a few lengths from the enemy. Then he sat up in the saddle and cried his war-cry, 'Tallal, Tallal', twice in a tremendous shout. Instantly their rifles and machine-guns crashed out, and he and his mare, riddled through and through with bullets, fell dead among the lance points.

Auda looked very cold and grim. 'God give him mercy; we will take his price.' He shook his rein and moved slowly after the enemy. We called up the peasants, now drunk with fear and blood, and sent them from this side and that against the retreating column. The old lion of battle waked in Auda's heart, and made him again our natural, inevitable leader. By a skilful turn he drove the Turks into bad ground and split their formation into three parts.

The third part, the smallest, was mostly made up of German and Austrian machine-gunners grouped round three motor-cars, and a handful of mounted officers or troopers. They fought magnificently and repulsed us time and again despite our hardiness. The Arabs were fighting like devils, the sweat blurring their eyes, dust parching their throats; while the flame of cruelty and revenge which was burning in their bodies so twisted them, that their hands could hardly shoot. By my order we took no prisoners, for the only time in our war.

At last we left this stern section behind, and pursued the faster two.

They were in panic; and by sunset we had destroyed all but the smallest pieces of them, gaining as and by what they lost. Parties of peasants flowed in on our advance. At first there were five or six to a weapon: then one would win a bayonet, another a sword, a third a pistol. An hour later those who had been on foot would be on donkeys. Afterwards every man had a rifle, and a captured horse. By nightfall the horses were laden, and the rich plain was scattered over with dead men and animals. In a madness born of the horror of Tafas we killed and killed, even blowing in the heads of the fallen and of the animals; as though their death and running blood could slake our agony.

Just one group of Arabs, who had not heard our news, took prisoner the last two hundred men of the central section. Their respite was short. I had gone up to learn why it was, not unwilling that this remnant be let live as witnesses of Tallal's price; but a man on the ground behind them screamed something to the Arabs, who with pale faces led me across to see. It was one of us — his thigh shattered. The blood had rushed out over the red soil, and left him dying; but even so he had not been spared. In the fashion of to-day's battle he had been further tormented by bayonets hammered through his shoulder and other leg into the ground, pinning him out like a collected insect.

He was fully conscious. When we said, 'Hassan, who did it?' he drooped his eyes towards the prisoners, huddling together so hopelessly broken. They said nothing in the moments before we opened fire. At last their heap ceased moving; and Hassan was dead; and we mounted again and rode home slowly (home was my carpet three or four hours from us at Sheikh Saad) in the gloom, which felt so chill now that the sun had gone down.

However, what with wounds and aches and weariness I could not rest from thinking of Tallal, the splendid leader, the fine horseman, the courteous and strong companion of the road; and after a while I had my other camel brought, and with one of my bodyguard rode out into the night to join our men hunting the greater Deraa column.

It was very dark, with a wind beating in great gusts from the south and east; and only by the noise of shots it tossed across to us and by occasional gun flashes, did we at length come to the fighting. Every field and valley had its Turks stumbling blindly northward. Our men were clinging on. The fall of night had made them bolder, and they were now closing with the enemy. Each village, as the fight rolled to it, took up the work; and the black, icy wind was wild with rifle-fire, shoutings, volleys from the Turks, and the rush of gallops, as small parties of either side crashed frantically together.

The enemy had tried to halt and camp at sunset, but Khalid had shaken them again into movement. Some marched, some stayed. Many dropped asleep in their tracks with fatigue. They had lost order and coherence, and were drifting through the blast in lorn packets, ready to shoot and run at every contact with us or with each other; and the Arabs were as scattered, and nearly as uncertain.

Exceptions were the German detachments; and here, for the first time, I grew proud of the enemy who had killed my brothers. They were two thousand miles from home, without hope and without guides, in conditions mad enough to break the bravest nerves. Yet their sections held together, in firm rank, sheering through the wrack of Turk and Arab like armoured ships, high-faced and silent. When attacked they halted, took position, fired to order. There was no haste, no crying, no hesitation. They were glorious.

At last I found Khalid, and asked him to call off the Rualla and leave this rout to time and the peasantry. Heavier work, perhaps, lay to the southward. At dusk a rumour had passed across our plain that Deraa was empty, and Trad, Khalid's brother, with a good half of the Anazeh, had ridden off to see. I feared a reverse for him, since there must still be Turks in the place, and more struggling towards it up the railway and through the Irbid Hills. Indeed, unless Barrow, last reported to us as delayed in Remthe, had lost contact with his enemy, there must be a fighting rearguard yet to follow.

I wanted Khalid to support his brother. After an hour or two of shouting his message down the wind, hundreds of horsemen and camel men had rallied to him. On his way to Deraa he charged through and over several detachments of Turks in the star-blink, and arrived to find Trad in secure possession. He had won through in the later twilight, taking the station at a gallop, jumping trenches and blotting out the scanty Turkish elements which still tried to resist.

With local help the Rualla plundered the camp, especially finding booty in the fiercely burning storehouses whose flaming roofs imperilled their lives; but this was one of the nights in which mankind went crazy, when death seemed impossible, however many died to the right and left, and when others' lives became toys to break and throw away.

Sheikh Saad passed a troubled evening of alarms and shots and shouts with threatenings from the peasantry to murder the prisoners as added price of Tallal and his village. The active sheikhs were out hunting the Turks, and their absence with their retainers deprived the Arab camp of its experienced chiefs and of its eyes and ears. Sleeping clan-jealousies had awaked in the blood thirst of the afternoon of killing, and Nasir and Nuri Said, Young and Winterton, had to strain every nerve in keeping peace.

I got in after midnight and found Trad's messengers just arrived from Deraa. Nasir left to join him. I had wished to sleep, for this was my fourth night of riding; but my mind would not let me feel how tired my body was, so about two in the morning I mounted a third camel and splashed out towards Deraa, down the Tafas track again, to windward of the dark village.

Nuri Said and his staff were riding the same road in advance of their mounted infantry, and our parties hurried together till the half-light came. Then my impatience and the cold would not let me travel horse-pace any longer. I gave liberty to my camel – the grand, rebellious Baha – and she stretched herself out against the field, racing my wearied followers for mile upon mile with piston-strides like an engine, so that I entered Deraa quite alone in the full dawn.

Nasir was at the Mayor's house, arranging a military governor, and police; and for an inquisition of the place; I supplemented his ideas, putting guards over the pumps and engine sheds and what remained of tool shops or stores. Then in an hour of talk I built up publicly a programme of what the situation would demand of them, if they were not to lose hold. Poor Nasir stared in bewilderment.

I inquired about General Barrow. A man just ridden in from the west told us he had been fired on by the English, as they deployed to attack the town. To prevent such an accident the Zaagi and I rode up the Buweib, on whose crest was visible a strong post of Indian machine-gunners. They trained their weapons on us, proud of such splendidly dressed prizes. However, an officer showed himself, with some British troopers, and to them I explained myself. They were indeed in the midst of an enveloping movement against Deraa, and, while we watched, their aeroplanes bombed the luckless Nuri Said as he rode into the railway station. This was his penalty for losing the race from Sheikh Saad: but, to stop it, I hurried down to where General Barrow was inspecting outposts in a car.

I told him we had spent the night in the town, and the shooting he heard was joy-firing. He was short with me; but I had little pity for him, because he had delayed a day and night watering at the poor wells of Remthe, though his map showed the lake and river of Mezerib in front, on the road by which the enemy were escaping. However his orders were Deraa, and to Deraa he would go.

He told me to ride beside him: but his horses hated my camel, so the General Staff bucked along the ditch, while I soberly paced the crown of the road. He said he must post sentries in the village to keep the populace in order. I explained gently that the Arabs had installed their military governor. At the wells he said his sappers must inspect the pumps. I replied welcoming their assistance. We had lit the furnaces and hoped to begin watering his horses in an hour. He snorted that we seemed to be at home; he would take charge only of the railway station. I pointed to the engine moving out towards Mezerib (where our little Sheikh had prevented the Turks from blowing up the Tell el Shehab bridge, now become Arab property) and asked that his sentries be instructed not to interfere with our proper working of the line.

He had had no orders as to the status of the Arabs. Clayton did us this service, thinking we should deserve what we could assert: so Barrow, who had come in thinking of them as a conquered people, though dazed at my calm assumption that he was my guest, had no option but to follow the lead of such assurance. My head was working full speed in these minutes, on our joint behalf, to prevent the fatal first steps by which the unimaginative British, with the best will in the world, usually deprived the acquiescent native of the discipline of responsibility, and created a situation which called for years of agitation and successive reforms and riotings to mend.

I had studied Barrow and was ready for him. Years before, he had published his confession of faith in Fear as the common people's main incentive to action in war and peace. Now I found fear a mean, over-rated motive; no deterrent, and, though a stimulant, a poisonous stimulant, whose every injection served to consume more of the system to which it was applied. I could have no alliance with his pedant belief of scaring men into heaven: better that Barrow and I part at once. My instinct with the inevitable was to provoke it. Therefore, I was very spiny and high.

Barrow surrendered himself by asking me to find him forage and food-stuffs. Indeed, soon we got on well. In the square I showed him Nasir's little silk pennon, propped on the balcony of the charred Government office, with a yawning sentry underneath. Barrow drew himself up and saluted sharply, while a thrill of pleasure at the General's compliment ran round Arab officers and men.

In return we strove to keep self-assertion within the bounds of political necessity. On all Arabs we impressed that these Indian troops were guests, and must be permitted, nay helped, to do anything they wished. The doctrine took us into unexpected places. Every chicken disappeared from the village, and three sowars carried off Nasir's pennon, having coveted the silver knobs and spike of its dainty staff. This pointed a contrast between the English General who saluted and the Indian trooper who stole: a contrast welcome to the Arab race-hesitation towards the Indians.

Meanwhile, everywhere we were taking men and guns. Our prisoners could be counted in thousands. Some we handed over to the British, who counted them again: most we boarded-out in the villages. Azrak heard the full news of victory. Feisal drove in a day later, our string of armoured cars following his Vauxhall. He installed himself in the station. I called with my record of stewardship: as the tale ended the room shook with a gentle earthquake.

CHAPTER CXVIII

Barrow, now watered and fed, was due to leave for his meeting with Chauvel near Damascus, that they might enter the city together. He asked us to take the right flank, which suited me, for there, along the Hejaz line, was Nasir, hanging on to the main Turkish retreat, reducing its numbers by continuous attack day and night. I had still much to do, and therefore waited in Deraa another night, savouring its quiet after the troops had gone; for the station stood at the limit of the open country, and the Indians round it had angered me by their out-of-placeness. The essence of the desert was the lonely moving individual, the son of the road, apart from the world as in a grave. These troops, in flocks like slow sheep, looked not worthy of the privilege of space.

My mind felt in the Indian rank and file something puny and confined; an air of thinking themselves mean; almost a careful, esteemed subservience, unlike the abrupt wholesomeness of Beduin. The manner of the British officers toward their men struck horror into my bodyguard, who had never seen personal inequality before.

I had felt man's iniquity here: and so hated Deraa that I lay each night with my men upon the old aerodrome. By the charred hangars my guards, fickle-surfaced as the sea, squabbled after their wont; and there to-night for the last time Abdulla brought me cooked rice in the silver bowl. After supping, I tried in the blankness to think forward: but my mind was a blank, my dreams puffed out like candles by the strong wind of success. In front was our too-tangible goal: but behind lay the effort of two years, its misery forgotten or glorified. Names rang through my head, each in imagination a superlative: Rum the magnificent, brilliant Petra, Azrak the remote, Batra the very clean. Yet the men had changed. Death had taken the gentle ones; and the new stridency, of those who were left, hurt me.

Sleep would not come, so before the light, I woke Stirling and my drivers, and we four climbed into the Blue Mist, our Rolls tender, and set out for Damascus, along the dirt road which was first rutted, and then blocked by the transport columns and rearguard of Barrow's division. We cut across country to the French railway, whose old ballast gave us a clear, if rugged, road; then we put on speed. At noon we saw Barrow's pennon at a stream, where he was watering his horses. My bodyguard were near by, so I took my camel and rode over to him. Like other confirmed horsemen, he had been a little contemptuous of the camel; and had suggested, in Deraa, that we might hardly keep up with his cavalry, which was going to Damascus in about three forced marches.

So when he saw me freshly riding up he was astonished, and asked when we left Deraa. 'This morning.' His face fell. 'Where will you stop to-night?' 'In Damascus,' said I gaily; and rode on, having made another enemy. It a little smote me to play tricks, for he was generous towards my wishes: but the stakes were high, beyond his sight, and I cared nothing what he thought of me so that we won.

I returned to Stirling, and drove on. At each village we left notes for the British advance guards, telling them where we were, and how far beyond us the enemy. It irked Stirling and myself to see the caution of Barrow's advance; scouts scouting empty valleys, sections crowning every deserted hill, a screen drawn forward so carefully over friendly country. It marked the difference between our certain movements and the tentative processes of normal war.

There could be no crisis till Kiswe, where we were to meet Chauvel, and where the Hejaz line approached our road. Upon the railway were Nasir, Nuri Shaalan and Auda, with the tribes; still harrying that column of four thousand (but in truth nearer seven) marked by our aeroplane near Sheikh Saad three busy days ago. They had fought ceaselessly throughout this time of our ease.

As we drove up we heard firing, and saw shrapnel behind a ridge to our right, where the railway was. Soon appeared the head of a Turkish column of about two thousand men, in ragged groups, halting now and then to fire their mountain guns. We ran on to overtake their pursuers, our great Rolls very blue on the open road. Some Arab horsemen from behind the Turks galloped towards us, bucketing unhandily across the irrigation ditches. We recognized Nasir on his liver-coloured stallion, the splendid animal yet spirited after its hundred miles of a running fight: also old Nuri Shaalan and about thirty of their servants. They told us these few were all that remained of the seven thousand Turks. The Rualla were hanging desperately on to both flanks, while Auda abu Tayi had ridden behind Jebel Mania to gather the Wuld Ali, his friends, and lie in wait there for this column, which they hoped to drive over the hill into his ambush. Did our appearance mean help at last?

I told them the British, in force, were just behind. If they could delay the enemy only an hour . . . Nasir looked ahead and saw a walled and wooded farmstead barring the level. He called to Nuri Shaalan, and they hastened thither to check the Turks.

We drove back three miles to the leading Indians, and told their ancient, surly Colonel what a gift the Arabs brought. He seemed not pleased to upset the beautiful order of his march, but at last opened out a squadron and sent them slowly across the plain towards the Turks, who turned the little guns their way. One or two shells burst nearly among the files, and then to our horror (for Nasir had put himself in jeopardy, expecting courageous help) the Colonel ordered a retirement, and fell back quickly to the road. Stirling and myself, hopping mad, dashed down and begged him not to be afraid of mountain guns, no heavier than Very pistols: but neither to kindness nor to wrath did the old man budge an inch. We raced a third time back along the road in search of higher authority.

A red-tipped Aide told us that over there was General Gregory. We blessed him, Stirling's professional pride nearly in tears at the mismanagement. We pulled our friend aboard and found his General, to whom we lent our car that the brigade major might take hot orders to the cavalry. A galloper hurtled back for the horse artillery, which opened first just as the last of the light fled up the hill to its summit and took refuge in the clouds. Middlesex Yeomanry appeared and were pushed in among the Arabs, to charge the Turkish rear; and, as the night fell, we saw the break-up of the enemy, who abandoned their guns, their transport and all their stuff and went streaming up the col towards the two peaks of Mania, escaping into what they thought was empty land beyond.

However, in the empty land was Auda; and in that night of his last battle the old man killed and killed, plundered and captured, till dawn showed him the end. There passed the Fourth Army, our stumbling-block for two years.

Gregory's happy vigour heartened us to face Nasir. We drove to Kiswe, where we had agreed to meet him before midnight. After us came the press of Indian troops. We sought a retired spot; but already there were men by the thousand everywhere.

The movement and cross-currents of so many crowded minds drove me about, restlessly, like themselves. In the night my colour was unseen. I could walk as I pleased, an unconsidered Arab: and this finding myself among, but cut off from, my own kin made me strangely alone. Our armoured-car men were persons to me, from their fewness and our long companionship; and also in their selves, for these months unshieldedly open to the flaming sun and bullying wind had worn and refined them into individuals. In such a mob of unaccustomed soldiery, British, Australian and Indian, they went as strange and timid as myself; distinguished also by grime, for with weeks of wearing their clothes had been moulded to them by sweat and use and had become rather integuments than wrappings.

But these others were really soldiers, a novelty after two years' irregularity. And it came upon me freshly how the secret of uniform was to make a crowd solid, dignified, impersonal: to give it the single-ness and tautness of an upstanding man. This death's livery which walled its bearers from ordinary life, was sign that they had sold their wills and bodies to the State: and contracted themselves into a service not the less abject for that its beginning was voluntary. Some of them had obeyed the instinct of lawlessness: some were hungry: others thirsted for glamour, for the supposed colour of a military life: but, of them all, those only received satisfaction who had sought to degrade themselves, for to the peace-eye they were below humanity. Only women with a lech were allured by those witnessing clothes; the soldiers' pay, not sustenance like a labourer's, but pocket-money, seemed most profitably spent when it let them drink sometimes and forget.

Convicts had violence put upon them. Slaves might be free, if they could, in intention. But the soldier assigned his owner the twenty-four hours' use of his body; and sole conduct of his mind and passions.

A convict had licence to hate the rule which confined him, and all humanity outside, if he were greedy in hate: but the sulking soldier was a bad soldier; indeed, no soldier. His affections must be hired pieces on the chess-board of the king.

The strange power of war which made us all as a duty so demean ourselves! These Australians, shouldering me in unceremonious horse-play, had put off half civilization with their civil clothes. They were dominant to-night, too sure of themselves to be careful: and yet: — as they lazily swaggered those quick bodies, all curves with never a straight line, but with old and disillusioned eyes: and yet: — I felt them thin-tempered, hollow, instinctive; always going to do great things; with the disquieting suppleness of blades half-drawn from the scabbard. Disquieting: not dreadful.

The English fellows were not instinctive, nor negligent like the Australians, but held themselves, with a slow-eyed, almost sheepish care. They were prim in dress, and quiet; going shyly in pairs. The Australians stood in groups and walked singly: the British clung two and two, in a celibate friendliness which expressed the level of the ranks: the commonness of their Army clothes. 'Holding together' they called it: a war-time yearning to keep within four ears such thoughts as were deep enough to hurt.

About the soldiers hung the Arabs: gravely-gazing men from another sphere. My crooked duty had banished me among them for two years. To-night I was nearer to them than to the troops, and I resented it, as shameful. The intruding contrast mixed with longing for home, to sharpen my faculties and make fertile my distaste, till not merely did I see the unlikeness of race, and hear the unlikeness of language, but I learned to pick between their smells: the heavy, standing, curdled sourness of dried sweat in cotton, over the Arab crowds; and the feral smell of English soldiers: that hot pissy aura of thronged men in woollen clothes: a tart pungency, breath-catching, ammoniacal; a fervent fermenting naphtha-smell.

CHAPTER CXIX

O UR war was ended. Even though we slept that night in
Kiswe, for the Arabs told us the roads were dangerous, and
we had no wish to die stupidly in the dark at the gate of
Damascus. The sporting Australians saw the campaign as a point-to-
point, with Damascus the post; but in reality we were all under Allenby,
now, and the victory had been the logical fruit solely of his genius, and
Bartholomew's pains.

Their tactical scheme properly put the Australians north and west of
Damascus, across its railways, before the southern column might enter
it: and we, the Arab leaders, had waited for the slower British partly
because Allenby never questioned our fulfilling what was ordered.
Power lay in his calm assumption that he would receive as perfect
obedience as he gave trust.

He hoped we would be present at the entry, partly because he knew
how much more than a mere trophy Damascus was to the Arabs: partly
for prudential reasons. Feisal's movement made the enemy country
friendly to the Allies as they advanced, enabling convoys to go up without escort, towns to be administered without garrison. In their
envelopment of Damascus the Australians might be forced, despite
orders, to enter the town. If anyone resisted them it would spoil the
future. One night was given us to make the Damascenes receive the
British Army as their allies.

This was a revolution in behaviour, if not in opinion; but Feisal's
Damascus committee had for months been prepared to take over the
reins when the Turks crashed. We had only to get in touch with them,
to tell them the movements of the Allies, and what was required. So
as dusk deepened Nasir sent the Rualla horse into the town, to find
Ali Riza, the chairman of our committee, or Shukri el Ayubi, his
assistant, telling them that relief would be available on the morrow, if
they constructed a government at once. As a matter of fact it had been
done at four o'clock in the afternoon, before we took action. Ali Riza
was absent, put in command at the last moment by the Turks of the

retreat of their army from Galilee before Chauvel: but Shukri found unexpected support from the Algerian brothers, Mohammed Said and Abd el Kader. With the help of their retainers the Arab flag was on the Town Hall before sunset as the last echelons of Germans and Turks defiled past. They say the hindmost general saluted it, ironically.

I dissuaded Nasir from going in. This would be a night of confusion, and it would better serve his dignity if he entered serenely at dawn. He and Nuri Shaalan intercepted the second body of Rualla camel men, who had started out with me from Deraa this morning; and sent them all forward into Damascus, to support the Rualla sheikhs. So by midnight, when we went to rest, we had four thousand of our armed men in the town.

I wanted to sleep, for my work was coming on the morrow; but I could not. Damascus was the climax of our two years' uncertainty, and my mind was distracted by tags of all the ideas which had been used or rejected in that time. Also Kiswe was stifling with the exhalations of too many trees, too many plants, too many human beings: a microcosm of the crowded world in front of us.

As the Germans left Damascus they fired the dumps and ammunition stores, so that every few minutes we were jangled by explosions, whose first shock set the sky white with flame. At each such roar the earth seemed to shake; we would lift our eyes to the north and see the pale sky prick out suddenly in sheaves of yellow points, as the shells, thrown to terrific heights from each bursting magazine, in their turn burst like clustered rockets. I turned to Stirling and muttered 'Damascus is burning', sick to think of the great town in ashes as the price of freedom.

When dawn came we drove to the head of the ridge, which stood over the oasis of the city, afraid to look north for the ruins we expected: but, instead of ruins, the silent gardens stood blurred green with river mist, in whose setting shimmered the city, beautiful as ever, like a pearl in the morning sun. The uproar of the night had shrunk to a stiff tall column of smoke, which rose in sullen blackness from the store-yard by Kadem, terminus of the Hejaz line.

We drove down the straight banked road through the watered fields, in which the peasants were just beginning their day's work. A galloping horseman checked at our head-cloths in the car, with a merry salutation, holding out a bunch of yellow grapes. 'Good news: Damascus salutes you.' He came from Shukri.

Nasir was just beyond us: to him we carried the tidings, that he might have the honourable entry, a privilege of his fifty battles. With Nuri Shaalan beside him, he asked a final gallop from his horse, and vanished down the long road in a cloud of dust, which hung reluctantly in the air between the water splashes. To give him a fair start, Stirling and I found a little stream, cool in the depths of a steep channel. By it we stopped, to wash and shave.

Some Indian troopers peered at us and our car and its ragged driver's army shorts and tunic. I was in pure Arab dress; Stirling, but for his head-covering, was all British staff officer. Their N.C.O., an obtuse and bad-tempered person, thought he had taken prisoners. When delivered from his arrest we judged we might go after Nasir.

Quite quietly we drove up the long street to the Government buildings on the bank of the Barada. The way was packed with people lined solid on the side-walks, in the road, at the windows and on the balconies or house-tops. Many were crying, a few cheered faintly, some bolder ones cried our names: but mostly they looked and looked, joy shining in their eyes. A movement like a long sigh from gate to heart of the city, marked our course.

At the Town Hall things were different. Its steps and stairs were packed with a swaying mob: yelling, embracing, dancing, singing. They crushed a way for us to the antechamber, where were the gleaming Nasir, and Nuri Shaalan, seated. On either side of them stood Abd el Kader, my old enemy, and Mohammed Said, his brother. I was dumb with amazement. Mohammed Said leaped forward and shouted that they, grandsons of Abd el Kader, the Emir, with Shukri el Ayubi, of Saladin's house, had formed the government and proclaimed Hussein 'King of the Arabs' yesterday, into the ears of the humbled Turks and Germans.

While he ranted I turned to Shukri, who was no statesman, but a beloved man, almost a martyr in the people's eyes, because of what he had suffered from Jemal. He told me how the Algerians, alone of all Damascus, had stood by the Turks till they saw them running. Then, with their Algerians, they had burst in upon Feisal's committee where it sat in secret, and brutally assumed control.

They were fanatics, whose ideas were theological, not logical; and I turned to Nasir, meaning through him to check their impudence now from the start; but there came a diversion. The screaming press about us parted as though a ram drove through, men going down to right and left among ruined chairs and tables, while the terrific roaring of familiar voice triumphed, and stilled them dead.

In the cleared space were Auda abu Tayi and Sultan el Atrash, chief of the Druses, tearing one another. Their followers bounded forward, while I jumped in to drive them apart; crashing upon Mohammed el Dheilan, filled with the same purpose. Together we broke them, and forced Auda back a pace, while Hussein el Atrash hustled the lighter Sultan into the crowd, and away to a side room.

Auda was too blind with rage to be fairly conscious. We got him into the great state-hall of the building; an immense, pompous, gilded room, quiet as the grave, since all doors but ours were locked. We pushed him into a chair and held him, while in his fits he foamed and shouted till his voice cracked, his body twitching and jerking, arms lunging wildly at any weapon within reach, his face swollen with blood, bareheaded, the long hair streaming over his eyes.

The old man had been hit first, by Sultan, and his ungovernable spirit, drunk with a life-time's wine of self-will, raved to wash out the insult in Druse blood. Zaal came in, with the Hubsi; and the four or five of us united to restrain him: but it was half an hour before he calmed enough to hear us speaking, and another half-hour before we had his promise to leave his satisfaction, for three days, in the hands of Mohammed and myself. I went out and had Sultan el Atrash taken secretly from the town with all speed; and then looked round for Nasir and Abd el Kader, to set in order their Government.

They were gone. The Algerians had persuaded Nasir to their house for refreshment. It was a good hap, for there were more pressing public things. We must prove the old days over, a native government in power: for this Shukri would be my best instrument, as acting Governor. So in the Blue Mist, we set off to show ourselves, his enlargement in authority itself a banner of revolution for the citizens.

When we came in there had been some miles of people greeting us: now there were thousands for every hundred then. Every man, woman and child in this city of a quarter-million souls seemed in the streets, waiting only the spark of our appearance to ignite their spirits. Damascus went mad with joy. The men tossed up their tarbushes to cheer, the women tore off their veils. Householders threw flowers, hangings, carpets, into the road before us: their wives leaned, screaming with laughter, through the lattices and splashed us with bath-dippers of scent.

Poor dervishes made themselves our running footmen in front and behind, howling and cutting themselves with frenzy; and over the local cries and the shrilling of women came the measured roar of men's voices, chanting, 'Feisal, Nasir, Shukri, Urens', in waves which began here, rolled along the squares, through the market down long streets to East gate, round the wall, back up the Meidan; and grew to a wall of shouts around us by the citadel.

They told me Chauvel was coming; our cars met in the southern outskirts. I described the excitement in the city, and how our new government could not guarantee administrative services before the following day, when I would wait on him, to discuss his needs and mine. Meanwhile I made myself responsible for public order: only begging him to keep his men outside, because to-night would see such carnival as the town had not held for six hundred years, and its hospitality might pervert their discipline.

Chauvel unwillingly followed my lead, his hesitations ruled by my certainty. Like Barrow, he had no instructions what to do with the captured city; and as we had taken possession, knowing our road, with clear purpose, prepared processes, and assets in hand, he had no choice but to let us carry on. His chief of staff who did his technical work, Godwin, a soldier, was delighted to shelve the responsibility of civil government. His advocacy confirmed my assumption.

Indeed, it was confirmed in Chauvel's next words, which asked liberty for himself to drive round the town. I gave it so gladly that he asked if it would be convenient for him to make formal entry with his troops on the morrow. I said certainly, and we thought a little of the route. There flashed into my head the pleasure of our men at Deraa when Barrow saluted their flag — and I quoted it as an example good to follow before the Town Hall when he marched past. It was a casual thought of mine, but he saw significance in it: and a grave difficulty if he saluted any flag except the British. I wanted to make faces at his folly: but instead, in kindness I kept him company, seeing equal difficulty in his passing the Arab flag deliberately not noticed. We stumbled round this problem, while the joyful, unknowing crowd cheered us. As a compromise I suggested we leave out the Town Hall, and invent another route, passing, let us say, by the Post Office. I meant this for farce, since my patience had broken down; but he took it seriously, as a helpful idea; and in return would concede a point for my sake and the Arabs. In place of an 'entry' he would make a 'march through': it meant that instead of going in the middle he would go at the head, or instead of the head, the middle. I forgot, or did not well hear, which: for I should not have cared if he had crawled under or flown over his troops, or split himself to march both sides.

CHAPTER CXX

WHILE we discussed ceremonial antics a world of work waited, inside and outside, for each of us. It was bitter, playing down to such a part: also the won game of grab left a bad taste in my mouth, spoiling my entry much as I spoiled Chauvel's. The airy birds of promise so freely sent to the Arabs in England's day of need were homing now, to her confusion. However, the course I mapped for us was proving correct. Another twelve hours, and we should be safe, with the Arabs in so strong a place that their hand might hold through the long wrangle and appetite of politics about to break out about our luscious spoil.

We sneaked back to the Town Hall, to grapple with Abd el Kader: but he had not returned. I sent for him, and for his brother, and for Nasir: and got a curt reply that they were sleeping. So should I have been: but instead four or five of us were eating a snatch-meal in the gaudy salon, sitting on gold chairs, which writhed, about a gold table whose legs also writhed obscenely.

I explained pointedly to the messenger what I meant. He disappeared, and in a few minutes a cousin of the Algerians came up, very agitated, and said they were on their way. This was an open lie, but I replied that it was well, since in half an hour I should have fetched British troops and looked carefully for them. He ran off in haste; and Nuri Shaalan asked quietly what I meant to do.

I said I would depose Abd el Kader and Mohammed Said, and appoint Shukri in their place till Feisal came; and I did it in this gentle fashion because I was loath to hurt Nasir's feelings, and had no strength of my own if men resisted. He asked if the English would not come. I replied Certainly; but the sorrow was that afterwards they might not go. He thought a moment and said, 'You shall have the Rualla if you do all your will, and quickly'. Without waiting, the old man went out to muster me his tribe. The Algerians came to the tryst with their bodyguards, and with murder in their eyes: but, on the way, saw Nuri Shaalan's massed lowering tribesmen; Nuri Said, with his regulars in the square; and within, my reckless guardsmen lounging in the antechamber. They saw clearly that the game was up: yet it was a stormy meeting.

In my capacity as deputy for Feisal I pronounced their civil government of Damascus abolished, and named Shukri Pasha Ayubi as acting Military Governor. Nuri Said was to be Commandant of troops; Azmi, Adjutant General; Jemil, Chief of Public Security. Mohammed Said, in a bitter reply, denounced me as a Christian and an Englishman, and called on Nasir to assert himself.

Poor Nasir, far out of his depth, could only sit and look miserable at this falling out of friends. Abd el Kader leaped up and cursed me virulently, puffing himself to a white heat of passion. His motives seemed dogmatic, irrational: so I took no heed. This maddened him yet more: suddenly he leaped forward with drawn dagger.

Like a flash Auda was on him, the old man bristling with the chained-up fury of the morning, and longing for a fight. It would have been heaven, for him, to have shredded someone there and then with his great fingers. Abd el Kader was daunted; and Nuri Shaalan closed the debate by saying to the carpet (so enormous and violent a carpet it was) that the Rualla were mine, and no questions asked. The Algerians rose and swept in high dudgeon from the hall. I was persuaded they should be seized and shot; but could not make myself fear their power of mischief, nor set the Arabs an example of precautionary murder as part of politics.

We passed to work. Our aim was an Arab Government, with foundations large and native enough to employ the enthusiasm and self-sacrifice of the rebellion, translated into terms of peace. We had to save some of the old prophetic personality upon a substructure to carry that ninety per cent of the population who had been too solid to rebel, and on whose solidity the new State must rest.

Rebels, especially successful rebels, were of necessity bad subjects and worse governors. Feisal's sorry duty would be to rid himself of his war-friends, and replace them by those elements which had been most useful to the Turkish Government. Nasir was too little a political philosopher to feel this. Nuri Said knew, and Nuri Shaalan.

Quickly they collected the nucleus of a staff, and plunged ahead as a team. History told us the steps were humdrum: appointments, offices, and departmental routine. First the police. A commandant and assistants were chosen: districts allotted: provisional wages, indents, uniform, responsibilities. The machine began to function. Then came a complaint of water-supply. The conduit was foul with dead men and animals. An inspectorate, with its labour corps, solved this. Emergency regulations were drafted.

The day was drawing in, the world was in the streets: riotous. We chose an engineer to superintend the power-house, charging him at all pains to illuminate the town that night. The resumption of street lighting would be our most signal proof of peace. It was done, and to its shining quietness much of the order of the first evening of victory belonged: though our new police were zealous, and the grave sheikhs of the many quarters helped their patrol.

Then sanitation. The streets were full of the debris of the broken army, derelict carts and cars, baggage, material, corpses. Typhus, dysentery and pellagra were rife among the Turks, and sufferers had died in every shadow along the line of march. Nuri prepared scavenger gangs to make a first clearing of the pestilent roads and open places, and rationed out his doctors among the hospitals, with promises of drugs and food next day, if any could be found.

Next a fire-brigade. The local engines had been smashed by the Germans, and the Army storehouses still burned, endangering the town. Mechanics were cried for; and trained men, pressed into service, sent down to circumscribe the flames. Then the prisons. Warders and inmates had vanished from them together. Shukri made a virtue of that, by amnesties, civil, political, military. The citizens must be disarmed — or at least dissuaded from carrying rifles. A proclamation was the treatment, followed up by good-humoured banter merging into police activity. This would effect our end without malice in three or four days.

Relief work. The destitute had been half-starved for days. A distribution of the damaged food from the Army storehouses was arranged. After that food must be provided for the general. The city might be starving in two days: there were no stocks in Damascus. To get temporary supplies from the near villages was easy, if we restored confidence, safe-guarded the roads, and replaced the transport animals, which the Turks had carried off, by others from the pool of captures. The British would not share out. We parted with our own animals: our Army transport.

The routine feeding of the place needed the railway. Pointsmen, drivers, firemen, shopmen, traffic staff had to be found and re-engaged immediately. Then the telegraphs: the junior staff were available: directors must be found, and linesmen sent out to put the system in repair. The post could wait a day or two: but quarters for ourselves and the British were urgent: and so were the resumption of trade, the opening of shops, and their corollary needs of markets and acceptable currency.

The currency was horrible. The Australians had looted millions in Turkish notes, the only stuff in use, and had reduced it to no value by throwing it about. One trooper gave a five hundred pound note to a lad who held his horse three minutes. Young tried his prentice-hand at bolstering it with the last remnant of our Akaba gold: but new prices had to be fixed, which involved the printing press; and hardly was that settled when a newspaper was demanded. Also, as heirs of the Turkish Government, the Arabs must maintain its records of fisc and property: with the register of souls. Whereas the old staffs were taking jubilant holiday.

Requisitions plagued us while we were yet half-hungry. Chauvel had no forage and he had forty thousand horses to feed. If forage was not brought him he would go seek it and the new-lit freedom puff out like a match. Syria's status hung on his satisfaction; and we should find little mercy in his judgements.

Taken all in all, this was a busy evening. We reached an apparent end by sweeping delegation of office (too often, in our haste, to hands unworthy), and by drastic cutting down of efficiency. Stirling the suave, Young the capable, and Kirkbride the summary backed to their best the open-minded power of the Arab officers.

Our aim was a façade rather than a fitted building. It was run up so furiously well that when I left Damascus on October the fourth the Syrians had their *de facto* Government, which endured for two years, without foreign advice, in an occupied country wasted by war, and against the will of important elements among the Allies.

Later I was sitting alone in my room, working and thinking out as firm a way as the turbulent memories of the day allowed, when the Muedhdhins began to send their call of last prayer through the moist night over the illuminations of the feasting city. One, with a ringing voice of special sweetness, cried into my window from a near mosque. I found myself involuntarily distinguishing his words: 'God alone is great: I testify there are no gods, but God: and Mohammed his Prophet. Come to prayer: come to security. God alone is great: there is no god — but God.'*

At the close he dropped his voice two tones, almost to speaking level, and softly added: 'And He is very good to us this day, O people of Damascus.' The clamour hushed, as everyone seemed to obey the call to prayer on this their first night of perfect freedom. While my fancy, in the overwhelming pause, showed me my loneliness and lack of reason in their movement: since only for me, of all the hearers, was the event sorrowful and the phrase meaningless.

* I have not seen this cry put exactly into English; indeed it will not go, for hidden in the Arabic there lurks a quantification of the predicate for which our accidence has failed to provide.

CHAPTER CXXI

QUIVERINGLY a citizen woke me, with word that Abd el Kadir was making rebellion. I sent over to Nuri Said, glad the Algerian fool was digging his own pit. He had called his men, told them these Sherifs were only English creatures, and conjured them to strike a blow for religion and the Caliph while there was yet time. They, simple retainers with an ingrained habit of obedience, took his word for it, and set out to make war on us.

The Druses, for whose tardy services I had this night sharply refused reward, listened to him. They were sectaries, caring nothing for Islam or Caliph or Turk, or Abd el Kadir: but an anti-Christian rising meant plunder, and perhaps Maronites to kill. So they ran to arms, and began to burst open shops.

We held our hands till day, for our numbers were not so great that we could throw away our advantage in weapons, and fight in the dark which made a fool and a man equal. But when dawn hinted itself we moved men to the upper suburb, and drove the rioters towards the river districts of the town's centre, where the streets crossed bridges, and were easy to control.

Then we saw how small the trouble was. Nuri Said had covered the parades with machine-gun sections, who, in one long rattle of fire, barraged them across to blank walls. Past these our sweeping parties urged the dissident. The appalling noise made the Druses drop their booty and flee down side alleys. Mohammed Said, not so brave as his brother, was taken in his house, and gaoled in the Town Hall. Again I itched to shoot him, but waited till we had the other.

However, Abd el Kader broke back into the country. At noon it was all over. When things began I had called up Chauvel, who at once offered his troops. I thanked him, and asked that a second company of horse be drafted to the Turkish barracks (the nearest post) to stand by against call: but the fighting was too petty for that call.

Its best consequence was among the pressmen in an hotel whose wall was the stop-block of one barrage. They had not dipped their pens in much blood during this campaign, which had run faster than their cars; but here was a godsend at their bedroom windows, and they wrote and telegraphed till Allenby, away in Ramleh, took fright, sending me a Press despatch which recalled two Balkan wars and five Armenian massacres, but never carnage like to-day's: the streets paved with corpses, the gutters running blood, and the swollen Barada spouting crimson through all the fountains in the city! My reply was a death-roll, naming the five victims, and the hurts of the ten wounded. Of the casualties three fell to Kirkbride's ruthless revolver.

The Druses were expelled from the city, and lost horses and rifles at the hands of the citizens of Damascus, whom we had formed for the emergency into civic guards. These gave the town a warlike look, patrolling till afternoon, when things grew quiet again, and street traffic normal; with sweetmeats, iced drinks, flowers, and little Hejaz flags being hawked round by their pedlars as before.

We returned to the organization of the public services. An amusing event for me, personally, was an official call from the Spanish Consul, a polished English-speaking individual, who introduced himself as Chargé d'Affaires for seventeen nationalities (including all combatants except the Turks) and was in vain search of the constituted legal authority of the town.

At lunch an Australian doctor implored me, for the sake of humanity, to take notice of the Turkish hospital. I ran over in my mind our three hospitals, the military, the civil, the missionary, and told him they were cared for as well as our means allowed. The Arabs could not invent drugs, nor could Chauvel give them to us. He enlarged further; describing an enormous range of filthy buildings without a single medical officer or orderly, packed with dead and dying; mainly dysentery cases, but at least some typhoid; and, it was only to be hoped, no typhus or cholera.

In his descriptions I recognized the Turkish barracks, occupied by two Australian companies of town reserve. Were there sentries at the gates? Yes, he said, that was the place, but it was full of Turkish sick. I walked across and parleyed with the guard, who distrusted my single appearance on foot. They had orders to keep out all natives lest they massacre the patients — a misapprehension of the Arab fashion of making war. At last my English speech got me past the little lodge whose garden was filled with two hundred wretched prisoners in exhaustion and despair.

Through the great door of the barrack I called, up the dusty echoing corridors. No one answered. The huge, deserted, sun-trapping court was squalid with rubbish. The guard told me that thousands of prisoners from here had yesterday gone to a camp beyond the town. Since then no one had come in or out. I walked over to the far thoroughfare, on whose left was a shuttered lobby, black after the blazing sunlight of the plastered court.

I stepped in, to meet a sickening stench: and, as my eyes grew open, a sickening sight. The stone floor was covered with dead bodies, side by side, some in full uniform, some in underclothing, some stark naked. There might be thirty there, and they crept with rats, who had gnawed wet red galleries into them. A few were corpses nearly fresh, perhaps only a day or two old: others must have been there for long. Of some the flesh, going putrid, was yellow and blue and black. Many were already swollen twice or thrice life-width, their fat heads laughing with black mouth across jaws harsh with stubble. Of others the softer parts were fallen in. A few had burst open, and were liquescent with decay.

Beyond was the vista of a great room, from which I thought there came a groan. I trod over to it, across the soft mat of bodies, whose clothing, yellow with dung, crackled dryly under me. Inside the ward the air was raw and still, and the dressed battalion of filled beds so quiet that I thought these too were dead, each man rigid on his stinking pallet, from which liquid muck had dripped down to stiffen on the cemented floor.

I picked forward a little between their lines, holding my white skirts about me, not to dip my bare feet in their puddled running: when suddenly I heard a sigh and turned abruptly to meet the open beady eyes of an outstretched man, while 'Aman, Aman' (pity, pity, pardon) rustled from the twisted lips. There was a brown waver as several tried to lift their hands, and a thin fluttering like withered leaves, as they vainly fell back again upon their beds.

No one of them had strength to speak, but there was something which made me laugh at their whispering in unison, as if by command.

No doubt occasion had been given them to rehearse their appeal all the last two days, each time a curious trooper had peered into their halls and gone away.

I ran through the arch into the garden, across which Australians were picketed in lines, and asked them for a working-party. They refused. Tools? They had none. Doctors? Busy. Kirkbride came; the Turkish doctors, we heard, were upstairs. We broke open a door to find seven men in night-gowns sitting on unmade beds in a great room, boiling toffee. We convinced them quickly that it would be wise to sort out living and dead, and prepare me, in half an hour, a tally of their numbers. Kirkbride's heavy frame and boots fitted him to oversee this work: while I saw Ali Riza Pasha, and asked him to detail us one of the four Arab army doctors.

When he came we pressed the fifty fittest prisoners in the lodge as labour party. We bought biscuits and fed them: then armed them with Turkish tools and set them in the backyard to dig a common grave. The Australian officers protested it was an unfit place, the smell arising from which might drive them from their garden. My jerky reply was that I hoped to God it would.

It was cruelty to work men so tired and ill as our miserable Turks, but haste gave us no choice. By the kicks and blows of their victor-serving non-commissioned officers they were at last got obedient. We began operations on a six-foot hole to one side of the garden. This hole we tried to deepen, but beneath was a cement floor; so I said it would do if they enlarged the edges. Near by was much quicklime, which would cover the bodies effectually.

The doctors told us of fifty-six dead, two hundred dying, seven hundred not dangerously ill. We formed a stretcher party to carry down the corpses, of which some were lifted easily, others had to be scraped up piecemeal with shovels. The bearers were hardly strong enough to stand at their work: indeed, before the end, we had added the bodies of two to the heap of dead men in the pit.

The trench was small for them, but so fluid was the mass that each newcomer, when tipped in, fell softly, just jellying out the edges of the pile a little with his weight. Before the work finished it was midnight, and I dismissed myself to bed, exhausted, since I had not slept three hours since we left Deraa four days ago. Kirkbride (a boy in years, doing two men's work these days) stayed to finish the burying, and scatter earth and lime over the grave.

At the hotel waited a bunch of urgent matters: some death sentences, a new justiciary, a famine in barley for the morrow if the train did not work. Also a complaint from Chauvel that some of the Arab troops had been slack about saluting *Australian* officers!

CHAPTER CXXII

BY morning, after the sudden fashion of troubles, they were
ended and our ship sailing under a clear sky. The armoured
cars came in, and the pleasure of our men's sedate faces heartened
me. Pisani arrived, and made me laugh, so bewildered was the good
soldier by the political hubbub. He gripped his military duty as a
rudder to steer him through. Damascus was normal, the shops open,
street merchants trading, the electric tramcars restored, grain and
vegetables and fruits coming in well.

The streets were being watered to lay the terrible dust of three
war-years' lorry traffic. The crowds were slow and happy, and
numbers of British troops were wandering in the town, unarmed.
The telegraph was restored with Palestine, and with Beyrout, which the
Arabs had occupied in the night. As long ago as Wejh I had warned
them, when they took Damascus to leave Lebanon for sop to the French
and take Tripoli instead; since as a port it outweighed Beyrout, and
England would have played the honest broker for it on their behalf in
the Peace Settlement. So I was grieved by their mistake, yet glad they
felt grown-up enough to reject me.

Even the hospital was better. I had urged Chauvel to take it over,
but he would not. At the time I thought he meant to overstrain us, to
justify his taking away our government of the town. However, since,
I have come to feel that the trouble between us was a delusion of the
ragged nerves which were jangling me to distraction these days.
Certainly Chauvel won the last round, and made me feel mean, for
when he heard that I was leaving he drove round with Godwin and
thanked me outright for my help in his difficulties. Still, the hospital
was improving of itself. Fifty prisoners had cleaned the courtyard,
burning the lousy rubbish. A second gang had dug another great
grave-pit in the garden, and were zealously filling it as opportunity
offered. Others had gone through the wards, washing every patient,
putting them into cleaner shirts, and reversing their mattresses to have a
tolerably decent side up. We had found food suitable for all but critical
cases, and each ward had some Turkish-spoken orderly within hearing,

if a sick man called. One room we had cleared, brushed out and dis-
infected, meaning to transfer into it the less ill cases, and do their room
in turn.

At this rate three days would have seen things very fit, and I was
proudly contemplating other benefits when a medical major strode up
and asked me shortly if I spoke English. With a brow of disgust for my
skirts and sandals he said 'You're in charge?' Modestly I smirked that
in a way I was, and then he burst out, 'Scandalous, disgraceful, outrageous, ought to be shot . . .' At this onslaught I cackled out like a
chicken, with the wild laughter of strain; it did feel extraordinarily
funny to be so cursed just as I had been pluming myself on having
bettered the apparently hopeless.

The major had not entered the charnel house of yesterday, nor
smelt it, nor seen us burying those bodies of ultimate degradation,
whose memory had started me up in bed, sweating and trembling, a
few hours since. He glared at me, muttering 'Bloody brute'. I hooted
out again, and he smacked me over the face and stalked off, leaving me
more ashamed than angry, for in my heart I felt he was right, and that
anyone who pushed through to success a rebellion of the weak against
their masters must come out of it so stained in estimation that afterward nothing in the world would make him feel clean. However, it
was nearly over.

When I got back to the hotel crowds were besetting it, and at the
door stood a grey Rolls-Royce, which I knew for Allenby's. I ran in
and found him there with Clayton and Cornwallis and other noble
people. In ten words he gave his approval to my having impertinently
imposed Arab Governments, here and at Deraa, upon the chaos of
victory. He confirmed the appointment of Ali Riza Rikabi as his
Military Governor, under the orders of Feisal, his Army Commander,
and regulated the Arab sphere and Chauvel's.

He agreed to take over my hospital and the working of the railway.
In ten minutes all the maddening difficulties had slipped away. Mistily
I realized that the harsh days of my solitary battling had passed. The
lone hand had won against the world's odds, and I might let my limbs
relax in this dreamlike confidence and decision and kindness which
were Allenby.

Then we were told that Feisal's special train had just arrived from Deraa. A message was hurriedly sent him by Young's mouth, and we waited till he came, upon a tide of cheering which beat up against our windows. It was fitting the two chiefs should meet for the first time in the heart of their victory; with myself still acting as the interpreter between them.

Allenby gave me a telegram from the Foreign Office, recognizing to the Arabs the status of belligerents; and told me to translate it to the Emir: but none of us knew what it meant in English, let alone in Arabic: and Feisal, smiling through the tears which the welcome of his people had forced from him, put it aside to thank the Commander-in-Chief for the trust which had made him and his movement. They were a strange contrast: Feisal, large-eyed, colourless and worn, like a fine dagger; Allenby, gigantic and red and merry, fit representative of the Power which had thrown a girdle of humour and strong dealing round the world.

When Feisal had gone, I made to Allenby the last (and also I think the first) request I ever made him for myself — leave to go away. For a while he would not have it; but I reasoned, reminding him of his year-old promise, and pointing out how much easier the New Law would be if my spur were absent from the people. In the end he agreed; and then at once I knew how much I was sorry.

DAMASCUS *had not seemed a sheath for my sword, when I landed in Arabia: but its capture disclosed the exhaustion of my main springs of action. The strongest motive throughout had been a personal one, not mentioned here, but present to me, I think, every hour of these two years. Active pains and joys might fling up, like towers, among my days: but, refluent as air, this hidden urge re-formed, to be the persisting element of life, till near the end. It was dead, before we reached Damascus.*

Next in force had been a pugnacious wish to win the war: yoked to the conviction that without Arab help England could not pay the price of winning its Turkish sector. When Damascus fell, the Eastern war — probably the whole war — drew to an end.

Then I was moved by curiosity. 'Super flumina Babylonis', read as a boy, had left me longing to feel myself the node of a national movement. We took Damascus, and I feared. More than three arbitrary days would have quickened in me a root of authority.

There remained historical ambition, insubstantial as a motive by itself. I had dreamed, at the City School in Oxford, of hustling into form, while I lived, the new Asia which time was inexorably bringing upon us. Mecca was to lead to Damascus; Damascus to Anatolia, and afterwards to Bagdad; and then there was Yemen. Fantasies, these will seem, to such as are able to call my beginning an ordinary effort.

APPENDIX I

NOMINAL ROLL:
HEJAZ ARMOURED CAR COMPANY

M.G.C.

Gilman Dowsett Grisenthwaite Wade Greenhill

D. M. Grant	E. Palmer	H. Comery
G. V. P. Kenknight	J. L. Pender	R. Fairgrave
G. S. Bond	W. Rowe	W. A. Holdsworth
F. J. Davies	H. M. Shackleton	V. Holden
A. Frost	A. Tunnicliffe	R. P. Jones
H. Mann	G. Westwater	D. M. Murray
D. Anderson	J. Wilson	R. McKenzie
G. Barton	J. Goodchild	H. E. Parker
T. W. Beaumont	H. Wareham	G. A. Pikett
H. W. Bailey	G. Williams	E. Stoller
G. A. Draper	H. J. Ingram	W. Thacker
A. Hancock	E. Featherstone	H. W. Twiner
J. H. Hurd	F. Wilson	F. Whitelegg
Jackson	W. Axup	A. Woodburn
E. Lowe	C. J. Bird	
W. McDonald	F. Brander	

R.A.S.C.

H. Monks	J. W. Ramsbottom	W. Hurst
A. Barnes	S. C. Rolls	W. W. Kidd
W. Coxon	T. R. Robinson	E. J. Keslake
A. Duff	J. O. Seddon	L. Matthews
S. Evans	J. E. Wadland	J. McKechnie
F. Garnett	A. Wainwright	W. Page
S. Haymes	R. B. Arnott	E. Rawcliffe
R. W. Hurst	G. Buckle	S. D. Ross
H. H. Helme	D. Dickson	J. E. Sanderson
A. Knowles	G. T. Elphick	C. W. Thomas
J. Mackay	J. E. Exton	W. E. Wells
O. McCarnen	H. R. Green	
F. Mudd	H. Hosker	

NOMINAL ROLL:
TEN-POUNDER TALBOT BATTERY

R.F.A.

Brodie

Pascoe

L. W. Parsonage

J. Black

T. Richardson

W. Bassett

A. Catley

C. W. Sorton

H. Iverson

H. E. Drewitt

J. Smail

H. B. Eccles

E. Garrett

R. Sneddon

W. Stanford

C. H. Hare

P. Stokes

J. Shaw

A. Lynn

A. Fawcett

R. Nicol

W. McInnes

J. Baxter

H. M. Palmer

R.A.S.C.

J. Bourne

A. Davies

R. Guthrie

M. Harper

Harrison

Draycuf

A. G. Frankis

A. Bentley

Puffer

J. Douglas

D. P. Quentin

J. W. Holyoak

W. Johnson

Heysed

APPENDIX II

The following table of our movements or position-at-night is from my skeleton diary. Accident, preoccupations, and prudence were responsible for gaps. My book follows the strict order of time: but leaves out many by-plays. The dates here do not altogether agree with its text. Memory sometimes assists me with moonlight, on a new-moon night: and I have preferred memory to the calendar. Arabic names are spelt anyhow, to prevent my appearing an adherent of one of the existing 'systems of transliteration'.

1917

Jan.	1	Nahkl Mubarak	Apr.	1	Abu Markha	June	1	Wadi Bair
	2	Nagb Dhifran		3	Magrah el Semn		2	Ageila
	3	Yenbo		4	El Fershah		3	Nebk, etc.
	14	In *Suva*, etc.		5	Km. 1121		19	El Wagf
	17	Bir Waheidi		6	El Fershah		20	Bair
	18	Semna		7	Bir el Amri		21	El Ghadaf
	19	Harrat Gelib		8	Abu Markha		22	Wadi Mishnag
	20	Wadi Dhulm		10	Wadi Geraia		23	Hemme
	21	Abu Zereibat		11	Wadi Hamdh		24	Minifir
	23	Kurna		14	Wejh		25	Ifdein
	24	Habban		27	Magrah Raal		26	Dhaba
	25	Wejh		28	W. Hamdh		27	W. Maghara
	27	In *Hardinge*	May	1	Mellaha, etc.		28	Bair
	28	Cairo, etc.		3	Wejh		29	Rijt el Herar
Feb.	1	Suez		6	Wadi Hamdh		30	El Jefer
	4	In *Arethusa*		7	Wejh	July	1	Km. 479
	6	Wejh, etc.		9	Kalaat el Zereib		2	Fuweileh
	20	In *Arethusa*		10	El Kurr		3	Nagb el Shtar
	22	Cairo, etc.		12	Wadi Arnoua		4	Guweira
Mar.	2	In *Lama*		13	Abu Saad		5	W. Yitm
	3	Wejh, etc.		14	Abu Raga		6	Akaba
	10	Seil Arja		17	El Shegg		7	Bir Mohammed
	11	Abu Zereibat		18	Wadi Aish		8	Sudr Heidan
	12	Wadi Kitan		19	Dizaad		9	Suez
	13	Wadi Gara		20	Wadi Abu Arad		10	Cairo
	14	Wadi Tleih		21	Bir Fejr		12	Alexandria
	15	Abu Markha		22	Khabrat Ajaj		13	Cairo, etc.
	26	Wadi Serum		23	El Jaala		15	Alexandria
	27	Wadi Meseij		24	Kaseim Arfaja		16	Cairo
	28	El Jurf		25	Arfaja		17	In *Dufferin*
	29	Aba el Naam		26	Maiseri		19	Jeida
	30	Wadi Turaa		27	Isawiya		20	In *Dufferin*
	31	Bir el Amri		30	Abu Tarfeiyat		22	Jidda

Aug.	1 Jidda	Oct.	1 Wadi Hafir	Nov.	7 Tell el Shahab
	2 In *Hardinge*		2 Batra		8 Abu Sawana
	4 Wadi Itm, etc.		3 Shedia		9 Minifir
	6 In *Hardinge*		4 Km. 489		11 Abu Sawana
	7 Cairo		5 El Kasr		12 Azrak, etc.
	14 Alexandria		6 Imshash Hesma		23 Wadi Butm
	16 In *Hardinge*		7 Rumm		24 Bair
	17 Akaba, etc.		8 Wadi Itm		25 Jefer
	21 Kuntilla		9 Akaba		26 Akaba
	22 Akaba, etc.		11 Suez		30 Wadi Itm
Sept.	7 Wadi Itm		12 Kelab	Dec.	1 Wadi Hawara
	8 Wadi Medeifein		13 Ismailia		2 Wadi Itm
	9 Guweira		14 Suez		3 Akaba
	10 Hesma		15 Akaba, etc.		8 Kantara
	11 Rumm		24 Wadi Itm		9 Gaza
	12 Akaba		25 Rumm		10 Suafa
	13 Rumm, etc.		26 Wadi Hafir		11 G.H.Q., etc.
	16 Wadi Dumma		27 Shedia		12 Gaza
	17 Mudowwara		28 El Jefer, etc.		13 Cairo
	18 Km. 587		30 Shegg		21 Suez, etc.
	19 Mudowwara		31 Bair		25 Akaba
	20 Rumm	Nov.	1 Wadi Dhirwa		26 Guweira
	21 Itm el Imran		2 Ammri		27 Abu Sawana
	22 Akaba		3 Ain el Beidha		28 Akaba
	26 Wadi Itm		4 Hamad		29 Guweira
	27 Hawara		5 Kseir 'Hallabat		30 Ramleh
	28 Rumm, etc.		6 Ghadir Abyadh		31 Tell el Shahm

1918

Jan.	1 Abu Tarfeiya	Feb.	20 Wadi Araba	Apr.	4 Wadi el Jinz
	2 Akaba, etc.		21 Beersheba		5 Wadi el Hafir
	10 Wadi Itm		22 Ramleh, etc.		6 El Atara, etc.
	11 Guweira		27 Jerusalem		11 Jurf el Derawish
	15 Nagb Shtar		28 Rafa		12 Odroh
	16 Aba el Lissan	Mar.	1 Cairo		13 Guweira
	18 Wadi Musa		4 Akaba		14 Waheida
	19 Shobek		6 In *Borulos*		18 Retm
	20 Tafileh, etc.		8 Cairo		19 Shahm
	28 Mezra, etc.		12 Suez		20 Ramleh
Feb.	4 Odroh		13 In *Borulos*		21 Disi
	5 Guweira		15 Akaba		22 Aba el Lissan
	8 Khabr el Abid		16 Guweira		23 Waheida
	9 Basta		17 Akaba		25 Aba el Lissan
	10 Shobek		18 Nagb Shtar		27 In *Arethusa*
	11 Tafileh, etc.		19 Shobek		29 Cairo
	13 Buseira		20 Sadaka	May	1 Sinai
	14 Ghor el Safi		21 Akaba, etc.		2 G.H.Q.
	16 Wadi Dhahal		30 Guweira		3 Jerusalem
	17 Seil Hesa	Apr.	1 Khabr el Abid		4 Aba el Lissan
	18 Hesban, etc.		2 Aba el Lissan		5 G.H.Q.
	19 Tafileh		3 Aneyza		6 Sinai

May 7 Cairo
14 Sinai
15 G.H.Q.
16 Wadi Hafira
17 Cairo
19 In *Imogen*
21 Akaba
22 Aba el Lissan
23 Akaba
24 Disi
25 Mudowwara
26 Akaba
27 Aba el Lissan
28 Fagair
29 Towani
30 Hesa, etc.
June 1 Sultani
2 Um el Rusas
5 Themed
6 Wadi Mojeb
7 Jurf
8 Aba el Lissan
10 In *Arethusa*
12 Suez
13 Cairo
15 Alexandria
17 Cairo
18 Sinai
19 G.H.Q.
20 Cairo

June 21 In *Mansurah*
25 Jidda
July 1 In *Mansurah*
3 Wejh
4 In *Mansurah*
6 Cairo
8 Alexandria
9 Cairo
11 Palestine
13 Cairo
26 In *Borulos*
28 Akaba
29 Aba el Lissan
31 Akaba
Aug. 1 Akaba
2 Wadi Itm
3 Wadi Nejd
4 Rumm
5 Akaba
6 Aba el Heiran
7 Akaba
8 Aba el Lissan
11 Jefer
12 Um Kharug
13 Amri, etc.
15 Bair
17 El Hadi
18 Wadi Ghadaf
19 El Umdeisisat
20 Muaggar

Aug. 21 Kusair el Amr
22 Azrak
23 Ammari
24 Um Kharug
25 Thlaithukhwat
26 Aba el Lissan
Sept. 1 Aba el Lissan
5 Bair
6 Azrak, etc.
13 Gian Khunna
14 Umtaiye, etc.
16 Mezerib
17 Nasib
18 Umtaiye
19 Ifdein
20 Azrak
21 Ramleh
22 Um el Surab
24 Umtaiye
25 Nueime
26 Sheikh Miskin
27 Sheikh Saad
28 Deraa
Oct. 1 Damascus
4 Kuneitra
5 Sebaste
6 Ramleh
7 Sinai
8 Cairo

INDEX TO PLACE NAMES

PERSONAL INDEX

READ MORE IN PENGUIN

In every corner of the world, on every subject under the sun, Penguin represents quality and variety – the very best in publishing today.

For complete information about books available from Penguin – including Puffins, Penguin Classics and Arkana – and how to order them, write to us at the appropriate address below. Please note that for copyright reasons the selection of books varies from country to country.

In the United Kingdom: Please write to *Dept. EP, Penguin Books Ltd, Bath Road, Harmondsworth, West Drayton, Middlesex UB7 ODA*

In the United States: Please write to *Consumer Sales, Penguin Putnam Inc., P.O. Box 12289 Dept. B, Newark, New Jersey 07101-5289.* VISA and MasterCard holders call 1-800-788-6262 to order Penguin titles

In Canada: Please write to *Penguin Books Canada Ltd, 10 Alcorn Avenue, Suite 300, Toronto, Ontario M4V 3B2*

In Australia: Please write to *Penguin Books Australia Ltd, P.O. Box 257, Ringwood, Victoria 3134*

In New Zealand: Please write to *Penguin Books (NZ) Ltd, Private Bag 102902, North Shore Mail Centre, Auckland 10*

In India: Please write to *Penguin Books India Pvt Ltd, 11 Community Centre, Panchsheel Park, New Delhi 110017*

In the Netherlands: Please write to *Penguin Books Netherlands bv, Postbus 3507, NL-1001 AH Amsterdam*

In Germany: Please write to *Penguin Books Deutschland GmbH, Metzlerstrasse 26, 60594 Frankfurt am Main*

In Spain: Please write to *Penguin Books S A , Bravo Murillo 19, 1ª B, 28015 Madrid*

In Italy: Please write to *Penguin Italia s.r.l., Via Benedetto Croce 2, 20094 Corsico, Milano*

In France: Please write to *Penguin France, Le Carré Wilson, 62 rue Benjamin Baillaud, 31500 Toulouse*

In Japan: Please write to *Penguin Books Japan Ltd, Kaneko Building, 2-3-25 Koraku, Bunkyo-Ku, Tokyo 112*

In South Africa: Please write to *Penguin Books South Africa (Pty) Ltd, Private Bag X14, Parkview, 2122 Johannesburg*

READ MORE IN PENGUIN

Published or forthcoming:

A Clockwork Orange   Anthony Burgess

Fifteen-year-old Alex enjoys rape, drugs and Beethoven's Ninth. He and his gang rampage through a dystopian future, hunting for terrible thrills, until he finds himself at the mercy of the state and the ministrations of Dr Brodsky, the government psychologist. *A Clockwork Orange* is both a virtuoso performance from an electrifying prose stylist and a serious exploration of the morality of free will.

On the Road   Jack Kerouac

On the Road swings to the rhythms of 1950s underground America, with Sal Paradise and his hero Dean Moriarty, traveller and mystic, the living epitome of Beat. Now recognized as a modern classic, its American Dream is nearer that of Walt Whitman than F. Scott Fitzgerald, and it goes racing towards the sunset with unforgettable exuberance, poignancy and autobiographical passion.

Zazie in the Metro   Raymond Queneau

Impish, foul-mouthed Zazie arrives in Paris from the country to stay with her female-impersonator Uncle Gabriel. All she really wants to do is ride the metro, but finding it shut because of a strike, Zazie looks for other means of amusement and is soon caught up in a comic adventure that becomes wilder and more manic by the minute. Queneau's cult classic is stylish, witty and packed full of wordplay and phonetic games.

Lolita   Vladimir Nabokov

Poet and pervert Humbert Humbert becomes obsessed by twelve-year-old Lolita and seeks to possess her, first carnally and then artistically. This seduction is one of many dimensions in Nabokov's dizzying masterpiece, which is suffused with a savage humour and rich verbal textures. 'You read Lolita sprawling limply in your chair, ravished, overcome, nodding scandalized assent' Martin Amis